EFFECTIVE BUSINESS COMMUNICATIONS

Third Edition

EFFECTIVE BUSINESS COMMUNICATIONS

HERTA A. MURPHY
Professor Emeritus of Business Administration
University of Washington

CHARLES E. PECK
Late Professor of Business Administration
University of Washington

McGraw-Hill Book Company

New York   St. Louis   San Francisco   Auckland   Bogotá   Hamburg
Johannesburg   London   Madrid   Mexico   Montreal   New Delhi
Panama   Paris   São Paulo   Singapore   Sydney   Tokyo   Toronto

Library of Congress Cataloging in Publication Data

Murphy, Herta A.
  Effective business communications.

  Bibliography: p.
  Includes index.
  1. Commercial correspondence. 2. Communication in management. I. Peck,
Charles Edwin, date, joint author. II. Title.
HF5721.M85 1980   651.7'4   79-22225
ISBN 0-07-044080-8

EFFECTIVE BUSINESS COMMUNICATIONS

 2 3 4 5 6 7 8 9 0 DODO 8 9 8 7 6 5 4 3 2 1 0

This book was set in Press Roman by Allen Wayne Technical Corp.
The editors were John F. Carleo and David Dunham;
the designer was Charles A. Carson;
the production supervisor was Richard A. Ausburn.
New drawings were done by Allen Wayne Technical Corp.
R. R. Donnelley & Sons Company was printer and binder.

Contents

PART FIVE   NONWRITTEN COMMUNICATIONS

APPENDIXES

CHECKLISTS

Preface

This third edition, like its widely adopted predecessor, emphasizes that the purpose and the receiver of every message profoundly affect content, organization, and style of presentation. In keeping with this theme, the book's broad content is practical and thorough, with substantial additions, updates, and revisions. Its organization, visual aids, cross-references, and clear, conversational style make meaningful reading easy. Abundant teaching and learning aids demonstrate key concepts for written and oral communications.

Purpose and Approach

Anyone preparing for or already in a business or management job that requires effective communication will find this book useful as both a text and a reference guide. Its goal is to help you communicate through sound written and oral business messages that receivers can easily understand and to which they will react favorably. It acquaints you with typical business communication problems, basic principles, planning steps, organizational patterns, legal cautions, and modern media. It is designed to develop a better understanding of human behavior and to improve abilities for analyzing, researching, organizing, writing, and speaking.

Explanations suggest *what* to do and *why*. Hundreds of examples show *how*. Chapter title pages list main topics, helpful for both preview and review. Checklists provide summary guidelines. End-of-chapter exercises range from simple to complex thought-stimulating activities.

This book is written for students in universities and colleges, community colleges, business schools, continuing-education centers, and special training programs for middle-management or supervisory personnel. Whether you communicate as a business executive, professional person, government employee, administrative assistant, club officer, or an individual consumer, the book has useful material for you. It is ample for one- or two-semester courses, and adaptable for short courses that cover only selected chapters pertinent to particular student needs.

Special Features

The third edition contains these features and major changes:

1. New materials on legal aspects, showing how some laws and sensitive situations affect recommendations; resumes, job applications, pre-employment interviews; credit, collection, and sales messages.
2. In reports chapters—new and revised illustrations of proposals, abstracts, documentation, graphs, short reports, and analytical long reports.
3. New suggestions, examples, and exercises for nondiscriminatory (nonsexist) expressions.
4. Updated text wherever desirable, in all chapters.
5. New checklists on source footnotes, openings, and closings. These are in addition to the popular, unique 39 capsule checklists and various outlines in the second edition. Together they provide concise summaries for most types of messages. They are to be used only as *guidelines and reminders—not* as *"recipe lists,"* because each message requires careful planning depending upon circumstances and purpose.
6. A total of 345 exercises—many new or revised—adaptable for community college as well as university students and business people.
7. Improved presentations on the communication process, organizational plans, report headings, and listening.
8. More aids for editing, revising, dictation, and cost cutting.
9. Some reorganized chapters for better readability and classroom use.
10. Deletions or shortening of some examples to provide space for new materials.
11. Examples of 324 complete messages plus numerous other paragraph and sentence illustrations. (Though examples are based on actual business situations, most names, figures, and products have been changed—to protect anonymity.)
12. Marginal notations that analyze significant parts in many examples of well-written messages.
13. Additional emphasis on integrity and ethics.
14. Updated bibliographies footnoted in some chapters, for further readings on related topics.
15. New motivating material on how effective business communication "pays off."

Plan of Organization

This 19-chapter text begins with six background-for-communicating chapters, which constitute Part One. They introduce you to the importance, process, "C" principles, planning steps, deductive and inductive organization, costs, and media of written and oral business communications.

In Part Two each of the four chapters presents letters and memos organized by a basic pattern—direct request, good news, bad news, or persuasive request. Included are inquiries, claims, recommendations, adjustments, credits, orders, favors, sales announcements, and transmittals.

Part Three features both written and oral special messages—job applications, interviews, follow-ups, collections, goodwill. You will see how the four plans and various media are adaptable to these message types.

Part Four consists of three expanded chapters on business reports. They cover planning steps, research, organization, visual aids, essential parts, documentation, format, and qualities.

In Part Five two chapters on nonwritten communications present guidelines for conference leadership, oral reporting, platform speaking, listening, interviewing, instructing, and dictating.

Appendixes include a brief discussion on legal aspects, writing mechanics, style, and symbols for checking papers.

Acknowledgments

To the many persons who have made suggestions and contributions I am heartily grateful. My sincere thanks go to the executives and staff members who have provided hundreds of illustrative materials from business and industry; to my American Business Communication Association colleagues, whose ideas, preferences, research, and writings along with those of other scholars through the years have enriched my knowledge and influenced the scope of this book; and to students who have brought numerous examples from their employment and organizational experiences.

Among those deserving special acknowledgment and thanks are the conscientious reviewers who offered helpful constructive comments for this edition. I am indebted to: John E. Binnion, Cleveland State University; Norma Carr-Smith, San Francisco State University; Marilyn A. Lewis, Arapahoe Community College, Colorado; Nancy B. Moody, Sinclair Community College, Ohio; Lou Mooney, Central State University, Oklahoma; Muriel Rada, Metropolitan Technical Community College, Nebraska. As one can expect, a few suggestions contradicted others. Because courses necessarily vary in scope and length, some topics that most instructors emphasize and value highly, others must omit entirely. So I have tried to include in this comprehensive text as many useful materials as space allows for both basic and management-oriented courses.

Also I am deeply grateful and extend special thanks to four professors at Cleveland State University who wrote challenging new exercises for eight chapters: John E. Binnion, Bella G. Clinkscale, Kenneth R. Mayer, Edward G. Thomas. My appreciation is expressed too to three of my colleagues at the University of Washington: L. R. Goldberg for reviewing and improving the updated appendix on legal aspects; Virgil Harder for his thoughtful views and examples; and Phyllis A. Needy, placement coordinator, for her specific suggestions on current sensitive issues regarding employment matters. Furthermore, to the authors and companies that have given permission to quote from their writings and whose names are mentioned in footnotes, I express sincere thanks.

In appreciation of the thousands of students who have given reliable feedback about text content and assignments, I dedicate this revision to all its users who want to improve their oral and written communication ability.

Herta A. Murphy

ONE

BACKGROUND FOR COMMUNICATING

chapter 1

Importance of Effective Communication in Business

You have an important, highly valued skill if you can communicate effectively, orally and in writing. Executives of American business, industry, and government have repeatedly expressed their concern regarding the need for better communication. In numerous surveys business executives have ranked ability to communicate in first place among the personal factors necessary for promotion to and within management. And they have selected business communication as one of the most useful college studies in their work.

This chapter includes answers to the following questions regarding the importance of effective communication in business:

How does effective business communication "pay off"?

What is the volume and cost of written business communication in the United States?

How can you meet the challenge of communicating for business?

HOW EFFECTIVE BUSINESS COMMUNICATION "PAYS OFF"

Effective communication is the "life blood" of every organization and a key to success in your business career as well as in your personal life.

"Life Blood" of the Organization

So important is communication that without it an organization cannot function. Since an organization is a group of people associated for business, political, professional, religious, athletic, or other purposes, its activities require human beings to interact and react; to exchange information, ideas, plans, proposals; to coordinate; to make decisions. Because this book is concerned primarily with effective *business* communication, the discussions and illustrations you will read pertain mainly to business firms. However, you can apply them also to other organizations and to the professions.

Both within and outside the organization, effective business communication pays off and is its life blood.

Internal Communication

Effective "downward" and "upward" internal communication is a vital means of attending successfully to matters of company concern. It helps decrease absenteeism, grievances, and turnover as well as increase job satisfaction, productivity, and profits.

When employees receive appropriate downward communication from management, they can be better motivated and more efficient. They want and need honest information about their company's current business problems and successes that concern them. They appreciate receiving not only clear task directions but also facts about organizational goals, procedures, viewpoints on important controversial issues, relevant management decisions, and employee benefits the company provides.

Likewise, upward internal communication has become increasingly more significant. Many executives sincerely seek frank feedback from employees and stockholders. They listen more closely to opinions, new ideas, complaints, and suggestions—especially when these are clearly and effectively stated.

External Communication

Communications to persons outside the company—customers, inquirers, suppliers, and the public—can have a far-reaching effect on the reputation and ultimate success of the company. The right letter, telephone call, or personal conversation can win back a disgruntled customer, create a desire for a firm's product or service, can negotiate a profitable sale, help an inquirer who is a potential customer, and in general create goodwill.

Reputable organizations are also seriously concerned about enhancing their public image through various communications. Among these communications are public speeches by their executives, tactful replies to comments and criticisms from consumer groups, free informative pamphlets, interviews with news media. All these forms of communication are transmitted with a greater emphasis on truthfulness.[1]

Thus employees who communicate effectively can contribute in a variety of ways to the life blood of their organization. Successful messages eliminate unnecessary additional correspondence, save time and expense, build favorable impressions, enhance goodwill, and help increase company profits.

Advantages for Your Career

Your jobs, promotions, and professional reputation often depend upon the success or failure of your written and oral communications. Especially if your career requires mainly mental rather than manual labor, your progress will be strongly influenced by how effectively you communicate your knowledge, proposals, and ideas to others who need or should receive them.

A Valuable Job Requirement

Preference for communication skills is found in the job descriptions listed by numerous companies wishing to employ college graduates. For example, Dr. Francis W. Weeks, Executive Director of the American Business Communication Association,[2] found in a six-year study of job listings at the University of Illinois Coordinating Place-

---

[1] Vernon M. Buehler and Y.K. Shetty, "Managerial Response to Social Responsibility Challenge," *Academy of Management Journal,* 19(1):66–78, March 1976; Sandra L. Holmes, "Executives Should Be Seen and Heard," *Business Horizons,* April 1977, pp. 5–8; John F. Steiner, "The Business Response to Public Distrust," *Business Horizons,* April 1977, pp. 74–81.

[2] The American Business Communication Association, organized in 1935, with its national office at the University of Illinois, Urbana, has members in major colleges and universities as well as in businesses across the United States and in 15 other countries.

ment Office that 340 jobs in 30 fields required communication ability. Among the specific descriptions were requirements like these:

Must be able to communicate effectively with all levels of management.

Must have substantial experience and/or training in oral and written presentations and must demonstrate good writing skills.

Will prepare special analyses, research reports, and proposals.

Needs ability to compose effective correspondence.

Must have ability to communicate and "sell" ideas.

Must be able to cultivate and maintain good customer relationships.

Needs skills in gathering, analyzing, and interpreting data and in writing analytical reports.[3]

Job and career opportunities in which effective communication is the *main* responsibility are available in various areas, such as customer relations, labor relations, marketing, personnel, public relations, sales, teaching. Also, technical fields need editors, producers, researchers, and writers. Advancement can be made to management, research, training, and consulting positions. Furthermore, new job positions are being established in public offices. In demand are people who can work specifically on written communications and eliminate foggy "double-talk" from government reports.

Even if your work is mainly with figures, as in the accounting profession, the ability to communicate to those who read your financial reports is essential. The *Journal of Accountancy* emphasized to the profession the importance of writing, by an experiment cited in *Horizons for a Profession.* A group of accountants who were considered "the most knowledgeable and forward looking segment of the accounting profession" ranked 53 subjects that a beginning CPA should be familiar with. First place went undisputedly to written and oral English—even over accounting theory and practice.[4]

An Essential for Promotion

Subscribers to *Harvard Business Review* have affirmed that the prime requisite of a promotable executive is "ability to communicate." Notice that it is the top rung of the

---

[3] Francis W. Weeks, "Communication Competencies Listed in Job Descriptions," *The ABCA Bulletin*, September 1971, pp. 18–37, and December 1974, pp. 22–34.
[4] Betty Ann Stead, "Communication and the Accountant's Responsibility," *The Journal of Business Communication*, Spring 1977, p. 24; with citations from Editor's Notebook, "The CPA and the Second 'R,' " *The Journal of Accountancy*, November 1969, pp. 39–40, and Robert H. Roy and James H. MacNeill, *Horizons for a Profession.* New York: American Institute of Certified Public Accountants, Inc., 1967, pp. 14–15.

ladder in Figure 1-1.[5] Too often those who cannot communicate effectively remain buried in lower, dead-end jobs. Members of management spend about 90 percent of their working day communicating—receiving and sending messages.

[5] John Fielden, "What Do You Mean I Can't Write?" *Harvard Business Review,* May-June 1964, pp. 144–145. Figure 1-1 adapted from original article.

Figure 1-1   Requisites for a promotable executive.

During the past 30 years, many surveys and articles have confirmed the statement that effective communication is essential for success and promotion in business. They have included, altogether, responses from thousands of executives and university business graduates across the United States. In answer to the question, "What has been the most valuable subject you studied in college?" such titles as Business Communications, Business Letter and Report Writing, and Written and Oral Expression were always listed among the top three. Respondents—including top, middle, and operations managers—have repeatedly asserted that business communication skills significantly influenced their advancement to executive positions.[6]

As a trainee on a new job, you have opportunities to discuss problems with co-workers and to submit memos, reports, and letters that test your ability to communicate clearly and quickly. A frequent complaint of managers is the inability of college graduates to make themselves heard, read, or understood. Your messages can reveal how well you are doing your job, and they help management to evaluate your fitness for a substantial promotion. For example, imagine that you are one of several highly trained employees in an organization that requires everyone to submit frequent reports to clients or company personnel. If there is an opening for promotion and you each rate about the same except that you alone can write effective reports, then clearly you have the advantage over the others. One alumnus who had five promotions in five years emphasized that her success was based on her ability to prepare concise reports for senior management.

[6] The following is a representative list of references: William Arthur Allee, "A Study of the Graduates of the College of Commerce. State University of Iowa, 1921–1951," Ph.D. dissertation, Iowa City, 1951; James C. Bennett, "The Communication Needs of Business Executives," *The ABCA Journal of Business Communication,* Spring 1971, pp. 5–11; Garda W. Bowman, "What Helps or Harms Promotability," *Harvard Business Review,* Jan.-Feb. 1964; William P. Carr, "An Evaluation of Accounting Curriculum Subjects" (Loyola University of the South, New Orleans), *Collegiate News and Views,* October 1952, pp. 5–10; Homer Cox, "The Voices of Experience: The Business Communication Alumnus Reports," *The Journal of Business Communication,* Summer 1976, pp. 35–46; Samuel D. Deep, *Human Relations in Management,* Glencoe Publishing Co., Encino, Calif., 1978, Chapter 1; H. C. Edgeworth, "Business Communication and Colleges of Business," *The ABCA Bulletin,* September 1978, pp. 34–36; William Grogg, "The Importance of Business Writing to the Student—A Businessman's Viewpoint," *The ABCA Bulletin,* June 1972, pp. 1–5; J. M. Hunter, Anthony Koo, and R. F. Voertman, "What Happens to Our Economics Majors" (Michigan State University, East Lansing), *Collegiate News and Views,* March 1954, pp. 11–13; R. R. Kay, "To Manage You Must Communicate," *Iron Age,* July 15, 1965, p. 55; Raymond V. Lesikar, *A Summary of Needs of Education for Small Business Based on a 1959 Survey of Louisiana Businessmen,* Louisiana State University Press, Baton Rouge, 1959; Charles E. Peck, "Survey of Curriculum Opinions of Business Administration," *University of Washington Business Review,* Seattle, 1958; Bill Rainey, "Professors and Executives Appraise Business Communication Education," *The ABCA Journal of Business Communication,* Summer 1972; C. Wilson Randle, "How to Identify Promotable Executives," *Harvard Business Review,* May–June 1956, pp. 122–124; Rollin H. Simonds, "Skills Businessmen Use the Most," *Nation's Business,* November 1960; J. B. Steinbruegee, T. J. Hailstones, and E. E. Roberts, "Personnel Managers Evaluate a College Business Program" (Xavier University, Cincinnati), *Collegiate News and Views,* May 1955, pp. 7–11; Stella Travaek, *An Opinion Report of the College of Business Administration, The University of Texas, 1917–1954,* Bureau of Business Research, University of Texas, Austin, 1954; Clarence E. Vincent, "Personnel Executives Examine the College Graduate," *Collegiate News and Views,* March 1966, pp. 12–16.

Advantages in Your Personal Life

Effective communication also helps you to better accomplish certain aims as an individual in society. You will sometimes need to write letters and reports or to present your views orally as committee chairperson, club officer, or private citizen. In these various roles you might communicate with public officials, business firms, suppliers, or club members. Whatever your purposes, you will usually achieve them more effectively when you apply the same skills that help you communicate effectively in business.

Additional benefits that enthusiastic students of business communication have gained are better grades in some of their other business courses that require analytical problem solving and high-quality, well-organized reports.

VOLUME AND COST OF WRITTEN BUSINESS COMMUNICATION IN THE UNITED STATES

No one knows just how many billions of dollars United States industries spend on communications, but the amount is enormous. Thousands of hours are devoted daily to interviews, conferences, meetings, in addition to the time for planning and writing letters, memos, reports, employee manuals, advertising aids, news articles, and bulletins. The following discussion is intended to give merely an estimate of the volume and costs of *some* phases of *written* communications in American business.

According to Lou Kriloff, president of Letterpower Institute, if all the letters written in the United States in one day were laid end to end, they would circle the country nine times.[7]

The Postmaster General's office has reported that in a recent year Americans mailed about 96 billion pieces of mail; of these about 80 percent—76.8 billion pieces—were *business* mail.[8] Even if only one-third of these business messages were personally dictated and typewritten, that would mean 25.6 billion pieces during the year.

How much does an individually dictated and typewritten "average" business letter cost? According to The Dartnell Institute of Business Research, *average* costs for a face-to-face dictated letter climbed from 30 cents in 1930 to $2.54 in 1968 to $4.77 in 1978. (In contrast, the cost of an "average" letter transcribed from dictation equipment was $3.74 in 1978.)[9]

Some cost consultants have asserted—after considering stopwatch timings and misuse of expensive machines—that too many business and government letters cost as much as $15 to $20 each. These estimates include the expenses of:

[7] Lou Kriloff, statement in *The ABCA Bulletin,* September 1974, p. 21.
[8] Figures courtesy of C. Neil Benson, Acting Senior Assistant Postmaster General, Operations Group, United States Postal Service, Washington, D.C., January, 1979.
[9] The average length of the business letter in 1940 was "around 240 words; in 1977 it was 135 words." Figures courtesy of R. S. Minor, Public Relations Director, Institute of Business Research, The Dartnell Corporation, Chicago, January 1979, and *Target Survey*, published by the Institute in 1978.

Total time devoted to the message by the executive who composes and dictates it. (The executive's salary is the chief element in overall message cost.)

Total time of secretary, mail-room employees, and file clerks working on correspondence.

Inefficiencies necessitating revisions, lags, idleness of expensive equipment, use of higher-paid employees than desirable for routine tasks.

Fixed charges (heat, rent, light, depreciation).

Material costs (stationery, carbons, postage).

To get a conservative idea of the estimated total annual cost of individually dictated mailed business messages in the United States, we can multiply the 25.6 billion by the $4.77 average. The result is a staggering $122 billion in one year. (This amount increases every year as total volume and costs increase.)

These figures do not, of course, reveal the cost of *ineffective* letters—those that require additional messages of clarification or that lose a customer because of various faults. Why are faulty letters mailed? Usually it is because the writers do not know how to express themselves effectively; or they think they cannot afford the time to revise, and they hope their message will be acceptable. If executives find on their desks piles of mediocre letters written by their aides, they must decide whether to sign them or to scrawl comments in red ink and return the messages to those who drafted them. Rejecting letters sometimes wastes the efforts of five or six persons involved in writing them. The recipients will have to wait another week for replies. Delays cost companies money. So, more often than not, managers sign letters that are clumsy, imprecise, choked with jargon. Often these poor messages are, indirectly, more costly because they destroy goodwill, alienate customers, and decrease profits.

If the $122 billion business correspondence costs were decreased even 10 percent because of improvements in message preparation, American business could devote an estimated $12.2 billion annually to other productive services. The savings could benefit the companies, employees, customers, and perhaps the general public. Many firms and government offices that have communication improvement programs report significant savings. For example, Mutual of New York reported saving an estimated $85,000 a year for 10 years by reducing both the number and length of letters written. A federal commission report to Congress regarding paperwork stated that for every $1,000 the federal government spent on correspondence management, it saved $32,000 in net operating expense.

THE CHALLENGE OF COMMUNICATING FOR BUSINESS

Because communication plays such a major role in the operation of a firm and in possible promotion for the individual, communicating for business should be a challenge meriting your best efforts. Like any other worthwhile activity, the quality of communication is affected by the individual's attitude and preparation.

Developing the Right Attitude

The "personality" or image of your company is an extension of many individual personalities. You are one of these important personalities, whether you are an executive or a new clerk responsible for merely minor routine messages. With the right attitude, you—as well as other communicators—have opportunities to build goodwill and get favorable responses.

Help Your Company Image

Ask yourself if your company's image is a little better because of you. Some communications are so important to a firm that they can win thousands or even millions of dollars worth of business or goodwill. If you were working on such a message (for a letter, report, speech, or crucial interview), you would probably devote several hours—perhaps days or weeks—to your best thoughts, imagination, and planning. But what about the other messages—especially the minor, routine kind that you will be handling daily? They may not be individually worth a million dollars, but each is part of the life blood of your organization. Each is an opportunity to build goodwill. Furthermore, such messages might lead to major business transactions. Collectively, the effect of thousands of routine messages is far-reaching.

"To the customer, you are the company," is good advice that public relations officials often give to their employees. AT&T's board chairman forcefully expressed this view when he urged all the firm's employees to be responsive to their customers' needs and concerns:

> If you were to sit at my desk and read and answer the mail I get about telephone service, you'd come to realize, if you don't already, how much "little things" mean; how sometimes lifelong impressions of the character of our business are formed on the basis of a single contact with just one employee. Rather significant, I'd say, when you consider that the Bell System employs more than a million men and women. . . .
>
> The key element in all the letters . . . I get is how the customer was treated by an employee of the company. . . . Intermixed with complaints are a goodly number of commendation letters . . . about how an employee treated the customer in a manner so unusually satisfying that the customer felt compelled to write to me about it.[10]

Be Enthusiastic and Competent

Doing an honest job enthusiastically and competently helps both the doer and the receiver. Need routine messages be boring? The following examples from a correspondence consultant emphasize why writing for business should and can be a challenge:

---

[10] John D. deButts, "When We Tell Customers, 'We Hear You,' We'd Better Be Listening," *Bell Telephone Magazine,* September–October 1973.

Letter writing is a boring job. It's also exciting and invigorating. Sounds like a paradox, doesn't it? But that's just the way two correspondents described their work to us recently. Both of them write letters for the same department of an insurance company. Yet one found his job as dull as last week's newspaper, while the other thought it interesting and challenging. Why such contradictory reactions? Could the identical job be both dull and exciting at the same time? And why? We thought we knew the answer. But to prove it to ourselves and to the correspondents, we tried a little experiment.

We gave each writer the same letter to answer as an exercise. It was a case of a policy owner who had asked what to do about his lost insurance policy.

First, here's the response of the correspondent who said he was bored with his job:

```
Dear Sir:

With regard to lost policy #23456, we are enclosing a lost policy
form.  Kindly complete this form and send it to us as soon as
possible.

Upon receipt of the above requirement, this company will consider
the issuance of a replacement policy.

                    Very truly yours,
```

Now let's see what the other correspondent wrote:

```
Dear Mr. Robinson:

Your lost policy can be easily replaced.  Please don't let it worry
you.  I've enclosed a form that will help us replace it for you.

All you need do is fill in the requested information and send it back
to us.  We'll see that you get your policy within 3 days after this
form reaches us.

                    Sincerely yours,
```

The first writer let a routine situation lull him into a routine attitude which made his response mechanical and impersonal. He didn't realize it, but he was boring—himself and his readers—with his own routine-sounding messages.

The second correspondent, on the other hand, had a different outlook. He viewed the routine question as a challenge to make his answer less routine. After all, though lost policy cases were familiar to him, they certainly weren't to the reader. This approach gave him incentive to put more effort into his work. And he had the satisfaction of writing a message that was warm, personal, and not the least bit boring for either the reader or himself.

Moral? While some of the work in business correspondence may not be terribly exciting, it need never be boring. If you catch yourself writing stale, repetitive messages, it may mean that it's time to try a new—and in many cases a more personal—

approach. Like any other job, letter writing is only as interesting or as dull as the individual makes it.[11]

Preparing Adequately

Most individuals can learn to communicate effectively for business if they desire to do so and are willing to devote whatever effort is necessary to prepare themselves adequately.

In addition to the right goodwill-building attitude, it is desirable to have the following requisites:

Intelligence and sound judgment in the choice of ideas and facts

Good humor and understanding—even in dealing with the unjustly insulting person

Integrity, backed up by a sound code of ethics

Reasonable facility with the English language

The effective message for business pays off. If you thoroughly understand the basics of business communication and then diligently apply these basics with a liberal dose of common sense, you will continue to improve your ability to communicate effectively. With that goal in mind, you should find a challenge in every message you prepare.

In the following chapters you will study various typical business communication situations. Your communications will involve thinking, analyzing, solving problems, planning, and organizing messages according to acceptable contemporary procedures and central principles which are the basis for effective business communication. In so doing, you should gain a better understanding of people, learn how to win favorable responses from them, and make friends for your company. The background provided should give you the confidence to tackle almost any task you might face in writing letters, memos, or reports and in communicating orally.

---

[11] From *Effective Letters,* New York Life Insurance Company, November–December 1962.

The Process of Communication and Miscommunication

Communication is a process of transmitting a message so that the recipient understands it. The communication is considered effective when it achieves the desired reaction or response from the recipient. Simply stated, communication is a two-way process of exchanging ideas or information between human beings.

In actual practice, however, the communication process is not simple. Sometimes quite complex and imperfect, it malfunctions easily and may result in miscommunication. This chapter includes a brief overview of communication elements and basic general principles relative to communication and its problems. The information presented is adapted from various studies in such fields as psychology, sociology, semantics, communications, and human relations.

ELEMENTS OF COMMUNICATION

The process of communication consists of four elements or factors:

1. Sender—writer, speaker, encoder
2. Message
3. Medium—letter, memo, report, speech, chart, etc.
4. Receiver—reader, listener, perceiver, decoder

Role of Sender and Receiver

The interrelationship of message sender and receiver profoundly influences communication effectiveness, as shown later in this chapter and in subsequent chapters.

When you send a message, you are the writer or speaker, depending upon whether your communication is written or oral. You are likewise the "encoder"; you try to choose symbols—usually words that will correctly express the purpose of your message and get the desired response from the recipient. The words must be adapted to your receiver's vocabulary so that they are appropriately meaningful. In addition to using words (the verbal symbols), you may also communicate with nonverbal symbols, to a lesser extent. These symbols include facial expressions, handshakes, bodily movements, job status, appearance.

The receiver of your message is your reader or listener. In all cases the receiver is also the perceiver and "decoder." Your communication is not complete until you, the sender, get feedback from the receiver. If the receiver incorrectly perceives (decodes) your message, you have miscommunicated. The success or failure of your communication is measured by the feedback you get.

The Message and Medium

The message is a written or oral communication that expresses ideas the sender wishes to convey to the receiver. Both the content of the message and the medium (or form) used depend upon the interrelationship of sender and receiver.

When you communicate with persons *inside* your organization, the written media are usually memos or reports. To persons *outside* your organization—customers, prospective customers, suppliers, job applicants, and others—your written media may be letters, reports, telegrams, Mailgrams, cablegrams, radiograms, postcards.[1] Oral media to persons both inside and outside your firm include interviews, telephone conversations, speeches. You can also communicate visually by charts and pictures.

SOME GENERAL COMMUNICATION PRINCIPLES AND PROBLEMS

No two people in the world are alike mentally, physically, or emotionally. Thus the innumerable human differences plus cultural, social, and environmental differences may cause problems in conveying the intended messages.

Each person's mind is a unique filter. What is already in this mental filter affects the meanings a person places on messages and, to some extent, determines the new ideas the person chooses to accept or reject. Communication difficulties are more likely to occur when the communicators' filters are sharply different. The message sender's meanings and the receiver's response are affected in numerous ways. Among them are their:

Interpretations of words

Perceptions of reality

Attitudes, opinions, and emotions

The consequences of miscommunication may range from mild or humorous to extremely serious and costly, as revealed in the following examples and suggestions for improvement.

Interpretations of Words

A fundamental general communication principle is that the symbols the sender uses to communicate messages must have essentially the same meaning in both the sender's and the receiver's minds. If the symbols are misunderstood or misinterpreted, miscommunication results.

Another basic truth is that meanings are in people. The knowledge a person already has in mind regarding any given subject affects the meaning placed on words. Different word interpretations are often especially noticeable in "bypassed" instructions and in reactions to denotations, connotations, and euphemisms.

---

[1] Other media, outside the scope of this book, are: *internal*—employee manuals, bulletins, job descriptions, commendations, policy statements, company magazines, news sheets, posters, and notes in pay envelopes; *external*—brochures, advertisements, news releases, circulars, bulletins, sales presentations.

"Bypassed" Instructions

When the message sender and receiver attribute different meanings to the same words or use different words though intending the same meanings, bypassing often occurs. Many words have several dictionary definitions; a few have over 100. For example, in one abridged dictionary the little word *run* has 71 meanings as a verb, another 35 as a noun, and 4 more as an adjective. Moreover, for some words people have their own unique meanings which are not in a dictionary. Thus, confusion sometimes arises easily, as these incidents illustrate:

1. An office manager handed to a new assistant one letter with the instruction, "Take it to our stockroom and burn it." In the office manager's mind (and in the firm's jargon) the word "burn" meant to make a copy on a company machine which operated by a heat process. As the letter was extremely important, she wanted an extra copy. However, the puzzled new employee, afraid to ask questions, burned the letter with a lighted match and thus destroyed the only existing copy!
2. An equipment supervisor told a new night-duty employee, "You'll have to crack all the valves before you clean the settling tank." The next morning the supervisor found a floor full of smashed castings. "Crack" to the supervisor meant opening each valve just enough to allow minimum flow. You may be surprised that the supervisor was discharged because of the inadequate instructions that resulted in costly miscommunication.
3. A superintendent (Jane) said to Tim, a maintanance worker, "Plant 2 is having trouble with its automatic control. Whatever the trouble is, go out there and get rid of it." The next day, after receiving angry complaints from Plant 2, Jane berated Tim for yanking out completely and discarding the entire control unit and installing a new one, even though Plant 2 had purchased the original unit only five months before. The company had a new, rigid cost-cutting program with rules to repair, rather than replace, all salvageable equipment whenever possible. But Jane had failed to inform Tim of that rule. Thus Tim thought that because the control unit was causing the trouble, that's what he should "get rid of." Jane had wrongly assumed that her instructions were clear, but Tim's meaning was entirely different from Jane's.

Bypassing occurs not only in business and industrial offices but also among government officials, professionals, and all of us in our everyday contacts. To avoid communication errors of bypassing when you give instructions or discuss issues, be sure to ask yourself whether the words and sentence structure you are using will convey the intended meaning to the recipient. What that person thinks the message means is of crucial importance, regardless of what you think it should mean. Also, when you are the recipient of unclear instructions, before acting on them, ask questions to determine the sender's intended meaning.

Reactions to Denotations, Connotations, and Euphemisms

Almost everyone has at some time been surprised that a remark intended as a compliment, matter-of-fact statement, or joke was interpreted by the receiver as an insult. A statement intended as a good deed can be distorted into something evil or self-serving. Some of these communication problems may occur because words have both denotative and connotative meanings, and the sender has not been thoughtful of the receiver's probable interpretations and reactions.

Denotations. The denotative meaning is the literal word meaning on which most individuals will probably agree. It informs the receiver, and it names objects, people, or events without indicating positive or negative qualities. Such words as *car, desk, book, house, water* convey denotative meanings (provided, of course, the communicators understand the English language).

Connotations. In addition to the literal denotative meanings, connotations arouse qualitative judgments and personal reactions. The term *meeting room* is denotative. *Director's lounge, executive suite, rickety firetrap, rat-filled joint*—though they each denote a meeting place—also have connotative meanings. The word *student* is denotative; *book worm, scholar, dropout, school dummy* are connotative. They tell how the sender evaluates the subject. Some words—such as *efficient, gentle, prompt*—usually have only favorable connotations. Others—such as *lazy, cowardly, rotten, delinquent*—usually have only unfavorable connotations. Some words have favorable connotations in some contexts, but unfavorable meanings in other instances. Compare, for example, *fat check* and *fat girl; free enterprise* and *free* (rude, bold) *manners; sucker* (customer) and *sucker* (candy); *cheap product* and *cheap price.* In common usage, words which usually have opposite meanings can sometimes have the same meaning, as in the two expressions *slim chance* and *fat chance.*

The connotative meanings for words and labels are also affected by the communicators' different backgrounds and interests. Words such as *amnesty, unions, generation gap, speed, grass, hippies, gay, fair wages, women's liberation* may arouse mixed feelings and arguments, depending on people's associations with them.[2]

Euphemisms. Tactful writers and speakers use euphemisms whenever possible to replace words that might have blunt, painful, lowly, or distasteful connotations. Euphemisms are mild, innovative expressions with which most people do not have negative associations.

Expressions like the following have obvious connotative advantages: *maintenance worker* or *staff member* instead of *janitor; slender* instead of *skinny; Salisbury steak* or *hamburger* instead of *choice ground dead steer.* Instead of saying an employee was *fired* a communicator may use such euphemisms as *laid off, terminated,* or *victim of reorganization* or *staff cutbacks.*

[2] For additional examples of connotations, see also the discussion on "slanting" (page 21) and "sexist language" (83–88).

Euphemisms and any expressions that have pleasant associations for the recipients are especially helpful in advertising and selling. Usually, mass-produced consumer items—like soap, lotions, toothpaste, soft drinks—have similar functions and ingredients though made by different manufacturers. Advertisers then market their products by associating them with pleasant experiences the users will gain—popularity at social functions, physical attractiveness, enjoyment at sports events, etc. Advertising slogans or labels can help make or break a product's effectiveness. For example:

> One basically sound product—a vibrating mattress, which could have been a great help to sufferers of insomnia and industrial fatigue—failed mainly because the advertisements stressed, "Shake yourself to sleep." The connotation of the word *shake* was the deathblow to the marketing effort.

To communicate effectively you need to be aware of the usual connotative meanings of various terms and also to realize that some people may have their own unique meanings because of their experiences and background. Thus, choose your words carefully, considering both their connotations and their denotations to convey the idea you want and to achieve the desired results. Whenever possible, choose words with positive (favorable) rather than negative connotations.

Perceptions of Reality

The world of reality is complex, infinite, and continually changing. Also, human beings' sensory perceptions—touch, sight, hearing, smell, taste—are limited and each person's mental filter is unique. Therefore, people perceive reality in many different ways. Our statements about an object, event, or person are necessarily incomplete—and sometimes also inaccurate. We make various kinds of abstractions, inferences, and evaluations.

Abstracting

The process of focusing on some details and omitting others is *abstracting*. In countless instances, abstracting is necessary and desirable—for both written and oral communication. However, the alert, honest communicator should also be cautious about at least two semantic traps of abstracting—the "allness" fallacy and "slanted" statements.

Justifiable Abstracts. Whether you write a memo, letter, or report, or converse by telephone, you will be limited somewhat by time, expense, space, and/or purpose. You will need to select—honestly—facts that are pertinent to accomplish your purpose and to omit the rest (as you do, for example, in a one-page job application letter about yourself). Also, when preparing a business report you may—after gathering perhaps a "mountain" of data—have to abstract and condense it into a "molehill."[3]

The chapter you are now reading is also necessarily an abstract; it condenses into

---

[3] For illustrations of report abstracts, see pages 637 to 639.

these few pages some highlights of numerous studies relating to communication and miscommunication.[4]

You, as the communicator, must also anticipate the likelihood that others may not be abstracting as you are. Their points may be as important as yours though they select differently from the infinite details in reality. For example:

> When reporting on an event—a firm's new-store dedication ceremony, a factory explosion and fire, a football game, a traffic accident—no two witnesses give *exactly* the same descriptions. Their knowledge and backgrounds affect what they perceive. The participants will have a different view than the observers, and all those within each group will perceive different details or parts, though some parts of the whole may be mentioned by all or several observers.

Differences in abstracting occur not only when events are described but also when persons describe objects, animals, projects, people. No two people perceive reality exactly the same way or choose exactly the same points when they abstract.

"Allness" Fallacy. We should not yield to the *allness fallacy*—the attitude that what we know or say about something or someone is all there is to know or say. The more we delve into some subjects, the more we realize there is so much more to learn and to consider. Semanticists suggest that we at least mentally add "etc." to remind us that statements are incomplete and to keep from making incorrect, unfounded judgments.

Even authorities on certain subjects humbly admit they don't know all the answers. Though they sometimes disagree among themselves on various topics, they continue to study all available facts. So do conscientious, open-minded business executives, government leaders, educators, students.

Unfortunately, it is true of some people that "the less they know, the more sure they are that they know it all." Perhaps you have worked with such persons.

---

[4] If you wish to read more details about communication and human relations, semantics, processes of speaking, listening, writing, reading, or group dynamics, you might begin with the following books plus any bibliographies they contain: David K. Berlo, *The Process of Communication: An Introduction,* Holt, Rinehart and Winston, Inc., New York, 1960; Richard W. Budd and Brent D. Ruben, *Approaches to Human Communication,* Hayden Book Company, Inc., Rochelle Park, N.J., 1972; James H. Campbell and Hal W. Hepler, *Dimensions in Communication: Readings,* Wadsworth Publishing Company, Inc., Belmont, Calif., 1970; Stuart Chase, *Power of Words,* Harcourt, Brace and Company, New York, 1954; William V. Haney, *Communication and Organizational Behavior,* Richard D. Irwin, Inc., Homewood, Ill., 1973 (comprehensive bibliography pp. 529–570); Thomas A. Harris, *I'm OK – You're OK,* Avon Books, New York, 1973; S. I. Hayakawa, *Language in Thought and Action,* Harcourt, Brace and Company, New York, 1949; Richard C. Huseman, Cal M. Logue, and Dwight L. Freshley, *Readings in Interpersonal and Organizational Communication,* Holbrook Press, Inc., Boston, 1969; Wally D. Jacobson, *Power and Interpersonal Relations,* Wadsworth Publishing Company, Inc., Belmont, Calif., 1972; Alfred Korzybski, *Science and Sanity,* Institute of General Semantics, Lakeville, Conn., 1948; Irving J. Lee, *Handling Barriers in Communication,* Harper & Brothers, New York, 1957; Gail E. Myers and Michele T. Myers, *The Dynamics of Human Communication,* McGraw-Hill Book Company, New York, 1973; Bess Sondel, *The Humanity of Words: A Primer of Semantics,* The World Publishing Company, Inc., Cleveland, 1958.

A conspicuous example is that of the high school sophomore chatting casually with a man who (unknown to the student) was a distinguished scientist devoting his lifetime to studying botany. The smug sophomore commented, "Oh botany? I finished studying all about that stuff last semester." As Bertrand Russell stated, "One's certainty varies inversely with one's knowledge."

Another unfortunate tendency of some people is to identify a person or a group by the obvious, undesirable, or worst attribute. When a person sometimes drinks heavily, he or she is labeled a drinker—though that person may also be a helpful neighbor; kind, generous parent; neat gardener; dependable accountant. If a company has one executive who is convicted of fraud and extortion, that individual's misdeeds may harm the reputation of the entire firm though its other executives and thousands of employees may be honest and law-abiding. Likewise, one insulting letter writer may adversely affect the image of the company that person represents.

Thus, it is best for us all to try not to judge the whole by a part. Otherwise we will have an inadequate, erroneous impression of the whole, as did the six blind men who each felt only one part of an elephant. The one who felt only the swinging tail thought an elephant was like a rope. The others' ideas of an elephant—based on the part they felt (shown here in parentheses)—were: a spear (its tusk), a wall (its broad side), a snake (its trunk), a tree (its knee), a fan (its ear).

"Slanted" Statements. Conscientious communicators—as both senders and receivers of messages—should try to determine whether the facts they are acquainted with are truly representative of the whole. Are they slanted with intentional bias and opinion? Slanting is unfair in factual reporting. The reporter should be careful to include quoted statements in context and exclude connotative expressions of personal approval or disapproval of the persons, objects, or occurrences being described. For example:

> The reporter is not permitted to write: "A small crowd of suckers came to hear Superintendent Jones yesterday noon in that rundown hotel that disfigures the central area." Instead, the write-up may state: "Between 100 and 150 people heard an address yesterday noon by Superintendent Jones in the auditorium at the Edgemont Hotel on Center Street."

Likewise, the voting secretary who writes minutes of meetings must be careful to avoid slanted reporting. To omit some items merely because they may seem less important or are contrary to the secretary's personal biases is both unfair and inaccurate. He or she must not allow personal preferences to influence perception and reporting.

Inferring

Every day most of us find it necessary to act on some inferences. We make assumptions and draw conclusions even though we ourselves do not (or cannot) directly see, hear, feel, taste, smell, or otherwise immediately verify the evidence. Statements that go beyond the facts our senses report and conclusions made by reasoning from evidence or premises are called *inferences*. Some inferences are both necessary and desirable; others are risky, even dangerous.

Necessary, Desirable Inferences. For business and professional persons inferences are essential and desirable in analyzing materials, solving problems, and planning procedures. Systems analysts, marketing specialists, advertisers, architects, engineers, designers, and numerous others all must work on various premises and make inferences after they have gathered as much factual data as possible. Even our legal procedures allow inferences from experts as acceptable evidence. However, when nonexperts attempt to argue on professional matters about which they have no facts, they—deservedly—get into communication troubles. Also, as consumers in our daily activities, we may make inferences that are necessary and usually fairly reliable.

When we drop an airmail envelope into a mailbox, we infer it will be picked up, flown by plane(s), and ultimately delivered to our intended reader(s). We assume that the gas station attendant pumps gasoline (not water) into our car's tank, that the restaurant's kitchen is sufficiently sanitary (and free from poisons!), that the elevator in our building is capable of taking us to the desired floor, and so on.

When we base our inferences on direct observation or on reasonable evidence, they are likely to be quite dependable; but even so, there are disappointing exceptions. Conclusions we make about things we have not observed directly may be true or untrue.

Risks of Inferences. As intelligent communicators we must avoid faulty inferences. We must realize that inferences may be incorrect, unreliable, and the causes of miscommunication. We need to anticipate risks before acting on the bases of inferences.

Suppose that a personnel manager notices that Sue Jones, a new management trainee, has been staying at least an hour after closing time every evening for the past two weeks. He might infer that Ms. Jones is exceptionally conscientious, that she is incapable of doing the required work within the regular time, that she has been given more responsibility than should be expected of a new trainee, or even that she is snooping around for confidential materials after others have left the office. Before acting on any of these inferences, the manager should get more facts!

In some industries executives may make a disastrous decision that ultimately causes loss of lives as well as money if they assume wrongly that an inference in a report is a verifiable fact.

On any job you do—for an employer or others—be sure to consider the bases of inferences. Inform those who may be acting on your inference what portions of your statements are mere assumptions. If you are presenting or receiving a report on which an important executive decision may rest, be especially careful to distinguish clearly among verifiable facts, inferences based on facts, and mere "guesstimates."

Making Frozen Evaluations

Another drawback to effective communication is the *frozen evaluation*—the stereotyped, static impression that ignores significant differences or changes. Stereotyping is often based on faulty generalization. To help assure that your comprehension of reality will be correct, you need to recognize that any person, product, or event

May be quite different from others in the general group

May have significant differences today when compared with characteristics yesterday or some time ago

May deserve more than a two-valued description

Individual Differences within Groups. In reality no two elements of a general group or classification are exactly alike. When people ignore significant individual differences and consider all parts of a group to be the same, they have formed a frozen—stereotyped and unfair—evaluation. Customer 1 is not customer 632. Even manufactured assembly-line products differ under a microscope. Flashlight $\#F320_1$ is not exactly the same as $\#F320_2$ or $\#F320_{1020}$. Though you may have trouble with one F-brand flashlight, that does not necessarily mean all flashlights of that brand are also defective.

Often, people adhere to their faulty stereotypes and communicate them to others. You have probably heard statements that all politicians are undependable, auto dealers are high-pressured "gyps," students are slow-paying customers, redheads are hot-tempered, fat people are jovial, people with close-set eyes are stubborn, and so on. Such stereotyped generalizations—based merely on assumptions that all parts of a whole are alike—unjustly disregard important differences in individual characteristics.

Differences within Time Periods. Frozen evaluations are also made when people disregard the possible changes that may have occurred over a period of time. Everything and every person in the world changes. No one, no thing remains static; neither should our evaluations remain static.

Perhaps you've known a customer who asserts, "I'll never again buy any coat with the Realex label! The one I bought last year came apart at the seams." He or she should realize that (1) probably not all Realex coats last year ripped at the seams; Realex $coat_1$ is not exactly the same as Realex $coat_{10,500}$; also (2) Realex coats last year may not be the same as Realex coats this year or next year.

A customer's payment record this year is not necessarily exactly the same as last year. Nor can you be sure that a successful sales campaign this month will again be successful next month. Furthermore, though a certain area may have been ideal (or disappointing) for skiing the past several weeks, its weather may be quite different next week.

In all, we should remember to avoid frozen evaluations made on the basis of what was true at one time. Changes occur in products, people, laws, business conditions, organizations, environment, and so on.

Differences in Degree. The communication practice of making only a strict, two-valued, "either-or" evaluation may be a source of miscommunication. If communicators designate people, products, or statements as either good or bad, strong or weak, honest or dishonest, hard or soft, large or small, fast or slow, black or white, true or false, they may be *polarizing.* They are overlooking important areas in between the extremes. To be fair and accurate, communicators should be specific in each case, using details and figures whenever possible.[5]

In short, to be discerning communicators, we must consider significant differences for a unit of any group—and also changes in any one unit during a period of time. We must ask *which* person, *which* product, *which* event, *to what extent* and exactly *when* any particular statement is true. This caution is useful for all communicators. It is also especially applicable for report writers, who must be able to identify their sources, dates, and specific details of important facts.

Influence of Attitudes, Opinions, and Emotions

The effectiveness of communication may be strongly influenced also by the attitudes, opinions, and emotions the communicators already have in their mental filters.

Attitudes and Opinions

When the information we read or hear agrees with our views and attitudes, we tend to accept it and react favorably toward it. The accepted information fits comfortably in the filter of our mind. On the contrary, when the information disagrees with our views, habits, and attitudes—or appears to be disadvantageous to us—we tend to react negatively toward it and/or toward the informer.

Rejecting, distorting, and avoiding are three common undesirable, negative ways that a receiver reacts to unfavorable information. For example:

Suppose some employees perceive that a recently announced change in company policy is contrary to their beliefs or benefit. In reacting, they may reject or resent the company and/or their boss, perhaps falsely accusing them of being unfair. Or they may, instead, distort the meaning and misinterpret the true purpose of the policy change. Or they may avoid the message, situation, or people by putting off acceptance, hoping that the delay will somehow prevent the change and protect them.

[5] For examples of ways to be specific, see Concreteness in Chapter 3, pages 50–55, and in Chapter 15, pages 562–563.

Another significant truth is that people tend to react according to their attitude toward a set of facts, rather than to the facts themselves. For instance, a customer may be happy over an adjustment or a loan which a company extends, but angry when learning that a neighbor received a better deal for what the customer assumes (perhaps wrongly) to be the same circumstances.

An added problem occurs if the receiver has a suspicion about or a prejudice against the message sender. People tend to react more according to their attitude toward the *source* of facts than to the facts themselves. A staunch Democrat will be less likely to accept an idea from a Republican than the same idea from a fellow Democrat. A conservative executive may be less likely to accept statements from the "office grapevine" than from the department manager.

Stated positively, employees, customers, and people in general will react more favorably when a communicator has credibility—when they respect, trust, and believe in the communicator. Also, when an adult must present a disagreeable message to another adult, the recipient will usually be more open to suggestions and less defensive if the sender communicates on an adult-adult basis instead of like a critical parent to a child, for such communications often arouse negative responses.

If you can predict the probable attitude, opinion, or prejudice the receiver already has about a certain matter or person, you can better focus your communication in ways to reduce tension and resistance. Also, if you are the receiver, try not to let your personal, biased viewpoints affect your perception of a message. Observe, read, and listen to various sources, because useful information may come from almost anyone.

When both sender and recipient are open-minded, each may find areas in which the other person is right, so that a compromise can be reached. In the words of an old Indian prayer, "Let me not criticize my neighbor until I have walked a mile in his moccasins."

Emotions

Another influence on communication effectiveness is the emotional state of the communicator's mind at the time the message is sent or received. When personal or business upsets occur, people sometimes unjustly take out their problems on others.

Undesirable emotions—such as worry, anger, fear, despondency, hatred—even when due to circumstances entirely unrelated to the particular message, can adversely affect it. On a day when everything at home is wrong and disturbing, a person's written and oral communications at the office might sound unusually gruff, gloomy, or uncooperative. On the contrary, when everything is rosy in an individual's personal life, that person's business communications may also reflect this better emotional condition. In an emotionally charged situation, words must be chosen extremely carefully, for even one slip may trigger an emotional reaction and ruin the success of a message.

To be good communicators we must realize that people may react inconsistently when they are influenced by their emotions. We will have better communication when we catch people in the right frame of mind. Admittedly, it is often difficult or impossible to know just when is the best time. We need also to try not to allow our own personal emotions and sore spots to affect our messages.

The *closed-minded* emotional person is one of the most difficult persons to communicate with. This person seemingly has a closed mind on a certain subject, refusing to consider any new facts, no matter how objectively and tactfully the sender presents them. Typically, this person has only inadequate and mainly incorrect knowledge of the subject. Yet this type of individual vehemently rejects additional information, even from an expert who has made a long, careful study of the problem and the proposed change. The closed-minded person says in essence, "My mind is made up. Don't bother me with facts. I want what I want." Sometimes he or she goes a step further and—even before reading or hearing the documented facts—unjustly labels them or the sender's views as distorted, or calls the sender a liar. In all, closed-minded individuals stubbornly reject, distort, and/or avoid a viewpoint before they know the facts.

Unblocking the minds of such people in an attempt at effective communication is far from easy. They may be reluctant to make any changes, yet they will not state why. They may argue, wrongly, that because something was good last year, it will be all right this year; or because a store, procedure, or machine has been operating satisfactorily one way for x years, why change now?

Sometimes there is hope for better communication if these adamant persons can be encouraged to state their reasons for rejecting a concept. They may reveal deep-rooted prejudices, opinions, and/or emotions. However, if they react only with anger and refuse both to give reasons as well as to consider the other person's facts, effective communication will be impossible. To settle such a dispute, the intervention of a mediator or even a court of law may be necessary.

SUMMARY

Effective communication depends to a large extent on insights into human nature and on the ability to get desirable responses. For most people, effective communication does not come naturally. It is a skill, to be learned and practiced. This chapter has included merely an introduction to the complex process of communication. Its aim has been to give you helpful ideas of why communication problems can occur and how, in general, they may be decreased or avoided.

To be an effective communicator, realize that human beings' mental filters differ. Try always to consider differences in word (and sentence) interpretations, keep an open mind for getting as many accurate facts as possible about reality, admit there is always more that can be said, and allow for the influences of attitudes, opinions, and emotions. Above all, try to better understand the people with whom you communicate. This ability will be useful and developed further as you apply the principles in the remainder of this book.

EXERCISES

1. Review the factors of the communication process, and discuss where errors are likely to occur.

2. Select an object that you are familiar with; then look for characteristics you have not noticed in it before. How can you explain your discovery in terms of a communication principle?

3. Consider three of the following names: John, Eleanor, Barbara, Ronald, Jackie, Liz, Virginia, Mary, Jimmy, Walter. Prepare to share with the class your thoughts, opinions, experiences (and emotions, if any) about each. Using communication terms in this chapter, explain how and why details of your reactions are different from those of classmates.

4. The comment "Gerald Joiner is a member of five business clubs and two athletic clubs" may be intended as a compliment. Why might some listeners interpret it as derogatory?

5. Suppose you see Alice (the tenant who lives alone in an apartment directly above you) leaving at 8 p.m. from the front of the building. You have observed that she leaves at the same time each weekday evening. Last week she told you she is a doctor in a downtown hospital and her shift started at 8:30 p.m. Tonight at 8:55 p.m. you hear footsteps in the apartment above you. You might infer spontaneously that a burgler has entered. Will you call the police? the apartment house manager? the hospital? Discuss reasons why your inference may be right or wrong.

6. Describe the room in which your class meets. How does your description differ or agree with those of your classmates? Why might an electrical engineer, interior decorator, and a flooring salesperson select even more and different details than any of the students?

7. Give two examples of how the opinions and prejudices in your mind affect your communication.

8. Last Monday Jean Carlson, a clerk in the credit department, talked a few minutes to a company vice president in his office regarding a credit problem. Within three days, several secretaries in the company applied for a job in the vice president's office, because the grapevine rumor was that he was interviewing for a new secretary. The vice president was surprised, for he had no such intention.
   a. Explain how this miscommunication may have occurred.
   b. Can you share with the class another example of a faulty grapevine rumor within a company you are acquainted with?

9. Discuss: "Communicators with similar mental filters are more likely to communicate effectively." Why? Give examples from your own experiences.

10. Assume you are assistant sales manager for the Widget Company. One of your new sales representatives, a recent college graduate, won top place last year selling the most tickets to a special campus event. Now she wants to use the same tactics she used for that college campaign. You are skeptical. Who's right? Discuss the viewpoints as part of the communication process.

11. You are manager of a six-unit apartment house. The rental agreement for one-room studio apartments states they shall be occupied by one person only. One of your tenants—Tom—has no car, but his friend Mike drives a 1979 Rabbit. For the past two weeks you have seen this Rabbit parked in front of the building

every night; it is still there each morning until 8 a.m. Can you infer that Tom is breaking the rule about one-person occupancy? Explain why or why not.

12. Draw two rough outline "maps" (using an atlas if you prefer) of (a) the state in which you live, and (b) one of the other 52 states in the United States or of a foreign country. These outlines are symbols. Why does almost everyone know the meaning of your first map a, and few, if any, find that your second drawing b has any meaning for them? Explain in terms of the communication process.

13. A popular humorist and actor has stated that sometimes the same jokes which cause one audience to laugh spontaneously don't even get a chuckle another night in a different town. Discuss this comment in terms of a communication principle.

14. Yesterday you attended a banquet at which the speaker was a state senator. You liked what she said. In this morning's newspaper you read a quotation from her speech, and you consider it contrary to the main point the speaker was making. Explain the discrepancy in terms of topics discussed in this chapter.

15. On television this morning you and a friend heard a public officer confess that he had lied both under oath and in his recent popular book. Your friend commented: "You just can't believe what you read in books these days." Using communication principles, discuss the truth of this statement.

16. Discuss whether each of the following statements is an inference or a verifiable fact based on observation:
    a. The boss is a "swinger".
    b. Employees under 20 and over 65 are inefficient.
    c. The union requested double pay for each hour of overtime.
    d. The union requested too much money.
    e. XYZ skis are no good.

17. What general communication principles do the following statements and incidents illustrate? Discuss each briefly.
    a. A friend of yours states: "I'll never buy our groceries from Tiptop Market. Haven't been there since the first week after they opened four years ago. Their produce department is a mess and prices are too high."
    b. In a public utility, an order went out setting up a new procedure; on the basis of that order, five different powerhouses set up five different procedures.
    c. This comment made to each of two employees caused one to be pleased and the other hurt: "Your report is very good today . . . what there is of it."
    d. An article in tonight's newspaper states that a nationwide strike appears all but certain after union negotiators walked out of contract talks and accused management of forcing a strike. But the chief negotiator said he couldn't "conceive how anyone could say what we gave them was a provocation for a strike."

18. Suppose your boss asks you to revise parts of a 70-page report because of various minor errors and omissions in two sections. You and Harold Lazybones worked together on that report the past two weeks. Harold is on vacation now. The portions to which the boss refers were written entirely by Harold, although the boss doesn't know this. (Incidentally, Harold's salary is $100 a month more than

yours.) How will your reaction to the boss's request be influenced by your attitude toward the set of facts rather than to the request itself? Explain.

19. Discuss the advantages and risks of making inferences in business.

20. Bring to class a picture, cartoon, or an intricate gadget. Show it to your class for one minute (if possible, use an overhead projector); then hide your illustration. Ask three volunteers to leave the room. One at a time each will reenter the room and describe to the class what you displayed. Does any one student cover *all* the details? How many more can the rest of the class add to the three students' descriptions? Discuss reasons for differences in perception.

21. After three of your college friends returned from a football game (which your team lost, 28 to 31), you asked each individually for impressions about game highlights. Susan commented in detail on the excellent defensive work and on "your" team members who made the touchdowns. Ron stressed the fumbling, incomplete passes, the poor stadium seat he had, and the cold weather. Nick— whose favorite sport is *not* football—enjoyed seeing the "cute" costumes of the cheerleaders, their unusual baton twirling, the marching bands. Then Scott—who stayed home—boasted that he saw everything on TV. Did he really? How do these different "reports" relate to some concepts of the communication process?

22. Can you share with the class an example of (a) bypassed instructions, (b) a closed-minded person, or (c) judging the whole by a part? Discuss the causes and consequences.

chapter 3

Business Writing Principles I

30

To help you communicate effectively in your letters, memorandums, reports (and oral communication), you need to apply certain specific writing principles. They tie in closely with the basic concepts of the communication process. Commonly called "the seven C's," they are: completeness, conciseness, consideration, concreteness, clarity, courtesy, correctness. This chapter covers the first four C's and Chapter 4 discusses the remaining C's.

COMPLETENESS

Your business message is "complete" when it contains all facts the reader needs for the reaction you desire. To achieve both the specific purpose of your message *and* the long-term purpose—maintaining goodwill—you need to consider carefully just how much information is enough for each reader. Remember that communicators differ in their mental filters; they are influenced by their backgrounds, viewpoints, needs, attitudes, and emotions.

Completeness is necessary for several reasons. First, complete messages are more likely to bring the desired results without the expense of additional messages. Second, they can do a better job of building goodwill. (Incomplete messages can lead to ill will, lost customers, and hence decreased sales income and profit.) Third, complete messages can help avert costly lawsuits which may result if important information is missing. Finally, papers that seem inconsequential can be surprisingly important if the information they contain is complete and effective. In high-level conferences, in courtrooms, and in governmental hearings, the battle often centers around an ordinary-looking message that becomes important because of the complete information it contains.

As you strive for completeness, keep the following guidelines in mind:

1. Answer all questions asked.
2. Give something extra, when desirable.
3. Check for the five W's and any other essentials.

Answer All Questions Asked

Whenever you reply to an inquiry containing one or more questions, answer all questions—stated and implied. A prospective customer's reaction to an incomplete reply is likely to be unfavorable. The customer may think the respondent is careless or is purposely trying to conceal a weak spot. In general, "omissions cast suspicions," whether you are answering an inquiry about your product or recommending a former employee for a new job. If you have no information on a particular question, you must say so clearly, instead of omitting an answer. If you have unfavorable information in answer to one or more questions, handle your reply with both tact and honesty.

In the three situations described here, ineffective communication developed from messages in which the writers failed to answer all the questions.

Situation 1

A distributor of model trains, when replying to an inquirer's letter, answered only three out of seven questions. Because they were unnumbered and somewhat buried in five long paragraphs, the respondent apparently overlooked or disregarded four questions. The reply, which was both incomplete and unfriendly, caused the distributor to lose the business and goodwill of a potential customer.

Sometimes before you can answer an inquiry, you need certain specific information from the inquirer. Then it is a good idea to list the needed details on a reply form which the inquirer can fill out and return to you. In this way both your answer and that of your respondent will be complete. In situation 2 the eight messages about one transaction resulted in delay and annoyed, disappointed customers. Had the bank supplied a reply form, the desired sale could have been completed promptly with four messages: the first inquiry; the bank's reply with an enclosed form to be filled out; the owner's authorization (on the form); and the bank's final liquidation notice and check.

Situation 2

On August 8 the owner of mutual fund stock wrote to a New York bank's investment department that he wanted to sell his shares. He asked "Just how does your bank want me to authorize this sale?" and he received the following reply:

> If you wish to terminate Account #99998 and liquidate the shares held
> by this bank, we need a letter of instructions signed by both you and
> your wife just as the account is registered. Please be sure to give
> us the name of your fund, your account number, and to whom proceeds
> are to be mailed.

The customer's reply, signed by both himself and his wife, included the fund name, account number, and this statement:

> Please sell our 37 shares effective this date (August 23, 19_) and
> send proceeds to us.

On August 28 they received the following telegram:

> RE MLF FUND A/C 99998 UNABLE ACCEPT INSTRUCTIONS TO LIQUIDATE ON A
> SPECIFIC DATE FORWARD NEW SIGNED INSTRUCTIONS.

After asking for clarification from a local broker, the Browns wrote essentially the same letter as their second; however, this time they omitted the words "effective this date." A week later they received from the bank another request—this time to include in their reply both the name and address *to which the proceeds were to be mailed! (The bank had not asked* specifically *for the address, and the customers assumed the proceeds would be mailed to their home address.) The next day they wrote their fourth letter. Finally—on October 8, two months after their original question—the Browns received a formal notice of liquidation with an attached check for the proceeds. However, during the delay, the price of the stock had fallen considerably and they lost money on their sale.*

The replies in situations 1 and 2 were incomplete because the respondents omitted the answers to one or more questions or omitted important information in an explanation that answered a question. The next situation is an example of an incomplete response that *entirely* ignores the writer's real request. Be sure to avoid such gross carelessness in answering inquiries.

Situation 3

An insurance policyholder had read and studied her policy but could not understand the meaning of a particular paragraph. She inquired about its meaning and in doing so quoted the entire paragraph in her communication. In response to her letter she received one from the company, informing her that if she would refer to paragraph 4, page 3, of the policy (the one she quoted!), she would find a complete explanation. (The correspondent added that the paragraph was clear and unambiguous.)

Give Something Extra, When Desirable

In writing letters you must sometimes do more than answer the customer's specific questions. They may not know what they need, or their questions may be inadequate.

For example, suppose you are president of the regional business executive's league for your industry and receive the following inquiry from an out-of-town member:

```
I think I'd like to attend my first meeting of the League, even though
I'm not acquainted in your city.  Will you please tell me where the
next meeting will be held?
```

If you answered only this one question, your letter would be incomplete. Realizing that your reader is a newcomer to your city and to your league's meetings, you should include in your reply a welcome plus such needed details as directions for reaching the building; parking facilities; day, date, and time of meeting; and perhaps also the program for the next meeting. Your message will then have the "something extra" that a reader really needs and appreciates.

Sometimes the "something extra" is a detailed explanation instead of a mere brief statement. The last paragraph of letter 1, below, contains an invitation that is meaningless for any new depositor who does not know what "facilities" are at his or her disposal. Letter 2, on the contrary, clearly explains the services offered and thereby makes the invitation meaningful. (If a writer can enclose a descriptive brochure, the letter can be shorter and still complete if it merely mentions the services and refers to the enclosure for details.)

Letter 1

Incomplete letter to a new savings depositor.

Thank you for the confidence you have shown us by the account you recently opened.

All our facilities are at your disposal, and any time we can be of service please feel free to call upon us. Our appreciation is best expressed by our being of service to you.

Letter 2

Revised, complete letter to the new savings depositor.

Thank you for the confidence you have shown in First Federal by the savings account you recently opened. Our goal is to make all our services to you both pleasant and helpful.

Among the conveniences and services available to you at First Federal, you may be especially interested in these:

10-DAY GRACE PERIOD each month on your deposits means that your savings earn 5% interest from the 1st day of any month if they are deposited by the 10th day of that month.

SAVE-BY-MAIL POSTPAID SERVICE helps you to add to or withdraw from your account entirely by mail.

SPECIAL PURPOSE ACCOUNTS such as Christmas and Vacation Clubs enable you to save for a special purpose.

MORTGAGE LOANS help you to buy, build, or refinance a home or to borrow for property repairs and improvements.

FREE CUSTOMER PARKING is provided in the lot north of our office. The teller stamps your parking check, entitling you to free parking while doing business here. Office hours are 9:30 a.m. to 3:00 p.m. weekdays except for Friday, when the doors remain open until 6:00 p.m.

You are most welcome to come in whenever we can assist you. Please consider this association your financial headquarters for your savings and borrowing needs.

Check for the Five W's and Any Other Essentials

Another way to help make your writing complete is to answer, whenever desirable, the "five W" questions—*who, what, where, when, why*—and any other essentials, such as *how*.

This method is especially useful when you write requests, announcements, or other informative messages. For instance, to order (request) merchandise, make clear *what* you want, *when* you need it, to *whom* and *where* it is to be sent, and *how* payment will be made. To reserve a hotel banquet room, specify type of accommodations needed (*what*), location (*where*), sponsoring organization (*who*), date and time (*when*), function or event (*why*), and other necessary details (*how*).

For some letters—especially those that bring bad news, make an unusual request, or announce a special meeting—answering the question *why* may be important. Remember this general communication principle:

> A message that answers the question *why* is more likely to motivate the receiver to take the desired action than one that does not explain why. But not everyone is motivated for the same reasons.

When you must refuse customers' requests for a refund or ask them to pay a higher bill than they expected, they will probably be less angry if you explain *why,* from *their* viewpoint.

To sell a product by mail, you need also to answer these five W's and the H (*how*). The example below shows the embarrassment and needless expense that can result when an omitted essential fact makes the action request of a sales letter incomplete. In fact, in this case a costly sales campaign failed because of incompleteness.

The sales department of a retail company decided to sponsor a direct-mail campaign to 100,000 prospects. The sales letter was to be personalized with a typed inside address and personal salutation. A special price offer was to be good for a limited time only. The letter ended with this request:

```
So that you can enjoy the advantages of (product) at this special
price, send your order--but no money--today.  Just take these two
easy steps--

     Write your initials in the upper right-hand corner of this
     letter.

     Then mail it back to us in the addressed, stamped envelope
     that is enclosed.
```

However, to save the expense of having typists insert the 100,000 inside addresses and personal salutations, a budget-minded official requested that the entire message be printed and that all inside addresses be omitted. And the salutation was changed to the general, printed, "Dear Customer." The result was that the company received over 11,000 of the letters back, but no one had the slightest idea to whom the 11,000 initials in the upper right-hand corners belonged! Because all inside addresses had been omitted, the letters were incomplete for the action requested; they failed to answer the questions who *and* how.

An attempt to find out from whom the orders had come would have necessitated the expense of a second letter to the same 100,000 people and the embarrassment of admitting the serious slipup. Instead, the decision was made to abandon the entire campaign. No one knows the resulting disappointment and perhaps ill will caused among the 11,000 prospects who received neither a reply nor the product they had ordered. In addition, the company wasted the cost of the first 100,000 letters and lost the profits from 11,000 orders.

In summary, make your messages complete by answering all questions asked, giving something extra when desirable, and checking for the five W's and H as well as any other essentials.[1]

CONCISENESS

Many business executives believe that conciseness is the most important writing principle, because a wordy message requires more time (and money) to type and to read. Conciseness is saying what you have to say in the fewest possible words without sacrificing *completeness and courtesy.* Conciseness contributes to emphasis. By eliminating unnecessary words, you help make important ideas stand out.

To achieve conciseness—the opposite of wordiness—try to observe the following suggestions.

1. Omit trite expressions.
2. Avoid unnecessary repetition and wordy statements.
3. Include only relevant facts . . . with courtesy.
4. Organize effectively.

This section discusses the first three suggestions. Later chapters cover organization. (For check points on conciseness and for additional trite expressions see also Appendix B.)

Omit Trite Expressions

Trite expressions (also called hackneyed words, clichés, stereotyped expressions, deadwood, whiskered words) are usually longer than necessary and have become stiff, formal, and relatively meaningless because of overuse.

The left-hand column below lists some of the many clichés that should be avoided in business letters, memos, and reports; the expressions in the right-hand column are generally shorter and certainly more conversational.

Not this	*But this*
above-captioned loan	this loan; Mr. Smith's loan
advise (unless you mean "to counsel")	tell; inform
enclosed herewith	enclosed
enclosed please find	enclosed is

---

[1] To make your *action request* complete in various types of letters, try suggestions concerning the five W's and the H discussed under Closing Paragraphs, pages 108 to 109.

it has come to my attention	I have just learned; Mr. Jones has just told me
Our Miss Smith	Miss Smith, our credit manager
please be advised that	(4 wasted words)
please don't hesitate to call upon us	please write us
pursuant to your inquiry	as you requested
under separate cover	by June 1; tomorrow; separately; by parcel post; by Railway Express
the undersigned; the writer	I; me

A letter loaded with trite expressions can give the reader an unfavorable impression of the sender. Compare, for example, these sentences:

Trite:

In accordance with your request of recent date, we are enclosing herewith our cashier's check in the amount of $103.60, representing a withdrawal of said savings account #12345.

Improved:

It's a pleasure to fulfill your request of July 19 by enclosing our cashier's check for $103.60. This amount represents a withdrawal from your savings in account #12345.

Avoid Unnecessary Repetition and Wordy Statements

Unnecessary Repetition

Sometimes repetition is necessary for emphasis. But when the same thing is said two or three times without reason, the message becomes wordy and boring. The following letter from a business executive to a firm the company had dealt with for five years shows unnecessary repetition at its worst:

Will you ship us sometime, any time during the month of October, or even November if you are rushed, for November would suit us just as well, in fact a little bit better, 300 of the regular 3" by 15" blue felt armbands with white sewn letters in the center.

Thanking you to send these along to us by parcel post, and not express, as express is too stiff in price, when parcel post will be much cheaper, we are . . .

The writer took 81 words to say what is said in 25 below:

```
Please ship parcel post, before the end of November, 300 regular 3" by
15" blue felt armbands with white sewn letters in the center.
```

Here are three additional ways to eliminate unnecessary repetition:

1. Use a shorter name after you have mentioned the long one once: Instead of the "Inter-Allied Johnson Manufacturing Company," use "Johnson Company."
2. Use pronouns rather than repeating long names: Instead of "The East Coast Fire Insurance Company, Inc." again and again, use "it" or "they."
3. Omit unnecessary articles, relative pronouns, prepositions, and conjunctions.

Article:	`The evidence we have`	`Evidence we have`
Relative pronoun:	`He said that he agreed`	`He said he agreed`
Prepositional phrase:	`date of the policy`	`policy date`
Conjunction:	`and`	`Omit "and."  Use a semi-colon or a period.`

Wordy Statements

Some expressions and sentences are wordy *gobbledygook*, words that waste the reader's time. Notice how expressions in the following *Concise* column save words without changing meanings:

Wordy	*Concise*
`a long period of time`	`a long time`
`along the line of (salary)`	`about (salary)`
`at this time`	`now`
`consensus of opinion`	`consensus`
`due to the fact that`	`because`
`during the time that`	`while`
`during the year of 1981`	`during 1981`
`endorse on the back of this check`	`endorse this check`
`for a price of $200`	`for $200`
`for the purpose of`	`for; to`
`for the reason that`	`since; because`
`from the point of view of`	`as`
`have need for`	`need`
`in accordance with your request`	`as you requested`
`in due course`	`soon`
`in many cases`	`often; frequently`
`in most cases`	`usually`
`in order to`	`to`
`in some cases`	`sometimes`
`in spite of the fact`	`although`
`in (for) the amount of $200`	`for $200`
`in the city of Chicago`	`in Chicago`

```
in the event that                if
in the neighborhood of           about
in view of the fact that         because
under date of                    dated
```

Regarding sentences, note that in the following examples the concise sentence eliminates from half to two-thirds of the words in the lengthy sentence. (Figures in parentheses are the total words.)

Wordy: I am writing you at this time to enclose the postpaid appointment card for the purpose of arranging a convenient time when we might get together for a conference. (*29*)

Concise: Will you please return the enclosed card and name a convenient time for an interview? (*15*)

Wordy: The picture which is enclosed will give you an idea of the appearance of this home. (*16*) (*Whenever possible, talk in the present tense.*)

Concise: The enclosed picture illustrates this home. (*6*)

Wordy: We hereby wish to let you know that we fully appreciate the confidence you have reposed in us. (*18*)

Concise: We appreciate your confidence in us. (*6*)

Include Only Relevant Facts . . . with Courtesy

A third way to be concise is to include only those ideas that develop the purpose of the message. How long should a message be? Just long enough to do the job effectively. The relatively short letter about armbands was wordy, not concise. Yet a two- or three-page letter about a complicated situation may be concise—if it includes only relevant facts and omits the irrelevant. Furthermore, a short letter may be brief but not concise if it lacks completeness and courtesy.

Relevant and Irrelevant Facts

Given below are two extremes. The first example shows how writers can be so brief that they eliminate relevant facts. The second is an example of irrelevant comments and excessive wordiness.

Example 1

Once upon a time, a fish dealer was planning a new sign for his store. It was to read: Fresh Fish for Sale Here Today. *A critical friend, however, had some suggestions:*

"You don't need the word 'here,' " she said. "People can see where the store is. And you don't need 'for sale' either. They know you're not giving things away."

The friend continued: "And how about 'fresh fish' and 'today'? Do you want customers to think this is the only day you have fresh fish? That you sell old fish on other days? Take out 'fresh.' And while you're at it, take out 'today.' People know you wouldn't be open if you weren't selling something today.

"You might as well drop 'fish' too. Anyone within half a mile can smell what you're selling."[2]

The moral of our fish story? Write concisely but don't destroy your message.

Example 2

The following very wordy letter is from a person who graduated from a university the previous year, and has had difficulty since graduation in finding a satisfactory place in the business world. As you read this letter to the placement office in the school of business administration, try to figure out why he's having so much trouble.

The university Placement Office has sent me at periodic intervals a form inquiring as to my current employment status. As you may recall from our discussion last spring I was most desirous of making a favorable change in vocational locale. After following up several recommendations made by your office (Goodwin, etc.) I was unable to negotiate an immediate change, and upon receiving suave assurances of rapid promotion from my superiors promptly regressed into the torpid

[2] From *Effective Letters Bulletin,* New York Life Insurance Company, Spring 1967, p. 1.

complacency which characterized my thinking upon graduation. However my present intention to move is more than a harbinger of that most fragrant of seasons but rather stems from a feeling of disillusionment and inadequacy with my vocational environment.

May I once again prevail upon you to assist me in this undertaking by informing me at your convenience of any job opportunity for which you think I would be well suited. As indicated in my last reply to your office, I no longer look to accounting as my forte but instead am seeking a selling situation which is both challenging and remunerative.

Thank you for your patience and understanding in this matter. You may reach me at 555-1234 during the day or at 564-4321 in the evening.

Few employers would risk hiring this person because he might talk and write to customers in the same way he did in this letter. The reader or listener reacts negatively toward him because he uses pompous words and irrelevant material.

In contrast to this unfavorably pretentious message, the message can be informal and relevant if it reads as follows:

Will you please tell me about any sales opening which is both challenging and remunerative? I am no longer interested in an accounting job.

You can reach me at 555-1234 during the day or at 564-4321 in the evening. I will appreciate your suggestions.

The major causes of irrelevancy include:

1. Not sticking to the purpose of the message.
2. Including information obvious to the reader—such as regurgitating at length what the reader told you.
3. Using big words to make an impression.
4. Beating around the bush—not coming to the point.
5. Using excessive adjectives (good writing uses concrete nouns and verbs that show action, but avoids excessive numbers of adjectives and adverbs).
6. Being excessively polite.
7. Writing long, involved introductions.
8. Not limiting the scope of the material.
9. Including too much explanation.
10. Not revising the first draft of a long, complicated message.
11. Including unnecessary background information.

Brevity without Courtesy

It is false economy to write brief letters which omit words and sentences needed for completeness and courteous tone. Such messages are abrupt, not concise.

Abrupt letter

```
Have you emptied your safe deposit box?  If you have, sign the
enclosed cancellation form and return it with the keys to the box.

If you are using the box, send us your check for $6 to pay the rent
from September 15, 1980, to September 15, 1981.
```

Concise letter

```
This is just a reminder that the rent on your safe deposit box has
expired.

If you wish to use the box another year, please send in your check
for $6.  You'll then be paid up until September 15, 1981.  If you
have no further use for the box at this time, just sign and return
the enclosed form with the keys.

Whenever we can help you with any of our other customer services,
please let me know.
```

It is true that the concise letter just given requires more words than the brief, abrupt message. But the end result is what counts—how the reader reacts. A reader might respond to the first sentence of the abrupt letter mentally by saying it's none of your business, but would not respond that way to the other message. Also, the "please" in the revision helps the reader feel he or she is not being ordered to do something. Always remember the reader expects sufficient facts and courteous treatment.

In summary, conciseness is a writing principle that the business executive considers especially important. By avoiding trite expressions as well as unnecessary repetition and wordy statements, and including only relevant facts with courtesy, the concise message helps emphasize important points. Also, it saves time, which is—or should be— scarce to anyone who spends a large part of the workday dictating and reading letters. memos, and reports.

CONSIDERATION

As discussed in Chapter 2, the interrelationship of the message sender and receiver profoundly affects communication effectiveness. Consideration means that you prepare every message with the recipient in mind and try to put yourself in his or her place. Try to visualize your readers (or listeners)—with their desires, problems, circumstances, emotions, and probable reactions to your request. Then handle the matter from *their* point of view. This thoughtful consideration is also called "you-attitude," empathy, the human touch, and understanding of human nature. (It does *not* mean, however, that you should overlook the needs of your organization.)

In a broad but true sense, consideration underlies the other six C's of good business writing. You adapt your language and message content to your reader's needs when you make your message complete, concise, concrete, clear, courteous, and correct. However, in four specific ways you can indicate you are considerate of your reader:

1. Focus on "you" instead of "I" and "we."
2. Show reader benefit or interest in reader.
3. Emphasize positive, pleasant facts.
4. Apply integrity to your messages.

Focus on "You" instead of "I" and "We"

Your readers are usually more concerned about themselves than about you or the company you represent. They are more likely to read your message when they see their name and the pronoun "you" rather than "I, we, us." Remember, the word *b-u-s-i-n-e-s-s* contains both "u" and "i," but the "u" comes before the "i."

Usually it is desirable to get your reader into the first paragraph. (Exceptions are presented later in this section.) If psychologically desirable, begin with "you" or "your," and keep your reader in the message (tactfully) until you finish. The opposite of the you-attitude is the we-attitude, in which the writer views every matter from his or her own (or the organization's) standpoint rather than from the reader's:

We-attitude	*You-attitude*
I want to send my congratulations . . .	Congratulations to you on your . . .
We will ship your May 4 order today.	You should receive the Apex screen you ordered May 4 on or before May 9.
We have enclosed a reply envelope.	Just mail your check in the enclosed envelope.

The we-attitude department store letter, below (letter 1), contains 20 "we-our-us-I-my" pronouns (underlined) and only three "you's" (in italics).

Letter 1

We-attitude.

May I take this opportunity to express my thanks for the account *you* recently opened with our store. We are pleased to furnish a wide variety of products for the home or individual.

We want *you* to take full advantage of our store services, for we have the largest stock in the city. Also we make deliveries of our customers' purchases free of charge within 30 miles of our store.

We always like to receive visits from our customers, but we also fill orders by phone. Our customer service department aims to fill every order within the same day we receive it.

When shopping at our store downtown, customers are invited to use the free customer parking privilege provided just across the street from us.

We welcome *you* to Bekinson's. If we can be of additional service in any manner, please call on us.

In contrast, letter 2—rewritten for more you-attitude—contains 18 "you's" and "your's" (in italics) and only two "we-our-us" pronouns (underlined):

Letter 2

You-attitude.

Thank *you* for the account *you* recently opened at Bekinson's. Serving *you* with *your* needs for clothing and home furnishings is a pleasure.

You will find 32 departments at Bekinson's stocked with a variety of quality items. And courteous sales clerks are here to assist *you* in selecting the merchandise that best meets *your* requirements.

If *you* prefer to shop within the comfort of *your* home, instead of coming to the store, *you* need only to telephone 882-5555 and ask for "Personal Shopping Service." A Personal Shopper will gladly take *your* order for any number of items, answer *your* questions about brands and sizes available, and see that the goods *you* order reach *you* by store delivery within a few days.

When *you* shop at *our* store downtown, *you* are invited to use the free customer parking privilege provided just across the street.

You are always welcome at Bekinson's. Please call on *us* whenever *you* need additional service.

As the foregoing examples illustrate, a letter is likely to have better you-attitude when it contains more "you's" than "I's." But there are notable exceptions! An extreme example is the collection letter with "you" or "your" in almost every sentence; yet if those sentences are insulting, sarcastic, tactless, or untrue accusations and threats against the debtor, the letter surely lacks you-attitude.[3]

In two kinds of situations it is advisable not to use "you."

1. When the reader has made a mistake:

---

[3] See also discussion under Courtesy, Chapter 4.

Poor:	You failed to enclose your check in the envelope.
Better:	The envelope we received did not have your check in it.

Poor:	Your contract tells you plainly that . . .
Better:	I am glad to explain more fully about the contract terms.

2. When the reader has expressed an opinion different from your own:

Poor:	You are entirely wrong in your attitude.
Better:	The proposed plan has three aspects which are extremely important and which we need to explain now.

Show Reader Benefit or Interest in Reader

Whenever possible and true, show how your readers will benefit from whatever the message asks or announces. They will be more likely to react favorably and do what you suggest if you show that benefits are worth the effort and cost. In situations where actual direct reader benefit is impossible or irrelevant to the subject matter, the message should at least show interest in and concern for the reader's needs or viewpoint.

Even a simple request gets better response when a reader-benefit plug accompanies it. For example, an insurance company that wanted to update its address files sent to one-half of its policyholders a double postcard with this message:

> Since we haven't written you in some time, please help us bring our records up to date by filling in and returning the other half of this card.

Only 3 percent of these cards came back. To the remaining half of its policyholders the firm sent the same request—reworded to show reader benefit:

> So that dividend checks, premium notices, and other messages of importance may reach you promptly, please fill out and return the other half of this card.

This request brought 90 percent of the cards back in a few days!

Merely inserting the word *you* does not ensure you-attitude, as shown in this sentence:

> You will be glad to know that we now have a Walk-Up Window open 7-9 a.m. and 3-8 p.m. every weekday.

The reader may wonder, "So what?" The revised sentence includes reader benefit:

You can now take care of your banking needs also at our new Walk-Up
Window, open to serve you 7-9 a.m. and 3-8 p.m. Monday through Friday.

Reader-benefit appeals help collect payments on bills, soften the blow in a turndown, and sell products. Though your company is in business to make a profit, you omit that selfish-sounding idea; the reader assumes it anyway and is motivated only by what benefits he or she receives. Reader-benefit appeals are desirable also in job applications, favor requests, and announcements to your customers, prospective buyers, stockholders, and employees. Whether you are writing to one person or to large numbers, try to personalize the reader benefits (as in Letter 2) instead of stating them in a general way ("our customers," as in Letter 1).

If your organization provides employee benefits—such as health insurance and various retirement plans—management should make every effort to assure that all employees understand and appreciate those benefits. Many may be unaware that their employer spends more than one-third of the total payroll on employee benefits. To inform employees effectively, management can use such media as memos, employee manuals, bulletins, policy statements, company magazines, news sheets, reports, posters, films, and notes in pay envelopes.

Emphasize the Positive, Pleasant Facts

A third way to show consideration for your reader (or listener) is to accent the positive. This means (1) stressing what *can* be done instead of what cannot be done and (2) focusing on ideas your reader can view favorably.

Statement of What Can Be Done

The reader wants to know what you *can* do for him or her. For most people negative words like *no, won't, cannot, never, impossible* trigger unpleasant emotional reactions. By making clear what you *can* or *will do,* you (by implication) often make clear what you *cannot do,* without using a single negative word. Furthermore, whenever possible and helpful, tell the recipient why or how.

Negative—Unpleasant	*Positive—Pleasant*
It is <u>impossible to open</u> an account for you today.	As soon as your signature card reaches us, we <u>will gladly open</u> an . . .
We <u>don't refund</u> if the returned item is <u>soiled and unsalable</u>.	We <u>refund</u> when the returned item is <u>clean and resalable</u>.
When you travel on company expense, you will <u>not receive</u> approval for <u>first-class</u> fare.	When you travel on company expense, your <u>approved fare</u> is for <u>tourist</u> class.
To <u>avoid</u> further <u>delay</u> and <u>inconvenience</u>, we are sending this report by special delivery.	So that you will <u>get</u> this report <u>as soon as possible</u>, we are sending it special delivery.

Ideas Your Reader May View Unfavorably

When a customer closes an account, try to begin your follow-up letter to the former customer with a favorable, positive paragraph. A negative opening emphasizes ideas you'd rather not have the reader think about. For example:

```
We regret that, since you closed your account, your name will be
missing from our long list of satisfied customers.  We sincerely
hope that, despite the best efforts of our fine staff, there was no
occasion on which you felt we failed to serve you properly.
```

A better opening would show appreciation for the customer's patronage and welcome him or her to other services, as in these two paragraphs:

```
It was a pleasure to have had you as a member of Federal Savings.
Thank you for giving us the opportunity to serve you.
```

```
We noticed recently that you closed your account with us.  Perhaps you
reached that particular goal for which you were saving, or it may be
that an emergency arose which called for a large outlay of cash.  What-
ever the reason, we are happy to have played some small part in your
financial program.  You are cordially invited to use our other profit-
able, timesaving services as occasion may require.
```

Avoid words like *hope, trust, if*—whenever they are likely to give readers unfavorable ideas or cause them to doubt your confidence. The following lists indicate how these words can be changed to emphasize positive, favorable ideas:

Unfavorable Connotation (negative)	*Favorable Idea (positive)*
If we can help, don't hesitate . . .	Please call on us when we can help.
I trust (hope) this is the information you wanted.	We're glad to give you this information; or: Should you need additional facts, please telephone me at . . .
Thank you for your trouble.	Thank you for your help.

Apply Integrity to Your Messages

To be truly considerate, you need also to apply integrity—high moral standards, personal honor, truthfulness, sincerity—to your messages. In our day-to-day living, in our jobs, in business transactions, in everything we do, integrity is indispensable. Without it, business communications would prove worthless and our confidence in people would be shattered.

Leadership demands integrity, be it leadership of a social or political group, a business, an athletic team, or a charitable bazaar. The leader's ethical standards, naturally, reflect on the organization he or she represents.

Because you are an agent of your company, always remember that your messages help build your company's image. And to make this image one of integrity requires consistently fair treatment of customers and emphasis on basic honesty instead of insincerity and bluffing.

Consistently Fair Treatment

As preceding sections indicate, when you show concern for your readers, you try to let them know you are aware of and are doing something about their interests. This does *not* mean, however, that you yield to the temptation of showing favoritism, allowing deviations for one customer that you would not allow for all other customers in similar circumstances, or arranging money kickbacks and bribes to obtain government or commercial business. Particularly troublesome (and tempting) are the demanding customers who threaten to withdraw their large-volume business unless they get special privileges which they know are against company policy and not granted to your other customers. If they insist that "everyone else does it," the temptation to comply with their wishes may be difficult. Nevertheless, widespread existence of evil does not make evil right.

High ethical standards are the basis of consistent, fair treatment and consideration for everyone. They may require "doing the harder right instead of the easier wrong." A paragraph from *Fortune* magazine published long ago is still completely true and applicable today.

> Language is not something we can disembody; it is an ethical as well as mechanical matter, inextricably bound up in ourselves, our positions, and our relations with those about us. When a businessman doubletalks, for example, it is often for reasons deeper than mishandled prose—hypersensitivity to criticism, fear of the competition, fear of getting out of line with trade-association policy, fear of a government suit, a serious split in the corporation policy—or . . . lack of any policy.[4]

How do unfair and unethical practices affect you and all other business communicators? Pertinent suggestions are in the following excerpts from "Corporate Morality and the Crisis of Confidence in American Business" by Phillip I. Blumberg:

> Corrupt practices corrupt personnel, impair the integrity of the corporation, challenge the corporate chain of command, and threaten the free-market system itself. . . . Corporations should establish internal codes of honest conduct for the guidance of company personnel and internal procedures for their effective enforcement. It should be made plain by the board and by management that economic results will not excuse violations of the code. . . .
>
> In the end, the problem comes down to individuals and their personal sense of

---

[4] "The Language of Business," courtesy of *Fortune,* November 1950, p. 138.

morality. . . . All acts are those of individuals, although they may be acting in the name of, and on behalf of, corporations. As individuals, they are subject to the inescapable imperative of morality. . . . There is no obligation to shareholders that requires management to steal or bribe for them. . . .

Further, we must recognize that unless this moral imperative is generally accepted by business leaders, business will inevitably suffer further decline in the confidence of the public and that its survival in its present form will become increasingly unlikely. Honesty is not merely the best policy. It is the *only* policy.[5]

Honesty instead of Insincerity and Bluffing

Is business bluffing ethical? This question has been widely discussed because reputable business managers feel strongly on the subject of ethics. They realize too that many times there are gray areas involving fine decisions between what is the complete truth and a partial falsehood. An honest business writer needs a strong conscience as well as knowledge of writing principles and company policies.

The old values of honesty, sincerity and trust, sometimes dismissed as Sunday school sentimentality, are actually Monday morning business realism in the quest for better communications. They create the climate in which communications grow. Where they do not exist, communications will be faulty, no matter how they are fertilized with methods and techniques. A man's character seems to have more influence than his personality in improving communications.[6]

In the long run the ethical way is also the most effective way. Buyers have the right to expect that clothing, food, equipment, and services will be as represented by advertising, the seller's agents, and/or in the sales letter they received. Insincere, misleading, exaggerated, or otherwise dishonest statements do not belong in a high-quality business message. For example, though the following sentence sounds "you" centered, was the manager who wrote it honest or insincere? His action is stated in parentheses.

"Your request will be given our careful attention, and we assure you our objective is to be fair." (This writer merely threw the case into a file folder, and told his secretary he had no intention of working on it or assigning anyone else to do so. He hoped that after a long wait the customer would forget.)

A sentence like the following, adapted from a sales message, is misleading and exaggerated: "Nationwide, three out of four people prefer this amazing new XYZ widget." (Actually, the product was *not* nationally known, and only three persons in each of four states were surveyed!)

[5] Phillip I. Blumberg, Dean of the School of Law and Professor of Law and Business at University of Connecticut, from his *Invited Essay to Beta Gamma Sigma*, "Corporate Morality and the Crisis of Confidence in American Business," January 1977. Beta Gamma Sigma, national scholastic honorary for students pursuing degrees in business and management, has endeavored to foster integrity in business practice since its founding in 1913.

[6] A. W. Lindh, "Plain Talk about Communicating in Business," courtesy of *Business Management*, April 1964; copyrighted by CCM Professional Magazines, Inc.

For the many business problems that involve delicate bad-news decisions, honest communicators need not choose between two evils—the white lie (outright untruth, but "harmless") and the blunt, crushing turndown. They can effectively avoid these negative alternatives by tactfully focusing on the morally positive goal of the message—to serve the customer well and also protect company profits.

Consideration involves the golden rule—showing to others the same fairness and honesty we expect for ourselves. Remember, both your own integrity and that of your company are revealed in the business messages you write.

In summary, consideration means you are genuinely thoughtful of your message recipients and consider their probable reactions to your messages. You can indicate you-attitude by focusing on "you," the reader; by showing reader benefit or interest in the reader; by emphasizing positive, pleasant facts; and by applying integrity—with consistently fair treatment, honesty, and sincerity.

CONCRETENESS

Writing concretely means being specific, definite, and vivid rather than vague and general. The following guidelines should help you write concretely:

1. Use specific facts and figures.
2. Put action in your verbs.
3. Choose vivid, image-building words.

Use Specific Facts and Figures

Whenever you can substitute an exact fact or a figure for a general word to make your message more concrete and convincing, do so.

Vague, general, indefinite	*Concrete and convincing*
These <u>brakes</u> stop <u>a car</u> within a <u>short</u> distance.	These <u>Goodson power brakes</u> stop a <u>2-ton car</u> traveling <u>60 miles an hour</u>, within <u>240 feet</u>.
Please send your check for the <u>full amount soon</u>.	Please send your check for <u>$753.50 on or before June 5</u>.
A <u>quick</u> shave.	A <u>three-minute</u> shave.
Our product has won <u>several</u> prizes.	(Name) product has won <u>first prize</u> in <u>four national contests within the past three years</u>.
Your savings earn <u>high compound</u> interest.	Your savings earn <u>5 percent</u> compound interest (<u>added to your account every three months</u>).
After traveling an <u>enormous distance</u>, the lunar module landed <u>almost on time</u>.	After traveling <u>240,000 miles</u> and circling the moon <u>18 times</u>, the lunar module landed <u>within 1 minute 17 seconds</u> from the pre-planned time.

This computer reproduces sales campaign letters fast.	This computer types 1,000 personalized 150-word campaign letters in one hour.

Often vague, general words are *opinion words;* they may have different meanings to the sender and the receiver. For instance, how fast is fast? A bicycle rider and a racing-car driver will have different meanings for this word. How large is large? A person reared in a village of 150 people may consider a population of 15,000 large; yet to a native of a city with 10 million inhabitants, 15,000 is very small. The list that follows gives words which can lead to uncertainty, misunderstanding, or confusion.

a few	low	most	several	small
high	many	nice	short	soon
large	more	quick	slow	tall

Using plenty of examples, prefixed by phrases like "for instance," "for example," "such as," also helps make your writing concrete as well as clear. (You will notice that this book uses this technique often.)

In certain cases it is, of course, permissible—and even desirable—to use general expressions. *Exceptions* to the "facts and figures" rule occur:

1. When it is not possible to be specific, for you may not have nor be able to get definite facts or figures.
2. When you want to be diplomatic. Thus, instead of writing, "We have sent you *five* notices of your overdue payment," you may be more tactful (to a usually prompt paying customer) by writing, "We have sent you *several* reminders of this. . . ." Also, when refusing credit to a potential consumer, you may feel it is more diplomatic to give a general rather than a specific reason.
3. When you want to allow the reader to form his or her own opinion, or when exact figures are unimportant, as in: "A *few* (or *many*) of our employees attended the parade."

Put Action in Your Verbs

Strong verbs can activate other words and help make your sentences definite. To write strong sentences, you should (1) use active rather than passive verbs and (2) put action in your verbs instead of in nouns or infinitives.

Active versus Passive Voice

When the subject *performs* the action which the verb expresses, the verb is said to be in the *active* voice. In "Mr. Jones *repaired* the computer," the subject (Mr. Jones) did the repairing; the verb *repaired* is active.

When the subject benefits from or otherwise *receives* the action the verb expresses, the verb is said to be in the *passive* voice. In "The computer *was repaired* by Mr. Jones," the verb *was repaired* is passive.

A passive verb has three characteristics: (1) The subject doesn't do the acting; (2) the verb consists of *two or more* words, one of which is some form of "to be" (is, is being, am, are was, were, will be, has or have been, had been, or will have been); and (3) the word *by* is expressed or implied ("by whom" or "by what"). The examples below show the difference between passive and active voice.

Passive (Subject receives the action)	*Active (Subject performs the action)*
Tests <u>were made</u> by us.	We <u>made</u> tests. Tests <u>showed</u> that . . .
A full report <u>will be sent</u> to you by the supervisor.	You <u>will receive</u> a full report from the supervisor. The super-visor <u>will send</u> . . .
It <u>is contemplated</u> by the com-mittee . . .	The committee <u>thinks</u> . . .
Your figures <u>are checked</u> by the research department.	The research department <u>checks</u> your figures.

Generally you should use active rather than passive verbs, because active verbs help make your sentences more:

1. *Specific.* "The board of directors decided" is more explicit than "A decision has been made."
2. *Personal.* "You will note" is both personal and specific; "It will be noted" is impersonal.
3. *Concise.* The passive requires more words and thus slows both the writing and reading. Compare "Figures show" with "It is shown by figures."
4. *Emphatic.* Passive verbs dull action. Compare "The child ran a mile" with "A mile was run by the child."

Occasionally, however, you may prefer the passive voice instead of the active, as in the following situations:

1. When you want to avoid personal, blunt accusations or commands. "The July check was not included" is more tactful than "You failed to include. . . ." "Attendance at the meeting is required" is less harsh than "You must attend. . . ."
2. When you want to stress the object of the action. In "Your savings account is insured up to $40,000," you have intentionally stressed "your account"—not the firm that does the insuring. Also, "You are invited" is better than "We invite you."
3. When the doer isn't important in the sentence. In "Three announcements were made before the meeting started," the emphasis is on the announcements, not on who gave them.

Action in Verbs, Not in Nouns

Seven verbs—*be, give, have, hold, make, put,* and *take* (in any tense) might be designated as "deadly" because the action they introduce is hidden in a "quiet noun." The examples below show how these "deadly" verbs can be changed to action verbs which shorten the sentences.

Action hiding in a "quiet noun"	*Action in the verb*
The function of this office <u>is</u> <u>the collection</u> of accounts and the <u>compilation</u> of statements.	This office <u>collects</u> accounts and <u>compiles</u> statements.
Mr. Jones will <u>give considera-</u><u>tion</u> to the report.	Mr. Jones will <u>consider</u> the report.
The contract <u>has a requirement</u> that . . .	The contract <u>requires</u> that . . .
They <u>held</u> the <u>meeting</u> in the office.	They <u>met</u> in the office.
He <u>made</u> his first installment <u>payment</u>.	He <u>paid</u> his first installment.
The chairperson <u>puts</u> her <u>trust</u> in each committee member.	The chairperson <u>trusts</u> each committee member.
We will <u>take a look</u> at your record.	We will <u>look</u> at your record.

Action in Verbs, Not in Infinitives

Action can also be concealed by infinitives. Notice, in the following example, that both main verbs in the left-hand sentence follow "is" (or some form of "to be") plus the preposition "to," and they don't convey much action.

Action hiding in infinitive	*Action in the verb*
The duty of a stenographer is <u>to check</u> all incoming mail and <u>to record</u> it. In addition, it is his or her responsibility <u>to keep</u> the assignment book up to date.	A stenographer <u>checks</u> and <u>records</u> all incoming mail and <u>keeps</u> the assignment book up to date.

Choose Vivid, Image-building Words

Among the devices you can use to make your messages forceful, vivid, and specific are comparisons, figurative language, concrete instead of abstract nouns, and well-chosen adjectives and adverbs.

Comparisons

Sometimes adding a comparison helps your reader to build a meaningful picture. Consider the vague "sense" images you get from the sentences in the left-hand column below as contrasted with the vivid impressions gained from those at the right.

Abstract	*Vivid*
There are a great many solder joints in the spacecraft, and each must have just the right amount of solder.	The spacecraft has 2½ million solder joints. If an extra drop of solder had been left on these joints, the excess weight would have been equivalent to the pay-load of the vehicle.
This is pure clover honey, made by honeybees.	Honeybees have gathered nectar from approximately 4½ million clusters of clover and traveled about 150,000 miles--or equal to six times around the world--to deliver this package of Bradshaw honey to you.

Figurative Language

Figures of speech often express an idea more vividly than literal language.

Literal (and dull)	*Figurative*
She is usually the one who gets things started in the organiza-tion.	Jean Jones is the spark plug of the organization.
X product helps you lose your double chin in four weeks, if you use X as directed.	If two chins quarrel constantly for a place on your collar, X product helps settle the argu-ment. Only one chin remains after you use X just four weeks as directed.

In employing figurative language, however, beware of mixed and inconsistent fig-ures of speech, for they may confuse the reader, or seem foolish and corny:

At the meeting our president's remarks hit the bull's eye right on the nose.

You deserve a nice bow for sticking to your guns right down the line.

You must also be careful not to use figurative speech which can be interpreted literally or negatively or which sounds inappropriate:

As you enter our new lobby, your eye will first be struck by the bright stainless steel lighting fixtures. (*Does this make you think, "Ouch"? Better: Your eyes will first* notice. . . .)

Good roasts are tough to get, but we have them.

If you want new dollar bills for Christmas gifts, come to us. We have as many as a dog has fleas.

Concrete instead of Abstract Nouns

Still another way to enliven your writing is to use concrete nouns instead of abstract nouns, especially as subjects of your sentences. Concrete nouns represent subjects your reader can touch, see, smell, feel, hear, or taste. Abstract nouns as subjects bring only vague, if any, "pictures" to a reader's mind.

Abstract	*Concrete*
Consideration was given to the fact that. . . .	The committee considered. . . .
Termination of the insurance contract will be in June.	The insurance contract ends in June.
Analysis of the situation suggests that Mr. Smith is right.	I think Mr. Smith is right.

Be exact in your titles, subjects, and references. Don't force your reader to guess. One more caution: If you are referring to an inanimate object, avoid using the neutral word *thing* whenever possible. Use a more specific word that is related to the "thing"—such as event, element, fact, idea, condition, method, plan, purpose, principle.

Adjectives and Adverbs

You can often build a more realistic and interesting word picture by adding well-chosen adjectives and adverbs. In the list below, adjectives are underlined; adverbs, in capitals.

Colorless	*Realistic, vivid, interesting*
The camera has a system that gives you good pictures.	The Poney camera has an UNCANNILY precise metering system that assures you PROPERLY exposed, true-color pictures.
This cookware is guaranteed to withstand changes in temperature.	Because Creston cookware can withstand extreme changes in heat and cold, the guarantee assures you that you can SAFELY move any piece from your freezer to your microwave oven.

In your search for vivid, picture-building words, be careful not to go to extremes with adjectives or with superlatives such as "the most," "the largest," "the greatest," and "the best."

Good concrete writing includes specific facts and figures; action verbs; and forceful, interesting, vivid, image-building words.

EXERCISES

1. Discuss orally what is needed to make each of the following postcard requests complete. (Some lack other C qualities in addition to completeness.)

   a. The red coat you had in your window last Thursday is exactly the style I would like to have. Please send it to me on my charge account.

   b. I am interested in the portable TV you advertised in yesterday's newspaper. Will you please tell me more about it? (*The firm advertised one television set in the city's morning paper and a different set in the evening paper.*)

   c. Please reserve three seats for the opera <u>Turandot</u> on Saturday evening.

   d. My daughter and I wish to repaint two bedrooms, each of which is 10' x 12'. Please send us the right amount of paint--in pink-- to do this job, and charge my account.

   e. The next meeting of the chapter will be held Monday at 8 p.m.

   f. Please send me c.o.d. five more shirts exactly like those I bought from you three months ago. (*From a cash customer.*)

2. Choose an active verb to replace each "deadly" verb hiding in some of the following nouns.

   a. Be of assistance.
   b. Make substitution.
   c. Have intention.
   d. Become an imposition.
   e. Improvement in quality has been made.
   f. Evaporation of the liquid takes place.
   g. Make a decision.
   h. Take action.
   i. We will give thought to your proposal.
   j. Put on a demonstration.

3. Which of the following verbs are passive and which are active voice?

   a. Each member was given a copy of the annual report.
   b. The printer is planning to expand operations on Monday.
   c. Each courteous clerk wins goodwill for Mace Department Store.
   d. Final preparation will be made by the planning committee.
   e. The finance committee has been making a careful study.
   f. By January, the committee will have interviewed all applicants.
   g. Mr. Thom's secretary has completed the assignment.
   h. The contract will be signed next week.
   i. A farewell banquet has been planned in honor of Miss Bray.
   j. Many customers are reached by television advertisements.
   k. An account was opened by Mrs. Simms.
   l. It is suggested that you come early.

4. Revise the following sentences to eliminate the negative aspects.

   a. To avoid the loss of your good credit rating, please send your $130 check this week.

   b. This information is being sent to you now so that we will avoid later misunderstandings about our credit terms.

   c. We know you will agree that our prices are not any higher than those of competitors.

   d. On c.o.d. orders we require a 20 percent deposit to safeguard ourselves against loss in case of refusal of merchandise.

   e. We will hold shipment of this hardware until we receive your confirmation.

   f. Unfortunately, I will not be able to give you any definite price until you let me know the size and quantity of cartons you need.

   g. We are sorry that we cannot add a car to the policy without a specific description of the vehicle.

   h. There will be a delay of four days in filling your order because the material for your coat has to be ordered from Chicago. We are sorry about this delay, but there is nothing we can do about it.

   i. Because of shortages of material, we will not be able to ship before June 10.

   j. I am sorry I cannot send you the booklet you requested, as we have not received it from the publishers.

   k. Your bicycle has been repaired and we hope you will have no further trouble with it.

   l. We regret that we cannot extend your payment date for more than two months.

   m. You won't be sorry you made this decision.

5. Change the following sentences so that they emphasize "you-attitude" instead of "we-attitude."

   a. We allow 2 percent discount for cash payments.

   b. This is just the kind of job I am looking for, since it offers me a chance to get practical experience in personnel work.

   c. We value your patronage, for satisfied customers are the foundation of our success.

   d. Since we have our own obligations to meet, we must ask your immediate attention to your past-due account.

   e. We do not send receipts because of the extra work involved for us; of course, you have your canceled checks anyway.

   f. Our pamphlet is designed to help its readers get the most out of raising beautiful roses.

   g. We hope to have the pleasure of showing you what we think is the finest assortment of Italian boots in the city.

   h. To help us improve our production schedule, we would appreciate your ordering two weeks in advance.

   i. I wish to tell you that we are sending your new coat tomorrow.

6. Assume that the following letter is a reply to a customer who asked for a copy of the free booklet the company had advertised on television a month ago. Is this reply concise or abrupt? Improve it in every way you can.

This is to inform you we cannot comply with your request regarding
booklets. We're out of stock and in the process of revising same.

7. Revise the following wordy sentences.

   a. You will note when you study the cost of stationery that the
      expenditure of stationery gradually and steadily increased for
      1976, 1977, 1978, and 1979.
   b. I have your letter of October 14 and wish to say that we'll be
      glad to give you a refund for the blouse you bought here last week.
   c. Permit me to take this opportunity to call your attention to the
      fact that we have brought your account up to date.
   d. For your information we are attaching hereto a carbon copy of the
      letter sent to Mr. Ava Knocash under date of April 25.
   e. Please find enclosed herewith a copy of the report which is 15
      pages in length.
   f. I wish to take this opportunity to sincerely acknowledge receipt
      of your order for one bushel of Washington Red Delicious apples
      and thank you for placing it with our company.
   g. Please be assured that we are now rechecking and reviewing all of
      our specifications as it is our earnest and most sincere desire to
      be certain and for sure that this machine gives you satisfaction
      and good service in every possible way in the future.
   h. In addition, will you please permit me to state in this letter
      that we will welcome any suggestions or comments that you may
      have at any time if you think of any methods for the improve-
      ment of our service to our customers.

8. Two months before his honorable discharge from overseas military service, a college
   graduate wrote to the largest university in your state asking about requirements for
   entrance into its law school. He said he wanted to make his home in your state and
   practice law there; therefore he preferred to take his law training in the area. Evaluate the following reply he received from that university. The letter was signed by
   "Director, Program for Servicemen." What improvements does it need?

   Blank University does not have a law school. If you are interested in
   such training, you should apply to a university where such work is
   offered.

9. Revise the following sentences to eliminate the faulty expressions:

   a. At the meeting, Mr. Johnson's remarks hit the bull's eye right on
      the nose.
   b. You deserve a nice bow for sticking to your guns right down the
      line.

chapter

4

Business Writing Principles II

The preceding chapter discussed four of the seven business writing principles: completeness, conciseness, consideration, concreteness. To make your writing easily understood, friendly, and accurate, you should also apply the remaining C principles: clarity, courtesy, and correctness.

CLARITY

Clarity means getting your message across so the reader will not misunderstand what you are trying to convey. You want your reader to interpret your words with the same meaning you have in mind. Accomplishing that goal is difficult because, as you know, individual experiences are never identical; and words have different meanings to different persons.

Here are some specific ways to help make your writing clear:[1]

1. Choose words that are short, familiar, conversational.
2. Construct effective sentences and paragraphs.
3. Achieve appropriate readability.
4. Include examples, illustrations, and other visual aids, when desirable.

Choose Short, Familiar, Conversational Words

The section on conciseness has already emphasized that good writing eliminates trite and wordy expressions. Omitting these expressions usually helps not only conciseness but also clarity. Furthermore, when you have a choice between a long word and a short one, use the short, familiar word, since you can usually be more sure your reader will understand it. Remember, your reader is busy and doesn't have time to run to the dictionary for meanings. Instead, the reader will guess what you mean (sometimes incorrectly) or will disregard some or all of the message.

Here is a story that involves clarity. A plumber wrote the National Bureau of Standards to tell them hydrochloric acid is good for cleaning out clogged drains. (Before you go any further into the story, visualize the plumber. Assume you don't know him or have never exchanged correspondence. It is a pretty good guess he isn't a college graduate—maybe he didn't finish high school. But he probably is a good plumber—at least conscientious—because he's writing to the bureau to tell them something he thinks will help other people.)

In reply to the plumber's message, a technical specialist of the bureau wrote:

```
The efficacy of hydrochloric acid is indisputable, but the corrosive
residue is incompatible with metallic permanence.
```

The plumber then wrote to thank the bureau for agreeing with him—when, of course, the bureau was actually disagreeing with him. Sensing the plumber didn't understand, another member tried to set the man straight by writing:

[1] See Chapter 2 and the checkpoints on clarity in Appendix B.

We cannot assume responsibility for the production of toxic and noxious residue with hydrochloric acid and suggest you use an alternative procedure.

Again the plumber thanked the bureau. Then, in desperation, the head of the department wrote:

Don't use hydrochloric acid. It eats hell out of the pipes.

The moral of this story is to write on—not above or below—the level of the reader's understanding.

Whenever possible, avoid technical jargon when you talk or write to a person who is not acquainted with such words. If you must use technical words, define them briefly and clearly. If you don't, you'll confuse, embarrass, or irritate the reader, and perhaps be forced to explain later. Here are a few technical words and the synonyms a layperson is more likely to understand:

Technical jargon	*Expressions familiar to the layperson*
abstract	history of the property
annual premium	annual payment
assessed valuation	value of property for tax purposes
charge to your principal	increase the balance of your loan
compound dividends	dividends earned on your deposits and added to your account, which then earns more dividends and deposits
easement for ingress and egress	agreement allowing passage in and out
escrow account	reserve account for taxes and insurance
maturity date	final payment date
per diem	daily

Notice that each sentence below (with technical words underlined) is much clearer in the revision.

1. The <u>conversion privilege</u> of this term policy <u>terminates</u> June 5, 1981.

   Revision:

   Your right to change this policy to permanent insurance ends June 5, 1981.

2. <u>Days of grace</u> under this policy <u>expire</u> May 15, 1980.

   Revision:

   The extra 30 days allowed you to pay your premium without interest end May 15, 1980.

A politician—using "big, unfamiliar words to fool little people"—helped defeat the opponent by telling audiences:

> Are you aware that this candidate is known all over Washington as a shameless extrovert? Not only that, but this man is reliably reported to have practiced nepotism with his sister-in-law, and he has a sister who was once a thespian in wicked New York. He matriculated with co-eds at the University, and it is an established fact that before his marriage, he habitually practiced celibacy.

To help make your business writing clear, use short, familiar, conversational words.

Construct Effective Sentences and Paragraphs

Arranging your words in well-constructed sentences and paragraphs is also an important task that requires adaptation to your reader. Generally, the *average* length for sentences should be about 17 to 20 words; for paragraphs, about four to five lines in letters and eight to nine lines in reports. Even more important than length is quality. Aim for unity, coherence, and emphasis.

Unity

In a sentence—whether simple, complex, or compound—unity means that you have one main idea, and any other ideas in the sentence must be closely related to it. "I like you" and "George Washington died in 1799" obviously don't belong together. Also, in a complex sentence, the main idea belongs in the main (independent) clause.

In a paragraph, unity likewise means that you have one main idea or topic. It should be expressed in a topic sentence, usually at either the beginning or the end of the paragraph. The following sentence from an insurance letter is confusing primarily because the main point is not emphasized clearly. Isn't the revised paragraph—with topic sentence at the beginning—clearer?

> We have been advised that the allotment for the above-numbered policy was filed effective April 1980, but inasmuch as the premium due March 1, 1980, of $9.91 has not been remitted and inasmuch as allotment payments are not applicable to premiums due and payable in advance of the effective date of allotment, we hereby request that you contact the insured directly and request payment of this premium due.

> *Revision:*
> Allotment payments can be applied only to premiums falling due after the effective date of allotment. Since the allotment did not become effective on this policy until April 1980, it cannot pay the March 1980 premium of $9.91. May we ask you to collect it?

In most business writing the preferred position for the topic sentence is at the beginning, where it receives the best emphasis. The sentences that follow it contain details to help develop the main idea. However, if you think that your main topic will be considered unfavorable or unclear by your reader, you may be wise to place the supporting details first and then lead up to the topic sentence at the end.

Coherence

In both sentences and paragraphs, coherence is the quality of hanging together in such a way that the intended meaning is clear. It involves showing the reader the relationships within a sentence, as well as pointing the way from one sentence to another. Place every modifier as close as possible to the word it is supposed to modify; otherwise, the meaning may be unclear.[2]

Unclear:	The car is in the garage that he smashed.
Clear:	The car that he smashed is in the garage.
Unclear:	Being a top lawyer, I am sure you can help us.
Clear:	Being a top lawyer, you can surely help us.
	or
	As you are a top lawyer, I am sure you...
Unclear:	Walking into your office, a bus hit the east wall.
Clear:	Walking into your office, I saw a bus hit the...

Lack of coherence in a classified newspaper ad caused embarrassing problems for the poor fellow mentioned below.

For sale: R. D. Smith has one sewing machine for sale. Phone 543-1111. Call after 7 p.m. and ask Mrs. Kelly who lives with him, cheap.

Naturally, the paper was more than willing to clear things up. Next day's retraction read:

We regret having erred in R. D. Smith's ad yesterday. It should read: For sale, R. D. Smith, one sewing machine for sale. Cheap. Phone 543-1111 and ask for Mrs. Kelly who lives with him after 7 p.m.

Still trying gamely, the paper printed another clarification:

R. D. Smith has informed us he has received several annoying phone calls because of an error we made in his classified ad yesterday. His ad stands corrected: For sale, R. D. Smith has one sewing machine for sale. Cheap. Phone 543-1111 after 7 p.m. and ask for Mrs. Kelly who loves with him.

---

[2] See also Dangling Participles in Appendix B.

Final version:

> I, R. D. Smith, have no sewing machine. I smashed it. Don't call 543-1111; the phone has been taken out. I have not been carrying on with Mrs. Kelly. Until yesterday, she was my housekeeper.

Emphasis

The quality that gives force to important parts of your sentence is *emphasis.* You can emphasize by position, space, and repetition. For instance, important ideas deserve the most important position in the sentence—at the beginning or at the end; they should not be buried in the middle. You can also emphasize important ideas by giving them extra space or by repeating significant words or phrases. Too much repetition, however, can result in a wordy sentence; too little repetition or the use of indefinite words such as *it* and *there is* can result in an unclear sentence.

Unclear:	Our association recommends Mr. Johnson's article on credit, but <u>it</u> says that in <u>it</u> he makes <u>it</u> seem easier than <u>it</u> is.
Clear:	Our association recommends Mr. Johnson's article on credit, but says that in the article he makes credit seem easier than it is.
Unclear:	(*In a letter promoting a laundry's special dry cleaning process that practically eliminated ironing by the customer.*) When your clothing is returned, <u>there is</u> very little left to iron....We don't mangle your clothes by machinery; we do <u>it</u> carefully by hand.
Unclear:	It is necessary, for technical reasons, that these warheads should be stored upside down. That is, with the top at the bottom, and the bottom at the top. In order that there may be no doubt as to which is the bottom, and which is the top, for storage purposes it will be seen that the bottom of each warhead has been labeled with the word "TOP."

Achieve Appropriate Readability

Besides aiming for qualities of unity, coherence, and emphasis, you should adapt your business writing so that its readability will be appropriate for your recipient's general education level.

Among several guides that measure readability is Robert Gunning's well-known Fog Index.[3] It is based on two factors: length of sentence and percentage of hard words.

---

[3] Robert Gunning, *The Technique of Clear Writing*, McGraw-Hill Book Company, revised edition, 1968, p. 38. Used with permission of author, copyright owner.

By using the Fog Index, you can determine the educational level of your writing—whether it is for a reader who has an equivalent of a ninth-grade education (first-year high school), twelfth-grade (senior in high school), thirteenth-grade (first-year college), and so on.

To find the Fog Index of a passage, take the following three simple steps:

1. *Determine average sentence length.* Use a passage of words (beginning preferably with the first word of a paragraph) in consecutive sentences which end nearest the 100-word level.[4] Divide the total number of words in this passage by the number of complete thoughts. (A simple or complex sentence has one complete thought; a compound sentence contains two complete thoughts.) Your quotient gives the average sentence length.

2. *Figure the percentage of "hard" words.* Count the number of words of three syllables or more in the passage, and include any unexplained abbreviations (CMO, BSD), but don't count words:
   a. That are (correctly) capitalized
   b. That are combinations of short, easy words (like *bookkeeper, butterfly*)
   c. That are verb forms made into three syllables by adding *ed* or *es* (like *created* or *trespasses*)
   Divide the number of hard words by the total number of words. Your quotient is the percentage of hard words.

3. *Add the average sentence length and the percentage of hard words and multiply by 0.4.* The product, called the Fog Index, is the reading level required for the same number of years of education.

This readability formula is especially useful when you want to determine if "average" Americans will clearly understand what you are writing to them. Who are these persons? They are the cross section of all the people in the United States. They have finished the eleventh grade—maybe even graduated from high school. They are probably typical customers. Therefore, your level of writing should be no higher than the twelfth grade—preferably even lower.

Whether highly educated or not, everyone appreciates easy reading with a Fog Index of between 7 and 12. (*Reader's Digest* and *Time* have indexes, between 9 and 10; *Scientific American* averages 11 or 12.) If your writing level to the average person is on the thirteenth level or higher, your message runs the danger of being ignored or

---

[4] These additional guides from Robert Gunning may help you: (1) Count anything as a word that has space around it. Thus *March 1, 1980,* is 3 words; *one thousand dollars* is 3 words; *5 1/4* is 2 words; *five and one quarter* is 4 words; but *5¼* is 1 word; *twelve-month* is 1 word; *$5,000* and *$9,752,461* are each 1 word; if spelled out, the latter figure is 10 words. Exception: Do not count the numbers (I, II, 1, 2, 3) or alphabetic letters (A, B, a, b, c) that precede items or paragraphs. (2) Count hyphenated words as polysyllables only if one part is a word of 3 syllables or more. For example, *seventy-two* is 4 syllables. (3) Do not regard numerals as polysyllables regardless of pronunciation. Example: $987,652,431.50 is 1 syllable.

misunderstood. Among the writings and documents that especially need simplifying to be understood by the average reader are those from legal, insurance, medical, and government offices. Also, in many other large companies the employee grapevine has indicated that management's messages are too often misinterpreted.

As you read the following portion of a letter, try to guess its readability level. (The underlined words have three or more syllables.)

> Thank you for your nice letter of March 1, 1980. Since you will be moving back to Pomona in the future, we look forward to meeting you then. To answer your questions <u>regarding</u> a savings plan, we have two types for your <u>consideration</u>.
>
> 1. <u>Regular</u> passbook savings yield 5 1/2 percent <u>dividends</u> compounded <u>quarterly</u>. You can make <u>deposits</u> and <u>withdrawals</u> by mail, with postage paid by us both ways.
> 2. Our Savings Certificates yield 6 1/4 percent <u>dividends</u>. <u>Minimum</u> amount for <u>opening</u> this type of account is $5,000 and then upward in amounts of $1,000. They can be six-month or twelve-month Certificates and are <u>automatically renewable</u> unless you advise us to the <u>contrary</u>. (*110 words*)

This example has 110 words in the first 7 sentences, or an average sentence length of 15.7 words. The 13 hard words (underlined) are 11.8 percent of the 110 words. From these figures, you can compute the Gunning Fog Index—11, the educational level of a high school junior.

Words in example	110	
Sentences	7	
Average sentence length (110 ÷ 7)		15.7
Percentage of hard words (13 ÷ 110)		11.8
Total		27.5
Multiplier		0.4
Grade level (Fog Index)		11.0

In contrast to the letter paragraphs shown above, the following from a letter to certificate depositors has a Fog Index of nearly 27—fifteen school years beyond a high school graduate:

> RESOLVED, That in <u>accordance</u> with the <u>provisions</u> of Section 545.3-1 of the rules and <u>regulations</u> of the Federal Savings and Loan System, and the charter and by-laws of this Association, there be and hereby is <u>established</u> this date a <u>separate</u> class of savings accounts <u>evidenced</u> by Separate Certificate <u>designated</u> as Class "C" which accounts shall be in a <u>minimum</u> amount of $10,000 and in <u>additional</u> <u>multiples</u> of $1,000. Said Class "C" accounts shall have earnings for the <u>period</u> <u>beginning</u> October 1, 1980, and ending December 31, 1980, and <u>maintained</u> for a <u>continuous</u> <u>period</u> of at least six months, declared <u>payable</u> at the rate of 6 1/4% per annum. (*108 words*)

Words in example	108	
Sentences	2	
Average sentence length (108 ÷ 2)		54.0
Percentage of difficult words (15 ÷ 108)		14.0
Total		68.0
Multiplier		0.4
Grade level (Fog Index)		27.2

Though average sentence length should be about 17 to 20 words, a pleasing variety of length is desirable. You can use a range of, say, from 3 to 40 words; but when a sentence exceeds 40 or 45 words, ask yourself how you can rewrite it into more than one sentence. Also, if *all* sentences are short (for instance, under 10 words) the result is monotonous, primerlike language—choppy and undesirable.

Mr. Gunning considers his Fog Index a "simple warning system"—not a cure-all for any writing problem. He wants you to use this formula "to check to see if your writing is in step with that which has proved easy to read and understand."[5]

Readability formulas are popular and helpful in improving clarity, but there are limitations and cautions. First, a writer must be careful not to use too many simple words and short sentences, for the writing would be monotonous, elementary, choppy. Second, some "long" words really aren't as difficult as some two-syllable words (for example, *employee* versus *avid*). Also, you must count the same word as many times as it appears in the passage. Finally, a message with crude, harsh, unethical, insulting words may still get a desirable Fog Index. Used with discretion, however, the formula will serve the purpose of a *guide* to the readability of letters, reports, books, magazine articles, or any other business writing.

Include Examples, Illustrations, and Other Visual Aids, When Desirable

When you have a complicated and/or lengthy explanation to make in a letter or a report, you'll often find that you can improve the clarity of your message by giving your reader an example, an analogy, or an illustration. Furthermore, visual aids—such as headings, tabulations, itemizations, pictures, charts—are definite aids to clarity and easy reading.

Whenever you have more than one set of figures, you'll make them much clearer to your reader if you itemize, tabulate, or set them off in some attractive way. Throughout this text—especially the section on reports—are examples of writing that use illustrations and visual aids to help clarify the material for the reader.

In summary, make your writing clear by using words that are familiar to your reader. Watch the quality and length of your sentences. Organize paragraphs and your entire message so that the purpose is clear. Itemize and tabulate figures to make them

---

[5] Robert Gunning, "The Fog Index after Twenty Years," *Journal of Business Communication,* vol. 6, no. 2, p. 3, Winter 1968.

stand out clearly. And give your reader helpful examples with appropriate, easy-to-read headings whenever you need to explain complicated material.

COURTESY

Courteous messages help to strengthen present business friendships, as well as make new friends. Courtesy stems from sincere you-attitude. It is not merely politeness with mechanical insertions of "please's" and "thank-you's." To be courteous the considerate communicator should follow—in addition to the four guidelines discussed under Consideration (Chapter 3)—these suggestions regarding tone and promptness of messages:

1. Be sincerely tactful, thoughtful, and appreciative.
2. Omit expressions that irritate, hurt, or belittle.
3. Grant and apologize good-naturedly.
4. Answer your mail promptly.

Be Sincerely Tactful, Thoughtful, and Appreciative

A truly courteous person sincerely likes people, is thoughtful of their feelings, and tries honestly to help them. One of the top copywriters in advertising, Walter Weir, has published a statement that is good advice for all letter writers as well as for advertising copywriters:

> I believe one best prepares himself for communicating by learning to love and genuinely loving all the countless other human beings with whom he inhabits the earth. I do not believe one can be a cynic and communicate effectively.[6]

The courteous communicator tries to make messages tactful instead of blunt, and she or he shows thoughtful appreciation in special messages as well as in everyday communication.

Tact instead of Bluntness

Though few people intentionally want to be abrupt or blunt, these traits are a common cause of discourtesy. Sometimes they stem from negative personal attitudes; sometimes from a mistaken idea of conciseness. A time to be especially wary of bluntness is on those days when everything seems to go wrong. At such times, you are in danger of allowing your pent-up feelings to come through in your messages. Avoid

[6] Walter Weir, *On the Writing of Advertising,* McGraw-Hill Book Company, New York, 1969.

expressions like those in the left-hand column below; rephrase as shown in the right-hand column.

Tactless; blunt	*Tactful*
Your letter is not clear at all; I can't understand it.	If I understand your letter correctly...
Obviously, if you'd read your policy carefully, you'd be able to answer these questions yourself.	Sometimes policy wording is a little hard to understand. I'm glad to clear up these questions for you.
Apparently you have already forgotten what I wrote you two weeks ago.	As mentioned in my May 15 letter (or memo) to you, *(continue with the facts)*. . .
Pat, get your list to me pronto.	Pat, may I have your list by tomorrow at 10? Then I'll include it in our report at the meeting.

Writing a letter to a customer generally requires more conscious "niceties" than writing a memo to a fellow employee. In letters to customers, you usually avoid a one-sentence body like the following, because it sounds blunt.

Before we can replace the safety lock on the trunk of your 1980 Ford, it will be necessary that you give us the number of it.

Instead, you need to add a few tactful words, as in this example:

We will be glad to replace the safety lock on the trunk of your 1980 Ford.

So that we can know the right lock to fit your trunk, please send us the casting number. You'll find it imprinted on the side of the lock.

Within the same morning we receive your reply, a new lock will be on its way to you.

But in a memo to someone within your organization, you can omit the public relations pitch. A one-sentence body like the following is all right to an employee or colleague if it adequately covers your particular message:

Tom,
Please call me (Ext. 312) to tell me the casting number on the side of the trunk safety lock you need for that '80 Ford.

When a reader has had sorrow, bereavement, or hardship, the writer should be especially considerate of feelings and emotions. Tactlessness may not only be blunt but also (unintentionally) cruel. For instance, when writing to a policyholder who had recently had one leg amputated, a heartless correspondent included this sentence:

Because you have lost only one leg, your policy doesn't entitle you to the full $30,000 payment. This amount is paid only when both legs are amputated.

Thoughtfulness and Appreciation

Writers who send cordial, courteous messages of deserved congratulations and appreciation (to persons both inside and outside the firm) help build goodwill.[7] The value of goodwill or public esteem, can be recorded on the balance sheet in thousands (or even millions) of dollars. Much money is spent on advertising to attract new customers and to keep desirable old customers. While advertising may bring buyers into the front door of your firm, discourteous letters can drive customers out the back door!

An unpretentious, sincere courtesy note can have far-reaching, favorable effects. Remember, customers indirectly help pay your salary; you should let them know you appreciate their orders, payments, inquiries. Even for routine payments a printed "Thank you" or "We appreciate your prompt payment" can be added to the flap or under the window of the company envelope in which you return to the customer your bill marked "paid."

Omit Expressions That Irritate, Hurt, or Belittle

The thoughtful business writer should avoid expressions that might offend the reader. Such expressions are discussed here in three groups: irritating, questionably humorous, and belittling statements.

Irritating Expressions

The following list contains irksome expressions to be avoided, particularly when used with "you" and "your."

contrary to your inference	you are delinquent
delinquency (delinquent)	you are probably ignorant of the
due to your questionable credit	fact that
we are unable to	you claim that
I do not agree with you	you did not tell us
if you care	you failed to
I'm sure you must realize	you forgot to
inexcusable	you have to
irresponsible	you leave us no choice
obnoxious	you neglected to; (overlooked)
obviously you overlooked	you say
simply nonsense	you should know
surely you don't expect	you surely don't expect
we are confused	your apparent disregard of our
we don't believe	previous request leaves us no
we expect you to	alternative
we find it difficult to	your complaint
believe that	your failure to
we must insist	your insinuation
we take issue	your neglect
why have you ignored	your stubborn silence

---

[7] For examples of goodwill messages see Chapter 14.

Questionable Humor

Humor is often quite effective in business writing. However, before you try to be funny, be sure your humor is good-natured and appropriate for the situation. A flippant attitude can be in poor taste, as letter 1 indicates. Letter 2 conveys the same message informally but courteously.[8]

Letter 1—Offensive rather than humorous

```
Dear Mr. and Mrs. Smith:

     We were mighty happy to learn about the package the stork
brought you.  And what a distinguished tag you put on him...
Joshua Gerald Smith II.  You tell Josh: that as soon as he's ready,
his Prudential agent will be around to help him set up his insurance
program.

     In the meantime, I guess it's up to us to take care of the
little fellow's insurance needs for a while--you know, educational
funds and a little nest egg to help him start his journey through
life.

     I'll phone you in a couple of days to find out when it will
be convenient for you to talk about insurance for your new bundle
of joy.  Till then, keep his powder dry!
```

Letter 2—Courteous

```
Dear Mr. and Mrs. Smith:

     Congratulations on the birth of your son, Joshua.

     Like other thoughtful parents, you no doubt want him to have a
happy, well-protected future.  It may seem early to be concerned
about financing his college education.  But we at Prudential have
seen too many youngsters miss out on college because their parents
put off the problem too long.

     If it is convenient, I would like to call at seven o'clock Fri-
day evening to show you how Prudential can help you solve this prob-
lem.  I'll phone Thursday to confirm the appointment or to arrange a
different time that you prefer.
```

Two other examples of humor in questionable taste are the following paragraph in a customer's letter to a department store and the store's reply. (The customer had received a lamp with the wrong base.)

```
The lamp I selected was sold to me by a highly untrained person in
your lamp department.  For some reason he was designated as sales-
person number 1.  If it is impossible to send me the right base for
```

---

[8] From *Dear Sir,* vol. 3, no. 1, Correspondence Improvement Section, Public Relations Department, Prudential Insurance Company of America, Newark, N.J., 1961–1962.

my lamp, perhaps you could send me salesperson number 1. That should
help your sales department, I would think, as he would make a better
lamp base than a salesperson.

The store correspondent apparently tried to be funny too; here is the reply:

Our records show that the base you wished was sent to you on May 10.
We are surprised you have not received it.

Having examined salesperson number 1 from all angles, we feel rather
reluctant to think he would make a good lamp base. We are gratified
this didn't involve the cheese department, for you might have suggested that we put him in the showcase.

We are sending you another lamp base. If the one we originally sent
should reach you in the meantime, we would appreciate your returning
it to us. We might have to use it in a pinch as a salesperson.

Belittling Statements

Talking down to or belittling a reader is another form of discourtesy that can have a
profoundly unfavorable effect, as in the following case:

*To substantiate a railroad claim, the accountant of the AMC company needed the
exact charges on certain returnable drums in which the XYZ Chemical Company
annually shipped thousands of dollars worth of chemicals to AMC. AMC's accountant
checked with the local representative of XYZ Company for this information, but was
asked by him to contact Mrs. Lancaster in Diamond, California. After writing to her,
the accountant received the following reply, which he said caused "a much greater
explosion within our department than could have all XYZ chemicals combined."*

In reply to your letter of October 10th addressed to Diamond, California, attention Mrs. Lancaster, you made two mistakes. In the
first place we have no Mrs. Lancaster, and in the second place Diamond is not a place to send mail.

We make a charge of $8.50 on the Carbon Bisulphide-Carbon Tetrachlo-
ride Mixture drum to AMC Company, in your city. That is for the
drum only. We trust this is what is meant.

Grant and Apologize Good-naturedly

Whenever you have occasion to comply with a customer's request, begin your letter
with the best news first and inject a courteous, ungrudging tone. Notice the difference
in tone of the following two paragraphs:

Grudging:

Your request causes a great deal of extra paper work to change monthly payments. However, in compliance with your request we hereby reduce your monthly interest and principal payments called for in our
note to $_____, plus $_____for taxes and insurance; effective
(month-day-year) your total monthly payment will be $_____.

Good-natured:

> As you requested, we will reduce the monthly interest and principal
> payments called for in your note to $_____ , plus $_____for taxes
> and insurance. Thus, starting (month-day-year) your total monthly
> payment will be $_____ .

If a request has caused you extra work, you may tactfully tell the customer somewhere in the letter—but not the first paragraph—to notify you by a certain time if he or she again wishes to change something.

Occasionally you may get a "nasty" letter from a customer, who is wrong in his or her accusations. A courteous reply can lead not only to an apology from the customer but also future staunch loyalty as a booster for your organization. For example:

An irate father severely criticized a savings association for not paying dividends on his young son's two deposits—30 cents and $10. He stated (discourteously), "Your failure . . . is inexcusable. . . . I am calling this discrepancy to the attention of the State Banking Department." Instead of responding with anger, the bank correspondent mailed the following courteous letter:

> Enclosed is your passbook for account #R 000 posted to date.
>
> Your desire to have the account earn dividends is certainly natural
> and understandable. I am glad you've given me the opportunity to ex-
> plain why the account has not yet earned dividends, so that you can
> bring the account to the desired balance in the future.
>
> A little over six years ago, starting January 1, 1974, the board of
> directors of the Association raised the minimum balance required to
> earn dividends to $50. In the preceding month a notice of this
> change of policy was mailed to all savings account holders; and also
> posters and counter cards with this information were displayed in
> all our offices for the entire year of 1974. In addition, in April
> of 1974 another letter was sent to all savings account holders whose
> balances were less than $50, reminding them of the change in policy.
>
> You can see, therefore, that we really tried to convey this new in-
> formation to our savings members. We're sincerely sorry that for
> some reason you were unaware of this policy change. It has always
> been our practice to fully inform savings account holders of any
> changes that take place.
>
> Your continued loyalty to the Association is very much appreciated.
> We invite you to continue adding to this account; one of these days
> soon your son will see that his money does grow when deposited with
> Ninth Federal Savings Association.

When someone in your organization makes a mistake, you can apologize and correct the error perhaps even before the customer discovers it. Sometimes a small, printed form like the following (used by a bank) is useful to admit an error promptly and courteously.

```
Date _____ 19_____ Account No. _____

            PARDON US ... IT WAS OUR ERROR!

    An incorrect entry was made. Please return your passbook in the enclosed
envelope for the following reason:

Interest
not entered ☐                              Balance incorrect ☐

    Thank you.


                        By _____
                                        (Name of bank)
```

Of course, if the matter is more serious, a special letter may be more appropriate, as you will see in later chapters.

Answer Your Mail Promptly

For courtesy as well as better results one should answer a business inquiry promptly— in two or three days if possible. Even a reply on the bottom of the inquiry or a hand-written note on a postcard is usually better than a late (or no!) reply. If you need time to gather information, or have a stack of other urgent work, before you can answer a request, sending a short note like the following distinguishes you as a courteous person:

```
I'll gladly send you the information you need.  It may take a few
days to assemble the facts.  You will hear from me by...
```

The next two examples illustrate the value of promptness.

Example 1

A certain retailer in fine china tried an experiment in promptness. For one week she "dumped" all incoming inquiries (many inspired by her regional advertising) into two piles without sorting of any kind. One pile she answered within 24 hours; the others, in three weeks. Result? The prospects who had been answered promptly turned in almost 70 percent more orders than those who had to wait.

Example 2

Customers pleased with a company's courtesy often comment on the promptness of its messages. The following paragraphs quoted from The Better Letter Gazette *of Teachers Insurance and Annuity Association illustrate well the effect that promptness had on a policyholder:*

But what impressed me still more was the extraordinary speed with which TIAA handled my claim. . . . It seems that special comment is called for when one of your policyholders sends in a claim one day, the check is made out the following day and he has it in his hands two days later. If this is typical of your operations, I can see why TIAA is regarded by the academic profession as a fairy godmother. So please accept my hearty congratulations along with my grateful thanks. . . .

I want you to know that I have policies with several different insurance companies. In no other instance have I received the prompt, courteous attention given me by TIAA. . . .[9]

Sometimes promptness can be achieved by unusual methods. For example, when the owner of a retail men's store in the Dakotas asked a Chicago manufacturer to check his previously submitted order and let him know when it would arrive, the manufacturer sent the following message:

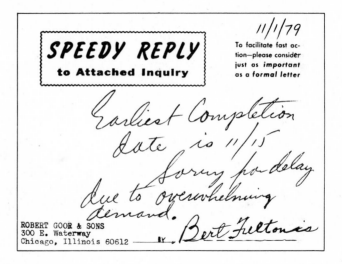

In this situation the manufacturer saved time by not dictating and sending a letter, and the retailer accepted the reply favorably. (Note that the printed explanation in the upper right-hand corner shows reader benefit.) If you are, however, writing to a new customer or if you don't know whether your customer would react favorably to such a reply, be safe and write a courteous card or letter instead!

CORRECTNESS

Some people have a distorted concept of the correctness principle. They think it comprises only proper grammar, punctuation, and spelling. The truth is that a message may be perfect grammatically and mechanically but still insult or lose a customer and fail to achieve its purpose.

[9] *The Better Letter Gazette,* TIAA and CREF, New York, August 1960.

In its broadest sense, the term *correctness,* as applied to a business letter or report, means the writer should:

1. Use the correct level of language
2. Include only accurate facts, words, and figures
3. Maintain acceptable writing mechanics
4. Choose nonsexist expressions
5. Apply all other pertinent C qualities[10]

Use the Correct Level of Language

As Figure 4-1 shows, there are three overlapping levels of language. These levels overlap because of our ever-changing language. Some words once considered substandard have moved into the informal level, and some once informal words are now acceptable on a formal level. The first two—formal and informal language—are both correct; but they are quite different from one another, have different uses, and should not be interchanged.

Figure 4-1

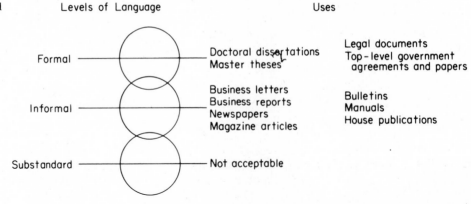

The formal level of language is used for writing a scholarly dissertation, a legal document, or other material for which formality is expected. The expressions used are often long, unconversational, and impersonal—just what the term *formal* implies.

In contrast, the informal level refers to the language of business—for letters, reports, newspapers, and other business communications. Instead of formal words, you will use short, well-known, and conversational words, as the following list illustrates:

Formal	*Informal*	*Formal*	*Informal*
anticipate	expect	endeavor	try
ascertain	find out	interrogate	ask
conflagration	fire	procure	get
deem	think (believe)	remunerate	pay

[10] See also Appendix B for checkpoints on correctness.

domicile	home	terminate	end
edifice	building	utilize	use

Phrases and sentences should likewise be expressed in conversational, informal language. For example, compare the stiff, wordy expressions in the *Formal* column below with the shorter *Informal* expressions.

Formal	*Informal*
We thank you in anticipation of this courtesy and assure you that it will be a pleasure to serve you in a similar manner.	I'll appreciate your helping us. Let me know when I can return the favor.
Should the supply of stickers sent you not be sufficient to meet your requirements, application should be made to this office for additional copies.	Pete, if you need more stickers, just call me (at Extension 521).
In order to substantiate our desire to accommodate our guests, we would appreciate your cooperation to anticipate your credit requirements before departure.	Please let us know in advance if you want us to cash a check as you leave.

The following poem by Enid C. Stickel provides a humorous example of how people try to formalize their language.

Readability Gap
Colleges aren't schools,
They are learning institutions;
Problems don't have answers,
They have viable solutions.
People don't spend money,
They re-allocate resources.
Newsmen don't use tipsters,
They rely on informed sources.

Speakers don't make speeches,
They give oral presentations.
Bosses don't set quotas,
They just indicate objectives.
Workers don't take orders,
Though they implement directives.

Machinery can't break down,
But components can malfunction.
A court does not command
It just issues an injunction.
Programs don't have failures,
They have qualified successes.
And jargon doesn't hurt you—
It just constantly distresses!

The third level of language—substandard—is the one you want to avoid, because people generally don't accept it. If you use words on this level in writing (or in speaking), your reader(s) will begin to question your ability to use good English. Here are a few examples:

Substandard	*Acceptable*	*Substandard*	*Acceptable*
ain't	isn't, aren't	haven't got	don't have
between you	between you	in regards to	regarding
and I	and me	irregardless	regardless
can't hardly	can hardly	nohow	anyway
hadn't ought	shouldn't	should of	should have

The following sentences illustrate the three levels of language discussed above—formal, informal, and substandard:

Formal: Although item 21 is enumerated in the report, the writer has ascertained that it is currently not in the organization's inventory or in the writer's possession.

Informal: Although item 21 is listed in the report, it's not in our stock now and I don't have it either.

Substandard: Irregardless of the report that item ain't on our shelves now, and I haven't got it either.

Include Only Accurate Facts, Words, and Figures

Doubtless you already know how important absolute accuracy is for written messages. One erroneous digit (for example, $65,000 instead of $75,000) can make a difference of thousands of dollars. Even small errors of a few cents can be annoying to customers and undermine goodwill, as various examples in this text will show. And a wrong figure in an account number muddles up records and leads to untold problems.

To be sure of the accuracy of your facts, you should verify all statements before writing and again before you sign or approve the message. Of course, you also need to be up-to-date on laws that affect your organization. Guessing or assuming that you are right can be costly. Just because a certain fact was true about a customer last year—or even last month—does not assure it is true now, as the following case illustrates:

Mr. Henry Simson sent in a claim for medical benefits to his insurance company. In turn, the correspondent handling the case wrote back to Mr. Simson, saying, "We are pleased to enclose a check for $277.54 for benefits due you because of your confinement at the Mountain View Hospital." Unfortunately this correspondent shouldn't have sent the check because that hospital was not certified as a full "general" hospital, a requirement under the terms of Mr. Simson's policy. Innocently, Mr. Simson cashed the check.

A month later the mistake was discovered and a notation made on Simson's file to the effect that no future payments were to be made because of confinement to the Mountain View Hospital.

Two months afterward Mr. Simson again sent a claim for medical benefits because he once again had been a patient in that same hospital. The person who handled the claim this time consulted Simson's file, found the notation, and wrote a letter refusing the claim.

However, this refusal was wrong because between Simson's two admissions the Mountain View Hospital had been certified as a full "general" hospital. Had the correspondents at the insurance company checked all the facts, such a mix-up would not have happened.

The good business writer must be continually alert to accuracy because of changing rates, regulations, laws, and conditions locally, nationally, and within his or her organization.

You should also realize that, like most things in life, English is alive and ever-changing. Even the dictionaries can't keep up with its fast pace, but they can usually help you choose correct words to convey your intended meaning. Below are a few of the many words that are often confused in usage.

a, an	Use *a* before a word that begins with the consonant sound or long "u" sound. Use *an* before a word that begins with a silent "h" or a vowel sound.
agree to, agree with	You *agree to* a plan and *agree with* a person. One thing *agrees with* another thing.
all ready, already	*All ready* means entirely ready; *already,* previously.
advise, tell	You give counsel when you *advise,* and you inform without counseling when you *tell.*
a.m., A.M.	*a.m.* is easier to type and seems less noticeable than the capital letters. Save A.M. and P.M. for headlines and tables.
amount, number, quantity	Whenever you count the units, use *number. Amount* and *quantity* refer to bulk, weight, or sums.
anxious, eager	*Anxious* implies worry, whereas *eager* conveys keen desire.
between, among	As a rule, *between* involves two people or two groups; *among,* three or more.
claims, says	*Claim* as a verb means "to ask for what is due one": He claimed his baggage at the station.
continual, continuous	*Continual* means to occur frequently. *Continuous* means without stopping.

data	You can safely use a singular verb (data *is*) with this word when you are considering all the facts as a unit. (Those who regard data as a Latin plural of datum use a plural verb—data *are*.)
different from, different than	Although both are acceptable, *different from* is preferred.
effect, affect	In business usage only *effect* is a noun; it means result, condition, or influence. Both words are verbs— to *effect* is to bring about, to *affect* is to influence.
fewer, less	If you can count the items, use *fewer; less* refers to amount or quantity.
healthful, healthy	*Healthful* means giving health; *healthy* means having good health.
imply, infer	*Imply* means to insinuate, or suggest; *infer* means to conclude. A writer *implies,* whereas the reader *infers.*
lay, laid, laid lie, lay, lain	A person or a rug *lies* on the floor, but a person *lays* the book on the table or *lays* oneself on the floor. If you can substitute *place(s)* and answer *what?*, use the proper tense of *lay.*
loan, lend	Although these words are interchangeable as verbs, some people prefer to use *lend* as a verb and *loan* as a noun.
party, customer	A *customer* is an individual or person. *Party* is a legal term for an individual or a group of people.
please, kindly	As a rule, use *please. Kindly* means "in a kind manner." If you say, kindly tell me, you are really asking someone to tell you something in a kind way.
principal, principle	*Principal* means "chief" or "main." Whenever you can substitute *rule,* use princip*le.* In all other instances, use princip*al.*
provided, providing	*Provided* means "if"; otherwise use *providing.*
we, I	*We* refers to the organization; *I* refers to the individual.
which, that, who	*That* refers to persons or things; *who* to people; *which* only to things.

Maintain Acceptable Writing Mechanics

This area of correctness includes effective use of the letter and memo parts (covered in detail in Chapter 6) and of reports (shown in Chapters 15 through 17). Envelopes, too, must be correctly addressed; if not, they may cause enormous waste. (See, for example, pages 140 and 141.)

Acceptable writing mechanics also includes correct sentence and paragraph structure, punctuation, capitalization, syllabication, spelling, and appearance.

This book does not attempt to teach you grammar and the numerous other components of mechanical correctness. Years of training in English throughout grade school, high school, and college should have taught you to write grammatically acceptable sentences and paragraphs. But if you need review on the dangling participle, numbers as words or figures, punctuation, and other details that seem to plague writers, you'll find helpful suggestions in Appendix B. And if you need help on the parts of speech and sentence structure, be sure to consult an excellent, up-to-date grammar book.[11]

Two common weaknesses in writing mechanics deserve special, though brief, mention here: the inability to spell correctly and careless omissions.

Spelling Errors

Business executives and customers expect you to spell correctly and may begin to question your overall ability if you misspell—especially the customer's name and everyday words like *convenience, questionnaire, stationery, dessert,* and *accommodation.* Errors of transposition (*nad* instead of *and* or *recieve* instead of *receive*) are also spelling errors that show carelessness.

The following letter is an example of a communication that led the receiver (Lt. *Bowser*) to doubt the ability of the sender (a motel manager) and even assume that carelessness could be the reason for many mistakes that might occur in that motel office.

```
Dear Lt. Booser

I'am writing this letter telling you how sorry I'am about the mis-
take this office and myself made concerning our business tranaction
on May 30th and the letter wich was send to you.

Please accept my apology for the mistake made to you.  Your bill
was paid in full, but the two checks tranaction were mis-led.  My
nite cashier remembers very clearly that you paid the bill, but my
nite man did not sign the bill paid, which was place on the book-
kepper's deck.
```

[11] You will find any of the following helpful: Erwin Keithley and Margaret Thompson, *English for Modern Business,* Richard D. Irwin, Inc., Chicago, 1977; Arno Knapper and Lola Newcomb, *A Style Manual for Written Communication,* Grid, Inc., Columbus, Ohio, 1974; Glenn Leggett, C. David Mead, and William Charvat, *Handbook for Writers,* Prentice-Hall, Inc., Englewood Cliffs, N.J., 1974; Porter G. Perrin, (Editor Jim Corder) *Handbook of Current English,* 1978; and Wilma Ebbitt, *Writer's Guide and Index to English,* 1978, both Scott, Foresman and Company, Glenview, Ill.

```
Again I'am sorry about this situation, and will you please come in
the next time you are this way, and wish to thank you personally
about the whole deal.
```

If you are one of the many educated men and women who are better able to solve complicated business problems than spell correctly, you can take two precautions: refer to a dictionary often, and hire a top-notch assistant who's a whiz at spelling! English spelling does have many inconsistencies, as the following anonymous poem entitled "Pluralistics" highlights:

Pluralistics
We'll begin with a box and the plural is boxes,
But the plural of ox should be oxen not oxes.
Then one fowl is a goose but two are called geese,
Yet the plural of mouse should never be meese.
You may find a lone mouse or a whole set of mice,
But the plural of house is houses not hice.
If the plural of man is always called men,
Shouldn't the plural of pan be called pen?
If I speak of a foot and you show me your feet,
And I give you a boot would a pair be called beet?

If one is a tooth and whole set are teeth,
Why should not the plural of booth be called beeth?
Then one may be that and three would be those,
Yet hat in that plural wouldn't be hose.
And the plural of cat is cats and not cose.
We speak of a brother and also of brethren,
But though we say Mother we never say Methren,
Then the masculine pronouns are he, his, and him,
But imagine the feminine, she, shis, and shim.
So English I fancy, you all will agree.
Is the funniest language you ever did see.

Incorrect spelling frequently results in ambiguity or misunderstandings, as these sentences illustrate:

Pierce Eugene Puckett, Assistant Professor and Aching Head, Department of Education—was the principle speaker.

In a newspaper column on advice to teenagers: "Keep jewelry to a very minimum—and leave errings to your older siblings."

Careless Omissions

Another way to maintain correct writing mechanics is to double-check for any careless omissions of punctuation marks or words needed for grammatical accuracy. Sometimes even small omissions can lead to costly miscommunication, as this example illustrates:

A traveling client had instructed his stock broker to buy for him as many shares of a certain company's stock as was possible and desirable. One day the broker found an opportunity to purchase 3,000 shares. Because the price had risen considerably, he asked the client to wire his decision—whether or not to buy. The client considered the price exorbitant. He wired:

NO.   PRICE TOO HIGH.

Unfortunately, the period was omitted after the first word; and the broker bought the unwanted shares.

Choose Nonsexist Expressions

Another important—comparatively recent—requirement for correctness is nondiscriminatory "equal treatment of the sexes." In a broad sense, *sexism* indicates any arbitrary stereotyping of males and females on the basis of their gender. Conscientious business communicators (as well as authors) should be continually alert to treat men and women primarily as people and not mainly as members of opposite sexes. They should use nondiscriminatory, nonsexist expressions whenever possible.

The discussion in this section is adapted mainly from "Guidelines for Equal Treatment of the Sexes in McGraw-Hill Book Company Publications." The suggestions selected here are guidelines that can be particularly useful for your written and oral business communication. Try to choose nonsexist language when you refer to occupational roles and achievements, personal characteristics, physical and mental attributes, humanity at large, names, and various title designations.[12]

Occupational Roles and Achievements

Neither sex should be stereotyped or arbitrarily assigned to a leading or secondary role. Both include individuals in a variety of professional work at all levels—doctors and nurses; principals, professors, and teachers; lawyers, judges, and social workers; bank presidents and tellers. Women should be shown at all professional levels, including the top levels.

Persons should be recognized for their own achievements. All work should be treated as honorable and worthy of respect, none downgraded. Instead, men and women should be offered more options than were available to them when work was stereotyped by sex. Women as well as men should be shown as accountants, engineers, pilots, plumbers, bridge-builders, computer operators, astronauts. Men as well as women should be shown as grade school teachers, secretaries, baby-sitters, file clerks. Work should never be stereotyped as "woman's work" or as "a man-sized job." Generic terms, such as *doctor* and *nurse,* should be assumed to include both women and men; modified titles such as "woman doctor" or "male nurse" should be avoided. Both men and women should be shown engaged in home maintenance ranging from cooking and housecleaning to washing the car and making household repairs.

[12] For a bibliography of 16 publications about sexist and nondiscriminatory communication, see "Some Guidelines for Nondiscriminatory Communication," *The Journal of Business Communication,* vol. 16, number 2, Winter 1979, pp. 75–76.

Personal Characteristics

Women and girls should be shown as having the same abilities, interests, ambitions, strengths and weaknesses as men and boys. Both sexes include people who are industrious, active, strong, independent, courageous, competent, decisive, assertive, persistent, serious-minded, successful. Both include logical thinkers, problem solvers, and decision makers pursuing career goals.

Stereotypes of the logical, objective male and the emotional, subjective female are to be avoided. In descriptions, the smarter, braver, or more successful person should be a woman or girl as often as a man or boy. Characteristics that have been traditionally praised in women—such as gentleness, compassion, sensitivity—should also be praised in men. Characteristics that have been praised in men—such as boldness, initiative, assertiveness—should also be praised in women.

Physical and Mental Attributes

Men and women should be treated with the same respect, dignity, and seriousness. Neither should be trivialized or stereotyped. Women should not be described by physical attributes when men are described by mental attributes or professional position.

Not this:	Henry Harris is a shrewd lawyer and his wife Ann is a striking brunette.
But this:	The Harrises are an attractive couple. Henry is a handsome blond and Ann is a striking brunette.
OR:	The Harrises are highly respected in their fields. Ann is an accomplished musician and Henry is a shrewd lawyer.
OR:	The Harrises are an interesting couple. Henry is a shrewd lawyer and Ann is very active in community (church; civic) affairs.

In descriptions of women, a patronizing or girl-watching tone should be avoided, as should sexual innuendoes, jokes, and puns. Among stereotypes to be avoided are: scatterbrained female, henpecking shrew, apron-wearing mother, frustrated spinster, and nagging mother-in-law clichés. Here are suggestions for changing some other undesirable expressions into acceptable ones:

No	*Yes*
girl, as in: I'll have my *girl* check that.	I'll have my *secretary* (my *assistant*) check that. (Or use the person's name.)
the *fair sex;* the *weaker sex*	*women*
female-gender word forms, such as *authoress, poetess, Jewess*	*author, poet, Jew*

the better half; ball and chain	*wife*
career girl or *career woman*	name the woman's profession: *Attorney Ellen Smith; Marie Sanchez, a journalist* (*editor; business executive; doctor; lawyer;* or *agent*)
Housewives are feeling the pinch of higher prices.	*Consumers* (*customers* or *shoppers*) are feeling the pinch of higher prices.

In descriptions of men, especially men in the home, references to general ineptness should be avoided. Men should not be characterized as dependent on women for meals, or clumsy in household maintenance or self-care, or as objects of fun (the henpecked husband).

Humanity at Large

In references to humanity at large, language should include women and girls. Common problems encountered when trying to meet this goal stem from "*man*-words" and singular pronouns.

Man-Words. The word *man* has long been used to denote not only a male person, but also, generically, humanity at large. However, to many people today the word *man* has become so closely associated with "a male human being" that they consider it no longer broad enough to be applied to any person or to human beings as a whole. In deference to this position, alternative expressions should be used whenever such substitutions do not produce an awkward or artificial construction. In cases where man-words must be used, special efforts should be made to ensure that pictures and other devices make explicit that such references include women. The following are some possible substitutions for man-words:

No	*Yes*
mankind	humanity; human beings; human race; people
If a man drove 50 miles . . .	If a person (or driver) drove 50 miles . . .
the best man for the job	the best person (or candidate) for the job
man-made	synthetic; manufactured; artificial; constructed; of human origin
manpower	human power; human energy; workers; workforce
grow to manhood	grow to adulthood; grow to manhood or womanhood

Singular Pronouns. Because the English language lacks a generic singular pronoun signifying "he or she," it has been customary and grammatically sanctioned to use masculine pronouns in expressions such as "anyone . . . *he*," and "each customer . . . *his* bill." Nevertheless, we should avoid whenever possible the pronouns *he, him,* and *his* when referring to the hypothetical person or humanity in general. Here are possible alternatives to consider:

Alternative	*No*	*Yes*
1. Reword to eliminate unnecessary gender pronouns.	The average American drinks *his* coffee black.	The average American drinks black coffee.
2. Recast into the plural.	The average *American* drinks *his* . . . . The shopper . . . *she*	*Most Americans* drink *their* coffee black. Shoppers . . . *they*
3. Alternate male and female expressions and examples.	Supervisors often say, "*He's* not the right man for the job," or "*He* lacks the qualifications for success."	Supervisors often say, "*She's* not the right person for the job," or "*He* lacks the qualifications for success."
4. Replace the masculine pronoun with *one, you, he or she, her or his.* (Use *he or she* and its variations sparingly to avoid clumsy prose.)	This sale benefits every charge customer. He may purchase up to	This sale benefits every charge customer. *One* (or *he or she*) may purchase up to . . . .
5. Repeat the noun (or a similar noun) if at least a few words intervene.	The executive benefits from this policy every month. *He* may choose from	The executive benefits from this policy every month. Each *executive* (or *manager*) may . . . .
6. Sometimes change to passive voice instead of active voice.	Every employee has an assigned parking place. *He should park* his car in	Every employee has an assigned parking place. Each car *should be parked* in . . . .

7. In long reports, to avoid severe problems of repetition or inept wording, it may sometimes be best to use the generic *he* freely; but you should add, in the preface and as often as necessary in the text, emphatic statements that the masculine pronouns are being used for succinctness and are intended to refer to both men and women. Each communicator must use good judgment regarding which alternatives to choose.

Names, Titles, and Parallel Language

Expressions used to designate men and women should, whenever possible, treat the sexes equally—by using their own names, nonsexist titles, and parallel language.

Own Names. Women should be referred to by their own names in the same ways that men are. Both should be called by their full names, by first or last name only, or by title. Unnecessary reference to a woman's marital status should be avoided. Whether married or not, a woman may be referred to by the name by which she chooses to be known, whether her name is her original or her married name.

No	Yes
Ron Smith and Helen	Ron Smith and Helen Brown
Helen and Smith	Helen and Ron
Mrs. Brown and Smith	Ms. Brown (because she prefers Ms.) and Mr. Smith
Mrs. Kohn and David Green	Hilda Kohn and David Green or Mrs. Kohn and Dr. Green

Occupational Terms Ending in "Man". Whenever desirable, occupational titles should be nonsexist. Terms ending in "man" may be replaced by terms that can include members of either sex unless they refer to a particular person.

No	Yes
businessman	business executive; business manager
congressman	member of Congress; representative (but Congress*man* Koch and Congress-*woman* Swanson)
cameraman	camera operator
fireman	firefighter
foreman	supervisor
insurance man	insurance agent
mailman; postman	mail carrier; letter carrier
policeman or policewoman	police officer
salesman	sales representative; salesperson; sales clerk
steward, stewardess	flight attendant

Regarding "chairman," many women as well as men still prefer this title and use it for all heads of committees or departments regardless of sex. The nonsexist communicator, however, can use various alternatives. Among them are: chairperson, chairman and chairwoman, head, leader, coordinator, moderator, the person presiding at (or chairing) a meeting, presiding officer, or the chair.[13]

Parallel Language. Such words as *lady* and *gentleman, husband* and *wife, mother* and *father* are role words. *Ladies* should be used for women only when men are referred to as *gentlemen.* Like a male shopper, a woman in a grocery store should be called a *customer* not a *housewife.*

No	*Yes*
the men and the ladies	the men and the women
	the ladies and the gentlemen
	the girls and the boys
man and wife	husband and wife

The foregoing discussion and examples have introduced you to ways you can reconstruct, substitute, or omit expressions in order to correct discriminatory sexist communication. However, always remember that good judgment is necessary. Before you change any words, check their meanings and roots to be sure they need to be changed. For some expressions changes could be unnecessary and ridiculously incorrect.

In summary, for overall correctness in business communications you should always watch for the little things as well as for the big things. And never leave checking for correctness solely to your secretary. Once you sign your name or initials to the message, you assume responsibility for everything on the page—correct language level, facts, figures, words, mechanics, nondiscrimination, and also all the other pertinent C qualities discussed in this book.

SUMMARY CHECKLIST OF BUSINESS WRITING PRINCIPLES

Completeness: Answer all questions asked
Give something extra, when desirable
Check for the five W's and any other essentials

Conciseness: Omit trite expressions
Avoid unnecessary repetition and wordy statements
Include only relevant facts . . . with courtesy
Organize effectively

---

[13]For decades the accepted procedure at meetings when addressing a female presiding officer has been "Madam Chairman." Ardent nonsexist communicators have asked, humorously, how a male presiding officer would feel if he were addressed as "Sir Chairwoman."

Consideration:	Focus on "you" instead of "I" and "we"
	Show reader benefit or interest in reader
	Emphasize the positive, pleasant facts
	Apply integrity to your messages
Concreteness:	Use specific facts and figures
	Put action in your verbs
	Choose vivid, image-building words
Clarity:	Choose short, familiar, conversational words
	Construct effective sentences and paragraphs
	Achieve appropriate readability
	Include examples, illustrations, and other visual aids, when desirable
Courtesy:	Be sincerely tactful, thoughtful, and appreciative
	Omit expressions that irritate, hurt, or belittle
	Grant and apologize good-naturedly
	Answer your mail promptly
Correctness:	Use the correct level of language
	Include only accurate facts, words, and figures
	Maintain acceptable writing mechanics
	Choose nonsexist expressions
	Apply all other pertinent C qualities

EXERCISES

1. Revise the following sentences so that meanings are clear. If necessary, use more than one concise sentence.

   a. During a job interview the executive wants to hear what you can do in a few seconds.
   b. Enclosed are your contracts on Gary Green in triplicate.
   c. Mr. Jones visited the factory yesterday and lectured on "Destructive Pests." A large number were present.
   d. Your Memorial Day speech will be followed by the firing squad.
   e. Next Monday we will see a program about mothers who give birth to babies that are alcoholics.
   f. From the mayor of a city to the county engineer:
   I have reviewed the plans of Metro, their ability to finance, and in some areas, realizing a great number of years may elapse, because of financial conditions and the build-up of areas, before construction is warranted of sanitary trunk lines for sewers, I think it is very appropriate at this time that the county enter into a study and possibly use their ability given to them under the County Services Act of operating lagoons and serving areas that can develop only if sanitary sewers are constructed.

g. From one insurance company to another insurance company:

```
Frankly, the information we have while it may disclose some con-
tributory negligence on our assured's part which, of course, is
questionable, we still feel that your assured had he not been
driving at the high rate of speed that he was could have swerved
to his right and avoided our assured's vehicle but due to the
fact he was coming down a hill at such a tremendous rate of
speed with no control over his car and struck our assured, there
was enough room to the right of your assured to have turned
slightly and, therefore, avoided the accident.
```

h. `Working in a grocery, several professors chat with him daily.`

i. `She wanted a policy for her house that cost $100 a year.`

j. `Although working full time on an outside job, Tom's grades re-`
   `mained good.`

k. `Thank you for your letter concerning the 10 pianos we received`
   `by airmail this morning.`

l. `When only four years old, this customer's mother died.`

m. `Inform me of your intentions as to the liquidation of this bal-`
   `ance.`

n. `To reinstate your policy will require proof of insurability as`
   `to physical condition.`

2. Check the Fog Index of two pieces of business writing—one that you consider easy to read and one that is difficult. Then tell the class how the Fog Index of each agrees with your readability level. Use examples from this list:
   a. Letter from a company to a customer
   b. Annual report
   c. Magazine read by the masses or members of a certain profession
   d. *The Wall Street Journal*
   e. Article on front page of your daily newspaper
   f. Report or textbook. One sample selection for a 500-word report, article, or booklet is sufficient. In long reports (or books) five or six separated samples may be desirable.

3. Assume you are writing to the average citizen. What synonyms for the following words would be better understood?

accelerate	contingent	rescind
aggregating	default	validity
allegation	discrepancy	terminate

4. Encircle the correct choice of "a" or "an" before each entry in the following list.

a an hotel	a an heroic effort
a an honorary degree	a an hour
a an unit	a an heir
a an historical event	a an union
a an honest opinion	a an unanimous decision
a an unique method	a an humble opinion

5. Correct the errors in the following message from a savings association to a real estate corporation:

In rgard to your letter of the fifteenth, let me explain our policy on our Certificates of deposit. Your certificate comes due on November 9, 198_. At this time the interest check will be dispersed as you indicated at the time of your initial deposit and the certificate will be automaticly renewed unless you give us instructions to the contrary.

In your letter you asked that the certificate be "rolled over for another 30 days." As I have explained our certificates have a life of 6 months, if you want the certificate renewed it will automaticaly be done. If you wish the certificate to be dispersed please contackt us prior to the experation date.

6. *Exercises on choice of words:* Choose the word or words that should be used in each sentence listed below. (For choice of words in some sentences you might need to consult a dictionary or grammar book in addition to the rules for word usage in this chapter.)

a. This act will not (effect, affect) my confidence in you.
b. I am (anxious, eager) to (tell, advise) you that you are correct.
c. This (party, customer) is (well known, well-known) in town.
d. We assure you (its, it's) a pleasure to do as you suggest.
e. We (shall, will) gladly handle the order (providing, provided) the firm is willing.
f. Enclosed (please find, is) my check for ($100.00, $100).
g. We have a large (quantity, amount, number) of suits on hand.
h. It will be (all right, alright) if you come later.
i. The dissension (between, among) the five departments has been settled.
j. The man (who, which, that) was crossing the street was struck by a car (who, which, that) Mr. Smith was driving.
k. Will you please see that (the undersigned, the writer, I) (is, am) notified of any changes in prices.
l. We sold (fewer, less) fans last month.
m. We had (already, all ready) received the dress when your letter arrived. I am (already, all ready) to write this customer.
n. Your rug should (lie, lay) (smooth, smoothly) on the floor. Please (lay, lie) the files on my desk.
o. The (principal, principle) officer of this company is Ms. Jones. The (principal, principle) of honesty should be evident in our letters. Now that you've been paying on your house for three years, how much (principle, principal) have you accumulated? The (principle, principal) of the school criticized the boy because he didn't know the (principal, principle) river in the United States is the Mississippi.
p. Of the two plans, the second is (least, less) expensive.
q. Do you know (who, whom) the manager promoted yesterday?
r. The credit for this sale goes to (you, yourself).
s. The chief engineer and (myself, I) inspected the factory.
t. I never knew anyone could be so slow in answering when a person wrote to (them, her or him).

u. Be courteous to (whomever, whoever) comes to your desk.

v. A large number of bills (is, are) outstanding.

w. The large number of employees (prevent, prevents) us from adhering to this suggestion.

x. We understand (you, your) wanting to be a sales representative.

7. Assume the following words appear in the letters and reports your secretary has typed for your signature. Without the help of any source, determine which words are misspelled and correct the errors. Then check all words (in a dictionary or in class) to see how many you had right.[14]

1. accommodation	31. insistance
2. aquainted	32. interupt
3. attatched	33. it's (possessive)
4. attendence	34. knowlege
5. attornies	35. labled
6. batchelor's degree	36. manageing
7. benefited	37. mispelled
8. brosure	38. occured
9. compliment (meaning supplement)	39. oppurtunity
10. catalog	40. payed
11. childrens'	41. paralel
12. colledge	42. personnel
13. consede	43. pertinent
14. concensus	44. preceed
15. corps	45. prefered
16. congradulate	46. proceedure
17. convience	47. proceed
18. correspondant	48. questionaire
19. defendent	49. recieve
20. descendant	50. referance
21. desert (meaning cake)	51. referred
22. develop	52. recind
23. dissadvantage	53. reccomodation
24. disatisfaction	54. resistence
25. envelop	55. salesbility
26. excellant	56. seperate
27. existance	57. sargeant
28. Febuary	58. servicable
29. heighth	59. stationary (paper)
30. incessent	60. writting

[14] If you need a handy pocket-size dictionary to help you spell correctly, try *20,000 Words,* compiled by Louis A. Leslie, McGraw-Hill Book Company, New York, 1977.

8. Collect two or more business letters or memos (that you, friends, or relatives have received)—each preferably 100 words or more. If possible, try to get messages that are individually typed—not processed forms. Evaluate each message by:
   a. Underscoring once all trite and wordy expressions
   b. Underscoring twice all technical language that the reader might not understand
   c. Placing parentheses around all negative expressions
   d. Encircling all words and expressions that produce an unpleasant tone—such as cutting words and abrasive language
   e. Checking for violations of mechanics—misspelled words, confusing punctuation, vague or incomplete sentences, number of sentences exceeding 45 words, "goozling" words (unnecessarily big words), incorrectly used words, and sexist expressions.

   Be sure to keep these letters after this assignment is completed, because you'll be using them again and again for other purposes.

9. Suggest acceptable nonsexist alternatives, if desirable, for the following words:

bellboy	crewman	manhole
cattleman	furnaceman	manpower
checkroom girl	layman	showmanship
committeeman	lumberman	spaceman
craftsman	maiden name	unionman

10. For the following interdepartmental memo (a) list all sexist statements and (b) opposite each statement write a nonsexist version. Number the paragraphs and your corrections in each.

```
TO:       Mrs. Erica Cosmos           DATE:  May 10, 198_
FROM:     Tom Grant
SUBJECT:  CPC Staffing Requirements


I would like your support along with that of Charles to serve as co-
chairmen of our Staffing Requirements Committee for the Communica-
tions Planning Centers.  As you know, the CPC's are a most important
sales tool and we need highly qualified manpower with top salesmen.

The other committeemen I have appointed to work with you are: Scott
Durke, Fred Picker, Miss Helen Jaynes, and Mrs. Thoms.

One of the important jobs at the centers is that of a professional
sales demonstrator, which requires many man-hours of work.  This man
will be an entry-level group manager, responsible for all equipment
sales demonstrations.  He must of course be extremely knowledgeable
about all our products and services.  Currently this assignment is
being handled by Miss Carolyn Mayer at our XY Center and by Kermit
Smith at ABC Center.  Both are doing a superior job.

We would like this task to be a one-year rotational assignment and
be filled with the best available candidate--man or lady.  This job
experience can greatly benefit the assigned individual and make him
```

more valuable to our company on future reassignments. Please get
your committee together this week to begin an extensive search for
good people that are available for these assignments. If you need
help typing announcements or other materials, I've asked the gals
in the typing pool to be available for you.

chapter

5

Planning before Communicating

Whether you are preparing an oral or a written business communication, you need to think and plan before presenting your message. Though you may understand the communication process and know the C qualities, your careful planning of the message is most important for effective communication. Your goal is to gain the desired reaction or action from the recipient.

Your letter on company stationery or your telephone call as a company representative to a customer can create in the receiver's mind a favorable or unfavorable attitude toward your entire organization. Even after you have communicated orally on an important matter, you are often asked to "put it in writing." Your message then becomes a permanent record which the recipient can reread anytime. Also, if geographical distance separates you and the person with whom you are communicating, or if the material is complex, technical, or lengthy, writing is often the only effective means of communication. A well-organized letter is like a bridge that spans the gap between you and the receiver of your message.

This chapter discusses the planning steps, basic organizational patterns, and openings and closings—all essential to good business communication. Though the ideas presented here and in later chapters can be useful for both written and oral communication, the discussion and examples focus on written messages, because most communicators need more help on them.

SIX PLANNING STEPS

To communicate effectively, you should go through the following six steps before you transmit your message:

1. Know the purpose of the message.
2. Visualize your reader (or listener).
3. Choose the ideas to include.
4. Get all the facts to back up these ideas.
5. Organize your ideas in the most effective order.
6. Write, revise, and proofread.

Know the Purpose

When you receive a letter, what runs through your mind—even before you begin to read? Usually you're wondering what the writer wants or what the purpose is. In fact, it's rather difficult for you to grasp all the various ideas of a particular message until you do know the purpose.

For example, suppose you receive a form letter[1] in which the first five paragraphs mention, in general, economic conditions, inflation, labor disputes, strikes, segregation, religious tolerance, and Americans' responsibilities for change. As you read the

---

[1] Form letters are identical messages reproduced from one master draft and sent to two or more persons. See Form Messages in Chapter 6, pages 152–154.

message, you cannot figure out why the writer sent it or what purpose the various facts are supposed to support. Then comes the last paragraph:

```
My business, of course, is to sell hosiery, underwear, and knit
goods.  Please think of me when you have need for these products
and let us not forget our obligation to every other fellow Amer-
ican.
                     Sincerely yours,
```

That letter could have started with a statement like: "Here is another newsy message to keep you posted on the crucial domestic happenings of our times." Then you would have known why the message was being sent. At least you wouldn't be in a quandry as you read the rest of the letter.

Like you, your reader appreciates knowing the purpose of your message. Sometimes you may have several reasons for your communication. Your first step is to determine your main purpose. For instance, is it to get an immediate replacement for a damaged article or just to be angry and complain? Angry accusations against readers may antagonize them and delay your desired action. As you will see later when studying organizational plans for various messages, you should mention the main purpose of most, but not all, letters and memos in or near the first paragraph. For all reports, state the purpose in the introduction.

In addition to the specific purpose of each message, all communications have, of course, an underlying general purpose—to build goodwill. For example, in a refusal or a collection letter, the purpose should be twofold—not only to refuse a request or ask for money, but also to maintain the customer's goodwill.

Thus, be sure to keep both your specific and the general purpose in mind as you plan every message.

Visualize Your Reader

After reading about the communication process (Chapter 2), you realize how important it is to better understand the people with whom you communicate. If you are well acquainted with your readers—or even if you have met them at least once—you can actually visualize each individual as you write. And you can better adapt your message to fit each individual's mental filter.

Most of your writing, however, will probably be directed to people you have never met. If you are sending a message to one person, you should try to classify that person the best ways you can—business or professional person or laborer; superior (boss), colleague, or subordinate; man or woman; young, middle-aged, or elderly; new or long-time customer; and so on. If you are addressing a form message to many people, remember the caution that every person within any group has a unique filter and special interests! You should try to discover characteristics common to all of them and then imagine you're talking to one individual within that group. For example:

1. In upward communications (to your superiors), you should support factual statements with detail (but not to the degree that the boss becomes impatient), curb personal opinion, and tactfully give only conclusions unless you're requested to include recommendations.

2. In downward communications (to your subordinates), be diplomatic—never overbearing nor insulting. When you give instructions, be sure you supply all needed information clearly and give reason(s) for an order whenever desirable. Also (if you can), point out how your order benefits those it affects.

3. In communications to successful retailers, assume they know their business well. You'd insult them if you talked down to them by saying, for example, that the right markup and an adequate turnover of merchandise will give a profit.

4. If you write to strangers for information, you must tell them how you intend to use it, particularly if the information is confidential or tends to be confidential.

5. Older persons may be especially interested in security, while younger persons look more toward the future.

6. Some people are more sensitive to tone (cutting words, negative words, and curtness) than are others.

7. To anyone not familiar with terminology of the business, you need to use easy-to-understand words and explain any technical terms.

To help get the desired response, you must also be sensitive to the feelings of your readers, as the following examples illustrate:

1. A chamber of commerce president included this sentence in his reply to a woman who had inquired about accommodations in and near his resort town:

   ```
   You can wear anything you choose and wearing nothing is approximated
   so closely at times that I think you could get by with that if you
   were so inclined.
   ```

   The woman who received this reply was a business woman in her fifties who was anything but a "swinger." She definitely forgot about staying at that place.

2. A university professor received from a leading corporation a complicated, unclear letter to stockholders; she wrote the chairperson suggesting the need for simplifying communications to the average stockholder. Here's part of the chairperson's reply:

   ```
   Yours is the first criticism we have had from the many thousands of
   stockholders who have already sent in the proxies saying that the
   purpose of the meeting was not understandable to them.  I do not see
   how I can state the facts any more clearly and simply than was done
   in my letter of January 18.
   ```

   Not only did the chairperson insult the professor but the reply itself was unclear. The wording gives the reader the impression that the *proxies* said "the purpose of the meeting was not understandable."

3. Finally, the writer of the following angry message about a mail-order firm's collection letter forgot that the person receiving his message was perhaps innocent of everything relating to the mix-up and misunderstanding:

   ```
   I just mailed to you bunch of idiots a check in the amount of $42.00.
   This morning from L.A., Cal, I received this piece of paper similar
   to the pile of junk I received yesterday from the same source.  I am
   ```

```
getting plenty tired of all this boloney you knotheads are pulling
off because I have cancelled checks from away back 20 yrs.  I also
have a copy of the last contract and my payments are not due til the
25th of the month.  I have typed a copy of that contract and along
with other proof I am mailing the whole package to Chicago to see if
I can't talk them into tying the can to about half of you numbskulls.
```

This disgruntled individual should have realized he was insulting innocent people who, in turn, had to act upon his message! Being called an idiot, knothead, and numbskull hardly makes a person willing to go all out to help someone.

In short, when you write you must visualize your reader as well as you can, and write with the individual in mind.

Choose the Ideas

After you have decided on the purpose and visualized the reader, you can begin to choose the ideas that go into the message. If you let only the purpose and reader govern what is included in your letter or report, you're more likely to avoid irrelevant ideas and overall wordiness.

In simple messages that discuss one or two points, you can make mental notes of the subjects you want to include. In more complex messages, you'll probably want to underline key words in the letter to be answered or jot down suggestions in the margin or on a memo pad. In a complicated letter or report, you may need a full outline of the major headings and subheadings.

Naturally, the ideas that you will include in your communication depend upon the type of message you're considering. For example, take a welcome letter that a savings and loan association sends to a new customer. What is the purpose of this kind of letter? If you say the only purpose is to welcome the customer, then one or two sentences should suffice. They might merely thank new customers for selecting your association and welcome them. But should the purpose of this message be *only* to welcome? Shouldn't you also help them know your policy concerning savings accounts, the overall services available to them, and your association's eagerness to be their financial headquarters? If so, then the following ideas should be included in your welcome letter. (List ideas as they come to you; rearrange them after you choose the right organizational plan.)

1. Welcome the customers and thank them for opening an account.
2. State some of your services—free parking, save-by-mail, mortgage loans, special accounts.
3. Tell them the hours you're open to serve them.
4. Mention percentage of interest they earn.
5. Assure them you're ready to help with their problems or wishes.

After you have decided on these ideas and completed the other planning steps, you can mail a good welcome letter. (See, for example, letter 2, page 34.)

Get All the Facts

Having determined what ideas to include, ask yourself if you need any specific figures, facts, or quotations. Be sure you know your company policy, procedures, and product details if this message requires them. Perhaps you should check with your boss, colleague, subordinates, or the files for an exact percentage, name of an individual, date, address, figure, or statement. Also, in reports that include tables or other illustrations, you should have these visual aids finished (or at least in rough draft form) at this stage.[2]

Organize Your Ideas

Before you write the message, outline it (in your mind or on paper). The order in which you present your ideas is often as important as the ideas themselves. "The discipline of translating thoughts into words and organizing these thoughts logically has no equal as intellectual training. . . . Disorganized writing reflects a disorganized, illogical (and untrained) mind."[3]

Choose the organizational plan after you have determined your purpose, collected all needed facts, and asked yourself "How will the reader react to these ideas?" The basic plans are discussed later in this chapter, briefly, and more specifically in other chapters.

Write, Revise, and Proofread

For the routine, short communications, you will usually be able to dictate (or write) quite easily with little or no revising. Try to compose rapidly from your outline and get down the main framework of ideas. Temporarily forget about mechanics of spelling, punctuation, sentence structure, but perhaps make notes in the margin to check certain places after you've finished the first draft. If you dictate your messages, see page 698 for additional suggestions.

For other writing—especially complex, longer messages and reports, new form letters, and any communication that is to be published—you should expect to revise, sometimes substantially. Top correspondents and authors have confirmed again and again that the best writers rewrite and rewrite and rewrite. Tolstoy revised *War and Peace* five times; James Thurber rewrote his stories as many as fifteen times.

A business writer can't and needn't rewrite everything 15 times. . . . But he does have an obligation—to his reader and to his employer—to reread what he has written before it is mailed and to rewrite it when necessary. . . . It may take time, but it's part of his job. . . . The hardest part is making each word and sentence say exactly

---

[2] You'll find further discussions on this planning step in Chapters 3 and 15 under Completeness.
[3] John Fielden, "What Do You Mean I Can't Write?" *Harvard Business Review*, May–June 1964.

what you want it to say so that your reader will interpret it correctly and react as you want him to.[4]

To revise effectively, you must read your draft objectively, from the viewpoint of your recipient. Make sure the message meets all principles of good business writing. Is it *complete, concise, considerate, concrete, clear, courteous, correct*—in content and all mechanics?[5] Read paragraph by paragraph for the continuity of ideas. Then check sentence by sentence and every word, figure, and punctuation mark for the other C qualities.

Whenever desirable, consider suggestions from knowledgeable associates. At times you may feel like the doubtful report writer who remarked to his supervising editor: "You mean you want the revised revision of the fifth revised revision revised?"[6]

Careful proofreading is also essential. After your best revised business message is typewritten—and before it is mailed!—you or other dependable persons should read it. Any error should be corrected so that your paper will reflect favorably on you and your company.[7]

BASIC ORGANIZATIONAL PLANS

Your choice of organizational plan depends upon how you expect your reader to react to your message. And that reaction, of course, depends to some extent upon what is already in your reader's mental filter, as well as on the content of your message.

Business letters, memos, and reports can be arranged by the direct (deductive) approach or the indirect (inductive) approach. For letters and memos you can choose one of four basic organizational plans: the direct-request, good-news, bad-news, and persuasive-request plans. The first two of these use the direct approach; the last two, the indirect approach. All these plans are to be considered as *flexible guides only, not as rigid patterns.* Your own judgment must help you decide the best organization and content of each message.

Direct (Deductive) Approach

When you think your reader will consider your message favorable or neutral and the information understandable (without any obstacle), you can use the direct approach. You begin with the main idea or best news. *After* the opening, you include all necessary explanatory details—in one or several paragraphs—and end with an appropriate, friendly paragraph.

---

[4] Adapted from *Dear Sir:,* vol. 4, no. 1, Correspondence Improvement Section, Public Relations Department, Prudential Insurance Company of America, Newark, 1962.

[5] See Chapters 3 and 4.

[6] Time-wasting retypings can be eliminated by using a machine such as the magnetic-card or magnetic-tape typewriter on which you can make changes or additions easily without having an entire report draft retyped. Text as originally draft-typed is "played out" automatically to each point of revision. Changes or additions are typed manually, and then automatic playout of the corrected copy resumes.

[7] See Correctness in Chapter 4.

The direct-request and good-news plans both have three basic parts, shown in the following sketch and brief outlines:

ORGANIZATIONAL PLANS USING THE DIRECT (DEDUCTIVE) APPROACH

Direct-Request Plan

1. Main idea
   a. Request, main statement, or question
   b. Reason(s) if desirable

2. Explanation
   a. All necessary and desirable details
   b. Numbered questions, if helpful
   c. Easy-reading devices

3. Courteous close, with motivation to action
   a. Clear statement of action desired
   b. Easy action
   c. Dated action, when desirable
   d. Appreciation and goodwill

Good-News Plan

1. Best news or main idea

2. Explanation
   a. All necessary and desirable details
   b. Resale material*
   c. Educational material
   d. Sales promotion material*

3. Positive, friendly close, including, if appropriate:
   a. Appreciation
   b. Clear statement of action desired, if any
   c. Easy action
   d. Dated action, when desirable
   e. Willingness to help further
   f. Reader benefit

Resale material is usually favorable information about a product or service the reader has already bought or is planning to buy. *Sales promotion material* usually includes suggestions for additional products or services the customer may find useful.

Use the direct-request plan when the main purpose of your message is to make a request that requires no persuasion, because the reader will say "yes" readily. Chapter 7, devoted exclusively to direct requests, gives you a variety of examples for such letters and memos. Some direct-request messages are also included in Chapters 12 and 13.

Use the good-news plan for messages that grant requests, announce favorable or neutral information, or exchange routine information between companies. In Chapters 8, 12, and 14 you will have opportunities to study numerous examples of good-news messages that are favorable replies or favorable unsolicited messages.

For reports you can also use this direct, deductive approach, as discussed in Chapter 15.

Indirect (Inductive) Approach

When you think your reader will probably react unfavorably (negatively) to your request or information, you should not spring the main idea in the first paragraph. Instead you will need to begin, preferably, with some relevant pleasant, neutral, or reader-benefit statements; then give adequate explanation *before* you introduce the unpleasant idea(s). You will also need to be especially careful of your word choices and tone, which will influence the reader's reaction.

The bad-news and persuasive-request plans both use the indirect approach. Notice that each has four instead of three parts. You need to take a little longer to present bad news and to persuade!

Main idea

ORGANIZATIONAL PLANS USING THE INDIRECT (INDUCTIVE) APPROACH

Bad-News Plan	*Persuasive-Request Plan*

1. Buffer (pleasant or neutral statements to "get in step" with reader)	1. Attention
	  a. Reader benefit
	  b. Reader-interest theme

2. Explanation
  a. Necessary details, tactfully stated
  b. Pertinent favorable, then unfavorable, facts
  c. Reader-benefit reasons
	2. Interest
	  a. Descriptive details
	  b. Psychological appeals
	  c. Reader benefits

3. Decision (implied or expressed), along with offer of additional help or suggestions

4. Positive, friendly close
   a. Appreciation
   b. Invitation to future action
   c. Clear statement of action desired
   d. Easy action
   e. Dated action, when desirable
   f. Willingness to help further
   g. Reader benefit and goodwill

3. Desire
   a. Statement of request
   b. Conviction material to help create reader's desire to grant request

4. Action
   a. Clear statement of action desired
   b. Easy action
   c. Dated action, when desirable
   d. Special inducement
   e. Reader-benefit plug

The bad-news message is one of the most difficult to write because your reader will consider it unfavorable. In Chapters 9 and 12 you can study various problems and examples that handle bad-news replies and unsolicited messages.

Use the persuasive-request plan when you feel that your readers will probably find obstacles and react negatively unless they are persuaded. Thus you try to show them how they or someone in whom they are interested will benefit from the granting of your request. In Chapter 10 you will find a variety of uses for this plan. In addition, Chapters 11 and 13 also illustrate persuasive requests.

This indirect, inductive plan is adaptable also to report writing, when you have reason to present facts in a "logical" arrangement. (See Chapter 15.)

OPENING AND CLOSING PARAGRAPHS

Two of the most important positions in any business message are the opening and closing paragraphs. You have probably heard the old sayings: "First impressions are lasting" and "We remember best what we read last." Whenever possible, place the main favorable ideas at the beginning and ending of a message. (This advice applies also to business sentences and paragraphs.)

Because openings and closings are so significant, this section gives you an overview so you can concentrate on common essentials before studying various message types in later chapters. (Remember also that the C qualities, discussed in Chapters 3 and 4, apply to *all* paragraphs of messages.)

Opening Paragraphs

Often the opening of a message determines whether the reader continues reading, puts the message aside for later study, or discards it. The following checklist and examples include suggestions for good openings that help make favorable impressions:

CHECKLIST FOR OPENING PARAGRAPHS

1. Choose an opening appropriate for the message and reader. You can begin with:
   a. Main idea or good-news subject—for direct-request, neutral, and good-news messages.
   b. A buffer—for bad-news messages.
   c. Attention-getting statements relevant to letter's purpose—for persuasive requests.
2. Be considerate and courteous.
   a. Get reader into opening.
   b. Focus on the positive.
   c. Use courteous, never irritating, expressions.
3. Make the opening concise and interesting.
   a. Keep first paragraph relatively short.
   b. Use conversational words.
   c. Avoid unnecessary repetition.
4. Check for completeness.
   a. In sentence structure.
   b. Regarding date of letter you're answering.

Choose Openings Appropriate for Message and Reader

Main Idea or Good-News Subject First. Begin directly with the main idea or subject when (1) doing so does not unfavorably affect the relationship between reader and writer, and (2) you are sure the information is considered favorable or neutral by the reader. It is, of course, also important that the reader will understand the main idea if it is in the first paragraph.

Request:	So that the account of Mr. A. B. Smith, deceased, can be transferred to your name as Executor, will you please return to us the following:
Granting:	You will be pleased to know that your recent application for open credit has been approved.
Good news:	Three copies of *Brown's Garden Book* were sent to you today by parcel post as you requested.
Announcement (five W's):	You and your family (*who*) are invited to a machinery demonstration (*what*) next Saturday from 10 a.m. until noon (*when*) in the ballroom of the Statler Hotel (*where*). The purpose of this demonstration is to show and explain to management the operation of the latest data processing equipment (*why*).

Buffer First. When you have bad news for the reader, begin with a buffer. Don't spread gloom with your first words; at least pave the way.

Poor:
> We regret your loan application did not meet our reg- ulations and board policies for approving a loan.

Good:
> Your application for a loan has received our careful attention. It is evident you are doing your best to provide a comfortable home for your family.

Attention-Getting Statements First. When you have a persuasive request (sales letter), begin with relevant statements that will induce the recipient to read further, as in this opening to a licensed dog owner:

> Like most conscientious dog owners, you know that proper food is just as important to a dog as it is to a human being. And you know, too, that if you are trying to make up a scientifically balanced diet for your dog, it involves more time and effort than you can spare. And that's where Muskies can help!

Be Considerate and Courteous

Get Reader into the Opening. Don't emphasize the writer.

Poor:
> We have your letter of June 10 and we have referred it to our legal department and they...

Good:
> You are right! Your insurance does fully cover...

Focus on the Positive. Mention the pleasant and what can be done. Avoid anything you do not want the reader to think about at the beginning. (See also examples on pages 46-47.)

Negative:
> We <u>regret</u> to learn from your letter of September 10 that you found a <u>foreign object</u> upon opening a can of Seacrest oysters.

Positive:
> Thank you for taking the time to tell us about your experience when opening a can of Seacrest oysters.

Use Courteous, Never Irritating, Expressions. Avoid an opening that might anger the reader.

Poor:
> I have your letter of (*date*) and I can't understand why you had difficulty in seeing that our action was correct.

Good:
> Thank you for your courtesy in letting us know your candid feelings regarding action on your claim.

Make the Opening Concise and Interesting

Keep First Paragraph Relatively Short. The first paragraph should be short enough— around six typewritten lines or less—to entice the reader to start reading. The first sentence should average about 17 words and not exceed 20 or 25 words. An inexcusably long opening sentence is the following:

> As doing so may be of possible service to you, I take sending the en-
> closed on-press tear sheet of your sketch as a convenient opportunity
> to recall to you that the privilege--
>
> as a biographee who has cooperated with our compilers by supplying
> and checking data published in it--
>
> which you now still have to an advance of publication subscription
> discount of 25 percent from the regular retail price of the shortly-
> to-issue new edition of Who's What in the United States.
>
> will soon expire on the formal announcement of the actual date of
> publication, for thereafter the standard price at retail must, as a
> matter of inflexible trade usage, invariably apply. (*113 words*)

Use Conversational Words. Avoid trite beginnings. Begin as though you were talking to the reader.

Poor:	Please be advised that we have written the above-captioned policy for this party.
Good:	You'll be glad to know that effective March 15, Mrs. Mary Ryan's fire and theft policy is in force.

Avoid Unnecessary Repetition. Don't begin with sentences that merely repeat what the reader told you.

a. I have your letter of the 21st, in which you informed me that Mr. John Smith called on you for the first time a few weeks ago and that he appealed to you as a capable and intelligent young person.

b. Your letter of March 13, 198_, requested comments and suggestions regarding proposed working papers for the second Technical Panel, 6023.

Check for Completeness

In Sentence Structure. Here are examples of incomplete openings:

1. Reference your letter of January 4, 198_, to Mr. Yokohoma of Japan Air Lines Company, Ltd.

2. Received your letter of January 26, 198_, concerning Ms. Helen M. Smith's application for Associate Membership in the Society of Real Estate Appraisers.

Regarding Date of Letter You're Answering. If the date is *beneficial* to either the reader or writer, include it *but don't stress the date.* The first words in your opening should begin to unfold the most important idea(s).

Poor:	As per your letter of October 10, we have shipped your order today by Railway Express.
Good:	The five dozen Conform hats you ordered October 10 were shipped to you today by Railway Express.

Closing Paragraphs

The closing is more likely to motivate the reader to act as requested if it is appropriately impressive. Here you have the opportunity to bring final focus on the desired action and leave a sense of your courtesy with the reader. What you say in the closing depends upon the purpose of the letter and the ideas in previous paragraphs.

The checklist and examples below again focus on ways to apply the C qualities in closings for various letter and memo situations.

CHECKLIST FOR CLOSING PARAGRAPHS

1. Make your action request complete with the five W's and the H if you want your reader (or someone else) to do something.
   a. Clearly state what action you desire and who should do it. (*what* and *who*)
   b. Make action easy. (*how* and *where*)
   c. Date the action, if desirable. (*when*)
   d. Show reader benefit, if possible. (*why*)
2. End on a positive, courteous thought.
   a. Include any apologies and negatives before last paragraph.
   b. Be friendly.
   c. Show appreciation.
   d. Occasionally add a personal note.
3. Keep last paragraph concise and correct.
   a. Avoid trite expressions.
   b. Omit discussion and worthless details.
   c. Use relatively short and complete sentences.

Make Action Request Complete with Five W's and H

Whenever you are requesting action by your reader or someone else, your closing paragraph will usually be more effective if you make clear *what, who, how, where, when,* and (if appropriate) *why.*

1. *What and Who?: Clear statement of the action you desire your reader (or someone else) to take.*

Should the reader: Phone your office for an appointment? Sign a card or a document? Return it? To whom? Come to your office in person? Send you certain details, merchandise, forms, payments, or opinions? Ask another person to do something?

2. *How and Where?: Easy action.*

Include your phone number (with area code) and extension if you want the reader to phone you. If you are often away from your desk or office, you might mention the best times the reader can reach you.

Enclose a form (card, order blank, questionnaire, document) and an addressed reply envelope (perhaps with postage paid) if you want the reader to furnish information or sign and mail something.

Give complete instructions regarding *where* and *how* if you don't include a form and/or an envelope.

Enclose an envelope large enough to hold and protect the contents whenever you want the reader to return something bulky, confidential, and/or valuable (a document, a check). Have your secretary address the envelope, and, if desirable and possible, affix the necessary postage.

State your office hours and location if you want the reader to come to you in person. When, if at all, is your office open evenings? Do you have a free parking lot? Where?

3. *When?: Dated action.*

Name the date (and the time, if pertinent) whenever you need the reply by a certain time. Tactfully state the reason you need it then—perhaps to meet a printer's deadline or for a speech you are giving at a certain meeting.

4. *Why?: Special inducement to act by a specified time.*

When appropriate, mention some benefit(s) the reader will gain by prompt action. A reader-benefit plug in the ending paragraph(s) is a stimulus to action.

In the following examples, notice how the vague action requests are improved by insertion of some or all the W's and the H:

Vague:	Please take care of this matter at your earliest convenience.
Better:	So that we can discuss suitable arrangements for your meeting, please call me at 323-9900, Ext. 25, before Thursday, June 2.
Vague:	I would appreciate your adjustment soon.
Better:	Please return my repaired EZ camera at no cost to me, according to your guarantee, and thus continue your fine reputation of customer satisfaction. I will need the camera for my trip, beginning August 10.

End on a Positive, Courteous Thought

Include Any Apologies and Negatives before Last Paragraph. Finish with positive statements. Beware especially of endings with *if, hope, trust* (as illustrated on page 47), and *why not.*

Negative: I regret we cannot be more helpful in the study you are making.

Positive: The best of success with your term paper. You have an interesting topic to research.

Negative: <u>Why not</u> fill out and mail the enclosed order blank?

Positive: So that you can enjoy this XY widget on your trip, fill out and mail the enclosed form today.

Be Friendly. Offer to help the reader further or again if that is appropriate. Remember, this is the last thought you're leaving with the reader. An abrupt, demanding, commanding, or angry remark causes unfavorable reaction. Words like *please* or *will you* help soften commands.

Good: Should you have further questions concerning this procedure, Max, please write or call me. My number is 555-4422.

Poor: Send us your check today.

Good: To keep your credit in good standing, please send us your check for $123.94 today.

Poor: I am sorry you had to write two letters, but of course you realize this action wouldn't have been necessary if you had supplied all the necessary information the first time.

Good: Thank you for giving us the opportunity to explain . .

Show Appreciation. Everyone likes sincere praise when it has been earned, but don't thank in advance. As a rule, it is presumptuous to ask people to do something and then thank them for doing it before they have agreed to do so.

Poor: I thank you in advance for your cooperation in informing your employees of these tours.

Good: I will appreciate your cooperation in informing your employees of these tours.

Occasionally Add a Personal Note. When unrelated to the subject discussed in the message, a personal note is appropriate sometimes as a last paragraph or preferably as a postscript.

1. You're fortunate to be at Estes Park this month. The thermometer registered 103° at 3 p.m. here yesterday.

2. Congratulations on the excellent paper you presented to our group last week. I thoroughly
   enjoyed what you said about...

Keep Last Paragraph Concise and Correct

Avoid Trite Expressions. In the examples below, the trite expressions are underlined.

Poor:	Enclosed <u>you will find a self-addressed</u> stamped en-velope <u>for your convenience</u>. (*It's okay to mention the envelope, but tie it in with a more important idea.*)
Good:	Please fill out this form and return it in the en-closed envelope by (*date*).
Poor:	If we can be of service to you in the future, please <u>do not hesitate</u> to contact us as <u>we stand ready</u> to serve you.
Good:	Whenever we can assist you again, please let us know.

Omit Discussion and Worthless Details. You can avoid a long final paragraph by
completing your discussion beforehand. Also, don't tack on a statement already mentioned in the message. Try to confine your ending to five or fewer lines.

Poor:	Again, we thank you for your inquiry.
Good:	Please let us know when we can help you again.

Use Relatively Short and Complete Sentences. Avoid especially those incomplete
endings that begin with an "ing" participle and end with "we are" or "I remain."

Poor:	Trusting this information will prove helpful, I re-main...
Good:	Please let us know if you need additional informa-tion.
Poor:	Hoping to hear from you in the affirmative, I re-main (*or I am*) ...
Good:	Please sign and return the enclosed form. Then you can soon begin to enjoy the comfort of...

SUMMARY

Before transmitting any message, consider carefully the six planning steps; they furnish
the basis for an effective message. Choose a direct or indirect organizational plan, depending upon your reader's probable reaction to the message. And when expressing
your ideas, pay particular attention to the opening and closing paragraphs because of
their strategic importance.

EXERCISES

1. What is your reaction to each of the openings below: Is it good, fair, or poor? Why? If there is more than one opening to consider (indicated by *versus*), which do you prefer? Why?

   a. You made several errors on the reply form you submitted, and you neglected to answer three questions.

   b. Jean Doe, about whom you inquired in your letter of July 6, has kept an account with us since August 13, 1965.

   c. As requested in your letter of June 3, we are very pleased to enclose herewith three copies of our latest administrative directory.

   versus

   Enclosed are three copies of our latest administrative directory that you requested in your letter of June 3.

   versus

   It is a pleasure to comply with your request and enclose three copies of our latest administrative directory.

   d. Our concern about your mortgage payment is not altogether selfish--we see too many people who practice paying late suddenly having to face unexpected bills, and then before they realize it, they are two months past due. Many never fully recover and eventually lose their home.

   versus

   You have failed to correct the existing delinquency on the above-captioned loan, and furthermore, you have made no arrangements for repayment.

   versus

   No reply has been received to our letter of November 8, and your above-numbered loan is in default since October.

   e. We are in receipt of your memo regarding the four #1111 Cragston wheels which you say are defective.

   f. Good news! After reviewing the facts again, we are issuing the desired policy.

   versus

   This is in reply to your letter of March 19, requesting us to review the application which was previously declined.

   g. We will be pleased to consider issuing the desired policy provided you submit a new application by November 15.

   versus

   A new application must be submitted by November 15; otherwise we cannot consider issuing the desired policy.

   h. Congratulations on making the final payment on your home improvement loan #4-5555. We are sure that you had a real happy feeling of satisfaction when you could finally say to yourself, "Well, that debt is paid in full."

versus

> Our records show that the balance on the loan account above has been paid off.

2. What is your reaction to each of the closings below? Is it good, average, or poor? Why?

   a. Thank you for coming to see us. We are sorry we could not grant your request.
   b. We hope our error has not inconvenienced you too much.
   c. When it is convenient, please let me know your decision.

   versus

   > I trust you will avail yourself of the opportunity of making either of these changes and when your decision is reached, notify me at your earliest convenience. I await the pleasure of your reply.

   d. You are never too young or too old to begin saving for a comfortable, financially worry-free retirement. Start today by opening a Check-A-Month Retirement Income savings account at State Federal and let us help you reach a sound retirement goal.
   e. We are sorry that we are unable to be of service to you and hope that we can help you at some time in the future.
   f. Please let us know when we can help you again.
   g. When you opened an account here, this became your bank. Please let us serve you in any way which will add to your convenience.
   h. We appreciate your interest and will keep you informed of all developments.
   i. Hoping to hear from you, I remain...
   j. Fill out this form and return to me.
   k. Trust that this will answer your question.
   l. We regret that we are unable to be of further assistance to you.
   m. As soon as you return the four completed forms, I'll airmail one to Chicago for prompt rating. In this way you will receive the renewal as quickly as possible.
   n. Again, let me repeat how sorry I am to have not answered sooner.

3. The following set of letters consists of an inquiry from a church to a bank and a reply to the inquiry.
   a. Which organizational plan does the inquiry follow?
   b. Evaluate the opening and closing paragraphs of the inquiry.
   c. What is the purpose of the reply? What organizational plan should be used?
   d. Evaluate the opening and closing paragraphs of the reply.
   e. Does the reply include the ideas necessary to fulfill the purpose? Are the ideas organized effectively? What improvements can you suggest?

Inquiry

Gentlemen

We would like to request your permission to post a church directional sign (First Christian Church) with directional arrow at the edge of your property parking lot on First Avenue, near Central.

This is an attractive, small sign on a neatly painted post. This is very important to our church because of the fact that Central Street is probably the shortest street in (*city*). The size of the sign is about 15" x 15".

The exact location of the sign will be specified to us as soon as we bring written permission from you from our office to Mr. Smith at City Hall. He will then advise us as to how and where to place the sign so that it will give a good appearance and not interfere with either traffic or your business operations.

Please indicate your permission hereon and return your reply to this office as soon as possible.

We appreciate your cooperation.

Reply

My dear Reverend Glouster

Thank you for your recent letter requesting permission to post a church directional sign in the corner of our parking lot on First Avenue near Central.

Unauthorized parking in the lot during our business hours has been a continuous problem for our bank. The parking lot already has several signs posted for different purposes. An additional sign in this corner of the parking lot could cause the public confusion regarding the use of the parking area. We, therefore, find it necessary to decline your request.

Your parishioners are welcome to continue to use this parking lot on Sundays and at other times that you have church services which do not conflict with the business hours of the bank. We appreciate and wish to continue the cordial relationship with you and members of your church.

4. The following reply is from the Blank Oyster Company, Anytown, to an out-of-state customer who complained that she found two "ugly specimens" in her favorite brand of canned oysters.
   a. What is (should be) the purpose of this message?
   b. What organizational plan should be used?
   c. Evaluate the opening and closing paragraphs and the explanation.
   d. Point out the portions that are "resale" material and "apology." Are they well placed? Discuss.
   e. Do you think the letter helps restore the customer's confidence? Why?

Thank you for giving us the opportunity to reply to your experience with Blank Brand oysters. We appreciate your thoughtfulness in writing.

Your enclosure turned out to be small pieces of the root section of a common seaweed which grows on the oysterbeds in great abundance. We are stumped how this substance could stick to an oyster through three successive washings and inspections in the canning process and still escape detection by our packers. But it did, and we are sorry that it happened.

It is of little help to explain that this harmless vegetable substance became totally sterile when the oysters were cooked in the can. You did exactly the right thing when you wrote about the incident.

Today we are sending you by parcel post two cans of Blank Brand oysters with our compliments. You are the discriminating consumer we want to please.

5. An office supply firm sends the following letter to parents of graduating high school seniors who have completed college entrance requirements. (For parents of a daughter, the word *son* is changed to *daughter*.)
   a. What is the purpose of this letter?
   b. What organizational plan does the message use?
   c. Evaluate each paragraph in terms of the suggested organizational plan for this type of letter.

Dear Mr. and Mrs. (*name*)

With high school graduation just four weeks away, you may be searching for an appropriate present for your son. The Butler portable typewriter is a practical gift for the college-bound student, one which will provide him with continuous benefits throughout his college years.

Your son will find that a typewriter, like paper and pen, is a necessary part of his college equipment. Nowadays, instructors usually demand that written assignments be typewritten. Typed reports are neat and legible, and they accurately reflect student effort. Furthermore, a typewriter can work to reduce the time pressure students experience by enabling them to complete notes and outlines more rapidly than they could by hand. And, of course, a portable typewriter is especially well suited for campus use simply because it's portable.

Unlike other machines, the Butler portable combines the quality features of an office typewriter with the storage and transportation convenience of a portable. Your son will find that the Butler copyset dial will allow him to make up to 10 clear carbons; that the extra large carriage will enable him to type on oversize paper; and that changeable type bars will permit him to include a variety of technical signs and symbols in his typing. You'll find these and many additional Butler features fully described in the booklet enclosed.

The Butler portable is a value in price as well as features, for it costs just $130. And, if you like, we'll be glad to arrange the payment plan that best suits your budget.

For your convenience our offices will remain open to 9 each week night from now until May 28. Ample parking is available on the west side of the building. We would enjoy meeting both of you and showing you why more people choose a Butler portable than any other make--and why it is a most useful and timely gift for your son.

6. Below is a wordy memo from the auditor of disbursements in Seattle to the auditor of disbursements in Los Angeles. Both people work for the same organization. Your job is to revise this monstrosity. The revision should be no longer than four or five sentences. (A *rear support* is a metal holder for a large ledger or dictionary you usually find only in libraries.)

We previously sent you copies of our correspondence with the Albert M. Hunter, Inc., relative to the Hunter Wage Charts. Particular attention is directed to our comments relative to the rear supports 4½ inches in length, which in our opinion were too long, in our letter dated April 8. As a result of our comments, Albert M. Hunter, Inc., developed rear supports 2½ inches in length which they furnished us to replace supports 4½ inches in length.

On July 19 we sent you by express 26 sets of the rear supports 2½ inches in length. We are of the opinion that the rear supports 2½ inches in length are a considerable improvement over the rear supports 4½ inches in length and have accordingly replaced the rear supports 4½ inches in length on the Hunter Wage Charts in use by us with rear supports 2½ inches in length.

We assume that you will also wish to replace the rear supports 4½ inches in length on the Hunter Wage Charts in use by you with the rear supports 2½ inches in length. If you make the replacement, please return the rear supports 4½ inches in length to us in order that we can return them to Albert M. Hunter, Inc., in accordance with their request.

For your information, the rear supports 2½ inches in length to replace the rear supports 4½ inches in length were furnished by Albert M. Hunter, Inc., free of charge with the understanding that the rear supports 4½ inches in length would be returned to them.

If you prefer to continue using the rear supports 4½ inches in length, please return the rear supports 2½ inches in length to us in order that we can return them to Albert M. Hunter, Inc.

7. Revise the following letter—from a college bookstore to a small manufacturer. Though the purpose is stated at the beginning, the letter rambles and seems artificially friendly. Improve it wherever desirable.

Once again with your kind permission, will you please make for us four armbands, blue felt, white sewn letters, and white chain stitching as per the attached layout, and if you please Mr. Cowell, we have marked on the layout for the operator to kindly make these up just as we show them, and not change them. What we mean by that, in a most friendly way, this is a little order which you made up for us a few days ago, and the operator, thinking it would be perfectly all right, transposed the position of some of the lettering, so that they were not uniform all the way, and too, inadvertently on one or two of them left one or two of the letters out, and we are not complaining about that at all, all we want to say sincerely is that we are grateful for your taking care of these little things for us, and we are not registering any complaint at all, for we are using them for samples and do not expect you for one moment to do this again without your regular charge, for you make nothing on it, and you are just like us, we know, doing this to satisfy a customer, we being a customer, for other things, and if we weren't we would not have the nerve to ask you to make these, so therefore, if you please, this is for a bunch of women and they are a little bit more particular then men, and if the operator will just follow what we have laid out everything will be fine.

Thanking you so much, and with best wishes and kindest regards, we are...

8. Discuss the purpose and weaknesses in each of the following letters. Then revise one to improve it in every way you can.

Letter A

Reply from a motel manager to a husband and wife who requested accommodations for two weeks starting one month from today.

Dear Sir and Madam

Your letter of the 23d. inst was received on the 25th, and in reply will say, I can give you two rooms for time you desire them, and can make you very comfortable with the exception of hot water.

My wife is away on a vacation and shut off the gas water heater, but the few guests here at present find the water warm enough for a shower bath. Sea bathing is close by, and we are in a very desirable location and very central. You could come and stop with me for a day or so and if it meets with your approval stay for the two weeks.

The price would be $15.00 per person per day or $99.00 per week each. Please let me know if you decide to be my guest and the time you expect to arrive. Thank you kindly.

Letter B

Reply from a sardine cannery in Canada to a college student who wrote that he especially liked the sardines but to please improve the can.

We thank you for your letter of April 28th and might say that we have a letter before us from our broker in Seattle wishing to purchase a carload of our sardines. After we received your letter we were a little uneasy about shipping him another car; however, on thinking the matter over if you had not liked our sardines we presume you would not have taken the trouble to write us.

We know the cans do not open right; it seems they will go alright for awhile and then we get a run of cans that everything seems to be wrong; the last thing we found out was that the grain in the tinplate had been changed without our knowledge. We have a special dye maker chasing this trouble all the time but let me tell you it is a

headache. Don't think for a minute that you are the only one that
writes in; we have good customers all over the country and when we
get a run of cans that don't open right you can bet your life we
get a lot of letters but we are going to keep trying and we hope in
the meantime our customers will not be too hard on us.

We are going to send you a few tins from the new pack and will just
pray that the dye maker has got the cans opening alright. With
kindest regards.

9. Assume that letters A and B were written by two correspondents in your insurance company to the widowed mother of a young man who was killed in an airplane crash. Which do you like better? Why? Revise the better of the two letters to make it excellent.

Letter A

The policy under which you have filed claim contains aviation
restrictions which limit the company's liability if the insured's
death occurs under certain circumstances.

As the evidence received indicates the insured's death came
within these restrictions, the company's liability is for the restricted amount. Our check representing the company's liability
will be sent shortly to our Chicago office for delivery to you.

Letter B

May I extend to you my sincere sympathy in your bereavement.

When your son applied for his insurance, he was a pilot in the
RCAF. He stated he did not want to pay an extra premium for the additional aviation hazard. Thus, the policy provided for payment of
a restricted amount should his death result from nonpassenger travel
or flight in any kind of aircraft. The restricted amount is a sum
equal to the premiums paid to the company, together with compound
interest at the rate of $2\frac{1}{2}\%$ yearly.

Because the evidence received shows that your son was pilot of
the plane that crashed, I am sorry to say the company's liability is
for the restricted amount.

Our check for the company's liability will be sent shortly to
our Chicago office for delivery to you.

10. The sales manager of Right Fite Hanger, Inc., recently wrote to three television stations asking if they would like to handle her product on a commission basis. She had heard that some stations occasionally used their open time in this manner. Which of the three replies below do you think adheres best to the writing principles for business? Why? Compare your choice with the other two replies.

Reply A

I don't know where you got your information as stated in the opening
sentence of your letter, "I have been informed that your station pro-

motes items on a commission basis," and we don't appreciate it. If you want to do business with us, buy; if you don't, don't write us.

Reply B

This will acknowledge your recent letter of offering your ladies' all plastic dress hanger on a commission basis.

I am quite sure that you did not run your advertisement in the Sunday newspaper supplement on a commission basis. By the same token, we will not accept business on a percentage or per inquiry basis.

For your information, I am attaching our rate card.

Reply C

Your information must have been somewhat misleading inasmuch as NUTZ has never promoted items on a commission basis.

We would be delighted to handle the Right Fite hanger, and I personally think it is an item of great demand.

Enclosed is our rate card so that you can choose the time, frequency, and length of message which will promote your product as you wish it.

As soon as your reply to these points reaches us, we will be glad to put all our resources at your disposal.

11. For the following, refer to the letters or memos you collected and have been studying for various purposes. (Or use any other letters as your instructor directs.) Study the body of each message for the following:
    a. Purpose—is it clear?
    b. Organizational plan—does the message use the right plan?
    c. Are opening and closing paragraphs appropriate?
    d. Notice the length of paragraphs. Do the first and last each have fewer than seven lines? Are other paragraphs under ten lines in length? What improvements, if any, are needed?

chapter

6

Appearance and Uses of Business Message Media

Among the various media you can choose for your written messages are letters and memorandums—plus such special timesaving media as memo-letters, postcards, Mailgrams, telegrams, radiograms, and cablegrams.[1] This chapter focuses on the appearance and uses of these media and on form messages—discussed from the writer's viewpoint.

BUSINESS LETTERS

The medium used most often for written messages to persons outside the firm is the business letter. It is judged on content, presentation, and physical appearance. Planning the content and presentation is your responsibility; typing the message so that it is neat, accurate, and attractive is usually your secretary's job. But when you sign your name at the bottom of the letter, you assume final responsibility for everything—mechanics, proper layout, content. If the message contains misspellings or grammatical errors, or if its appearance is poor, the reader judges you, not your secretary. Therefore, you and your secretary must work as a team to produce effective and attractive messages.

Recipients of your business letters form their first impressions even before reading your messages. Elements of appearance that help produce favorable reactions are appropriate stationery, correct letter parts and layout, and properly addressed envelopes. (In addition to these elements, neat typing also helps make favorable impressions. Poor appearance caused by strikeovers, dirty keys, light ribbon, smears, or poor erasing reflects on you as much as on your secretary.)

Stationery

Although your organization's stationery may be selected by your purchasing department, if you have an opportunity to make a choice or suggest a change, keep the following guidelines in mind.

Quality, Size, Color

To help build an image of quality and stability, the paper you use should have at least 25 percent rag content. Weight of general correspondence stationery ranges from 16 to 20 pounds; and of airmail stationery, from 13 to 15 pounds. (Each of the figures is the actual weight of four reams of standard-sized paper.) The standard-sized sheet is 8½ by 11 inches, but other sizes are also appropriate for various uses. White is the most popular color, although many firms achieve a distinctive and warm touch by using pastel stationery and envelopes.

Good-quality paper is not only more attractive, but it permits easier and neater erasing. The difference in price is nominal. Even the best stationery costs usually less than 3 cents a sheet—very little, considering the average cost of a letter.

[1] For reports, see Chapters 15–17.

Letterhead

Every business, even if it is a one-person operation, should use letterhead stationery for the first page of a letter. Only when you are writing a business letter for yourself (not as an agent or representative for any organization) will you use paper without a letterhead.

Figure 6-1 Illustrations of modern letterheads. (All these letterheads are printed in black, except the following: TWA initials, circles, and horizontal lines, in red; Weyerhaeuser outer triangle, in dark green; Allenite, all printing in medium green.)

The modern letterhead (see Figure 6-1) usually occupies no more than two inches at the top of the page. Printed, embossed, or engraved in this area are name and complete address of the firm, including ZIP code, and sometimes the telephone number, cable address, nature of the business, and name of the department or branch office sending the correspondence. Optional details are names of officers and directors, trademark or symbol, slogan, starting date of the firm, and an appropriate picture—perhaps of the building, product(s) or a familiar landmark.

Standard Parts of the Letter

Most business letters have seven standard parts: (1) heading, (2) inside address, (3) salutation, (4) body, (5) complimentary close, (6) signature area, (7) reference section. (See Figures 6-2 to 6-7; be sure to read these letters, because they include additional essential explanations.)

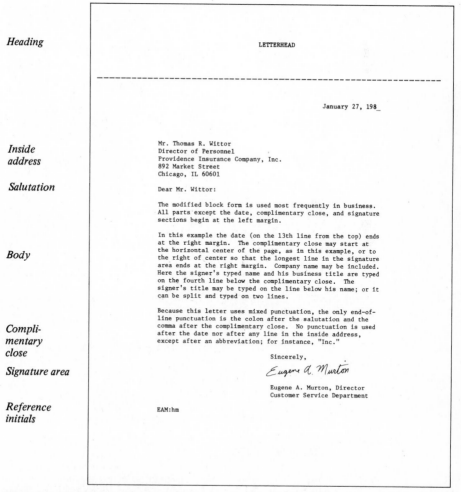

Figure 6-2 Modified block; mixed punctuation. Length, medium; side margins, 1¾"; line length, 5".

Heading

The letterhead and typewritten date comprise the heading. It shows where the letter comes from and when it was written (or dictated). Usually the date is typed two lines below the last line of the letterhead—at left margin, centered, begun at center, or placed so it ends with the right margin.[2] (The letter style and letterhead help determine which placement to choose. See Letter Layout, pages 136-138.) When you type a business letter on blank paper (for yourself, not an organization), type—at

LETTERHEAD

December 1, 198_

2 blank lines

Accounting Department
Eastern Register Company
1969 Fourth Avenue NE
Sometown, Anystate 99999

Attention Mr. Johnson

Ladies and Gentlemen:

    This modified block form is like that in Figure 6-2 except that its paragraphs are indented five or more spaces. The date may be centered or placed so it does not extend into the right margin. In this example the date begins at the horizontal center of the page.

    The attention line here is at the left margin, two lines below the inside address, and underlined. It could also have been centered and typed in all capital letters without underscoring. If you wanted Mr. Johnson's name in the salutation, you would type his first name (or two initials) and his surname above Accounting Department. Then you would omit the attention line and use "Dear Mr. Johnson" in the salutation. If you know him well and address him by his first name (Bill), your salutation could be "Dear Bill."

    In this example the complimentary close, like the date, begins at the center of the page. The company name is omitted, but it could have been included. Also the signer's name--instead of being at the left--could have been typed above the "General Manager" and reference initials (like "MM:hw") could then have been used at the left margin.

    The term "Enclosures 3" in the reference section shows that three additional items are being enclosed in the envelope. Each different item is counted as one, regardless of the number of pages it may have. The notation "cc" indicates that a carbon copy is being sent to Mr. Jami and Miss Krown. Names are in alphabetical order or by rank. The address of each may be included if doing so will help the typist in sending the carbon copy or if it is needed for filing information.

Very truly yours,

Millard M. Morrison

*3 blank lines
for signature*

Millard M. Morrison/hw   General Manager

Enclosures 3
cc: Mr. Thomas Jami
    Miss Helen Krown

Figure 6-3 Modified block with paragraph indentations; mixed punctuation. Length, long; side margins, 1¼″; line length, 6″.

---

[2] The date sequence in American business letters is always month, day, year. The names of the months should be spelled out, and the days (in figures) following the month should not be followed by *st, nd, rd,* or *th.* The same rule applies in the body of the letter. But when the date or the day stands alone, add *st, nd, rd,* or *th;* for example, "The goods arrived on the 15th of this month."

least two inches from the top—your return address and the date, but *not* your name (see Figure 6-7).

Inside Address

Always blocked at the left-hand margin, the inside address of a letter to an individual includes that person's courtesy title, name, business or executive title, and address—as in Figure 6-2.

In a letter addressed to a group, the inside address consists of the group name and the address (see Figure 6-3). In form letters to several or many people the inside address is sometimes omitted and replaced by a few eye-catching words (as, for example, in Figure 6-6).

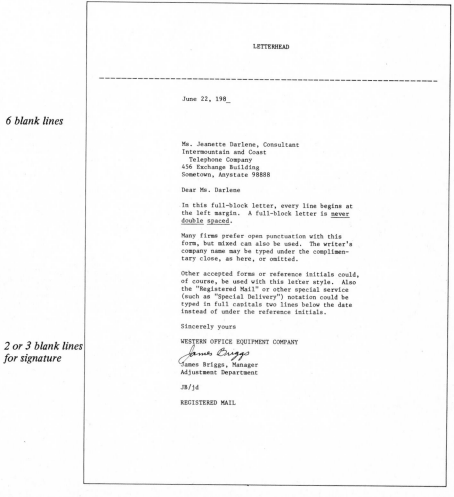

Figure 6-4   Full block; open punctuation. Length, short; side margins, 2¼″; line length, 4″.

Courtesy Title and Name. If the addressee has no professional title—such as "Doctor" or "Professor"—the traditional courtesy titles are "Mr.," "Mrs.," "Miss," or "Ms." Yet labeling women (but not men) by their marital status ("Mrs." or "Miss") is considered an invasion of their privacy. Thus many women prefer the courtesy title "Ms.," which stands for either "Miss" or "Mrs." Others, however, insist on the traditional "Miss" or "Mrs." When you write to a married woman who prefers "Mrs." coupled with her husband's name ("Mrs. John Jones"), address her that way. When in doubt about a woman's preference, use "Ms." plus her own first name and surname. The trend is to use "Ms." as the courtesy title for all women, regardless of their marital status, unless of course they have a professional title that takes precedence (or they

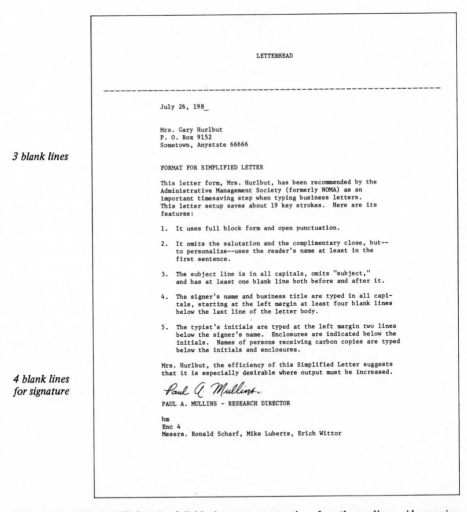

Figure 6-5 AMS simplified style; full block; open punctuation. Length, medium; side margins, 1¾"; line length, 5".

insist on "Mrs." or "Miss"). For business and professional men and women, include after their courtesy title their full first name or two initials[3] plus surname.

Business or Executive Title. Depending upon relative length of lines, the business or executive title may be typed (1) on the same line as the addressee's name, (2) on the second line preceding the company's name, or (3) on a line or two by itself. Any of these is correct:

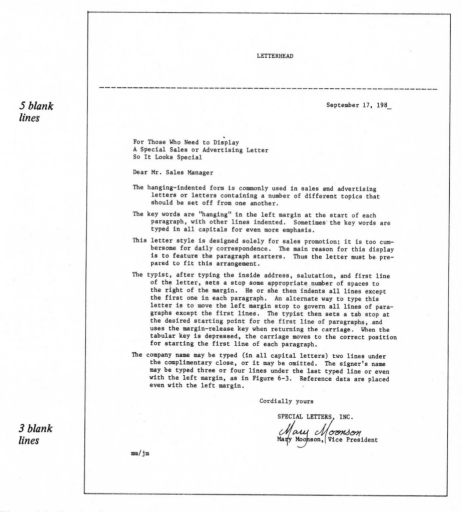

5 blank lines

3 blank lines

Figure 6-6 Hanging (or inverted) paragraph style; open punctuation. Length, long; side margins, 1¼"; line length, 6".

[3] When you do not know the sex of the addressee, you can use "Mr. or Ms." for the courtesy title —or omit it.

1. Mr. William Stassen, President
   Western Construction Company

2. Ms. Marietta R. Worthington
   Treasurer, Ace Credit Company

3. Mr. Harry M. Fitzsimmons
   Vice President and General Manager
   Building Services, Inc.[4]

1½" from top

3 blank lines

1½" from bottom

1524 17th Avenue
Seattle, WA 98102
October 4, 198

Mr. Joseph M. Albrecht
Manager, Jupiter and Jones, Ltd.
815 Fourth Avenue East
Vancouver, B.C.
Canada V5T 1E9

Dear Mr. Albrecht:

Subject: Letters with Quotations and Tabulations

The subject line (if given) is typed on the second line below the salutation. It may be at the left margin, indented the same as paragraphs, or
centered--as in this example. It may be typed either in all capital
letters or in capital and small letters that are underscored. The word
"Subject" often precedes the actual subject.

When you have quoted matter, numbered paragraphs, tabulations, or other
material that you want to emphasize in the body of your letter, your
secretary should always double space before and after such material. For
instance, here is a quotation from an article in a handbook:

When a quotation occupies more than three lines, give
it special display (use a shorter line length than
that used for the remainder of the material) and type
it single spaced, instead of using quotation marks.

When you want to set off listed items or tabulated material, your secretary should indent the left and right margins equally and single space
such material.

	1979	1980
Gross income	$550,972	$588,974
Expense and taxes	390,004	392,593
Net income	$160,968	$196,381

To bring out points more forcibly, the items may be indented an equal
number of spaces from the left and right margins and numbered. These
methods help to bring material to the reader's attention quickly and
artistically.

1. Your profit will increase 10 percent.
2. Your savings are insured up to $40,000.

Figure 6-7 Personal business letter, modified block with mixed punctuation. First page of a two-page letter typed on blank paper (with no letterhead). Side margins, 1¼"; line length, 6".

---

[4] If you need suggestions on when to spell out and when to abbreviate words, see Abbreviations in Appendix B.

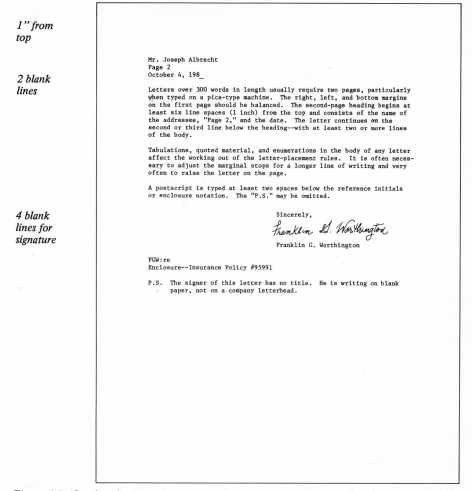

1" from top

2 blank lines

4 blank lines for signature

Mr. Joseph Albrecht
Page 2
October 4, 198_

Letters over 300 words in length usually require two pages, particularly when typed on a pica-type machine. The right, left, and bottom margins on the first page should be balanced. The second-page heading begins at least six line spaces (1 inch) from the top and consists of the name of the addressee, "Page 2," and the date. The letter continues on the second or third line below the heading--with at least two or more lines of the body.

Tabulations, quoted material, and enumerations in the body of any letter affect the working out of the letter-placement rules. It is often necessary to adjust the marginal stops for a longer line of writing and very often to raise the letter on the page.

A postscript is typed at least two spaces below the reference initials or enclosure notation. The "P.S." may be omitted.

Sincerely,

Franklin G. Worthington

Franklin G. Worthington

FGW:re
Enclosure--Insurance Policy #95991

P.S. The signer of this letter has no title. He is writing on blank paper, not on a company letterhead.

Figure 6-7 (Continued) Second page of a two-page letter. Side margins, 1¼"; line length, 6".

Avoid duplication of titles.

Wrong: Dr. Herbert Moore, M.D.
Right: Dr. Herbert Moore <u>or</u> Herbert Moore, M.D.

Order of Arrangement. The various elements of the inside address are arranged like a pyramid. On the top line you place the smallest unit (an individual's name). The remaining items progress downward to the largest unit, as the pyramid below illustrates:

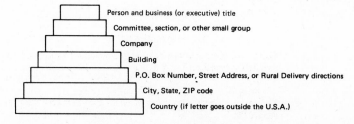

Person and business (or executive) title
Committee, section, or other small group
Company
Building
P.O. Box Number, Street Address, or Rural Delivery directions
City, State, ZIP code
Country (if letter goes outside the U.S.A.)

The number of lines usually ranges from three to six, as the following five-line addresses illustrate:

```
Mr. James Bengstone, Manager      Dr. Alicia Browne, Associate Dean
Southwest Title Company           School of Business Administration
1601 Tower Building               109 Commerce Hall
2973 Lerpson Boulevard            University of Anystate
Los Angeles, CA 90020             Anytown, ST  ZIP
```

Salutation

The salutation is the friendly greeting that precedes the body of the letter. This section presents various acceptable salutations and salutopenings for business letters.

Acceptable Salutations. The following list includes both traditional and comparatively recent salutations, all of which must be *appropriate for the first line of the inside address*. Each salutation is typed at the left margin, two lines below the inside address and two lines above the body. You have these choices:

1. Dear Mr. (or Ms., Mrs., Miss) Doe—when the first line of an inside address (FLIA) is the name of a customer, acquaintance, prospect, stockholder, supplier, or stranger. The courtesy title for the salutation is the same as for the inside address.
2. Dear John (or Mary or nickname)—when writing to an individual you'd address this way in person and when it is appropriate for you to do so in your letter on this occasion. In the following examples notice that whether you choose a salutation like those in item 1 or item 2, each should agree with the first line of the inside address (FLIA).

```
Mr. James Smith      Ms. Mamie Brite      Mrs. (or Miss) Helen Way
. . . . . . .        . . . . . . .        . . . . . . .
. . . . . . .        . . . . . . .        . . . . . . .

Dear Mr. Smith:      Dear Ms. Brite:      Dear Mrs. (Miss) Way:
(or Dear James       (or Dear Mamie)      (or Dear Helen)
 or Dear Jim)        (or Dear nickname)   (or Dear nickname)
```

3. Dear Mr. or Ms. Doe (or Dear Manager or Executive or Director or an appropriate variation—when the FLIA names a person whose sex is unknown (because the name has only initials) or the FLIA is a position within an organization. (Avoid "Dear Sir" and "Dear Madam.")

```
R. L. Macon                         Manager, Service Department
. . . . . . .                       . . . . . . . .
. . . . . . .                       . . . . . . . .
. . . . . . .                       . . . . . . . .

Dear Ms. or Mr. Macon:              Dear Manager:
                                    (or Dear Mr. or Ms. Manager)
```

4. Ladies and Gentlemen (or reverse, or Gentlemen and Gentlewomen, or Dear Members of . . . , or Dear People, or Gentlewo/men, or Gentlepersons, or other innova-

tions)—when the FLIA is a committee, company, or group of men and women; "Gentlemen" if all are men, and "Ladies" ("Mesdames") if all are women.

```
ABC Toy Company                          Public Relations Committee
. . . . . . .                            . . . . . . . .
. . . . . .                              . . . . . . . .
                                         . . . . . . .
Gentlemen and Gentlewomen:               Gentlemen and Gentlewomen:
(or others, as above)                    (or Dear Public Relations
                                         people, or others, as above)



Professional Women's Club                XYZ Fraternity
. . . . . . .                            . . . . . . .
. . . . . . .                            . . . . . . .

Mesdames (Ladies):  (or                  Gentlemen:
Dear professional women:)                (or Dear Members of XYZ)
```

Most of the suggestions under item 4 are innovations since the women's rights movement has advocated eliminating the all-male plural salutations when females may be within the group. Some of these new salutations are not yet widely used. If you don't like them, or you feel your recipients may dislike any of your choices, *omit* the salutation and get right on with the message. See AMS Letter Style, p. 137, and Figure 6-5. In general it is courteous to address people the way they feel comfortable. Some are less likely to miss an omitted salutation than they are to be annoyed by one to which they object.

For messages that omit the inside address—as in sales letters, announcements, or other identical letters to more than one person—various salutations may be used. Among them are: "Dear Customer"; "Dear Homeowner"; or "Dear Executive," "Student," "Occupant(s)," "Member(s)" of name group; or similar expressions. Often such letters also omit the salutation entirely. In place of both the inside address and the salutation they include an eye-catching statement to attract the reader's attention.

Salutopenings. Some business executives prefer "salutopenings" when they feel a salutation such as "Dear Mr. Brown" is not appropriate because he is a stranger, or "Dear" just seems unnatural, or they merely want a change. When you use a salutopening, type it on the salutation line, but omit "Dear" and begin with the first few words of your opening paragraph plus reader's name. After the name, the sentence continues a double space down to the first line of the letter body, as below:

Salutation line	What do you think, Mr. Brown,
Body	of the enclosed suggested arrangement for. . .?

and

Salutation line	Thank you, Miss Smith,
Body	for writing us so promptly about your new address.

If you use the Administrative Management Society (AMS) "simplified letter" (see Figure 6-5), you omit the salutation line and place the reader's name near the beginning of the first sentence (as in a salutopening).

Body

This book discusses in detail the content and presentation of the message body; thus only general guidelines are summarized here. In the body you try to:

1. Organize according to an appropriate plan.
2. Keep your first and last paragraphs short—preferably less than seven lines.
3. Vary the intervening paragraph lengths.
4. Make the average length of your sentences about 17 to 20 words.
5. Achieve the C qualities.

Generally all letters should be typed single space, with double spacing between paragraphs, before and after the salutation, and before the complimentary close.

When the body of a letter is two or more pages, each page beyond the first is headed by a combination of addressee's name, page number, and date. This information is typed 1 to 2 inches from the top of the sheet in any of the following ways:

```
Mr. John Jones
Page 2
May 3, 198_
```
or
```
Mr. John Jones                    2          May 3, 198_
```
or
```
Mr. John Jones-2-May 3, 198_
```
or
```
General Supply Corporation        2          May 3, 198_
Attention Mr. John Jones
```

Complimentary Close

The complimentary close should agree, with respect to formality or informality, with your salutation. Most business letters use one of three key words—*sincerely, truly,* or *cordially.* Only the first letter in the first word of any complimentary close is capitalized. The following salutations and complimentary closes are appropriate together:

```
Dear Mr. (Ms., Miss, Mrs.) Smith,    and    Sincerely, Sincerely
Gentlemen (Ladies), or various              yours, Yours sincerely,
acceptable innovations                      Very truly yours, Yours
                                            very truly [5]
```

---

[5] Business executives' views differ widely on the use of "yours" and "very" in the complimentary close. Many writers prefer to omit both these words with "sincerely" and "cordially," because they feel that adding them makes these friendly closes sound stilted or inappropriate. On the contrary, with "truly" many prefer both "very" and "yours," for just plain "Yours truly" has fallen in disfavor because of jokes about this expression. Thus they use "Yours very truly" or "Very truly yours." Still others dislike all the "truly's." The choice is up to you.

Dear John (Mary, or a nickname)   *and*   Sincerely, Cordially, or
some more familiar phras-
ing in good taste--such as
Best regards

At times, you may want to use a complimentary close that ties in with your message or product, for example:

Warmly   Yours for fashion   Yours for extra profits

Gratefully   Yours for cleaner air   Season's Greetings

[But avoid inappropriate "gimmick" complimentary closes, like the following: "Gastronomically yours" (from a restaurant), "Hopefully yours" (from a collector), or "Saltily yours" (from a salt processor).]

The AMS simplified letter (Figure 6-5) omits complimentary close and salutation.

Signature Area

You can include in the signature area four separate identifications—name of your company, your signature, your typewritten name, and your business title.

Company Name. If printed on the letterhead, your company name need not be repeated after the complimentary close (except in legal documents and negotiable instruments). Even though the firm name is not typed in the signature lines, the firm is considered responsible for the content of the message written by one of its agents (only when it concerns business the agent is *authorized* to handle). However, if you wish to include the company name (many firms require it, for various reasons), type it in capital letters a double space under the complimentary close, as in Figure 6-4.

Signature, Typewritten Name, and Business Title. Your signature is penwritten above your typed name, which appears three to five lines under either the company name (if included) or the complimentary close. The typed business title usually follows the typed name.

Very truly yours,   Yours sincerely,   Cordially yours,

Thomas L. Sutton   THE BRONSON COMPANY   *Roy*
Thomas L. Sutton   Roy Layton, President
Manager, Plant 2   *Mary P. Tracy*
                         Mary P. Tracy
                         Personnel Manager

Usually the signature is the same as the typed name. An exception is that if you have used your reader's first name for the salutation, you will usually sign only your first name above your typed name, as Roy Layton did in example 3, above.

If you prefer, instead of having your name typed under the complimentary close, it may be typed flush with the left margin, usually on the same line with your title, which appears four lines under the complimentary close. You sign above your title, as in Figure 6-3.

As discussed earlier in this chapter and in Chapter 4 under Nonsexist Expressions, for business and professional women unnecessary reference to their marital status should be avoided. In the signature area a married woman always signs *her* first name and not her husband's. Thus for Mary P. Tracy, Personnel Manager (example 2 above), though she is the wife of William R. Tracy, her professional messages are never signed (nor addressed to her as) "Mrs. William R. Tracy." If her name before marriage was Mary Pullman, she may sign either "Mary P. Tracy" or "Mary Pullman Tracy." (Of course, when she writes about a personal charge account, for instance, that is listed as "Mr. and Mrs. William R. Tracy," she should include the latter name in parentheses so as to correctly identify herself.)

It is also noteworthy that many married women, especially professionals, do not use their husbands' surname. Their signatures continue as before marriage, and they prefer the title "Ms."

Another noteworthy nonsexist trend is that both men and women may prefer to omit the courtesy title from both their typewritten names and their signatures. However, if a man or a woman uses only initials before his or her surname, or the first name is not clearly male or female (for example, Chris, Robin), then it is helpful to the recipient for the man to include "(Mr.)" and the woman to include "(Ms.)" in front of their typewritten names.

Reference Section

Your initials as dictator of the message, and those of your typist, usually appear at the left margin on the same line with the last line of the signature area (your name or title) or one or two lines below that. If your name is typed at the left margin instead of in the signature area (Figure 6-3), the typist's initials follow it. Among the common forms used are:

```
KLM:tr              KLM:TR              klm/tr
K.L.Morning:TR      KLMorning-tr        K. L. Morning:tr      tr
```

If someone other than the signer of the letter composes it, practice varies regarding reference initials. Many firms show at least on the file copy the initials of signer, writer, and typist (KLM:JC:tr); the original, to the addressee, may omit all or the writer's initials, to avoid showing that the signer did not dictate the letter.

Optional Parts of the Letter

When appropriate, any of these optional parts can be included: (1) attention line, (2) subject line, (3) enclosure(s), (4) copy notation, (5) file or account number, (6) mailing notation, and (7) postscript.

Attention Line

Considered part of the inside address, the attention line directs a letter to a particular person or title or department when the letter is addressed to a company. It is useful when the writer (a) doesn't know an individual's name but wants the message to go to a particular title (sales or adjustment director) or department (personnel), (b) knows only the individual's surname and thus cannot use that name on the first line of the inside address, or (c) expects that the addressee travels often, and the writer wants the letter to be attended to promptly by whoever takes care of the addressee's business.

Because the first line of the inside address is to a company (or group), the salutation should be plural. The intervening attention line does not change the salutation.[6]

The usual placement of the attention line is between the inside address and salutation (a blank line before and after it), flush with the left margin, indented with the paragraphs, or centered. (See also Figure 6-3.)

```
Mallory Equipment Company
(Street address)
(City), (State)   ZIP

                            ATTENTION: Mr. Jones, Purchasing Manager

Dear Mallory people:
(or other choices in #4, page 130, or omit the salutation)
```

Subject Line

Considered part of the body of the letter, the subject line helps to tell your reader at a glance what your letter is about. It also helps in filing. The subject line may include or omit the word *subject* or *about*. It is usually placed either on the same line with the salutation or double-spaced below the salutation and centered. (See Figures 6-5 and 6-7.)

Enclosure Notation

To remind whoever prepares your envelope for mailing that something is to be enclosed, the enclosure notation is usually typed a single or double space under the reference initials. This notation also alerts the addressee's incoming mail department to check for enclosures. An enclosure is anything in the envelope other than the message itself. One enclosure is a unit that can consist of one or more pages (for example, a two-page resume with an application letter is only one enclosure). When more than one item is enclosed, your secretary should indicate the number: "Enclosures 3" or "Enc. 3." When the enclosures are especially important (checks, legal documents, or blueprints), it is desirable to list in the enclosure notation exactly what the enclosures are, as in Figure 6-7.

Copy Notation

When you want other persons to receive a copy of the letter you have written to the addressee, the names of these persons (arranged in order of importance or alphabet-

---

[6] Some business executives do not use this rule. If they must begin the inside address with the organization name and must also have an attention line to an individual, they personalize the salutation, using, for instance, "Dear Mr. Jones." As an alternative, if you feel strongly that you want to use Mr. Jones's name in the salutation and it's agreeable with your firm, then add his full name (first name or initials and surname) on the inside address, above the company name, and omit the attention line.

ically) should be typed after "cc" (carbon copy), "xc" (Xerox copy), or a similar notation just below the reference initials or the enclosure notation (if any):

```
cc:  Mr. Sims          Copies to A. E. Brown and R. J. Sims
```

If you do not want the addressee to know that other recipients are getting a copy of the letter, your secretary can type "bcc" (blind carbon copy) and the recipients' names *on the carbon copies only*.

File or Account Number, and Mailing Notation

To aid in filing and quick recognition for both the sender's and the reader's company, some firms require that file, loan, or account numbers be typed above the body of the letter in a conspicuous place.

Mailing notation words such as *Special Delivery, Registered,* or *Certified Mail,* when applicable, may be typed either below the copy notation (or whatever is the last notation) or on the second line below the date.

Postscript

To emphasize a point already in your letter or to include a personal brief message unrelated to the letter, a postscript (typed or handwritten) may be added—below everything else typed on the page. However, if you forgot to include an important idea in the letter body, it is usually better to retype the letter than to add the information in a postscript. (See Figure 6-7.)

If you have occasion to use several notations after the signature area, the initials RECMP may help you remember the proper order for arranging them vertically at the left margin: reference initials, enclosures, copy notation, mailing notation, postscript.

Letter Layout

Although the layout of the letter is primarily the typist's responsiblity, it is covered briefly here to give you a basis of choosing the style(s) you prefer. Many progressive companies have adopted a format used throughout the company, so that all their letters contribute to an attractive, uniform image—regardless of dictator, department, or stenographer.

Punctuation Styles

The two forms of punctuation most used in business letters are "open" and "mixed." In open punctuation, no line of any of the seven standard letter parts (except the body) has any punctuation at the end unless an abbreviation requires a period. Mixed punctuation—the most popular style today—is like open except that a colon follows the salutation and a comma follows the complimentary close.

Letter Styles

Business letters are usually arranged in one of the letter styles described briefly below. They are single spaced with double space between paragraphs. You will find additional details discussed within the letters illustrated in Figures 6-2 to 6-7.[7]

1. *Modified block* form is currently the most popular style. All parts are blocked; there are no paragraph indentations. The date, complimentary close, and signature sections begin near the center of the page; the other parts, at the left margin. (See Figures 6-2 and 6-7.)
2. *Modified block with paragraphs indented* is also popular. (See Figure 6-3.)
3. *Full block* begins every line at the left margin. (See Figure 6-4.) This is the fastest style to type, especially when used with open punctuation. To offset a lopsided appearance at the left, some firms use a letterhead with most of its printing at the right side.
4. *AMS simplified style*, adopted by the Administrative Management Society, uses full block and open punctuation; omits the salutation and complimentary close; and includes a subject line without the word *subject,* typed in all capital letters a triple space after the inside address. The first paragraph contains the reader's name. (See Figure 6-5.)
5. *Hanging (or inverted) paragraph style* is unsuitable for daily correspondence, but distinctive for a sales or advertising letter in which you want to emphasize the first words of each paragraph. All lines of the letter body are indented except the first line of each paragraph. The letter could use a personal inside address and salutation or replace these with an attention-getting statement and general salutation, as in Figure 6-6.

Public and government officials—as well as businesspersons writing formal messages—often use what is called the *official letter style.* Its general layout may be blocked or semiblocked, but the inside address—instead of being placed above the salutation—is typed at the left margin two to five lines below the last line of the signature section. Reference initials and other notations, if any, then appear after the inside address. (Some writers also use this style with informal letters that begin with a first-name salutation.)

Tips for Letter Placement

The easiest way to achieve a pleasing appearance for all your letters is to have a competent secretary. However, most students—and even many young businesspersons—

---

[7] The discussion in these letters is adapted from Ruth E. Gavin and William A. Sabin, *Reference Manual for Stenographers and Typists,* McGraw-Hill Book Company, New York, 1970, and from Doris H. Whalen, *The Secretary's Handbook,* Harcourt Brace Jovanovich, Inc., New York, 1978. For additional details about typing mechanics and numerous other helpful tips, consult these or similar manuals.

find it necessary to type some letters themselves. To save time and money, some firms use the same line lengths—usually 5 inches—for all messages, regardless of length. (In short messages they sometimes double-space the message and triple-space between paragraphs.)

Nevertheless, for the most attractive-looking letters, it is advisable to use line lengths of 4, 5, or 6 inches, depending on letter length. Though there are other good placement guides, the following table is easy to use. It assumes a fixed vertical position for the date—on about the 14th line from the top of the page. Before using the guide, you should:

1. Estimate the approximate number of words in your letter.
2. Place the typewriter paper guide at 0.
3. Know whether your typewriter has elite (E) or pica (P) type. With pica type you get 10 characters to the horizontal inch and 85 across the 8½-inch page; with elite, 12 to the inch and 102 across the page. Both have 6 vertical lines to the inch.

(The letters in Figures 6-2 to 6-7 are based on this guide, for elite type.)

Letter length	Words in body	Line length in		Margins		Number of lines between date and inside address
		Inches	Spaces	Width in inches	Machine settings*	
Short	Under 100	4	40 P 50 E†	2¼	22–62 P 26–76 E	6–10
Medium	100–200	5	50 P 60 E	1¾	17–67 P 21–81 E	3–8
Long	200–300	6	60 P 70 E†	1¼	12–72 P 15–85 E	2–6
2-page	Over 300	6	60 P 70 E†	1¼	12–72 P 15–85 E	2–6

*To allow for the ringing of the typewriter bell and to avoid frequent use of the margin release key, add five spaces to the settings for the right margin. For suggestions on how to divide words correctly at the right margin, see Syllabication in Appendix B.
†Rounded off.

Envelopes

Your organization's envelopes not only get your messages to their destination but also help, indirectly, to advertise your company. The quality of the envelope paper (preferably the same as the letter stationery) and the pictures and slogans, if any, all contribute to your organization's image. Each envelope should show the sender's return address, which is usually printed (in a format identical with that of the letterhead), or typewritten if necessary, in the upper left corner.

The inside address of the letter is the outside address on the envelope. To quicken the processing of your mail at the post office, your company should keep up to date

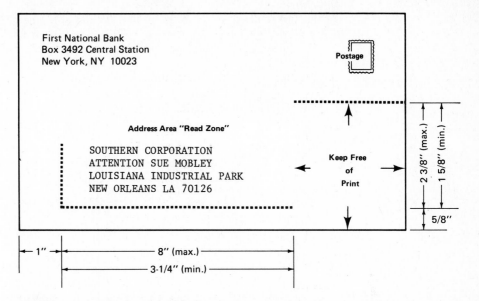

Figure 6-8 Sample envelope—showing placement of address for OCR readability.

on post office-recommended location and legibility of the address on the envelope and the layout of information within each address. You can get from your local post office various pamphlets and guidelines published by the United States Postal Service to help answer questions about addressing mail for automation, and various special services.

Recommended Address Location and Legibility

Your return address should be printed or typed in the upper left corner of the envelope, about ½ inch from the top and left edges.

The addressee's name and address must be completely in the *lower section*—the "read zone"—because the post office electronic mail sorters, Optical Character Readers (OCR), are programmed to scan this specific envelope area. (See Figure 6-8.) To be read by the OCR, the envelope address should be clearly imprinted with dark print (or typewriter type) on a light background. The address should be parallel (within five degrees) to the bottom edge of the envelope; slanted or crooked lines can confuse OCR recognition.

Recommended Address Layout

To be processed quickly and accurately by OCR, the envelope address should meet these requirements (see also Figure 6-8):[8]

---

[8] Most information in this section is adapted from *Guidelines for Designing and Printing Envelopes for Machine Processing,* Notice 23E, March 1973; and *Memo to Mailers,* U.S. Postal Service, June 1978 and December 1978.

1. **The format** must be single-spaced and blocked, not indented. Uppercase (all capitals) typewritten characters without punctuation are recommended.
2. **City, state,**[9] **and ZIP code,** in that sequence, must all be on the bottom line.
3. **Street name—correctly spelled—or box number** should be on the line immediately above the city, state, and ZIP code.
4. **Number of an apartment, room, suite, or other unit of multiunit unnamed building** should appear immediately after the street address on the same line—never above, below, nor in front of the street address.
5. **On-arrival instructions** such as "Confidential," "Attention Mr. Drake," "Please forward," and account numbers should be typed inside the read zone on any line above the second line from the bottom of the address (as shown in these examples and in Figure 6-8).

```
654-7589-23F34MAR78      MR H M JONES           MS KATHY STEVENS
H E BROWN                ACCOUNTING DEPT        CLIFTON TOWERS APT 952
342 HIGH ST ROOM 56      ABC CORP               SACRAMENTO CA  95816
WASHINGTON DC   20017    3645 E INDUSTRIAL PKWY
                         CLEVELAND OH  44106
```

Some firms use layouts like these only for monthly billings and large quantity mailings. When appearance is more important than speedy delivery, you may prefer to have envelopes addressed in the usual format—with upper- and lower-case typewritten characters (NOT all capitals), with punctuation, and few if any abbreviations except states.

To give you an idea of the wastes that occur from inadequately addressed mail, here are some figures from the Postmaster General's office:

45,000,000 pieces of mail went to the dead-letter offices in 1976.

$460,000 in checks, drafts, and cash was found in letters sent to the dead-letter offices during this year.

---

[9] Although you can use any of the traditional spellings and abbreviations for states, the Post Office recommends use of the following two-letter abbreviations—two capitals without periods or spaces.

Alabama	AL	Louisiana	LA	Ohio	OH
Alaska	AK	Maine	ME	Oklahoma	OK
Arizona	AZ	Maryland	MD	Oregon	OR
Arkansas	AR	Massachusetts	MA	Pennsylvania	PA
California	CA	Michigan	MI	Puerto Rico	PR
Colorado	CO	Minnesota	MN	Rhode Island	RI
Connecticut	CT	Mississippi	MS	South Carolina	SC
Delaware	DE	Missouri	MO	South Dakota	SD
District of Columbia	DC	Montana	MT	Tennessee	TN
Florida	FL	Nebraska	NE	Texas	TX
Georgia	GA	Nevada	NV	Utah	UT
Hawaii	HI	New Hampshire	NH	Vermont	VT
Idaho	ID	New Jersey	NJ	Virginia	VA
Illinois	IL	New Mexico	NM	Washington	WA
Indiana	IN	New York	NY	West Virginia	WV
Iowa	IA	North Carolina	NC	Wisconsin	WI
Kansas	KS	North Dakota	ND	Wyoming	WY
Kentucky	KY				

$35,000   could not be restored to rightful owners because of lack of information on or within the envelope.

$5,000,000   —approximately—is spent by the Postal Service each year trying to find correct addresses for inadequately addressed mail.[10]

MEMORANDUMS

In contrast to the letter, which is directed outside your organization, the memorandum (memo) goes within your organization. It is an informal, written communication from one person or department to another person, persons, or department. The stationery, parts, layout, and envelopes of the memo are somewhat different from those of the letters described in the preceding section.

Stationery

Memorandum stationery often differs from letter stationery in quality, color, size, and printing.

Quality, Color, Size

Because the memo goes to employees within the firm, consideration of public relations is not necessary. Memo stationery is usually of a much less expensive quality paper than that for regular letters; also, instead of white, memo paper is often in pastel colors—yellow, cream, pink, blue—for easy identification. Sometimes each color indicates the department to which a particular copy should go. Sizes of sheets range from the standard 8½ by 11 inches to small slips 4 by 5 inches.

Printing

At the top of the full-page memorandum are usually printed such words as OFFICE MEMORANDUM and the company's name (but not address). Along the left margin (or in various other locations) are printed: TO, FROM, SUBJECT, DATE—and sometimes also MESSAGE. In some memos FROM is omitted and the writer signs at the end—as on a letter. Some memos also include such printed words as File number; Telephone; For your: approval, information, comment. Printing at the bottom sometimes includes various instructions and reminds employees of the risks of oral messages (see Figure 6-9).

The combination *message-and-reply memorandum* form is an especially good time- (and expense) saver for both sender and recipient. A packet of three or more sheets of paper (white and colored), plus carbons (unless special "carbonless" paper is used), makes up a message-reply packet. Printed instructions at the top or bottom tell the sender and the reader how to use the sheets. Printed lines may aid those who commu-

---

[10] C. Neil Benson, Acting Senior Assistant Postmaster General, Operations Group, Washington, D.C., January 1979.

MEMORANDUM (Company name)

DATE:_____

TO:_____ FROM:_____

DEPT:_____ TELEPHONE:_____

SUBJECT:_____ *For your*
☐ APPROVAL ☐ INFORMATION ☐ COMMENT

Message, Comment, or Reply

WRITE IT • DATE IT • SIGN IT   Oral messages waste time, cause annoying interruptions and are likely to be misunderstood or forgotten.

Figure 6-9 Office memorandum. (Jagged line indicates a portion of actual sheet removed here only to save space.)

nicate in handwriting. Each packet is perforated near the top for easy removal of sheets, and each sheet is divided into two sections—one labeled MESSAGE, for the sender, and one marked REPLY, for the recipient. These two sections may be side by side or one above the other. (See Figure 6-10.)

Parts of the Memorandum

The standard parts of the memorandum are: to, from, subject, date, and body. Optional are such items as reference initials, enclosure(s), file number, routing information, and the department and telephone number of the sender. Most of these parts are printed on the memo stationery, as illustrated in Figures 6-9 and 6-10. Unlike the letter, the memo requires no inside address, salutation, complimentary close, or full signature. The combination message-reply forms do, however, provide lines for both the writer's and the reader's signatures. (See Figures 6-10 and 6-11.)

What you write after the TO, FROM, and DATE will vary with the situation and your organization's practices. A courtesy title—Mr., Mrs., Miss, Ms.—before your reader's name (after TO) may be used or omitted, depending upon your relationship with the reader (superior or subordinate) and the degree of informality within your organization. You omit the title before your name. Also, if the memo is a temporary message, not to be filed, and if you and the writer work together regularly, you may merely use initials, first name, or nickname after TO and FROM, and all figures or abbreviations for the date:

Figure 6-10 Interoffice memorandum packet containing carbons under sheets of paper (white, yellow, pink) with sections for both the message and the reply.

TO:	J.E.H.		**TO:**	Jack
FROM:	T.R.M.	*or*	**FROM:**	Ted
DATE:	2/10/8_		**DATE:**	Feb. 10, 198_

However, if the memo will be filed, these parts should be spelled out:

TO: Mr. (optional) James E. Hill, Personnel Manager
FROM: Theodore R. Murdock, Accounting Department
DATE: February 10, 198_

If you are sending the same message to several persons, their names and/or titles should be typed after TO. If you write to the same persons often, you might have a form prepared with their names printed (or dittoed, Xeroxed, or mimeographed) after the TO. When you have only one copy of a document, book, or other important papers that you want everyone in a certain group to read and comment on, circulate a covering memo—the single original, with no copies for readers to keep—among those on your list. Brief instructions (printed or typed) tell the readers what to do. Their names are listed alphabetically or in order of importance.

DATE: May 2, 198_

TO: Tom Brehm____   Please initial and pass on; last

          James Brown____   reader please return memo and attach-

          Anita Jones___   ment to sender.

          Searl Lichen____

          Harry Green____

FROM: Kermit Hobson, Personnel _K.H._

SUBJECT: <u>Your suggestions on attached Procedures Manual</u>

FROM

TO

Best Products Co.
PO Box 0000
Sometown, Somestate 47777

RELIABLE Furniture Mfr's., Inc.
1742 FIRST AVE.
SEATTLE, WASHINGTON 98104
(206) 563-1440

SUBJECT   Our order No. 8203 of March 2   DATE: March 26, 198_

FOLD ↑   **MESSAGE**

On Mar. 2 we placed an order for 36 #20000-RR's, 24 #2900's, and 36 #500-CLS's, and sent it along with a note to Tom Jears in Los Angeles (asking to ship either WASH-ORE. SHIPPERS COOP ASSN - Chicago or E. St. Louis, whichever was less expensive for your truck or auto freight to deliver to the above depots).

As of this date we have had no confirmation. PLEASE ADVISE.

JD:hw

PLEASE REPLY TO ⟶   SIGNED   John L. Doe

    REPLY

We have been temporarily out of rug rollers. However, we should be able to ship your order this week by Washington Oregon Shippers.

DATE   March 31, 198_   SIGNED   Jim Rebessa

GRAYARC CO., INC., BROOKLYN, N.Y. 11232   **THIS COPY FOR PERSON ADDRESSED**   (1st page: white)

GRAYARC CO., INC., BROOKLYN, N.Y. 11232 **PERSON ADDRESSED RETURN THIS COPY TO SENDER** (2d page: pink)

DETACH THIS COPY — RETAIN FOR ANSWER.
SEND WHITE AND PINK COPIES WITH CARBONS INTACT.   (3d page: yellow)

Figure 6-11 Memo-letter stationery for routine short messages—usually going outside your company. (Jagged lines indicate a portion of actual sheet removed here only to save space.)

The body of the memo, as for the letter, is its most important part because it contains your message. *In general, you can use the same guidelines, principles, and organizational plans for the memo as for the letter;* the few differences are pointed out in succeeding chapters.

Layout of the Memorandum Body

The memo body, unlike that of a letter, is not centered on the page. The first line usually begins a triple space under the subject line regardless of message length. Left margins are usually lined up evenly below the TO. The body is typed single space, with double spacing between paragraphs.

For memo pages beyond the first, headings are the same as those for the business letter, namely, reader's name, page number, and date. Reference initials are typed a few spaces below the body, at the left margin. If only your title appears in the FROM line, or if the FROM line is omitted, you should sign your name a few spaces below the body of the memo. If your typewritten name follows FROM above the body, you may place your handwritten initials above or to the right of your name, to indicate that you have read the memo.

Copy notations (cc or xc) in memos may be placed after the reference initials (as in letters) or near the top of the memo between the TO and the FROM.

Envelopes

How your memo is routed to the addressee depends partly upon where you and the reader are located. If you are in the same building, the memo might be inserted into the reader's mailbox, put on her or his desk by a messenger, or routed through compressed-air tubes. If you are in different buildings, your memo may be mailed in a manila or regular company envelope. The envelope address contains your name and department in the upper left corner and the reader's name, department, and address according to your organization's procedures.

SPECIAL TIMESAVING MESSAGE MEDIA

Included in this section are various message media that save time for both the sender and recipient. They can be useful in certain situations when speed is essential *and* the messages are relatively short (though, of course, there are exceptions). The media that merit at least a brief discussion here are memo-letters, postcards, Mailgrams, telegrams, cablegrams, and radiograms. (Form messages are also time-savers; their advantages and types are discussed in the next section.)

Memo-letters

In the interest of speed and lower costs, many firms (especially wholesalers, publishers, and manufacturers) use a combination message-reply or memo-letter form for routine short messages directed *outside* their organization. Compare the reply message memo-letter packet in Figure 6-11 with the interoffice memorandum shown in Figure 6-10. The main differences are that in the memo-letter: (1) after the FROM, the full name and address (perhaps also phone number) of the sender's company are printed (some-

---

J. W. MICROELECTRONICS CORPORATION
REGIONAL TECHNOLOGY PARK - BLDG. C
4901 STENTON AVENUE • PHILADELPHIA, PENNSYLVANIA 19144 • PHONE 215-329-8681

REQUEST FOR INFORMATION

TO: _____   DATE _____   REQUEST NO. _____

_____   P.O. NO. _____   INV. NO. _____

_____   INV. DATE _____   INV. AMOUNT _____

PLEASE REPLY TODAY VIA   ☐ THIS FORM   ☐ WIRE   ☐ TELEPHONE   ☐ RETURN ENVELOPE ENCLOSED

☐ 1. PLEASE ACKNOWLEDGE OUR ORDER AND GIVE SHIPPING DATE
☐ 2. PLEASE CHANGE ORDER AS NOTED BELOW AND ACKNOWLEDGE
☐ 3. PLEASE ADVISE WHEN ORDER WILL BE SHIPPED
☐ 4. MUST HAVE MORE SPECIFIC SHIPPING DATE
☐ 5. CAN YOU MEET OUR SHIPPING DATE?
☐ 6. GOODS NOT RECEIVED, PLEASE TRACE SHIPMENT
☐ 7. IF SHIPMENT HAS BEEN MADE, PLEASE MAIL INVOICE TODAY
☐ 8. WHEN WILL BALANCE OF OUR ORDER BE SHIPPED?
☐ 9. PLEASE RUSH PRICES REQUESTED
☐ 10. PLEASE SEND A SHIPPING NOTICE
☐ 11. PLEASE SEND A RECEIPTED FREIGHT BILL
☐ 12. PLEASE SEND A CERTIFIED WEIGHT SLIP
☐ 13. PLEASE SEND ACCEPTANCE COPY OF OUR P.O.
☐ 14. RELEASE SHIPMENTS AS SHOWN UNDER "REMARKS" BELOW
☐ 15. PUT OUR P.O. NUMBER ON ALL SHIPMENTS
☐ 16. SHIP THIS ORDER TO ADDRESS BELOW
☐ 17. WE HAVE NO RECORD OF TRANSACTION COVERED BY YOUR INVOICE. PLEASE GIVE US ORDER DATE, DATE SHIPPED, P. O. NUMBER, NAME OF PERSON PLACING THE ORDER AND/OR SIGNED DELIVERY RECEIPT.

☐ 18. YOUR INVOICE IS RETURNED FOR REASON CHECKED:
☐ 19. WE REQUIRE_____COPIES OF EACH INVOICE
☐ 20. PRICES DO NOT MATCH YOUR QUOTATION
☐ 21. TERMS DO NOT MATCH OUR P.O.
☐ 22. QUANTITY DIFFERS FROM OUR P.O.
☐ 23. UNIT PRICE IS INCORRECT
☐ 24. EXTENSION PRICE IS INCORRECT
☐ 25. OUR P.O. NUMBER IS LACKING OR INCORRECT
☐ 26. SALES TAX DOES/DOES NOT APPLY
☐ 27. ORDER SHOULD BE BILLED F.O.B. DESTINATION
☐ 28. ORDER MUST BE SHIPPED VIA _____
☐ 29. _____
☐ 30. _____
☐ 31. _____
☐ 32. _____
☐ 33. _____
☐ 34. _____

OUR REMARKS   **YOUR REPLY**

Form R-R113 The Drawing Board, Inc., Box 505, Dallas, Texas

Figure 6-12 Printed request-for-information packet (three sheets) with numbered requests for easy check-off; also spaces for remarks and for recipient's reply.

times in the same format as the firm's regular letterhead); and (2) after the TO, a larger space is provided so that the typist can insert the full name and address of the recipient, because he or she is outside the sender's firm. Some firms have the word *memo-letter* printed near the top of the sheet.

A further time-saver is the printed request-for-information form, as illustrated in Figure 6-12. Notice that besides the printed 28 requests this firm commonly uses, the form leaves spaces for 6 others to be inserted if desired. The bottom of this memo-letter form allows space for comments by both the sender and the receiver. This form, like the interoffice memo packet shown in Figure 6-10, is a packet of three sheets with carbons preinserted.

The memo-letter is mailed in the same kind of envelope as a regular business letter or in a window envelope (in which the address after the TO serves also as the envelope address).

Postcards

For short messages that are not confidential, you can often save time and expense by using postcards. These media do not require folding, sealing, or inserting in envelopes, and the postage is less than for letters sent first class.

On the stamped side of the card, usually only the reader's name and address are typed. The message side includes the name and address of the sender, the date, salutation, message, complimentary close, and signature. (To save both space and time, some

---

ORDER CARD

Please send me

_____ copies of *Two Studies in Automobile Franchising*   @ $9.50= $ _____

_____ copies of *Institutional Holdings of Common Stock*   @ $9.00= $ _____

_____ copies of *Antitrust Policy and Economic Welfare*   @ $6.00= $ _____

total $ _____

Name _____

Address _____

City _____ State _____ Zip _____

Payment enclosed _____   Bill me _____

Prepaid orders are sent post paid. Foreign orders must be prepaid.

Figure 6-13 Business reply order postcard. The reverse side is addressed to the seller; the firm's name, address, and postage permit number are printed in appropriate places for address and stamp.

H & S BUILDING MAINTENANCE, 2916 Commons Ave., Boston, MA 02109

November 10, 19 —

Dear Customer:

Thank you for writing us regarding the adjustment on your account.

The search you requested is being made and should be completed before the end of this month. Any corrections will be shown on your next month's statement.

Very truly yours,

a. H. Mason

Customer Services Department

Figure 6-14 Seller's postcard acknowledgment of a customer complaint.

business firms have their name and address *printed* in one line, usually across the top of the postcard's message side.)

As a customer you can use a postcard, for example, to inquire, to request a free advertised booklet, or to order a product that is to be charged to your account. As a representative of a business firm you can send postcards and reply cards for a wide variety of uses, three of which are illustrated in Figures 6-13–6-15.

Figure 6-15 Seller's "miss-you" postcard, asking to serve customer soon.

Mailgrams

When you need to reach any number of people predictably, simultaneously, in writing, with impact, the *next business day*—you can use Mailgrams. These media have urgency and prestige value similar to telegrams, but at much lower cost.

Uses and Appearance

You can use Mailgrams in many ways—to announce important news to sales representatives, distributors, stockholders, employees—speedily, simultaneously; quote special prices; acknowledge orders; congratulate; collect delinquent payments. Figure 6-16 illustrates Mailgram format and tells some advantages in the words of Western Union's Vice President John E. Cochran.[11]

Methods of Sending

Your Mailgram can originate from a telephone, IBM Communicating Mag Card or Redactron Communicating typewriters, Telepost terminal, Telex, TWX, computer, or tape. Each message is routed electronically by the Western Union network to a post office near your addressee and printed out individually. It is delivered in a Western Union blue and white envelope (Figure 6-17) the next regular mail, usually the day after it's sent, sometimes the same day.

To send one or a few Mailgrams, you can phone Western Union toll-free, day or night. An operator types each message, as you dictate it, onto a cathode ray tube, makes any corrections electronically, and presses a button that transmits your message to the computer. Then the computer automatically switches your message to the appropriate post office.

If your company has a Telex, TWX, or Infocom system, your operator can type your messages directly from your teleprinter into the Western Union computer. To send 100 or more Mailgrams at a time, you can get Western Union assistance regarding computerized address lists and messages—for lowest tariff rates.[12]

Telegrams, Cablegrams, Radiograms

You can send a message by telegram within the continental United States and by cablegram or radiogram for overseas communication.[13] The format of telegrams and

---

[11] Additional information in this section is from Western Union brochures and courtesy of Marlene D. Copans, Administration Manager, Western Union, Seattle, Washington.

[12] Cost of a Mailgram originating by phone (in 1979) was $2.95 for 100 words or less ($1.50 each additional 100 words). For a Mailgram originating from Telex, TWX, or computer, costs are significantly less—depending on the sending method and length of message. Words in the message plus the address, salutation, and signature are counted in Mailgrams—six characters per word.

[13] Information and examples in this section are included courtesy of Ms. Marlene D. Copans, Administration Manager, Western Union Office, Seattle, Washington.

```
MGMNWKB NWK
2-205617E158 06/07/79
ICS IPMMTZZ CSP
2018251100 MGM TDMT UPPER SADDLE RIVER NJ 100 06-07 0929A EST
ZIP 07834
```

western union **Mailgram**

```
MR.ACTION COMMUNICATOR
1 MAIN STREET
ANYWHERE U.S.A. 07384



DEAR MR.COMMUNICATOR:

MAILGRAM IS THE ACTION COMMUNICATION.

MAILGRAM'S TELEGRAPHIC FORMAT AND IMPACT GET QUICK READERSHIP.
IT'S EASY TO USE, MAY BE PERSONALIZED,GETS ATTENTION, AND MOST
OF ALL IT GETS RESULTS.

WESTERN UNION WILL GLADLY ASSIST YOU IN PREPARING YOUR MESSAGE
AND LIST FOR TRANSMISSION IN VOLUME ORDERS SO THAT YOU MAY OBTAIN
THE LOWEST RATE POSSIBLE.

THE WRITTEN RECORD MAKES YOUR MEANING CLEAR. MAILGRAM MAKES SURE
THAT EVERYONE GETS NOTIFIED IMMEDIATELY. THE MEDIUM SAYS THE
MESSAGE IS IMPORTANT.

JOHN E COCHRAN
VICE PRESIDENT, MARKETING
WESTERN UNION TELEGRAPH CO.
ONE LAKE STREET
UPPER SADDLE RIVER,NJ 07458

0932 EST

MGMNWKB NWK


THIS SAMPLE MESSAGE IS 700 CHARACTERS IN LENGTH (or 116 WORDS).
```

Figure 6-16 Mailgram.

cablegrams is similar to that of the Mailgram. Most telegrams today are delivered by telephone; cablegrams are transmitted by transoceanic cable; radiograms are wireless messages (usually delivered to ships).

Telegrams

For domestic telegraphic service, you can choose full-rate telegrams or overnight telegrams. The fastest domestic service, for transmission within two hours, is the full-rate telegram. The minimum charge is for 15 words. The more economical overnight telegrams are messages accepted up to midnight for delivery not earlier than the following

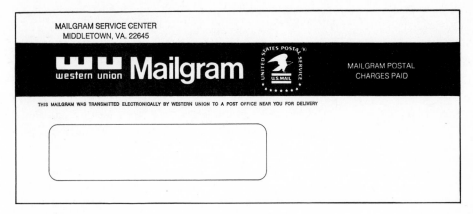

Figure 6-17   Mailgram window envelope (3¾" × 9").

morning.[14] The minimum charge is for 100 words between points within the United States. If your firm sends numerous telegrams, you should be sure to get a copy of Domestic Telegraph Service Rules. These sheets contain highly useful, money-saving, specific details on how to count words, figures, forms of money, symbols, and punctuation.[15]

Cablegrams and Radiograms

Because transmission of messages outside the continental United States is necessarily costly, it is extremely advisable to be well informed on rules for international word count. If you communicate frequently with representatives overseas, you might develop mutually understood code symbols to save costs. For example, notice how the following cable text from an insurance agent in Greece to her home office in the United States can be cut from a word count of 25 to only 10 words. (Words in the address count extra.)

(25 words)   CUSTOMER HAS TODAY ACCEPTED A NEW INSURANCE POLICY IN-
CLUDING FIRE EXTENDED COVERAGE AND VANDALISM ALSO PUBLIC
LIABILITY AND PROPERTY DAMAGE AS WELL AS WORKMEN'S COMPEN-
SATION

[14] Cost of an interstate 15-word telegram (in 1979): $4.95, if delivered by telephone; $7.95 by messenger; 15 cents for each additional word over 15 up to 50 words; 9 cents, each word over 50. Cost of an interstate overnight telegram: $4.25 for 100 words or less, if delivered by telephone; $7.45, by messenger; 3 cents for each additional word over 100. Only words in the message (not the address or signature) are counted.

[15] Chargeable words in a domestic telegram are a total of (a) dictionary words, (b) full words in proper names, and (c) matter subject to the five-character word count. Under the five-character rule, combined figures, signs, or alphabetic letters count one word for each five characters or fewer. For example: these are one word: urlet (your letter), 9-16-79, #415(A). Punctuation marks— including , . ; : - () — though transmitted, are neither counted nor charged for. Spaces automatically separate matter into word groups: AT&SF is one word; A. T. & S. F. is five words. These are counted as one word each: # $ % & / " indicating inches or seconds; thus these are each two words: 112-3/4 and 15".

(10 words)   CUSTOMER TODAY ACCEPTED NEW POLICY INCLUDING FECVM PLPD
                  AND WC

FORM MESSAGES

Whenever you want to send an identical message to at least two persons, you can write what is called a "form letter" or a "form memo," based on a master draft. These messages have various uses and advantages, a few disadvantages, and four kinds of forms you can choose.

Uses, Advantages, and Disadvantages

Form messages are useful when you need to (1) announce news to customers, employees, stockholders, suppliers; (2) seek information on credit or job applicants; (3) answer often-recurring inquiries; (4) acknowledge orders; (5) make simple adjustments; (6) acknowledge payments; (7) sell a product or service by mail; (8) collect payments on charge accounts; (9) promote goodwill.

Why use forms? The main advantages are these:

1. *They save time.* After a master draft is prepared, it can be duplicated (by automatic typewriter or other timesaving machines), used again and again, and thus help speed up correspondence. If the form is designated by a code number, marked in the customer's folder, an actual copy of the form need not even be filed in the folder. Thus forms can save the time of executives, secretaries, and (in some cases) file clerks.
2. *They save money.* Mainly because they save time, messages processed from a master draft may cost only a few cents each, instead of several dollars for individually dictated and typewritten messages.
3. *They can be better quality.* Sometimes if routine messages are prepared by inexperienced, hurried, or disgruntled writers (and overworked typists), they are mediocre or poor both in content and appearance. In contrast, when experts prepare the master forms, the messages can be of higher quality and more effective.
4. *They make possible wider mass mailings.* If desired, thousands of copies can be duplicated quickly from a master draft and mailed the same day to persons over a wide area. The impact of such a mailing campaign could not be achieved as quickly (or economically) without forms.

The few disadvantages of form letters can be avoided when the sender uses good judgment.

1. "Complete" form messages are impersonal. Though this characteristic can be an advantage—as in early-stage collection reminders—it can also be a serious disadvantage whenever a personal letter is advisable. Consider your readers and their needs!

2. Be sure the chosen form message really applies to the people who receive it. Even excellent form letters can drive away customers if incorrectly used. Much goodwill built up by thousands of dollars spent on advertising can be nullified by carelessly chosen forms. For example, if a potential customer living 3,000 miles from a company inquires about its services, he or she will be disappointed and angry upon receiving a processed sales letter that merely asks the reader to "drop in the office tomorrow" and answers not one specific question.

Kinds of Forms

Four kinds of form messages are: complete form, fill-in form, guide form, and paragraph form.

Complete Form

Messages identical in every word are *complete forms,* especially useful for announcements, some collection reminders, and large-scale campaigns when being *impersonal* is desirable. They may be reproduced on a printing press, computer, multigraph, mimeograph, ditto, Xerox, or other types of duplicating machines.

In a complete form *memo* the word TO is followed by such terms as "All Employees" or "Management Personnel." In *letters* a general salutation (Dear Customer, Homeowner, Sports Buff, Student) is chosen to fit the type of individuals getting the letter. Sometimes the first few words of the opening sentence are placed where the inside address and salutation usually are:

Faked	The last time you had
inside	a chance like this
address	to get World and Home News
Faked	at a big savings . . .
salutation	
	. . . business was coasting along without any serious
Body	worries, the war in Asia seemed to be cooling off,
	the President had . . .

Fill-in Form

A message prepared in advance to meet a specific kind of situation may have spaces left for filling in variable information. The date, customer's name and address, account number, payment due date, and so forth are inserted in the right spaces on each individual letter. The fill-ins should be made on a machine with matching type and ribbon.

Some fill-in forms—like, for example, Figure 6-12—are obviously forms. They are useful in routine situations when both the writer and the reader consider forms acceptable.

However, when it is desirable to personalize each letter, fill-in forms can be reproduced by computer, automatic typewriter, or other high-speed automatic machines with magnetic tape capacity for inserting variable information at the time each form is reproduced. Thus, each person on your mailing list will receive a letter containing his or her name in one or more places and all the specific variables that apply to his or her case. The "fill-ins" are almost unnoticeable. If your firm uses a word-processing system, form letters can be run automatically at 1,000 wpm.

Guide Form

Sample letters prepared in advance for various situations can be kept on hand (usually in an office correspondence manual) and referred to whenever a communicator writes similar messages. The communicator uses any sample as a guide only, inserting personal phrasing wherever desirable.

Paragraph Form

An office booklet or a magnetic disc for storing paragraphs to meet various situations is often an efficient way to save the letter writer's time. The writer does, however, need to use good judgment in selecting appropriate paragraphs.

The booklet or disc usually contains various sections covering the frequently written messages. An airline, for example, may group its paragraphs under Passenger Fares, Flight Schedule Inquiries, Air Cargo, Adjustments, Charter Flights, and Goodwill. Each section contains numbered pages with various opening, closing, and intervening paragraphs that answer often-asked questions. Each paragraph may be marked by a number and a letter of the alphabet.

Thus, after choosing the appropriate paragraphs for your message, you need merely dictate the paragraph numbers; for instance, "2C, 5A, 9C, 15E." If you need a special paragraph that is not in the booklet (or on the disc), you dictate it. Your transcriber arranges the designated paragraphs and adds your specially dictated paragraph in the right order. (If an automatic typewriter programmed with magnetic tape or card is used, a letter can be completed in a few seconds.) Each customer gets an attractive, personalized letter composed of form paragraphs that exactly answer his or her questions and needs.

SUMMARY

Letters and memos are the most used written business message media. In addition, for special situations, memo-letters, postcards, Mailgrams, plus other telegraphic and wireless media are also effective.

Attractive appearance of a business letter is an important aid to the reader's favorable first impression. Stationery, parts and layout (format), and envelope addressing should follow certain guidelines. For memorandums (sent within the organization) the stationery, parts, layout, and envelopes are different from those of letters. Memo-letters have a format more similar to a memo than to a letter. Postcards have certain timesaving features. Though the formats of Mailgrams, telegrams, and cablegrams are similar, these messages differ in methods of transmittal, word count, and costs. All convey the impression that your message is important and urgent. To get the most economical rates, study the telegraph company's rules governing these services.

The four kinds of form messages offer advantages in time, cost, quality, and quantity mailings; but they must be used with good judgment to avoid possible disadvantages.

This chapter is your guide for *formats* of business letters, memos, postcards, telegraphic media, and form letters and memos. In Chapters 7 to 14, which focus on *content,* most illustrations include only the message *body*—to save space. Therefore, when typing your complete messages, you may want to refer regularly to this chapter for correct layouts.

EXERCISES

1. What are the standard and optional parts of a business letter?
2. **a.** What is the most popular layout style for business letters?
   b. Describe it and compare it with four other popular styles.
   c. Which do you prefer and why?
3. How do the standard parts of the memo differ from those of the letter?
4. What are the advantages of using postcards, when desirable, for business messages? What disadvantages can you name?
5. Describe briefly five features of the AMS Simplified letter.
6. Name three differences between a modified-block form and a full-block form of letter. Consider all standard and optional parts of these letters.
7. What are the advantages—and possible disadvantages—of (a) form messages? (b) Mailgrams? (c) telegrams? (d) cablegrams?
8. Each of the following parts of a letter has one or more faults. Treat each part as an independent unit. Correct errors and change all obsolete forms.

   In the heading (stationery that doesn't have a letterhead):

   a. 3 April 198_
   15,447 E. 5th St.,
   Seattle, Wn. 98155

   b. Mr. Ray F. Byfield
   15 Mt. Vernon Ave.
   New Orleans, La. 52345
   Jan. 5th, 198_

   In the inside address:

   c. Mrs. John E. Henning,
   4317-18 Avenue N.E.
   Chicago,
   Illinois

    d.   Professor Lee Stephenson, Ph. D.
          School of Business Administration
          University of California
          BERKELEY 94900

    e.   Campbell and Morris Furniture Co.,
          1,496 Westlake Ave.
          City

In the signature and reference section

    f.   (open punctuation)   Very Truly Yours,
                                       State Federal Savings Assn.,
          D.E.S./A.R.F.   Mr. Donald E. Smith
          INCLOSURE   President

    g.   (mixed punctuation)   Sincerely Yours,
          Richard E. Scroggs:ab   Credit Manager

    h.   (mixed punctuation)   Cordially yours
                                       MEURER & HOHANNES, INC.
          RAJ:AF   Raymond Jensen
          cc: Thomas Brown   Prod. Mgr.

In the inside address, salutation, and complimentary close (assume mixed punctuation for parts i through n):

    i.   Veterans Adm.
          Detroit, Mich. 23456

          Attention: Dr. Chester Allen Powers

          Dear Dr. Chester Powers

                             Respectively yours,

    j.   Dr. William Knapp, M.D.
          618 Wrigley Bldg.
          Chicago 14, Ill. 60667

          Dear Carl,

                             Sincerely yours

    k.   B.K. Renshaw
          17,672 3rd St., N.E.,
          New York City 10011

          Dear Sir:-

                       Yours

    l.   Gladyne Lucchesini
          644a Liberty Bldg.
          Des Moines, Ia. 8022

          Dear Miss Gladyne Luchesini

                      Yours truly

   m. Northwest Company, Inc.
       Accounting Department
       Phila, Penna. 33333

       Dear Ms. Swanson

                          Your faithful friend

                          Pasco & Co.

       Incl.   Clifford D. Bergerson
       al; cdb:TR   Personnell Mgr.

   n. HAVDAHL MANUFACTURING COMPANY
       Attention: Miss Helen Burgess
       Eleven South Fifteenth St.
       Kansas C'y, Mo. 76543

       Dear Sirs: RE: February Sale

9. Which of the following three memorandums is best? Why? How does even this memo need improvement? In your evaluation, be sure to consider the probable purpose of the message and whether the memo is likely to be filed.

  a.

```
Jack to Bob, 4-23-8_

B O O K L E T   S C H E D U L E

Johnson now says Saturday sure.
```

  b.

```
TO:     RJL
FROM:   JS
April 23, 198_
HEALTH BOOKLET SCHEDULE

I checked with Johnson and now have a definite promise that the
6,000 Standard "Your Health" booklets will be delivered Satur-
day, April 26.

This rescheduling will not affect our other production sched-
ules.
```

  c.

```
TO:         Dr. Robert Lawson, Vice President
FROM:       John Spam, Managing Editor
April 23, 198_
RESCHEDULING OF STANDARD "YOUR HEALTH" BOOKLETS

I talked with Thomas Johnson this morning in an effort to re-
schedule production of 6,000 Standard "Your Health" booklets
to permit delivery Saturday, April 26.

He indicated at first that such a rescheduling would delay
either the "Travel Plans" or the "Vacation Hints" booklets,
but after talking with his production manager he agreed to
```

```
make the schedule change without delaying our other pro-
duction.

Thus we can definitely count on delivery of "Your Health"
Saturday.
```

10. If you have an employer or know an organization that is willing to furnish the following specified materials, ask for them and then answer the questions:
    a. Bring to class a sample of a firm's letterhead stationery and envelopes and be prepared to evaluate them orally. If the firm has several sizes, qualities, and colors of stationery, evaluate them all and discuss briefly the uses of each.
    b. Bring to class a sample of memorandum stationery and any intracompany envelopes used for memos. Be prepared to evaluate them orally. Can you suggest improvements—perhaps timesaving additions or changes?
    c. Which of the standard styles of letter layout does the firm use? If the firm has not adopted a uniform style for all letters, try to collect—from various secretaries—as many different styles and layouts as you can. Be prepared to:
       (1) Illustrate those you like best and tell why.
       (2) Discuss those you like least and tell why.
       (3) Find out, if possible, why the secretaries and/or their bosses prefer the style they use.
    d. Find out from two or three secretaries in the firm what their pet peeves are concerning their bosses' use of letter parts or manner of dictating these parts.
    e. Be prepared to discuss the following aspects of memos in the firm you visited:
       (1) How frequently are memos used rather than telephone conversations?
       (2) Who writes memos? Only department heads? Nontitled employees? Others?
       (3) To whom do employees write memos?
       (4) Are memos usually routed through a superior? If so, through whom?
       (5) What is the average length of memos?
       (6) What standard and optional parts do the firm's memos contain?
11. Evaluate (in writing or orally, as your instructor assigns) the following, using the letters that you have already collected and been studying:
    a. Regular parts of each letter
    b. Optional parts
    c. Appearance—layout on page, strikeovers, type alignment, ribbon lightness
    d. Spelling accuracy

PART TWO

MAJOR LETTER PLANS

chapter 7

Direct Requests

When the main purpose of your message is to ask the reader to do something, you are writing a *request* letter or memo. Whether you organize your message according to the direct- or the persuasive-request pattern depends upon the nature of the request and, most of all, upon how you think the reader will react to that request. Generally when you make a simple inquiry or a routine request, you will *not* have to persuade your reader to do what you ask. You can usually handle the following types of messages with the direct-request plan:

Inquiries

Claims (complaints) and requests for adjustments

Requests for action related to routine business procedures

Invitations, orders, reservations

Requests pertaining to civic causes or public officials

Early-stage collection messages

This chapter presents the direct-request organizational plan, discusses the first five types of requests, then compares them briefly in capsule checklists. Chapter 13 discusses early-stage collection messages.

ORGANIZATIONAL PLAN

For a routine inquiry or request you assume that the reader will do as you request, once he or she understands what you want and why you want it. Thus you use the direct approach—introduce your main idea in the first paragraph. The direct-request plan has three basic parts:

---

1. Main idea
   a. Introduce your request, major statement, or question.
   b. State reason(s), if desirable, justifying the request.
2. Explanation
   a. Include details necessary to help the reader respond to your request correctly.
   b. Consider numbering your questions (if more than one) for easy reading and answering.
3. Courteous close with motivation to action
   a. State clearly what action you want the reader to take—and when.
   b. Make action easy, if appropriate, by including a postpaid reply envelope, your telephone number, office hours, or any other appropriate, helpful information.
   c. Express appreciation and, if appropriate, include a statement of goodwill or reader benefit.

INQUIRIES

To get facts that you need and cannot conveniently or economically obtain yourself, you write inquiries requesting information. Because the questions asked are important in all inquiries, this section begins with suggestions about phrasing and arranging questions. Then follows a discussion of direct-request messages that seek information about persons and messages inquiring about products, services, and other matters requiring no persuasion.

Wording and Arrangement of Questions

So that you can get exactly the information wanted, you must be especially careful when planning the questions to be included in your inquiries.[1] The following suggestions apply to all kinds of direct-request inquiries:

1. Make your questions specific. If the product about which you inquire is technical, include specific physical dimensions, technical specifications, exact intended use of the item, architectural drawings, or whatever else will help the respondent. A single general question such as "Will you give us any information you can on this applicant (or product)?" will probably bring a reply so general that it will be almost useless.

   The more penetrating your questions, the more likely you are to get the information you need. Most respondents who would not *volunteer* unfavorable facts (especially about a person) will be frank when asked specific questions, provided you promise confidential treatment.
2. Use a separate paragraph for each main question if the questions require explanation.
3. If you have more than one question, consider numbering them. If you have only two or three questions, you may place them in the body of your letter, but it is generally better to list your questions on the same sheet below the body. Then the respondent can answer directly in the spaces provided and need not write a separate letter.
4. When you have more questions than space at the bottom of your letter page, or when your questions require lengthy answers, place them on a separate sheet and be sure to allow enough space for adequate answers.
5. Keep your questions to a minimum and make them clear. A long or vague questionnaire decreases the number of returns.
6. Word your questions to get more than "yes" or "no" answers if you need a detailed opinion or description. For example a yes or no answer to: "Did the applicant have duties that required responsibility?" would probably be inadequate. To obtain a more helpful answer, you might ask: "What kinds of duties requiring responsibility did the applicant perform especially well?" In contrast, a yes or no

---

[1] See also Stanley L. Payne, *The Art of Asking Questions* (especially Chapter 14, which lists 100 considerations), Princeton University Press, Princeton, N.J., 1951; and Lyndon O. Brown, *Market Research and Analysis,* Ronald Press Company, New York, 1969.

answer would be adequate for such a question as: "Does the applicant have an account with you?"

7. Word some questions for simple checking of "Yes," "No," or "Don't know" if you plan to tabulate numerous answers (say, 50 or more).

8. If you wish the respondent to "rate" a person, product, or service, it may be better to define each category on your rating scale. For instance, the following example shows one of eight questions on an employer's questionnaire about an applicant for employment. Notice how both the squares and the definitions make responses easy. The best choices may be at the right (as in the example) or at the left, but consistent placement of best choices is more convenient for both the reference and you—especially if you must compare many replies.

```
ABILITY TO GET ALONG WITH OTHERS:
    Is the applicant a likable, friendly, and tactful individual, or
    an egotistical, unpleasant, or thoughtless individual?  Will this
    person attract the people with whom he or she deals or keep them
    at a distance?  Is he or she poised in normal social situations?
    (Check one.)

       □               □               □            □            □
    Egotistical,   Somewhat neutral,  Approach-   Likable,    Exceedingly
    unfriendly     does not easily    able        friendly,   pleasant and
    or tactless    attract friends                and tactful agreeable;
                                                               will attract
                                                               others
```

9. Carefully arrange your questions—generally with the easiest to answer first.

10. Word your questions in a neutral way so you will not influence the answers.

11. Consider sending to your reader two copies of the questionnaire if you think he or she might need one for personal records.

Inquiries about Persons

When you need information about a person, you usually direct your request to a reference—a responsible source of information. You ask the reference to give information about an applicant for a job, a loan, credit, membership in an organization, an award, or some kind of special training or insurance protection.

Inquiries to a reference may be written by the applicant or, more frequently, by the person who seeks information about the applicant.

Applicant's Request to a Reference

Sometimes an applicant asks references if they will send a recommendation direct to someone who needs confidential information about that applicant. For instance, suppose you are seeking admission into a graduate school that requires at least four confidential recommendations. Perhaps you can approach some of your selected references in person or by telephone. To others, however (if they are out of town or if you have a questionnaire they need to fill out), you will have to write a letter.

Because your request to a reference is asking a favor, it is best to state courteously in the first paragraph why you are writing to this person and what the recommendation is for. If you haven't been in touch with the references for some time, you may need to refresh their memory about who you are.

The explanation section of your request should include a brief summary of pertinent facts about yourself. Consider carefully the references' relationship to you and decide what facts they will need to grant the favor you are asking and to give a fair, helpful recommendation. (Sometimes an attached data sheet is useful.) If, for example, the reference is a former professor, you might include the following information:

1. The course you studied under the reference—when, where, and your grade.
2. Your major, and your grade point average (GPA) in the major.
3. Your overall GPA in college. If the professor will or might recall that you made poor grades, include perhaps an honest, brief explanation as to why your college GPA wasn't higher (for instance, number of hours each week you worked to provide finances; a bad first year or first two years, but higher GPA the last year; or whatever is pertinent).
4. Difficult related courses you studied (if grades are good), from whom you took the courses, and the grades you received.
5. Test scores—graduate record exam, law school admission test, admission test for graduate study in business or medical school, or any other pertinent scores.
6. Honors, honor societies (Phi Beta Kappa, Beta Gamma Sigma, etc.), studies in any special honors programs.
7. Scholarships awarded.
8. Leadership qualities; for example, offices held in living group, on campus, in political groups.
9. Activities—tutoring, United Nations Model Congress, etc.
10. Guidelines, if possible, for the recommendation. Enclose, if you can, a form or letter from the graduate school, stating what information it seeks from the reference about you—distinguishing intellectual traits or abilities, leadership capacity, quality of work done, character, integrity, or other personal traits.

Your closing paragraph should state to whom the letter or form is to be sent; be sure to state the full name and address, unless this information is printed on the form. And, of course, include a statement of appreciation.

If it is necessary for you to obtain recommendations about your work in specific courses or jobs in which your work was just mediocre, be sure to provide an explanation regarding the quality of your work, if possible. In inquiry 1 the applicant shows consideration for the reader by courteous tone, by the facts included about courses she studied, by mention of factors that influenced the quality of her chemistry studies, and by the reasonable time allowed for response.

Inquiry 1

An applicant's well-written request to a former professor.

Dear Professor Brown:

Introduction of request and reason

This letter is to reintroduce myself to you and to ask a favor of you. The University of Montana's Dental School has asked for a recommendation from my Organic Chemistry professor.

Explanation: details about past relationship

Almost four years ago--in winter and spring quarters of (*year*)--you were my chemistry professor here at the University of Montana. The courses I took from you were Chemistry 241 and Chemistry 242, both of which met at 3 p.m. daily. The grades I received were C's, but I believe I could have done better if circumstances had been a little different that year. Besides the lapse of two years between my inorganic and organic studies, there was my part-time job in the Applied Physics Laboratory until 3 p.m. four days a week. Because this work caused me to come to your class about 15 minutes late, I sometimes missed important laboratory work, a fact which necessarily affected my grade. In our several conferences, however, you often commented very favorably on my work.

More details, leading to reason for this request

Currently I am a senior, graduating this quarter with a grade point average of 3.02 (out of 4.0) in Business Administration. I am applying for admission to the Dental School at the University of Montana. To this date I have completed successfully all the pre-dental requirements, and would like to begin dental studies next fall.

Easy and dated action

The enclosed form is one the Dental School requires regarding my studies in organic chemistry. Professor Brown, will you please fill out and return this form in the enclosed envelope to the admissions officer? I will appreciate very much your mailing this information within the next two weeks--before the admissions deadline, March 1.

Inquirer's Request to a Reference

The most frequent requests to references are those written by persons who need confidential information about the applicant. Suppose, for example, that you are the employer, lender, creditor, insurance underwriter, or officer of any organization that is considering an applicant for a special reason. The letter of inquiry you write to each reference the applicant has listed can be organized according to the direct-request pattern.

Your opening paragraph usually includes the full name of the applicant you are considering, why you are considering the applicant, and why you are writing to the reader.

The explanatory section should include:

1. Sufficient details about the requirements of the job, loan, credit, scholarship, or membership for which the applicant is being considered. Such facts help the reference to visualize whether the applicant can meet the requirements. (The latter should, of course, be within current laws. Forbidden requirements are those that discriminate on the basis of race, color, religion, sex, or national origin. Also forbidden, depending on circumstances, are age, handicap, and marital or parental status discriminatory requirements.)

2. If appropriate, a few pertinent facts the applicant has already told you—such as length of time worked for the reference, job title, achievements. This way you can check on the applicant's accuracy and honesty.

3. Clearly stated questions (preferably numbered) asking exactly what you want to know about the applicant.

The ending paragraph usually includes appreciation, promise of confidential treatment of the reply, and (if appropriate) provisions for easy action,[2] and an offer to reciprocate.

Obviously, the content and processing of your inquiry to a reference will depend upon your purpose and your reader. If, for example, you are writing to references about an applicant for a unique position, you will no doubt compose a special message with special questions. Not only will your letter be individually typed, but also you will usually expect a letter reply from the reference. The letter below (inquiry 2) from a hardware store manager to a department store manager, is an example of such an inquiry.

Inquiry 2

Personalized request listing numbered questions in the letter.[3]

Name; why being considered; a few facts he has told	Mr. Victor L. Dryer, one of your former employees, has applied here as assistant manager of our electrical supplies department. He states that he was in charge of your electrical appliances section for about a year, and he has given your name as a reference.
Request	We need a qualified person who can, in about two years, become department manager. I will appreciate your frank answers to the following questions and any other pertinent facts you can include:

---

[2] When you write to a business executive at a business address, you can usually omit the enclosed reply envelope because many business executives prefer to use their own firm's stationery. However, when you write to a reference at home (for instance, to a personal reference whose business address is unknown to you) or to someone who may be in a one-person office or in a nonprofit organization, it is appropriate to enclose a stamped reply envelope.

[3] To save space, most examples in this and succeeding chapters include only the body of each message. You can assume the salutation is the usual "Dear Mr. (Mrs., Miss, Ms.) plus the reader's surname; and the complimentary close is one of those illustrated in Chapter 6, unless otherwise indicated.

Questions:

1. When was he in your employ and why did he leave?
2. How satisfactory were his services as a section head in your store?
3. Do you know of any personal habits or characteristics that might hinder or help his success in a position of responsibility?

A promise

Your statements will, of course, be kept confidential.

Inquiry 3 below is an exceptionally thorough, individually typed inquiry which interweaves explanation and unnumbered questions for each qualification. It is reproduced here as an example of the care that a reputable firm takes in placing an outstanding candidate.

Inquiry 3

Personalized request interweaving explanations with questions in the letter.

Full name; reason for request

We are seriously considering Ms. Barbara Rankin for a position in our research department here. She has given your name as a reference.

Details— applicant's work

As you may know, Ms. Rankin has been working in a clerical position for us part-time for about a year in our branch office in your city. Now she has expressed interest in getting into more professional work and pursuing her career in writing for our head office.

Details; specific request and explanation

Because of Ms. Rankin's outstanding record in college, to say nothing of the fine work she has done for us, we are making every effort to find, or create, a position for her here. And for that reason I am asking for help in finding out as much as possible about her relative strengths and weaknesses. In this way we can do a better job of fitting her talents to our needs and in assigning her work which is neither beyond her present capacity nor out of line with her interests and skills.

Two implied questions

I understand that Ms. Rankin worked about two years part-time in your advertising office, and I will welcome information about how effectively and concisely she writes, particularly how readily she can compose business letters to advertisers.

More questions with details

In addition, we would like to have your impressions of the attitudes and skills that Ms. Rankin can carry over from school to the business world--her ability to organize her work, her originality, initiative, reliability, and ability to work smoothly with others while under pressure. Under what degree of supervision and guidance is she likely to do her best work?

A promise

Any and all comments you may care to make will be a great help and, of course, confidential.

Easy action
(phone)

Your schedule is probably particularly heavy at this time of year--and I hesitate to call you when you may be busy. Perhaps it would be simplest for you to telephone me collect *(area code and phone number)* when convenient for you. I am usually at my desk between 9:00 and 11:30 Monday through Friday.

If you (for example, as personnel manager) need references on hundreds of new applicants, sheer volume will force you to plan a duplicated form that you can use again and again. For instance, inquiry 4, used by a national business machines firm, is printed with lines for typewritten fill-ins, including name and city of the applicant, in the opening. The questions on the lower half of the same sheet ask the reference to evaluate the applicant—from superior to unsatisfactory—on various personal qualities. (If you prefer to define each rating category, use a form with questions similar to that illustrated in suggestion 8, page 164.) As is customary and desirable, the last question gives the respondent additional space for "other comments." The information obtained from such open-ended questions can be extremely important and helpful.

Inquiry 4

Printed inquiry adaptable for any reference about any prospective applicant; evaluation form on same page below the request.

Name;
reason

M _____ *(name)* _____ of _____ *(city)* _____ states that he or she was employed by you as *(type of work)* from *(date)* to *(date)*. He or she has listed your name as a reference.

Type of work

We are making a careful study of the qualifications of this applicant to determine whether it would be in his or her best interests to consider a position as sales representative in our business of furnishing a complete line of *(type of machines are named here)*.

Request;
easy action

Will you please give us your answers and comments on the following points and any other comments which you feel will be helpful to the applicant in choosing a life's work? Just mail your reply in the enclosed stamped return envelope as soon as possible.

	Superior	Good	Average	Below average	Unsatisfactory	Comments
Potential ability to sell a quality product (your estimate) _____						
Personality _____						
Industry—determination _____						
Aptness in learning _____						
Creative ability—resourcefulness _____						
Dependability—cooperation _____						
Disposition—balance _____						

For what type of work do you think applicant is best fitted? _____

Would you strongly recommend that applicant enter sales work? _____

Other comments (you may also use reverse side): _____

(Signed) _____

Date _____   (Title) _____

Inquiries about Products or Services

Both as a consumer and as a business or professional person, you will have many occasions to seek information from the seller of products and services or from customers, employees, and others.

Direct Request to the Seller

When your inquiry goes to a seller—whether a manufacturer, retailer, investment broker, or hotel clerk—the addressee's self-interest should make him or her glad to comply with your wishes. Perhaps you want a free catalog, price list, or booklet about products, deliveries, or payment plans. At such times your complete direct request need be only one sentence, such as:

> Please send me your latest sporting equipment catalog and the descriptive folder you advertised in the April issue of <u>Sportsman Illustrated</u>.

If, however, you have a unique individual problem, you may need to ask questions for which the recipient does not have prepared answers. Following the direct-request plan, present your main idea (request and/or reason) in the first paragraph. For most inquiries to a seller concerning a product or service, it is entirely optional whether to present request or reason first. But if you think your request is somewhat unusual or will be time-consuming for the reader to answer, state the reason first. After the opening paragraph, include all needed explanations and/or questions. The final paragraph contains the action request.

Inquiry 5 is written by a purchasing manager requesting information from a manufacturer about a product he is considering buying. Notice that the letter begins with the major request; but if you prefer to begin with the reason, you might interchange paragraphs 1 (request) and 3 (reason).

Inquiry 5

Inquiry about an advertised product; numbered questions within the letter.

Major request   Your ads in <u>Good Business</u> magazine have attracted our attention, and we will appreciate your answers to the following questions:

Specific numbered questions	1. What is the price of each Quiktyper? 2. How long does it take an average typist to learn to operate this machine? 3. To what extent can your experts estimate how much money a company can save in a year with Quiktyper, if it uses--for instance--25 different one-page form letters and mails a total of 270,000 letters a year? 4. What guarantee do you offer?
Reason for request	Before deciding whether our firm should invest in one or more automatic typewriters, we should like as much information as possible about leading brands.
Suggested action	If you have a factory agent in this area, we welcome a demonstration any time within the next two weeks, preferably after receipt of your written reply to these four questions.

Direct Requests to Customers, Employees, and Others

As the seller of products or services, you can often use inquiries to win back "missed" customers who have not bought from your firm for some time or to obtain information about your firm's products or services.

"Miss-You" Messages. Simple "miss-you" requests are discussed below (see also Persuasive Requests, Chapter 10). Many firms have revived hundreds of unused accounts by mailing a series of direct requests—ranging from colorful postcards to form letters on specially designed stationery. Such messages concentrate on telling readers that they are missed, appreciated, and important, and asking them to come back. Specially designed letterheads and colors often aid in making visual the word pictures expressed in miss-you messages.

Inquiry 6, from a firm of auto specialists, includes a touch of humor on a descriptive letterhead that introduces the theme of the message.

Inquiry 6

A miss-you request designed mainly to get the customer to come back. A picture at the top shows a home hallway, a lighted lamp, a clock with hands at 2:15, and a person entering the front door cautiously on tiptoe while carrying a pair of shoes. A voice from upstairs calls:

"WHERE HAVE YOU BEEN?"

Main idea	We've missed you too! And we've been asking about you, because it's the repeat appearances of good customers like you that play the leading part in our business.

Reason

In fact, customers like you are the balance wheel, the spark plugs, the drive shaft that keep us going. With us, customers are about the whole works.

Suggested action

That's why we've been wondering about you. Remember that our door is always open for you--from 8 a.m. to 6 p.m. Mondays through Fridays. You won't have to tiptoe in. Every appearance you make in our shop is sincerely appreciated. DRIVE IN SOON, won't you? WE'LL DO OUR BEST TO PLEASE YOU.

Inquiry 6 is designed simply to get the customer to come back. Other miss-you letters may go a step further and ask what is wrong. Then if the former customers have a complaint, they feel they can express it; if they have none, they will probably say so and perhaps place another order. Either way the silence has been broken, and a dead account may be revived. Also, your firm may have gained useful information about its products or services.

When you ask your customer what is wrong, you have several ways to make replying easy. Some messages, like inquiry 7, merely ask the reader to jot down the reason on the margin or back of the letter. Others invite the reader to phone, and still others list a few possible reasons for the reader to check off. (This list may include some humorous unlikely reasons. See, for example, Figure 6-15, page 148. A later sentence then asks for another chance to serve the customer soon.)

Inquiry 7

A miss-you inquiry aiming mainly to get a reply that answers: "What is wrong?"

Main idea

Perhaps you have the answer to a question that has worried us. For a long time we have received no order or mail from you; and as we do not know why, we are concerned.

Explanation

We have missed the privilege of serving you--a good business friend. Often we have asked ourselves: "What did we do or say to offend this good customer?" What causes this absence? We've checked all the orders and correspondence from you plus our shipment schedules and prices to you--and everything looks OK.

Suggested reasons

But something must be wrong, to keep you from us so long. Please tell us about it frankly. If in any way our merchandise or service did not come up to your expectations, let us make amends. There may be some other reason why we have not heard from you; and if so, will you please tell us?

Easy action

Just write your note on the margin or back of this letter and mail it in the postpaid envelope addressed to me. I'll very much appreciate your reply.

Other Inquiries about Your Firm's Products or Services. Besides asking lost customers what is wrong, you can ask steady or new customers for their comments about your products which they have bought or returned. Then not only will you obtain valuable information, but you will also help build customer confidence in your genuine desire to maintain good service. (For examples of messages showing continuing concern, see Chapter 14.)

Often you will need information from employees, colleagues, or other persons *within* your organization. Inquiry 8, a *memo* launching an employee survey, can be adapted so that it is suitable for other types of readers—inside or outside your organization—whenever your questions are easy to answer and no persuasion is necessary.

Inquiry 8

A memo seeking employee needs and preferences about parking on company premises; questionnaire attached.

```
TO:        All employees          DATE:  May 1, 198_.
FROM:      Parking Division, Personnel Department
SUBJECT:   Your preferences about parking permits
```

Reader-benefit reason

In an effort to improve the parking situation for all employees, your parking division is conducting a survey of your needs and preferences.

Request and dated action

Will you please fill out the attached questionnaire and return it, unsigned, to your supervisor by Friday, May 1, at 5 p.m.? Then you will be sure that your feelings are included in the survey. The results of employee opinions and suggestions will be tabulated and announced at the next employee meeting, May 15.

CLAIMS (COMPLAINTS) AND REQUESTS FOR ADJUSTMENTS

Whenever you are dissatisfied with a product, service, or policy, it is to your advantage—and the company's—to communicate with the right person promptly about the desired correction. Oral complaints to sales representatives or clerks often do not bring results; a much better procedure is to write an effective letter to the proper company official who does care when a problem exists and who can and will do something to correct it.

When you state your complaint, you usually make a claim or request for some kind of adjustment. All such requests are grouped together in this section and labeled *claim letters.* Claim letters should be organized by the direct-request pattern whenever they involve a routine matter that is covered by a guarantee or by established procedures for customer relations.

Typical situations for direct-request claims about merchandise involve defective materials or workmanship, malfunctioning parts, soiled or shopworn items, or products not as represented. Claims about services include delivery mix-ups, broken promises, discourtesy, carelessness, clerical or bookkeeping errors, and minor inconveniences relating to violation of published company policies. (For those claims that involve controversial issues, substantially large sums of money, repeated errors, and other serious matters, you will need to write a persuasive request, as discussed in Chapter 10.)

Characteristics of Well-written Claims

To be fair to the seller, product or service, and yourself—write promptly. Also, be sure your letter has all the C qualities. Show by your attitude and wording that *you have confidence in the readers' fairness*—confidence that they will make the adjustment after they get the facts. Omit any statements that sound like appeals or threats.

When you complain about the poor condition of a product, for instance, state all the pertinent facts logically, courteously, and impersonally, without exaggeration or irrelevant material. Guesses and opinions about who may be to blame are unwise and unhelpful. Let the reader determine causes; you present facts as you see them. And when your purpose is to call attention to employees' poor service, make clear you are doing so because you think the behavior is not representative of the firm's usually good customer relations policies. Cite phone-call records of dates and times each call was made as well as the name of the person spoken to.

Anger and name-calling are, of course, taboo. Remember that the reader is not the person who made the mistake. A writer who antagonizes the recipient merely lowers the chances of satisfactory adjustment—or at least of being considered a reasonable person. One extra caution: When you write as an agent for your employer or business, you must be even more careful to avoid tactless, intemperate accusations. Such outbursts not only reflect unfavorably upon you *and* your company, but they also may place you in danger of a libel suit.[4]

It is often a good idea to state both sides of the case—for example, you might comment on something you *like* about the firm's products or service. Such a statement can be in the opening paragraph or in the explanation. Even humor (not sarcasm) is appropriate when the matter is relatively small.

Organization and Content of the Simple Direct Claim

Begin your direct claim with the main idea—namely, the need for an adjustment or correction of an error. Do not waste the reader's time with details or background information in the first paragraph.

In the explanatory paragraph(s) include all facts the reader will need to understand your claim clearly. For instance, if you wish free repairs on an item that is malfunctioning within the guarantee period, present evidence of the date of your purchase, make clear that you followed carefully the operating instructions (if you did), and state clearly what is wrong.

In your action paragraph, ask for what you want or leave the decision to your reader. Depending on circumstances, you will usually request one or more of the

---

[4] See Appendix A, about legal aspects of letters.

following. (The numbers in parentheses after each request refer to the claim-letter examples illustrated in this section.)

1. Refund—for all or part of purchase price (1)
2. A new shipment with the correct item(s) ordered (1)
3. Free replacement of the defective part(s), the whole item, or the whole shipment, or service (2)
4. Free repairs (3)
5. Reduction in the price (because of a product or service defect) (3)
6. Free inspection, leading to redecorating, complete overhaul, etc.
7. Explanation and/or change in policy or procedure (3)
8. Credit to your account (or a credit slip)
9. Cancellation of an order or part of an order
10. Correction (and perhaps explanation) of a billing error

If you need the adjustment by a certain time, state why, as in the last paragraph of the following claim. You should also consider (and perhaps ask) whether the defective or incorrect product should be returned to the seller. Although the claimant in the letter below returned the wrong-sized item without asking, often it is better not to return goods until you have the seller's instructions.

Claim 1

A courteous claim (dated June 9) to a sportswear department manager from an out-of-town cash customer who needs an exchange or a refund.

Main idea; request	Enclosed is the sweater which Nelson's delivery truck left yesterday and which I wish to exchange for the correct size or a refund.
Explanatory details	When I selected and purchased this Hudson sweater in your department last week (for $30.50 cash), I asked that a size "L" be sent to my home. The size I received is only an "S", and of course I can't wear it. My sales check is #7902, dated June 4, written by salesclerk #801.
Specific request *Dated action*	Will you please send me the correct size "L" in exactly this same style and color or, if this is not available now, a cash refund of $30.50? As I am leaving on a one-month trip June 17, it is necessary that I receive the sweater or the check before that date.

Sometimes you may have to present your direct-request claim a second time. A second request usually goes to a higher official, and your letter will probably have a dual purpose—to obtain the desired action and to complain about the lack of response (or incorrect response). For example, suppose that instead of receiving the sweater or cash refund you requested by letter in claim 1, you receive only a credit slip which you don't want. Or suppose that instead of writing your first claim, you returned the sweater in person to the sportswear department, and there both the salesperson and the department manager rudely insisted that you accept a credit slip. If you know the refusal is contrary to the store's published policy, you will justly feel that a higher official should know about the situation.

For such a dual-purpose direct-request letter, you might begin with a paragraph similar to one of the following:

> The purpose of my letter is to ask you for a cash refund which I am unable to obtain through normal channels. Also I'm sure you will want to know about the discrepancy between the treatment I received in your sportswear department and your advertised company policy of customer satisfaction or a full refund.

> *or*

> You will be interested, I think, in the experience I had with a wrong-sized sweater I received from your store June 8. I believe I am entitled to a cash refund, though two of your employees refused to give it to me.

Your explanatory paragraph should tactfully present all pertinent facts about your purchase and the department employees' statements; you should also enclose a copy of the credit slip or its date and number. The ending paragraph will be a forthright request for the refund.

The next two examples are written by business executives for claims concerning their companies. Claim 2 concerns faulty products; claim 3, faulty service. Notice that in both letters the writers present all needed facts without anger and with a good you-attitude.

Claim 2

A considerate complaint from a gift store owner to a wholesaler, about faulty merchandise.

Main idea; request
Our shipment of Swedish tumblers was checked in yesterday and put on sale, then hurriedly withdrawn when the stock room reported it to be a completely defective shipment. We are asking you for an adjustment on these tumblers.

Details
The news about this shipment was especially disappointing to me because we had already advertised that the sale was to begin today. I personally washed and examined a dozen glasses of each size, four each (and not necessarily the worst) of which we are sending you by express for your examination and comment.

There is no regularity in the mars, scratches, and abrasions, or whatever the defects should be termed, to indicate faulty moulds. In fact, I've never seen anything in domestic or imported glass to equal the variety of imperfections apparently present to some degree in every glass of this shipment.

You-attitude

I realize fully that you had no opportunity to check this merchandise and that it is only through your customers that you learn of its condition and can in turn seek an adjustment from the factory.

Action

We are withholding sale of the glasses and payment of the bill until we hear from you.

Claim 3

A considerate complaint (May 18) from a restaurant manager to a laundry, about faulty service.

Main idea: something is wrong; compliment too

What has happened to Spic's starching and mending service? You may recall my April 19 letter complimenting you on the neat appearance of the uniforms Spic sent then. But the last three shipments have contained both torn and incorrectly starched garments.

Details

On May 10, nine of our twenty waitresses' uniforms came back as limp as though they had not been starched at all. On May 14, all twenty uniforms came back again limp--in collars and cuffs. Also, four had unmended rips. That morning, on our outgoing laundry bag I pinned a note for the driver, asking if the laundry would please again observe the following request, which had been overlooked the previous week: EXTRA HEAVY STARCH ON ALL COLLARS AND CUFFS.

More details

Good-natured attitude

Today--same thing happened. All collars and cuffs were limp. But this time five of the cotton slacks of our men waiters were so stiff they stood up alone! It took a bit of persuading to get the men to wear them; we had a good laugh each time.

More you-attitude

Yet all this mix-up hurts the image of our restaurant. We like our employees to look neat. As you know, I'd much rather compliment than complain. But the change has been so abrupt that I'm sure you want to know. Will you please:

Specific request

Reduce your charges for the 49 unstarched uniforms
  and the overstarched five pairs of slacks,
Make free repairs on the four torn uniforms, which
  we will return to your driver on his next call,
  and
Let me know whether we can count on the usual good
  mending as well as starching service in the future.

REQUESTS FOR ACTION RELATED TO ROUTINE BUSINESS PROCEDURES

The messages in this section include business or professional people's requests that are directly related to routine business procedures within their firm. The discussions and examples are grouped in two categories—according to whether the requests go to persons outside or within the organization.

Requests to Persons outside Your Organization

As a business or professional person you may need to ask your customer, supplier, transportation company, or others to sign an enclosed signature card or form or document. Or you may need missing answers on a customer's credit application, or the return of a budget payment book, or a correction of an irregularity in a check sent to your firm. These and numerous other routine matters can be handled by direct-request messages.

You can use form letters, either processed or individually typed, but it is often a good idea to personalize the letter by individual typing, as in request 1 below. However, even processed form messages—for example, requests 2 and 3—are satisfactory when the messages are clearly the same for all members (customers) in a group.

Notice that all the following letters are concise, clear, and courteous. And they all begin with the reason or the request (or a major statement that leads to the request) either in the first paragraph or at the beginning of the second.

Request 1

A bank's trust department asks the executor of an estate to return an affidavit, signature card, and passbook; individually typed message.

Reason; request

So that we can transfer the account of Mr. R. S. Roe, deceased, to your name as Executor, will you please do the following:

Numbered specific requests

1. Sign the enclosed affidavit.
2. Fill out the enclosed card and sign it.
3. Return to us the signed affidavit, card, and your passbook #222-222.

Reader benefit; easy action

The same day these important materials reach us, we will transfer the funds to a new account, with no loss of earnings. Please use the enclosed air-mail envelope to speed your reply.

Request 2

Request from a mortgage loan company to a borrower regarding insurance premium payments; personalized form letter signed by the company's president.

Main idea

The valuable benefits your Homeowner's Mortgage Protector Plan provides become effective on the date the certificate indicates--if you have paid the insurance premium for the plan.

*Request, with
specific payment
amounts*

In case you have already mailed your mortgage installment for the month in which your protection is to become effective, please send the premium--$ --to us
now so that you will be fully protected for the
month.

Next month and for all future payments please be sure
to combine your mortgage and insurance payments into
one check for $.

Reader benefit

We are pleased you have secured this protection for
yourself and family. Many of our customers have
found this is a very valuable and worthwhile program.
After you have read the certificate carefully, please
file it with your other valuable papers.

Whenever common errors—for instance in checks, order forms, registration—occur
frequently among your customers, a well-worded form request is a time-saver. Request
3 illustrates a simple, concise form. (See also Figure 6-12 for another timesaving form
for handling routine requests.)

Request 3

*Multipurpose printed form (7" x 3½") to inform customers of needed check correc-
tion.*

Request

Your check is being returned with the request that
you please make the correction(s) indicated below.
This check . . .

*Details (what
should be done
instead of what's
wrong)*

____Should be signed by maker.
____Should be properly endorsed.
____Needs an individual endorsement.
____Must have the written amount agree with the fig-
ure.
____Should be made payable to us.
____Needs the correct date.

*Action;
reader benefit*

As soon as you have made the correction(s), please
return this check or a new check, and we will be
glad to credit your account.

Requests to Persons within Your Organization

The memos included here are straightforward requests exchanged between employees,
colleagues, supervisors and subordinates, and others, such as stockholders, who are
part of an organization. (Most memos of authorization for special studies and reports
also fall in this direct-request group.)

The next two examples illustrate well-written requests to persons within the writer's organization. As you read request 4, notice its good features—the six numbered details for easy reading and the definite, courteous instructions about the desired action. Enclosed with the memo was a two-page sample report with a detailed discussion of each of the six headings.

Request 4

A division manager's memo asking field representatives to send monthly reports.

TO:	Jim Inkley	Emma Koontz
	Ruth Lindquist	Dick Dubuque
	Tom Sedlock	
CC:	Ralph Smith	
	B. J. Loners	
FROM:	James Pearson	

SUBJECT: <u>Monthly Reports</u> DATE: September 10, 198_

Request

Starting October 1, will each of you please submit to this office on the 21st of the month a monthly report including:

Numbered details

1. Major orders received during the month
2. Anticipated major orders for the following month
3. New business activity
4. Lost orders
5. Industrial trends
6. General comments

Helpful sample

A copy of the form I would like you to use is attached.

Clear statement of where and when report should be sent

By no later than the 21st of every month, please mail your monthly report to me, with copies to the following:

1. Each of the other sales representatives
2. Gail Rankin, Sales Manager

I will appreciate your cooperation.

Request 5, to stockholders, includes both a reader-benefit reason and two suggestions for easy action. Notice the "faked inside address" and omission of salutation.

Request 5

A corporation secretary's second request to stockholders for a proxy; printed message.

Second Request
For Proxy for
Annual Meeting of Stockholders May 9, 198_

Main idea	At the close of business on April 25, we had not received a proxy from you for the Annual Stockholders Meeting to be held May 9.
	Perhaps you have already mailed that proxy. If so, we thank you and ask that you disregard this request.
Request; *easy action*	If you have not yet returned your proxy, however,-- or are doubtful whether you did so--will you please fill out either the enclosed proxy form or the one we sent to you April 8 along with the meeting notice and invitation?
Reader benefit; *easy action*	So that you will be represented at the meeting, please mail your proxy today in the enclosed reply envelope.

INVITATIONS, ORDERS, RESERVATIONS

Though quite different from each other, invitations, orders, and reservations are similar in that the reader is asked for participation, merchandise, or facilities.

Invitations

Invitations that require no persuasion can be classified as both good-news announcements (Chapter 8) and simple requests. Regardless of how you classify them, they are organized according to the same three-part plan: main idea, explanation, action.

The main idea in the first paragraph is the invitation request, and you should try to include in it as many of the five W's as you can. The following sample openings are representative of two kinds of invitations you may need to send in business.

Memo

To all employees (from the company's house-organ editor).

Do you have an item of news or a suggestion you would like to share with other employees in our company? If so, you are invited to submit it for inclusion in our Semiannual Company House Organ before March 1.

Letter

To all customers (from an administrative officer).

You are cordially invited to attend the open house of our Topname Airplane Company . . .

Sunday, June 10, from 2 to 5 p.m.
in Plants 2 and 3.

In the explanation paragraph of your direct-request invitation, include all details that your reader(s) will appreciate and need. The ending paragraph clearly states the desired reader action and makes the action easy. If you need a reply by a certain date, be sure to say so.

The letter below invites business executives to a luncheon meeting.

Dear ALTRUA member:

Request	The next meeting of Altrua is one you are especially invited to attend. As your yearbook shows, this is the
What *Who*	FORUM LUNCHEON, sponsored jointly by the Chamber of Commerce and our club
	to be held
Where	at Lake City Community Hall, *(address)*
When	on Thursday, April 21, 198_ 12:15 p.m.
A detail about the program	A highlight of the program is the panel discussion on the topic, "Problems of the Small Business Executive in King County." You will find the discussion timely, challenging, and thought provoking.
Easy action	To make your reservation, please call either Trish Norden (823-7777) or Mike Browne (349-9999) before Tuesday, April 19, 5 p.m. How about phoning right now while you think of it?
Reader benefit	We look forward to seeing you April 21 at the luncheon. For your convenience, free parking is available on the north side of the Hall.

Orders and Reservations

When you are ordering supplies or equipment and do not have an order blank or purchase form of the company with which you are placing the order, you can accomplish your purpose by writing a letter according to the direct-request plan. The same is true when you wish to reserve hotel accommodations, a meeting room, parking facilities for a conference, or any other premises.

Order letters include three kinds of facts: details about *what you are ordering or reserving, directions for shipment,* and *manner of payment.* In both order and reservation messages, the main idea in the first paragraph is that you are ordering or reserving something. Your explanatory paragraphs give whatever details the order or reservation requires—about quantity, color, style, size, price, payment, location, shipment date, place—plus any special instructions your reader might need. The last paragraph invites prompt shipment and dated action, if desired.

The following letter illustrates the organization and content of an order letter with items tabulated for easy reading. You can use a similar organization plan for reservations.

Request Please ship the following supplies to reach our main office at 9251 Grand Avenue (*City, State, Zip*) by Wednesday, June 3:

Details

Quantity	Description (and or catalog number)	Unit Price	Total
		Total	$_____

Payment These items are to be charged to our account on the usual 2/10, net 30 terms.

Shipment; courtesy As we plan to distribute the ball-point pens for customer gifts on the opening day of our new branch, June 5, it is imperative that this shipment arrive on time. We count on your company's usual promptness in filling orders.

REQUESTS PERTAINING TO CIVIC CAUSES OR PUBLIC OFFICIALS

Public officials need and appreciate suggestions from enlightened business executives, professionals, and concerned citizens. Often, when an important issue is up for debate, they welcome direct communications that are not part of an organized drive.[5]

When you have a request, plan, or information that you sincerely believe is in the best interests of the community—or at least of your business or industry—remember the power of a good letter to the proper officials. As the late President Kennedy said, "Everyone's vote counts in America, but those who write letters to express their opinions make their vote count more often."

Messages regarding civic causes or to public officials can involve any of the previously discussed four types of common situations—inquiries, complaints, requests for action related to routine business procedures, or invitations. But because of their special nature, they are grouped separately in this section. Letters of this type are generally best handled by the direct-request plan. The busy official receiving your letter will welcome the message that states the purpose in the first paragraph. The following opening paragraphs about various issues should give you ideas on how to begin your request with the main idea:

1. *From a business executive to a Senator in Washington, D.C.:*

   The proposal to increase the truck weight and sizes on the interstate highway system deserves your serious consideration. I believe such an increase would be extremely unwise and wish to join the many others who ask that you oppose such a measure.

2. *From a store owner to the City's District Engineer:*

   This letter protests the proposed underpass at 60th Street and Highway 409. This change would cause an undue hardship on small-business owners who have invested their savings to build businesses convenient to the community in this area.

[5] For special forms of address and salutation when you write to civic, state, and national public officials, see Robert L. Shurter, *Written Communication in Business,* McGraw-Hill Book Company, New York, 1971, pp. 603–614.

3. *From a citizen to a county highway commission:*

> The newspapers have stated that your department is installing numerous directional signs, in an attempt to help people (especially strangers) find their way around (*city name*). This action is a tremendous and useful job. My suggestion concerns how to help the many people who miss the right exits and need to get back to the freeway again.

4. *From a member of the Air Force to a home-state senator:*

> This letter respectfully requests your assistance for my early release to accept employment because of family hardship.

As with all other direct requests, after you have introduced your main idea (request and reason), continue with adequate explanation. You may also find it desirable to enclose drawings, printed summaries with documentation, or any other visual material pertinent to your explanation. End with a forthright request such as, "We will appreciate whatever you can do to urge that Congress will legalize . . . during the current session."

The Capsule Checklists on pages 202 and 203 provide a quick summary of each type of direct request discussed in this chapter—inquiries, complaints, requests for action related to routine business procedures, and orders that require no persuasion.[6] As you study these direct-request plan lists, notice that you introduce your main idea at or near the beginning, include whatever details your reader needs, and end courteously with easy and dated action, if appropriate.

Caution: Remember that these Capsule Checklists—and all others in this text—are to be used *only as guidelines and reminders, NOT as "recipe lists."* In every message, use your best judgment for planning and content after you have considered purpose, reader, and pertinent circumstances.

EXERCISES

Inquiries about Persons, Products, Services

1. Comment orally on the good and poor qualities of the following inquiries about persons (sent to references). Which ones do you think will best accomplish their purpose? Why?

   a. From a national oil company:

   > We are considering Mr. Larry R. Terrill, for a position with this company, and he has given your name as a personal reference.
   >
   > May we have your frank comment both as to his ability and personal qualities? Do you know of any reason for our not

---

[6] For every direct request pertaining to a civic cause or public officials, follow the checklists on whatever type of situation best applies. If you prefer, merely follow the *Direct-Request General Plan* in the first column and use your good judgment about what details to include.

giving him full confidence? We shall appreciate any additional
comments which will help us in reaching a correct decision, and
also in adapting him to our organization in the event of our
employing him.

Since this matter is very active at present, we shall
appreciate a prompt reply and are enclosing a stamped and self-
addressed envelope for this purpose.

b. From the Big Brother volunteer service organization of a city: (This is an
obviously processed form letter.)

Dear Mr. Willman:

About: Robert Zurbach

The above-named gentleman has applied to us to serve as a Big
Brother. He has given your name as a reference.

We feel you, in your contacts with him, would be able to advise
us as to his stability and moral character. As a Big Brother,
he will be working with a young, fatherless boy, establishing a
friendship and offering moral and character guidance to the boy.

We would like your frank appraisal, which will be held in
strict confidence. Since your evaluation is necessary to complete the application, we will appreciate hearing from you soon.

c. Night letter telegram from an agency of the United States Government:

PATRICIA M. MONELL DATE OF BIRTH 5/18/52 BEING CONSIDERED FOR
EMPLOYMENT AS VETERAN'S CLAIMS EXAMINER QUASI-LEGAL POSITION HAS
GIVEN YOUR NAME AS REFERENCE. REQUEST EVALUATION BY RETURN
NIGHT LETTER COLLECT WITH APPLICANT'S DEMONSTRATED POTENTIAL TO
PERFORM SUCH DUTIES, AND PERSONAL CHARACTERISTICS EXHIBITED DUR-
ING EMPLOYMENT WITH YOU. DO YOU HAVE ANY ADVERSE INFORMATION?
WOULD YOU RECOMMEND FOR FEDERAL EMPLOYMENT?

2. Messages a and b are forms used by two law schools to get information about the
   many applicants who seek admission. Compare them for completeness, clarity of
   questions, information sought, and ease of action. Which will probably be more
   effective?
   a. The above named person has applied for admission into (school name) Law
   School. Because your name was listed as a reference, we will appreciate a letter
   of recommendation from you.

   No special form is required. Letters should be detailed, with frank appraisals
   of the applicant as to (1) qualities of intellect, (2) communication skills, (3)
   character, (4) maturity, and (5) personality. Comparisons of the applicant with
   other students known by the writer to have been admitted to the law school
   are helpful.

b. Mr.

Ms.

Mrs. _____

Miss (LAST NAME)   (FIRST NAME)   (MIDDLE NAME)

is an applicant for admission to the (school name) Law School. Each year the number of applicants to the school far exceeds the number that can be accepted. You will greatly assist this applicant and the school by providing specific and candid answers to this inquiry. The information you provide will be treated as confidential. Prompt completion of this form will be appreciated by both the applicant and the school, for the application cannot be acted on until this form is received from you. Thank you for your cooperation.

1. How well do you know the applicant? _____

2. Has the applicant performed in an honorable and trustworthy manner in

   academic work and social relationships? _____

3. Has the applicant been the subject of disciplinary action or proceedings (for

   misconduct) or of academic censure (for deficient scholarship)? _____
   If so, please explain. (Please use the reverse side if this space is insufficient.)

   _____

   _____

4. Has the applicant any physical handicap or any illness, physical or mental,

   that in your opinion bears on his or her ability to do law school work?_____

   If so, please explain. _____

   _____

5. In classes with you, how have you graded the applicant's academic perfor-

   mance (percentile, if possible)? _____

6. What is the applicant's approximate rank for all work taken in your college?

   _____

   _____

7. To what degree did the applicant's scholastic achievement measure up to

   capacity? _____
   □ Fully realized capacity.   □ Had capacity to do considerably
   □ Performed reasonably in view   better.
     of capacity.   □ No basis for judgment.

   Remarks: _____

   _____

   _____

8. Please furnish any other information that will be of assistance to a consideration of the applicant's transcript and college record as a whole. Helpful remarks can relate to, but need not be limited to, unusual time-consuming

extracurricular activities, leadership performance, motivation, capacity for interpersonal relations, and significant participation in outside employment. We will also appreciate your estimate of the applicant's grades, courses taken, and major field as a reliable measure of academic capacity. (Please

use the reverse side if this space is insufficient.) _____

_____

_____

9. Do you recommend the applicant for admission to the (name) Law School?
   ☐ I recommend with enthusiasm.   ☐ I recommend with reservation.
   ☐ I recommend.   ☐ I do not recommend.

Signature _____

Name (Please type or print) _____

Title _____

Date _____ Address _____

3. Prepare to discuss orally the strengths and weaknesses of the following letters designed to get information. Comment particularly on organization, clarity, completeness of explanations, and motivation for action.

a. To subscribers of a magazine (salutation is "Dear *Journal* Reader"):

You're right. Another questionnaire.

But we feel it's an important one, and the short time required to complete it should be well spent, for it will help shape the course YOUR magazine, the Journal, will take in the important years ahead.

We say YOUR magazine because it's written and edited with readers like you in mind. That's why the editors would like to take stock of what you like and dislike about the Journal. What parts are good? What needs improvement? What might be cut down or eliminated? What might be added?

Your answers will help the Journal keep in step with the rapidly changing field of (*name of field*).

You will note that we have not provided a space for your signature. This is by design. We believe that anonymity will produce more straight-from-the-shoulder opinion and constructive criticism. Thank you for your help.

b. From a firm of research counselors in New York to an addressee in a state 2,500 miles away. Addressee is an employee of a city light company (letter is an obvious form with a "Dear Sir" salutation):

May we ask a favor that takes only a minute of your time?

We are conducting a special study to help determine how familiar people in industry are with one of our clients.

We would appreciate it very much if you would answer the questions on the attached sheet and return the questionnaire to us
in the enclosed stamped envelope. Your reply will be confidential, of course, and the results of the study will be shown in
statistical form only.

c. To a real estate agent (salutation is "Dear Mrs. Aimes"):

I have clients very much interested in the Sand & Surf in (*town
name*).

They are prepared to make an offer of $110,000.00. This seems to
be in line for a restaurant that grosses between $115,000.00 and
$118,000.00 a year. My clients have a background in this type of
business, restaurant and lounge. They have been wanting to locate this side of the mountains and preferably in (*town name*)
area.

4. Assume the role of purchasing manager for an industrial firm with over 2,000
employees. You have a desire to install a word processing center in your company
to cut down on the cost of processing your daily paper load. You will need equipment to take care of (1) *original input* (longhand, shorthand, machine, handwritten, or central dictation); (2) *reproduction* [spirit, fluid (ink); offset; carbon
copy; composer systems such as magnetic tape typewriters, magnetic card typewriters, paper tape typewriters; or copying machines] ; (3) *delivery system* (personal, messenger, PBX, dial system, private wire, telephone, or machine dictation
options); (4) *storage file* [magnetic tape, magnetic cards, paper tapes, computer
storage (punched cards, discs), microfiche, microfilm, or office storage file cabinet
(alpha numeric, geographic, library indexing system or mechanized system)] .

Select several equipment suppliers that handle word processing equipment. Request the following information, to be presented to your board of directors one
month from the date of your letter: different models available; special features
of each model; estimated price of equipment; service policy cost; in-service training availability; portability; facility needed to house equipment; and noise level
when in operation.

You are to prepare the information you have requested from the various suppliers, make a decision in two months on what equipment you will purchase for
your firm, and present this to your board of directors. Write a letter that can be
sent to several companies, requesting the information you will need.

5. You are personnel director in charge of training for Meyer Stores, Inc., a chain
of retail hardware stores with headquarters in San Francisco and with branches
in Washington, Nevada, Arizona, and Oregon. Yesterday you interviewed James
Uperno (age 24), who seeks to join your management training program. His application form indicates he graduated from the University of Ohio three years ago
and that he served in the Coast Guard for the next two years. He says he worked
"for a while" at the Midwest Appliance Company in Detroit. He thought he
wanted to work up to top management with that firm but finally decided he'd
rather live on the Pacific Coast, because he enjoys the ocean and water sports. He
seemed to be very enthusiastic about working up into a branch store management
position with your firm.

His application letter—and his comments during the interview—indicated that he also worked part time as a sales representative in a men's clothing store two months, while attending the university; one-half year in a service station, part time; and "also in several other places."

His scholastic record—with a major in marketing—is excellent (he says), although you don't have the transcript of his work. You are more concerned right now about his disposition to stick with a two-year training program. Your company's usual procedure is to place young trainees in the smaller towns, most of which are inland. (Some are over a hundred miles from the ocean.) You wonder if Uperno would stick with the company during the years (perhaps up to six or seven) that he would be situated inland. Also, as you talked with him you noticed that he interrupted you several times to tell you about his views, and he knocked two of his former employers, including Midwest Appliance Company. One of the references to whom you will write today is Mr. Karl Dunn, personnel director at Midwest Appliance Company. Try to find out whether his experience with Uperno indicates that he has the qualifications to do effective work—first as a management trainee and later as a branch store manager. He'd also be in the customer service and adjustment departments for a while. Is he sufficiently tactful and courteous? Be careful that your questions are within the laws regarding fair preemployment inquiries.

6. You are an assistant marketing manager for a manufacturer of pharmaceuticals. Your sales staff markets prescription drugs to drug stores, hospitals, and physicians and dentists in private practice. Every year from five to seven new sales representatives must be trained in your two-month sales instructional program. Experienced sales representatives are brought back to the main office for periodic one- or two-day professional development workshops.

One training procedure which has been effective is the videotaping and playback of sales role-playing situations and sales presentation simulations. Training lectures are other items which are taped for viewing by sales trainees. Your organization has one videotape recorder, a tripod-mounted black-and-white camera, and a 19-inch monitor—all of which are scheduled for replacement. The marketing manager has authorized you to investigate new videotape equipment and recommend replacements.

In the latest issue of *Pharmaceutical World* you noticed an advertisement for equipment manufactured by Video-Eye Corporation, 1980 South Michigan Avenue, Chicago, IL 60616. Write them requesting product, service, and price information. You are considering switching to color equipment for more realism but are wary of cost and dependability. You are interested in converting from reel-to-reel to cassette equipment; however, you are concerned about higher cost, capability of tape cassettes, and reliability of the mechanically more complex cassette equipment. Finally, service is extremely important because you have no backup equipment and require minimum downtime.

Indicate to the Video-Eye Corporation that you will be trading in your present equipment. An equipment choice decision must be made within three weeks, so you must request specific follow-up to this request. Create other relevant supporting details, if necessary.

7. As executive administrator of staff personnel at City Hospital, you are currently searching for the right person to be chief pharmacist. One of the applicants you interviewed yesterday is Helen Tinsel (age 34), who worked at the Excello Pharmacy in Omaha from January 1975 until July 1979. She has given the name of Vivian Hollan, chief pharmacist at Excello, as a reference.

Your hospital, one of the leaders in the country, established a new 300-bed teaching and research wing two months ago and now plans to open a new pharmacy five months from today. Both personal qualifications and technical skill are important for the responsible job of chief pharmacist. You need to know whether Ms. Tinsel has the ability or potential to organize from scratch a pharmacy in your modern, well-equipped hospital. You need a frank evaluation of her as a worker, because this job will demand a tremendous amount of initiative, drive, and sustained working capacity. Also, because she will have people working under her direction, she must be able to organize them into a tightly knit and happy working group. You'd like to know if she is liked and respected by subordinates, associates, and supervisors. Also, it would be helpful to know what duties she performed at Excello Pharmacy. Write a tactful, well-organized inquiry to Ms. Hollan for the information you need. Keep your questions within the laws regarding fair preemployment inquiries.

Claims (Complaints) and Requests for Adjustment

1. Evaluate the following opening paragraphs of claim letters, and tell how to improve the poor ones. Which one(s) do you consider effective? Why?

   a. In the past year I have ordered nearly $200 in goods from your store, by mail. Two weeks ago I came there in person and bought a gray overcoat. As I was heavily loaded with packages, I asked the clerk to send the garment to me by store delivery. When the overcoat arrived, I was busy and so I didn't open the package until two days ago.

   b. Never in my life have I been treated so rudely as I was the other day in your store, by two jerks you call employees. I tell you, the way I was insulted gave me a good indication of what kind of people you're hiring these days. I'm so mad I will never go back to your store again.

   c. In line with your policy on consumer satisfaction published in your recent catalog, I am requesting a cash refund of $39.38 for a toaster I purchased two weeks ago for cash. The reason I have directed this request to your office is that your department manager said such a refund would not be possible. (*Written to the adjustment department manager.*)

2. You are a student at (use the name of your own college or university) and are often tempted to buy some of the merchandise which is advertised on the school bulletin boards. You are also a camera fan and have been looking for ways to cut down on the cost of your hobby.

One of these opportunities came your way just four weeks ago—at least, you thought it did. A firm in East Vancouver, Idaho, has advertised 35mm film for an outstandingly low price: ASA 64 daylight film, 36 exposures, similar to the best known American and Japanese brands, for only $3.50 per roll. As a complete package, the cost is spectacular, because it also includes processing the film into 35mm slides *if* additional film is ordered at the time the used film is sent in for processing.

The offer sounds too good to be true, but you sent your $3.50 to the Leslie Film Company in East Vancouver to see if the film and the processing were any good. You have waited and waited, but no film has yet arrived and you are anxious and just a little angry. Write to the Leslie Film Company to find out about the delay (your check was cashed) and ask for immediate action. Also remind the Leslie Company that permission to post such coupon notices must come from the Office of the Dean of Students and that if a reply does not come immediately you will report the action to the Dean and suggest that further posting be disallowed.

Be careful that you do not issue any threats or make any accusations. It could be an error in the Leslie shipping department or a loss in the U.S. mails, and if so the company will surely make amends. *Do* ask for immediate action.

3. Comment on the following claim letters. Consider tone, organization, clarity, accuracy, and probable effectiveness in getting the desired result. What changes, if any, do you recommend? Please be specific. Try to determine first what each writer really wants.

a. From a business firm in Detroit to Air Freight Corp. in Pittsburgh, Pa.:

> Re your Airbill #54663, we originally shipped this same amount of mdse. to Cincinnati UPS (United Parcel Service), got overnight delivery, and it cost only $10. Now your shipment from Cincinnati to us took over 15 days to get to us and you want $42.38. Now if you want to rebill and charge ICC surface rates, we will pay you, but if you think 15-day delivery is Air Express. . . better check the rubber bands on your airplanes or start feeding those pigeons better.

b. From a charge customer to a department store with five branches: [This handwritten letter had merely the date at the top and the writer's signature ("Mrs. Joan M. Smith") at the end. Her envelope had no return address. (The store has 250 Smiths and no Joan M. Smith.)]

> I cannot understand your statement each month showing that our account has a past due payment. This is very irritating since our payments have been:
>
>   1/10/8_ - $25.00
>   2/3/8_ - $30.00
>   3/4/8_ - $25.00
>   4/3, 5/6/8_ - each $50.00
>
> It is my understanding that our payments each month are to be only $20.00 per month. As you can see ours have been much more than that--so where do you get this "overdue" bit?
>
> I am at this time sending another $50.00 check, which I'm sure you will agree does not make my account past due. Please get my records straight as I don't believe this makes my credit rating look too good.

c. From a landlord to apartment tenants:

```
It seems some of your typing late at night disturbs some tenants.
Perhaps when all is quiet it is easier to hear.

I was wondering if you type on the nook table--as that is bad be-
cause the table is fastened to the building.  A felt pad will
help if you do not already have one.  The university bookstore
has them just for that purpose.

I know your typing is important to your schoolwork, however I
would like to keep everyone happy.
```

d. From a college student in a small town to a discount house in another state:

```
To whom it may concern:

     I don't know who packs your boxes but they sure blew this
order.  (A)  I ordered ice bucket 86103NF gld w/blk trim, & re-
ceived ice bucket 86-118NF Tahitian Holiday pattern w/ivory trim.
(B)  I ordered a trip nip bottle tote 416VT & get a Deluxe Car-
ry-all Diaper bag 516HR.

     Now listen I'll keep the ice bucket OK.  But the diaper bag
has got to go.  I'm a senior in college & single.  I don't have
a wife or baby.

     Please send me my trip nip bottle tote & advise me on what
to do with the diaper bag.  Come on give me a break; this is a
small campus what are you trying to do--start rumors?
```

4. Your local chapter of Zeta Theta Omega national sorority has planned to do a dramatic skit presentation at their regional conference in order to invite the convention to their city next year. This requires that all members wear the uniform dress. Therefore, as chairperson of the sorority social committee, you were given the assignment of ordering twenty-five floral pink dresses from the Arts Company in California. You placed your order for these dresses and requested the following sizes: five dresses in size 9; two in size 10; four, size 12; four, size 14; five, size 16. This is a total of twenty dresses.

The other five dresses you ordered were in special sizes, as follows: two in size 18½; one, size 7; and two, size 9 for tall girls.

When you received the shipment, you discovered that the order had been partially filled. Twenty of the twenty-five dresses ordered were shipped to you, and the other five dresses were promised within one week. Today, one month after arrival of the first shipment, you received the other five dresses; but they are all damaged so much that the girls cannot wear them. An explanation for the delay was enclosed with the order, stating that because of the irregular sizes, the dresses had to be specially made. There are now only two days left before your convention, and you do not have time to return the dresses to the company for replacements.

The members, disappointed, have voted to return all twenty-five dresses. You have packed and shipped them back to the Arts Company today. Now it is your responsibility to write the claim letter requesting refund for the complete order—the twenty dresses in excellent condition and the five that are damaged. After discussing the circumstances and reasons in class, decide whether you should also ask for reimbursement on the shipping charges.

5. Last Saturday you took a 7:30 a.m. Transcontinental bus to Mount Vernon, a city 200 miles from where you live. The bus was scheduled to make five stops along the way and to arrive in Mount Vernon at 11:30 a.m. This would be just in time for you to attend an important regional luncheon at the Marlborough Hotel, starting at 12 noon. (You were to be a panel speaker at this function and had accepted the appointment two months ago. You planned to return the same afternoon on the 5 p.m. bus.)

    At about 10 a.m. the driver of your 7:30 a.m. bus, after making four scheduled stops to pick up passengers, turned off the freeway for an *unscheduled* stop at a roadside snack bar—a 6-foot open-air counter with no chairs and no roof. He told passengers they would be there "a few minutes to stretch and have a snack if they wished." As your hands were sticky after eating a candy bar, you stopped in the rest room to wash them. About two minutes later when you came outside, the bus was gone! The driver had apparently left without a warning toot or a count of noses! Thus you were stranded off the freeway, 15 miles from any scheduled bus stop; and no other bus was to pass on the freeway ½ mile from the snack bar for three hours. You would surely miss the entire function. What could you do?! (You're not a hitchhiker.) The snack bar operators stated this was the second time in a week that the same bus driver had left a passenger stranded at the same place. Rather than have you miss your luncheon, one of the operators generously offered to drive you in her car until she caught up with the bus. You both hoped it would be just a few miles, because she had to get back to her job. However, after 25 miles you reached the next town—the fifth scheduled stop—just as the bus driver was starting the motor, ready to leave for the last lap of his trip. You hurriedly pressed $9 cash into the hand of your Good Samaritan and hopped on the bus. Not one word of apology came from the bus driver! At the luncheon all your friends agreed with you that the driver should be reported.

    Write an effective letter to the customer service manager at Mount Vernon requesting whatever adjustment (and explanation) you think is fair. Send a copy to the bus company's head office in Austin, Texas. Make your message as concise as possible; assume whatever is necessary for completeness.

6. Last Tuesday you took an interesting tour with a group of 15 other businesspeople through the Ace Lumber Mills. All of you had attended a conference and the tour was scheduled as part of the conference. After walking from one building to another, you happened to be the target for a glob of tar that dripped from a roof of one of the mills as you entered. It fell on your left shoulder, on your new suit. One of the employees suggested that after the suit was cleaned you should send the bill to that lumber mill. Now you have had the suit cleaned and you want reimbursement. Write a courteous letter to get the desired refund ($9.50).

7. The person who delivers your daily newspaper folds the paper and hurls it at your home as she speeds past on her bicycle. Last summer you had to replace the wire

screen on the door because of the repeated impacts. You spoke to the girl about the damage, and she promised to be more careful. Now, on January 18, you find that she has broken a pane of glass in one of your living-room windows.

Write to the North End News Agency and endeavor to have the situation righted. You cannot speak to the girl directly because you are away from home at the time she delivers the paper. Telephoning would mean a long-distance charge, because your work requires you to travel out of town every day.

8. As the chairperson of your company's social committee, you called several committee meetings to decide on the entertainment for your company's annual Valentine Day dance. After considering several suggestions, the committee voted to contract with a new local company for the evening's music. The company, called Dance Machine, Inc., specializes in providing recorded music and a special light show for parties and dances.

Specifically, the company brings in a sound system with records and tapes for any type of music desired. Two disc jockeys are provided so that you may have continuous music with commentary; the D.J.'s also provide some special events, such as dance contests. In addition, the company also has a computerized light show which is synchronized to the music for added effect.

You asked Dance Machine for the names of two clients who have used them for parties. When you checked with the references, the reports were good. Apparently, the company had delivered everything as promised and the clients were completely satisfied. You signed a contract with Dance Machine for their standard service (recorded music, professional quality sound system, two disc jockeys, and the light show). You stated your preferences as to the music to be provided and agreed to make the meeting room (the ballroom of a large local hotel) available five hours prior to the scheduled starting time for the dance. Your contract with the hotel guaranteed that your event would be concluded by a specific time and, because of union agreements, hotel cleanup personnel would be entitled to overtime pay if you exceeded your time limit. The company, in turn, agreed to have the equipment set up and checked out at least one hour prior to the starting time.

On the day of the dance the company's technicians arrived only two hours before the scheduled starting time for the dance. Consequently, the equipment was still being set up when the first party-goers arrived. Also, while checking the sound levels, the technicians generated high-pitched squeals (feedback) through the speakers, causing considerable irritation to the guests. A tall technician named Mark seemed to be in charge. When you asked him how long it would require to complete the preparations, he gave you a menacing look and growled "Leave us alone, Mac. We'll be done when I'm satisfied with the sound." The disc jockeys arrived on time, but the dance got started 30 minutes late.

Among the party-goers who arrived on time was the president of your company. He remarked that he hoped things would soon begin to run more smoothly. He also commented that because the dance was delayed, he thought you should get some adjustment in the fee charged by Dance Machine. After the equipment problem was solved, the dance started and the evening was enjoyed by everyone. The disc jockeys were professionals who were able to generate excitement and make the attendees forget the earlier problems.

Because of the delay, the dance was not over by the deadline, and you were subsequently billed by the hotel for $56 in overtime charges for the cleanup personnel. You believe that the overtime charges were the direct result of Dance Machine's failure to have the equipment set up and operating properly by the agreed-upon time and that you are justified in asking Dance Machine's manager for an adjustment in the fee to compensate for the overtime charges. Also, because you had to listen to several complaints about the late start and the irritating noises made by the technicians, and because the sharp comments made by the head technician were overheard by several of your company colleagues, you feel some apology from Dance Machine is in order. After all, you kept your part of the bargain and booked the hotel ballroom early enough to provide sufficient time for Dance Machine's technicians to do their work.

Make sure the tone of your letter is correct. Remember that the company's reputation indicates that this is not their usual mode of operation. Also, you should remember to praise the disc jockeys for their professionalism and their ability to salvage what could easily have become a disaster. Address your claim to Mr. Edward C. Harris, Manager, Dance Machine, Inc., 1983 E. 24th St., Cleveland, OH 44115.

9. You are accounting department manager of Flowers by Hardley, a reputable florist. Today (April 2) you received a $104.50 bill from Airway Freight Corporation, 947 Columbus Building, Indianapolis. The bill shows two deliveries—Airbill #18692 and #25479—unpaid since January 15 and February 5, respectively. You have canceled checks and invoices showing that both these shipments were paid when delivery was made. In fact, your firm always pays freight when it arrives. You resent the computerized statement across the bottom of today's bill: "THIS IS OUR FINAL REQUEST BEFORE REFERRING THIS TO A COLLECTION AGENCY. REMIT NOW." This is the first billing you have received. Your firm's general manager has decided that as of today he is switching to another airfreight company that takes better care in bookkeeping. He says that any company this careless in keeping records probably is no less careless in handling freight. Write to the general manager of Airway Freight Corporation after you have determined your purpose and what evidence you need to enclose with your message. Use good judgment in the tone and content of your letter.

Miscellaneous Requests, Orders, Invitations

1. The following messages deal with routine business situations. Analyze each situation and then decide whether the message is adequate. Suggest improvements.
   a. A printed form letter from the president of a savings association to customers; it has no salutation, but the customers' names and addresses are inserted at the top:

   _____ Please sign the enclosed withdrawal slip and return to us.

   _____ Would you please send us your signature card. _____

   _____ Would you please send us your social security (reporting) number.

_____ We need your *original* hazard (fire) insurance policy (with extended coverage) in at least the amount of $ _____ .

_____ An error was made on your last transaction, which has already been corrected on our records (we'll correct your passbook the next time we have it).

_____ We are returning your check because _____ .

_____ Your construction interest payment starts _____ , 19 _____ in the amount of $ _____ ; thereafter, interest payments will be $ _____ until regular payments ($ _____) start _____ , 19   . YOU MAY MAKE FULL PAYMENTS AT ANY TIME AND RECEIVE CREDITS TOWARD FUTURE PAYMENTS.

Thank you.

b. *Memo* from the company's social director to all supervisors.

SUBJECT: Christmas gifts for our departmental secretaries

With Christmas just around the corner, it's time for me to raise my ugly head above ground once again to remind you it's time to consider our departmental secretaries.

If you wish to contribute toward a gift for each gal, please leave your donation in my box by December 10. A dollar from each of you will be adequate.

2. You are social chairman for the (choose a name) Club. Write to all members inviting them to your club's Preholiday Luncheon, November 16, at the Highpoint Country Club. Cost is $8.50 including tax and tip. Make clear all necessary details as to time, location, directions for reaching the country club, parking facilities, and deadline for reservations. Also ask who needs a ride and who can furnish rides. Ask that they call Jane or Dick Jones at 850-3000. For luncheon reservations provide an easy-to-fill-out form at the bottom of your announcement, instruct as to whom their check should be made payable, and remind them to enclose a stamped, addressed envelope with their check so you can return tickets to them. The speaker will be Rybald Plummer, on "Knocking around the Orient."

3. *(Memo)* Your employer encourages young executives to enroll for additional university training whenever possible, and the firm pays tuition for desirable programs. You (assistant personnel manager) would like to attend the Graduate School of Business Administration Management Program at the State University (in the same city). Because most classes meet Monday evenings and a few on Saturdays, they will not interfere with your job. You believe the course will definitely make a graduate more knowledgeable in the management field, thereby

increasing his or her worth to the company. Some of the topics you foresee as particularly valuable to your present job are: Management Communication, Performance Appraisals, and Basic Human Motivation. The course, over one academic year, costs $1,500; $300 required to be submitted with your application and the remaining $1,200 by October 8. Today is August 13. Enclose your application with your memo to Mr. D. J. Heinrich, Executive Vice President, for his approval.

4. *(Memo)* You are area coordinator for your company's blood bank. Last year, through the cooperation of various departments, your blood bank had ample credits to provide the 289 withdrawal units requested by employees. Now the annual drive is approaching again. On March 3 and 4 your company's employees are to participate in this worthwhile cause, from 10 a.m. to 4 p.m. (You decide on the place and on other necessary details.) You want donors to sign up for the time most convenient for them. Provide sign-up sheets in convenient places, and write a memo to all 200 employees, attaching a folder about the blood bank and on donor qualifications.

5. *(Memo)* To conserve fuel, because of the current fuel shortage, you—as operations manager of a large company—want to request all employees to observe certain simple fuel-saving steps. Without fuel your plant cannot operate; so it is to everyone's interest that as much gas and diesel fuel be saved as possible.

   You ask that all vehicles must be shut off when idle. Examples include: during lunch periods and break times; when chip trucks are under bunker for any time (diesel manufacturers recommend engines should not idle for more than five-minute periods); when trucks are being loaded with lumber, logs, or other materials; when trucks are standing idle at any other times not in use. Also, you want all employees having company cars to obtain fuel at outside sources. And you request that operators run machines in such a manner as to conserve fuel without loss of efficiency. Excessive speed where not necessary consumes more fuel. You believe that cooperation of all employees could result in a 5 to 10 percent savings. Ask the superintendent and shop stewards to make sure proper steps are being carried out. Mention in your memo that you will make personal inspections periodically. Plan an attractive, easy-to-read format for your requests.

6. *(Memo)* You are purchasing manager of the ABC Products Company. In a recent survey you made of the purchase requisitions prepared by the manufacturing department, you found that in several instances the wrong merchandise was ordered. In searching for causes, you found that in every case the discrepancies were the result of typing errors or illegibility in the requisitions. You are convinced these could have been avoided by more careful preparation of the requisitions. In the past many were made in pencil and the handwriting was small and indistinct. Some items that required several lines of description were run together with other items; double spaces should have been placed between them. Some requisitions included the names of several suppliers, whereas only one name should be on each requisition. Write a concise, courteous, well-planned memo to the superintendent of manufacturing. Include tactful, clear, positive suggestions that will help eliminate such errors and improve final results.

7. *(Invitation)* You are the local sales manager for an office equipment company which has a new line of word processing machines. Since this is your company's first entry into the word processing field, you have decided to display your new equipment at a business show sponsored in your city by the Administrative Management Society. An admissions fee is charged to defray the expense of the show, but you have purchased a block of tickets to distribute to your regular customers and to other good prospects for your products. The three-day event starts one month from today. At the show, you will display your company's new Wordpro I electronic disc typewriter; the Wordpro II Computerized CRT machine; and your new line of dictating equipment, the Wordbank machines.

Write a letter, which will be personalized and typed on your new Wordpro I machine, to invite your customers to see your machines at the business show in your city's convention center. The letter will go to purchasing agents, office managers, administrative managers, and word processing supervisors. Enclose a ticket to the show and give them the exact dates and exhibit times. You will be happy to furnish more tickets if there are others from a company who wish to attend. All they need to do is call your office (give your number). You will send the extra tickets immediately.

8. The following is the first draft of a form letter request from a mortgage loan company to borrowers. The improved revision which was mailed is illustrated in request 2, page 178. Which do you think should be more effective and why? Compare the two letters' organization, openings and closings, paragraphs, action requests, clarity, completeness, and consideration. Be specific.

Dear Homeowner:

We wish to inform you that the Homeowner's Mortgage Protector Plan Certificate which you recently received is to be read carefully and then filed with your other valuable papers. The benefits provided by the plan are very valuable.

The protection will become effective on the date indicated on the certificate after the premium has been paid. The premium which is shown on the enclosed certificate should be added to your future monthly payments.

If your mortgage payment has already been made for the month the protection is to become effective, the premium should be sent now so that you will be fully protected for the month. Next month, combine the payments.

We are pleased you have secured this protection for yourself and family. The acceptance of this plan by so many of our customers indicates to me that it is certainly a valuable and worthwhile project.

9. *(Memo)* You are the owner of a small retail business which specializes in household appliances and the repair of those appliances (mixers, vacuum cleaners,

waffle irons, toasters, and similar items). When you started your business about five years ago, you operated the store yourself and received help from your wife in keeping records and waiting on customers during busy times.

Business has been good, and you have expanded your stock of sales items. You now have one full-time salesclerk and one part-time repairperson to help. Even the bookkeeping and accounting records are now done by an outside firm on a part-time basis. (The firm that does your accounting comes in once a month for routine affairs, does your year-end closing, prepares tax returns, and is responsible for the annual inventory.)

In recent months you have been wondering about the advertisements you have read in the newspaper and heard on radio and television about "small computers" and their value to a small business. All that you have heard sounds good, but you really know little about computers and will need some advice on how you could use them.

Write a memorandum to your accountants (the Northeast Accounting and Management Service) and ask them to investigate this matter for you. You will want to know the cost of such a small computer, what specific bookkeeping and accounting functions it can perform for you, what special training your employees will need in order to be able to use it, how it can help Northeast, and other business matters. You will also want to be certain that the accountants understand that you are not trying to replace them—that you only want to know if the small computer will provide you with more information than is currently possible and, if so, whether the additional information is worth the cost of the equipment, maintenance, and training. Be specific in your request for information.

10. As administrative assistant to the president of Benson Savings Association, write a letter inviting customers and their families to be your special guests at a grand opening of your new quarters on Thursday, Friday, and Saturday, the last three days of this month. There will be handsome gifts for both ladies and gentlemen, special door prizes with drawings every two hours, and refreshments. Children will receive balloons. Also, each current passbook holder will receive a special present. Your new building is graciously furnished, with a number of authentic period antiques. A SPECIAL GUEST name tag which you will enclose with your invitation letter entitles customers to their gifts.

11. *(Memo)* You are assistant director of your company's regional office. You need to write a memo to all 15 plant managers asking them for a report by July 30 of this year. In this report—for the past fiscal year, July 1 through June 30—you want them to be sure to cover the following points: the major accomplishments of their plant during the past year, major problems facing them for next year, objectives for their plant for next year, plans for accomplishing them, and anticipated difficulties. Also, you want a brief summary—one paragraph on each subject—covering their plant's operations last year in the areas of: organization planning, quality performance, production and scheduling performance, com-

munity relations, personnel management, costs of operation, health and safety, product development, and any other matters they think significant. If they will please organize their report in this manner, they will be especially useful to you in preparing your Annual Division Report and in making plans for next year. You feel the company has had a good year and you look forward to an even better one next year.

Arrange your request in an easy-to-read format (perhaps consider some tabulating?) and achieve a pleasant tone.

12. One of your duties as circulation manager for *Hike and Bike,* a special interest monthly magazine aimed at hiking and biking enthusiasts, is to control the spiraling costs of delivering this magazine to your 50,000 subscribers all over the country. Some magazine publishers have been experimenting with alternative home-delivery methods which are less costly and faster than the third-class mail service that *Hike and Bike* has always used.

Compose a memo of authorization to your administrative assistant requesting an informational report. Ask your assistant to gather and organize data on the following: types of alternative delivery modes, such as private mail carriers; publishing companies which have experimented with or adopted alternative delivery methods; and an analysis of their experience, examining such factors as reliability and promptness of delivery; coverage of urban, suburban, and rural subscribers; cost, etc.

You will need to make conclusions and recommendations based on the report's contents at a staff meeting in 30 days. Suggest that the report be based on information gathered from recent articles in trade and business publications (provide several leads) and from telephone and in-person conversations with circulation staff members of similar periodicals (suggest the names of a few of your professional contacts).

13. Assume you are the new assistant manager of the Central Life Insurance Company's office in your city. Your company will be holding interviews on a nearby college campus January 30 for winter and spring quarter graduates. You want to send a concise, personalized form letter to graduating seniors inviting them to sign up for an interview (whenever you specify) or to call you for further information. You will also grant off-campus interviews. You believe your company has jobs that graduates might be interested in. They can be in the fields of accounting, marketing, computer programming, personnel, and administration. Graduates can build a business career with no capital investment, they can get comprehensive training to develop their talents, and a monthly life income after 20 years of qualified service. Is there anything else you should include?

14. As customer relations director of Custodial Services, Inc., you now have the pleasure of announcing your firm's three-day housekeeping seminar. Your letter is to be a form, individually addressed to local and regional directors of large firms that

employ custodial supervisors (caretakers, janitors, maintenance people). Make clear that from each firm one or more custodial supervisors may attend. Enclose with your announcement a formal seminar folder, giving cost and detailed program. Make clear in your letter the place, dates, and highlights of the training sessions, and create a pleasant, goodwill-building tone.

I	II Inquiries about Persons		III
Direct-Request General Plan	To Reference by Applicant	To Reference by Person Interested in Applicant	Inquiries about Products or Services

1. MAIN IDEA
  a. Request, main statement, or question
  b. Reason(s), if desirable
	1. Main idea
	  a. Reason for writing to this person
	  b. Introduction of request
	  c. Memory refresher
		1. Main idea
		  a. Applicant's full name
		  b. Why you are considering this applicant
		  c. Why you are writing to this reader
			1. Main idea
			  a. Major request and/or
			  b. Reason(s) for interest in product or service

2. EXPLANATION
  a. All necessary and desirable details
  b. Numbered questions, if helpful
  c. Easy-reading devices
	2. Explanation
	  a. Summary of pertinent facts about yourself: courses, major, GPA, outside work, tests, scores, honors, scholarships, leadership
	  b. Guidelines for the recommendation: kinds of information the inquirer needs
	  c. Enclosure of form(s) and resumé, if helpful
		2. Explanation
		  a. Requirements for job, loan, credit, scholarship, membership (legal?)
		  b. A few pertinent facts applicant told you about him- or herself
		  c. Specific questions for:
		    (1) More than "yes, no" answers
		    (2) Explanations if necessary
		    (3) Itemization— in body, underneath, or on separate questionnaire
			2. Explanation
			  a. Specific questions
			    (1) More than "yes, no" answers
			    (2) Explanation, whenever necessary
			    (3) Itemization if more than one and desirable for clarity and/or ease of response
			  b. Promise of anonymity, if desirable

3. COURTEOUS CLOSE, WITH MOTIVATION TO ACTION
  a. CSAD[1]
  b. EA[2]
  c. DA[3]
  d. Appreciation and goodwill
	3. Courteous close
	  a. CSAD,[1] to whom recommendation should be sent
	  b. EA[2]
	  c. DA[3]
	  d. Appreciation
		3. Courteous close
		  a. Appreciation
		  b. Promise of confidential treatment
		  c. EA[2]
		  d. DA[3]
		  e. Offer to reciprocate, if appropriate
			3. Courteous close
			  a. Suggested or specific action desired
			  b. DA[3]
			  c. EA, when appropriate[2]
			  d. Appreciation and courtesy

[1] CSAD = clear statement of action desired
[2] EA = easy action
[3] DA = dated action, if desirable

DIRECT REQUESTS

IV Complaints, Claims, Requests for Adjustment	V Requests for Action Related to Routine Business Procedures	VI Invitations	VII Orders and Reservations

1. Main idea
  a. Purpose(s)
    (need for
    adjustment or
    correction of
    error or
    procedure)
	1. Main idea
	  a. Reason and
	  b. Request (inter-
	    changeable)
		1. Main idea
		  a. Invitation
		    request with
		    all pertinent
		    5 W's: who,
		    what, when
		    (day, date),
		    where, why
			1. Main idea
			  a. Statement of
			    order or
			    reservation

2. Explanation
  a. Something good
    about reader,
    product, or ser-
    vice, if true
  b. All facts perti-
    nent to claim
  c. Omission of
    anger, threats,
    sarcasm,
    exaggeration,
    persuasion
  d. Desirable quali-
    ties: prompt-
    ness; faith in
    reader's fairness;
    good humor,
    when appropriate
	2. Explanation
	  a. Desired details
	    and, if helpful,
	    instructions
	  b. Itemization,
	    preferably when
	    more than two
	    items are
	    requested
	  c. Reader benefit,
	    if any
		2. Explanation
		  a. All necessary
		    details–if to a
		    function:
		    program, time,
		    apparel, costs,
		    refreshments,
		    location, direc-
		    tions, parking;
		    if to submit
		    material:
		    length, method,
		    format, etc.
		  b. Setup and
		    enclosures as
		    needed for
		    easy reading
			2. Explanation
			  a. Details about:
			    (1) Needed items
			      or facilities–
			      quantity, size,
			      color, style,
			      catalog num-
			      ber, price
			      (or rate)*
			    (2) Payment–
			      method,
			      time, deposit
			      (if any)
			    (3) Shipment–
			      date and place
			    (4) Special in-
			      structions,
			      if any
			    *If reservation:
			    function, number
			    in expected attend-
			    ance, requirements

3. Courteous close
  a. CSAD:[1]
    Free replacement,
    free repairs,
    refund, credit,
    price reduction,
    inspection, expla-
    nation, apology or
    change, new ship-
    ment, or adjust-
    ment left up to
    reader
  b. EA[2]
  c. DA[3]
  d. Appreciation
    and courtesy
	3. Courteous close
	  a. CSAD[1]
	  b. EA[2]
	  c. DA[3]
	  d. Courtesy
		3. Courteous close
		  a. CSAD[1]
		  b. EA[2]
		  c. DA[3]
		  d. Courtesy
			3. Courteous close
			  a. CSAD[1]
			  b. EA[2]
			  c. DA[3]
			  d. Courtesy

[1] CSAD = clear statement of action desired
[2] EA = easy action
[3] DA = dated action, if desirable

chapter

8

Good-News and Neutral Messages

A message that conveys good news is usually easy to write, because you are giving or telling your reader something that is pleasant. A neutral-reaction letter is also relatively easy to write, because the message is about something that the reader considers neither good nor bad news—just information that may be useful.

You can adapt the good-news plan to a variety of situations. Use it whenever you answer a request or when you initiate an unsolicited message yourself, if the news will be favorable or neutral—at least not unfavorable—to your reader. Among the many kinds of letters and memoranda you can organize with the good-news plan are the following:

Favorable replies

Answering inquiries for information related to sales

Answering inquiries for information unrelated to sales

Granting adjustments on claims and complaints

Approving credit

Acknowledging orders

Granting favors

Accepting invitations

Granting any other requests—pertaining to business, government, and organizational procedures or individual needs

Accepting job offers or franchises, and other negotiations

Favorable unsolicited messages

Announcements about:
    Sales and events
    Procedures, policies, and responsibilities
    Honors and activities of people

Transmittals

Congratulations, appreciation, and other expressions of goodwill

This chapter discusses the good-news organizational plan, the first six types of favorable replies listed above, and all the listed favorable unsolicited messages except the last entry (Congratulations, etc.). Additional illustrations of messages adaptable to the good-news pattern are included in Chapters 12 and 14. Reports can also be organized by this (direct, deductive) good-news plan, as discussed in Chapter 15.

ORGANIZATIONAL PLAN

The direct approach—putting the best news or the main idea (if it is favorable or at least not unfavorable) in the opening paragraph—is the most effective plan to use for good-news and neutral messages. As with direct requests, the organizational structure of these messages has three parts. Hereafter, this good-news neutral pattern is called simply the *good-news plan:*

---

1. Best news or the main idea
2. Explanation, which includes one or more of the following, when desirable:
   a. All necessary details
   b. Educational information
   c. Resale material
   d. Sales promotion
3. Positive, friendly ending
   a. Appreciation
   b. Clear statement of action desired and motivation to action
   c. Willingness to help further

Because the items in the explanation section form the basic core of your message, you must use good judgment in deciding which items to include. The following discussion highlights the content and uses of these four items:

1. *All necessary details:* Include whatever facts, terms, reasons, and other explanations pertain directly to the best news or the main idea. Consider, for instance, whether the reader needs specific details on the why, what, when, who, where, and how of the news or main idea.
2. *Educational information:* Include instructions for use and other educational facts about a product or service the customer has bought if such information is necessary to help the customer get the utmost benefit from the purchase or from the relationship with your firm. If you enclose an instruction booklet, a short paragraph within the letter may call special attention to certain pages in that booklet.
3. *Resale material:* Include appropriate favorable information about a product or service the reader has already bought or is planning to buy, or about your organization. Such material usually answers the question, "What will this do for me?" and strengthens the reader's confidence. Write concisely and with restraint. Avoid exaggeration and superlatives (such as "sensational," "perfect," "out-of-this-world value") because most readers react negatively toward them. Good resale keeps the customer "sold" on the product and company and helps to encourage repeat orders.
4. *Sales promotion:* Include suggestions about other products or services related to those the customer has bought or is considering buying. Whenever you do so, you indicate your desire to be of further service to the customer. This material should be presented without sales pressure; the emphasis should be on what the customer may need or appreciate and not on a desire to get more business. Also you need to consider the reader's probable mood before you decide to include or omit sales promotion. For instance, near the end of a good-news message—when you are fairly sure the customer will be in a receptive frame of mind—sales promotion may be quite appropriate.

FAVORABLE REPLIES

To help build goodwill, any progressive organization replies to all reasonable requests courteously, helpfully, and promptly (within two days, if possible). If you know there will be a delay, a brief acknowledgment should state why and then tell the inquirer approximately when to expect a complete answer. In such a message you can still begin with the best news first—information that is useful to the reader or shows you are doing something. Don't start with such negative statements as: "We are sorry we cannot answer your request here. . . ." Emphasize the positive, for example:

> Your request for information about solenoids has been forwarded to our Chief Systems Analyst, Mr. Richard Hacket, in our Chicago offices.
>
> You can expect to receive his helpful comments regarding your special needs soon after he returns from Alaska next week.

In every good-news reply your compliance with the reader's request is more important than any expression of gratitude or pleasure. Depending upon circumstances, you can begin by saying that you have done it (the preferred beginning), that you are doing it, or that you will do it. Thereafter the material you select for the explanation and ending varies significantly with the circumstances.

The discussion in this section includes guidelines and examples of favorable replies to requests for information (both related and unrelated to sales), adjustment, credit, orders, and favors, and provides a basis for deciding how to answer all other types of good-news replies.

Answering Inquiries for Information Related to Sales

Requests for information about services or products you sell are inquiries related to sales. Included are questions about catalogs, prices, terms, discounts, deliveries, products, manufacturing methods, types of accounts available, sources of supply, and similar information.

Replies to many of these inquiries are actually sales letters and are often called *solicited,* or *invited,* sales messages.[1] The inquirer is often already your customer, or a potential buyer, who may become a steady, satisfied customer *if* you send a reply that impresses favorably. This section discusses content of the three good-news parts and suggestions for handling inquiries prompted by advertising.

Positive Opening Paragraphs

The best way to begin these letters is by courteously doing one of the following:

1. *Sending the requested material*

> Enclosed are three samples of the nylon materials you asked about. We are glad to send these to you with our compliments.

[1] For a discussion of *unsolicited* sales messages, see Chapter 10.

2. Answering favorably one of the inquirer's questions

   a. Yes, Ms. Jones,
      You can use Latex Enamel paint in your bathroom with complete
      assurance that it is washable.
   b. You're right! Model XL2, about which you inquired, can eas-
      ily become an exceptionally good profit maker for you. Our
      dealers have reported it to be their most popular do-it-
      yourself maintenance kit.

3. Introducing the main idea(s) that your letter will cover

   a. Thank you for giving us the opportunity to tell you about the
      two insured savings plans available to you at First Federal.
   b. I am glad to explain to you the differences in the three Por-
      table Vibration Monitors you asked about in your January 5
      letter.

Answers to All Questions

In your explanation section, you should answer all questions—direct or implied.[2] In many cases, you will also provide educational, resale, or sales promotion information. Arrange your answers so that the favorable responses are at the beginning and end of your explanation section, to accent the positive and "embed" the negative aspects. Maintain a you-attitude; keep the reader in every paragraph if possible.

    Embedding the negative does not mean that you should omit or twist the truth. It means that you can emphasize what something *is* rather than what it is *not*. Like a good salesperson, you try to determine what the customer really needs. Contrast, for instance, the negative and the positive answers to the following four questions:[3]

1. Question:

Is the raincoat sprayed with ABC liquid so that it will be waterproof?

Negative reply:

No, I'm sorry to say the raincoat is not sprayed with ABC liquid.
However, the material itself is made of durable vinyl which is
completely waterproof.

Positive reply:

The material in this raincoat is made of a durable vinyl which is
permanently and completely waterproof. Thus you need never bother
with any spray even after the garment has been cleaned many times.

2. Question:

Do you carry the Bronson tape recorder? If so, how long would it
take for you to send one to my office if I should decide to order
it? (*The inquirer lives 500 miles from the seller, and only 100*

---

[2] See also the section on answering all questions asked, pages 31–33.
[3] You may also wish to reread examples on stressing positive and pleasant facts, pages 46–47.

miles from the factory. The seller is out of the item today, but notice that the inquirer has not yet ordered it.)

Negative reply:

We are temporarily out of stock of the Bronson, and so we couldn't send you one right away. If we reorder especially for you, it will take 10 days after we receive your request.

Positive reply:

Yes, we do carry the Bronson tape recorder, and we can usually send it to you within one day after we receive your order. As it is an extremely popular model, we sometimes run out of it temporarily. In such a case, we will gladly reorder immediately so you can expect delivery within 10 days. Occasionally, for a rush order, we could have the item sent to you direct from the factory within two days after your request reaches us.

3. *Question:*

Do you send these washing machines c.o.d.?

Negative reply:

No, we don't send c.o.d.

Positive, helpful reply:

Instead of c.o.d., which would require you to pay the full amount upon delivery of the machine, you have a choice of several payment plans. With every purchase the required down payment is 10 percent sent at the time of the order; the balance is payable in convenient monthly installments which you can arrange with our representative, Mr. Jepson.

4. *Question:*

Will you refund our money if we buy these draperies by mail and then find they don't blend with our other room colors?

Negative reply:

No, we don't refund all your money; you must pay for shipping charges.

Positive reply:

If you should wish to return the draperies within two weeks from the invoice date, you will get a full refund less shipping charges.

When quoting prices, be sure to use the same positive psychology by considering your reader's needs and circumstances. Unless the price of a particular product is a bargain, mention it only *after* you have stated most selling points and reader benefits.[4]

---

[4] For additional suggestions on methods of handling price quotations honestly as well as effectively, see Chapter 10.

Effective Action-Getting Paragraphs Leading to Sales

To get the desired action from your invited-sales reply, remember to make action clear, easy, dated if necessary, and beneficial to the reader when possible.[5] Sometimes, itemizing the steps that the reader should take is effective, as in the following example:

Action, clear and easy

> To start either account, you need take only three easy steps:
>
> 1. Complete the enclosed application card. Be sure to check which plan you prefer, indicate which name or names should appear on your account and what address we should send your mail to, add your social security number, and sign your name at the bottom of the card.
> 2. Enclose--in the prepaid envelope provided--both this application card and your money order or check that you wish to deposit.
> 3. Drop the sealed envelope into the nearest mailbox. As soon as your application card and deposit reach us, we will open an account which will begin earning 5% or 5 1/2% dividend immediately for you.

Reader benefit

Letter 1 below is a helpful reply to an inquiry related to sales.[6] It can be sent to any consumer who writes to this manufacturer for information and prices on the firm's interior home furnishings products—floor coverings, ceiling materials, furniture, and wall coverings. Notice that the consumer services manager includes specific suggestions for finding helpful retail merchants who can give the consumer needed information. The letter focuses on positive aspects instead of on negative regrets that the manufacturer can't quote retail prices.

Letter 1

A well-written reply that answers questions tactfully, encloses a booklet containing decorating ideas, and suggests where to go for additional help.[7]

Best news first; reader benefit

> Thank you for your recent request for information about Armstrong products. We appreciate your interest and are enclosing for you various pamphlets showing how these products can help make a home easier to care for as well as more attractive.

[5] To refresh your memory about other suggestions for all good closings, you might wish to reread pages 108-111.
[6] Regarding salutations and complimentary closes used for examples in this and following chapters, please see footnote 3, page 167.
[7] Courtesy of Armstrong Cork Company, Lancaster, Pennsylvania.

Further help available

For retail information and addresses of nearby Armstrong merchants, we suggest that you refer to the Yellow Pages of your telephone directory. You will find Armstrong products listed under "Floor Materials," "Carpet," and "Ceilings." For additional information on our Thomasville and Founders furniture, please write to Thomasville Furniture Industries, Inc., P.O. Box 339, Thomasville, NC 27360. Retail sources for Armstrong Cork Wallcovering can be obtained by writing to Katzenback and Warren, 950 Third Avenue, New York, NY 10022.

Educational information

Your local retail firms selling our products will gladly supply retail cost information. We do not establish retail prices. Because of shipping and other considerations, prices necessarily vary in different zones of the country. In addition, when floors, carpet, or ceilings are professionally installed, your real cost is the "installed" cost, which, again, we cannot anticipate. We suggest that you obtain such information from local retail firms selling our products, most of whom will gladly give you estimates without obligation to you.

Suggested action

So that you can see the newest in products, designs, and colors, visit Armstrong retail merchants near you. From them you can get complete and up-to-date information on current offerings. We wish you every success with your selections.

Suggestions for Handling Inquiries Prompted by Advertising

Whenever a firm advertises, it should be prepared in advance for various kinds of inquiries. To save time and expense, you can compose pertinent form paragraphs, and even entire messages, as guides for answering the most asked questions. Some messages should look personalized and individually typewritten, even though the body may be essentially the same for other inquirers who asked the same questions. (The cost of personalized messages can be decreased considerably by using automatic typewriters, computers, or other word processing equipment.)

On the other hand, many favorable replies do not need to be personalized—especially in routine situations when you are sure your reader will not object to a processed form. Most readers would rather receive promptly a high-quality, courteous form that is complete than a poor, personalized letter that is late, incomplete, or perhaps even inaccurately—and hurriedly—typewritten. Letter 2 is typical of the well-written processed sales-oriented replies that accompany booklets, samples, or other free information sent in response to a coupon or inquiry.

Letter 2

Processed sales promotion reply (without inside address) with easy action order form.

Good news with courtesy; no salutation	Here is your . . . Foremost Radio catalog to aid you in your selections. Thank you for requesting information on Foremost communication receivers.
Resale *Reader benefit*	You will find much useful data in the section on "precision construction and advanced design." Other sections show you why Foremost sets are the world's finest receivers. They are the choice of radio amateurs, shortwave listeners, industrial and scientific users. A Foremost set places the whole world at your fingertips.
Reader benefits	All communication receivers listed in your catalog are in stock now for prompt shipment at the prices shown. You can get liberal trade-in allowances on standard communications receivers (Hallicrafters, National, Apex, and Howell). If you prefer a time-payment plan, the attached sheet gives you details.
Easy action	To assure delivery within 10 days, just enter your order on the enclosed order form and mail it now in the postage-free envelope. Your order may be accompanied by a deposit as low as 10%, with shipment to be made c.o.d. for the balance due, or you may include full remittance if you prefer.
Reader benefit	You can begin to enjoy the unusual reception of a famous Foremost set by placing your order now.

Answering Inquiries for Information Unrelated to Sales

Among the most frequent nonsales-related inquiries you might need to answer are requests for information about personnel and credit applicants. Other inquiries may be from students, researchers, educators, and the general public—about a variety of subjects. The following section focuses on recommendation letters (about personnel and credit applicants), but also briefly discusses other replies to nonsales-related inquiries.

Letters of Recommendation

When you furnish pertinent information about an applicant's qualifications, character, and/or general conduct, you are writing a recommendation. It should preferably be addressed to the specific person interested, instead of "To whom it may concern."[8]

---

[8] A to-whom-it-may-concern letter is sometimes given to a satisfactory employee before she or he leaves the company; but because it must necessarily be general and not confidential, it carries much less weight than the confidential, specific recommendation.

You have a *fourfold responsibility* when you write recommendations. You must be fair (1) to the applicants, so they can get what they are best qualified for, (2) to the inquirers (prospective employer, creditor, landlord, or whoever), for they are depending on your frank comments, and (3) to your own conscience and reputation for integrity. Also, (4) you must abide by civil rights laws and be aware of possible legal problems.

Basically, a recommendation is a confidential personnel report.[9] Recommendation letters are included in this section, however, because they are important good-news or neutral replies to nonsales inquiries. Discussed below are the expanded good-news outline, recommendation letters on outstanding candidates, and recommendations on candidates with shortcomings.

Expanded Good-News Outline. The following suggestions serve as a basis for confidential recommendation letters when facts are mainly favorable or neutral.

1. Main idea
   a. State the applicant's full name and what his or her relationship was to you—employee, customer, friend, tenant, club member. Mention dates, length of time, and type of job, credit, tenancy, or whatever is pertinent that he or she held under you. Use facts; don't guess.
   b. Include an expression of pleasure, if sincere, in your statement of purpose for the letter: *replying confidentially to a request.* A subject line can cover part of item b with such words as "Confidential report by request, on Thomas W. Jones as a prospective field representative."
2. Explanation
   a. Answer all questions—direct or implied—unless doing so would be legally risky.
   b. Arrange answers in the best psychological order, depending upon facts.
   c. Back up your statements of evaluation (excellent, outstanding, and so on) with specific facts about performance record. For a job applicant:
      (1) Tell specific job duties that applicant performed.
      (2) If the inquiry states requirements of the job for which the applicant is being considered, talk about those duties that will be significant.
      (3) When desirable, mention work habits that show personality characteristics.
   d. Be honest and fair with negative material.
      (1) Include it *only* if pertinent to the inquiry and likely to affect the applicant's fitness to perform the particular job. (See five points, p. 215.)
      (2) Embed and subordinate it through amount of space and word choice.
      (3) Know the legal aspects of recommendations (see Appendix A).
      (4) If you prefer to omit pertinent negatives, invite the reader to phone you; then present the facts orally and discreetly.
3. Ending
   Include if possible a candid statement of your personal opinion about the applicant's probable fitness for the position (or whatever the applicant is being con-

---

[9] See Chapter 16 for additional discussion on letter reports.

sidered for—lease, credit, membership) and your recommendation, qualified or unqualified.

Recommendation Letters for Outstanding Candidates.   When everything you want to say is favorable, the recommendation is easy to write, as in letters 1 and 2 below.

Letter 1

A Marine Corps commanding officer writes a good solicited recommendation to the regional manager of a nationally known business firm about a corporal seeking a management trainee position.

Pleasure; purpose; name; job; length of time	I am glad to answer your inquiry about Wayne S. Prochas. Because Wayne has worked with me nearly two years as a correspondence clerk, I know him well.
Answers to questions	During this time he has demonstrated outstanding abilities in both general office and management work. In twenty years of military service I have only once before made such a high recommendation, and presently I have over 800 officers and men in my command.
Duties performed	With speed and efficiency Wayne has attended to the administrative correspondence of more than 800 men attached to this command, and he has never once complained of the work load or poor conditions under which he has had to work.
Personality *and* *character*	I recognize in this man a great potential because he is intelligent, industrious, and so well liked by all who come in contact with him. Corporal Prochas does his work with no supervision and can be relied upon to deliver a finished product at all times. Also I get the very definite impression that he could, if placed in a position to do so, generate ideas as well as process those of others.
	As to conduct, personal habits, and ability to handle himself properly this man has no faults, to my knowledge. He doesn't appear to have to work at being a gentleman. It seems to come natural to him. His loyalty is unquestionable and by his practices he has influenced others to a great extent.
Unqualified recommendation	I have two regrets: first, I can not take this man to my next command and, secondly, I do not possess the word power necessary to describe this man. But I do say this; my information is accurate and I am sincere. He will make a real contribution to any organization which he may choose to join. I recommend him very highly without any reservation.

Though the statement following "secondly" in the last paragraph above seems overdone (and could be revised), this commanding officer is to be commended for his sincerity and for including more than mere glowing adjectives to describe a man he considers outstanding.

Letter 2

A retailer courteously answers an inquiry about a credit applicant.

Name and relationship	Mrs. George L. Wardman, about whom you inquired in your May 2 letter, has been a customer of ours for the past eight years.
Answers to questions	She has used our credit facilities with a limit of $400. Her orders have been placed, on the average, about twice a month. I am pleased to report that she has always paid her bills promptly according to invoice terms.
Candid opinion	We consider Mrs. Wardman one of our preferred customers, thoroughly responsible with her financial obligations.

Notice that in letter 2 the reference correctly refrains from making unwarranted statements about the applicant's probable ability to shoulder any other debt. She merely reports on Mrs. Wardman's past credit record with her (the reference's) firm; she does not (and cannot) promise future payments elsewhere.

Sometimes an inquiry will contain a question which you can't answer—either because you don't know or because you can't reveal the information. In either case be sure to tell the reader why, instead of ignoring the question.

Recommendations for Candidates with Shortcomings. You must decide whether to include or omit negative material. If the candidate has the needed good qualities, you may be able to give a qualified or even an unqualified recommendation without stating the shortcoming. In any case, you should mention a weakness only if it meets these conditions:

1. It is pertinent to the job (or credit, etc.) for which the candidate has applied.
2. *It is sufficiently serious* to affect the applicant's probable fitness for that responsibility.
3. It is true (not hearsay or stated because of your personal prejudice, jealousy, malice, or discrimination).
4. It occurred often enough (and recently enough) to be worth mentioning.
5. It answers a specific question asked or implied, and/or you mention it in a spirit of goodwill based on items 1 to 4.

Recommendations are misleading and useless as personnel reports if they omit truthful, pertinent, helpful information. Nevertheless, many employers have been reluctant to make any negative—though truthful—statement (in writing or orally) for fear of a costly lawsuit or unfavorable publicity if the applicant should sue. Others, however, feel they have a moral duty, when responding to a legitimate inquiry, to state what they honestly and in good faith believe to be true and pertinent to the questions asked about a former employee. Basically, one should have no fear of stating the *truth prudently.*

For instance, an applicant who was discharged, after warnings, because he was caught three times stealing from the cash drawer should probably not be employed in a job handling company funds. But he may be a fine employee in other work. Likewise, such serious shortcomings as the following, unless corrected, will probably affect an employee on the next job, too: excessive drinking or drug use, poor health causing frequent absences, unwillingness to cooperate or to obey laws, dishonesty, extreme emotional instability. If you prefer not to present them in writing, you can write a short letter acknowledging the request and inviting the reader to call you. To protect yourself whenever you must make negative statements, you should know the legal aspects of recommendations (see Appendix A).

If you are writing a recommendation letter about a candidate who, apart from one serious shortcoming, is satisfactory (or excellent), organize your letter so that you establish the applicant's more favorable characteristics before you mention the defect. In letter 3, for example, the negative facts answering two questions are embedded; the message ends with a candid, qualified recommendation. (Three lawyers and an assistant attorney general have declared this letter "absolutely legal.")

Letter 3

A department manager comments on a former employee who had a serious shortcoming. (This letter, dated July 28, answers inquiry 2, page 167.)

Full name and brief summary

Confidential Appraisal by Request on Victor L. Dryer

Mr. Dryer worked hard for us as a salesperson in the electrical appliances section for about a year. He was such a dependable salesperson that when the section manager resigned to go to the East, we placed Vic in charge and found him well qualified for the job. He was with us 22 months--until June 30 this year.

Answer to part of question 1

As section manager, Vic had much responsibility. Besides ordering all merchandise for the section, he was also in charge of the five salespeople working under him. He was well liked by subordinates and customers. He had a knack of being tactful and thoughtful with every customer. Because of his personality and his knowledge of the stock, he pleased a good many steady patrons and helped increase total sales within his section.

Answer to question 2

Vic's work at the store was entirely commendable for about 16 months. Then he developed a personal problem, which noticeably affected his disposition and his attendance. When I talked with him about the change, he mentioned serious worries. He tried to lick the problem and did so for three weeks. But after he had missed at least a day's work every week for six months, I regretfully had to let him go.

Favorable comment before and after the negative answer to part of questions 3 and 1

*More about
question 3*

Vic's other personal habits are good. His personality, honesty, and physical appearance are an asset
to any company. He takes an active part in outdoor
sports and, except for the problem I mentioned, is
in fine health. It is quite probable that his move
to your town will be a definite advantage to his
family and himself.

*Qualified
recommendation*

Vic is intelligent and well educated (a marketing
graduate of Broadway College). Because he knows the
electrical appliance business well and has so many
other fine qualities, he can be a top-notch department or section manager especially in the electrical field.

Other Replies to Nonsales Inquiries

Answering the nonsales inquiries that business executives receive from various people
often takes a good deal of time. Nevertheless, to build goodwill and give genuine service, helpful replies like letter 4 are desirable.

Letter 4

*A collection manager replies with a personalized letter to a college student who re-
quested information.*

Dear Mike:

Courtesy; best news

It is a pleasure to return to you the completed form
as requested in your letter of April 12.

Comments

I was very favorably impressed with the sample collection series you enclosed. As a whole, the letters
are courteous and also appropriately firm. Achieving
the right tone in this type of letter is very important, and I believe you have done so.

*Offer of
further help*

Any further information you may need from us will be
gladly forwarded.

*Interest
in survey*

The recap you offered to send showing your survey results should be interesting. I will appreciate receiving a copy.

If, in its advertising, your firm offers free information pamphlets not related to
sales, you can handle replies with processed form messages, which cut costs substantially.

Granting Requests for Adjustment

An *adjustment letter* is the reply to a complaint (called a claim letter). In general, the
best attitude is to give the customer the benefit of any doubt. Most persons are honest

in their claims, and it is usually better to make the desired adjustment than to risk losing a customer.

Even though your firm's adjustment policy may be generous, the ultimate success of your good-news adjustment letter depends upon not only what you say but also how you say it. The discussion in this section concerns (1) the tone of adjustment-granting messages, (2) organization and content when the seller is at fault, (3) variations when the buyer or a third party is at fault, and (4) organization when the fault is not yet determined and will be investigated.

Tone of Adjustment-granting Messages

Consideration and courtesy are exceptionally important when you grant an adjustment. Because your reader has been inconvenienced, irritated, and perhaps angered, he or she is especially sensitive to the tone of your message. Even when the letter grants a request, it can lose a friend and destroy goodwill if its tone is poor. Compare, for example, the following "poor" sentence (in which the antagonizing expressions are underscored) with the suggested "better" version:

Poor:

Nevertheless, <u>so that we can keep you as a satisfied customer</u>, we are <u>willing to allow you</u> to exchange these toys. (*The motive sounds selfish; "willing to" and "allow you" sound condescending and grudging; the sentence lacks you-attitude.*)

Better:

Because we want you to be completely pleased, we will gladly exchange the toys for you.

When you (or anyone else in your firm) are definitely at fault, saying "I'm sorry," "We apologize," or even "Please forgive us" is quite disarming. You are more likely to lose face by *not* apologizing than by doing so. One apology (preferably in the *explanation* section) is enough, for most situations.

Organization and Content When Seller Is at Fault

You should, of course, always grant the adjustment when your company is at fault. In general, the best organization is:

Begin with the best news—what is being done about the claim.

Include whatever explanation and details are desirable concerning the cause of the mistake; resale on the product, service, or your firm; sales promotion and/or educational material.

End courteously, showing a desire to cooperate, please, and assist.

The following discussion aims to help you avoid common pitfalls and plan carefully. After reading about various parts and paragraphs of adjustment grants, you will see examples of complete letters.

Opening Paragraph. Try to begin with whatever you think the reader will consider the best news. If the customer asked for something specific—like a refund, exchange, credit memo, or speedier service—you should grant or promise immediately. However, if the nature of the request or attitude makes a "granting" opening inadvisable, you will try to get in step with the customer in some other appropriate way. For example, if a customer has found a bug in a jar of oysters and vows never to buy your products again, you can't very well *begin* by saying you're sending another jar of oysters to replace the faulty one! Instead, you might express appreciation for the thoughtfulness in writing and/or agree with a comment made in the complaint.[10] In the following examples, the first two grant immediately and the last three open with various statements to get in step with the reader.

Customer's request or complaint	*Suggested opening*
1. That you "eliminate the delays" in your merchandise shipments or risk losing business.	You will be glad to hear that we have found a new way to speed deliveries of fresh vegetables to you. From now on your produce can reach you within two hours after we receive your order.
2. That you replace immediately five defective copies of a book needed by May 15.	Today five copies of (*book title*) were sent to you by air express, shipping charges prepaid. You should receive them three days before May 15.
3. That you refund to a friend the $30.50 purchase price because of your firm's "inexcusable error." (Your customer bought a wedding gift for a friend. Instead of charging it to your customer's account, your store incorrectly sent the "gift" to the friend c.o.d. That was two months ago; the friend does not yet know about the mix-up.)	(*To the customer's friend*). You have had the unusual experience of paying for your own wedding gift—much to the embarrassment of our mutual friend, James L. Lamson. The mix-up is due entirely to our inexcusable error, for which we extend to you our sincere apologies. (*Note: In this case the refund check is mentioned only after the explanation.*)
4. That two special toys ordered four weeks ago did not arrive in time for Christmas.	We have disappointed you and your children at what is usually the happiest time of year, and we are truly sorry! Now I want to do everything possible to make amends.
5. That the service of a certain waiter in your restaurant was disappointing, and the customer's guests were embarrassed.	You are perfectly right to feel that you should receive prompt and courteous service from our waiters. That is exactly our goal for every guest, and we thank you for taking time to write us.

---

[10] Later in the letter, after appropriate explanation and resale, you can tell the customer you are sending a gift replacement. See, for example, letter 1, page 222.

Explaining What Caused the Mistake. When your firm is at fault, admit it frankly. How much explanation to include depends upon the kind of mistake and the customer's probable interest, but generally it is desirable to include at least *some* explanation.[11] Paragraphs such as the following—from two different adjustment grants—help the reader understand how the error occurred:

```
1. You guessed correctly.  Apparently all the shipping papers, includ-
   ing the original ones that should have been kept for our use, were
   sent to you.  As a result, we have no record of the ordered paint.
   We are certainly sorry that you were inconvenienced by our slipup.
   We always try to be careful in processing every customer request
   accurately and promptly.
2. Sometimes we find that a package miscarries in the mails.  This oc-
   casionally happens because of an error in addressing the label, or
   damage to the label in the mail, obliterating the address.  Appar-
   ently that's what happened with your parcel.
```

Avoid the following pitfalls in your explanations:

1. Don't blame an inexperienced clerk. Your firm should have trained the clerk adequately; thus it is better that the company ("we") assumes the mistake rather than the individual.

2. Don't suggest that your employees are careless or inefficient. Describe your normal businesslike methods to indicate that this error was an exception.

3. Don't say, "mistakes are bound to happen" or that because of the size of your firm there will naturally be frequent errors.

4. Don't promise the error will never happen again. If it *does* happen again, the situation will be doubly embarrassing. Better show the care you are taking to assure correct service in the future.

Sometimes an explanation isn't necessary, for example, when the mistake merely involves a small routine clerical error between two business firms. Also, if the matter is complicated (or perhaps even confidential), or if for no good reason someone just "goofed" several times, no explanation at all is sometimes better than a lengthy discussion which may sound like an alibi or which will be filled with negatives.

Resale. If the person complaining seems to be losing faith in your firm, resale is desirable. If possible, include concrete evidence of your efficient service, safe and correct shipments, and/or your care in producing or selecting high-quality products. If certain steps have been or will be taken to prevent recurrence of whatever the customer is complaining about, mention them. Sometimes you can honestly state that a new procedure is developed "on the basis of helpful comments like yours."

```
Because of your excellent suggestion, we plan to install the "right
turn only" sign to improve the parking lot exit at Emmett Street.
Thank you for your interest in suggesting a practical way to help
traffic move smoothly.
```

---

[11] See, for example, letters 1 and 2 pages 222 and 223, which include careful explanation plus resale.

When you grant a customer's request to exchange unsatisfactory goods, you can strengthen confidence in the replacement you send by including a resale paragraph.

```
This new flowering quince is a choice plant from our sturdy Penbrook
stock.  It is hardy enough to withstand zero temperatures and re-
quires little care.  You will be delighted with its deep-pink blos-
soms twice each year--at Christmas and in midsummer.  In size it
fits beautifully with the other trees you selected last month.
```

Sometimes it is desirable to resell the customer on keeping both the replacement you are sending *and* and the original slightly defective shipment. (You save return-shipping charges and the bother of processing the damaged merchandise.) A consumer may be glad to keep slightly damaged articles if you substantially reduce their price. Likewise, a dealer customer may be willing to accept a below average shipment which can be used for a special sale and quick profits if you give sufficient inducement—price reduction, consignment terms, or perhaps longer payment time.

Sales Promotion Material. If a retailer sells only one type of costly product (like furnaces, home insulation, or roofing), which the average consumer buys only once in a great while, sales promotion material would be out of place. On the other hand, if the seller carries a variety of often-replaced items, sales promotion may be desirable. Without sounding greedy, you want to encourage the customer to continue to buy other goods from you.

Also, if the customer returned the original shipment and is receiving credit or a refund, she or he really needs a different replacement. Sales promotion material is then appropriate, as in the following paragraph:

```
Your nephew Tommy may be happier with toys designed especially for
his age group.  Tillman's carries many toys just right for 4-year-
olds, as the enclosed folder illustrates--on pages 12-14.  Tommy
may enjoy our alphabet puzzle (#R-6322), which is sturdy, enter-
taining, and educational.  Other toys he will like are the plastic
set of modern cars (M-8909), the metal boat kit (B-6222) that can
be assembled easily, and our small-size sing and play piano.  All
these and others shown are educational toys to help Tommy learn as
he plays with his friends.
```

With a genuine desire to serve the customer well—and *not* mainly to make a sale—you can sometimes also include informal, no-pressure sales talk regarding products useful with goods you have just shipped. This information focuses the customer's attention on your thoughtfulness and gives a feeling of a pleasant future relationship.

Ending Paragraph. For a pleasant close you may (1) tie suggested action in with sales promotional material; (2) comment on the pleasure the reader will gain from the high-quality new article you have sent; (3) express appreciation that the reader took time to write; and/or (4) issue a cordial invitation that the customer continue to come to your firm for top service. Omit negative thoughts, such as an apology or a reminder of the inconvenience the mistake caused. Don't suggest future trouble or imply that the customer may stop buying from your firm.

Now that you have read about the parts of adjustment grants when the seller is at fault, you are ready to analyze and compare complete messages.

Letter 1 concerns a situation in which the seller is at fault. The disappointed customer stated the intention of never buying a canned food product again. Notice that the writer does not begin by "granting" or even giving the free assortment; the main idea is appreciation and resale. The assumption is that only after reading the explanation—and more resale—will the customer be in a mood to accept the replacement. The last paragraph effectively ties in a gift with a hint of sales promotion.

Letter 1

A good adjustment-granting letter from the assistant manager of the quality control department of a national packing corporation to an out-of-state customer who found a fly in the can.

Main idea: thanks; resale

Thank you for writing us of your experience upon opening a can of DeMona spinach. We are very concerned about this because of the particular care taken in the preparation of all DeMona products to assure you of receiving a wholesome and high-quality food item.

Explanation, with resale

Upon arrival at the packing plant, the spinach is run through a large perforated cylinder where it is tumbled and shaken apart to eliminate particles of soil, etc. From there, it is transferred to wide traveling belts where inspectors remove all imperfect leaves and any other defects present. The spinach then goes into the washers in which a series of paddle wheels keeps it in a state of constant agitation while high-pressure jets of water wash, rewash, and rewash. After that, it is subjected to a further careful inspection as it is placed in the cans; therefore, you can see we do everything possible to produce a clean, wholesome product.

Easy action; apology

To further investigate this incident, we will appreciate your sending us the code mark which was embossed on the lid of the can in question. This will enable us to refer the matter directly to the plant where the spinach was packed. If you made a note of it, please send it to us on the enclosed reply card. We appreciate your bringing this situation to our attention and offer you our sincere apology.

Gift to regain goodwill and promote sales

Within a few days you will receive an assortment of DeMona fruits and vegetables. We want you to enjoy them so thoroughly that you will continue to be a regular DeMona satisfied customer.

In letter 2 the customer service manager's main purpose is to regain Mrs. Larson's confidence in the store's desire to serve promptly. Thus the manager begins with an idea calculated to please this, or any, reader—a sincere indirect compliment and appreciation.

Letter 2

A tactful reply to a department store customer's complaint about not being waited on in turn.

Compliment implying granted request	You were thoughtful to write us about the service you have received in our store. Your letter helps us in our constant effort to improve and make Gill's a place where you and others can enjoy shopping.
Explanation	Your friendship and goodwill mean a lot to us and we have thoroughly investigated the incident about which you write. Miss Simkins feels her error keenly, Mrs. Larson, because she has always assisted our customers to the utmost of her ability. In all sincerity, she said she did not know you were ahead of the other customer at her hosiery counter. Miss Simkins will be most appreciative if you permit her to see and talk with you, for she feels a personal apology is the least she can offer you.
Sincere apology; resale	Though an apology will not take the place of the good service you should have received, we do want you to know that we are sorry the incident happened. Prompt and courteous service is Gill's pledge--a pledge every salesperson in the organization must follow.
Courtesy; forward look to service	My office is on the third floor, Mrs. Larson, to the left of the elevator. On your next trip to Gill's, won't you stop in just for a minute or two. Your interest in Gill's is highly valued, and we look forward with pleasure to seeing and serving you again soon.

Variations When the Buyer or a Third Party Is at Fault

When someone other than the seller is at fault, you may be justified in refusing—instead of granting—the request. Nevertheless, firms will occasionally grant a buyer's claim even though the buyer or a third party is at fault.

Buyer at Fault. If you decide to grant the adjustment claim, though the buyer is at fault, you have two choices for letter organization. You can begin with the best news (granting the claim) and continue with the usual pattern or you can begin with a statement that gets in step with the reader, then explain the mistake, and after that grant the claim. The reason for the latter alternative is that sometimes the psychological effect on the reader is better if you allow the claim *after* you have shown tactfully that the buyer, not your firm, is at fault. The next two letters handle the same situation in these two different ways: letter 3 begins with the refund, and letter 4 begins with a buffer. Both have a "Dear Mrs. Hamilton" salutation.

Letter 3

A sales manager grants a refund on a blouse that faded because someone washed it incorrectly; best news first.

Best news: refund

We are very concerned to hear of your experience with the Lady Marlow blouse you purchased recently at our downtown store. As a result, you are receiving the enclosed cash refund for the original purchase price, plus sales tax, totaling $21.50.

Resale, with tactful (impersonal) explanation of necessary washing care

The Lady Marlow is one of the finest lines of ladies blouses made. The synthetic fibers and the special dyes which make possible the beautiful colors in these blouses do, however, require special care. Whenever these blouses are laundered, washing in a solution of very mild detergent and lukewarm water gives the best results. As the instruction tag on every blouse states, these garments are very sensitive to heat and should therefore always be dried at room temperature, never in an automatic dryer. Furthermore, any staining substance which comes in contact with the material must be loosened in cold water, because hot water often causes a chemical change that loosens the dye and results in fading.

Resale; additional emphasis on care; educational enclosure

Although the Lady Marlow line does require special care, I'm sure you will agree that its beauty and elegant fashion lines outweigh the special care required by the fine fabric. Because of the many new materials on the market, I think you will find the enclosed booklet on the laundering of all types of synthetics both interesting and educational.

Sales promotion, with implied action and courtesy

As you are one of our regular customers, we invite you to our upcoming June sale. A complete line of summer fashions, including new pastel and print blouses, will be waiting for your inspection. The sale begins June 12, but the general public will receive an announcement on June 14.

It's been a pleasure to help you.

Letter 4

An alternate for letter 3; explanation before the best news.

Resale on the firm (buffer)

As a regular customer of Finestein's, you know that we are proud to guarantee the quality of each of our garments. In light of this, we were very concerned when we received your Lady Marlow blouse in the mail.

Resale on blouse; explanation

(*Resale and explanation paragraph may be similar to paragraph 2 in letter 3*).

Tactful statements showing seller not at fault	Since our laboratory tests show that the fading in the trim of the blouse is not due to defective dye, the stripes have apparently come in contact with some other chemical agent, water that is hotter than luke-warm, or excessive heat. Although we cannot assume responsibility for the fading in this blouse, we are
Best news: refund with sales promotion	glad to give you the opportunity to replace it. Enclosed is a check for $21.50, covering the purchase price plus sales tax.
Sales promotion; invited action	We invite you to visit the blouse department again soon to select your choice from any of the newest arrivals. Besides the popular Lady Marlow you will find several other famous-name brands. And of course you may also be interested in the new summer fashions in dresses and coats.

Third Party at Fault. Many firms accept responsibility for adjusting claims and seek reimbursement from the third party. This method is customary with wholesalers shipping to small dealers or retailers sending to individual customers who are unfamiliar with claim-filing procedures.

Letter 5

A gift shop owner replaces a lamp damaged in shipment.

Best news: replacement	A new Brighton lamp should reach you in a few days to replace the one you received in damaged condition. We sent it today by prepaid express.
Explanation showing seller not at fault	As the (*name*) Railroad gave us a receipt acknowledging that they received the original lamp perfectly crated, the porcelain base must have been cracked in transit. We are sorry this happened, for we know how much you want this beautiful gift for your cousin's wedding anniversary. Although our responsibility ended when the railroad accepted the package, we are glad to make this replacement for you.
Suggested action to help claim with carrier	Will you please give the original lamp to the express driver when the second lamp is delivered? We will then enter a claim with the railroad.
Courtesy; resale	Thank you for writing promptly. Our main concern is that you receive the lamp in time for the anniversary, and in perfect condition.

Organization When the Fault Is Not Yet Determined

Sometimes the final adjustment decision cannot be made until the seller determines who is responsible for the mistake. In such cases, let the buyer know promptly that you want to investigate the claim. Your letter should have a neutral effect on the reader, for you are neither granting nor refusing the request. The best organization is: express interest in the problem, assure the customer you are looking into the matter, include brief resale if desirable, and courteously state that you will give the facts as soon as they are available.

Letter 6

A hatchery manager promises to investigate.

Interest in problem

Thanks very much for your report on the N&H "Nick Chick" Leghorn pullets delivered to you on March 29. I sympathize with you, for pullets you buy from Nerving's should meet the high standards of previous lots. We want to do everything possible to cooperate with you.

Possible causes of problem; promise of investigation

Tints, egg size, broodiness are characteristics both genetic and environmental. That fancy phrase simply means pullets can be influenced by both breeding and rearing, management, etc. Because there are so many factors involved in the conditions you describe, we are asking our Oregon field representative, Mr. Vern Jackson, to call on you within the next few days. You will find him cooperative and helpful.

Resale

Most hatcheries would be satisfied if 90% of their stock were good 90% of the time. Not Nerving's. We are aiming for 100% on both counts and won't rest until we reach that goal. Of course, when you are dealing with "life", there are numerous variables making this difficult. But, we keep trying. That's why letters such as yours help in pointing out where improvements can be made.

Courtesy

We want you to be a satisfied customer, Mrs. King. If we are at fault in any way, you are assured we'll do our level best to make amends. Thanks again for writing; you help us take steps to make things right.

Approving Credit

The message telling the customer of your granting credit[12] often includes all parts of the basic good-news plan—best news first, then terms,[13] resale, sales promotion, and appreciation.

---

[12] Every city has a credit bureau—an association of credit grantors (stores, banks, car dealers, credit unions, and so forth). The function of the credit bureau is to collect the credit records of their customers and consolidate the information of each individual. Then, when a credit grantor receives a request for credit, it asks the credit bureau for the applicant's record and forms its own conclusions. The larger credit grantors are linked to the bureau by teletype, which enables them to get a printed record in seconds.

[13] You can place the terms either before or after the resale and sales promotion. If before, you're more certain the reader will notice them because you're emphasizing the terms; if after, you seem to be stressing the other person and not "what's in it for me."

Decision or Shipment in First Paragraph

If the customer has not yet ordered any merchandise on credit, begin with the credit-granting decision and a cordial welcome. If an order was sent with the request for credit, begin with the date and method by which the goods are being shipped (thereby implying the credit grant). Make clear the purchase details (name and quantity of goods sent, item prices, freight, and total charge); for more than two or three items, attach an invoice copy. Mention cordially that the shipment has been added to the customer's new account.

Explanation of Credit Terms

In your explanation section, mention briefly the basis on which credit was earned, and clarify the terms. If, for instance, an applicant's references all speak highly of prompt-pay habits, it is psychologically a good idea to mention them. The applicant is then encouraged to continue to live up to this good reputation in dealing with you.

Your explanation of the credit terms must be clear and concrete to help reduce collection problems later. Suppose, for example, your wholesale firm's terms are 2/10, net 30. You must be sure that every new credit customer (dealer) knows whether your terms are based on invoice date, shipping date, delivery date, or from the end of the month (e.o.m.). Misunderstanding on this important detail can cause a customer's payments to be as much as a month off. Compare these vague and clear statements regarding credit terms.

Vague:	Our credit terms are the usual 2/10, net 30.
Vague:	Under our credit terms of 2/10, net 30, you earn a 2 percent discount if your payment is made in 10 days. (*10 days after what?*)
Clear:	Our credit terms are the usual 2/10 net 30, based on invoice date.

To an *inexperienced* business owner, or one whose payment record has been shaky, you might write:

> Under our credit terms of 2/10, net 30, you earn a 2 percent discount if your payment is postmarked within 10 days of invoice date; the full amount is payable in 30 days. On the enclosed March 28 invoice you save $12.40 by mailing your check on or before April 7--a saving to you almost equivalent to the cost of two shirts.

Of course, if all wholesalers within your industry abide by the same standard interpretation and your new customer is experienced in this industry, you need merely state your terms.

Besides stating terms clearly, you need also to use positive wording about a credit limit, if any, as these examples show:

Negative:	We are limiting you to $500 maximum credit each month (each credit period).

Positive: In any credit period you are welcome to (you may) purchase up to $500 of merchandise on your new account.

If you are in a retail firm, you must likewise make your billing and payment obligations clear to the consumer. Are you opening a monthly charge account,[14] a budget account,[15] or a revolving credit account?[16] Do all statements (bills) from your firm go out on the same day each month or do you have cycle billing? Be tactful in telling the customer when payments are due. Compare, for example, the poor tone in, "We expect you to pay" or, "You are expected to pay" with the improved tone in, "Payments are due within 10 days after the billing date" or, "Please send your payment within 10 days."

Resale and Sales Promotion

The credit-granting message should include customer-benefit resale information on the firm's services. Also, it is sometimes desirable to include sales promotion material (in the next-to-last or last paragraph) about such news as a forthcoming sale, new seasonal merchandise, or products allied to those ordered (if any). Such news encourages the customer to use credit.

To keep your letter short, you can enclose a leaflet describing departments and services such as the following:

For the consumer
   Free parking, mail and telephone shopping, personalized services for men, home-planning bureau, bridal consultants, tearoom, other restaurants, child-care, gift wrapping, free and frequent deliveries, special discount or purchase privileges.

For the intermediary (retailer or wholesaler)
   Nearby warehouses, factory representatives, quantity discounts, free window or counter displays, national advertising, cuts and mats for newspaper and other advertising, repair services, manuals, factory guarantees, prompt and speedy deliveries, research department.

---

[14] With a monthly charge account, the customer may charge purchases during any month and is required to pay for them in full usually upon receipt of a statement (or within 10 days of its receipt) the month following the date of charge. Some retailers mail all statements the same day each month. Others use *cycle billing*, which helps to level out the billing department's load over a 30-day period. For example, customers whose names begin with A–C may be billed for 30-day purchases through the 5th of a month and statements may be mailed on the 10th; those whose names begin with D–F may be billed through the 8th and statements mailed on the 14th; etc.

[15] With a budget account (a time-payment plan) the customer makes a down payment (usually 10 percent) on the purchase and agrees to make monthly repayments on the unpaid balance. Purchases on home furnishings, appliances, and electronic equipment usually must be paid within 18 months; apparel and other "soft" items, within 12 months.

[16] With revolving credit the customer and the store agree on a maximum amount of credit, and then the customer agrees to pay a certain monthly amount according to the store's established terms (ranging from $10 to $25, usually, on account balances from $100 to $150). The customer usually pays an interest and service charge on the unpaid balance. Additional purchases may be made at any time, provided they do not raise the total balance beyond the agreed limit.

Future-Service Ending

Close your credit grant with statements which indicate your desire to serve the customer well in the future, or which specify particular services. Inviting readers to a special sale, for example, helps to get them to use their accounts. The tone must in no way sound greedy for orders, and you must observe the usual suggestions for easy action and courtesy.

Each of the following two letters establishes a pleasant and clear relationship with the new credit customer—letter 1 to a consumer and letter 2 to a wholesaler.

Letter 1

A retailer uses a processed form letter to grant credit to a consumer; the applicant's name and address are typed in the inside address and salutation.

Best news: welcome; new account

We welcome you as a Nelson credit account customer. Your new charge plate is enclosed and we invite you to use it often. This plate will identify you at all Nelson stores; so please sign it in ink before putting it into your wallet or purse.

Credit terms

You will receive your statement soon after the first of each month, showing purchases up to the 23d of the preceding month. Bills are payable by the 10th of each month. (Unpaid bills are subject to a 1 percent finance charge.)

Resale on store services

As one of our regular charge customers, you will receive announcements of all our sales before they are advertised for the public. If you should wish sometimes to shop in the comfort of your own home without a trip to town, you can do so conveniently by phone. Just ask for "personal shopping services," tell your needs to the shopping assistant, and then just say, "Charge it to my account."

Invitation to future use of account

The enclosed leaflet explains the numerous Nelson services available for your convenience. Do use them often to save yourself both time and money. We look forward to giving you friendly, courteous service in any of our colorful stores . . . for many years to come.

Letter 2

A wholesaler grants credit (and ships merchandise) to an established hardware store owner; the letter is individually typed.

Best news: shipping goods; new account

The Topskill tools you ordered April 3 are on their way to your store today by B&L Motor Freight. You can count on having them for your gardening customers by Saturday. This merchandise, as itemized on the

enclosed invoice, has been added to your newly opened
account.

Explanation
of terms

We are pleased to extend to you our most favorable
terms of 2/10, net 30 (based on invoice date). The
information we received about you is completely complimentary to you personally and as a business owner.

Resale on products

We appreciate your choosing us to supply you with our
nationally advertised hardware and gardening products.

Resale on
wholesaler's services

Packed with your order is our latest assortment of
window display materials with full directions for making them attractive. Our representative, Ms. Carla
Webber, will call on you about twice a month and
gladly assist you in asnwering any questions you may
have about Topskill. If you would like free envelope
stuffers to mail to your customers and mats for your
newspaper advertising, indicate your wishes on the
enclosed illustrated checklist.

Resale on product

You will notice the enthusiasm customers express for
your new line of tools. Their durability and precision is appreciated by both the craftworker and the
amateur do-it-yourselfer.

Easy action
for orders

To place your future orders, just use the easy-mail
order forms at the back of your catalog. You can expect deliveries within three days after we receive
your orders. You may be assured of our cooperation
at all times.

Acknowledging Orders

An order acknowledgment performs several important functions. It lets the buyer
know that his or her order has been received, is appreciated, and is given attention.
It helps to build goodwill. Furthermore—and very important—by identifying and accepting the order, the acknowledgment completes a valid contract between buyer and
seller. For these reasons the acknowledgment must be definite and complete, in keeping with the situation.

Orders that your firm can fill immediately fall into two types—first orders and
repeat orders. Although the acknowledgment for both types should identify the shipment and show appreciation, the message contents will be quite different.

Acknowledgment of First Order

The new customer needs to know that his or her order is being filled promptly and
correctly, that it is appreciated, and that—because of your products and services—
dealings with your firm will be pleasant and profitable.

Sending the Ordered Items. Usually the best beginning for your first-order acknowledgment is to state what, when, and how you shipped. If possible, state approximately

when the shipment should reach its destination. Express appreciation for both the order and remittance (if you received the latter).

Then take care of any needed details about shipping charges and payments. If you opened a new credit account for this customer, you will of course explain the credit terms.

Here are a few overworked expressions to avoid in first-order acknowledgments; they are followed by comments and/or suggested revisions:

Vague, trite, and a little inaccurate: "We have shipped your order. . . ."
Comment: The order is really a piece of paper on which the customer authorizes you to send requested items; your firm fills the order and ships merchandise, groceries, livestock, or whatever was ordered.

Better: "The bedspread (#204) and the electric blanket (#B43) which you ordered September 4 were sent to you today by parcel post. You can expect them in a few days. Thank you for your order and your enclosed $58.20 check in full payment.

Trite: "Welcome to our long list (or family) of satisfied customers."
Comment: Omit such statements and show elsewhere in your letter by actions—prompt service, reader-centered resale, sincere thoughtfulness—instead of by empty words that you appreciate the order and want to please the customer.

Specific Resale Material.   Resale on company services (as listed on page 228) is appropriate for both the consumer and the retailer. Resale on products ordered is usually more desirable for the consumer than for the retailer. Before ordering, the business manager who will resell your products has usually studied their merits carefully—through sales literature, catalogs, and perhaps information from your sales representative—and you generally need not repeat what has already been read. However, the manager may appreciate a few additional facts and any special product features he or she can emphasize to customers.

To a consumer, resale material from the "home office" is sometimes extremely helpful. After placing a first order with a firm (either by mail or through a house-to-house sales representative), the consumer may regret having signed the contract—especially when the item purchased is a luxury. For example, suppose that you bought a 20-volume deluxe encyclopedia for $450 and gave the traveling sales representative a $50 down payment. Afterward you have "buyer's remorse," and feel that you can't really afford such a purchase. Now, suppose you receive from the publisher a three-paragraph order acknowledgment devoted entirely to your payment obligations. Such a letter would hardly be reassuring!

On the other hand, suppose that instead of the letter just described, you received one like letter 1 below. Notice that eight of its nine paragraphs contain reader-benefit and resale material and only one mentions payments. Don't you agree that such a letter would help reinforce your confidence in your purchase? Depending upon circumstances, adequate resale may range from one sentence to several paragraphs.

Letter 1

Resale in a completely processed acknowledgment to a consumer purchaser of an encyclopedia (and perhaps other educational materials).[17]

Contract acceptance; thanks; resale

With sincere thanks we accept your contract covering the items listed on the enclosed Summary of Purchase. By placing your order with us, you have joined hundreds of thousands of parents, teachers, and children to whom these outstanding educational materials have become an important part of daily living.

Resale

In addition to these fine products that you will soon receive, there are several important and exclusive supplemental benefits and services that we want to tell you about:

Summary of purchase; payment details

Your Summary of Purchase lists all the items you ordered on your contract and total price of the order less your down payment. If you have chosen our budget plan, it also states the payment terms. If you paid for your order in full, this summary will serve as your paid-in-full receipt.

Reader-benefit suggestions

Also included on your Summary of Purchase is your account number. If you should have occasion to write us, stating your account number will help us quickly identify your account and give your inquiry prompt handling.

Reader benefits; sales promotion

The enclosed Exchange Certificate offers you the opportunity to purchase at a discount, another set of World Book under the conditions specified. In addition, you can choose other learning and teaching aids prepared for children and adults.

Reader-benefit suggestion

Be certain to look at these enclosures very carefully, and then put them in a safe place. They are most valuable and important to you, and will be helpful if it is necessary to answer questions about your account.

Reader benefits

As a World Book purchaser you will be able to keep your set up to date with The World Book Year Book, an annual supplement which reviews the important events of the preceding calendar year. You will also find our Science Year Annual very helpful and informative. You'll receive an announcement regarding these supplements before they are published each year.

We congratulate you on your decision to purchase this marvelous encyclopedia which has been serving American education for more than five decades. The pres-

[17]Courtesy of Field Enterprises Educational Corporation, Chicago.

Resale

ent World Book is the result of years of planning under the supervision of an editorial advisory board of specialists and was produced by more than 1400 noted scholars and authorities. It includes all the features on which the World Book has built its reputation.

A confidence-building close

A year from now, I feel certain, you will agree that this purchase has proved one of the most satisfactory investments you have ever made. It will serve you well for many years to come.

Looking Forward to Future Orders and Reader Satisfaction. To end the first-order acknowledgment, you can tie your suggested action in with resale or sales promotion. Be sure your reader has order blanks or whatever else is needed for easy action. If you wish, you may invite the cash customer to fill out and return a credit application form; but avoid suggesting that credit will be automatic.

Letter 2 on page 229 is typical of a good first-order acknowledgment to a dealer buying on credit. With a few changes, that letter could be adapted for a dealer who sent a check with a first order. Letter 2 below, to a cash customer, includes a credit application form.

Letter 2

Personalized acknowledgment of a first cash order from a dealer.

Restatement or order

You can expect to receive the two dozen Topskill lawn edgers, #L592, and the five manual mowers, M 687, in time for your garden sale Monday, May 15. They were shipped by prepaid express this afternoon.

Appreciation; check acknowledgment

Thank you for your order and for your $425.50 check, which exactly covered the items as priced in your new dealer catalog. As you know, the suggested markup on these items is 30 percent.

Resale on services for dealer; customer benefit

Your customers will be pleased with these highly popular Topskill tools. Currently they are advertised in special 1/2-page, two-color ads in House and Home and Western Garden magazines, April through July. You can assure your customers that every Topskill is factory guaranteed according to the contract that accompanies each tool. A special feature of the Topskill edger is its ability to trim neatly within one inch of flower beds and rockeries. On the mower, a simple twist of the dial knob adjusts both wheels and roller for precise cutting height and ease of operation.

Services to dealer

Illustrations of counter and window displays and other free sales helps are sent with this letter. Just let us know your needs on the enclosed checklist.

Suggestion for credit   You may be interested in our regular credit terms of 2/10, net 30 on future orders. If so, just fill in and return the enclosed form; we will gladly consider your credit application. Also, if you have any ques-

Courtesy   tions with which we might be able to help, just write us. We'll do our best to serve you promptly.

Acknowledgment of Repeat Orders

Most orders come from repeat customers who know and like a firm's products and services, and who don't expect a typewritten letter acknowledgment. Usually the goods can be sent as quickly as an acknowledgment can be mailed. In some cases standard purchase order forms give complete instructions about terms and delivery date, and they stipulate that the buyer will be notified only if the order cannot be filled as requested. In others, an adequate good-news order acknowledgment is an inexpensive (perhaps printed) form, a carbon copy of the shipping invoice, or a postcard as illustrated below. Various rubber stamps enable clerks to insert pertinent comments (such as the one shown here referring to the "will-call").

Though most repeat orders are filled without letter acknowledgments, an unusually large order may occasionally warrant a personalized letter. This message may include appreciation, a statement of how the order is being handled, and perhaps a few cordial comments about your past relationship and future plans to supply the customer's needs.

Granting Favors

Whenever you decide to grant a favor, you have a comparatively easy letter to write. Whether the favor is serving on a committee, speaking without pay at a convention, donating money, or lending your firm's equipment without charge, the good-news plan is the best to use. Usually all you need is the acceptance first, pertinent comments or explanation, and a cordial ending—as in the following letter in which a business executive accepts an appointment:

Acceptance	I will be glad to serve as a panel member on the program of the National (*name*) Association's 198_ regional convention in Chicago.
Comments	The date--March 25--has already been circled on my calendar. Also, my employer warmly approves of this participation. Arrangements have been made so that I can be away from the office three days.
Comments on the assignment and participation	The topic you suggest is one I've been interested in for some time. If they will work in, I might bring several charts which our company has been using this past year with some success. With four members on the panel, however, and one hour allotted to us I know I should limit my comments to no more than 12 minutes, as you suggest. Then we'll have time for questions and answers.
Courtesy	I'm looking forward to working with you and the other panel members toward putting on a stimulating panel discussion.

By following the good-news plan plus the suggestions and cautions discussed in this section, you can also write effectively favorable replies to all other kinds of requests—from customers, employers, employees, friends, government officials, or anyone else.

UNSOLICITED FAVORABLE MESSAGES

The previous section considered messages that are written because someone inquired. This section discusses *unsolicited* favorable and neutral-reaction messages—specifically, announcements and transmittals. Good-news unsolicited messages that congratulate, thank, welcome, and show continuing concern are covered in Chapter 14.

Announcements

Favorable and neutral-reaction announcements should follow the good-news plan—best news or main idea first; then adequate explanation, resale, or educational material; and, finally, the appropriate ending. Some messages combine an announcement with an invitation. How should you classify them? Either way. Whether you call them announcements (discussed in this section) or invitations (Chapter 7), you use the same three-part organizational structure.

Included in this section are group and personal announcements about sales and events; procedures, policies, and responsibilities; and honors and activities of people.

Announcing Sales and Events

Whenever you wish to announce a sale or an event (luncheon, conference, celebration, meeting, or other function) about which you need merely to inform your readers, you can use the good-news plan. The opening paragraph usually includes as many of the five W's as possible.

An excellent way to build and strengthen goodwill with regular customers is to let them know you appreciate them. For example, message 1 announces a sale before newspaper publication.

Message 1

(Letter) *A store's preannouncement to charge customers about a forthcoming sale; a processed form without an inside address or salutation, but with a "Cordially" complimentary close and the signature of the district manager.*

Reason;
best news;
five W's

Because you are a regular (*store name*) customer, we are glad to announce to you a special sale of an unusual collection of spring coat values . . . in one of the Designer Room's greatest coat events. This announcement comes to you now so that you can make your selection during a three-day period before newspaper ads appear.

Displayed items
for emphasis

PREANNOUNCEMENT SELLING
Wednesday, Thursday, and Friday
February 6, 7, and 8
NEW SPRING COATS BY OUR FOREMOST MAKERS
all priced far below regular
$69 $109 $149

Details

FINE COATS FROM OUR BEST MAKERS . . . IN MISSES AND PETITE SIZES. Coats such as you'll see at much higher prices after this great selling. Every one a new, just-arrived 198_ fashion!

EXCITING FASHIONS AND COLORS including white coats, neutrals, and bright colors, town tweeds, dressy and casual styles, various shapes, coats that wrap or button.

Easy action

TAKE ADVANTAGE OF THIS OPPORTUNITY FOR FIRST CHOICE AND SUPER SAVINGS! Come in early...February 6, 7, 8...to choose your coat. Prices will return to regular immediately after this outstanding coat event.

Announcing Procedures, Policies, and Responsibilities

Some business firms commonly use "directives" to announce to employees official statements of company policy, procedures, and employee responsibilities. They provide loose-leaf policy manuals for all employees to file every current directive (usually typed in memo form) and to remove those that are outdated. The manual may cover a wide variety of topics ranging from assigned parking facilities and office hours for employees to policies about salary increases, retirement benefits, overtime, handling inflammable goods, and treatment of customers.

Two cautions to remember when you write directives are: (1) be sure your statements are absolutely clear to all levels of your employees, from the top executive to the part-time janitor, and (2) avoid a bossy or threatening tone. Show confidence that all will cooperate if they understand what they are supposed to do. For example, see request 4, page 180.

Of course, many messages about procedures, policies, and responsibilities are not directives. They can be processed announcement letters to customers (and others) or memos like message 2, to employees. Or they may be individually typed memos—or letters, like message 3.

Message 2

(Memo)   *Announcement to all employees about enrollment for company insurance plans.*

```
TO:        All Kenmore employees  DATE: Feb. 22, 198_
FROM:      John K. Wood, Retirement and
           Insurance Officer[18]                JKW
SUBJECT:   Open Enrollment Period for Company
           Insurance Plans
```

The annual open enrollment period for employee insurance plans will be between March 4 and 27 at the retirement and insurance office. During that time, you may

Why; when; for whom; where; what (itemized)

1. Enroll in medical, life, salary continuation, or accident insurance plans for the first time,
2. Transfer from one basic medical plan to another, or
3. Add previously uninsured dependents to medical insurance plans.

Effective date

Changes and additions made during the open enrollment period will take effect April 1, 198_.

Enclosure; instructions

Please refer to the attached individual Insurance Program Summary, which shows the premiums, company contributions, and payroll deductions for the plans in which you are presently enrolled. Then refer to the rest of the attached material, which explains just what to do if you wish to make changes in your coverage.

Offer of more help

Brochures describing the plans and individual counseling services are available at the retirement and insurance office, 4th floor; or phone extension 9876 if you wish one mailed to you.

---

[18] Some officers omit the FROM line and sign above their typed signature and title at the bottom.

Message 3

(Letter) *A lending officer's message to a new loan customer about payment responsibilities; individually typed. (Salutation: "Dear Mr. and Mrs. Mooney")*

Congratulations; main idea
Several days ago it was our pleasure to congratulate you on your plans to improve your home. Now we are pleased to give you details concerning the loan you received from Central Loan Association to provide the funds you need.

Here is the important data pertaining to your home improvement loan:

Details tabulated for easy reading

Date of loan	May 15, 198_
Amount of loan	$1,349.88
Number of payments	60
Monthly installment	$25.40
First payment begins	June 1, 198_

Offer of further help
Should you have any questions or inquiries as to any of our services, please come in, or just give us a ring at 222-2222. We are always glad to help you.

Though the preceding message is individually typed, it can be based on a guide form, since all paragraphs except the figures and dates in paragraph 2 will be the same for every borrower.

Announcing Honors and Activities of People

To inform employees and customers about promotions, awards, honors, new appointments, retirements, and other recognition-deserving activities of various persons, it is thoughtful to send announcements. The memo below is one way to tell employees of a colleague's promotion to manager.

Message 4

(Memo) *Announcement of an employee's promotion to an office.*

MEMO TO:	All employees Copy to:[19] Richard W. Bram
	Lois Glass
	Elaine B. Wells
FROM:	James T. Camp
DATE:	February 15, 198_
SUBJECT:	<u>Bernard S. Galston</u>, new <u>St. Paul Manager</u>

Best news first
We are very pleased to announce that Bernard S. Galston has been promoted to the position of St. Paul manager. He will be responsible for all aspects of

---

[19] Though the usual position for copy notations is at the end of the message (a double-space under the reference initials), some firms have a standard procedure to indicate the copy routing in the memo heading, especially if the persons receiving copies are officers.

the St. Paul–Minneapolis warehousing and trucking operations.

Details about the new officer

A native of St. Paul, Mr. Galston was graduated from the University of (*name*) in (*year*) with a BA degree in business administration, emphasizing transportation. He has had extensive experience in all phases of transportation and in all phases of our own company's operations. Also, he is a captain in the United States Army Reserve and a member of the National Guard Association.

Suggested action

We know you will all join us in congratulating Mr. Galston on his promotion and in wishing him success in his new position.

A letter of introduction announcing a new field representative who will be calling on customers is often printed on the company's letterhead or on a special card. Another use for this type of letter (individually typewritten, usually) is to introduce a friend or acquaintance to a business executive you know in the city the friend is moving to or visiting.

Message 5

Letter of introduction from a business executive to a business acquaintance.

Full name; why being introduced

This note is to introduce to you Rhoda M. Parker, the daughter of a dear friend and customer of ours. Ms. Parker is doing a survey among business firms in your city. Her interest concerns problems of the small-business executive.

Explanation

She has just finished college and is expecting to enter the Graduate School of Business at the University of (*name in another state*) next fall. In the meantime, Ms. Parker is donating her summer to this voluntary study.

Request; courtesy

I would consider it a great favor if you would give this person a few minutes of your time and open the door for her to meet other business leaders in your community. You'll find her appreciative and bright. Both her father and I will be grateful to you for any courtesy you show to Ms. Parker. I really think you'll find her quite interesting.

Courtesy

The next time you get to our city, give me a call. I'd be delighted to have you as my guest for lunch or dinner.

Transmittals

Transmittals differ from announcements in several ways. Announcements always include an explanation whose main purpose is to convey information. Transmittals may or may not include explanation; their main purpose is to transmit something, which is usually mentioned in the first paragraph. This section discusses two types of transmittals—those without discussion and those with discussion.

Transmittals without Discussion

Many times you will need to mail something, such as a check, document, form, passbook, booklet, or map, to a consumer or a business house. If your action is routine, you can transmit the item without explanation. Such transmittals don't even have to be individually typewritten, or even in the format of a letter. They can merely be in the form of a cordial, short note. Given below is an example of an acceptable processed fill-in transmittal to which a typist adds the missing usual parts.

Transmittal 1

(Processed fill-in form) *Document transmittal letter.*

                    Dear   :

Main idea: SUBJECT: _
transmittal
and reason   We are enclosing the following instruments for
                    your file regarding the above property:

                    ( ) Owner's policy
                    ( ) Warranty deed conveying property to your
List for   name
easy checking   ( ) Cancelled note and deed of trust, loan #___
                         Payable to_____
                    ( ) Copies of closing papers
                    ( )

Courtesy   Thank you for allowing us to be of service to you.

Transmittals with Discussion

When you include discussion in a transmittal, your message may be quite similar to favorable replies to requests.[20] The main difference is that in the transmittal the writer is sending the enclosure of his or her own volition, not because the reader asked for it. These messages may be personally typewritten or processed, depending upon the circumstances. Transmittal 2 is individually typed.

Transmittal 2

Individually typewritten form transmittal of savings certificate's first dividend. (Salutation: "Dear Mr. and Mrs. Briggs")

---

[20] See also the discussion of transmittal letters with reports, Chapter 17.

Best news:
transmittal

Six months have gone by and your savings certificate
has earned its first dividend. Enclosed is a check
for the amount earned.

Explanation;
news of increased
earnings

As agreed, your certificate will be renewed automatically for another six-month period. At the same
time, we are glad to announce that as of January 1,
198_, dividends on savings certificates will be computed at the rate of 6 1/2% instead of 6%. Because
each account is now insured up to $40,000, you might
want to increase your account.

Easy action; thanks

If you wish to purchase another certificate--and saving by mail is more convenient for you--just state
your wishes on the enclosed signature card and mail
it with your check in the postpaid envelope. Thank
you for saving here at State Federal.

Whenever you answer favorably a request or announce news that will be favorable
or neutral to your reader, keep in mind the three-part organizational good-news plan.
The Capsule Checklists on pages 258 to 260 give you a review of both the basic plan
and various adaptations when you answer requests for information, adjustment, credit,
order filling, favors, and when you announce or transmit something.

EXERCISES

Favorable Replies to Inquiries for Information Related to Sales

1. Letters **a** and **b** below are replies to routine, direct requests. Suggest improvements
   where needed in opening and closing paragraphs, you-attitude, and adequacy of
   resale material. Which of the two do you like better? Why?
   a. Individually typed reply from a steam specialty company:

   Gentlemen:

       Replying to your letter of 30 Sept. 198_, please be advised
   that we are mailing to your attention, under separate cover, four
   copies of our current #57 General Catalog describing products of
   our manufacture, at no charge to your company.

       Appreciating your inquiry and hoping to be favored with
   your orders, we remain...

   b. Processed form reply from a clock manufacturer;[21] personalized address and
   salutation:

   Here is the Seth Thomas booklet which you recently requested.

   As you look over the wide variety of styles offered for your
   choice, we are sure you will find the Seth Thomas clock you have

[21] Courtesy of Seth Thomas Clock Company, Thomaston, Connecticut.

always desired--either for your own home or for that certain
someone who appreciates an outstanding gift. There are distinguished period designs, charming colonial reproductions, and
smart moderns for those who appreciate this mode of furnishing.

All clocks illustrated represent the finest in designing achievement and are truly the creations of experts in the craft of fine
clockmaking. Their friendly presence in your home is a tribute
to your appreciation of fine living.

May we suggest that you visit your local Seth Thomas dealer.
Many appliance stores handle Seth Thomas self-starting elec-
trics--while keywound and electrics are offered by better jewelry and department stores.

For gifts that will surely become treasured possessions, select
Seth Thomas clocks--they are always appropriate. And, for finer,
friendlier living in your own home, be sure to choose an authentic Seth Thomas--"The Finest Name in Clocks."

2. The following is the reply a motel manager in a small resort town sent to a young
man who inquired about rates and accommodations. He wrote that he and his wife
were planning a three-week automobile trip and they expected to stay five nights in
the town (Lagina) "sometime in July."

Comment orally on the good and poor qualities of this reply. How many errors
can you find? (The crossed-out words appeared that way on the mailed letter.) Rewrite it so that it is accurate and contains appropriate you-attitude and resale material. Make any necessary assumptions.

Thank you for your postal card regarding rates for Summer.
Our rates for two are $180.00 per week & ~~xxxxxxxx xxxxxxxx~~
Oceanview are $190.00 per week.
These Apartments consist of Bed Sittling room, fully equipped
kitchen, bathroom and Shower and Garage.
We are located in the North section of Lagina about a mile from
the main business District. The market is a block away and we are
about two hundred yards from Crescent Bathing Beach.
We do not allow Pets.
On receipt of $15.00 deposit we will be pleased to reserve the
accomodation you require.
Thanking you for your courtesy, I am,

3. As customer service manager of American Business Forms, Inc., you just received
an inquiry from Mary C. Hunt, Purchasing Agent, Cardinal Machinery Company,
24101 Lakeshore Blvd., Euclid, OH 44123. Ms. Hunt wants to know if your company prints custom stationery (letterhead and envelopes). If so, she would like to
know how a customer submits the design, what types of paper are available, what
your prices are, and how long it will take for delivery.

American Business Forms does sell custom stationery so the customer may be its
own "image maker." The customer may choose a logo from your stock selection
or Cardinal Machinery may submit its own design. (You will accept a sketch or a
printed sample.) The customer has a wide range of choices in paper and ink color.

The best idea is for the customer to send a sketch or sample of the exact letterhead and/or envelope format desired and let you do the rest. Your answer to Ms. Hunt will include a catalog which shows all the choices and the exact prices. You should direct the customer to page 22 for information on custom stationery. Remind the customer that you have a minimum order quantity of 1,000, but prices for larger quantities are discounted.

Make sure that Ms. Hunt knows about the order form and postpaid envelope in the catalog. Also, let her know that orders may be called in on your toll-free number (1-800-527-2678). Finally, your company has a 30-day free trial policy. If, for any reason, a customer is not completely satisfied, she or he need only return the merchandise within 30 days and the payment will be refunded or the invoices canceled.

4. As correspondent for the Patton Electric Products Company, manufacturers of electric mixers, toasters, and other kitchen appliances, you need to answer an inquiry from Mason Electric Company, one of your new distributors in Phoenix, Arizona. They carry your complete line of eight products in their two stores, and they need the free newspaper mats to use in their local advertising campaign and also window display materials. Also, they would like to see a sample of the envelope stuffers (illustrative sales leaflets) that they might enclose with their customers' monthly statements. These leaflets are not free, although of course the one sample you're sending today is free. These colorful leaflets cost $8.80 per thousand but customers get good ideas from them. This is the first inquiry you have had from this new distributor since the welcome letter you sent 10 days ago.

5. Assume you work in the passenger department of Central Airlines, whose planes fly in and out of your city, Houston, Texas. Answer the following letter from Mrs. Matilda Oldtimer, who lives in a rural area about 60 miles north of Houston.

For several years now I've been wanting to get up courage to take an airplane trip from Houston to Los Angeles. I have saved up the money and the bus to downtown Houston goes right by our house. Now I'm 78 and I guess that is supposed to be old. My family has been urging me to come. My favorite grandson is getting married in L.A. and I want to attend his wedding, and I want to go the safest and fastest way. How long does the plane take?

There are a few things I want to know first. I've heard that lots of people get sick on airplanes. I also hear that you serve alcohol and I can't drink anything but milk or tea. I suppose, too, that nothing but cold food is served, and I have to have hot meals. Oh, and one more thing, would we be too high up to see objects on the ground?

If you can clear up these points, I think I'd like to take the trip.

Here are the facts: Fewer people get airsick than get sick in trains or autos. You don't serve cold meals. Hot meals are prepared and served individually by the stewards—not just lunches but full dinners. Also, there is no charge for the meals. You don't serve alcohol free in economy and tourist classes. Champagne cocktails are served free in first-class travel, but for those who don't want champagne, there's tomato or fruit juice. Jet planes between Houston and Los Angeles fly at between

30,000 and 39,000 feet altitude, from which passengers can see the ground when the weather is clear. One stop is made in Phoenix, Arizona—the plane swoops down smoothly before it lands. Scenery is gorgeous along the way. Flying time is about three hours. Airport bus picks up passengers at Sleepeze Hotel in downtown Houston and takes them to the Houston Airport in 35 minutes; the charge one way to the airport is $2.50. Give all the information Mrs. Oldtimer needs to make a reservation. Your goal is to try to encourage her to travel by air *on your line*. Skillfully combine reader-benefit sales talk with your answers to all her questions, implied and stated. Assume any other needed pertinent details.

Favorable Replies to Inquiries for Information Unrelated to Sales

1. *(Memo)* As staff supervisor in the test support division of RMX factory, you have been asked by the personnel department to write your recommendation on Thomas J. Sackman, Clock #3-409. Today is August 31. Your statement about Tom's summer employment will become part of the permanent personnel records. A carbon copy of your memo is to be sent to Janet Bore and Max Taylor, both department heads in your firm. Tom arrived in your department on June 12 this year and was assigned to your most tedious job—#5477 (you can decide what this job is)—which lasted two months. Tom is returning to college next month, as agreed when he was hired in June. Tom reasons well and has the ability to organize his work load. Should he apply for reemployment next summer, you would gladly welcome him into your group. Tom learns quickly and has adapted himself to your methods with minimum difficulty. His attitude, attendance, and cooperation are excellent. He is highly thought of by his lead personnel and supervisors. Write a recommendation, using correct *memo* format.

2. You—personnel manager for Aceline Insurance Company—have just received the night letter telegram in Exercise 1c, page 185, about Patricia M. Monell. Pat worked in your claims department 20 hours a week for two years while attending the university, in the school of business administration. She was meticulously accurate, unusually conscientious, and tactful with customers. Although only a part-time employee, she earned two promotions during the two years. She thrives on responsibility. From the telegram inquiry you don't know what duties she will be expected to do in a quasi-legal position. You do recall that she took three university courses in Business Law, and she happily told you she received two A's and a B. You know no adverse information (except that while working in the claim filing section she dressed quite shabbily; her interest was not in clothing). Write your night letter telegram in 100 words, choosing only pertinent facts. (See footnote 15, page 151, for chargeable words.)

3. Assume that you are a training manager in the XYZ Manufacturing Company, a large, successful firm. A group of managers in your company, during the past year, conducted a survey on various management techniques that had proved to be successful. Much of the information received formed the basis for a booklet on *How to Become an Effective Manager.* Your company has decided to provide additional

funds to the project for printing, postage, and publicizing in order that you can share this information with other companies and distribute the booklet free of charge.

Included in the booklet are tips on motivating employees, enforcing company policy effectively, dealing with employee resistance, flexible time scheduling, and other techniques used by your company's various department and/or division managers.

You have already received a request for the booklet from a training manager in another company who is new on the job. Write a letter to this training manager at the CAC Company and send a copy of the booklet. In addition, offer any help or materials your company can provide.

4. Assume you received from the Big Brother Volunteer Service Organization the same letter that was written to Mr. Willman in Exercise 1b, page 185. Robert Zurbach is one of your best friends. You've known him nine years and have the highest regard for his stability as well as his moral character. Assume pertinent details and perhaps a specific example showing why you believe he would be ideal for giving character guidance to a fatherless boy. Add any other needed details to make your letter complete and effective.

5. You are assistant manager of the loan department of the Central National Bank, your city, and you have received a letter of inquiry from Ms. Helen Mack, Public Relations Director of the National Environmental Council. She is considering Nathan Rohn for a field representative job and asks your recommendation of Rohn, who worked for your bank as a field collector of unpaid loan installments. Rohn's job was to call at debtors' homes and collect their payments which were past due. In the new job he would work with business executives to upgrade environmental conditions.

Nathan worked for your bank from May 16 to December 17 last year and quit on impulse with one week's notice after a disagreement with an immediate supervisor. This supervisor happens to be the strictest of all your supervisors in his collection policies. He insists that every item of property should be promptly repossessed when a debtor is delinquent in his payments. Nathan Rohn, on the contrary, believed in the gentle "soft sell" method. He was pleasant, honest, and extremely patient with customers, often much more so than the supervisor wanted. With one customer in particular, Nathan and the supervisor clashed; it was finally the cause of Nathan's leaving. The customer had borrowed $6,000 to lease a fleet of trucks for an out-of-state construction job. Although he was financially able to pay the monthly installments, he was habitually late; furthermore, he threatened to transfer all his business—including his checking and savings accounts—to a competing bank unless the collection department stopped harping about his late payments. Rohn sided with the customer, arguing that as long as the customer cheerfully paid extra interest on all his late payments and because he always did pay (though late), the bank should "go easy" in its dealings with him, to save his goodwill. One day the supervisor angrily told Rohn to repossess his customer's trucks or quit; Rohn chose the latter, for he refused to compromise what he thought was the right course of action.

When you heard about the incident, you called Nathan back to your office and tactfully told him that his record had been very satisfactory with the bank and you hoped he would reconsider and stay. Nathan's collection record for the six months he was with your bank was second to the top for your 12 collectors in the field. He was exceptionally well liked by customers and fellow employees. Rohn thanked you for your invitation to return and said he would like to; but, because he would have to remain under the same stern supervisor, he thought it best to return fulltime to his university studies and give up the job until another opening might occur the following summer.

Nathan is a sociology and English major at the university, and an ardent supporter of social justice. He spoke occasionally about his desire to do something worthwhile in the community to help improve environment and help the underprivileged. You honestly believe he will be happier in the type of work for which Ms. Mack is considering him. Write a tactful, frank recommendation, after you have sorted out the important and the irrelevant facts.

6. On the top of your incoming mail this morning is a letter from a good friend, Jack "Rooster" Crowe. You have known Rooster for more than 10 years and have sometimes had some doubts about his future in business—he has changed jobs often and has never seemed to make the right kind of advancement.

His letter this morning tells you that he has just quit his job as sales manager of a local firm in order to take a public relations position in a different field of business. Furthermore, his new firm has had more than its share of troubles; Rooster will be spending half his time on the public relations position and the other half on another job (with the same firm), about which he knows little. You are worried, puzzled, and sorry that he has made this sudden change to what he considers a glamorous position.

The letter also asks if you will help him with his communication problems on the new job: letters going outside the firm, speeches before community groups, gimmick advertising (such as calendars), in-house memorandums, and similar items. You are ambivalent about the request because although you really do not have the time, your friendship is such that you want to see Rooster make a success in his new position.

Write to your friend and tell him that you will be willing to help him for a total of two hours a week for the next three months, and for one half day each month after that time. Also tell him that you want this to be a contract position at an annual salary of $1 per year—and stress that as a consultant you will expect him to pay attention to your suggestions and use them unless they differ with company policy or unless you misunderstand the situation.

Make it a tight agreement, but be certain that Rooster understands that you truly want to help him succeed in his new position. Of course, you will also want to congratulate him on the new position and wish him every possible success.

7. Assume you are consumer services director of Stop-and-Save Supermarket, a 20-store chain in your state. Prepare a favorable reply to the following letter from a local teacher who requests an interview.

May I have 30 minutes of your time to conduct an interview to obtain your opinion on consumer reaction to nutritional labeling, and your suggestions for increasing consumer use of nutritional information? The information you provide, along with similar data from consumer affairs specialists employed by the 10 largest supermarket chains in the state, will be used to complete my master's thesis in consumer education at Central State University. Your responses will be confidential, and you will receive a summary of the study within three months.

I can conduct the interview at your convenience during the next 10 days. Please contact me at (216) 226-9675 to complete the arrangements. By cooperating you will improve the caliber of consumer education in our schools and obtain information to help your customers use nutritional labeling to the utmost.

Although you will be leaving town this afternoon to attend a conference, you will be pleased to be interviewed when you return—if that is not too late. Ask the teacher to call you the following Tuesday to set up an interview. Send copies of informational pamphlets your office has prepared for consumers about using nutritional information properly. Also send a copy of your company's most recent annual report which contains an illustrated section on your consumer services office and which may be useful to the writer in his or her research.

Convey a helpful attitude, because you and the management of Shop-and-Save Supermarkets view strengthening relationships with consumer educators as a major objective of your office.

Granting Adjustments

1. Evaluate the following adjustment letters. What do you like and dislike about each? Suggest specific improvements where needed—in the tone, organization, accuracy, and adequacy of explanation and resale.

   a. From the Chicago (head office) Service Department of a national electrical appliances firm to a customer in a city 1,000 miles away. The letter is mimeographed; the customer's name and "Coffeemaster" (at the bottom) are obvious typewritten fill-ins.

   We are concerned with your report about your appliance.* Our service work is guaranteed and if our service person failed to repair the appliance correctly, we want to see that the proper repairs are made without further expense.

   We would suggest that you return the appliance* to us and use the enclosed shipping label on the package so that it will be connected with this correspondence when it arrives here. If we failed to make the correct repairs, we will not only take care of that for you without charge, but we will also pay the postage both ways.

   * Coffeemaster

b. From a manufacturer to a retailer.

Thank you for telling us of the problem you have had with the coats you purchased.

Some time ago, a batch of material having bad formulation escaped detection by our quality control people. The line inspectors caught most of the finished coats before they were invoiced. However, some were shipped. Apparently your order was among them.

The situation has since been corrected and we don't believe you will have this problem with a replacement. Accordingly, a special shipping label is enclosed for returning your defective merchandise to us. It will be promptly exchanged upon receipt. Please let us know if we may be of further service.

2. You are the sales manager of a local hotel which is a member of a large, national chain of hotels and motels—the Hudson Inns. The Harrisburg chapter of the Administrative Management Society (AMS) was host to the annual spring district meeting; approximately 80 officers and spouses were present. The meeting started on Thursday night for the early arrivals, but the main meetings began on Friday and lasted until Saturday noon.

   In making preliminary arrangements the Hudson Inn agreed to provide two suites for the meeting (one for the international president and his wife and one for the district president and her husband) at a special price of $120. As these were connecting suites, with a large meeting room between, complete with meeting tables, a beautiful view, and a wet bar, the price was most attractive.

   The meeting was a success and everything was fine until the final accounting from the Hudson Inn was presented to the Harrisburg chapter. The charge on the suites was $160 and there was also one long distance telephone charge of $2.65 billed to AMS which was made in the afternoon after a member checked out in the morning. The treasurer of the Harrisburg chapter, of course, appealed the two charges.

   As sales manager of the local Hudson Inn, write a letter to Mrs. Bette O'Brien, treasurer of the Harrisburg chapter of AMS, admitting to the error and telling her to disregard the two charges ($40 for the suite and $2.65 for the phone call). Remind her of the excellent facilities, good meals, extra service, and other good reasons for the Harrisburg chapter to use Hudson Inn for another AMS meeting sometime in the future.

3. Assume that two months ago Mrs. Frank Espy, one of your long-time good customers, bought a dual-control, four-slice, chrome-plated electric toaster from your store and asked that it be sent as a wedding anniversary gift to her out-of-state friends, Mr. and Mrs. Robert Giffin. Since then she has found no charge for the $39.50 on her monthly statements from your store; neither has she received a thank you from the Giffins. Last weekend, as a guest at the Giffin home, she noticed they were using the exact toaster she had sent them. To her chagrin they called it their "mystery toaster" because it had reached them c.o.d., although

neither of them had ordered it. Because they needed one, they kept it. Mrs. Espy then told them of her gift. She is furious with your store and wants you to make a proper adjustment immediately. This situation requires two letters—one to the Giffins and one to Mrs. Espy. Will you send her a copy of your message to the Giffins? Also, should your letter to the Giffins mention the refund in the opening paragraph? Why or why not? The salesclerk forgetfully omitted Mrs. Espy's name on the sales slip. Finding only the name and address of the Giffins (who have no account at your store), the shipping department sent the toaster to the Giffins c.o.d.

4. You are adjustment correspondent for the R. L. Buck Co., a mail-order firm with nationwide distribution. Three weeks ago today Mrs. John Morton, of your city, placed an order (in person) for one galvanized steel Tower Climber with flying trapeze (#79 FP 3077, priced $30.99, shipping weight 51 pounds). She wanted your store to send it to her grandson, Donald Brawn, 417 North Sixth Street, Billings, Montana. She paid you $30.99 plus 94 cents sales tax. She left emphatic instructions with your mail-order department to bill *her* for all shipping charges, because at the time the clerk who waited on her could not determine the exact charges to Billings.

   Today you received the following letter from Mr. Dennis Brawn, 417 Sixth Street, Billings, Montana:

   ```
   If the enclosed material exemplifies the efficiency of your op-
   eration, I'm glad I don't patronize your firm! You sent this
   bill to Donald Brawn, our 5-year-old, who can't write you him-
   self.

   Enclosures:
   Order blank
   Due slip for $4.03
   ```

   Across the address on the order blank is clearly written "Send due to customer Mrs. John Morton, 1439 East Spruce Street (your city)." Under the caption "shipping charges" at the bottom of the order blank is another notation: "Send due to cust." Both these notations were made at the time the clerk first took the order. Therefore, it's quite obvious that someone slipped up. Since you want to try to keep the goodwill of Dennis Brawn (he may trade at your Billings store), write a letter trying to erase the bad impression he no doubt has of the efficiency with which your store seems to operate, especially regarding the $4.03 due slip.

5. As assistant manager in the customer service department of A. B. Atle Company, "jewelry's finest craftsmen," in Hartford, Connecticut, you need to answer today (February 3) a special delivery complaint from Olaf Lampson, vice president of Beta Gamma Sigma, business honorary, at the University of Nebraska chapter. He asks what happened to the order he mailed to you almost three months ago (November 5). The chapter needs 35 crested pins for an initiation to be held three weeks from today. Your records show you received his official order and that the pins were shipped to him December 9 by first-class mail. Since the package has not been returned to you unclaimed, you can only assume it was lost in the mail.

Company procedure requires that the customer complete the enclosed insurance affidavit so that you can file a claim and tracer with your insurance company. Upon receipt of the affidavit properly executed, you will immediately enter a no-charge replacement order. Write a goodwill-building adjustment. (This chapter has bought jewelry from you for many years.) You'll rush the pins to reach him before initiation.

6. As circulation manager of the North End News Agency, in your city, answer the complaint in Exercise 7, page 193. Because the newsperson who broke the customer's pane of glass is one of your employees, you assume responsibility and agree to pay for replacement of the living room windowpane. You've also taken the necessary steps to see that the paper deliverers understand how they should deliver papers in the future. Make clear what the customer is to do so that you can pay for the glass promptly.

7. Step into the position of customer service manager of Transcontinental Buslines. Today you are to answer the complaint in Exercise 5, page 193, from the passenger who was left stranded at an unscheduled stop. You are very disturbed about this matter and glad the customer wrote to you. You did not know that this particular driver had left another customer stranded last week. The company has strict rules for bus drivers and for safety of passengers. One of them is that they stop only at scheduled places. Another is that they make sure each passenger is back on the bus when it is time to depart from each stop. This driver is usually very dependable, and he regrets the inconvenience he caused the passenger. Make whatever reasonable adjustment you think will please the passenger. Try to keep goodwill for future trips on your busline. (The passenger also has friends who have heard of the incident.)

8. From Ms. Lillie Jons you (customer service manager) received today a complaint letter that the boots your store sent by mail last week are too small. These boots were on special sale for $28.50. The usual store policy is to accept no returns on special sale merchandise. (This rule is one reason that you can offer goods at such low prices.) However, in this case you will make an exception to the rule because she did not know (and your store did not inform customers) that this style of boot must be larger than for dress shoes. You'll be glad to take the boots back and you will credit her account for $28.50. Ask her to pack them in the same box in which they came and to mail them with your name on the address label. If she wants a larger size, you will send it to her for the sale price.

9. You are correspondent for National Commemorative Stamp Society, Philadelphia, PA 19122, an organization which sells first-day covers and albums. A *first-day cover* is an envelope bearing a commemorative stamp and related illustration postmarked on the first day of issue at a designated post office. Prepare a response to this letter from a novice stamp collector:

> I am returning this album because it is not suitable for my first-day covers. Please credit my account for the $21.40 which I was charged. A copy of the invoice is enclosed.

The album holds my U.S. covers but not my British covers. I
looked through the album catalog again, but I am still not sure
which album would best accommodate all my first-day covers--the
U.S. and British covers I now own and additional future covers I
may purchase which may be of assorted sizes.

What National album would best store my growing collection of
covers of different sizes? Do you have a suggestion?

Indicate that you will credit the customer's account immediately. Even though
the customer received exactly what he ordered, it is National's policy to accept
returns and refund the purchase price if the item is undamaged and does not suit
the collector's needs.

You can give the customer a choice of two suitable albums. One is the Lafayette,
which holds 96 first-day covers in crystal-clear vinyl pockets arranged in two tiers
of 48 covers each. It is bound in tough, simulated Morocco leather, comes with a
matching dustcase, and is available in either blue or chestnut brown. The other is
the Jefferson, a convenient loose-leaf binder with fingertip controls for ease of
opening and 24 clear vinyl pages which will hold 48 covers. It, too, is bound in
simulated Morocco leather in either black or emerald green. Both are described
in the album catalog you are enclosing. The Lafayette is $20.50; the Jefferson,
$13.75.

Make ordering easy. Because this is a relatively new customer, include appropriate resale material about National first-day covers, display albums, and customer
service. Assume any other pertinent details consistent with the facts of the case.

Other Favorable Replies about Credit, First Orders, Favors

1. You are a correspondent in the credit department of the leading department store
   in a city of 100,000 population. Several weeks ago Mrs. Ima Rich wrote you, saying
   she just moved to town from a distant city and wants a credit account with your
   store. In turn, you sent her an application form to fill out because the local credit
   bureau had no information available on Mrs. Rich. She filled out the form and returned it to you promptly. You checked her facts—including the references—and
   find she has an excellent credit reputation. The references complimented her for
   prompt payment throughout the years she traded with them. Your assignment is
   to notify her that you have granted her credit with your store. Assume your department store has the services you'd expect in a city of 100,000. In preparation for
   this assignment, you (or a representative from your class) might want to find out
   what services are available at a comparable department store and also the type of
   message the store sends to an individual like Mrs. Rich.
2. You are credit manager of the National Athletic Supply, Inc., a wholesale firm in
   Bloomington, Illinois. Today (January 25) you approved a credit request from
   Mr. Robert Ramstale, owner-manager of Bob's Sporting Goods in Muncie, Indiana.
   He has ordered:

20 Little League baseball bats, Catalog #BB987	$2.25	$ 45.00
30 baseballs with cork centers, BC 0716	1.75	52.50
10 Deluxe table tennis sets, #TT8106	8.00	80.00
Total		$177.50
Shipping charges		6.50
		$184.00

This is his first order to your firm. It came to you through your field representative, Lana Browne, who reports an exceptionally favorable location of Bob's Sporting Goods—within two blocks of both junior and senior high schools and in the heart of a residential shopping area catering to young families with children. Mr. Ramstale (a college graduate six years ago, majoring in recreation) bought the store three years ago with savings and a small inheritance. Although his capital investment is limited, he is a well-liked manager with progressive ideas. As a former captain of his college football team and as a Little League coach for four years, he is widely known and respected in the community. His character and ethical standards are above reproach. His references report that he has always paid his bills, although often payments have run past the 30-day periods. You decide to grant him credit on your usual 2/10, net 30 terms and to give him a little "education" (tactfully) on what he gains from paying within the discount period. You are setting a credit limit of $200 until you see how well he keeps his account up to date. The items he ordered were sent by Railway Express today; delivery will be within two days. The Little League bats (of white ash) are approved by the American Baseball Association; the Deluxe table tennis sets (with five-ply basswood paddles and sure-grip vinyl handle bindings), as well as the bats, are nationally advertised in *Sports Parade* and *Parents* magazines. You're enclosing with the shipment some counter and window displays, plus the needed order lists and blanks and your new spring catalog.

3. You are sales manager for American Wholesale Office Supplies Mart, Cincinnati, Ohio. Acknowledge a first order from Carson's Office Equipment and Supplies, 898 Second Avenue, Scranton, Pennsylvania. Ms. Julia Carson, owner-manager, has ordered by letter the following from you:

20 cartons of standard mimeograph stencils (MS952)	@ $2.25	$ 45.00
50 reams MP 621 mimeograph paper	@ $2.00	100.00
50 reams easy-erase typing paper EP 632	@ $2.30	115.00
		$260.00

Ms. Carson enclosed her check for $275, saying she was estimating the shipping charges and would forward more if necessary. You must refund the excess paid, because shipping charges are only $9.50. These supplies are being wrapped and shipped tomorrow afternoon by motor freight, and should get to Scranton the next morning. From her order, it appears that Ms. Carson has only your Paper and Duplicating Supplies Catalog. Send her your folder illustrating your new line of other office supplies, which ranges from letter scales and portable envelope sealers to typewriter erasers and 10 different colors of pens and pencils. Can you think of anything else you should send or tell her to make this retailer's future ordering from your firm easy and profitable? (Credit terms to charge customers are 2/10, net 30.)

4. Assume that in the five years since you graduated from college you have become active in the local chapter of a national business organization relating to your major work. (Assume a pertinent name.) Last month you were presented with the "Executive of the Month" award, and a short article appeared about you in this organization's national magazine. Today you receive a complimentary letter and invitation from the president of the organization's chapter in another city (100 miles away) to be dinner guest (6 p.m.) and banquet speaker (20 minutes) on Thursday evening, one month from today. Your spouse or a friend will also be a welcome guest, and the organization will provide for your car expenses and hotel overnight costs. There is no fee for speaking. After thinking the matter over, you decide to accept, even though you must be back at your office at 8 a.m. the next (Friday) morning. The topic suggested for your talk is one that's dear to your heart. Write your pleasant acceptance and make clear any details the president will need to know. Assume any additional necessary facts. The chapter's publicity will go to press 10 days from today, so of course you need to respond fairly soon. The earliest you can get to the banquet is 6:30 p.m.

5. As the credit representative for the Sampson Department Store, your job is to secure new customers and encourage them to accept an unsolicited credit card account with your store.

   You decide to find a new source for customers through your old credit applications which had been turned down for one reason or another according to your store's credit policy. Ms. Carla, a person identified as a prospective credit card customer, is in the group of old credit applications. She had been denied credit in the past because of her irregular payment record at other stores. However, upon recently checking with the credit bureau for her credit history, you discovered that Ms. Carla's credit payment habits have greatly improved.

   Write a letter to the prospective customer informing her that the credit application filed with your store several months ago, and turned down at that time, has been reevaluated. Inform her that the account has already been established in her name. All she needs to do is sign the enclosed form and return it by (date of one week). Explain the terms of the account in your letter as payable in full within 30 days from the date of the billing.

6. As customer relations manager, you have decided to write a personalized form letter that your firm (a chain of retail department stores) can send to each customer who reports that his or her credit card is lost or stolen. Acknowledge receipt of the notification and assure the customer that he or she will be protected, from the date you received it, against loss arising from its use by persons not authorized by the customer. Here is how your new security system works for the customer: You will mail a new set of credit cards to the customer as soon as they can be prepared. They will have a code number after the regular account number, but otherwise they

are the same as before. Once the new cards are received, the customer is to use only these cards and return any remaining old credit cards in an envelope which you have provided.

To reduce possible loss to your firm, you have in the meantime placed a "stop credit" notice on the customer's old credit cards, which means they will be accepted by all stores without question but only for charges under $10 each. The customer should therefore not attempt to make individual purchases larger than $10 between now and the time the new cards are received. The new cards may, of course, be used normally. For the time being, the customer will receive (as before) only one statement from your stores, and it will combine purchases made on both old and new cards. The customer is to examine the sales slips carefully. Should there be any discrepancies, the customer is to return the slips to your office at once for crediting to the account. Let the customer know that you appreciate the opportunity to be of service.

7. Assume you are the newly elected vice president and membership chairperson for your college alumni association. Your first form letter is to the alumni who have paid their membership dues for the current year. Welcome them and express your personal appreciation for their interest and support. Encourage each member to participate fully in the various alumni programs available (name them). Solicit suggestions at any time concerning your association. Address your sample form letter to Harold Harms, 983 Summit Avenue North, your town (city). All future letters you mail to members for this same purpose will have a body identical to the one you write today, but each will be typed on an automatic typewriter and will have a personalized inside address and salutation.

Good-News and Neutral Announcements

1. You have recently been appointed chairperson of your company's employee finance committee. One of your long-time employees—Tom Nielson—will retire September 30 this year after serving the company in various capacities for one-third of a century. For the past two years he has been editor of the employee newsletter, which goes to 100 employees. Known for his witty columns and good-natured humor, Tom is generally well liked. Last month when he returned from a trip to Spain he wrote (and told) ribald mouse stories to the delight of the office grapevine. His enthusiasm for improving the employee newsletter caused him to spend the whole biennial operations budget in the first year, but by special "know-how" he has done well this second year.

To honor his years of dedicated service there will be a reception from 3:30 to 5 p.m. (office hours) in a company meeting room you select. Your committee plans goodies, punch, and a minimum of maudlin speeches. To help "punch up" the punch, pay the caterer, and if possible, present a little token to Tom, you must now write a memo to all "friends of Tom Nielson." Let them decide how much to give, but tactfully set a suggested minimum. Some past and present department chairpersons will perhaps recall how Tom extricated them from problems from time to time. Spouses are welcome, too, at the reception. If you can, add a little light humor to your memo.

2. You are chairperson of the chamber of commerce second annual spring luncheon, and you've been working hard on plans for the past two months. A senator of your state, the Honorable Denise J. Doe, has accepted your invitation to be principal speaker. Because you anticipate that recent events in the state capitol will generate a high level of interest, you have moved the luncheon to a larger room at the local athletic club. You have decided to permit each member to bring one nonmember guest. The purpose of these luncheons is to provide an opportunity to get reacquainted with other business executives in your community and to hear a challenging and provocative message from a prominent public figure. The program this year should provide both. The date is Thursday, May 20, 198_. The total number you can accommodate is 175. Your cutoff date for reservations is May 16. Luncheon will begin at 12 noon. Write the letter announcing this event and make action easy for reservations. Be specific.

3. You are accountant for R&H Distributors. Today (February 28) you have discovered an error you made regarding freight bill #730015, dated November 11 last year, from Howard Carloading Company, 908 Utah Avenue, Salt Lake City, Utah. Through your oversight you have not yet paid this bill, though payment was due last November 18! Your firm tries always to pay its bills on time. It was an honest mistake and you want to apologize for it. You received freight bills 730015 and 72119 from Howard on the same day. Since these two freight bills were identical except for the bill number, you had put them together assuming that one was a copy of the other. You hope this incident will not hinder any future good relations your firm may have with Howard Carloading. Write an appropriate letter with which you transmit your check for the $50.98 that was due 3½ months ago.

4. As assistant manager of the credit department of Morgan Department Stores, you have been looking for ways in which the company can really show its appreciation to its prompt-paying customers. In the past, such customers received, once a year, a computer-printed message on their monthly statements thanking them for their good payment records.

   You have now instituted a more beneficial plan. During December of each year your good credit customers will receive a personalized letter which thanks them for their patronage and the excellent manner in which they have made their payments. The letter also extends them the opportunity to take advantage of your Skip Payment plan. Under this plan the customer may simply skip the monthly payment scheduled for January, thus giving some relief from the expenses associated with the holidays.

   Because of state fair trade laws Morgan will have to assess the normal finance charge for the month, but the account will not be considered delinquent. The charge will simply be added to the customer's balance and will be reflected on the February statement. To take advantage of the plan, the customer needs to do nothing; the finance charge will be computed on the unpaid balance, and regular payments will resume in February. Of course, if customers wish to make their regularly scheduled payments (and avoid the finance charge), they are free to do so.

The letter should end with a holiday greeting and a statement that the company looks forward to serving customers in the coming year. Your superiors have approved the plan and you have been asked to write the letter which will announce the Skip Payment plan to your prompt-paying credit customers.

5. As executive assistant to the president of Topeak Life Insurance, Tulsa, Oklahoma, you have the pleasure of writing an announcement today (March 1) to all Topeak stockholders. (It will be signed by the president.) The board of directors voted to declare a 10 percent stock dividend payable to all stockholders of record on April 15 this year. This is the first stock dividend declared by the company. It can be attributed mainly to the outstanding combined efforts of the board of directors, home office, and field marketing personnel. Since its inception, Topeak has been dedicated to growth, not for the sake of growth alone, but because the company recognizes growth as the primary instrument to be used in building a successful and progressive company. The president feels that stockholders can look upon the company's past growth with justified pride and toward its future growth with great optimism.

Tell the stockholders that if their home address has changed recently, they should notify the home office to prevent delay in receiving dividends. If a stockholder is currently holding Topeak stock which is not in his or her name, the stock should be forwarded to the home office so that a transfer can be made before April 15. Right after that date the dividend will be computed and sent directly to each stockholder of record. The stockholder need not send any verification to the home office. Your announcement is to be a complete form with the same salutation for all recipients.

6. Revise the following memo announcement so it has better you-attitude and more active than passive verbs. Correct any other errors. This company employs both men and women to sell its products.

```
DATE:            March 9, 198_
TO:              Customer Service Personnel
FROM:            Ron M. Jensen
SUBJECT:         Deposit and Cash Receipt Books
```

Effective March 9, 198_, the following changes will be made in the use and care of deposit and cash receipt books by our salesmen:

1. The deposit and/or cash receipt book(s) issued to a salesman will be used only by the client to whom the book is issued.

2. Whenever a deposit or other monies are collected, the salesman will remove from the receipt book(s) the customer's copy(s) and give this to the customer as is now done. In addition, at the end of his shift, each salesman will no longer turn in the reciept book(s) with the money and tickets for those transactions.

3. Deposit and reciept books are not to be left laying around in a vehicle or other places. They are to be under the strict control of the individual the book(s) is issued to.

Normally a salesman will have one deposit book and one cash receipt book. Additional books may be issued by a service supervisor.
All used up books are to be returned to the supervisor for forwarding
to the accounting department.

7. You are employed as assistant director in the school of drama on your campus. At the end of the present academic year (June 5) two popular professors, Anne Hansen and Gloria Sike, have elected to retire after a combined total of 58 years' dedicated service to your university. They have both directed numerous productions in the community and been active in the field of children's drama. The director has asked you to write a letter to their friends (both on and off campus) telling them about a bound volume of letters your school would like to present to each of them. Ask your recipients to send you any letter of appreciation they would like to write to either or both of them—only if they feel moved to do so. They could mention the influence the work of these people had in their own life. Give specifications of the paper size and due date for these messages. Today is May 10, so time is short.

CAPSULE CHECKLISTS FOR GOOD-NEWS MESSAGES

I Good-News (and Neutral): General Plan	II Answering Inquiries for Information Related to Sales	III Answering Inquiries for Information Unrelated to Sales—Letter of Recommendation

1. BEST NEWS
or
MAIN IDEA
	1. Best news or main idea
	  a. Positive opening with
	    one of these:
	    (1) Requested mate-
	       rial
	    (2) Favorable answer
	       to a question
	    (3) Introduction of
	       main idea(s)
	  b. Courtesy; appre-
	    ciation
		1. Best news or main idea
		  a. Applicant's full name
		    and relationship to
		    you; job(s) held
		  b. Reason for writing
		    (by request)

2. EXPLANATION
  a. All necessary
    details
  b. Resale material
  c. Educational
    material
  d. Sales promotion
	2. Explanation
	  a. Answers to all ques-
	    tions—direct or
	    implied
	    (1) Positive, helpful
	       tone
	    (2) Embedded nega-
	       tives
	    (3) Emphasis on
	       what something
	       is, what you can
	       do or have
	    (4) Reader benefits
	    (5) Prices after most
	       selling points
	       (unless price
	       is a bargain)
	  b. Resale (with reader
	    benefits), when
	    appropriate
	  c. Educational material
	    on product use, if
	    pertinent
		2. Explanation
		  a. Answers to all ques-
		    tions—direct or
		    implied
		  b. Best psychological
		    order for threefold
		    responsibility to:
		    (1) Applicant
		    (2) Person considering
		       applicant
		    (3) Your conscience
		  c. Specific facts about
		    (1) Applicant's job,
		       duties, conduct
		    (2) Applicant's work
		       or other habits
		    (3) Personality, etc.
		  d. Honesty and judgment
		    about negatives
		  e. Caution on legal aspects
		  f. Confidentiality
		  g. Offer, phone call

3. POSITIVE, FRIEND-
  LY ENDING
  a. Appreciation
  b. CSAD[1]
  c. EA[2] and motiva-
    tion
  d. Willingness to
    help further
  e. DA[3]
  f. RB[4]
	3. Courteous close
	  a. CSAD[1] (sometimes);
	    itemized steps, if
	    desirable
	  b. EA[2]
	  c. DA[3]
	  d. RB[4] and courtesy;
	    offer of further help,
	    if appropriate
		3. Courteous close
		  a. Candid statement of
		    your personal opinion
		    about applicant's
		    probable fitness for
		    whatever he or she is
		    being considered for
		  b. Positive (not negative)
		    attributes at end

[1] CSAD = clear statement of action desired
[2] EA = easy action
[3] DA = dated action, if desirable
[4] RB = reader benefit

CAPSULE CHECKLISTS FOR GOOD-NEWS MESSAGES

IV Granting Requests for Adjustment		V
Seller at Fault (A)	**Buyer of Another at Fault (B)**	**Approving Credit**

1. Best news
   a. Whatever will please buyer most
   b. Courtesy
	1. Best news or buffer
	   a. Same as IV, 1a
	       or
	   b. Get-in-step-with-reader, courteous comment and concern
		1. Best news
		   a. Credit grant (if no purchase)
		   b. Shipment (if goods ordered)
		     (1) Description
		     (2) Quantity
		     (3) Prices, costs
		     (4) Method, charges
		   c. Courtesy

2. Explanation
   a. Brief resale with tactful explanation of error (if desirable)
   b. Instructions for buyer action, if needed
   c. Concrete resale on firm, services, or goods, if desirable
   d. Cautions
   e. Sales promotion on replacement of returned item(s) or on allied goods
	2. Explanation
	   a. Brief resale with tactful explanation of error, showing seller not at fault
	   b. (If use of 1b above, best news after explanation)
	   c. Concrete resale same as IV, A, 2c
	   d. Cautions
	   e. Sales promotion same as IV, A, 2e
		2. Explanation
		   a. Basis for credit; compliment
		   b. Credit terms; payments, discounts, limits
		   c. Resale on services:
		     (1) *Consumer:* parking, shopping services, departments, conveniences, deliveries, price benefits
		     (2) *Middleman:* warehouses, discounts, selling aids, advertising, guarantees, repairs, deliveries
		   d. Resale on product choices
		   e. Sales promotion?

3. Courteous close
   a. Suggested action and forward look to future pleasant use of goods and services
   b. EA[2]
   c. Positive idea; help
   d. RB[4]
	3. Courteous close
	   a. Same as IV, A, 3 a–d
		3. Courteous close
		   a. Forward look to pleasant service and orders (not greedy)
		   b. Suggested action
		   c. EA[2]
		   d. RB[4]
		   e. Courtesy; suggestion of further help, if pertinent

[1] CSAD = clear statement of action desired
[2] EA = easy action
[3] DA = dated action, if desirable
[4] RB = reader benefit

CAPSULE CHECKLISTS FOR GOOD-NEWS MESSAGES (Continued)

VI Acknowledging First Orders	VII Granting Favors	VIII Announcements	IX Transmittals
1. Best news 　a. Shipment details same as V, 1b (1)–(4) 　b. Thanks for remittance and/or order	1. Best news 　a. Acceptance of favor, request 　b. Courtesy	1. Best news; main idea When appropriate: 　a. Five W's (all or most); reader in first and all other paragraphs 　b. Statement of pleasure, compliment, congratulations 　c. Admission of error, with good news	1. Best news; main idea 　a. Transmittal of specific item(s) 　b. A concise reason 　c. Courtesy
2. Explanation 　a. *For credit customer,* same as V, 2a and b 　b. *For cash or credit:* Resale on services same as V, 2c 　　Resale on products ordered; highlights on special features—adapted to buyer 　c. *For cash customer:* Perhaps credit application form enclosed, with invitation to return it for consideration.	2. Explanation 　a. Pertinent comments, and details regarding favor—what is being or will be done, etc. 　b. Questions, if necessary, pertaining to favor	2. Explanation 　a. Details to emphasize, reader benefits, if possible *In admission of error:* 　b. Explanation apology; emphasis on sincere desire to serve well 　c. Resale on firm, products, or services, as appropriate	2. Explanation, if needed: 　a. Comments 　b. Instructions
3. Courteous close 　a. Forward look to pleasant service and orders (not greedy) 　b. Suggested action 　c. EA[2] 　d. RB[4] 　e. Courtesy, suggestion of further help, if pertinent	3. Courteous close 　a. Cordial, pertinent comment; perhaps a forward look, good wish, compliment, or request	3. Courteous close 　a. CSAD[1] 　b. EA[2] 　c. DA[3] 　d. RB[4] and/or offer of further help 　e. Courtesy	3. Courteous close 　a. CSAD[1] 　b. EA[2] 　c. DA[3] 　d. Offer of further help or other items or RB[4] about items transmitted

[1] CSAD = clear statement of action desired
[2] EA = easy action
[3] DA = dated action, if desirable
[4] RB = reader benefit

chapter

9

Bad-News Messages

Whenever you must write a message that your reader will consider disappointing or unfavorable in some way, the situation requires special planning and careful choice of words. A competent letter writer can actually win or keep a friend for his or her company even when refusing an inquirer's request or transmitting other unfavorable facts.

Most of the bad-news letters and memorandums you may have to write can be grouped under the following unfavorable replies and unfavorable unsolicited messages:

Unfavorable replies

Answering sales-related inquiries when the information is undesirable

Answering nonsales-related inquiries when the information is undesirable

Refusing adjustments on claims and complaints

Refusing credit

Acknowledging orders you can't fill now or at all

Declining requests for favors

Turning down contract or work offers

Unfavorable unsolicited messages

Announcing bad news about prices and/or services

Requiring minimum orders and/or deposits

Penalizing for nonconformity with rules and procedures

Conveying other bad news

This chapter discusses the right attitude for transmitting bad news, suggests plans for bad-news messages, presents various examples of unfavorable replies and unsolicited messages, and provides capsule checklists. Additional illustrations of bad-news messages are in Chapters 12 and 13.

THE RIGHT ATTITUDE

Everything you learned in preceding chapters about the communication process, consideration, and courtesy toward your reader applies to bad-news messages.[1] In such messages it is especially important that the *tone* of your letter be appropriate. Because the right attitude toward your recipient will improve the tone and thus the effectiveness of your letters, keep the following additional suggestions in mind when you write bad-news letters:

[1] See especially pages 24–25 regarding attitudes and opinions, pages 42–50 about consideration, and pages 68–75 about courtesy.

1. *Remember that every letter you write can be considered a sales letter.* You are trying to sell your reader on the idea that your decision, though contrary to his or her request or action, is fair, necessary, and reasonable—and possibly even to his or her advantage in the long run.

2. *Try honestly to see things from the other person's point of view.* A statement such as, "It will be advantageous to you if you work it out this way...." is much more effective than the selfish, "It would be inconvenient for us (or against our policy) to do as you ask."

3. *Avoid leaning on company rules or policy;* it seldom soothes your reader. Include, if possible, the *customer-benefit reasons* that are behind your rules and procedures.

4. *Look for the best in the other person.* Although a customer may be mistaken, try to have confidence that she or he honestly wants to do the right thing. The following expressions show faith in the reader:

```
We are confident that you...
You are probably wondering how you can...
You will agree, I believe, that...
```

5. *When praising a person, single him or her out; when criticizing, put the person in a group.*

   Single out: You certainly made the right decision, Mr. Brown.

   As a group: Sometimes customers, unknowingly, make the wrong decision.

6. *Shield the reader's pride.*

   Tactless: If you had read the instructions I gave you, you would have noticed that they specifically state you had to sign the acceptance form within 30 days.

   Tactful: Our commitment was good for 30 days. In the instructions that you received with the...you will find...

7. *Talk with the reader; do not talk down to him or her.*

   Condescending: We are willing to look into this matter for you.

   Agreeable: Thank you for taking the time to tell us about . . . We always appreciate...

PLANS FOR BAD-NEWS MESSAGES

The underlying purpose of every bad-news message is to present the unpleasant facts with you-attitude—in such a way that the reader will consider you fair and reasonable and, preferably, remain a friend of the organization you represent. Your choice of message plan is influenced by the circumstances—your purpose, your relationship to the reader, and the particular facts in each case. You have two choices of plans: the indirect or the direct.

Indirect Plan

Before you read the suggested indirect pattern for stating bad news, try an experiment on yourself. Suppose you, as a customer, have been waiting for a reply to your request for something you want very much from a business firm—a refund or perhaps a loan important to you. How would you react if the reply began with a negative statement similar to these:

> We regret (are sorry, wish to state) that we are unable to refund the $300 down payment you made on the car.

or

> Your application for a loan (refund) has been denied (refused, rejected).

Wouldn't you feel more receptive toward the firm and its bad news if the reply had opened with at least a brief agreeable statement—like the following—and then presented an explanation *before* the bad news?

> ·We appreciate your letter telling us how you feel about the 198_ hard-top Mercury you purchased from us three months ago.

or

> Thank you for giving us the opportunity to consider your loan application for financing your proposed home purchase.

Most people appreciate hearing at least some explanation before the bad-news decision, especially if it seriously affects them. Usually a good rule to consider is: "Be quick to give good news, but take longer to tell the bad news." Thus, whereas the good-news message uses a direct approach, the bad-news message usually follows the indirect approach. Using this approach, the bad-news plan has the following four-part suggested organizational structure:

---

1. Buffer
2. Explanation and analysis of circumstances
3. Decision—implied or expressed—with resale and/or constructive suggestions
4. Friendly, positive close

Under each part of this bad-news basic pattern you have several alternatives, as shown in the expanded list below.

1. Buffer.

If possible, fill your first paragraph with mainly reader-interest information—to get in step with your reader. However, your buffer must begin close to the general subject of your letter; avoid irrelevant material. Also, avoid statements that might mislead the reader into thinking you are granting the request; such statements merely build the reader up for a sad letdown! Apologies are unwarranted if your firm is not at fault. One or more of the following buffers can help put your reader in a more receptive attitude:

a. *Agreement.* Agree with your reader on something, if possible (perhaps a matter-of-fact comment on which there is general agreement—business conditions, costs, or any other pertinent item).

b. *Appreciation.* Thank the reader (for a check, information, application, request, inquiry, cooperation, or whatever applies).

c. *Assurance.* Assure the reader of careful consideration and explanation of all available facts about the problem.

d. *Compliment.* Try to compliment the reader on something good about his or her past record or request (sincerity, careful listing of all pertinent facts, etc.).

e. *Cooperation.* Show a sincere desire to be as helpful as possible.

f. *Good news.* If you can grant any part of a request and you think your reader will be pleased, begin with that good news.

g. *Neutral courtesy.* Keep your opening paragraph noncommittal. For instance, if you must announce an unfavorable price increase or service decrease, use neutral words such as "needed change."

h. *Resale.* Begin with brief, appropriate resale (on your merchandise, services, or organization).

i. *Sympathy.* Express sympathy—if the matter is very serious and likely to be greatly disappointing to the reader.

j. *Understanding.* Show understanding of the reader's needs and problem (desire to have a dependable product, to pay at least a partial amount due, etc.).

2. **Explanation and Analysis.**

Include honest, convincing reasons why under the circumstances the matter must be handled differently from the way the reader wants it. In two types of situations, however, stating a reason is unnecessary: (1) when the matter is routine and obvious (clerical error) and (2) when you'd get mired in negative or confidential material if you tried to explain. When you decide to include an explanation, place it *before* the decision and remember these suggestions:

a. Try to convince the reader you are acting in his or her best interests in the long run, or at least according to a law that is enforced equally for all. Avoid the insincere: "Much as I would like to . . . however . . ." Also avoid reasons that suggest benefit only to your firm.

b. Explain courteously all pertinent facts behind your decision. Mention first the favorable factors, then the less favorable ones.

c. Don't dodge with such statements as: "Our policy prevents . . ." State, if possible, specific reasons (especially customer-benefit reasons) for your policy.

d. If the reason is confidential or too complicated to explain, then show—as a substitute—that the request has been carefully and sincerely considered (for the reader's benefit as well as your company's).

3. **Decision—Implied or Expressed—with Resale and/or Constructive Suggestions**

Make the decision clear, positive, concise; embed it in favorable material, if possible. You have these alternatives:

    a. If the reasons are so sound that your reader will conclude you *must* refuse the request, payment, or such, you can omit the negative entirely and make the bad-news decision clear by implication. For example, if you are already scheduled as luncheon speaker in Chicago on May 6, omit saying, "Therefore, I cannot attend your luncheon in St. Louis that same day."

    b. If an implied decision might be misunderstood, express your decision briefly and clearly, near the end of the explanation. Be careful never to mislead or cause your reader to be uncertain about your decision. The best place for a negative decision is in the middle—not the beginning—of a paragraph, and never in a paragraph by itself. Avoid "must refuse," "cannot grant," and similar negatives.

    c. If you can, offer a constructive suggestion, state a counterproposal, an alternative course of action, or a ray of hope for the future. By emphasizing what *can* be done, you may clearly imply what can*not* be done, without actually using the negatives. For instance, if you must refuse requested credit, you can offer a layaway plan; instead of a requested personal interview, you can enclose a helpful booklet to answer questions.

    d. If a compromise is desirable, suggest what your firm can do and what the customer can do.

    e. If desirable, resell the reader on your company's services and/or practices and policies.

4. Friendly, Positive Close.

End on a positive note, with one or more of these ideas:

    a. Assure the reader he or she is appreciated as a customer (or as an interested inquirer and possible future customer).

    b. Invite future patronage, cooperation, suggestions, and/or compliance with the decision. Include mild, no-pressure sales promotional material if you think your reader is in the right mood for it. (See page 206.)

    c. If you are awaiting his or her approval or if he or she should take some action, make clear what the customer is to do, when to do it, and how to do it easily. (See Closing Paragraphs, Chapter 5.)

    d. Express continued interest, service, and reader benefit.

Genuine sincerity must underlie whatever words you use to express your message. The writer who has a true feeling of goodwill toward every customer will find it easier to convey a bad-news message effectively and at the same time protect the interests of the company.

Direct Plan

Though you can use the indirect bad-news plan for most unfavorable messages, there are situations that may warrant the direct approach. Again, the choice depends upon the particular circumstances. You may decide to begin directly with the bad news if you have:

A routine or small matter on which the reader is likely not to be seriously disappointed or personally emotionally involved—especially a message between employees of two business firms or within the same firm (and perhaps also to a person who is known to prefer reading the bad news in the first paragraph!).

or

An urgent message that should be called to the reader's attention forcefully—as in the late stages of a collection procedure.

If you use the direct approach, the pattern is essentially the same as the direct good-news plan, except that the opening contains bad instead of good news.

---

1. Bad-news decision (with or without a brief buffer)
2. Explanation
3. Appropriate courteous ending

Most examples of bad-news replies and unsolicited messages in this chapter are organized by the *indirect* approach (hereafter referred to as the bad-news plan). For examples of messages organized according to the direct approach, you will find the words *direct plan* in the title.

UNFAVORABLE REPLIES TO REQUESTS

This section focuses on unfavorable replies to requests for information (sales- and nonsales-related subjects), adjustment, credit, orders, favors, and some kinds of contract offers.[2]

Answering Sales-related Inquiries When the Information Is Undesirable

If you have no honest favorable answer to your reader's direct question(s) regarding catalogs, prices, terms, products, and similar sales-related information, your reply should be organized by the bad-news plan. In some situations all four parts of such a message may be expressed adequately in four or five sentences, as in letter 1.

Letter 1

A concise, helpful bad-news reply about a product the writer's firm does not manufacture.[3]

---

[2] To embed negative material in replies that are chiefly good news, see pages 208–209.
[3] Adapted from a letter by Goodyear Tire and Rubber Co., Akron, Ohio.

Buffer: thanks	Thank you very much for your interesting letter concerning Little Tyke.
Explanation; implied decision	Goodyear does not make rubber sundry items such as balls and toys, and we have no molds with which to make up the item you need for Little Tyke.
Helpful suggestion	Some rubber company specializing in rubber drug sundries may be able to help you. You might try the Miller Rubber Company, Division of Goodrich, in Akron, Ohio.
Pleasant close: good wishes	The best of success to you in finding just what you need for your famous pet.

When the inquiry is about a complex or more serious matter, much more detail may be necessary, especially in the explanation and resale portions. The next example—from the president of a wholesale cement firm to a contractor who had asked why the firm's prices were so high—illustrates how tact and specific details can help to retain a reader's goodwill despite bad news.

Letter 2

A goodwill-retaining bad-news reply to an inquiry about high prices.

Buffer: thanks for inquiry and business	Thank you for your inquiry and concern over the amount we charged you for your concrete. Because your business is very much appreciated and valued highly, it is important to me as well as to you that you understand why we billed you $525.08 instead of $463.13.
Explanation *Decision* *Fairness to all; reader benefit*	Due to the $1.44 hourly employee wage increase, the increase in the price of cement, and overall increases in direct and indirect operating expenses, it was necessary to increase the price of our concrete. For the past 11 months our prices for 5 sacks of our concrete have been $19.90 to individuals and $19.40 to all contractors. If we lower the price to one contractor, all others would rightly expect equal treatment. By maintaining our price, we treat everyone equally and can assure you that you are getting the quality of material you order and expect.
Resale	I realize that you were able to buy concrete at a lower price in the past, but the company that you bought the concrete from is no longer in business just because their price was not sufficient to cover their direct costs and expenses. Neither you nor we would want this condition to happen to us. We are proud of our reputation for quality products and service and want to continue to serve you in the future.

Pleasant close: thanks; further service

Your letters are always welcome. Also, if you have questions or need supplies, please call me between 7:30 a.m. and 5:30 p.m. at 999-3333, or call evenings at 666-6666.

Answering Nonsales-related Inquiries When the Information Is Undesirable

Occasionally you may have to write bad-news answers to nonsales-related inquiries. Whenever you send bad news to anyone outside your firm, it is usually better to follow the bad-news plan.

When you receive a request for a recommendation on a person about whom you have only unfavorable information, and whom you honestly cannot recommend, you have four alternatives:

1. Call the inquirer on the telephone and discuss the matter (with prudence).
2. Write a brief refusal similar to the following:

   On the basis of my experience with Tom Dawson, I am sorry to inform you that I do not have sufficient favorable information to recommend him for the position (credit) for which you are considering him.

3. Omit the applicant's name throughout the reply (use: "the person about whom you inquire in your letter of April 10")[4] and include whatever facts are pertinent regarding employment, credit, or personal record.
4. Include both the applicant's name and an honest, frank report, as in letter 3. Because of libel laws it is imperative to be cautious and scrupulously accurate. (See also the five guidelines on page 215 and Appendix A.) The following letter to a counselor uses the bad-news plan. Notice the first paragraph is basically a buffer of neutral courtesy; it does not reveal the bad news. Only after stating facts does the writer state a decision. This person may become a truly desirable employee with benefit of a counseling service.

Letter 3

A frank confidential nonrecommendation of an unsatisfactory former employee.

Full name; work

Tom Zoe, about whom you inquire, was on our payroll five months--from April 197_ until two months ago. He was hired as a messenger and a sign painter's helper.

---

[4] Omitting the applicant's name is acceptable if you are sure your reader knows whom you are writing about. However, such a practice could be extremely confusing and lead to mix-ups if the same two firms happen to correspond about two or more persons on the same day! Employers who exchange information frequently might set up a file number for each person on whom they seek information. Replies would then be about a file number (known to the employer and respondent as a specific person).

Facts

Because his job with our firm was his first since he quit high school, we tried to be more understanding about his personal problems that affected his work. I must tell you confidentially that Tom had been victimized by unfortunate home experiences which caused him to drift into careless habits from the standpoint of responsibility and reliability.

Unfavorable work

Decision

His attendance record with us shows an average of one absence every six days. As both a messenger and helper he abused rules and privileges. Because each time he promised to do better, we gave him several extra opportunities to straighten himself out. Unfortunately the pattern became worse instead of better and we finally had to replace him. Thus, on the basis of our experience with him, I am sorry I cannot recommend him for responsible work. I am glad to see that he is now getting the help of your counseling service and sincerely hope he will develop right attitudes.

Hope for the future

Perhaps in time he will be able to establish himself with really worthwhile activities. You have my sincere good wishes.

The best overall policy is: be honest, tactful, and aware of your threefold responsibility—to the applicant, to the addressee, and to yourself.

When you're writing to someone in your own organization about a relatively small matter with which the reader is not emotionally involved, you probably should use the *direct* refusal plan, as in the memo below.

Message 4

(Memo) *A bad-news direct-plan memo about company equipment.*

TO: Ann Brown, Purchasing
FROM: Harry Mills, Plant 2
SUBJECT: New ventilating fans needed

Bad news

Today Jake Jones, representative of Ace Electric, told me that the noisy fans you asked about can't be repaired or adjusted again. He says they're a total loss. The only thing possible for ventilation is to buy new fans.

Details

Three fans, model XA22, should do the job well. They'll cost us $80 apiece installed. Jake says he can install these fans this coming Saturday.

Action request

If you approve, I'll go ahead and make arrangements. Jake needs two days' notice, because he'll order what we need from the factory. Will you give me a jingle by Wednesday afternoon?

If your firm is a nonprofit organization that gets large numbers of requests for free information—and if you often need to send bad-news replies—you may, to cut correspondence costs, even devise a form letter listing the most recurring negative facts.

Letter 5

Printed form letter to handle a nonprofit organization's multiple inquiries for which many answers may have to be bad news.

Buffer: thanks

Thank you for your recent inquiry. In the interest of economy your request is being answered by this form letter. Check marks and the comments below indicate the action taken.

Facts; implied decisions

1. The item or information you requested is
    (a) enclosed.
    (b) out of print. Copies are in many librar-
         ies.
    (c) not yet available; (___will be sent later),
         (___related material is enclosed).
    (d) not a publication of this organization.
2. Your request will be filled as soon as our sup-
    ply is replenished.
3. The free supply of this report is exhausted.
    Copies may be purchased from (name and address)
    for ___ cents a copy.
4. Your request has been referred to_____
    _____.

Suggestions for future action

If you write us again in regard to this request, please return the enclosed correspondence, since we have retained no record of it.

                        (Printed name and title of writer)

Comments:

Refusing Adjustments on Claims and Complaints

When you refuse a request for adjustment, realize that the customer is probably disgruntled and even irritated, and be particularly tactful when "selling" on the fairness of your refusal. Especially important material to include—besides your buffer and explanation—is resale material, constructive suggestions, and even sales promotion when appropriate.

This section discusses three kinds of unwarranted customer claims on which you may have to write a refusal: (1) when the customer is at fault regarding a product, (2) when the customer is mistaken in a complaint about an account or a service, and (3) when the customer makes an unjustified policy complaint.

When the Customer Is at Fault Regarding a Product

Often, customers who claim free replacement or repair of a "malfunctioning" product are at fault because they violated instructions for using it. Or a customer might return as "new" an article which cannot be resold because of something the customer did wrong. Also, many customers seek a refund or credit on items simply because they have changed their mind. The next three examples illustrate satisfactory adjustment refusals in such cases.

Misuse of a Product. Notice that in letter 1 the writer calls attention to the user's mistake indirectly and that she shields the reader's pride. She doesn't say, "You violated the instructions" or, "You obviously failed to read the directions." Instead, the message includes a tactful, logical explanation and an implied but clear refusal, followed by a constructive suggestion and easy-action, reader-benefit ending.

Letter 1

A mail-order house refuses to replace free a broken, misused garden hose.

Buffer: agreement, appreciation	When you buy a Widgeon product, you are right to expect high quality. We appreciate your returning the hose for our inspection so that we can meet our goal-- satisfying your needs.
Resale; assurance about honoring guarantee	To provide each of our thousands of Widgeon customers with the specific hose he or she needs, we carry a wide selection. Each type of garden hose described in the Widgeon catalog is guaranteed to give you the service it was designed for. We are always glad to replace a hose provided its defect lies with assembly or materials.
Reason for hose breakdown	As stated in the catalog, the Opaque Plastic Hose you bought is recommended only for use in mild climates and also it is not to be shut off at the nozzle. Since Mount Vernon's weather ranges in temperature annually from −15 to +105°F, you can see how these extremes may have affected the splitting of the hose. Laboratory analysis indicates that the damage was caused by excessive water pressure resulting from either shutting the hose off at the nozzle or from water pressure greater than that normally found in most cities. Because Mt. Vernon has the normal water
Implied refusal	pressure of 60 pounds per square inch, the split occurred because someone shut the hose off at the nozzle.
Constructive suggestion	Two Widgeon hoses--the Gold-Line Plastic and the Neoprene Rubber--are especially recommended for shutting off at the nozzle. In addition, you can use the Neoprene Rubber Hose even in harsh weather. Both are described on the enclosed copy of catalog page 977.

*Easy action;
reader benefit*

After you have decided which hose best meets your
needs, fill out the enclosed order form and mail it
in the envelope with your check or money order for
$9.97 or $11.98, which includes shipping costs; or
indicate that you wish c.o.d. shipment. Either way
you can be watering your garden again just three days
after we receive your order. And you can be sure of
many years' dependable service.

Unsalability of Returned Product. The customer who claims a purchase is no
longer wanted may be trying to return an item he or she has damaged or owned for
so long that the store can no longer resell it. Letter 2 is a retailer's refusal to a consumer; letter 3, a wholesaler's refusal to a new dealer.

Letter 2

*A retail clothing store adjustment manager refuses to accept a returned evening gown
for credit.*

*Buffer: assurance;
thanks*

To please our customers is the foremost aim of Bon-
James. Thank you for writing us explaining your
wishes about the evening gown you purchased here last
month.

*Reader benefit facts
about exchange
policy in general*

We want you and all our other customers to enjoy the
confidence of knowing that any purchase from us is
for merchandise of outstanding quality and style and
that it is absolutely clean, fresh, and new. Wearing
apparel may be returned for full credit anytime within 30 days provided the garment is in clean, resal-
able condition.

Findings in this case

To maintain the high standard on the goods we sell,
we carefully check returned merchandise before it is
again placed for sale. This examination of the gown
you mailed to us disclosed facial makeup at the
neckline and several brown spots near the hemline.

Implied decision

Because cleaning would render the garment "used" to
anyone wishing to repurchase it, the gown is unacceptable for resale.

Helpful suggestions

You can be sure that the skillful touch of our fit-
ter will make the sleeves of your Dior evening gown
just the length you like best. For this reason, we
suggest that you stop in to see Mr. Davis, who served
you when you purchased the gown. He will hold it for
you until you can come in for a fitting; or, if you
want us to send it to you without any changes, he
will arrange its prompt return.

Easy action

Please check and mail your preference on the enclosed
card. You can depend upon us to do everything possible to help you feel pleased with the gown. You
can wear it for several years with confidence that it

Resale

is a highly fashionable evening garment. As you may

recall, it was an outstanding success in the designer show held in New York on June 2.

Letter 3

A wholesaler refuses to accept returned out-of-season clothing from a new small retail shop owner (who started in business six months ago). The letter is dated December 13.

Buffer: courteous, neutral opening

The three suits and two coats which you returned to us arrived today. We appreciate the business you have done with us and, as you are new in the apparel field, we would like to inform you again about our policy of returns.

Explanation about wholesaler require-ments; reader benefit

Women's clothing is highly seasonable merchandise and items move very fast. No wholesale firm accepts re-turned clothing when it is out of season. As we ex-plained in our first letter to you, we must ask that any retailer who may wish to return anything on open order, do so within two weeks of purchase. Such a system of merchandising benefits you in the long run, because you are assured of top quality fashion cloth-ing at lower prices.

Specific facts on this case

Decision

All the five garments we received from you today have been out of our house almost seven weeks. You pur-chased them October 23, when we were selling fall and winter goods. In the present time of year, we in the wholesale business are going entirely into spring merchandise. Thus you will understand why we cannot accept these garments for credit and are returning them to you.

Suggestion

Resale

You will surely find appreciative customers for these suits and coats through a specially advertised sale before Christmas. As they are in popular colors and materials, your customers can get several years of good wear from them.

Future orders; service

When you are ready to select your spring stock, use the handy order blanks in the back of your Marco spring catalog. You can choose from a wide variety of leading spring fashions and expect deliveries within four days after we receive your order.

When the Customer Is Mistaken in a Complaint about an Account or a Service

In addition to refusing adjustments on returned merchandise, you may also have to write bad-news letters to customers who make erroneous claims resulting from a vari-ety of intangible grievances. Among them are unwarranted claims about their account balances and unjustified gripes about various aspects of your firm's service.

Unwarranted Claims about Account Balances. When customers think you have made an error and you find your records are correct, you must give the customers the bad news that they owe more than they claim. Be sure to explain each additional charge clearly, for your readers may have forgotten that a purchase or late charges were added or that some past checks were returned by the bank for various reasons. A tabulation of figures, as in letter 4, or a photostatic copy of the record may be helpful to your customers.

Letter 4

A loan company's credit manager explains why a borrower owes more than she thought.

Buffer: assurance; cooperation

As you requested, I have rechecked all your loan payments back to the first one you made after our company purchased your loan in June 1974. I'm glad to give you this summary so that it will help you reconcile your record with ours.

Your $87 check just received was credited as follows: Interest $1.50 and principal $85.50. The amount still past due is $138.93, made up of the following:

Detailed explanation

1978	August payment missed	$82.93
	October and December payments each short $2	4.00
1979	February payment short	
	March, April, May, June, July, August, September, October payments each short $2	16.00
	December interest	23.00
1980	February payment short $3	3.00
	Balance past due	$138.93

Suggested action

To make payment of this amount easier for you, you may add $11.58 each month for the next 12 months. In this way your monthly payments of $94.51 ($82.93 and $11.58) will help you pay the overdue balance within a year.

Insurance policyholders sometimes make unwarranted requests which the claims department must refuse. In these and similar instances, if you can grant any part of a claim, be sure to begin with that good news. After a positive good-news opening, the reader will be in a better frame of mind to accept whatever refusal is necessary. For instance, compare the following two openings to a policyholder who requested both an $825 refund (which she could not have) and a $55 annual reduction in future premiums (which she could have).

Negative:

We are sorry to inform you that we cannot refund the $825 you have paid us in extra premiums the past 15 years. As you were rated a substandard risk because

of high blood pressure, the additional premium was
mandatory.

Positive:

The good news from our medical examiner's report that
you no longer have high blood pressure now makes you
a standard risk in all respects. We are glad to tell
you that you will no longer need to pay the $55 an-
nual extra premium.

Even if a situation has no good news or alternative, careful organization and wording can help soften the blow. Notice how letter 5 (excessively negative and organized
by the direct plan) can be improved by emphasizing positive ideas and using the indirect plan, as in letter 6.

Letter 5

Direct plan. *A poor, negative liability denial sent by a death benefits division to a
policyholder.*

Bad-news decision

I regret to have to inform you that it is the company's position that no liability exists for this
benefit.[5]

*Negative
explanation*

It cannot be found that we have been furnished with
the due proof required by the policy contract that
death resulted directly and independently of all other causes from bodily injury effected solely through
external, violent, and accidental means. On the
contrary the proof of death furnished by you indicates that death was due solely to disease. Furthermore, the denial of the authorization for examination and autopsy has deprived the company of one
of its rights under the policy contract.

Negative decision

On these grounds liability for double indemnity is
denied. The amount of single indemnity already paid
represents the company's entire liability.

Letter 6

Indirect plan. *Improved revision of letter.*

*Buffer: assurance;
careful consideration*

Your claim for double indemnity has been given careful consideration. Our study included the evidence
you submitted and information obtained by the company through investigation.

The policy provides for the payment of the double
indemnity benefit upon receipt of proof that the

---

[5] Though the blunt bad-news opening in letter 5 was undesirable for the policyholder, a similar
direct opening *could* be used in a memo to the agent or to other employees concerned with the
case.

Explanation of policy's coverage

death of the insured resulted directly and independently of all other causes from bodily injury solely through external, violent, and accidental means; and, furthermore, that double indemnity shall not be payable if the insured's death resulted directly from infirmity of mind or body, illness, or disease.

Facts in this claim

The certificate of death you submitted in support of your claim gave the cause of death as disease. It does not refer to any accident. Moreover, information obtained through our investigation appears to confirm that death was due solely to natural causes. Also, refusal to furnish authorization for an autopsy deprived the company of substantial rights under the policy. In these circumstances, the company denies that it has any liability for double indemnity. I am sorry, Mrs. Smith, that our decision could not be more favorable to you.

Decision

Positive thoughts

The single indemnity payment that you have already received represents the company's entire liability under the policy. I am glad it is of some help to you, and wish you many years of continued good health.

Unjustified Gripes about Company Services. Careful and tactful explanation is desirable to establish your company's accuracy and resell the reader on its usual high-quality service. For instance, the printer who is wrongly accused of misspelling a name on the customer's stationery may have to enclose a copy of the customer's original handwritten order showing the identical spelling.

An unusually knotty problem concerning an unjustified gripe is handled by letter 7. A customer with two teenage sons had told a rug cleaning company's driver that though she had had the rugs 12 years, they had never before been cleaned professionally. The rugs were badly worn and extremely dirty; the cleaner devoted about four times the amount of care and time given the usual carpet. Yet the first time the rugs were delivered to the customer she refused to pay for the cleaning, saying they were "not clean enough." She paid after the second cleaning, but then asked for a refund, saying she was still not satisfied.

Letter 7

A rug cleaner refuses a request for refund.

Buffer: agreeable comment

It is often said that a carpet will more than double the comfort of a room, and a clean carpet does even more. It gives you longer service and is more attractive.

General

Carpet experts agree that the best care for a rug is to have it professionally cleaned about once in three years. The hardest wear and tear on a rug comes from grinding the dirt into it over a period

Educational facts about carpet care

of time. Sometimes it is hard to realize how worn and spotted a rug can become from 12 years of normal wear--especially with growing boys in the family. Some spots and dirt get ground in and just won't yield to even the best cleaning methods, like ours.

Specific facts on cleaning customer's rugs

I well remember your carpets as they were brought in. It was determined by our experts that to give you the best job possible, we would double the time and care given the usual carpet. When your carpets were returned to us, we were somewhat surprised; nevertheless we indicated to you on the phone that we would do the second cleaning free of charge.

More facts about service; resale

Decision

Altogether, your rugs received four times the amount of time and care given the usual carpets, and we only asked that you pay for one cleaning. With experienced workers skilled in modern cleaning and spot-removing processes, we try to satisfy all our customers. Because we have well earned the charge of $56.72 on your rugs--and in fairness to our other customers--we must charge you for an honest, reasonable cleaning job.

Sales promotion; easy action; reader benefit

Please allow us to place your name on our customer calendar, from which we automatically send you a rug cleaning reminder every third year. Just fill in and mail the enclosed postcard if you wish this exclusive service. We are glad to be able to give you free pickup and delivery and prompt, dependable service to keep your rugs in the best of condition through the coming years.

When the Customer Makes Unjustified Policy Complaints

Customers' incorrect complaints about company policies cover a wide range—from prices to employees' activities to merchandise displays. The main purpose of your reply is to explain and justify whatever policies and procedures the complainer finds undesirable, and to resell on your company. The suggestions in this chapter should help you handle such situations effectively, with the bad-news plan.

Often a "soft" answer can not only placate the customer, but even lead to an unexpected happy relationship. For instance, one new customer had the audacity to write a sarcastic complaint to a company president because a welcome letter to the customer referred to his friend, the salesman, as Mr. R. Brown instead of Ragmar Brown. Letter 8 is the courteous reply from the president, Mr. Plumb.

Letter 8

A good-natured reply to a sarcastic policy complaint.

Buffer: agreement; partial explanation

I agree with you that the name R. Brown sounds rather abbreviated. But in preparing these welcome messages to new customers, we abide by the wishes of each field representative concerned. Mr. Brown, in asking us to welcome you, directed us to refer to him as R. Brown.

More explanation

Now, if I had changed R. to Ragmar because I prefer it or because I surmised you might prefer it, then Mr. Brown might have informed me he detests "Ragmar" and thus requests that we use his initial.

A few "human" comments

I'm sorry the abbreviation upset you. You can be sure that "rushing off to a golf course," which you mention, is not within my day's activities. I haven't found how to run a nationwide company and still find time to play golf at all.

Pleasant resale

Please don't feel too unhappy toward us. At least we tried to welcome you as a new customer. I believe you'll even like us as time goes on.

The president's courtesy paid off. The customer wrote a pleasant apology, which ended with this paragraph:

> If you should ever visit my town, I would be honored to have you as my guest at the golf course. I'm going to take up that sport and discontinue writing nasty letters.

Mr. Plumb did visit the customer (Mr. Simpson) one day. The happy ending of this story is that Mr. Simpson later became an employee of the company—as field representative.

When customers write anonymous complaint letters, you usually have no way to reply. However, some business executives receiving anonymous complaints about matters that should be cleared up for all customers run both the complaint and the reply in local newspapers, or even magazines. Among complaints adaptable to such a procedure are, for example, those about store hours ("Why aren't you open evenings and Sundays?") or service ("Why do you have a self-service policy?"). A business executive's display reply underneath such a complaint can be an effective, excellent advertisement, filled with resale, customer-benefit explanations, and sales promotional material.

Refusing Credit

Even when you are refusing a credit application, you want to try to keep the reader's goodwill. A person's credit reputation is quite important. Therefore, a credit manager has responsibilities to make sound, informed decisions. In fact, there are federal laws concerning credit. If someone makes a wrong decision, his or her company could be involved in a lawsuit and unfavorable publicity. A credit manager must be careful about what he or she writes and how reasons are expressed.[6] Refusals of both retail and mercantile credit are organized by the bad-news plan, but since their content can differ, they are grouped separately in the following discussion.

Retail Credit Refusals

For various reasons, approving credit purchases of some customers may be undesirable or impossible. Also, sometimes a customer who has credit established must be told that further credit purchases will be stopped until a current balance is reduced or even paid in full. Other decisions may involve those people who move into the city and want credit immediately; unsettled divorce actions which bring different problems; young people who are just getting started in married life and who may be good risks, but yet have no established credit record; and others.

To an individual consumer, a refusal usually begins with a buffer that refers to the firm's appreciation or careful consideration of the reader's request for credit and/or to his or her interest in the store.

Explanation portions of retail credit refusals vary considerably, but four ways of handling the reasons for refusal are in common use:

1. Reason is omitted entirely (see letter 1).
2. "Insufficient information" is the only reason given (see letter 2).
3. Factors generally considered in evaluating credit applications are stated without indicating specifically which apply to the reader (see letter 3).
4. Specific reasons are stated (see letters 4 and 5).

The first three of these methods can be easily adapted by credit departments that find it necessary to use form letters because of a large number of applications (often over a wide geographic area)—for example, chain stores, national oil companies, travelers' card services. Because of similar names among the thousands of individual requests, mix-ups and errors do occur. Thus credit managers for firms which handle numerous requests find it safer to omit specific reasons, especially those that pertain to undesirable character and poor pay habits. From the customer's standpoint the refusal which omits the reason entirely is the least helpful (although it may save some embarrassment). The "insufficient explanation" reason is considered by some customers to be artificial and insincere; nevertheless both methods 2 and 3 are popular and usually acceptable under certain circumstances, provided the constructive suggestion is tactful and helpful.

Letter 1

No stated reason. An unhelpful retail credit refusal.

Buffer: appreciation   We sincerely appreciate your confidence in us as expressed by your recent credit application.

---

[6] Some credit departments use the telephone for all their refusals. Even if you work in such a department, you will find that you can apply many of the writing principles in this chapter to your oral refusals.

Decision	After careful consideration, we find that at this time it would be better for you to continue your purchases from us on a cash basis.
Forward look (weak)	We hope you will give us frequent opportunities to serve you from our wide selection in each of our stores.

Letter 2

Insufficient-information reason. A popular retail credit refusal inviting a conference as well as cash purchases.[7]

Buffer: thanks	Thank you for the preference you have shown Merrimack's by your application for a charge account.
Explanation: insufficient information *Decision* *Suggestions: conference; cash buying*	As you know, the usual custom before opening a new account is to get information which will serve as a basis for credit. Such information as we have thus far obtained is insufficient (or: does not permit us) to pass favorably upon your request at this time. If you feel there are other details which would favorably affect your credit, you are welcome to call on us so that we can consider all the facts.
Resale	In the meantime, please let us supply your needs on a cash basis. We will make every effort to serve you well with high quality merchandise and friendly service.

Letter 3

List of factors usually considered (general reasons). A popular retail credit refusal inviting reapplication and layaway (with no reference to cash buying).

Buffer: thanks	Thank you . . .
	for your recent inquiry regarding the status of your credit application.
Explanation: list of factors considered	A number of factors are taken into consideration when reviewing an application. Length of time at one residence and employment are of vital importance to us as well as income, assets, age, number of dependents, and the paying record of current and past obligations.
Implied decision; assurance; invitation	You are assured that all the above available information has been carefully analyzed in your case. Circumstances may change in the future, at which time we would be pleased to reconsider your new request for credit.

[7]The last paragraph of letter 2 refers to buying on a cash basis. Because some customers consider this suggestion obvious—maybe even offensive—you can avoid reference to cash by wording the last paragraph in a way similar to that in letter 3.

Invitation to purchase; no mention of cash
In the meantime, we invite you to save on your household and clothing purchases at Ranney's regular everyday low prices and frequent sales. Also, of course, you're welcome to use our easy layaway plan for bigger purchases.

The fourth method of refusing credit—stating specific reasons—is desirable when the following conditions exist:

The situation requires an individually typed reply (as in an application for a large loan).

The reason does not involve poor (dishonest, unreliable) personal character.

The desired relationship between the credit department and the applicant is somewhat personal.

The applicant cannot come for a personal interview and is likely to be offended with anything but an individual helpful letter.

Such letters are usually longer—and harder to write—than the first three types, but when tactful and accurate they are highly appreciated by the recipient because they indicate what must be done to earn (or restore) a good credit standing.

In stating your decision, avoid such negatives as "not able," "did not approve," "unfavorable," "does not meet," "must decline." Instead of stressing what is wrong, suggest (whenever possible) how the situation can be improved. Often you can combine resale and constructive alternatives with either the decision or the ending paragraph. In line with circumstances, the applicant may be invited to take one or more of these steps:

1. Come to an office to discuss the case if he or she has questions or thinks an error has been made
2. Examine his or her record at the credit bureau and write any needed corrections[8]
3. Apply again later when conditions have improved
4. Contact another lender or credit agency that you name
5. Use the layaway plan or another suitable credit plan
6. Continue buying from the company on a cash or c.o.d. basis

The ending usually ties in with one of these suggestions and, if possible, includes a reader benefit. Compare letters 4 and 5 for methods of handling reasons.

Letter 4

Specific reasons: inadequate income. An individually typed loan refusal.

---

[8] See footnote 12, page 226 about functions of city credit bureaus. It is customary that for 30 days after applicants have been refused credit because of a credit bureau report, they can see their report free. But they are charged a fee ($3.50 to $5) if they merely want to check its accuracy. If you are moving from one city to another, it is an excellent idea to check your current report, then request that it be sent to the bureau nearest your new home.

Buffer: compliment; favorable aspects

You are to be complimented on your desire to provide the best possible housing for your family. Also, both your loan application and credit report indicate that you have maintained a steady employment record. This too is commendable.

Explanation: reasoning from general to specific

In mortgage lending, however, extensive studies have revealed that a certain relationship between a person's income, fixed monthly expense, and loan amount should exist to make a loan advisable. Our maximum loan is 2½ times the annual income, or payments may not exceed 20 percent of the monthly income. Since your income at present meets neither of these requirements, you can understand why we feel that an additional financial burden will not serve your best interests.

Reader-benefit decision

Suggestion

If you would like to stop in my office, I will be glad to go over with you the minimum requirements for a smaller loan. This discussion might help you in setting and planning your desired goal for home ownership. As time goes on and your income increases, you will be able to improve your financial position to the point where we can help you buy a newer and larger home.

Future help

Feel welcome to come in any day between 9 and 5. We sincerely want to help you reach your desired goal.

Letter 5

Both general list of reasons and specific reasons. A processed form retail credit refusal by a firm handling a large volume of applications. (Salutation: Dear Customer)

Thanks

Thank you for your recent request for a charge account at Berry's.

Decision

Because of the reasons checked below, we regret that we cannot open an account with you at the present time.

Specific reason(s)

_____under age 18
_____age not indicated on application
_____short time on present job
_____unemployed at present time
_____unable to verify employment
_____application incomplete (returned once to be completed)
_____insufficient information for credit bureau to work with
_____inadequate response from credit references
_____references given are too new to rate
_____overextended
_____no banking

Forward look

When the checked condition is changed, please give us the opportunity to reconsider your application.

Mercantile Credit Refusals

Wholesale or mercantile credit is that which is extended by one business firm to another. The preferred organizational pattern for these credit refusals is the bad-news plan.

For the buffer you have choices similar to those used in retail refusals—appreciation, assurance of careful consideration, brief resale on products or services. If the firm sent an order, refer to it only incidentally, because you are not filling it now and should not detract attention from the main concern—credit.

The most noticeable difference between retail and mercantile credit refusals is that the latter are generally more forthright in the reasons for refusal and are individually typewritten. The decision is based on the firm's financial statement plus other credit ratings (by Dun and Bradstreet, special rating agencies, creditors, and sales agencies of the wholesaler or manufacturer considering the applicant). As with retail credit, the emphasis should be on the positive—the desirable goal—rather than on what is wrong now.

A mercantile credit refusal can include one or more reader-benefit suggestions:

1. Reduction of apparently excessively high inventory by special means
2. Ways to build up customer's volume of sales (and working capital, if pertinent); perhaps offering assistance of your firm's sales representative
3. Advantages of modest buying, local financing, and cash discounts
4. Cash purchases—smaller, more frequent orders
5. Cash on delivery or cash with orders earning discount privilege
6. Review of the applicant's credit situation at a future time

Which of these suggestions do you find in the following refusal?

Letter 6

Credit refusal from a wholesaler to a retailer.

Buffer

Thank you for promptly forwarding the credit information we requested on January 15. The statements provided by trade references are essential to our evaluation of each request for an open account.

Explanation

Without exception, the reports we've received strongly attest to your excellent character and integrity. Information regarding operations of the hardware store, however, has been somewhat less encouraging. The intense local competition you face apparently has had an adverse impact on your profit position. Understandably, meeting existing obligations as they fall due has been no easy task. Though these difficulties are only temporary, any additional credit purchases at this time would increase your obliga-

Implied refusal

tions to an unhealthy level. Of course, we want to do everything possible to help you regain the compet-

itive position that will allow us to arrange an open
account.

Offer of
additional help

I've asked our area representative, Ms. Erica Wittor,
to visit your store and discuss with you the programs
you can use to increase your volume of business. Our
experience with hardware outlets has enabled us to
assist many customers with their merchandising problems. For instance, effective promotion of leader
items can quickly expand store traffic, increase the
turnover rate of general merchandise, and help dis-
pose of excess inventory.

Offer of
additional help

In the meantime you'll need to maintain your stock of
necessary merchandise. By reducing your present
order about one-half, you should be able to obtain
the essential items your store requires. Of course,
you will be entitled to the 2% discount that applies
to all cash purchases.

Friendly, positive
ending

Just use the enclosed order form and mail it in the
envelope provided. Your shipment will be on its way
the same day we receive your instructions.

One good test for any letter is what your reaction to it would have been if you had
received it. Would you feel offended if you were the retailer? Would you buy from the
wholesaler? True, you're not getting credit, but the writer seems sincere and interested
in helping you.

Acknowledging Orders You Can't Fill Now or At All

Whenever you get an order which you cannot fill immediately, your acknowledgment
will be at least temporarily bad news to your customer. The customer is expecting the
goods ordered, and any intervening message from you may delay delivery and cause
some inconvenience. This section discusses bad-news acknowledgments regarding incomplete or vague orders, back orders, substitution orders, and diverted or declined
orders.

Many firms handle routine and repeat orders by preprocessed forms. These are acceptable when the firm sells cataloged, small, or low-profit items and when the situation does not require much detailed explanation. One common timesaving way to
indicate portions of routine orders that cannot be filled as requested is to use rubber-
stamped (or typewritten) comments inserted on printed acknowledgments (like the
stamped S7 comment regarding a substitution in "letter" 1 that follows).

"Letter" 1

*A printed order acknowledgment with stamped comment, used by a national retail
mail-order firm.*

COMPANY NAME OF SELLER		INVOICE NO. ____		
Thank you for your order. It received our careful attention. Any changes necessary in filling your order are explained by stamp impressions or by letters.	Catalog Current Number Price L5021 $3.85	VALUE OF GOODS		
		TAX		
PLEASE DO NOT DESTROY THESE PAPERS until you are satisfied that your order is all right in every respect.	Catalog Current Number Price L5053 $4.95 (S7) OUR SELECTION IS THE NEAREST TO YOUR CHOICE THAT WE CAN FURNISH. IT IS BETTER MERCHANDISE AT NO INCREASE IN PRICE.	SHIPPING CHARGES		
IF YOU WRITE US about this order, please be sure to return ALL these papers with your letter. It will help us give you prompt service.		TOTAL AMOUNT		
IF YOU RETURN ANY PART of this order, please glue the envelope containing these papers and your letter to the outside of the package and apply additional mailing postage for the envelope.	This is the amount charged by the post office for c.o.d. service. The delivering postmaster also collects a fee to pay for the money order sent to us. You can save the c.o.d. fee expense by including total remittance with future orders.	←U.S. MAIL C.O.D.—FEE		
		TOTAL AMOUNT OF C.O.D.		

Though processed form letters are time-savers, they are impersonal and cold. Many times the customer expects or deserves a more detailed explanation. Situations that require personal letters are discussed below.

Incomplete or Vague Orders

If an order that omits necessary information comes from a customer who has never before ordered the items in question, you probably cannot guess what is wanted. It is always better to write (or phone) the customer than to risk errors and annoyance. Your main goal is to keep the customer sold on your goods and to get whatever information is missing so you can fill the order soon.

If the order lists some items that you are sending now, mention them first, of course. If not, begin with a buffer—usually short resale on the product about which the order is incomplete, appreciation for the order, and, if a first order from a customer, welcome. Then, before you request the missing information or payment, state a reader-benefit reason—that you want to be sure to send exactly what will be liked best. Shield the reader's pride by omitting such words as "you forgot" or "you failed to." Be sure to include explanatory facts the customer needs to complete the order, such as sizes or color choice available. Include pictures, catalog numbers, sketches, swatches, and other helpful items when appropriate. Make the action easy and clear for the customer, and assure him or her of prompt shipment (if true), as in letter 2.

Letter 2

Acknowledging an incomplete rush order from a charge customer.

Buffer: resale	You have made a perfect choice in ordering the fashionable three-piece Adrien suit for your vacation. Smart styling, combined with sophisticated simplicity, 'gives you a suit you can wear for many activities in Alaska and elsewhere.
Reader-benefit request	So that we may send you the exact suit you have in mind, let's double check on the style and color. The enclosed leaflet pictures the two models available. You may choose each of these suits in pink,
Facts	aqua, light green, or white. Presently we have your size 12 in all of them.
Easy action	To help you get your reply to us easily and quickly, we are enclosing a telegram order form addressed to us, with spaces for your choices. Just fill in the model number and color you want and wire it to us collect. Your suit will be sent air express the same day we hear from you.
Prompt delivery; resale; courtesy	In less than two days you will be enjoying the use of your smart crease- and soil-resistant, no-iron Adrien for your pleasure in vacationing and traveling. Thank you for giving us this opportunity to serve you.

Often incomplete-order acknowledgments are much shorter—perhaps even postcard size. The opening might omit the resale and begin with "Thank you for your order for . . . ." The second paragraph then states the available sizes (or colors or whatever is pertinent); the last paragraph makes action easy and perhaps states a reader benefit.

Orders for Out-of-Stock Items to Be Back-ordered

If your stock of an ordered item is temporarily depleted and you expect a new shipment within a reasonable time (one or two weeks), you can usually back-order and assume the customer would rather wait than cancel the order.

As with the incomplete-order acknowledgment, your main goal in the back-order letter is to keep the customer sold on your goods and to serve him or her well. Because of the necessary delay in waiting for the return of the out-of-stock item, your message should again be organized by the bad-news plan.

Your buffer can be resale on the ordered item (to reinforce the customer's confidence in her or his choice), appreciation, and (if appropriate) a welcome.

Your explanation should focus on the positive aspects—the date the goods will or can reach the customer. Be sure to omit such negatives as "cannot send," "out of stock," "exhausted," "Won't have any . . . until." Instead, word your idea something like this:

> We will be able to ship these radios to you by May 15, when our re-
> ordered new shipment from the factory is expected here.

Your explanation should preferably include a reason for your being out of the item, so the customer won't think your firm is inefficient. If such reason(s) pertain to high popularity or exceptional demand, this even strengthens your resale and the customer's desire for the item. In your action-getting close, positive suggestion is again useful. The easiest way for the customer to "show" approval of the back order is to take no action. Thus back-order acknowledgments often include the positive:

> Shipment will be made as soon as we receive the new supplies, unless
> you instruct us to the contrary.

If the wait might be unreasonably long, you should ask the customer to let you know (perhaps by an easy-action reply card) whether he or she approves of your shipping on the later date. Your emphasis whenever possible should be on acceptance, not cancellation. Sometimes a bit of sales promotion material on seasonal or related goods is appropriate, if it is included clearly for the customer's benefit—as a service to the customer rather than just another sale for your firm.

A short message such as letter 3 is sufficient on an order for one temporarily out-of-stock item. Letter 4 shows how to mention the same item in a combination order.

Letter 3

Acknowledging an order from a long-time charge customer on an item be be back-ordered.

Buffer: thanks; acknowledgment	Thank you for your order for one dozen Perkup 26-inch Window Fans, at $42 each.
Resale; explanation	The demand for this newest three-speed reversible fan has far exceeded our most optimistic expectations at this time of year, with the result that we have twice reordered from the factory. The manufacturer has assured us that our new supply will be delivered within 10 days.
Decision: expected delivery date; reader benefit	You may plan on receiving a rush shipment of your fans before March 20. Your customers will like the way these automatic thermostatically controlled Perkups enable them to enjoy cool breezes indoors regardless of the heat outdoors.

Letter 4

Acknowledging a combination order that includes an out-of-stock item to be back-ordered for a business firm (long-time charge customer).

Items shipped	The following items you ordered March 8 are being shipped to you today by National Motor Freight:

```
10 Bellman Door Chimes, walnut grain      @ $15.50
 5 Hassock Fans, four-speed, woodtone     @  35.95
```

Resale; explanation on out-of-stock item; expected delivery date

Thank you for your order. You can expect to receive the one dozen top quality Perkup 26-inch Window Fans ($42 each) before March 20. The demand for this newest three-speed reversible fan has far exceeded our most optimistic expectations at this time of year, with the result that we have twice reordered from the factory. The manufacturer has assured us that our new supply will be delivered within 10 days.

Resale

We will rush your fans to you as soon as they reach us, so that you'll have them a good while before the usual hot weather spells in your area. You can assure your customers that these automatic thermostatically controlled Perkups will enable them to enjoy cool breezes indoors regardless of the heat outdoors.

Orders for Out-of-Stock Items on Which You Suggest a Substitute

When you get an order for a certain model or brand that you cannot supply soon enough by back-order or that has been discontinued, you can often suggest a substitute—provided you honestly think it will meet the customer's needs.

Usually it is safer to ask permission to substitute before you ship, as in letter 5, especially if the customer must pay a higher price for the newer line and if the items are breakable or otherwise costly to ship. (Unfortunate shippers who have sent large substitute shipments without permission have sometimes had to pay many dollars in express charges both ways for rejected merchandise returned by a displeased customer.)

Letter 5

Suggesting a substitute in place of an ordered discontinued item.

Buffer: thanks; brand resale

Many thanks for your order on June 27 for a Semco office storage cabinet. You can be sure that your decision to buy a Semco was a decision to buy the finest.

Explanation for new model (substitute)

Early this year, in line with business executives' increasing need for better internal security, the Semco factory came out with a new model storage cabinet, the C-402. Because it has all the features our customers have been asking for, we now stock this model exclusively. Though it's possible that George's Supply in North Center may

Where ordered item might be obtained

still have the model C-302 you ordered, we are sure you will want our newest after you check these improved features of the C-402:

Reader-benefit features of substitute

√ . . . HEAVIER GAUGE STEEL than any other cabinet on the market assures extra heavy duty for extra safety.

√ . . . REINFORCED DOORS and BASE provide added sturdiness.

√ . . . A DEPENDABLE YALE LOCK makes the cabinet tamper-proof for stored articles.

√ . . . ADJUSTABLE SHELVES--six of them--allow easy storage for almost any size supplies.

√ . . . NEW COLORS blend with your office decor: mint green, fog grey, or walnut brown.

Easy action

For all these advantages the C-402 is inexpensively priced at[9] only $94.95 delivered to your office. To give me your "OK" for shipment, just call me at 873-9999 any weekday between 8 and 5. I'll have your new Semco cabinet on its way to you the same day.

Reader-benefit resale

We'll be happy to deliver it on open account, giving you a full 30 days for payment. You'll be glad you bought the newest Semco: C-402.

Letter 5 exemplifies well the desired organization for the substitution letter. Notice that the buffer begins with appreciation and general resale—emphasizing the strongest point of reader appeal that the two articles have in common—the Semco brand. It omits any point of difference (model number, in this case) between ordered and substitute items.

The explanation and bad-news decision stress what the firm *does* have instead of what it does not carry. The new substitute—model C-402—is introduced with one of its merits *before* the bad news that the ordered item—model C-302—is unavailable. One good way to do this is to state that you now stock the substitute *exclusively* (if true), but don't use the word *substitute* in your letter because of its negative connotation. If the substitute is a different brand instead of merely another model of the same brand, do not mention the ordered item by brand name more than once (or at all), because you want the reader to focus attention on your product. However, don't knock your competitor's product; sell your product on its own merits. If you can mention where the ordered product may be obtained, subordinate your statement in a dependent clause, as in letter 5. If the price of the substitute is higher, be sure to state adequate selling points to justify the difference. If your substitute is lower in quality but an excellent value because of price or other reasons, stress these benefits.

Your ending paragraph asks for authorization to send the substitute—or tells why you have already sent it, as in letter 6. Then make clear that the item comes to the customer on trial or subject to approval. Although you are safer to get approval be-

---

[9] Instead of "is inexpensively priced at," you might write, "is well worth the small additional $5," or "is an excellent value even at $5 more than the older model," if you think your reader would appreciate knowing the price difference.

fore sending a substitute, many sellers (such as mail-order firms) substitute quite regularly in orders from repeat customers whose preferences they know. Sometimes substitution is also made in rush orders for very similar same-price inexpensive items or when the company absorbs the price difference. The writer of letter 6 mailed the substitute because it was identical to the customer's order in every way except the print, and he felt sure this buyer would like the one sent.

Letter 6

Sending a substitute before asking permission.

Buffer: thanks	Thank you for your order of May 20 for a Hailani Hawaiian sport shirt, size 40.
Facts about the substitute	We are sending you today by parcel post a Hailani shirt of the same high quality, casual style, and bright colors as the one specified. Though the printed design on the fabric is a little different from the one you described, we feel sure you'll be delighted with it as soon as you see it.
Resale	As you know, one of the distinctive features of Hailani sportswear is the great variety of fascinating exotic prints, with only a few in each size. We are fortunate to have the gay "tropic garden" pattern in your size. It is being sent to you on your
Return privilege	account for your approval, of course, on a money-back guarantee.
Resale	You'll appreciate this wash and wear shirt, we're certain, on many carefree days this summer.

Orders That Must Be Diverted or Declined

Some orders you will have to divert or refuse because the customer has come through the wrong marketing channel, does not meet your standards as to payment or other requirements, or has ordered goods or services that you cannot supply now or ever.

For instance, if your firm is a manufacturer or wholesaler and you cannot sell direct to a consumer, your refusal should preferably keep this consumer's goodwill. Convince the customer to buy your products from your authorized dealers. Your buffer thus will be basically resale, to build the customer's confidence in the choice of product or brand. Your explanation will give reader-benefit reasons for your merchandising policy —stressing how you do market your products (exclusively through authorized dealers) instead of how you don't. Make your refusal clear and combine it with a reader benefit. Among consumer benefits for local dealerships are:

Customer's privilege to see all goods before buying

Faster deliveries

Lower shipping costs—or none

Personal services

Provide for easy action by returning any check the reader sent you and including names and addresses of nearby dealers plus a reassuring statement about them. A last reader-benefit bit of resale will help keep customers sold on the product and encourage them to buy it.

Letter 7

Diverting a consumer's order from the factory to an authorized dealer.

Yes, Ms. Janette,

Buffer: resale

all those nice compliments you've heard about TOWER musical instruments are true. And you're right to insist on buying a TOWER for the first--and every-- guitar you own.

Explanation for local marketing

One of the reasons that so many musicians are en- thusiastic over their TOWER instruments is the spe- cial individual care they received before selecting just the right guitar for their own particular pref- erences. This is why we market all TOWER instru- ments exclusively through authorized music stores instead of by mail from our factory.

Easy action

The name and address of the authorized music shop that handles all TOWER products in your city is:

Polk Music Supply House
422 Broadway East

Reader benefit

Any of their experienced music representatives will gladly show you the different styles and sizes of TOWER guitars. They range from the slim, fast- action flat-top guitars to the mellow-sounding classic-type and electric guitars.

Motivation to action

So that you can select your favorite personally, we are returning your check. Do stop in at Polk's soon--to hear, feel, and buy the TOWER guitar you like best.

Sometimes you must refuse an order because you have no other choice. If you cannot supply the customer's needs now but want him or her to return to you for future orders, you will of course include resale on your product or service. In addi- tion you will mention where the customer can get what he or she urgently needs now— *if* you think such suggestion will be helpful. For instance, a hotel manager can mention to out-of-town customers other hotels (competitors) if her own hotel will be filled dur- ing a certain weekend. However, she should also include some resale on her own hotel and invite the customer to stay there on his next visit to the city. In contrast, the orchard owner in the situation handled by letter 8 finds it both unnecessary and unfeasible to mention where his repeat customer might buy apples elsewhere. Instead, he concentrates on reselling his own apples.

Letter 8

Refusing an order from an orchard's repeat mail-order customer.

Thanks; resale

Thank you for your order of one crate of Wilfred Orchard's red delicious apples. We are pleased that the popularity of our fruit extends into the eastern states to good customers like you.

Resale; reason

Decision

As a steady customer for five years, you understand the care we take in shipping our fruit nationwide. You may have heard that eastern Washington experienced a heavy storm during blossomtime, and an unusually cool summer. As a result, the fruit in our orchards is not up to the quality you have a right to expect. Therefore, I am returning your check at this time.

Forward look; resale

Next year I will notify you when the apple crop is ready. Then you can order the delicious apples you and your friends have enjoyed in the past.

Declining Requests for Favors

Customers, noncustomers, and employees may request various privileges or favors, other than information, which you have to refuse. The bad-news plan is usually the safest to use in most favor refusals. However, in some instances you may use the direct plan, placing the refusal in the first paragraph. This section illustrates a variety of favor refusals, both business-related and personal.

Declining Business-related Favors

Among the numerous favors that customers ask and that you may have to refuse are: changing requirements or payment due dates, transferring from one type of account to another, seeing your firm's confidential material, getting special reduced rates, or skipping several payments on a contract (as handled by the message below).

Message 1

A loan officer refuses a customer's request to skip several loan payments.

Buffer: thanks

Thank you for telling us your viewpoint regarding your loan payments during the summer.

Accommodating customers is one of our main objectives. This service involves fair treatment to

Explanation; appeal to fair play

every borrower with accepted business practice that also protects the investments of our depositors. Exceptions granted to one customer could rightfully be expected of others too, and thus eventually disrupt the entire credit structure. Therefore, the long-established rule is that all payments not made within 10 days of the due date are subject to an added "late payment" charge. When a loan becomes 90 days past due, the law requires that foreclosure action be started.

Implied refusal

Mr. Howe, when you obtained the loan last December, you agreed to repay it in regular monthly payments. Though you were a schoolteacher then there is no indication in our file that you requested any deviation from the usual 12-month payment schedule. Because most of the high school teachers in this area get their salary each of 12 months, we assumed the same was true for you. However, even on a 9-month basis a teacher does know in advance that he will receive no paychecks during the summer. Many other people have little or no advance indication when their source of income will cease.

Reader-benefit suggestion

The enclosed leaflet was prepared for persons who need to allocate earnings over a 12-month period. You will find it useful, I believe. For the present, you will save the late-payment surcharge if your check reaches us by June 10.

Action request

If you feel that mailing your June check before that due date would impose an extreme hardship on you, please call me at 772-7222. At that time we can make an appointment so that we can work out your problem with you.

When you must refuse to lend your company's supplies, premises, or other valuables, you should also use the bad-news plan (see message 2).

Message 2

A tactful goodwill-building refusal to lend a bank's lounge and parking facilities for a Cub Scout area meeting.

Buffer: appreciation; agreement; compliment

Your letter extending us the opportunity to contribute to the activities of your Cub Scout group is warmly received. As a den mother, you surely must share our high esteem for scouting and all it stands for.

Reasons

On November 20, the date of your scheduled meeting, our main office will host a group of visiting bank managers and board members from throughout Illinois, Missouri, and Indiana. Thus, for most of that day our lounge will be filled with business leaders.

Implied refusal

May I suggest, however, an alternative location for your meeting?

Suggestion	When I spoke to my friend, James Scott--building manager of the Lakeside Eagles--about your needs, he said he could offer their hall November 20. The room is large enough to easily accommodate 40 to 50 scouts and chaperones, and parking space is adequate. Mr. Scott suggests that you phone him soon
Easy action	(683-9992) on weekdays between 7 a.m. and 4 p.m. to confirm your plans and discuss necessary details.
Cooperation; good wishes	You may be assured that we at First National are sincere in our desire to help you and your group whenever we can. Best of success always with your group of scouts!

On somewhat routine matters between departments of the same firm it is quite permissible to begin directly with the bad-news decision, as in this memo:

Message 3

(Memo)   Direct plan.   *An acceptable direct-plan refusal of a specification change; message between two departments of a commercial airplane manufacturer.*

	TO: J. R. Lander
	FROM: T. M. Jepson
	SUBJECT: <u>Food</u> <u>and</u> <u>Beverage</u> <u>Elevator</u>
	REFERENCE: RPD-5244-12 dated 6-15-8_
Refusal	As shown on page 5 of the specifications, paneling for elevator walls remains a valid requirement. Thus the referenced request to use paint instead of vinyl paneling is unacceptable.
Explanation	Because of the particular uses for this elevator and the expected altitudes for flights, it is necessary that all walls have the extra protection of the exact vinyl as in the specifications instead of mere coats of paint.
Request	Will you please, therefore, see that the paneling requirement is met, according to specifications?

Declining Nonbusiness and Personal Favors

Requests concerning nonbusiness activities may involve donations of your time, money, property, or other assistance. In refusing a nonbusiness favor, include an appropriate buffer, reason(s) before your decision, and (if possible) a helpful suggestion.

Message 4

A refusal to accept the office of regional director.

Buffer: agreement;	XYZ Club has a great deal to offer businesspeople. I've always found it worthwhile. And so I appreciate

compliment; *appreciation*	even more the compliment you expressed in nominating me for the office of regional director.
Reasons	To perform this job adequately, I realize I should travel to the three State Days this coming year and correspond regularly each month with the 22 chapters in this region, before sending monthly reports to our national office. I've given your invitation a good deal of thought, in the light of my present responsibilities as executive trainee at the ABC Company here. My job requires that I devote long hours
Implied refusal; *emphasis on* *positive*	to the program daily. Often I work Saturdays, too. In addition, Sally and I must spend a great deal of time with our 3-month-old son. Considering everything, I'm convinced the job would be better filled by someone else for the coming year.
Suggestion	If you'd like a suggestion, you might find Herbert J. Smith would be interested in this type of chapter office. He's been active in XYZ for 10 years, two of them as our excellent president. He's an established accountant at the National Gadget Company and is unmarried. Herb enjoys being involved and in my opinion would be a perfect regional director. I'm enclosing a card with Herb's address in case you would like to contact him.
Cordial wishes	You have my best wishes, Jim, for getting the right person. You're doing a terrific job for the organization.

At times you may honestly feel that a request is extremely unreasonable and you're tempted to tell the reader so. If you must get some negative thoughts off your chest, go ahead and write the grumpy letter. But don't mail it immediately. Chances are that the next day you'll decide to soften the tone (which writer of message 5 didn't do but should have done, as in message 6).

Message 5

Tactless refusal from a manager of a marketing research firm to a college student.[10]

I have your request for advice and booklets regarding the practices and experiences of this company in consumer research and market testing. You list seven questions, each of which is so broad in scope that an adequate answer would require at least a written chapter. A comprehensive answer to all seven questions would comprise a thesis on marketing research. I would like to ask you a few questions:

---

[10] Though message 5 (which was actually mailed) is not tactful, its questions may deserve serious consideration by those who seek detailed information. Requests like "Please give us information about all the goods you sell" are so broad that they are impossible to fulfill.

1. Do students think a manufacturing company has any responsibility to contribute to their education? Do they think the company should help students prepare their thesis for the sake of building goodwill? or for the sake of securing a possible future customer?

2. If an affirmative answer is given to #1, what do students regard as a reasonable amount of cooperation?
    a. To check a few "Yes" or "No" questions?
    b. To furnish available and pertinent literature if available?
    c. To write a dissertation for them on one subject? on seven subjects?
    d. To write a thesis for them?
    e. To teach them by mail?

3. Do university instructors advise their students to request commercial companies to contribute their knowledge of market research to the students? You ask: "What effect do consumers' desires and needs have on the adoption of specifications and designs for a product?" Is this not in your textbook, or can it not be answered by your instructor?

4. How do university instructors think commercial companies would justify the time and expense involved in writing educational material for students in answer to specific but broad-scope questions?

You need not answer the above questions nor reply to this letter. My questions are rhetorical and I have no intention of writing a reply to your questions. My contribution to your education is this letter, and in my opinion it should be more valuable to you than an answer to your questions would be.

Message 6

An improved version of message 5.

Buffer: thanks	Thank you for your interest in our practices and experiences in consumer research and market testing.
Desire to help	We definitely want to share with you this requested information, and it's possible to do so if you limit yourself to specific questions which permit answering in a few minutes. A questionnaire form that allows us to fill in answers seems to be the best format. The seven questions you submitted to us are so broad in scope that each one requires a lengthy reply to cover the subject adequately.
Decision	
Alternate	
Suggested action; reader benefit	Please send your one- or two-page questionnaire to Mrs. Michael Leach, vice president of research in our organization. She is our authority on consumer research and market testing. Since she will not be

starting on her three-week survey trip for another
month, she will probably have time to fill out and
mail your material to you the same day she hears
from you.

Turning Down Contract or Work Offers

Grouped in this category are the refusals you may have to write to business firms,
clubs, and individuals that propose various jobs and services for a fee. Letter 1 illustrates a refusal to enter a bid on a business firm's project; letter 2 turns down a nonprofit organization's idea for raising money. Both use the bad-news plan. Refusals
by and to individual job applicants are covered in Chapter 12. Letters of resignation
are discussed in the section on bad-news announcements, pages 305–306.

Letter 1

Declining to bid on a construction job.

Buffer	Thank you for the opportunity to bid on the plumb-ing work for the 50 homes in the Highland Park development.
Reason *Refusal*	Because of other large commitments we have lined up for the coming year, our time schedule is such that we must reluctantly pass up the opportunity to compete on your job this time.
Suggestion; cordial close	Please keep us on your list for your next project. Best wishes for your satisfactory completion of the Highland Park plan in time for occupancy next fall.

Letter 2

*Refusing a nonprofit organization's proposal to earn funds by subcontracting services
for an out-of-state management corporation. (Letter was mailed to the president of a
university business honorary. Salutation is "Dear Ed.")*

Buffer	We appreciate very much your letter inquiring about the possibility that Milton Management Corporation might be able to subcontract some of our handwork through your chapter.
Explanation	Ed, if we were to ship any of our large mailings to your city from St. Louis in order for your chapter to complete the necessary work, we would encounter many difficulties. To give you an example, an annual report mailing for Milton funds weighs approximately 18 tons. You might also be interested to know that we no longer mail our annual and semiannual reports in envelopes because of the terrific expense involved with hand-stuffing. We now pack each report in a polyethylene bag electronically sealed, thus saving us a considerable amount of money each year.

Refusal	I do want to assure you that your request for obtaining work from our corporation has been given very careful consideration; but because of the distance involved between our home office and your university, it is not feasible. You might contact some of your larger printing companies or firms that do mailings in your local area and subcontract work from them.
Suggestions	You might also consider such fund raising projects as tuition dances, car washes, or bingo games.
Forward look	With your good leadership and your chapter's cooperation, you will surely reach your very commendable goal.

UNFAVORABLE UNSOLICITED MESSAGES

You may sometimes have to send unpleasant messages which are not in response to an inquiry. This section illustrates unfavorable announcements about prices and services, orders and deposits, rules and procedures, plus miscellaneous bad news. You are generally wise to use the bad-news plan whenever you think your readers will be seriously disappointed or even angered by your bad news. However, when you write to employees or other business associates on routine matters, you may use the direct plan.

Announcing Bad News about Prices and/or Services

When your firm finds it necessary to increase prices and/or curtail services to customers, a buffer opening followed by reasons before the unhappy decision will help break the news gently, as in message 1.

Message 1

A clear, acceptable announcement by a wholesaler, regarding limitations in services.

Buffer: neutral courtesy	In reviewing 198_ business and trying to plan for a future in which we can continue to give you good service, it has become evident that some modifications must be made.
Reasons	Our problems are not unlike yours or anyone else's in business today. All items of expense in business have been constantly increasing without a corresponding increase in profit margin on goods and services.
Decision	Rather than increase prices in general, the following changes as an alternate plan will become effective July 1 this year:
Details on the decision	(1) Free local delivery will be continued only on orders of at least $15. Orders for a lesser amount, if received by 1 p.m. can be delivered the next business day by United Parcel Service or can be sent by our regular delivery service if the customer wishes; but the actual cost of this service will be added to the invoice.

(2) Out-of-town shipments will continue to be
shipped as instructed by the customer, or instead
of instructions, will be routed by the least expensive of Parcel Post, United Parcel Service, or Auto
Freight. Actual shipping costs will be added to the
invoice.

(3) Collect telephone calls will be accepted only
in cases where we have been in error.

Fairness to customers; courteous invitation

A decision on these three changes was made after a
very careful analysis of our costs in relation to
service. We are sure you will agree that these
changes are minimal and fair to our customers. If
you have any suggestions on how we may improve our
service to you, we will greatly appreciate your
writing or calling us right now.

In contrast to the *buffer openings* of message 1, to customers, you can use *bad-news direct-approach openings* similar to the following when you announce the same decisions in *memos* to your employees. The first is an opening for a memo about a laundry's increased prices:

Because of increased costs of all materials and operations, TRIM now
finds it necessary to increase prices of laundry services. The following new prices will go into effect for all customers May 1, 198_.

And an opening for a memo about the wholesaler's limited services might be:

So that Gray's can continue to give good service without a general
increase in prices to our customers, the following restrictions in
delivery and telephone services will become effective July 1 this
year.

Even for employees, however, you should follow the bad-news plan and begin with a buffer when they are likely to be personally affected or seriously disappointed by your bad-news decision. Suppose, for instance, that your company management has decided to close the employee cafeteria food service mornings and evenings and to keep it open only during noon hours. To partially offset this decrease and to provide for changing employee food preferences, the snack bar service will be increased. Message 2 illustrates a poor way to announce these changes to employees; message 3, a good way. Notice the difference even in subject lines.

Message 2

(Memo)   Direct plan. *A poor negative, incomplete bad-news announcement to employees about decreased cafeteria service.*

TO: All employees of ABC   January 25, 198_
FROM: Karen Whitson, Food Services Director
SUBJECT: Closing of Cafeteria for Breakfasts and
          Suppers

Starting next Monday, February 1, there will be no
more breakfasts or suppers served in the cafeteria.

This facility will hereafter be closed every morning and afternoon. Lunches will be served in the cafeteria only between 11 a.m. and 2 p.m.

However, to provide continuing service to our employees, the snack bar will be open from 8 a.m. to 5:45 p.m. and offer a wider selection of food.

Message 3

(Memo)   Indirect plan.   *An improved version of the preceding bad-news announcement to employees.*

TO: All employees of ABC   January 25, 198_
FROM: Karen Whitson, Food Services Director
SUBJECT: <u>Changes in Company Snack Bar and Cafeteria
          Service</u>

*Buffer:
reader-benefit;
noncommittal
statement*

To keep food prices at their present level, in spite of rising costs, and to meet your changing needs--the snack bar and cafeteria services will be modified <u>starting</u> <u>Monday</u>, <u>February 1.</u>

Reasons

Changes are necessary because during the past three years fewer employees have been eating breakfasts and suppers in the cafeteria and costs of operating it have steadily increased. So that you can contin-

Employee benefits

ue to benefit from both low prices and good-quality food, we are altering the services and we believe you will like them.

*Decision: favorable
changes first*

<u>Snack Bar Services</u>--The snack bar will be expanded to offer a wider selection of food than ever before. From the semi-self-service counter and the vending machines you can choose:

Packaged Cereals	Fruits and Juices	Sandwiches
Doughnuts	Soft Drinks	Hamburgers
Rolls	Ice Cream	Salads
Coffee, Tea, Milk	Pies and Cakes	Potato Chips
Hot Chocolate	Candy Bars	Soup

*Decision: emphasis
on the positive*

<u>Cafeteria Service</u>--Each day a lunch special consisting of a hot main course, salad, dessert, and drink will be served, as before, for less than $2. The cafeteria will serve only lunches.

<u>New Hours</u>--The new hours effective February 1 are:
Snack Bar   -   8 a.m. - 5:45 p.m.
Cafeteria   -   11 a.m. - 2:00 p.m.

Employee benefits

In addition, the cafeteria doors will remain open between 8 a.m. and 6 p.m. for those of you wishing a meeting place during work breaks or to enjoy food brought from home or the snack bar.

You are invited to use these facilities whenever you can. They are available to you at no extra price on

Forward look:
employee benefits;
invited action

snacks or lunches. If you have any suggestions on
the new cafeteria or snack bar services, please jot
them on a slip of paper and drop them into the suggestion box, at the cafeteria door.

Occasionally for a relatively small matter, you can put across a bad-news decision
effectively by using good-natured humor:

Message 4

(Memo) Direct plan. *Humorous price-rise announcement to employees.*

TO: All employees   Date: December 2, 198_
FROM: Cafeteria Management
SUBJECT: An Invitation to a "Funeral Service"

Sad(?) news

On Friday, January 30, 198_, your company cafeteria
will bury a very dear servant, a veteran of 20 years
whom most of you enjoy every day.

Details

There will be no music, no solemn ovations, no (we
hope) violent outbursts of emotion. Instead, there
will be FREE COFFEE for everyone in the cafeteria
during the lunch period, January 30. We hope you
will attend the last rites of the 20 cent cup of
coffee. On Monday, October 3, the price will rise
to 25 cents. It has been decided that coffee ser-

Decision

vice should no longer be subsidized, and the current
cost of producing and selling a cup of coffee is
more than 20 cents.

A happy thought

We're sorry. We loved that 20 cent cup of coffee
too. But here is a cheery thought: Your pennies
still buy more when you use them in your company
cafeteria!

Requiring Minimum Orders and/or Deposits

At times you may need to tell a customer that he or she must either give your firm
more business or lose former privileges. For instance, a manufacturer may require his
authorized distributors to sell at least a certain minimum amount or lose their fran-
chise; a retailer may discontinue sending free catalogs if she does not receive orders; a
publisher may want to cut costs by decreasing the length of his "free" mailing list; and
a bank may have to announce bad news about minimum balances on dormant savings
accounts. For such messages the bad-news plan is advisable. Letter 1 erroneously follows the direct plan, while letter 2 correctly uses a buffer.

Letter 1

Direct plan. *A poor bad-news announcement from a large producer of fully prepared*
baking mixes to a wholesale firm.

We are sorry to see that your business with us has fallen down so that it does not pay to have you on our books any more, as we can only afford to have accounts on our books who sell merchandise right along.

We appreciate the Alaskan situation where it is seasonal buying, but your business has fallen off so that now there is practically nothing.

We would appreciate a line from you as to whether you think you could build this business up, or whether it would be best for all concerned for us to discontinue your company as one of our jobbers.

Will you please advise us by return mail so we will know what to do?

Letter 2

Indirect, bad-news plan. *An improved version of letter 1 (asking a wholesaler to increase his orders or drop off the list).*

Buffer: favorable past

In the past five years we have had the pleasure of filling your orders for prepared baking mixes. We have also appreciated the prompt manner in which you have always paid your account.

Explanation; minimums; reasons

When you first started trading with us, we extended jobbers' prices to you--on the condition that a minimum amount of merchandise be bought during the year. Setting our price structure on this minimum for jobbers enables us to sell at lower prices. In spite of seasonal buying from Alaskan customers, you have in the past sold the product well.

Concern; implied bad-news decision

Because during the last year your purchases fell far short of the agreed minimum of $300, we are concerned about ways that we might help you, rather than assigning your territory to another jobber. Pasty Cake Mixes are nationally advertised to help create a demand at grocery stores, and orders should be flowing your way. Homemakers use cake mixes the year 'round. Perhaps you would like to work out with our representative, Barbara Hempstead, a special plan adapted to your particular situation. During the

Suggestions

busy summer season your volume could be higher to offset the decreased size of orders during the slack winter months.

Requested action

Will you please let us know, in the enclosed envelope, within a week if you plan to continue to represent Pasty Cake Mixes? We want to have your firm distribute our products provided you meet your jobber's quota regularly.

Penalizing for Nonconformity with Rules or Procedures

Announcements about penalties for deviating from required procedures or disregarding previous notices quite often begin with the bad news. The direct plan should be used especially when the situation is urgent or when the writer wants the reader to be sure to read the main idea, as in this letter:

Dear Saver:

Main idea

A new federal ruling will drastically affect the status of your inactive account #111-1111.

Explanation

Effective August 28 of this year, federal regulations governing our operations were revised regarding a service charge on inactive savings accounts of less than $10. We are now permitted to charge $1 each year to maintain each account that has not been used in the last three years. As you realize, this minimum charge permits an association to just about break even financially in maintaining these small inactive accounts year after year.

Decision

Suggestion

May I suggest that you arrange to convert your account into an active one before (*date*) so that you earn a high 5% dividend with complete safety of your money. By doing so, you also avoid the $1 yearly charge on an inactive account. But, if you do not wish to add to this account, then you should close it immediately to avoid this charge.

Pleasant close

Please come in or call me at 222-2222 if you have any question concerning your account. We are here to serve you.

Conveying Other Bad News

You may have to write other bad-news unsolicited (and solicited) messages. As a rule, you can handle most of them well by the bad-news plan.

However, one exception to the usual rule for customer bad-news letters is when you must announce that you made a mistake which is not in the customer's favor. In such cases it is often better to admit your error in the opening, as in the next example.

Letter 1

Announcement of an error that unfavorably affects the reader.

*Tactful lead
to bad news*

We always appreciate the opportunity to be of service to our customers, but I'm sorry to tell you that last month we did you--and ourselves--a disservice.

Details

The correct amount of your February, 198_ premium was $125.61, and we billed you for only $120.55, a difference of $5.06.

We overlooked the difference in insurance premium between your former policy and the new policy, which
has given you additional coverage since January 1.

Request;
easy action

May we ask you to sign the attached form and send it
to us with your check for $5.06? Just slip it into
the enclosed envelope and mail it.

Goodwill

You can be sure we'll do our best to see that you get
accurate service in the future.

The letter of resignation is another bad-news announcement you may have to write.
Whether you resign from a job for which you have been paid or from an elective office, you consider your reader(s) and your relationship to them before you decide to
organize by the direct or indirect plan. Your letter should include your reason for resigning (ill health, better position, or whatever), appreciation and pleasant comments
about the people you are leaving, perhaps a statement of regret, a definite effective
date for the resignation, and a sincere, cordial ending. The following two letters of
resignation are both well written. In letter 2 the writer felt that the busy board of
directors would prefer reading the main idea (though it is bad news) in the first paragraph. Letter 3 gives the bad news *after* the reasons.

Letter 2

A direct-plan letter of resignation (to a board of directors).

Main idea:
bad news

With much reluctance and regret I must ask to be released from my position of state director of civil
defense.

Reason

Because I have developed a heart condition, my doctors have instructed me to move on a slow bell and
particularly emphasized my giving up civil defense.
While the condition is not dangerous at present, it
is of the "warning" type.

Pleasant comments

Date of resignation

As you may guess, this is pretty much of a blow to
me, but it isn't smart to ignore the advice of our
doctors. During the past four years I've greatly
enjoyed working with the many fine people of our
state organization. It is thus difficult for me to
request that you accept my resignation to become
effective immediately after your next month's board
meeting.

Good wishes

I'm convinced of the importance of our civil defense cause and assure you that my good wishes will
continue to go with you and the great work you are
doing.

Letter 3

*An indirect-plan resignation (to a college senior's employer, for whom he worked five
years); dated May 1.*

Buffer: agreeable statement	Just as each business must chart its course for the future, so must every individual ask: Where am I going and where do I want to be 15 years from now?
Appreciation	Over the past five years I have given serious thought to these questions. I will always remember how much your company has meant to me. You have given me not only valuable experience and a sense of perspective, but also work and earnings that helped pay my expenses through the university. As
Reason	both you and I realize, however, my chances for long-run advancement necessary to satisfy my goals are limited here at Ace Sign Company.
Reason	To make full use of my college training and in an effort to provide better benefits to my family, I am accepting a position in the finance department of the International Products in (*city*). As my reporting date will be June 11, please consider this resigna-
Resignation	tion to be effective June 5. In the meantime I am willing to work any necessary overtime, at no additional cost to you, to ensure an effective transition for my successor here.
Cordial close	Again, thank you for your many kindnesses during the years I have worked in your firm. I hope that you and all my coworkers at Ace will continue to be my personal friends in the years ahead.

In summary, whenever you must write unfavorable news—whether you are replying to a request or initiating an unsolicited message—you are usually safe to follow the indirect, four-part bad-news plan. If you use the direct plan, be sure that the type of message, the situation, and the relationship between yourself and your reader warrant that approach. The Capsule Checklists on pages 323–327 review both plans (column 1) and adapt the indirect plan to 10 kinds of bad-news messages.

EXERCISES

Answering Inquiries When the Information is Undesirable

1. Your new assistant has just laid on your desk the following letter he wrote (to a long-time customer) for your signature as customer service manager of your firm, Research Consultants. He admits he hasn't had much training in letter writing and says he'd appreciate your comments on his attempt. You decide to rewrite this one for him and let him compare the two versions of this bad-news message. Improve the letter in every way you can—especially the organization and you-attitude. Emphasize positive instead of negative aspects, and maintain goodwill toward your firm. Because you aim to assist this good customer as much as possible, you have asked your staff to contact other sources in addition to your own company files. Those sources may have some materials on plans that do fall into the class the customer discussed. As soon as they have something definite, you will write the customer again.

```
I am sorry to say that, unfortunately, our editors did not find any-
thing in our plan files that would apply to your problem regarding
pension plan summaries for trade association staff employees.

We have also not yet found any plan elsewhere that would fall into
the class you discussed.

I wonder if, when you looked through the reports, you did not notice
that there is a pension plan for the Employee Association League of
New York State?  I found this plan on pages 106-112.  I am not cer-
tain whether this is the type of plan you are interested in.
```

2. As purchasing assistant for a national life insurance company, answer Ms. Linda Mond's courteous request for literature about attitudes of drivers. She needs this material for a speech she will give at a community meeting of taxpayers. Your company does not handle any other insurance except life insurance. Therefore you do not have any material which will help her. What constructive suggestion(s) can you add to aid her? Can you name two or three firms that specialize in accident or car insurance? State and local law enforcement officers may also have useful information.

3. The following letter from a national manufacturer of party favors has several weaknesses. Rewrite it (to Tim White, chairperson of a college football banquet) to improve it in every way you can. Assume additional pertinent facts, if necessary, and try to be more helpful to this banquet chairperson. He wants individual souvenirs ("about 2 or 3 inches wide") to use as favors or place cards for the 250 persons expected to attend the banquet, five weeks from today. Although your factory does not have any such souvenirs in stock, you do manufacture special items to order. All you need is a design and three to four weeks' time; your skilled workers turn out really attractive novelties. Assume that your reader (the chairperson) lives 2,000 miles from your factory. Time is short. It is possible that the L. G. Baldwin Company (a retail supplier about 1,000 miles from Tim White's city) may have football souvenirs in stock. What can you say to be helpful?

```
Dear Sir:

We have pleasure in acknowledging your letter of 20 September con-
cerning your inquiry about small individual football souvenirs for
your banquet.  Though we note that you had been advised by Marcus
Company to approach us in this connection, we are sorry to inform
you that we do not have football novelties and thus cannot supply
the material which you need.

We regret we cannot be of service to you for this occasion.
```

Refusing Adjustments on Claims and Complaints

1. As consumer service assistant manager of the Bleachex Company, in Worcester, Mass., you have today received a complaint from Mrs. R. A. Layton, of Spokane, Washington. She writes that after using your Bleachex liquid to remove a stain from her new white nylon car seat belt, she found the belt turned "an ugly yel-

low." She wants you to pay the $10 for a new belt. However, from her description of the yellow discoloration, it appears that the nylon had been treated with a resin (for soil resistance and "body") that is not compatible with any dry or liquid chlorine bleach. Your label states that Bleachex removes fruit, vegetable, etc., stains from washable cotton, linen, nylon, and other synthetic materials. But you do not advocate Bleachex for stain removal unless the entire item can be immersed in the properly mixed solution and then rinsed well, which is important to stop the bleach action. Thus, Bleachex should not be used on a car seat belt because of the inconvenience of removing the belt and all metal trimmings before immersing the material in the right solution. Though you can't guarantee 100 percent results, she may wish to immerse the belt for a few minutes in a solution of 1 gallon water, 2 tablespoonfuls of sodium sulfite (from a drugstore or photo supply shop), and ½ cup of white vinegar, and then rinse thoroughly. Although you must refuse her claim, make your reply tactful, helpful, and positive.

2. You are customer service director for the telephone company in your region. One of the letters you must write today is a refusal to Sam Winter, a student at Central Community College (about 50 miles from your office). Here is his letter:

> The enclosed bill from you for $78.80 contains long-distance calls that I won't pay for. Apparently someone in your office got numbers screwed up and charged my account instead of someone else's. I know I made eight of the calls on this bill, but the other two I didn't make. I don't know anyone in those towns and therefore I refuse to pay the $17.95 charges on them.
>
> Your bill says I supposedly made those calls on March 19. Well, that day I'm sure I didn't make any long-distance calls, because I was busy planning for the little celebration party I had that same night. It was a special event. I didn't see anyone using my phone that night, either. Anyway, whoever made the calls should have to pay for them, not me.
>
> Enclosed is my check for $60.85, which I think is in full payment of what I owe you.

Your operations staff members have thoroughly investigated this claim. Your highly accurate equipment registers every call—whether it is directly dialed, or placed through an operator as a collect call. If it is the latter, the operator makes a definite, written report on each call. The two calls Mr. Winter questions were placed at 9:30 p.m. and 10:05 p.m. March 19; each was directly dialed; one was 16 minutes long, $8.10, and the other, 21 minutes, $9.85. The number from which these calls originated is definitely that of Sam Winter. As every phone book states near the front under "long-distance information and rates," any calls dialed must be billed to the number from which the call is made. Thus Sam must pay for the entire bill, including the $17.95 unpaid balance. Can you include one or two helpful suggestions for him? (Perhaps, now that he knows the date, time, town, length of each call, and the cost of each, he should check among his March 19 guests to see who placed the calls.) Your staff even checked all equipment and operations records, and found no equipment problems recorded for March 19.

Write Sam Winter a tactful refusal that will keep his goodwill and, you hope, get his full payment before your company has to disconnect his telephone! Remember to emphasize positive aspects.

3. You are the manager of the adjustment and claims department in a small department store with a relatively low volume of business. Therefore, it is the store's unwritten policy to grant few refunds and replacements on items returned 30 days after purchase.

    A customer, Mr. David Farmer, recently returned a sweater with which he was dissatisfied. The sweater was red knit, size 42, and contained a label which indicated that the sweater was wash and wear but must be washed by hand using a mild detergent. Mr. Farmer decided to return the red sweater because after he had washed it in his washing machine, using the wash and wear cycle, the sweater would no longer fit. He had no record of when it was purchased because he had misplaced his sales slip. However, when he came to the store, he stated that he bought the sweater over two months ago. He also indicated that he had washed it on several occasions, using the wash and wear cycle on his washing machine. The sweater, as returned, now appeared to be a size 40 instead of a size 42.

    The customer argued that the label on the sweater said wash and wear and that the store should be accountable. The settlement was not made when the customer came into the store, but you promised to respond to him in writing in a few days.

    Write a letter to Mr. Farmer refusing the request for a refund or a free replacement on the knit sweater, because the instructions said specifically to wash the sweater by hand and with a mild detergent. You believe the garment was not properly laundered. However, provide some other alternatives in your reply so that Mr. Farmer will be inclined to forget about the requested adjustment. You might offer an inducement such as an invitation to a special customer sale or a discount on another purchase.

4. Assume that you are customer service department manager of the Ketchum and Pleasam Department Store, in your city. Today you get a letter from Mrs. James Gleason, 919 North 20th Street, in a small town about 20 miles from your store. Attached to her letter is a package containing three pairs of ($7.50 each) faded blue jeans that she bought from your store when she was there in person. She describes exactly from which of your basement departments she bought the jeans, and she's right. Her complaint is that they have shrunk and faded so that she will not wear them. She wants you to send, without extra charge, three pairs of sanforized navy blue jeans that won't shrink or fade. She complains that she's surprised your store's merchandise doesn't stand washing.

    Here are the facts: To meet the demands of the numerous young people who insist on wearing jeans skintight, who prefer to cut them off at odd places, and who want them to look "grubby" soon, you carry a special brand that pleases these customers. On the counter at several places are signs stating: "These jeans are guaranteed to shrink and fade!" This is the counter from which Mrs. Gleason bought her jeans. Clearly, she just didn't read or see the signs, and you can't be responsible for her error. From your third-floor sports department you can send her three pairs of Topco brand sanforized navy blue jeans ($8.50 each) in her size, and they're guaranteed *not* to shrink. Of course, she'll have to pay for them. If your instructor approves, you may suggest a compromise to Mrs. Gleason; perhaps she won't suffer a complete loss on the faded jeans she returned. If you make no compromise, be sure to return the unwanted jeans and add a constructive suggestion.

5. As adjustment department manager of Otis Radio Company, manufacturers of portable radios, you need to write a refusal letter today to Mr. Swen Swenson. He sent his portable Bike Radio #95432 to you for repair because it ceased to function. He enclosed a copy of his $17.95 purchase slip dated six months ago and asks that you repair the radio free because the year is "not yet up." He lost the guarantee, but assumes it was for one year. Actually, however, these radios were guaranteed—on workmanship and materials—for 90 days. During that time you gladly make all repairs free of charge. However, since the guarantee period expired on this radio three months ago, Mr. Swenson will have to pay the $16.95 repair charges. You can get the radio into like-new condition.

Because your newest tiny portable radio costs only $18.95, you wonder if he wouldn't rather purchase the newer one instead of repairing his own. This new radio is guaranteed for one year. Though it is a little smaller than his present radio, its large controls assure adequate volume and tuning. The high-impact case clamps on the handlebar easily; it fits most bikes. It uses only one 9-volt battery. Though battery costs (50 cents) usually are extra, you would send one free of charge, if he should wish this new radio. Do not in any way high-pressure him, however; he'd be $2 ahead if he chooses to keep his present radio. But the new one is solid-state AM; measures just 5 x 6 x 2 inches; weighs less than 1 pound; and it can be detached from the handlebars and used as a portable to carry indoors whenever he wishes. It is your factory's newest model, and, you think, it's the best you have turned out for this low price. Write the letter that will be truly helpful to this customer, who must choose between paying $16.95 repairs or $18.95 for a new radio, even though he had thought all repairs would be free.

6. Your firm repairs cameras and electronic equipment. One of your out-of-town customers sent you for repair a GRAPHLIX camera, Model 512, bearing the serial number 59866. She claims the camera is defective and asks for free repairs, because she has had it only six months on a one-year guarantee. Examination shows that the camera is not defective, but it has been dropped and badly misused. These repairs are needed: replace broken lens, $35; repair range finder, $6.50; repair and readjust electronic eye, $5. These repairs will put the camera in first-class shape; it cost originally $165. Write to the customer, Ms. Jean A. Morton, letting her know why she will have to pay for these repairs. You are customer service manager. Your guarantee accompanying all cameras states they are guaranteed for workmanship and materials under normal operating (use) conditions, but *not* when immersed in water, dropped, or given other unusual "shock" treatment.

7. A customer returned his Superfonic automatic record changer, Model 940, for service to Stereo Outfitters, in your city. He wants the phono needle replaced and the turntable mechanism checked for speed fluctuations. The changer, which was purchased 18 months ago, is covered by a 24-month limited warranty, which states in part: "This warranty does not cover the cabinet, plastic parts, or phono stylus furnished with the set."

Your service technicians have examined the changer and determined that only one of the required repairs is within the scope of the warranty. As service manager, write the customer, notifying him that the deteriorating sound quality was caused by normal wear of the phono stylus. A new needle can be installed for $28.25, including labor. The replacement stylus also incorporates technical improvements which result in a noticeable improvement in sound quality over the original-equipment stylus. Try to imply clearly the bad-news decision.

Tell the customer that the speed fluctuations were caused by a defective drive mechanism which can be repaired under warranty terms. Interweave resale, on turntable quality, throughout the letter. Convince the customer that $28.25 is a small investment to return his record changer to like-new condition. Make it easy and convenient for the customer to indicate his instructions.

8. As head of the accounting department of Duro Business Forms Company, you have the responsibility of handling customer complaints. Today you received a request for an adjustment from Mr. James B. Olsen, Manager, Atco Produce Company, 1635 Ventner Blvd., Dallas, TX 75221. Mr. Olsen stated that he had just received a shipment of 3,000 voucher checks from Duro Business Forms.

Voucher checks are prenumbered bank checks with a voucher form attached, and a perforation between the check and the voucher. The check portion of the form has the company's name and address, the bank's name and address, a space for the amount of the check to be written in numerals, a space for the amount to be written out, a space for an authorized signature, and the MICR (magnetic ink character recognition) bank and customer code printed at the bottom. The voucher portion contains space for listing the check number, a description of the payment, invoice numbers, and similar information. The payee detaches the voucher portion before depositing the check.

Mr. Olsen states that the preprinted MICR code on his order is incorrect. The MICR code on the checks carries the bank's identification number and the company's bank account number. The bank account number for Atco Produce Company is 0138-0660-9. The MICR code printed on the checks was 0139-0660-9. Mr. Olsen asks that you replace the order free of charge, as Duro Business Forms made a mistake in the printing. The cost of the order of 3,000 checks was $145.20, including postage.

You routinely keep a copy of all orders for business forms, so you located Mr. Olsen's original order form. The bank account number which was typed on the order form was clearly 0139-0660-9. Thus, the error was not yours, but that of Mr. Olsen and/or his typist. You printed the number which was on the order, so reprinting the checks free of charge is out of the question.

However, you wish to keep Atco Produce as a customer. You can offer to reprint the checks with the correct account number at a 40 percent discount. The reason you can print the checks at this price is because you already have all the information, which was printed on Mr. Olsen's checks, on a computer tape. Your company has computerized type setting, and you normally retain the information from each printing job for 30 days in case of error or if the customer should want to reorder immediately. The job could be rerun quickly and inexpensively.

Write a letter to Mr. Olsen in which you must refuse his request for an adjustment. Enclose a copy of his original order form. Offer to reprint the checks with the correct bank account number at the discount noted above. Also, Duro will pay the postage for the new checks. Tell Mr. Olsen what he should do to let you know his decision.

Refusing Credit

1. Mr. and Mrs. James A. Self, 1444 Northwood Lane, Putnam, OR 97752, have been your credit customers for the five years they have lived in your city. Their account shows that average monthly purchases are about $50 and until two years ago their account was almost always paid on time. During the past two years, however, the payments have not been made when due. The account balance is now more than $500 and no payments have been received for four months.

In your today's mail was a letter from Mrs. Self which said that she had tried to purchase some furniture last week and the salesclerk told her that the items could not be charged. She left the store in an angry mood, and this letter from her is the result. Among all the things mentioned in the letter are two which are of importance: (1) she threatened to take the matter up with the local better business bureau and the local credit bureau; and (2) she said that she would never again purchase anything at your store.

Write to Mrs. Self and explain, in a tactful manner, why her recent credit purchase was turned down. Remind her, for example, of the current balance in the account; of the credit terms that she agreed to when the account was first opened; that neither the better business bureau nor the credit bureau will take any action, because your store has broken no laws; and anything else that will support your position. You will not, of course, resort to threats but will encourage immediate payment of the account so it can be reopened for her future convenience.

You will also want to include, as best you can, some statement of goodwill or concerning her future as a customer of your store. This is not, of course, the time to try to sell her anything; but you can remind her of the quality products you sell, the several convenient locations in the area shopping centers, the customer announcements which go out several days before sales are announced to the general public, and similar points. Tact and firmness are both important, but so is your effort to regain the Self family's goodwill.

2. As credit manager of a national oil company, you receive hundreds of applications for credit cards. One refusal which you must write often is to young people under legal age. Draft a goodwill-building form letter (which can be processed) to handle

such refusals. If the applicant could get an adult who would be willing to guarantee his or her account, you'd do your best to accommodate. Enclose a necessary form together with a second credit card application. The guarantor is to sign both forms and the applicant is to return them to you with a reference to his or her original application.

3. You are the assistant credit manager of Hammond-Bradley Plumbing Supply Company, wholesalers of bathroom fixtures and plumbing hardware. Compose a credit refusal to Mr. George Radden, owner of Reliable Plumbing and Heating, 19527 Clifton Boulevard, Lakewood, OH 44107.

   After examining the business's financial statements, credit ratings from Dun and Bradstreet and the credit bureau of Cleveland, and reports from two of Reliable's creditors, you must tactfully deny the credit application because of a slow open account payment record and the firm's low working capital ratio. Reliable has been making an average of $250 cash purchases monthly, and you want to keep them as a cash customer. You also feel that in a year or two the company may have improved its credit worthiness to meet your credit standards.

   Carefully consider these factors and use the most appropriate organizational pattern—direct or indirect. Provide several reader-benefit suggestions for strengthening Reliable's credit eligibility. Assume, as needed, other pertinent and realistic facts regarding Reliable's financial position.

4. You are the manager of a wholesale fabric business. You distribute fabrics to many stores in your state. You allow them 30 to 90 days to pay for goods and sometimes longer if necessary. Just recently you have run into a very difficult situation. You extended credit to one small fabric shop that was run by a very personable fellow, Mr. Greenfab. He has come in several times to your warehouse and ordered and picked up fabric. He seems quite at home with all the personnel in your company and everybody likes him. For these reasons, when he was unable to pay his bill in 90 days, you gave him an indefinite extension. He continued to place orders and his bill has become larger and larger. It has now been a year since he has paid for anything. Of course part of the blame is yours for letting it go on as it did, but you have decided that you can no longer extend credit to this man until he starts paying his past bill. You had explained that you had to stop credit and he said he understood, but when he called up on what he termed "emergency" situations, you always said, "Well, only this time." The situation is now out of hand, and you want your money. Decide on a course of action and write an effective letter.

5. As credit manager of the Fair Department Store, you have received a credit application from Mrs. George Bann, who seems to be doing a noble job of making the family ends meet on her $550 monthly wages. She and her husband and four children rent a $95-a-month cottage. Her husband has been unable to work for three months because of illness, but he hopes to get a job within two or three more months. You honestly feel that a charge account is not what this family should have now. Unexpected emergencies in their financial position could cause

them serious problems. Cash purchasing from your complete catalog, where they pay as they go, lets them know where they stand at any time. Also you have end-of-month sales regularly, with savings up to 50 percent. Send Mrs. Bann a catalog supplement with all the news about your sales. Perhaps when Mr. Bann is working you will reconsider her application for your monthly payment plan. Make your letter specific and genuinely helpful.

6. During the past 16 months you, credit manager of Eastern Building Materials, Inc., have noticed that Mr. Malcolm Build—a contractor customer of yours—has been running later and later in his payments. Instead of discounting his bills each month (paying them within 10 days and receiving 2 percent discount) as he had always done previously, he has been taking the full 30 days and longer. In fact, the last seven payments have been 60 to 90 days late. You realize that many buyers in the construction industry have been experiencing higher operating costs and fewer contracts. Nevertheless, it is essential to keep accounts receivable current. You must refuse to sell any more materials to Mr. Build on credit until his past statements are paid up and his financial condition has improved. Hopefully, this is only a temporary situation. Suggest smaller orders and cash payments—with the 2 percent discount to help him reestablish his former excellent credit standing. Have you any other suggestions to show that you want to cooperate with him?

7. For a credit refusal on a retailer's first order, see Exercise 14, pages 506-507.

Acknowledging Orders You Can't Fill Now or At All

Incomplete Orders

1. As customer service representative for Diller Department Store, Los Angeles, CA 90014, you have today (Tuesday, June 8) received an order from Ms. Rose Fair-well, 135 Third Street, Gardena, CA 90247. She writes that last Saturday evening on her way to a theater in Los Angeles, she happened to pass your store windows on the west side. In the center window she saw a pantsuit that she would like you to send her in size 12: in "white and blue. I think the price was $69.50; just charge it to my account. It's just the thing I'd like to take with me on a trip; we'll be leaving Tuesday, June 15. Will you please send it to reach me no later than Monday?" In checking with your window decorator, you learn that six pantsuits were displayed in the center-west window last Saturday. Worse yet, three of them were in blue and white: (1) horizontal stripes in the jacket top, with navy blue slacks, (2) vertical stripes for both the jacket and slacks, and (3) light blue jacket with navy trim on the collar, and white slacks. Which does she want? Your secretary tried today to reach her by phone, but discovered that Ms. Fairwell has either an unlisted number or no phone. You must now write her a letter which goes in the 5 p.m. mail pickup and should reach her tomorrow or Thursday morning. If she will get her answer to you by no later than Friday noon, you can be sure to send the right suit to her on the store delivery truck Monday morning. Devise easy

action for Ms. Fairwell, and also make sure you will get all the information you need to fill her order immediately.

2. From Mr. Sylvester Camp, assistant manager, Midwest Marine and Pool Supply, 910 Jetson Avenue, Detroit, MI 48214, you receive an order for:

10 Boarding ladders, 3 steps	@ $9.50 each
50 ft. #6314 Marine Mat and Dock Runner, red	@ 3.20 per ft
3 doz. deluxe #98145 Chaise pads, floral	@ 3.00 each

These items are to be shipped freight charges collect and billed on the firm's usual credit terms of 2/10, net 30. You can't ship two of these items, however, until you get more information. The boarding ladders come with 7- and 11-inch hooks —so they can clamp securely to boats, rafts, pools, or docks. Which size does he want? It is even possible that he might want five of each, but you think it is risky to guess. The ladder prices are the same for both sizes of hooks. These white vinyl-covered hooks turn a full 360 degrees for fast and easy fitting, and they fold so that the ladder is flat for convenient storage. The steps are varnished oak hardwood, 15 inches wide.

The Mat and Dock Runner #6314 is in aqua color, not red. The red is listed in your catalog (which Midwest Marine has) as #6315. Though he probably wants the red and just wrote the wrong catalog number, you want to be sure before you ship this heavy roll. (Shipping weight is 3 pounds per foot!) This is an excellent runner for deck or dock. It is made of all-weather, nonslip, brush-action polyester pile with heavy rubber backing and is 36 inches wide.

You do have the chair pads and can ship them today. They are a durable, waterproof vinyl floral pattern, ideal for outdoor patio use. Today is May 10. Decide whether you should ship the pads today or wait until you can send the other items too. Write for the needed information, make action easy, and cover all pertinent details. You are assistant sales manager for Pool and Patio Wholesale Company, San Francisco, CA 94101.

3. You are assistant research director of Travel Service, International. Members pay annual dues and get travel assistance as well as discounts on trips they book through their local chapters. Your organization publishes and mails (free) a *Quarterly Newsletter* to all members across the United States. Also you publish (for sale at cost) a few reports and booklets on various phases of travel. Because your organization has no credit department, none of these published booklets can be sent unless the member sends cash with the order. You do not send c.o.d. Part of the back page of every *Quarterly Newsletter* is devoted to announcements about new publications and their cost (which includes postage for mailing to any town in the United States). There is a clear statement on this back page about the cash-in-advance policy. Nevertheless, today you received an order from Mrs. Susan Land, Shelby, Illinois, asking that the following reports be sent c.o.d. (or that you bill her later):

2 "Money-saving Hints for Modern Travelers"   ($5 each)
1 "The Incredible Paradox of the '70s"   ($4.50)

You must hold up shipment of these booklets until you receive her remittance. Write a tactful acknowledgment of her order, explaining both your policy and the reason for it. Your prices on the pamphlets are at cost; the saving that your organization makes by operating without a credit and collection procedure is passed on to members in lower prices.

Back Orders

4. Mr. Harry Western, a charge customer at 855 Glenwood Drive, Eugene, OR 97401, orders five more rolls of the #TG3773 gold color, flocked, raised damask wallpaper ($16.95 a roll). He writes that he just finished papering the dining room with this pattern and his family likes it so much that they now want the hall to match. Your store (Galli's Interior Design Shop, Portland, OR 97208) is completely out of this pattern; you sold your last roll three days ago. You are the exclusive dealer for these distinctive wallpapers in Oregon and get them direct from the Mayberry Mills in Massachusetts. A wire from the mills yesterday promised that your special order of #TG3773 would reach your shop in 10 days. Write Mr. Western the appropriate letter to keep him convinced that this choice wallpaper is well worth waiting for. It is one of the most elegant you carry. Its beautiful flocked damask pattern has the lovely look and feel of velvet. Textured to simulate fine silk, all on tough vinyl, it is strong and won't tear even when wet. Also, it's prepasted and pretrimmed, and can be cleaned with soap and water. Shipping time between Portland and Eugene is one day.

5. In your Wholesale Camera Supply Company (Norman, OK 73069) you have just received an order from Angel's Photo Shop, 931 Wabash Avenue, Shawnee, OK 74801, for parts to repair a Model #35 box camera. Mr. Angel stated that his customer cherishes this old camera as an heirloom and wants to get it into good working order. Facts: This model of American camera is obsolete and new parts are no longer available. If Mr. Angel's customer desires, you will try to obtain these parts on special order; however, there will be a delay from four to five weeks and the parts may be used. The price also may be considerably higher than current material prices on similar parts for newer models. At this moment you have no way of knowing just what the prices may be. Write to Mr. Angel to get his approval of the back order and an understanding about what his customer considers the maximum she would be willing to pay. You will, of course, try to get them for the lowest price possible and assure Mr. Angel that such an old-model camera in top working order will be a possession to be proud of. Make action easy.

6. As a correspondent in the customer relations department of Outdoor World, Philadelphia, PA 19108, it is your job to write Mrs. Sydney Cline, Director of Rocky Creek Camp, Great Falls, MT 59401, that the new printing of the book she ordered—B9552 ($8.98)—has been delayed about one month. From your

catalog she ordered three copies of this book, which she says she wants for her camp counselors. She enclosed a check in full payment, including $1.20 shipping charges. As it is still early in the summer (today is May 26), you wonder if she would like you to ship the books when they come off the press. In case she needs books sooner, you do have other titles similar to the one she ordered. Enclose a new brochure from which she can select other books at the same price, any of which you can send so they'll reach her within a week. Ask Mrs. Cline whether she wants you to back-order B9552 and if she'd like you to send any other books to tide her over. In case she wants to reorder instead of or in addition to waiting for B9552, enclose an order form and make clear what you'll do about her check.

Substitution Orders

7. From Ms. Helen Mayson, owner of Southern Variety Store, Macon, GA 31201, you (Acme Closet Accessories, Inc., wholesaler, in Hartford, CT 06101) receive an order for:

3 dozen #25C538 12-pocket Todd shoe bags	@	$2.90	$104.40
2 dozen #25P862 16-garment Todd vinyl bags	@	3.40	81.60

   These are to be added to her account. You have today shipped by parcel post the shoe bags, but the particular garment bags she ordered are no longer manufactured by Todd Brothers. This item was discontinued last month. The new (#35P882) garment bag comes in three colors—sea green, sky blue, and pink—of electronically quilted vinyl instead of the clear plastic formerly used. The quilted vinyl wears better and is guaranteed to resist splitting at the seams. The zipper is 48 inches long instead of the former 40 inches and thus makes inserting garments easier. Because this bag was not included in last year's catalog, Ms. Mayson of course did not know about it.

   You are sending her the new spring catalog, just out. The bag in question is pictured on page 6. Its price is $4.10 each, but well worth the 70 cents difference over the clear plastic. A complete assortment of other color-mated closet organizers is also available. Her customers will like, for instance, the matching eight-suit bag and the five-shelf file, both with zipper front, sturdy steel frames, and see-through 1-foot square windows of clear vinyl. Though you're sure Ms. Mayson will be glad to carry the new #35P882 bags—and also the other accessories—you write to ask her approval before shipping the bags. Provide order blanks and any other information she may need.

8. You are the hotel reservation clerk for an ultramodern, very popular hotel in New York City. Every Thanksgiving holiday various tourist groups of holiday shoppers make plans to come into the city and want to stay specifically at your hotel. Your facility offers the finest restaurants, great entertainment, attractive meeting rooms, indoor shopping facilities including the leading department store outlets, health spa, swimming pool, ice skating rink, etc. This is a facility for any season in the year. Therefore, the name is the Four Seasons Hotel.

A request has been received from a group of "Golden Agers" who would like to stay at your hotel. They have done so in the past, but are late in sending their reservations for this year. Although your records show that this particular group has been your guest for the past six years, you must write them that your hotel cannot provide them with all the reservations they have requested. Offer them 30 of the 50 rooms requested, and confirmation on the other 20 rooms in another hotel close by. Give a deadline date for their response.

9. You are the manager of Training Systems, Inc., a firm which designs seminars and training programs for various companies in your city. You also conduct specialized training sessions in your own offices in the heart of the city. One of your most popular in-house programs is your C.A.M. (certified administrative manager) review seminars.

    The C.A.M. is a professional certificate program sponsored by the Administrative Management Society for Administrative Managers (those involved in office management, personnel management, computer systems and information management, and financial management). The tests are administered twice a year in your city (in April and November). You have set up your review sessions (two 3-hour sessions per week) so that they end during the week before the C.A.M. examinations are given. And, because you use C.A.I. (computer assisted instruction) extensively in your program, you are limited in the number of participants you can serve during each series of seminars. You only enroll as many clients as you have computer terminals for them to use.

    Your next training series is completely sold out. Today you received an application and a check for the full amount of the seminar from Ms. Evelyn Corder, 1326 Angas Ave., (your city). Obviously, you cannot enroll her in the seminar series which begins next week. However, on occasion you do have a cancellation from someone who has already enrolled. You are returning Ms. Corder's check now, but you will place her name at the top of the waiting list. If you get a cancellation before classes start, you will immediately call her (her phone number is on the application form, which you have retained).

    You should remind her that a new series of review seminars will be given before the next C.A.M. examinations. If she wishes to wait for the next series, all she has to do is send her check back and you will complete the processing of her application. You will be happy to use her application form for the next series and guarantee her a spot in the classes. Tell her that your former students have had remarkable success on the examination after attending your review seminars.

10. You are sales manager of National Confectionery Supplies. Your assistant has just composed the following draft of a bad-news message, which needs your signature before it is sent to Ms. Martina Roget, Roget Candy Company, Bedford, Indiana:

```
Thank you for your special delivery letter of January 10 ordering a
rush shipment of another supply of our Exel Cherry Syrup.

May we suggest item 12-B on page 10 of our catalog?  This is in stock
now and ready to be shipped to you immediately.  Item 12, "Jumbo
```

Ann," which you inquired about has been completely sold out; we will
be unable to fill any more orders for this particular item until
early February, about the 8th. The two syrups, 12-B and 12, are similar except that the former has a heavier syrup. We have found that
many of our customers prefer the heavier syrup since, by dilution,
they have been able to supplement their other syrups without appreci-
ably altering the original. As you will note in the catalog, the
price of item 12-B is 10 cents a case higher than the cherry syrup
which was the subject of your inquiry.

We believe you would be completely satisfied with the substitution
and shall await further instructions from you.

Today is already January 12. This letter overlooks the fact that Ms. Roget stated
in her "rush order" letter that she needs the syrup by January 16 at the latest,
because the factory has exhausted its supply and must fill large candy orders from
stores before the Valentine Day rush. Shipment time between your warehouse and
Bedford is two days minimum. Thus there is insufficient time for an exchange of
information by even special delivery. You need to get your message to her faster.
If you can get Roget's reply of approval by January 13 (tomorrow), you will ship
12-B in time to reach her by the 16th. Now try your skill in expressing the above
letter in these timesaving ways:
  a. A 15-word telegram. (See footnote 15, page 151, for word-cutting suggestions.
    Remember also the seven C's.)
  b. A 100-word Mailgram. (See pages 149–151.)

Declining Favors, Invitations, and Miscellaneous Requests

  1. Assume you receive the following letter from Mrs. Harry Gaylord, chairperson of
    the local United Way campaign for this year:

Dear Mr. (*or* Ms.) (*your name*)

As you know, our city conducts a United Way fund drive annually.
Many people volunteer their help to coordinate the campaign. Will
you be willing to serve as a captain this year?

Captains are responsible for a particular geographic area. Yours
would be a 10-block area bounded by _____ Street on the west, _____
Street on the east, _____ Street on the north, and _____ Street on
the south. You would be responsible for selecting workers in each
block, who in turn will canvass each house in their particular
block.

Needless to say, your effort will be for a most worthy cause. Will
you drop me a line . . . soon, saying you'll accept?

Unfortunately you must decline the request. Since the campaign is kicked off in
October and you will be out of the state on vacation (or company business) that
month, you won't be around to do your duty. Write a considerate reply.

  2. Mr. John Bold, 429 Ninth Street, North Platte, NE 69101, writes to you—loan officer of the Second Federal Loan Company, Lincoln, NE 68501—requesting a favor. He would like you to let him change the due date of his loan payments from the 1st of each month to the 10th, but you have to refuse his request. Mr. Bold borrowed from your company on a Government Guaranteed Loan and signed a Deed of Trust Note. The due date on such mortgage loans is determined by the date the mortgage is signed. It is written into the mortgage contract that his payments must be received within 15 days of his due date, which is the 1st of each month. His remittance must arrive by the 15th of that month to avoid a late charge. It is possible, of course, for him to use the payment date of the 10th of the month, but he would have to prepay one month in advance. You are unable to change due dates on Government Guaranteed Loans. Write the appropriate reply to Mr. Bold.

3. As the sports editor of the daily morning newspaper of a large city, you are the recipient of a large quantity of mail. Some of the letters are important; others could just as easily be answered by the writer, if that person would devote just a little time to the question. So it is with the current letter in your hands.

   Specifically, the writer wants to know how many times the Boston Red Sox have played in the World Series, how many times they have won, and in which year was their last win. There is obviously much information you could provide, but the writer (a girl of 14) should know where such information can be found so that she could look it up herself.

   Answer the young person in a polite manner, and tell her where she can easily find those answers and additional information about baseball: World Series games and scores, Cy Young Award winners, home run leaders, members of the Baseball Hall of Fame, and much more. One of the more common almanacs would be a place to start, but her librarian could also provide additional information, plus some interesting books about baseball.

   Be polite and wish her well, but remember that you are doing her a favor by giving her information about source material that she will be able to use for years to come. You might even want to give her the names of several references. Above all, you want to retain her as a reader of your column and your newspaper.

4. As chief clerk of the traffic department of the Washington State Ferries, you have to answer a request you received two days ago from Miss Jane Prat, Star Route 3, Box 95C, Bremerton, WA 98307. She asks if you would please make a special search for a pair of manicure scissors she lost on the ferry from Bremerton to Seattle, February 8. They were a gift from her friend who is now in the Navy, 3,000 miles away, and she will be heartsick until they are found. She was sitting by a window seat in about the middle of the ferry on the right-hand side and she thinks these scissors dropped either on the floor or into a crack along the wall. As she doesn't mention the name of the ferry nor the exact time of her trip, and as you have four ferries on this route, you had to search on all four ferries. So far no scissors have been found. But you'll keep this a matter of permanent record and if the item is found or turned in, you will notify her immediately. Write the bad news to Miss Prat; send copies of your letter to: Information Booth, Colman

Ferry Terminal; Dock Superintendent, Colman Ferry Terminal; and Agent, Bremerton—and indicate these copies on your letter to Miss Prat.

Bad-News Announcements

1. *(Memo)* Your company cafeteria, built 18 years ago to serve about 1,000 employees, is definitely too small for your 1,900 employees. As a remedial step you (vice president for food services and finance), together with the board of directors, have decided upon a temporary solution. You will close the directors' lounge as a lounge facility, starting September 5, 198_, and will no longer serve just officers and guests there. The plan is to convert the directors' lounge—which is a table service dining room of very limited capacity and use—to an employee vending-machine food service room, supplemented by short-order counter service during peak demand hours. Present patrons of the directors' lounge are mainly a few officers and a few guests; the average patronage daily has been less than 30 during the three hours a day the present table service is open. Economically this is a marginal operation that cannot be justified. This lounge is conveniently located so that it can easily be used by your swing shift during evening hours without keeping the rest of the building open.

   This planned change will of course greatly alleviate the pressing demands for additional food service facilities for employees. But the table service will be missed by the few who enjoyed it before. To them this announcement will be bad news. Word your announcement so that every loyal officer will accept your decision with understanding, and even approval. The new plan should help decrease employee lunch-hour tardiness and improve morale. The officers still have the officers' dining room on the twelfth floor. To partially offset the loss of table service from the directors' room, this officers' dining room now has additional private seating space. The recent enclosure of the south porch has been equipped with comfortable lounge facilities in the latest decor, and a modern sliding partition is usable for those officers who want a separate space for private conferences. Write your memo to all management members.

2. For many years your company has been sending free copies of a glossy magazine, *Improving Your Correspondence,* to anyone who requested to be on your mailing list. Seldom do you hear from your readers. The cost of this little publication is about $2.50 each. In an effort to try to pare unnecessary expenses, your firm's directors have suggested that the mailing list be revised to include only those persons and firms that still read and appreciate the publication. They realize that after a passage of years those who originally requested to be on the mailing list may no longer be reading the magazine. Write a pleasant, positive-sounding, processed message that will offend no one, even though it is basically bad news. Your goal is to find out which readers wish to keep the magazine coming. They'll help you keep your mailing list up to date by taking a certain action that you request. Can you word your announcement in such a way that the readers will be dropped from your mailing list if you don't hear from them?

3. *(Memo)* Announce to your employees in building B that all electricity will be turned off between 10 and 11 a.m. next Thursday morning, June 8. They will have to plan their work in such a way that they can get along without using any electric machines that hour; in fact they won't have any electric lighting either. However, as these are sunny days, lack of electricity for lighting should not be too much of a problem. Everyone will be responsible for getting out the amount of necessary work that day, and the electricity shutoff will not be an excuse for working overtime in the afternoon, for no extra pay will be allowed. The electricity shutoff is necessary while workers hook up a major power cable between building B and the highway. New fluorescent lighting will be installed within the next month. In organizing your memo, consider whether you should use the direct or indirect plan—and have reasons to defend your decision.

4. You are president of the Exchange Building Garage, Inc. Your company manages a 400-car garage used by business executives who occupy the Exchange Building. Because of steadily increasing operating costs (mainly wages) you have found it necessary to increase the monthly parking rates to $45 a month (instead of the former $40), plus the state sales tax. This increase will become effective January 1, 198—.

   For the past two years you have been absorbing the increased operating expenses, but cannot continue to do so any longer. After several conversations with Mr. J. L. Dorff, vice president of Commercial Properties, Inc., and with Exchange Building owners who lease to the business firms in the building and from whom you lease your garage facilities, you received permission for the rate increase. Now that you have decided on the rate and date, you will write two messages:

   a. A letter to Mr. Dorff, telling him your final decision regarding the monthly rate and the effective date. Inform him that you will notify all your parking customers before a certain date. You might restate to him briefly the reason for this increase, refer to your previous conversations, and show appreciation for his understanding. Will you organize this message by the direct or indirect plan? Why?

   b. A letter to all customers who have been renting monthly parking space from your garage. This increase comes to them as a bad-news surprise. Give them whatever details you think they will appreciate having. Will you organize the same way as for message a? Why or why not?

CAPSULE CHECKLISTS FOR BAD-NEWS MESSAGES*

I Bad News		II Answering Inquiries When the Information Is Unfavorable	
General plan (A) (indirect)	Exception (B)† (direct)	Sales-related (C)	Nonsales-related (D)

1. BUFFER
  a. Agreement
  b. Appreciation
  c. Assurance
  d. Compliment
  e. Cooperation
  f. Good news
  g. Neutral courtesy
  h. Resale
  i. Sympathy
  j. Understanding
	1. Main idea
	  a. Bad-news decision,
	    sometimes with a
	    brief buffer and/or
	    reason
		1. Buffer
		  a. Appreciation
		  b. Assurance
		  c. Resale
		  d. Understand-
		    ing
			1. Buffer
			*For unfavorable
			recommendations:*
			  a. Applicant's name;
			    relationship
			  b. Reason for writ-
			    ing; reply by
			    request
			*For other nonsales
			inquiries:*
			  a. Same as II C,
			    1a–d

2. EXPLANATION
  a. Necessary details—
    general to specific
  b. Favorable, then
    unfavorable facts
  c. RB[4] reasons
  d. Emphasis on
    desired goal
	2. Explanation
	  Same as I A, 2,
	  usually a and d
		2. Explanation
		  a. Answers to
		    all questions
		  b. Pertinent
		    facts and
		    details
		  c. RB[4] reasons
		    for company
		    policy
			2. Explanation
			  a. Answers to all
			    questions
			  b. Pertinent facts
			    (favorable and
			    unfavorable)
			  c. Caution on
			    legalities
			  d. Confidentiality
			  e. Offer, phone call

3. DECISION—implied or
  expressed—WITH
  RESALE AND/OR
  CONSTRUCTIVE
  SUGGESTIONS
  a. Embedded statement
    of bad news—with
    suggestion of what
    CAN be done
  b. Helpful counter-
    proposal, plans,
    alternatives
  c. Resale
  d. Sales promotion
	3. Decision omitted
	  (already in I B, 1)
	  Resale and suggestions
	  often unnecessary and
	  omitted; sometimes
	  same as I A, 3b
		3. Decision—with
		  resale and/or
		  suggestions
		  a. Same as I A,
		    3a
		  b. Ideas for help
		  c. Possible fu-
		    ture changes
		  d. Resale on
		    firm, prod-
		    ucts, services,
		    if appropriate
			3. Decision—with con-
			  structive suggestions
			About applicant:
			  a. Honest non-
			    endorsement
			  b. Possibility of
			    changes since
			    you last saw
			    applicant
			*About other non-
			sales-related in-
			quiries:*
			  a. Same as I A,
			    3a and b

4. POSITIVE, FRIENDLY,
  APPROPRIATE CLOSE
  a. Appreciation
  b. Invitation to future
    action
  c. CSAD[1]
  d. EA and motivation[2]
  e. DA[3]
  f. Willingness to help
    further
  g. RB[4]
  h. Good wishes
  i. Courtesy
	4. Positive, friendly,
	  appropriate close
	  Sometimes same as
	  I A, 4a–i
		4. Positive, friendly,
		  appropriate close
		  a. Good wishes
		  b. Appreciation
		  c. CSAD[1]
		  d. Willingness to
		    help further
			4. Positive, friendly,
			  appropriate close
			  a. Ray of hope for
			    improvement
			  b. Willingness to
			    help further
			  c. Good wishes

*All lists include possible content. For any one
message, choose only pertinent and appropriate
items.
†For uses of Direct Plan, see pages 266–267.
[1] CSAD = clear statement of action desired;
[2] EA = easy action; [3] DA = dated action, if
desirable; [4] RB = reader benefit.

See also pages 108–109 about action requests
and the five W's.

III	IV	
	Refusing Credit	
Refusing Adjustments on Claims and Complaints	**Retail Credit (E)**	**Mercantile Credit (F)**

1. Buffer
  a. Agreement
  b. Appreciation
  c. Assurance
  d. Cooperation
  e. Neutral courtesy
  f. Understanding
  g. If granting a part is good news, opening is on that part
	1. Buffer
	  a. Agreeable comment
	  b. Appreciation
	  c. Assurance
	  d. Brief resale on product and/or firm
	  e. Incidental reference to the order, if any
		1. Buffer
		  a. Same as IV E, 1a–e

2. Explanation
  a. Logical statements of reasons
  b. General RB[4] procedure, policy, instructions, guarantee
  c. Resale interwoven
  d. Education on use
  e. Impersonal facts on buyer's mistake
	2. Explanation
	  Choice of:
	  a. No reason
	  b. "Insufficient-information" reason
	  c. List of all usual reasons
	  d. Specific reason(s): same as I A, 2
		2. Explanation
		  a. Specific reasons
		  b. Favorable, then unfavorable facts
		  c. Emphasis on desired goal

3. Decision—with resale and/or suggestions
  a. Impersonal, expressed or implied, but clear refusal; positive language, perhaps RB[4]
  b. Clear indication if you are returning product
  c. RB[4] suggestion(s) for using rejected product and/or another
  d. Resale on product, service, and/or firm
	3. Decision—with RB[4] counterproposal and suggestion(s)
	  a. Same as I A, 3a
	  b. Suggestions:
	    Conference
	    Other lenders
	    Future review
	    Other credit plans available
	    Layaway
	    Cash or c.o.d. buying
		3. Decision—with RB[4] counterproposal and suggestion(s)
		  a. Same as I A, 3a
		  b. Suggestions:
		    Inventory reduction
		    Sales or capital increase
		    Local financing
		    Cash or c.o.d. buying; smaller, frequent orders
		    Help of sales representative
		    Future review

4. Positive, friendly, appropriate close
  a. CSAD (tactful suggestion without urging)[1]
  b. EA[2]
  c. Positive forward look
  d. RB and satisfaction[4]
  e. Courtesy
	4. Positive, friendly, appropriate close
	  a. Invitation regarding a suggestion; CSAD[1]
	  b. Forward look
	  c. Resale
	  d. RB[4] and EA[2]
	  e. Courtesy
		4. Positive, friendly, appropriate close
		  Same as IV E, 4a–e

[1] CSAD = clear statement of action desired
[2] EA = easy action
[3] DA = dated action
[4] RB = reader benefit
*S = substitute; O = ordered item

324

BAD-NEWS MESSAGES* (Continued)

V
Acknowledging Orders You Can't Fill Now or at All

Incomplete or Vague (G)	Back Orders (H)	Substitutions (J)	Diverted or Rejected (K)
1. Good news, if any, and buffer a. Shipment details, if sending anything b. Buffer: short resale on vaguely described item(s) c. Brief order acknowledgment (date, item) d. Appreciation e. Welcome, if new customer	1. Good news, if any, and buffer a. Same as V G, 1a b. Buffer: specific resale on ordered depleted item; no mention of depletion c. Same as V G, 1c–e	1. Good news, if any, and buffer a. Same as V G, 1a b. Buffer: broad resale embodies both substitute and ordered item; omits differences c. Same as V G, 1c–e	1. Buffer a. Resale, only if your products or services are to be bought elsewhere b. Brief order acknowledgment c. Appreciation
2. Explanation a. RB[4] reason for requesting missing information b. Facts about choices available (sizes, colors, models) c. Descriptive enclosures	2. Explanation a. Approximate date goods expected to reach buyer b. Reason unavailable now (RB?)[4] c. Resale	2. Explanation a. One or two merits of substitute (S)[5] before revealing unavailability of ordered item (O)[5] b. Sales point on why we carry S exclusively	2. Explanation a. One or two RB's[4] for your sales policy: selections, deliveries, shipping costs, extra services b. Any other pertinent facts
3. Decision—with resale and/or suggestions a. See G 2a, above—implied decision b. Perhaps brief resale on the item(s) in general	3. Decision—with resale and/or constructive suggestions a. See H 2a, above—implied decision b. Possibly mild sales promotion on allied item(s) to be shipped with back-ordered item c. Perhaps brief resale on back-ordered item	3. Decision—with resale and suggestions a. Unavailability of O—in positive terms (exclusively stock S[5]—if true) b. Passive statement on where O may be bought c. Price and quality justification of substitute; RB[4] d. Sales promotion	3. Decision—with resale and suggestions a. Positive statement of your policy, to clarify what you can and can't do b. Payment return, if any c. Justification of price difference at local dealer d. Help on where to get what reader wants
4. Positive, friendly, appropriate close a. CSAD[1] b. EA[2] c. DA[3] d. RB (prompt delivery?)[4] e. Courtesy	4. Positive, friendly, appropriate close a. If shipment in reasonable time: no action; assumption that back-order is OK b. If longer: CSAD[1]; EA[2]; DA[3] c. RB[4]	4. Positive, friendly, appropriate close a. If S[5] is already shipped: assurance of money-back "shipment on approval"; RB[4] b. If S is not yet shipped: CSAD[1]; EA[2]; DA[3]; RB[4]	4. Positive, friendly, appropriate close a. Resale b. CSAD[1] c. Future service d. RB[4]

[1] CSAD = clear statement of action desired
[2] EA = easy action
[3] DA = dated action
[4] RB = reader benefit
*[5] S = substitute; O = ordered item

325

VI Declining Requests for Favors and Invitations	VII Turning Down Job or Contract Offers	VIII Announcing Bad News about Prices and/or Services

1. Buffer
  a. Appreciation
  b. Compliment (to reader)
  c. Assurance
  d. Agreeable comment
	1. Main idea or buffer
	  a. If routine matter between
	    businesses, maybe I B, 1
	  b. Otherwise, I A, 1 buffer:
	    (1) Appreciation
	    (2) Agreeable comment
	    (3) Compliment
		1. Main idea or buffer
		  a. If routine (or reader not
		    emotionally involved),
		    I B, 1
		  b. Otherwise, I A, 1 buffer:
		    (1) Agreeable comment
		    (2) Neutral courtesy
		    (3) Brief resale

2. Explanation
  a. Facts and (sometimes
    personal) reasons leading
    to refusal
	2. Explanation
	  a. Reasons leading to turn-
	    down (already full sched-
	    ule in writer's firm; usual
	    requirements or qualities
	    sought, with or without
	    revealing reader's specific
	    lack)
		2. Explanation
		  a. RB[4] reasons and analysis
		    of increasing costs, etc.

3. Decision—with resale and/or
  suggestions
  a. Clear, tactful decision, im-
    plied or stated; emphasis
    on the positive aspects
    (desire to help, etc.)
  b. RB,[4] suggestions—when,
    how you *can* help
  c. Alternate sources of help
    to reader
	3. Decision—with resale and
	  suggestions
	  a. Clear tactful decision, im-
	    plied or stated—emphasis
	    on positive aspects (what
	    your firm *is* doing about
	    such work, etc.)
	  b. Invitation for possible
	    future reapplication and
	    review
	  c. "Filing" for future
	  d. Alternatives
		3. Decision—with resale and
		  suggestions
		  a. Effective date of new plan
		  b. Clear statement and item-
		    izing if needed
		  c. Enclosures or examples if
		    helpful
		  d. Resale on your firm's
		    products, services, prices

4. Positive, friendly, appropriate
  close
  a. CSAD[1]
  b. EA[2]
  c. DA[3]
  d. Good wishes
  e. RB[4]
  f. Courtesy
	4. Positive, friendly, appropriate
	  close
	  a. Good wishes
	  b. CSAD[1]
	  c. Courtesy
		4. Positive, friendly, appropriate
		  close
		  a. Forward look
		  b. Resale
		  c. Invitation to action
		  d. CSAD[1]
		  e. EA[2]
		  f. RB[4]
		  g. Courtesy

[1] CSAD = clear statement of action desired
[2] EA = easy action
[3] DA = dated action, if desirable
[4] RB = reader benefit

BAD-NEWS MESSAGES (Continued)

IX Requiring Minimum Orders and/or Deposits	X Penalizing for Nonconformity with Rules or Procedures	XI Conveying Other Bad News

1. Main idea or buffer
  a. If routine (or reader not emotionally involved), I B, 1
  b. Otherwise, I A, 1 buffer:
    (1) Agreeable comment
    (2) Neutral courtesy
    (3) Compliment on past
    (4) Hint of urgency or need for change
	1. Main idea or buffer
	  a. Same as IX 1a
	  b. Same as IX 1b
		1. Main idea or buffer
		  a. Same as IX 1a
		  b. Same as IX 1b

2. Explanation
  a. Tactful review of reader's record—favorable to unfavorable
  b. Emphasis on desired goal and helpfulness
	2. Explanation
	  a. Details about the requirements
	  b. Reasons leading to the penalty
		2. Explanation
		  a. Details on what is wrong

3. Decision—with resale and suggestions
  a. Clear, tactful statement of what will happen unless reader meets requirements
  b. Suggestions (improved advertising or merchandising; assistance of sales representative)
  c. Enclosures; aids
  d. Resale
	3. Decision—with resale and suggestions
	  a. Same as IX 3a
	  b. Suggestions for eliminating penalty in future
	  c. Forms and deadlines
		3. Decision—with suggestions
		  a. What needs to be done
		  b. How to do it

4. Positive, friendly, appropriate close
  a. Same as VIII, 4
	4. Positive, friendly, appropriate close
	  a. CSAD[1]
	  b. EA[2]
	  c. DA[3]
	  d. RB[4]
	  e. Assurance
	  f. Good wishes
	  g. Courtesy
		4. Positive, friendly, appropriate close
		  a. CSAD[1]
		  b. EA[2]
		  c. Goodwill
		  d. Courtesy

[1] CSAD = clear statement of action desired
[2] EA = easy action
[3] DA = dated action, if desirable
[4] RB = reader benefit

chapter

10

Persuasive Requests

Besides situations in which mere *asking* is sufficient (routine direct requests), you will face situations in which you need to *persuade*. The favor or action you ask—the reader's time, money, support, or agreement—is such that you anticipate some objection. To persuade your reader to take the requested action, you develop rational and/ or emotional appeals. Analysis of and consideration[1] for your reader's circumstances, needs, and emotions are especially important for effective persuasion.

You can use the persuasive-request plan for the following kinds of messages:

Requests for favors that—
    Require time, knowledge, or effort
    Ask donations of money or other valuables
    Urge cooperation on goals and projects

Other nonroutine requests:
    Adjustment
    Credit
    Changes in policy or performance

Unsolicited sales letters to—
    Make a direct sale
    Serve as stimulus to future sales
    Bring back lost customers
    Apply for a job

Collections (discussion and late stages)

This chapter discusses the persuasive-request plan and how you can adapt it to various requests for favors, other nonroutine requests, and sales. Job applications are covered separately in Chapter 11 and collections, in Chapter 13.

ORGANIZATIONAL PLAN

The persuasive request, like the bad-news letter, uses the indirect approach. You assume that if your request were stated directly at the beginning, it would be bad news to your reader, who would then react unfavorably. Thus, before you mention the specific request, you will have to prepare the reader for it, and, when possible, present facts to indicate that your proposal is beneficial or useful. Remember, your reader is not expecting your message, and you should attract his or her attention and arouse interest *before* revealing what you'd like done.

The basic structure for persuasive letters usually has four parts, commonly known as the AIDA formula for sales presentation:

[1] For a review of general ways to show consideration, see pages 42–50.

> **A**—Attract the reader's favorable *attention.*
> **I**—Arouse the reader's *interest.*
> **D**—Create *desire* and convince the reader.
> **A**—Make clear the *action* the reader needs to take.

Although attention, interest, and desire are listed here as distinct steps, they are usually combined or blended so smoothly in the well-written persuasive message that it is difficult—and unnecessary!—to separate them. Also, the parts do not always occur in the sequence given here; for example, it is possible to omit or deemphasize those points that have been covered in earlier letters, advertising, or personal contacts with the prospect. You-attitude content and reader benefits are most important. What you call the parts and whether you have three or four is unimportant. In fact, the persuasive-request plan is sometimes called the four P's—promise, picture, prove, and push—or discussed under *three* parts—star, chain, and hook. In the AIDA persuasive-request *general* outline below, the other names for the parts are indicated in parentheses.

1. **Attention** *(promise; star)*

   Attract favorable attention with a reader-interest or a reader-benefit theme. Begin with a relevant statement or a challenging question that entices the recipients to read on because they want to know: "What's in this letter for me?" Highlight a point that is close to the reader's interests or needs, instead of talking about yourself or your organization. Avoid exaggeration, foolish questions ("Do you want a steady income?"), and obvious statements ("Money helps you pay your bills").

   Because many people throw away envelopes that look like part of bulk mailings, even the envelope plays an important part in getting favorable attention. Among the devices used with varying degrees of success on envelopes are color, handwritten addresses, contest announcements, questions, and a few enticing words from the message printed on the envelope. Some firms conceal their identity on envelopes, omitting their name and address. However, because many people resent such tactics, this practice has questionable value.

   The letterhead can also be an effective, important attention getter. For favor and sales letters that are sent to numerous readers, letterheads can and do deviate from the usual simplicity suggested for other business letterheads. Some contain different pictures and colors to tie in with each favor or sales message. (Advertising agencies and stationery design specialists can help you with these needs.) The discussion in this text concentrates on the written message itself.

2. **Interest** *(picture; chain)*

   Build upon the theme started in the attention-getting opening. Begin to tell what your project, product, or service is and what it will do for the reader. Describe it clearly and specifically in two ways (not necessarily in this order):

   a. Its physical description—important features, construction, appearance, performance, beauty, functions (any or all of which may be omitted for a long-established subject well known to the reader).

b. Its value or benefits to the reader or others in whom the reader is interested. (Some writers call this material "psychological description.")

Of the various features and uses that the project, product, or service has, emphasize the central selling point—that point you think is most likely to make the strongest appeal to the prospect. For instance, will your proposal bring comfort? entertainment? health? recognition? security? Show the reader how your proposal gives one or more benefits like the following:

Appreciation (by others)	Pleasure
Approval (by others)	Popularity
Beauty or attractiveness	Position of authority
Cleanliness	Prestige
Comfort	Pride
Convenience	Profits
Cooperation	Protection for family, business,
Customer satisfaction	self, or others
Distinctiveness	Provision for the future
Efficiency	Recognition
Enjoyment	Reduced work
Entertainment	Respect
Extra earnings	Safety and security
Fair treatment	Satisfaction of helping others
Friendships	Savings
Good reputation	Self-preservation
Health	Solution to a problem
Improvement	Success
Love of home, family, others	Thrift habit
Money and other valuables	Usefulness
Peace of mind	

3. **Desire and Conviction** *(prove; chain)*

So that your readers will desire to do as you request and be convinced they (or others in whom they are interested) will benefit from your proposal, you usually present proof. Give evidence that your statements are true. Include needed facts, figures, testimonials, tests, samples, guarantees, and any other proof your proposal may call for. Be aware of your legal responsibilities for truth.

A descriptive folder permits you to avoid cluttering your letter with many details. However, if you have an enclosure, mention it only after stating most of your selling points and then motivate your reader to read further details in the folder. Link your reference to the enclosure with a sales point. Don't depend on the enclosure to do your selling.

Emphasize positive aspects, but be honest about stating costs when pertinent; minimize negative aspects, and write from the reader's point of view.

4. **Action** *(push; hook)*

Clearly state what the reader should do to comply with your request and thus to gain the benefits. Make action easy—by including a reply form, envelope, phone number, office hours, location, and so forth. Induce the reader to act now or within a certain time, and end on a reader-benefit plug, which may tie in with your opening statement.

PERSUASIVE REQUESTS FOR FAVORS

As a conscientious business or professional person you probably participate actively in various committees and organizations. And you have numerous opportunities to write (as well as to answer) favor requests that seek the recipient's donation of something—time, knowledge, effort, money, or cooperation. The AIDA plan helps you to ask a favor effectively, as described below.

Getting Attention for Favor Requests

To begin your favor request with something close to your reader's interest or benefit, consider what appeals are likely to be most meaningful to her or him. Try to introduce a direct or indirect benefit that you can develop as a central selling point more fully later in the letter. You want to get the reader's attention *before* stating your request, but you need to use good judgment in introducing benefits. Be careful that your statements don't sound like high-pressure appeals or bribes, as in this poor opening for a letter inviting a political candidate to speak: "How much would it be worth to you to influence the views of 2,000 voters?"

Effective openings you can use—with discretion—for various favor requests are:

1. Comments or assertions with which the reader will agree
2. Compliments—if sincere
3. Frank admission that your message is a request for a favor
4. Problem(s) that are the basis of your favor request
5. Question(s)—one or two rhetorical questions
6. Statement(s) of what is being done or has been done to solve or lessen a problem

Agreeable-Comment or Assertion Openings

To speak to students majoring in advertising:

Advertising is the spark plug of any business and a challenge to the creative thinker. Yet what advice can you give to the many students who cannot decide what area of advertising to enter?

To help in getting community support:

If there is one topic in which you and I share a special interest, it is the education of our children. The success of our school levy will determine the quality of education received by Bellevue students.

Sincere-Compliment Openings

Request to speak, without fee, to a local chapter:

Ever since your stimulating speech last year to delegates at KSA national convention in Atlanta, our TriCity chapter members here have wanted to meet you personally. We believe you could be a profound influence on our future program and growth.

Request to accept an important chairperson position:

Your exceptionally fine work in People-to-People projects, as well as your present council position, emphasizes that you deserve a place on this year's East Coast conference program of the National Personnel Association.

"Frank Admission of Favor" Opening

(Disarming frankness encourages some readers to discover for themselves how they will benefit from complying. Though these frank openings are like those used in direct requests, the remaining paragraphs of persuasive letters contain meaningful appeals.)

To accept an honorary state appointment:

The state needs your help!

As a prominent respected psychiatrist, you have been recommended to serve on the state board of three to conduct oral Civil Service examinations of applicants for psychiatric work in State Rehabilitation Centers.

To be moderator at a national convention:

To get and keep our 198_ NRMA convention program on the beam, we shall need three top-grade people to serve as moderators. You can no doubt guess why I am making this appeal to you.

To fill out and return a questionnaire:

WILL YOU HELP DMAA?
--AND HELP YOURSELF, TOO?

I'd like to ask a favor of you. It concerns the gathering of important facts and information regarding postal rates. Here, in a nutshell, is the story:

Basic-Problem Openings

To contribute to a lab fund:

DIAGNOSTIC LABORATORY IN DANGER!
INDUSTRY STANDS TO LOSE $60,000!
Contributions for the new diagnostic lab in (*town name*) have stopped coming in. Unless we can immediately raise $11,000, we will lose the $60,000 appropriated by the last legislature, on the condition we in the industry match it with $35,000. Only $24,000 of the necessary $35,000 has, so far, been pledged.

Question Openings

Request to participate in a six-month research project:

Have you ever had the fun of participating in a market research
study? As you know, market research is the study of consumer reactions and attitudes to products. This research is extremely useful
to manufacturers in helping them to give you and your family products
to better suit your needs.

Request to become a member of a university YWCA:

WHAT'S THE USE?
"What's the use of getting an education?"
  "What's the use of planning ahead?"
    "What's the use of living thoughtfully?"
      "WHAT'S THE USE OF ANYTHING?"

"What Has Been Done about a Problem" Openings

To send a gift to the Fund for the Blind:

Thousands of blind Americans wait eagerly each month for their copies
of the Braille or Talking Book edition of The Reader's Digest. It is
the only magazine of its kind available in Braille or Talking Book
form (long-playing records) which is exactly like the ink-print edition read by their sighted friends. This means something very special to them.
  With the help of friends like yourself, we can supply these...

To hire the jobless through the Millionair Club:

During the past year homeless and needy men, women, and children enjoyed 123,000 warm nourishing meals at Millionair Club; 3,088 adults
and children received clothing; men and women received 9,321 jobs,
406 units of blood transfusion, emergency hospital treatment, and
many other kindnesses.

Arousing Interest and Creating Desire to Do the Favor

Once you have decided on an opening that sets the theme and encourages the recipient
to read on, you can continue to build on your idea. To get both the reader's interest
and desire, you need to (1) include all necessary description—physical characteristics
and value of the project, (2) present facts and figures through which the reader can determine direct or indirect benefits he or she may derive, and (3) handle negatives positively. This material comprises the greater portion of your persuasive request.

Physical Characteristics and Value of Project

If your reader is not a member of your organization or familiar with it, you need to
give brief, but adequate information about its purpose, scope, and members. But be

sure not to *begin* your letter by talking about yourself and your organization, especially if the reader is an outsider! Place this material after a you-attitude opening.

In addition, you need to describe to all readers the problem or project to which the favor relates and to establish its values. For instance, if you are asking for funds to send underprivileged children to summer camp, you might describe (perhaps with the use of a folder) the physical camp facilities, size and number of buildings, surroundings, recreation areas, and number of children and counselors. Then you show the value of these facilities to the children—character-building, friendships, appreciation of nature, fun, and so forth. Sometimes you can effectively get readers to visualize themselves in the shoes of those their funds can help and in this way arouse their interest in your project.

Direct and Indirect Reader Benefits

Usually near the middle of your letter you explain how the reader is to take part in the project. So that readers will desire to do as you ask, be sure to include all necessary facts and figures to convince them that their contribution will be enjoyable, easy, important, and of benefit to them (as much as is true and possible). Try to show direct and/or indirect benefits.

Direct Benefits. To a person who does a favor, vary direct benefits with the type of favor. For example, if a person is to speak (without a fee and perhaps even without a traveling expense allowance) at a widely publicized convention, he or she may gain direct benefit from the favorable publicity as well as from personal contacts with the audience. If other prominent speakers are on the same program, say so; for this fact is an additional compliment to your reader. Both the speaker and his or her employer (who perhaps pays traveling expenses) can gain directly from recognition, prestige, and popularity—plus increased future sales of products or services. However, it is better not to actually state these benefits, but rather to let the reader determine them from the facts. Be sure to tell the reader when he or she is to speak, where (date, day, hour), on what topic (or if the speaker is to choose it), for how long, to whom, and to how many people.

Direct benefit may also come to the company that donates merchandise to, for instance, a charity or well-attended event. The people who see the company's name on the donated product will feel goodwill toward the donor and tend to buy its products when they need them. Again, it is better not to state such benefits specifically, but to let your readers determine them themselves. Stating obvious benefits bluntly may make the favor request sound like a bribe.

If your reader is to become a member of your club or to take part in a project, describe that club or project and tell how it will (directly) benefit the reader. Try to keep the reader in each paragraph and write from the reader's viewpoint.

In some favor requests the direct benefit offered may be a premium or gift or other small reward or token of appreciation. Those who participate in a questionnaire survey may gain, because the results will ultimately lead to improvements that make their work easier or help them to save money.

Indirect Benefits. The participant who helps the members of a group he or she is interested in or a member of, may receive indirect benefits. For instance, you can use indirect-benefit appeals to get a sales manager to speak (without a fee) to your school's marketing club or an auditor to talk to an accounting club. In each case, your reader's contribution may benefit him or her or the profession at least indirectly, because he or she helps a group of listeners whose interests are in a field of work he or she is interested in. Similarly, when you want to urge a busy person to accept a time-consuming office without pay, you can appeal to a sense of loyalty to the organization and the benefit his or her leadership can provide. Such indirect reader benefits are often persuaders.

In still other cases you can get a reader's cooperation by appealing on the basis of *altruism*—selfless devotion to the welfare of other human beings (or even animals). When persons contribute to a charity drive, for instance, they benefit by knowing they have helped bring happiness and hope to less fortunate people.

Though there may be times when you honestly cannot see or show reader benefits, try always to present every favor request from the reader's point of view.

Positive Handling of Negatives

With the persuasive-request plan you must not only use appeals and stress reader benefits, but you need to ask yourself, "To what will my reader probably object?" Then stress the positive aspects—what *can* be done—to minimize the negatives, as in the following examples:

Probable Objection	*Possible Points to Stress*
1. Allowance for traveling expenses and/or speaker's fee is inadequate	a. Will you gladly meet her at the airport or any other station? b. Will she be guest of honor at a banquet? Maybe her spouse too? c. Will a car be available for her use in your city? d. Is her part on the program so important that her employer will want to take care of her expenses? e. Are other famous functions, exhibits, or attractions available in your city? f. Can you arrange overnight accommodations? g. If she lives in the same city, will someone pick her up at home or office? h. If she'll drive her car, how about parking and easy access to the place where she'll be speaking?
2. Expected pledge or contribution is too large	a. Will you accept contributions in small installments? b. May he pledge now and pay after a future date? c. Can you compare the donation to amounts spent on luxuries? d. Can you show the great relief his gift will bring to those who need it?

3. Requested questionnaire looks long	**a.** Are the questions easy to answer? Why?
	b. Is taking part in the survey fun because . . . ?
	c. Can the entire questionnaire be finished within x minutes?
	d. Will the ultimate gain or reward be an incentive?

Asking for Action

Having included necessary facts, benefits, and positive aspects, you can confidently ask for the reader's acceptance. Make action clear, easy, and dated if necessary. If you need the reply by a certain date, tie this request in with reader benefit whenever possible—prominent billing on the program, adequate time for publicity, and so forth. Omit such negative statements as, "*If* you can donate anything, please . . . ." Better say, "To make your contribution, just return . . . ." Your last sentence often can tie in with an appeal or statement featured in the opening paragraph, as a last reader-benefit plug.

Asking Favors That Require Time, Knowledge, or Effort

By using the persuasive-request AIDA plan, you can urge a busy person to be speaker at an important banquet or conference for little or no pay—and even partly or entirely at his or her own (or employer's) expense. You can encourage people to accept time-consuming chairmanships or to serve without pay on long-term committees and boards. You can obtain answers to research questionnaires which require more than routine effort by the recipient. You can give employees or club members a pep talk about attending certain functions; and you can increase membership in a business, professional, social, or religious organization. All these favors require time, knowledge, and/or effort, as the next two examples illustrate.

Request for a Speaker

In letter 1, the president of an aircraft owners and pilots association invites an author (who is a member of the same nonprofit association in another city 500 miles away) to be principal speaker. The letter includes all needed details about date, time, place, audience, length and topic of talk. The underlying appeal or central selling point is the reader's ability to help in a serious crisis those of similar interests. Notice how paragraph 3 emphasizes positive aspects and also makes clear that the group *can* pay transportation expenses (but is not offering a speaker's fee). If you are writing for a nonprofit organization to a nonmember, you should explain the club's purpose and nonprofit nature before you state what you *will* pay for the speaker. (For some very large functions—with an attendance of several hundred persons—even a nonprofit organization might assess each member a small amount to cover both a speaker's fee and traveling expenses.)

Letter 1

Inviting a speaker to address a banquet, without an honorarium.

*Attention;
reader-centered;
compliment*

The article you wrote in the March issue of <u>Flying</u> has been of great interest to us in the Viewmont chapter of AOPA. We are currently involved in a battle to acquire a surplus Naval air station for general aviation use and find your ideas on airport facilities just the approach we need to convince those not familiar with general aviation problems.

*Interest;
the problem*

Three months ago we learned that the Highpoint Naval Air Station would be surplus in August of this year. It seemed at first that general aviation would easily acquire this badly needed airport. But recently much opposition has developed. The area residents simply do not understand why another airport for "small planes" is needed. We have planned a banquet for the leaders of the community to convince them of the genuine need for this facility and would very much like you as our dinner guest and speaker. Your views on the general crisis of airport congestion would be extremely helpful in presenting our case. Will you tell us

And the request

how you put the new program into effect last year in your city?

Reader benefit

You will enjoy, I'm sure, the dinner and entertainment we have planned. The banquet will be held at the new Century Hotel, Monday, June 20, at 7 p.m.; but the time can be changed if another hour is more convenient for you. You will, of course, be reimbursed for your traveling and overnight hotel expenses; and I personally will see that you are picked up and returned to the airport at your convenience. We expect about 100 persons to attend.

*Desire;
conviction details*

After two local speakers present their views, we would like you to speak for twenty to thirty minutes to conclude the arguments with an expert's opinion which will add much strength to our cause.

Dated action

A brief letter from you indicating acceptance will assure the success of this function. Also, please include your preference as to dinner hour. Because the program goes to press in three weeks, will you send your decision by May 20? The members in this

*Value of
reader's talk*

area will sincerely appreciate the contribution you can make to our obtaining another urgently needed general aviation airport in this area.

Request for Help in a Survey

Whether you are a student gathering firsthand information for a report, a business executive surveying your employees, or a research consultant working for numerous clients, you will get better cooperation from your readers when you write persuasively.

Letter 2, for example, stresses reader benefit throughout. This letter also illustrates one way you can save money if you have a slim budget and a long mailing list: in place of the personalized inside addresses and salutation, you can use a reader-centered attention-getting statement or question. A letter similar to the one below gained a 79 percent response.

Letter 2

A persuasive, effective request for return of a questionnaire by college teachers.

Attention; reader benefit	Would knowing what other college teachers are doing in their business communication courses help you?
Reader benefit or interest	Perhaps you, like many others, have wondered how the content, emphasis, and assignments of your basic course compare with those in other colleges that offer courses similar to yours in credit hours, size of sections, and prerequisites. Or you may have considered changing your courses and you could use tips on what others are including.
Interest; description of project	To gather this information about this rapidly expanding field of study, we are making a nationwide survey of business communication courses taught in schools holding membership in the American Association of Collegiate Schools of Business (AACSB). This study is planned to get specific details on the subject matter and written assignments in 1979–1980 courses.
Desire; facts; reader benefit	You are the only teacher in your institution receiving this letter and the enclosed form. All names of participants will remain confidential in the report of this study. By completing the questionnaire and returning it, you will be helping expand knowledge about the teaching of this vital subject matter. Also, you'll know how your courses compare with others. You will find the questions easy to answer, we believe, because most of them require only your check mark.
Dated, easy action; reader benefit	To make sure that your college is included in this study, please mail the form by May 1, in the stamped envelope provided. In appreciation of your cooperation in this study, you will receive a summary of the findings, if you wish,[2] before the information appears in print.

The benefits offered to the college teachers for mailing the questionnaire enclosed with letter 2 are mainly intangible, yet they are adequate because the readers are expected to have a keen interest in helping to improve their profession. On the other

[2] The respondent could indicate his or her wish—and also protect anonymity—by returning his or her name and address on an enclosed separate slip.

hand, when you ask information from persons who have no built-in interest in your questionnaire, you may—if your budget allows—also have to offer a tangible inducement. For instance, the director of consumer panels for a national market research firm, in a request to "Dear Homemaker," included a tangible gift (tableware), as well as intangible benefits (enjoyment, usefulness, safety, and anonymity). The following two paragraphs from the letter come after three paragraphs that describe this particular product study and how it helps manufacturers "to give you and your family products to better suit your needs":

> All we ask is that you keep a record of your purchases of these items. In addition to the fun you will have being a part of this interesting study, you will receive a place setting of, International Silver Company's Rogers Cutlery Stainless Tableware from their "Modern Living" group--for every month of diaries we receive. It will be important, however, that you return every diary for each of the six months so that you can continue on the panel.

> You will never be approached by a sales representative as a result of your participation in this study, nor will the purchase information you send us' ever be reported as coming from your family. Your information will be strictly CONFIDENTIAL.

Asking Donations of Money or Other Tangible Valuables

Many people are even more reluctant to part with material goods than they are to donate their time. Thus all you have learned about persuasiveness, appeals, factual presentation, and reader benefits is even more important for requests to donate valuables.

If you want your reader to donate money, describe the problem and tell what is being or has been done, what needs to be done, and what your organization is doing about the problem. After stating meaningful facts, tell what it will cost to do what your organization wants to do—and how the reader can help.

If the donation is for a cause from which the reader benefits directly—as in improved recreation facilities for a club of which he or she is a member—you can choose from appeals such as comfort, enjoyment, friendships, health, love of family. However, if the donation goes to charity, your main appeal is usually altruism. Action paragraphs like the following help the conscientious reader who wonders how much he or she should give:

1. A gift of $5 will buy vitamins for 25 children...$8 will provide a cup of milk to 500 children...$25 may keep a father and mother alive to care for their own children...$150 sends 1,000 pounds of medicines to our hospitals.
2. "What is a thoughtful contribution?" You can best answer this question, BUT we suggest that an amount approximating two hours' pay would be justified in light of...

In the next letter, notice how appealingly the boys' home director and the business executive present the problem, tell what has been done and needs to be done about it, and persuade the reader to help.

Letter 3

*A persuasive request before Christmas for a donation to charity—unusually senti-
mental, but especially appealing to readers who have a generous spirit at Christmas-
time. (A colorful letterhead shows two homeless boys in the snow peering forlornly
into a bright Christmas-decorated home living room in which a fire is glowing warmly
in the fireplace.)*

My dear Friend:

*Attention: what
has been done*

HOW MUCH IS A HOMELESS BOY WORTH? Today thousands of
proud, productive citizens who live in the cities and
towns across the nation were, only a few years ago,
homeless, destitute boys. Many are skilled mechanics
in the various trades; others are farmers, business
and professional men.

The problem

These men came to Boys Town as young boys, of all
races and religious creeds. They all had the same
qualification--they were homeless. They were sad,
sensitive, with many heartaches because some tragedy
had robbed them of their home and parents. Some wan-
dered along the crossroads of the nation, their only
home in some empty freight car. Others, who had
been in trouble, came to us with snarls on their
faces, with eyes that were hard, sullen, and suspi-
cious.

HOW MUCH ARE THEIR LIVES WORTH TODAY--TO THEMSELVES,
THEIR WIVES AND CHILDREN, AND TO THE NATION?

*What our
institution does*

Here at Boys Town we continue, year after year, to
rebuild the lives of homeless, deserted boys. We
give them a good home, good food, and a parent's
rightful attention which they have been denied. I
talk with them individually, discuss their problems,
and help them solve these problems. They are educated in our schools, and are taught a practical
trade in our well-equipped trade school, on our
farm and dairy. During their spare time they engage in athletics, music, Scouting, and many hobbies. Their mental and moral training, and our
self-government system teach them to become stal-
wart, wholesome citizens.

*What needs
to be done*

My boys need you, and there are many more to come.
As Christmas approaches, won't you help me provide
for more homeless boys who will come to Boys Town, and
who have no other place to go? I am enclosing your
19__ Christmas seals. Most contributions I receive
are in $2, $3, and $5 amounts, but any amount you
care to send will let me serve as your Santa Claus to

*Action request;
altruism appeal*

my family of almost 1,000 boys. Because they've already had life's share of grief and hardships, won't
you help them to be happy now?

Reader benefit   God bless you, and may your own Christmas be doubly
happy because you have brought happiness to a home-
less, helpless boy.

(*Complimentary close and signature area*)

Reader benefit   Your contribution is an allowable income tax deduc-
tion. We employ no solicitors or fund-raising organization; we pay no commissions.

Letter 4

(Memo) *An executive's persuasive request to employees to contribute generously to an annual fund drive.*

TO: All Members of the Wigget Staff
FROM: Alberta Jones, President
SUBJECT: An appeal for the UGN Fund . DATE: Oct. 15,
                                                19__

Attention: problem
All of you are aware that this year our community has
a larger number of needy, desperate, afflicted people
of all ages, creeds, and races.

What is being done
You know also of the fine work that the United Good
Neighbors Fund does to provide community services
through 82 Good Neighbor agencies. Hundreds of persons volunteer freely of their time and money to
make this drive successful each year, with no thought
of tangible rewards.

Reader benefit

Request
Your one contribution helps in many ways, and you are
spared from being dunned by separate agencies. I
would like to make a personal appeal this year that
all of us reassess our values of this program and
make an honest effort to give just a little bit more.
Each of us sets the figure our conscience dictates,
but I sincerely hope you can find it in your hearts
to join me in increasing our donation this year. Our
company's goal is $52,900.

Appeal to altruism
We are all most fortunate in not being on the receiving end of this program, and one way to count our
blessings is by helping those less fortunate, as described in the enclosed leaflet.

Easy action
Remember, UGN pledge cards make it possible to contribute in small monthly or quarterly installments, or if
you choose, you may pay by payroll deductions.

Appeal to pride, altruism
Let's give serious consideration to the amount we contribute this year and try to make it one of which to
be proud. Your support will be received with appreciation by the many agencies within UGN.

Urging Cooperation on Goals and Projects

As a committee chairperson or officer you may from time to time need to get your readers to support various goals and projects that your organization considers important. Letters 5 and 6, sent to members and voters respectively, illustrate how persuasive requests can help move readers to action toward which they would otherwise be indifferent.

Letter 5

A membership chairman appeals for help in boosting membership.

Attention: *agreeable* *comment* *and question*	NPRA MEMBERSHIP JUMPS 100% Wouldn't you be delighted to see that headline in the <u>NPRA Journal</u>? And you can . . . for it can be done easily . . . without gimmicks or strings or expense to you.
Reader-benefit goal	Increased membership will strengthen our effectiveness and benefit each of us as well as the entire field of public relations. If you--each member--will find us <u>one</u> new NPRA member, our size can double.
Easy-action request	The method is simple and effective. Go over your firm's executive roster, your list of business associates. Think of everyone you know who might be interested in public and customer relations. Write the names and addresses on the enclosed card and drop it into the mail. That's all you need to do! Our secretary, Mr. Jim Ark, will take it from there.
Tie-in with opening	Isn't that easy? Find one new member for NPRA . . . and look for that headline soon . . . NPRA MEMBERSHIP JUMPS 100%.

Letter 6

Four citizens (one expert each in engineering, medicine, business leadership, and law) persuade citizens to vote for a bond issue.

	Dear Southside resident:
Attention: *reader-benefit* *comment*	Each of us has the opportunity on May 19 to leave a legacy for the future when we vote on the Forward Move bond issue--rapid transit. This program will substantially improve the quality of your environment for many years to come.
	Rapid transit will reduce traffic congestion and air pollution, both of which are becoming increasingly

*Interest:
reader benefits*

difficult problems in the Southside area. In addition, it will be of enormous benefit to you as a
resident of Southside. To you and the employees in
this area rapid transit brings easy access to plants
and businesses plus increased mobility from the
south side to all parts of the greater (*city name*)
community.

Two paragraphs for "interest and desire" include reader-benefit facts about two new underground bus transfer stations and low taxpayer costs (less than 6 cents a day).

*Reader-benefit
request*

On the basis of the compelling need and an opportunity to preserve and strengthen your area, we ask
you to vote "yes" with us on May 19.

OTHER PERSUASIVE NONROUTINE REQUESTS

Adapting the AIDA Plan

You can also use the AIDA plan effectively when you must persuade your reader to grant your request for adjustment, credit, or a change in a policy or performance. For your attention-getting opening you can use any of the suggested six kinds discussed above for favor requests (pages 332 to 334). However, to present a concise logical argument, it is usually best to begin with an assertion. This statement often is a principle—a major premise on which both you and the reader agree or about which you wish to persuade the reader; for example, these two (which can also be considered agreeable-comment openings):

No doubt you expect your authorized dealers to uphold the good name
of your products.

I am sure you want your company to have a reputation for fairness
and honesty.

You will get the reader's interest and desire when you state all necessary facts and details—interwoven with reader benefits. Include whatever description the reader needs to see that his or her firm is responsible (if this applies) and that your request is factual, logical, and reasonable. Your action request should be a logical conclusion based on the major premise and the clearly stated facts.

Persuasively Requesting an Adjustment

When a product or service from a reputable firm is unsatisfactory but you know that your claim for an adjustment is outside the warranty or otherwise unusual, your message should follow the persuasive-request instead of the direct-request plan. You also need to be persuasive when your request is *not* unusual but the seller disregarded your first direct request.

In letter 1, because of unusual circumstances, the customer persuasively asks for a new camera and certain other expenses—even though the printed guarantee includes a statement that the firm will service the camera but "cannot assume responsibility for loss of film, for other expenses or inconveniences, or for consequential damages occasioned by the equipment." This is an unusually long letter, but the details included are necessary to achieve the goal. The writer did get essentially what she wanted, though in slightly different form—six free rolls of film with processing mailers and an exchange of her camera with one owned by the manager of the local Picturetronics, Inc.

Letter 1

A consumer writes persuasively to a manufacturer's adjustment manager, requesting an unusual adjustment.

Attention: assertion of major premise

"Let your Wessman camera preserve those precious moments for you." This appealing advertising slogan, plus your company's good reputation, helped me to choose a Wessman camera for my once-in-a-lifetime trip to South America. Because of unusual circumstances I now find it necessary to appeal to you.

Interest; facts about purchase

Six months ago I purchased my Wessman Instanshot camera from a reputable store here. That was two months before my trip, so that I would have time to become thoroughly familiar with the camera before traveling in a foreign country. (I was a member of a group representing the Foundation for International Understanding, and our long-planned trip was a goodwill tour which I wanted to preserve in good pictures.)

For Conviction, a paragraph states facts on malfunctioning and repairs of the electronic eye, bar indicator, and flash attachment by an authorized dealer twice before the trip.

Conviction: more on the problem

Reader in writer's shoes; writer's care and trust

Two days before my departure they called to report my camera was "now in excellent working order." Little did any of us guess the picture problems ahead. Nevertheless, the camera was again a disappointment only two days later--on my first attempt to take a picture before leaving the airport. Twice the flash did not go off. Because it was Sunday morning and only a few minutes before plane departure, there was of course no way to have further repairs then. Perhaps you can imagine how you would feel at this moment. I had depended upon your authorized dealer's word that my camera was in excellent condition! (Incidentally, I always handle a camera with care according to instructions, for I know it is a delicate precision instrument.)

Tie-in with major premise

Throughout my trip there were numerous "precious moments" I wanted to preserve with my new Wessman camera. Most of these were on indoor occasions-- receptions, dinners, and other functions with peo-

ple. I can buy postcards of buildings and nature.
But no one sells pictures of the precious moments
with other human beings who assembled just for our
group! Yet these moments are lost forever because
Writer's losses   the flash attachment failed numerous times. These
failures also resulted in my ample supply of Wess-
man film being exhausted much too soon. I thus
had to purchase additional film plus flashbulbs in
foreign stores, at much higher prices.

When my developed film was returned I found that
72 negatives were total blanks. In other words,
72 times that flash attachment failed; 72 precious
moments are lost instead of preserved, as your
slogan advertises.

Appeal to fairness   Picturetronics, Inc. have said they can't under-
and pride   stand what is the matter with this camera and
they've done all they can. Even they suggest that
my camera must be one of the very rare defective
products from your usually dependable high-quality
stock. Thus I am returning this camera to you for
your inspection. But after all the heartaches it
has given me--in losing instead of preserving pre-
Request   cious moments--I ask that you please keep this
camera and send me instead a new dependable Instanshot camera. Also, will you please reimburse
me for the $49.20 I paid for wasted film, processing,
and flashbulbs. Copies of sales slips are enclosed.

By making these fair replacements you will help to
restore my faith in Wessman. Also, not only I, my-
Tie-in with   self, but friends who share my disappointments, will
major premise   again believe that Wessman does "preserve those precious moments."

Letter 2—also long—is a persuasive request written after previous direct requests had
failed. Because of the seriousness of the situation, this writer (the dealer) uses some
negative appeals—*loss* of reader benefits—along with the positive benefits. The letter
is addressed to the production manager.

Letter 2

A dealer persuasively requests better deliveries of a manufacturer's products.

Attention-getting   Repetition is an accepted mechanism for achieving
assertion   emphasis. Although we have stated to you before our
situation with respect to Crown tools, we are writing
again now to emphasize to you the probable sad consequences of your current performance and alloca-
tions.

Interest; problem	Because of population influx in this area and the tremendous increase in construction here, we believe you are taking a serious hazard by overlooking your competitive position in _____ (*name of state*).
Risk of losing benefits	Too many new users of electric tools and too many established Crown customers are finding it necessary to turn to other brands. Come the day when you have more tools than orders, you'll be sorry, and we with you will suffer in pride and pocketbook.
Reader benefit	Our plea to you is certainly more deserving than most distributors you know, here or elsewhere. We sell Crown saws and no other handsaw; we sell Crown drills, not eight other kinds; your sanders, your grinders, your shears and even your good little nibbler are all we have. We have no connection nor do we seek one with any of your competitors.
Conviction; facts that affect reader benefit	Now, we have lots of lines, big equipment and small. We represent 84 manufacturers and we have 14 sales people outside, 4 inside. Whether on commission or on trainee salaries, these people get paid in direct proportion to the gross profit they bring in. Our total allocation of Crown tools for June was $2,800. Even if we had received these tools, which we didn't, each representative could have had $155 worth to sell, a maximum personal gain on Crown tools of about $14. What percentage of sales efforts do you
Description of problem	expect to command for a maximum monthly potential of this amount, especially if the representative had to wait 6 to 12 months after the sale to get delivery for a, by then, irate customer?
Appeal to fairness	How can we reasonably spend time training sales personnel in your line? We took about 115 down payments on saws, based on promises we made on your authority in good faith. So far, we have refunded 68, you have lost 68 customers at least temporarily, and our expense of handling these and other Crown tool orders has been serious. Should we continue booking orders even on extremely indefinite delivery? Please tell us.

Reader-benefit appeal is further developed in two paragraphs with specific facts on the backlog, cancellations, broken promises, and risk of Crown's losing major industrial and responsible contractor customers.

More risks	In conclusion, a word about competition. It is public information that Rall brand has made us and you look pretty foolish here. We have heard some mechanical complaints about Rall, but the difference of say 40% in the life of a saw is not noticeable to the man who has only Rall saws. Because of your unbalanced

and locally unfavorable allocation flow here, very
few people we know have been able to compare new
Ralls with any but old Crown saws. We cannot in
honesty divert Crown saws to rental for the present,
and the number we have to sell doesn't allow many
chances for comparison.

Request;
reader benefit

Therefore, please do everything you can to step up
your shipments to fill the backlog of orders while
you can still save this excellent market!

Persuasively Requesting Credit

Most credit applications are direct requests, made in the routine course of business. However, sometimes you may seek a special credit privilege which on the surface you appear to be unqualified for. In such cases a persuasive request is more effective. For instance, if you are just starting your own first store and your capital, inventory, and current income are barely adequate, you will need to convince prospective creditors that they can depend upon you to pay regularly. Or you may wish to ask for 120-day credit terms instead of the usual 30-day period. Whatever your unusual request may be, be sure to include sufficient facts and figures to show how you have planned carefully and perhaps how the reader will benefit—for example, from your expected expanding market.

Sometimes credit applicants' first direct request is turned down and they cannot understand why. If they still want credit with that firm, a persuasive request such as letter 3 may help accomplish that purpose. This letter brought a prompt, pleasant phone call, an apology, and the granting of a revolving credit account "gladly."

Letter 3

A persuasive request for credit after a turndown.

Attention:
assertion

Your form letter of January 31 refusing my request
for the Blank's Revolving Credit (BRC) account and
suggesting I consider an Easy Payment Account came
as a mild shock.

Interest;
applicant's work
and knowledge

Blanks, without a doubt, maintains certain
policies regarding credit applications from individuals. In my occupation as a bookkeeper and assistant manager of City Paint and Hardware Company, I
process many applications for credit. Therefore, I
feel that when you considered my application, either
sufficient information was not given or the fact
that I am renting a house, rather than buying, was
regarded as grounds for listing me as a person of
"questionable" credit standing. In either assumption, I believe the following information will give
you a clear picture of my "present circumstances."

Conviction facts

Employment and Income
(*7 lines*)

Assets and Liabilities
(*8 lines*)

References
(*11 lines*)

Reader-benefit request

The Easy Payment Plan you suggest is an expensive way to buy merchandise. To buy on this plan partially defeats the purpose of "SHOP AT BLANKS AND SAVE!" Small easy payments <u>do</u> <u>not</u> appeal to me. Nor does dragging out payments over a long period of time. Your BRC account would be one I would use frequently. And you can be sure that you will receive prompt payments. BRC fits my present needs and my ability to pay. Your extending this privilege to me will be greatly appreciated.

Persuasively Requesting Changes in Policy or Performance

Besides requesting nonroutine adjustment or credit, you may at times need to persuade a company to make other exceptions from its usual policy. Or you may wish to persuade individuals to change their actions; or to give employees a written pep talk, hoping to improve their future performance. The basic persuasive-request pattern is again applicable here.

Changes in Policy

In letter 4, an advertising consultant tries to persuade the public relations officer of ABC Company to deviate from its usual policy of not giving away or lending products. An outstanding magazine feature writer (renamed "Jake Edlis" in this example) had written for permission to borrow, free, ABC Company's new XX boating equipment—to use, photograph, and mention in his new series of feature stories on outdoor life.

Letter 4

An advertising consultant's persuasive request to deviate from the usual no-loan policy regarding company equipment.

Attention: assertion

Though I know it is ABC's policy not to loan or give away its products, I think sticking to it in the case of Jake Edlis would be a mistake.

Interest; conviction

There are very few writers in the recreation field for whom I'd take a stand on this issue. Among them are_____, _____, _____, and Jake Edlis.

Company benefit

First, lending your boating equipment is a relative-ly small expense for the publicity ABC is bound to receive in return. The space value could, conceiv-ably, amount to tens of thousands of dollars. As you know, his write-ups reach about 16 million readers each month.

More company benefit

Second, ABC is a big league now. Big leaguers play the game by getting respected writers like Edlis to use their products (many of them carrying big price tags) and write about them.

More company benefit

Third, as a member of the Outdoor Writers Associa-tion of America and a well-known feature writer, Edlis is bound to talk to a lot of other "influen-tials" in the field. He could, intentionally or not, start word that ABC is willing to take lots of free space, but unwilling to extend the accepted courtesy of letting legitimate feature writers try its products without charge. Ultimately, this could lead to poor press relations and a resulting drop in our publicity lineage.

Risk of harmful results if change is not made

Company-benefit request

In the interest of maintaining exceptionally good press relations, please reconsider your company's "no giveaway" policy when someone with the stature of a Jake Edlis offers his services. I'm sure you'll be glad you did.

Changes in Performance

Persuasion is necessary whenever you need to convince individuals to change their per-formance (which may include personal appearance and habits as well as business prac-tices) and if direct requests have been or would be unheeded.

The next two examples[3] illustrate how important the right tone and use of appeals are for getting reader cooperation. As you read letter 5, note these faults:

1. Overemphasis on negatives—"disturbed," "horrified," "will have to be removed," "senseless," "punishing," "destroying"
2. Overuse of "we"—meaning "Landlord, Inc.," rather than "all people (us) in the neighborhood"
3. Manager's domineering, threatening, discourteous attitude, which places all parents on the defensive and seems to blame their children, although the vandals may have been outsiders
4. Total lack of reader appeals

Letter 5

A poor, negative, unpersuasive request from a building manager to tenants.

[3] Courtesy of New York Life Insurance Company, *Effective Letters Bulletin*, Summer 1965.

TO ALL PARENTS LIVING IN 100 OAK AVENUE AND 50 ELM AVENUE

We have become seriously disturbed because of the recent vandalism in your neighborhood. Every day now, storage room doors are
being broken, tires removed from bicycles, parts of baby carriages
are taken off, etc. etc.; but today we were horrified to see a beautiful living tree (in front of 50 Elm Avenue) completely cut in half.
Now the tree will have to be removed.

We would like all the parents to have a good talk with their
children in order, to stop this senseless destruction.

We will start patrolling this section very closely from now on,
and if necessary, we will call in the municipal and school authorities of Metropolis, in order to start punishing children who are
found destroying property.

In contrast, letter 6 eliminates the main faults of letter 5. Its tone is friendly, courteous, and positive. Equally important, this letter emphasizes community spirit, mutual concern, and cooperation. Letter 6 appeals to the parents' pride, love of family,
health, and desire for security; and it includes the young people as citizens instead of
accusing them indirectly of being vandals.

Letter 6

An appealing, improved version of letter 5.

TO ALL FAMILIES IN THE ELM AVENUE SCHOOL DISTRICT:

*Attention:
a mutual problem*

I know you will be as sorry as I was to learn
that the lovely old elm tree which gave our school
its name was destroyed today. Its beauty and grace
are now lost to us forever, and all of us regret
this tragedy.

*Interest; need for
mutual effort*

The destruction of our landmark appears to be
another in a recent series of acts of vandalism in
our neighborhood--a problem which can affect all of
us unless we make a mutual effort to rid ourselves
of it.

*Conviction; appeals
to safety, health,
security, and civic
pride*

A number of residents of our community have
volunteered to do patrol duty in their off-hours,
protecting the safety of our families and our property. Though we appreciate their desire to help,
we need to ask ourselves if a patrol is what we
really want. Do we want our neighborhood to be a
prison for our children or a place of freedom and
healthful growth?

Shall we instead face this problem frankly and
constructively? Let us consider a few facts. Does
our community have adequate provisions for recreational activities, or should we be contributing more
to the creativity, growth, and culture of Metropolis?

Have we done everything possible to make this the city in which our young people will be proud to grow up?

Request

It has been suggested that we discuss these things both in our own homes and then together as a community. Will you meet with us next Monday evening, January 18, at 7:30 in the auditorium of Elm Avenue School so that we may plan a constructive program of progress? Perhaps we can form a Civic Pride Committee comprised of both young people and adults--a committee which can investigate our needs and help us plan a calendar of events to appeal to everyone. Our mayor and council members share our enthusiasm and have agreed to be present.

Appeals to pride and cooperation

Reader benefits

Let's make Monday evening "Family Night." Fill the auditorium with families, ideas, and appetites for cake, coffee, and sodas. See you at 7:30!

UNSOLICITED SALES LETTERS

Every year millions of dollars' worth of goods and services are sold through sales letters—both solicited and unsolicited—to consumers, businesses, and industries. Unsolicited sales letters are also known as "prospecting" and "cold turkey" letters. They are initiated by the seller for various reasons and are not direct answers to inquiries.[4] Direct mail[5] successfully urges people to buy products ranging from mail-order cataloged items to real estate. Not only large retail chains such as Montgomery Ward and Sears, but also thousands of lesser-known big-city and small-town merchants, wholesalers, and manufacturers sell effectively by mail. Many firms sell exclusively by mail. Even managers of shops selling services (for home and auto repair, health, beauty, protection, and others) stimulate their businesses by sales messages.

Although you should be aware of the enormous potential income that is possible using well-written sales letters, you need also to be aware of the strong resistance that many people have toward such messages. Common criticisms from readers who look unfavorably on sales letters are these: insincerity, appeals to the wrong group, hidden gimmicks, lack of personalization, excessive length, exaggeration.

In general, your success in sales letters will depend upon three factors: the mailing list, the right appeals, and the presentation. The first two of these factors are *prewriting* steps. The remainder of this chapter discusses the steps to take before writing unsolicited sales letters, gives suggestions for writing them, and offers examples of

[4] For solicited sales letters—which are answers to inquiries about products and services—see Chapter 8, pages 207–212.
[5] In general, the term *direct mail* refers to any printed matter, other than periodicals, that attempts to sell or promote sales by mail. It includes—in addition to letters—postcards, manuals, brochures, order blanks, pamphlets, leaflets, gadgets, and reply forms. These items usually supplement the letter and help create a favorable seller-buyer relationship.

various kinds of unsolicited sales letters. Appendix A includes various cautions regarding the seller's legal responsibilities in written and oral statements about the product or service. They can strongly affect the success of your sales messages.

Steps before Writing the Unsolicited Sales Letter

Because your sales letter may go to hundreds—even thousands—of people, you need to do exceptionally careful planning before starting to write it. The six planning steps—about purpose, reader, ideas to include, fact gathering, organization, and revision—are especially important. You usually first gather facts on your product and your prospective buyer and then give extra thought to the purpose, appeals, and presentation of your entire sales message.

Gathering Facts about Your Product

Before you write a sales letter, you first analyze thoroughly the product you want to sell. (The word *product* as used here includes both tangible products and intangible services.) You gather information through reading, observing, testing, using, comparing, questioning, researching.

If yours is a tangible product, what are its physical characteristics—size, color, shape, content, composition? How is it made and where did raw materials come from? How does it operate? What is its performance record? How does it compare with and differ from competitors' products in durability, efficiency, appearance, price, terms? What are its weaknesses? Strengths?

For your future buyers, benefits (psychological description) are usually much more significant than physical description. What will the product do for each user? What human needs or desires does it fulfill? For instance, a magazine may be a certain size, with *x* number of pages, on glossy paper, with hundreds of half-page pictures. But what information and enjoyment—even profits—does it bring to the user? What good does it do the buyer in business, home, family, and community contacts?

A new real estate subdivision may consist of 100 six-room brick, ranch-style houses on one-quarter-acre tracts. But why should the reader purchase in this subdivision rather than elsewhere? Perhaps living here is unique because of the climate and scenic beauty which allow year-round sun, fun, and sports, plus a plentiful supply of fresh water and fertile soil? Perhaps a trend of prolonged rise in real estate values makes this property a good investment? Perhaps it is an exceptionally good place to rear children?

Your vinyl jackets may have the same "rich grain as expensive buckskin leathers" and be available in 10 sizes. But of special interest to your customer are these facts about what a jacket *will do for her:*

It is completely water-repellent, so she will be dry in any downpour.

Though the jacket is fully lined, she can wear it in any weather all year round.

It's soft and pliable and never needs costly dry cleaning; she saves money.

Dirt and stains come clean with a damp cloth and a little mild detergent.

Its classic style won't go out of fashion.

She saves money also by buying direct from the factory, and no salesperson rushes or pressures her.

She can try the jacket on at home and wear it 10 days without obligation.

Whatever your product, you must know all its physical features and its reader benefits before you can confidently and effectively sell it.

Considering Your Reader and Mailing Lists

To sell your product effectively by letter requires also a knowledge of your reader and a selective, up-to-date, accurate mailing list. You'll use the mailing list both for a test mailing and for the entire mailing of one or several sales letters. *Testing* means mailing the letter to a small percentage (perhaps 5 to 10%) of the names on your list to see whether the letter brings the percentage of response necessary for you to make a profit.[6]

When your product has almost universal use, you may have several different, reasonably homogeneous groups of prospects. Thus if you want to sell lighting fixtures by mail, you need to know the tastes, problems, preferences, and conditions of your various prospective users—homeowners, architects, store or office managers, plant or hospital or school superintendents, and so forth—and you'll write different letters to each group.

Selectivity. Even an excellent sales letter about the best product in the world will not sell if the message goes to the wrong readers. You would not sell office filing cabinets to outdoor laborers, fishing boats to low-income people in a desert area, or Cadillacs to pensioners.

You can buy, rent, or make up a mailing list that includes the best potential buyers for your product. The more similar their characteristics and circumstances, the better. You can buy names and addresses of almost any kind of specialized group of people—classified by income level, age, marital status, sex, number of children, occupation, geographic location, color of eyes, height, education. However, you need to be cautious. For instance, even if your product is for people with above-average incomes, you must take other factors into account. For example, an individual with a $30,000 income and eight children may be less able to spend for luxuries than a childless person with a lower income.

If you wish to make your own list, you will find one or more of these sources useful: telephone books, directories, membership lists, vital statistics, newspaper articles,

---

[6] Previous discussions in this text on you-attitude and visualizing your reader also apply to sales letters.

replies to your advertising, and—sometimes best of all—your own company records.[7] Your credit and sales departments can give you lists of present and former customers; other departments can furnish lists of stockholders, employees, suppliers. Any or all of these may be good for your own company-prospect list.

Up-to-dateness and Accuracy. Postal authorities tell us that over one-fourth of all addresses change within one year. Names and titles may change too. The mailing list must be correct in addresses, spelling of names, use of prefixes (such as Mr., Miss, Mrs., Ms., Dr.), and titles (such as vice president or executive vice president). No matter how selective the list may be, it is good only when it is updated and correct.

Deciding on Purpose

The purpose of an unsolicited sales letter may be to make a direct sale, to serve as stimulus for future sales, or to win back lost customers.

To Make a Direct Sale. For relatively inexpensive convenience items or services the purpose of the sales letter is usually to make a direct sale. Sometimes even for more expensive or complex items your purpose may be to sell with only one letter, as you will see later in this chapter. More often, however, for such products the direct-sale letter follows previous groundwork laid by former letters (in a campaign series), by demonstrations, by advertising, or by sales representatives. The requested action to clinch the sale is that the prospect send for the article. In some letters—those offering a free trial or money-back guarantee—the requested action to send for the article is usually only a preliminary, conditional step. The sale is really not closed until the customer has examined and perhaps used the product within a specified time limit.

To Serve as Stimulus for a Future Sale. The long-range purpose of sales promotion messages may be to help build goodwill, supplement advertising, or give pep talks to distributors. Or they may serve as part of a campaign series involving complicated costly products (like factory machinery) or services (like mortgage lending) that require planning and/or individual consultation with a company representative before purchase. In these letters the purpose may be to introduce the product and then follow up with a salesperson. The requested action may be that the customer should: ask for a booklet, catalog, or other information; invite a representative to call; or come to the salesroom.

To Win Back Lost Customers. In other sales letters the purpose is: to let customers who haven't bought anything for some time know you miss them, to find out why they haven't been buying from you, and to sell them on coming back. The requested action is usually that the customer return a questionnaire; often an enclosed order blank brings a direct sale. And good follow-up can help bring in future purchases by presently dissatisfied customers.

---

[7] Among the many firms that have compared the pulling power of rented versus their company-prospect names is Merrill Lynch, Pierce, Fenner and Smith. They found that 10,560 rented names brought a 7.4% response; 10,900 company-prospect names brought a 24.9% response. (*The Reporter of Direct Mail Advertising Newsletter,* November 1966.)

Choosing Ideas and the Central Selling Point

After you have collected facts on your product, obtained a mailing list of likely prospects, and determined your purpose, you are ready to decide on ideas to include in your sales letter. Instead of cluttering your letter with a long list of facts about your product, you should select for emphasis a *central selling point* and translate it into user benefits. You stress *whatever appeal is most likely to convince the prospect that he or she should buy your product.* Often this is the feature or benefit that differentiates your product from competitors'. After you have stressed the central selling point, you can introduce other appeals about your product. (For a second letter to the same prospect, you can stress a second central selling point.)

Your central selling point is always based on what you estimate are the prospect's needs. Will the product cut his or her costs? protect him or her? make him or her more attractive? If your product will appeal to different groups of prospects for different reasons, you will write a different sales letter to each group. In each letter you will feature the central selling point and appeals that you estimate are most pleasing to the readers for whom you write it. For example, to dealers who expect to resell your product, you will emphasize quick turnover and profits. To consumers you may feature comfort, pride in personal appearance, safety, or any other appropriate appeals like those listed on page 331. Remember also that individuals within any group have different mental filters and situations, and may thus be motivated for different reasons (perhaps another central selling point which you stress in a later letter).

Suppose, for instance, you want to sell by mail the vinyl jacket described briefly on page 353. To readers living in rainy areas you might feature year-round comfort (dry in any downpour). To readers in arid regions your major appeal may be convenience (easily cleaned and wearable the year around). For students you might focus on both attractiveness (in style) and saving money (infrequent replacements, factory prices, no dry-cleaning bills).

Planning the Presentation and Making Revisions

The fifth and sixth planning steps—organization and rewriting—involve much more than deciding upon the organizational plan and final content of the letter itself. Consider your letter as part of an entire mailed sales presentation which includes the letter with all enclosures—whether it is to be a single sales effort or to be part of a campaign series.

Your presentation must move readers to take the desired action—and yield a satisfactory profit. The percentage of response needed for profitable returns may range from less than one percent to a much higher figure, depending upon various factors. For instance, the Mercedes-Benz letter mentioned in footnote 9 successfully achieved its goal, though only three-tenths of 1 percent of the readers purchased a car. The returns the mailing brings must be sufficiently greater than its total cost—for the list, plus planning, consulting (with direct-mail specialists),[8] writing, revising, reproducing, testing, and mailing the letter with all its enclosures.

[8] Many firms (except those with specially trained direct mail staffs) ask outside specialists to write their sales letters and plan the enclosure.

Ultimately, though the initial cost of these steps may be high, the cost per mailing may be as low as 10 to 50 cents or as high as several dollars each—and the resulting profits many times these amounts. Plans and decisions (by you and perhaps other executives and a consultant) are essential. You need to consider enclosures and also the length, appearance, and timing of the entire sales message. Your budget and numerous other factors enter into this plan.

Number and Kinds of Enclosures. Before writing your sales letter, plan the enclosures. Will the envelope contain any descriptive pamphlet, separate testimonials, pictures, samples, gimmicks, gadgets, order blank, and/or reply envelope? Gadgets and gimmicks should be used only if they help to dramatize a point, not if they merely attract attention. (Some readers dislike them; others become absorbed in them and fail to read the letter.) The usual enclosures are leaflet, order blank, and reply envelope.

Length of Sales Letter. If the enclosures adequately take care of all needed details, the letter should preferably be only one page. This is especially true if its purpose is to get action other than a direct purchase. If a catalog or booklet is to be sent later upon request, or if a demonstration or sales representative is to follow, these methods will help make the sale. On the contrary, if you do not have a separate enclosure—and especially if you want to make a direct sale—your letter may have to be longer than one page. Just be sure it is as concise as possible!

Many conflicting ideas exist about the desirable length of sales letters. However, direct-mail experts have proved again and again that long copy works—if it catches and holds the reader's interest and is sufficiently convincing.[9]

Appearance of Sales Letter. To a prospect a company is what it appears to be in its printed mailing. You need to decide (usually with the help of experts in direct mail, advertising, and/or processing) on the quality and color of paper to be used and also whether the printing will be in one or more colors. Other factors to be considered in your planning are these:

Should special pictures, designs, handwritten "teaser" statements, or other attention-getting devices or gimmicks be used on the outside envelope and the letterhead?[10] If so, they will to some extent affect the wording of your letter . . . and your costs too.

Should the letter be personalized with the reader's name and address? You will be well repaid for carefully comparing relative costs. If your mailing list is long, computerized letters with computerized matching fill-ins can be effective. Or you may have the name, address, and salutation processed in a different color from that of

[9] One of the more startling success stories is the case of the Mercedes-Benz company that sold 1,500 Model 190D Sedans for $4,068 each, one summer before Labor Day (1965)—entirely through a five-page letter which their advertising agency designed and mailed to 500,000 people. This letter's success was remarkable for another reason: these cars used diesel fuel, a hurdle because diesel fuel stations were scarce at the time. (Courtesy of Mercedes-Benz of North America, Inc., Fort Lee, New Jersey.)

[10] See also page 330, regarding the attention-getting importance of envelopes and letterheads.

the letter's body. Another alternative is to insert a catchy appropriate statement in place of the inside address and salutation, as illustrated on pages 153 and 374.

What about the sizes of the letterhead, envelopes, and other enclosures? Should any be oversize? Transparent? With what size and kind of type?

Should the envelopes have windows? Should part of the letter's message show through one or more windows?

Should you "dress up" the sales letter itself? You can add interesting variety and emphasis by occasional underscoring or capitalizing of important ideas, by indenting some sentences or paragraphs on both margins, by use of more short than long paragraphs, and by "inked" lines, arrows, or other marks to emphasize ideas.

Reproduction of your mailing pieces should preferably be done professionally. Using your company's duplicating machine may be all right for some small sales efforts, but professional jobs make the best impression. Also, it is best not to try to disguise direct mail with "cute" attempts to fool the recipient, for most people react negatively to them. The honest, well-written factual presentation that is reader-centered and pleasing always outpulls the others.

Timing of Sales Message. Consider what is likely to be the best time of the week, month, season, and year to launch a certain sales campaign. The time of your mailing will naturally affect the wording of your sales letter and sometimes your choice of appeals (as for certain seasons, holidays).

Figures released by the National Association of Manufacturers show that 80 percent of orders are placed after the sales representative's fifth call. Remember that a sales letter is a "sales representative" too. Some firms have effectively sent the same letter (perhaps on paper of a different color) to the same prospects two or three times and received orders only after the last mailing.

Suggestions for Writing the Unsolicited Sales Letter

After you have completed the prewriting steps about your product, mailing list of prospects, choice of ideas and main appeals, and the planned presentation—you are ready to develop the sales letter itself. This writing (and revising) will probably take hours, even days. If time and budget permit, you may decide—with the help of a consultant—to prepare several versions of your letter to test their pulling power before mailing one to the entire mailing list.

Your basic guide is the AIDA organizational pattern discussed on pages 329-332. Although the discussion below focuses separately on each part of the AIDA plan, the parts need not always be in this sequence, nor need all parts be in every letter. Some sales letters begin with desire-creating material such as testimonials or guarantees. Some start with action-inducing statements such as special offers or free trials. Some may skip product description and uses (the interest section) and devote most of the letter to proof—if, for example, the reader already knows the description and uses but needs conviction material to reinforce interest and create desire to buy the product. Circumstances vary—and so do sales letter content and organization.

Attracting Your Prospect's Attention

The best way to catch the attention of a busy reader is by promising—or implying a forthcoming promise—*to benefit him or her by satisfying a need.* Mention what the reader gains from the product before you name it. Even before the opening paragraph you can attract the reader's attention by inserting a benefit in place of the inside address. See for example letter 2, page 369 and letter 4, page 374. (Using the reader's name in the salutation also helps get attention.)

Though the letter may go to thousands of people, each copy must "talk" in a natural, sincere, friendly way to an individual human being. The opening should be appropriate, fresh, honest, interesting, specific, and relevant to the central selling point. Avoid tricky, exaggerated openings, which have been so overused that the American public is unmoved or annoyed by them. Of course, if you can think of a novel, catchy opening that honestly relates closely to your central theme, go ahead and use it.

Also be careful to avoid openings that may outdate your letter soon. For instance, one letter addressed to "Dear Graduate" began "Now that you are out of school for three months . . . ." Readers who had been out of school longer than that were of course annoyed by the inaccuracy.

Keep the first paragraph short, preferably two to five lines, sometimes only one. Short paragraphs look easy to read and thus are more likely to get the reader started. If unusual circumstances require you to have a long opening paragraph, it should be set up in an easy-to-read way—sometimes with double spaces between sentences or with some lines indented from both margins.

For the *content* of your attention-getting opening, you can choose from any of the following 10 kinds (arranged alphabetically).

1. An Agreeable Assertion
Offering a free brand-new handbook with a magazine subscription.

```
As a Westerner interested in boating, you know how different our
yachting and boating activities and opportunities are out here.
```

2. A Comparison or a (Short!) Story
Selling a secretary's handbook along with a free *kit:*
(Pictures of a cluttered and a tidy desk at top of letter)

```
It's really amazing!  Betty and Sue work side by side in the same
office.  They have the same secretarial training and skills...both
have identical workloads--yet Betty is usually putting away her
typewriter by 4:45 everyday, while Sue usually can't even find her
newspaper under the clutter of unfinished work still on her desk.
   And not only the janitor notices!  Their boss has noticed the dif-
ference too.  So besides the sheer delight of an easier day with
much less pressure, let's face it, Betty will be in line for pro-
motions, pay raises, and all the "fringe benefits" that go with
them!
```

3. An Event or Fact in the Reader's Life
Selling car insurance:

The fact that you are a college senior specializing in medicine and attending a well-respected university like (*name*) tells people about your character.

For instance, it may qualify you for a special low-cost auto insurance program that might not otherwise be available to you.

4. A Problem the Reader May Face

Urging use of a catalog to shop by mail:

During the next few weeks you and people all over the country will be doing Christmas shopping. Some will be early birds. Others will wait until the last minute; and if they are shopping in the stores, they will be pushed around and have to take what is left instead of being able to purchase just the items they had in mind.

5. A Quotation

Selling repair service:

"A stitch in time saves nine."

6. A Scare Opening[11]

Selling bank safe-deposit boxes:

(Picture of a burning home. Letter is on a simulated document from which a corner has been burned off.)

Let's JUST SUPPOSE
This was a valuable document in your home, destroyed because of fire. Not only could it mean a severe financial loss but replacing it might take months as well as a considerable amount of inconvenience.

7. A Significant Fact about the Product

Selling TV cable service:

More than 4,000,000 viewers in the UNITED STATES...

...and...

over 10,000 people in the (*city*) area alone enjoy sharp, clear, multichannel television reception by means of C.A.T.V. (Community Antenna Television).

8. A Solution to a Problem

Selling canned seafood:

Here's the solution to your Christmas present problem. Your relatives, friends, and business acquaintances will delight in receiving this taste treat from the North Pacific.

Selling hospital insurance:

You can receive a check like this, or even up to $5,000, when you or a member of your family goes to the hospital...IF you are protected by Hospital Plan.

---

[11] Scare openings are usually *not* recommended—except for some kinds of insurance and other services treating accidents or crime *if* the idea of harm or danger is already in the prospect's mind and the letter offers a solution. If, however, the idea of danger or harm is not likely to be on his mind, the opening should be positive and pleasant, stressing the solution rather than the danger.

9. **A Special Offer or a Gift**
   Selling book club membership:

   The extraordinary opportunity described in the big circular--for you
   to get this remarkable new major dictionary AT AN IMMEDIATE SAVING
   OF $20 (*capitals in red print*)--speaks pretty much for itself.

10. **Testimonials**
    Selling industrial cleaning compound:

    "XX is by far the best cleanser we have ever used," says Mr. Tom
    Brown, building superintendent at ABC Company.

Arousing the Reader's Interest

Having attracted the reader's attention, you now arouse interest by beginning to "picture" your product and telling what it will do for the reader. You begin to develop the central selling point.

As stated in the general outline on pages 329-332, you can picture your product in two ways—physical description and reader benefits. You can place the benefits first—as in example 1 below—or later, but usually they are interwoven with physical description, as in example 2.

Example 1

Stating benefits before physical description.

When you use <u>Family</u> <u>Investments</u> you find hundreds of ways to make
your money earn more and go further--for your home, clothing, food,
travel, taxes, and pleasure. You get a rich source of advice from
accountants, automotive specialists, real estate agents, tax consultants, life insurance experts, bankers, stockbrokers, lawyers.

This leatherbound book contains 467 pages, divided by subject into
15 chapters, 165,000 words. Sturdily built for continual use, the
book has 310 drawings, graphs, and tables to illustrate points and
clarify meanings. In essence, using the book will be like taking a
fascinating course in managing your family's money--from highly
paid professionals.

Example 2

Interweaving benefits and physical description.

The "heart" of your outfit is Bell & Howell's great Zoom-Lens Elec-
tric-Drive Super 8 Camera. You just pop in the Kodak cartridge of
Super 8 color film (it's fast and simple) . . . <u>aim</u> . . . and
<u>shoot</u>. That's all there is to it. And this camera is <u>electrically</u>
powered--no winding whatsoever. Pop the cartridge in and you are
ready to shoot a full 50-foot movie without interruption.

Just consider how every step virtually takes care of itself: the
camera sets itself automatically for different types of film--it
even adjusts automatically for indoor or outdoor filming--and the
Optronic Electric Eye sets the lens (also automatically), measuring
only that light reaching the film.

Creating Desire and Convincing the Reader

After getting your readers interested in one or several of your product's benefits, you need to create in them a desire to own it. Furthermore, if your purpose is to make a direct sale, you need to convince them that they should buy your product. Like the personal sales representative, your letter leads the prospective buyers through a "mental demonstration" so they imagine themselves already the owner—and it offers proof whenever necessary.

The reader's progression from interest to desire to conviction is usually gradual. It is not necessary to worry about exactly where one step begins or ends; these steps are parts of an integrated whole. Together they develop your central selling point and help urge the reader to take the requested action.

Desire for Your Product. Desire-creating material within the letter ranges from one paragraph—in a one-page letter with descriptive brochure—to several paragraphs if the letter itself is two or more pages long, with or without an enclosed brochure.

Emphasis on reader use and benefits is especially important if your product is valued mainly for its use and/or your prospect is familiar with its appearance (for instance, an electric iron, a camera, or a television set). But if the product is valued mainly because of its appearance (for example, an ornament or a blouse), its physical details must be fully described; usually an accompanying brochure also includes a colorful picture. If the product is machinery or technical equipment, your letter must clarify its sturdiness of construction, fine crafting, and other technical details in terms that the prospect values and can understand—whether the prospect is an ordinary citizen or a professional. Whenever desirable, you enclose with your letter technical sketches and meaningful pictures, charts, graphs. In all cases, be sure to emphasize the central selling point and show how the reader benefits. Work on one or more appeals, such as those listed on page 331.

The following example illustrates desire-creating paragraphs that develop the central selling point and benefits. Example 3 here follows example 2. Notice how it continues to stress the central theme—convenience—in order to increase the reader's desire. These paragraphs are part of a three-page letter.

Example 3

Developing the central selling point and benefit—convenience.

Breathtaking ZOOM shots from wide-angle to close-up[12]

And with this camera, the special fingertip-control ZOOM lens makes it possible for you to get the same kind of breathtaking zoom shots TV and movie directors use--you can actually shift from wide-angle shots to dramatic close-ups (and back again) while you're shooting. And there is still another tremendous design advance: you actually

---

[12] The headings in this letter were green, in contrast to the blue print used for the rest of the letter; in a subsequent mailing of the same letter, headings were orange and the rest of the letter print, brown.

view <u>through the lens</u> while you're filming--you get exactly what
you see. And for extra fun, you can get in the act yourself: you
just set the camera's special "Automatic Run Control."

<u>Bell & Howell Super-Bright Super 8 Projector Threads Itself</u>

With this Bell & Howell Super 8 Projector, threading is, at last,
outmoded--this projector does it all for you--easily, in just five
seconds! Just press a button, insert the film, and the film automatically <u>winds itself</u> through--and you sit back, relax and enjoy
your movies--up to 400 feet of film without interruption of any kind.

And this projector has other top-quality abilities: Imagine being
able to run your movies backward. You can! Simply flip a lever
and divers bounce backward onto the board or the family goes backward
into the car after just getting out.

Just flip a lever again and this projector practically turns into a
slide machine! Now you can view the hundreds of motion picture
frames you have taken <u>one at a time</u>--and look at them individually.

<u>You get a complete HOME MOVIE "ENTERTAINMENT CENTER"</u>--all these ex-
tras are included: (*The letter continues to list nine extras.*)

Evidence to Convince. Prove to your reader that the features and benefits you
describe are true. By convincing the reader you strengthen his or her desire to have the
product. Try to anticipate the reader's questions and objections—about the product
itself and/or its price—and answer them. You might not get another chance to do so!

The main proof about your product's features and benefits comes preferably from
evidence that persons outside your company determine. These outside sources include
satisfied users; recognized testing laboratories, agencies, and disinterested persons; and
the prospect himself or herself. Seven popular kinds of proof are illustrated below.

From Satisfied Users:

1. Facts about Users' Experience with the Product
These include verifiable reports and statistics from users.

The green page in the enclosed brochure itemizes the savings which
203 contractors have realized from EASI-POUR concrete mix. Notice
that their actual savings range from 45% to 85%. As you study the
table, note its specific facts about the size of each job. Then compare the figures with your own average costs for similar projects.

2. Names of Other Buyers and Users
*State how many persons or firms already are using the product. Better yet, when
appropriate, give the names of satisfied well-known users, or offer to send names
and addresses upon request.*

Among the hundreds of business firms that are pleased with their use
of ABC equipment are: Marshall Field and Company, Alcoa Aluminum,
Ford Motor Company, United Airlines, and Chase Manhattan Bank.

3. Testimonials
*Because testimonials have been abused (with phony quotations by nonusers who
are paid to make them), many people distrust them. To establish the credibility of*

the testimonials you use, select persons or firms that are bona fide users of your product and whose judgment the reader respects. And be specific. Avoid exaggerations and vague generalities.

"Since we've been using EASI-POUR concrete mix, six of our workers can place and finish a section of concrete street with curb--12 feet wide and a football field long--in only <u>one hour</u>. Its paving ability and its quality surpass any concrete mix we've used during our twenty years of operation." Gene Aimes, Project Superintendent, East Contractors, Inc.

From Recognized Testing Laboratories, Agencies, Disinterested Persons:

4. Performance Tests

Whenever recognized experts, testing laboratories, or authoritative agencies in a field relative to your product have made satisfactory performance tests on it, their evidence offers convincing proof. Also effective are statements, reports, and statistics compiled by impartial, reliable witnesses.

Learnfun electric toys have earned the endorsement and Seals of Approval from Underwriters Laboratories, Good Housekeeping Institute, American Medical Association, and National Safety Council.

In every performance test by the United Automotive Association, ALERT batteries ranked at the top of the list. Read in the enclosed brochure the details of qualities tested, and decide for yourself why ALERT is the battery for you.

From the Prospect:

5. Free Trial

If you have so much confidence in your product that you're willing to let the prospect try it on a free trial basis, your offer provides a very effective form of proof. The mail-order customer thus has the same opportunity to examine the product carefully as he or she would have before buying in a store. In fact, the customer gets the added privilege of using it before buying or paying for it.

For your use alone, we have enclosed a Reservation Certificate giving you the privilege of using the <u>Bell</u> & <u>Howell</u> <u>Super</u> <u>8</u> <u>Complete</u> <u>Home</u> <u>Movie</u> <u>Outfit</u> <u>for</u> <u>30</u> <u>full</u> days--<u>free</u> <u>and</u> <u>without</u> <u>obligation</u>. We supply the color film--a 50-foot Kodak Cartridge--and the movies you make are yours <u>free</u>--to show and to keep.

You'll have a full 10 days to use your new coats . . . to wear them walking, driving, working--without actually spending a single cent. . . . If for some reason, any reason at all, you don't like them, just send them back to me within 10 days, and we'll forget the whole thing. What could be fairer?

6. Guarantee

With the guarantee, the customer pays for the product before using it, but gets a written promise that if not satisfied he or she will get a refund (or credit), free repairs, or free replacement of the entire article.

With every ARTEX product you buy you get this firm, money-back guarantee: "All ARTEX products are Unconditionally Guaranteed to please.
If you are not completely satisfied with any ARTEX, return it for
full refund within 30 days."

7. Samples

Let the prospect examine, try, and/or use the samples that you send (for instance,
swatches of clothing or drapery materials; pieces of wire, rubber, or fireproof in-
sulation) or that he or she calls for personally (such as gasoline for the car, or a
food and beverage made fresh daily). The prospect is asked to perform some sug-
gested action to convince him- or herself that the product meets the writer's claims.

Look at the sample I've sent along. See the beautiful grain. Notice
how soft and pliable it is. No jacket leather was ever softer--or
more carefree. And notice the quilt lining. You'll be comfortable
no matter what the weather.

The placement of the proof section varies. Usually these statements come after the
desire-creating description and benefits. However, if the proof involved possesses the
necessary attention-getting qualities to justify placing it at the beginning, you may do
so.

Price of Your Product. Your presentation on the selling features, benefits, and
proof may have convinced the prospect that your product meets the need and he or
she should buy it. But is the product worth the price and can he or she pay for it?

If your price is a bargain, you might feature it as an attention-getting opening. If
the price doesn't justify this degree of emphasis, state it only *after* you have presented
most of the selling features, benefits, and proof. Of course, if your letter is part of a
campaign series to sell a costly item, the price might not be mentioned until near the
end of the series. Sometimes price is not mentioned in the letter at all. If the product
or service varies with the customer's needs (as for insurance or a complex heating installation in an industrial plant), the exact price quotation is given only after consultations with sales representatives.

If your prospect is likely to consider your price a drawback, try to bring the price
within reach. For example, in addition to stating the full price, you can use the following methods to deemphasize price and help convince the prospect that he or she can
pay it!

1. Break it down into "easy" weekly or monthly payments.
2. State it in terms of unit prices ($6 each book) instead of case lots, dozens, or sets
   ($160 for the encyclopedia set).
3. Interpret it on the basis of the benefits to be gained.
4. Emphasize its cost on a daily, monthly, or yearly basis—depending upon the product's estimated life and service (only 2 cents a day).
5. Compare it with the amount the average reader spends daily (monthly) for nonessentials or luxuries.

The discussion of price is usually presented just before the action paragraph(s)—if
price and action are clear-cut and distinct. Sometimes, however, they blend, as do

interest and desire. In some letters you will include price inducements with conviction details; in others, with action. Because offers of easy payment (as well as "no money down now" and credit card use) more often serve as special inducements to action, they are discussed in the next section.

Getting Action

Having convinced your reader that your product is valuable, needed, and worthy of purchase, you now must encourage the most important step—performing the action you request.

All previous discussions in this book about handling negatives, overcoming price resistance, and inducing action are applicable to sales letters and are not repeated here. You also already know that a complete action section should:

State clearly the action you desire.

Make action easy.

Date the action (when desirable).

Offer special inducement to act by a specified time (when desirable).

End with a last reader-benefit plug (when appropriate).

To induce the reader to act within a certain time instead of procrastinating, you can use one or more of the following methods (arranged here alphabetically):

1. Credit Cards

The convenience of merely charging a purchase to a nationally accepted credit card —bank, national oil company, travel agency, diners' club, or other cards—is an effective inducement to action. The holder of such credit card(s) need not write a check or send a money order now, but merely return an order blank listing a credit card number.

Send no money now. To order, just check on the enclosed form that you wish this purchase charged to your account with one of the acceptable national credit firms listed. Then be sure to fill in your account number as shown on your credit card.

2. Easy Payments and/or "No Money Now"

A budget plan or a future-payment plan by which the prospect pays nothing down now may serve two purposes—to convince the reader that he or she can afford to buy your product and to induce him or her to take the requested action. Thus, though the prospect may not have the entire price of the product, he or she will be able to order right away if the entire amount (or anything) is not required at once.

For as little as $10 down you can begin to reap the benefits of this useful encyclopedia before school starts. Easy monthly payments as low as $8 a month can be arranged at your convenience.

3. Free Gift[13]

If the prospect buys one item, two may be received for the price of one; or he or she may receive a free gift that is different from the item you are selling.

```
Agree to try them for 10 days on our No-Money-Down offer, and I'll
send you a matching leather-look vinyl Tote Bag FREE.  This gift is
yours to keep, even if you later return the jackets.
```

4. Free Trial

The free trial serves two purposes—to convince the reader of your sincerity about the product's merits, and to induce action now. The reader has nothing to lose; no money is spent now and he or she need pay later only if the article is found satisfactory.

5. Limit in Quantity or Time

If you can honestly state that supply of the product or the time for its production is limited, you have an effective inducement for prompt action.

```
The supply of this model is limited.  When our current stock is sold
out, no more will be available.  That's why I urge you to complete
and mail the Official Reservation Form before midnight of the date
shown.
```

6. No Obligation to Buy

When the purpose of your letter is to get the prospect to ask for more information, to come for a demonstration, or perhaps to ask a sales representative to call, he or she is more likely to act if you promise there is no obligation to buy.

```
Mailing the enclosed card does not in any way obligate you to buy
insurance, and no salesperson will call on you unless you invite him
or her.  To receive full details about this plan, with specific fig-
ures at your present age--and your free portfolio--just return the
postpaid card above.
```

7. Premium

A promise of higher earnings if the reader acts before a certain date is also a good incentive.

```
By sending your deposits in the enclosed envelope, so they reach us
by the 10th of May, you earn 5% dividends from the 1st of the month.
```

8. Special Price for a Limited Time

Setting a time limit for bargain prices (perhaps on out-of-season items), or for introductory prices on new items or to new buyers, effectively induces action. Offer a

---

[13] Sweepstakes and other games of chance have been powerful action inducements. The prospect may be "eligible for winning any one of 5,000 prizes" if an enclosed card is mailed before midnight of a certain date. However, such methods are prohibited in some states. Furthermore, studies have shown gross inconsistencies between the prizes that some companies advertise and the number they actually award. See "Games People Shouldn't Play," *Sales Management*, December 1969, pp. 17–18.

discount on the purchase price if the reader buys before a certain date or if cash in full is sent with the order.

This special introductory rate (for new subscribers only) brings you 40 big news packed issues of <u>World Reports</u> for only $4.97. That is down to half-price for 40 issues if you bought them a copy at a time. You get this special rate if your order is postmarked before November 1.

Writing an effective sales letter is a lot of work, but it can be greatly rewarding. Many a sales letter mailed to thousands of prospects has brought thousands—even millions—of dollars in returns. Even the expert writers "agonize" over their copy. Good selling presents the benefits and the proposition in such a way that the readers become convinced and "sell themselves." On the other hand, if the letter sounds like a high-pressure sales pitch, the readers may become defensive. To achieve your goal may require meticulous editing and rewriting, but the results will be worth the effort.

Examples of Unsolicited Sales Letters

This section illustrates letters that aim to: (1) make a direct sale, (2) serve as stimulus to future sales, and (3) bring back lost customers. As you read them, notice how description is mixed with and reinforces reader benefits, how the central selling point (labeled CSP in these examples) is developed, and how reader-benefit appeals are emphasized. Notice also which of the suggested ways these letters use to gain attention, interest, desire-conviction, and action.

Making a Direct Sale

When the product you want to sell is relatively inexpensive (from your prospective customer's viewpoint), you may be able to sell it effectively with one sales letter. (Even expensive items can sometimes be sold in this way.) All direct-sales messages ask the reader to buy now or within the near future.

The first letter below, sent to business owners, illustrates one way to sell relatively high-priced items successfully by one letter and detailed enclosures. The two items sold were priced at $170 and $295 (prices, though omitted in the letter, were in the enclosures). On a mailing of 4,500 this one-page letter brought in $45 in direct sales for every single dollar of costs.[14]

Letter 1

Selling radiator cleaning tanks to service-shop owners.
CSP: Less time to clean tanks.
Appeals: Reduced work; higher profits.

---

[14] Courtesy of Aeroil Products Company, West New York, New Jersey, and The Dartnell Corporation, *The Dartnell File of Tested Sales Letters.*

Attention

IF THREE RADIATOR REPAIR EXPERTS WALKED INTO YOUR
SHOP THIS AFTERNOON . . .

And the first one, the owner of Midtown Auto Radiator
Service of New York City, said: "We are cleaning 10
to 12 radiators in our tank and find that it requires
only 20 minutes to get them thoroughly clean."

Interest

And the second person, proprietor of the Bronx Radiator Service, said: "We clean nine radiators in one
tank in half the time it used to take to clean two."

And the third person, owner of Goldberg's Auto Service of St. Johnsbury, Vt., said: "We have found
this the most satisfactory way to clean radiators
that we have ever used."

Desire

. . . you'd certainly feel that you owed it to yourself to find out just what they used to bring those
people such new speeds and profits, wouldn't you?

Well, here is how they--and YOU--are in a position
to make such claims!

Conviction

You will find their explanations of exactly how they
do it (along with reports of other leading radiator
specialists from coast to coast) in the enclosed
Bulletin #308. In addition, you will find complete
specifications on two sizes of radiator cleaning
tanks that will enable you to clean up from 4 to 12
radiators at a time--probably in LESS time than it
now takes you to clean ONE!

Conviction; action

Don't just take our word for it - - - read the genuine letters and see the actual, unretouched photographs in the enclosed bulletin. Then prove these
new speeds and savings in your own shop by mailing
the Guarantee Order Form TODAY!

Letter 2 is two pages long and, like letter 1, also has an enclosed folder. To provide
variety and emphasis, letter 2 uses variations in color, margins, and type.[15]

Letter 2

Selling "Stick-Up" album pages to business persons.
CSP: An exclusive easy-to-use plastic product, guaranteed, at factory-to-you prices.
Appeals: Convenience, quality, savings of money and time.

---

[15] The first line and paragraphs 2, 6, 7, and 11 are in light brown type; all others are black. The signature is brown.

IT'S UNPRECEDENTED!

Attention

<u>an opportunity to</u>
<u>test a new product</u>
<u>right at your own desk.</u>

Reader benefit

Within the next few minutes you can prove to yourself, without leaving your desk, that our amazing
new STICK-UP--the instant press self-adherent album
page--does away forever with messy paste-up of
clippings.

Interest and proof
—by use of sample

Just pick up the enclosed STICK-UP page, pull back
the hardy Celanar protective sheet. Then place an
assortment of odd-sized clippings, ads, photos,
memos on the STICK-UP sheet in any arrangement you
choose. Finally, return the protective covering
and press down gently.

> Note how <u>sharply</u> and <u>clearly</u> you see every word
> through the transparent sheet, every shading of
> the material you've mounted on the STICK-UP
> page.

> <u>But note this, too</u>: If the arrangement you've
> set up doesn't please you, all you have to do
> is pull back the Celanar cover once again, pick
> up the clippings or photos, and rearrange them
> any way you desire.

Desire

With STICK-UP, you can do this as often as you
wish . . . and there's no mess, no fuss, no sloppy
paste pot! You save time and save money; you do
away with aggravation and frustration. And, what's
more, you always have a neat, clean, effective set

More reader benefits

of clippings or other materials for presentation or
record purposes.

Price advantages

STICK-UP is exclusive . . . you can obtain it only
from Transparent Industrial Envelope, Inc. And like
other high-quality, famous T.I.E. products, it comes
to you at great savings, because--like the <u>Hercules</u>
<u>Page Protectors</u> and <u>Hercules Ring Binder Sets</u> that
are described on the back of the enclosed folder--
it is offered to you directly by the manufacturer,
at low, low factory-to-you prices.

T.I.E.'s direct-sales technique means there's <u>no</u>
jobber, <u>no</u> retailer, <u>no</u> middleman. It means <u>no</u>
mark-ups--and <u>you</u> reap the benefits!

After you've product-tested the enclosed STICK-UP
instant press album page yourself . . . after you've
<u>proved</u> to yourself how STICK-UP ideally meets your
own needs . . . read the accompanying folder care-

More reader benefit   fully. It tells you in detail all about three great products available to you from T.I.E., <u>the world's largest direct-to-you producer of transparent protective plastic products</u>. Because we specialize in meeting your requirements for mounting, preservation, presentation, and protection of your sample materials . . . because we do this on a larger scale than any other firm in the world . . . because T.I.E. adheres strictly to the highest standards of design and construction, we offer you this firm, money-back guarantee:

Guarantee   "All Transparent Industrial Envelope products are <u>Guaranteed to please</u>. If you are not completely satisfied with any T.I.E. product, return it <u>for full credit within 10 days</u>."

Plus gift offer   You'll find this Guarantee repeated in the accompanying folder. And you'll find there, too, a most unusual Personalized Free Gift Offer, with full details of how you can obtain, without cost, a practical, convenient, prestigious gift for use in your office and at home.

Action request with reader benefit   So, take advantage now of T.I.E.'s low factory-to-you prices on STICK-UP, the new instant press self-adherent album page with protective Celanar cover. For your 8½ x 11" or 8½ x 14" sheets, order <u>Hercules Page Protectors</u>, the strongest page protectors available anywhere today; and <u>Hercules Ring Binder Sets</u>, built to take the toughest punishment you can give them.

Reader benefit   Send in your order today; remember, every T.I.E. product is <u>fully guaranteed</u> to give you complete satisfaction - or your money back!

Sincerely,

Easy action; reader-benefit proof   P.S. There's a handy postpaid Order Form enclosed for your convenience. But before you fill it in and mail it, pick up the material you've already mounted on the STICK-UP sample sheet and rearrange it. Then smooth the protective Celanar sheet back into position.

Isn't STICK-UP great?

In addition to prospective customers, you can also mail direct-sales letters, like the preceding two, to your present customers—about products they have not yet bought from you. Such letters can even get a "free ride"—thus saving you extra postage—if you enclose them with your monthly mailings to your customers. By this means hundreds of companies sell to their present customers goods ranging from books, magazines, and record albums to movie projectors, home furnishings, and clothing. Many of these letters are prepared by the manufacturer (with the assistance of advertising consultants) for use by dealers on their own letterhead stationery. They are especially effective because action is made easy; customers can charge their purchases on their own credit cards instead of dealing with distant manufacturers direct. Repeated tests have shown that an offer mailed equally to customers and prospects produced many times more business from customers than from prospects.

Another popular kind of direct-sales letter that stimulates present customers to "buy now" is the announcement about a special function "for our preferred customers only." Usually as a special inducement a substantial discount is offered on all items customers purchase that certain day or evening. Other effective inducements include inexpensive gifts, premiums, or refreshments. When these announcements do not require strongly developed appeals, they are really good-news letters rather than persuasive requests.[16]

Serving as Stimulus to Future Sales

Many sales letters urge action other than an immediate order for a direct purchase. Some of these sell products or services which are complicated or expensive, or which must be specially tailored to fit the buyer's particular needs. Others sell continual use of the customer's credit card which enables her or him to buy not only the firm's products but also other conveniences.

To Sell Complicated, Expensive, or Specially Designed Items. For some products the buyer will need more time, information, and personal observation. In this category are real estate, industrial equipment, insurance, costly installations, pleasure boats, cars, and products or services the reader may have considered unnecessary.

A campaign series of letters is a popular means of stimulating ultimate sales of such products and services. You decide in advance how many letters you should send, the time intervals, and the content of each. Some might ask the customer merely to request further information.[17] In other letters you might request that the reader call your office or store for a demonstration, or ask for a sales representative to visit, as in letter 3.

Depending upon the kinds of products you sell, you can sometimes get a highly satisfactory return by mailing only a relatively few letters. For instance, a manufacturer of bulldozing equipment mailed one sales letter to only 58 business executives. To the requested action "Write, wire, or phone for further details" 30 readers replied; they bought $250,000 worth of equipment. An example of an effective single letter is letter 3. Though mailed to only 100 sales managers, the letter sold one million caps! Each letter was individually typewritten on one page.

[16] See Announcing Sales and Events, page 236.
[17] Your replies to these respondents would be solicited sales letters—discussed on pages 207–212.

Letter 3

Urging sales managers to request a sales representative to give more information about an advertising gadget.[18]
CSP: Adjustable, lightweight, low-cost Paperlynen service caps for distinctive advertising.
Appeals: appearance, savings, comfort, distinctiveness.

Dear Mr. Gates:

Attention

Literally and figuratively you can <u>hit the top</u> with your advertising.

How? With Paperlynen Adjustable Service Caps.

Interest

Paperlynen Caps offer the ideal medium for placing your name constantly before the public eye. Worn by storekeepers and your own employees, these caps will not only help sell your products but are a constant goodwill reminder. And, as a means of cooperative advertising, they're excellent. In addition, Paper-lynen <u>Adjustable</u> Service Caps are preferred because of their:

<u>Appearance</u>
Adjustable to any and every head size; always fit; look like linen; sanitary-clean

<u>Low Cost</u>
Cost less than expense of having ill-fitting cloth caps laundered; this saving in addition to saving of initial cost of cloth caps

Desire

<u>Comfort</u>
Light in weight; porous nature of crown permits free, filtered ventilation

<u>Distinction</u>
Offer the opportunity of distinction through imprint-ing your firm's name or trademark in a manner not possible on ordinary caps. With cooperative adver-tising or as a dealer help, the storekeeper's name may also be added.

Conviction

Several samples of Paperlynen caps are enclosed. Look at 'em, try 'em, test 'em. We're sure you'll like 'em.

Action

When you are ready for more information, call XX3-628-1030 and one of our salespeople will be up to see you promptly.

[18] Courtesy of S. Posner Sons, Brooklyn, New York, and The Dartnell Corporation, *The Dartnell File of Tested Sales Letters.*

To Sell Continual Use of the Customer's Credit Card. From time to time you need to show the benefits that can be gained from the credit card, as in letter 4, which an oil firm's credit card promotion manager used "with a great deal of success."

Letter 4

Urging use of credit card for product purchases and other conveniences.[19]
CSP: Detergent gasoline for extra engine life and mileage at no extra cost; also additional advantages of the credit card.
Appeals: savings, safety, convenience.

Attention

> $1 of Mobil gasoline . . . Free! . . .
> with the enclosed certificate and
> your Mobil Credit Card.
> Nothing to buy.

Dear Fellow Motorist:

Attention

It may be surprising, but it's nonetheless true: The biggest single expense we are likely to have in our lifetime is for our automobiles. If you're like most Americans, you will spend even more money on your car (including insurance, depreciation, repairs and operating expenses) than on your home. And if your family has two cars, you'll spend a great deal more.

In either case, it's important to get the most for your money, to make your car serve as long as possible. One of the best ways to prolong the life of your car is to make sure the inside of its engine is clean.

Interest (in card and product)

This is why you should be happy that you carry a Mobil Credit Card. Because Mobil Premium and Mobil Regular both have a detergent that not only cleans carburetors . . . but also helps clean a number of vital engine parts. And it does it faster than gasolines without detergent action get them dirty.

If you keep on using Mobil Detergent Gasoline, its cleaning action will keep working for you automatically. And your cleaner engine will . . .

give you less frequent and smaller repair bills;
give you noticeably more engine power for safe
  acceleration;
give you faster starts and smoother running, both
  of which reduce wear and tear on your car.

[19] Courtesy of Mobil Oil Corporation, New York, New York.

Desire-conviction

And there's one more bonus--cleaner air. . . . We learned how to make this gasoline through a massive and continuous research program on the automotive pollution problem.

(*Five paragraphs, omitted here, explain how the special detergent additive helps your car release less pollutants into the air, cleans a dirty oil screen, and saves you money.*)

You can buy Mobil Detergent Gasoline at over 26,000 Mobil Dealer Stations, coast to coast. But with your Mobil Credit Card, you can do even better:

> You can use it to pay for tires, batteries, and all kinds of auto accessories on Mobil's new convenient Revolving Credit Plan.
> You can charge a stay at any one of some 2,200 really good motels all over America.
> And if you ever run into trouble on the road, you can use it to charge car repairs up to $75 . . . and use Revolving Credit too.
> You can reduce the amount of money you must carry, reducing the risk of loss or theft.

Action (continued use of card and product)

Your Mobil Credit Card brings you greater motoring pleasure and convenience, and Mobil Detergent Gasoline helps keep your engine clean (instead of making it dirty). We thank you for using them both and hope you'll continue to enjoy these important dividends every mile you drive.

A postscript on letter 4 tied in with the offer made at the beginning and served as a special inducement to action:

We're so pleased with Mobil Detergent Gasoline we'll buy your next dollar's worth. Simply hand the enclosed certificate and your credit card to your Mobil dealer, who'll put $1 worth of Premium or Regular gasoline in your car but not charge you a cent. It will be your first step toward a cleaner engine.

Bringing Back Lost Customers

Many businesses spend thousands of dollars on advertising to attract new customers and yet neglect regular customers. Studies have indicated that *indifference* on the part of the seller is the main reason customers leave one company for another. At least two-thirds of such customers drift away because they feel their business isn't appreciated, because they are treated discourteously, or because some grievances were unadjusted.

The best way to find out why customers haven't bought from you for, say, six months or more, is to ask them—either in person or by mail. Warm, sincere, friendly letters can help you to learn why you lost customers and can also help you win them back. (Of course, it is important that after you know customers' reasons, you take steps to correct any weaknesses!)

The secret for winning back lost customers is to tell them that you miss them—and to keep telling them. Patience and persistence do pay off. For instance, one department store in Chicago reopened 2,724 accounts with sales totaling $73,001.34; a retail store in Long Beach, California, brought in $30,000 from lost customers; and a Buffalo merchant regained 47 percent of his lost accounts with 30 mailings over a period of five years.[20] Numerous other firms have also had rewarding results (sometimes even with one letter!).

Your first miss-you letters may be simple (direct-request) inquiries without appeals. However, when direct inquiries bring no response, you need to mail persuasive requests that say, in essence:

We miss you.

Here are the benefits you get by coming back to us.

Please come back.

Sincerity, imagination, appropriate appeals, and sometimes good-natured humor characterize these messages, as illustrated below in letters 5 and 6.

Letter 5

A unique letter to win back "lost" hotel guests.[21]
CSP: High standard of personal service to "special guests."
Appeals: Enjoyment, comfort, convenience, prestige.

Dear Mr. Morgan:

Attention

Today we registered an ex-president; two senators; a congressman; several assorted corporation presidents; a foreign personage with party; generals by the one, two, and three star; plus a group of tourists. But not you.

Interest

I suppose you thought we'd be too busy to notice that you were among the missing. But that's not true. We haven't made The Mayflower the standard of personal service by forgetting our special guests the moment they leave the checkout desk.

What happened?

Desire

Have you sworn off roast beef when it's as succulent as our Rib Room specialty? Are you punishing yourself by giving up really comfortable, handsome, air-conditioned guest rooms for lesser accommodations?

---

[20] *The Reporter of Direct Mail Advertising,* September 1965, pp. 49–50.
[21] An award-winning letter created by Spiro & Associates, Inc., Philadelphia, for the Mayflower Hotel in Washington, D.C.

Do you feel guilty about staying at a hotel so perfectly located and so completely dedicated to your
convenience? Or have you just not been in Washington lately?

We hope it's the latter.

Action

Please write and end our suspense as soon as possible. Or, better yet, come back for a visit. Old
friends are best friends. And busy as we are, we
miss one of our very best friends: you!

Letter 6

*An unusual department store letter that brought an "excellent response in revived ac-
counts and much favorable comment," according to the credit manager.*[22] *(Beneath
the letter was a picture of a customer credit card, removed from Rosenfields Good
Customer File.)*
CSP: The magic of purchases and services through the credit card.
Appeals: Ease, convenience, friendly good service.

IF YOUR ACCOUNT CARD COULD TALK, HERE'S WHAT IT WOULD
SAY . . .

Attention

I'm getting lonesome - you haven't used me or your
charge account at Rosenfields in over 90 days.

Interest

Really, I'm not fussing, but I'm not just an ordinary
card. I'm full of magic!

Desire-conviction

Reader benefits

I can dress you up in clothes as glamorous as a queen
or movie star, yet priced to meet any budget. I can
supply you with beautiful lingerie, hats, shoes, accessories, and dozens of other clothing, household,
and personal needs, so easily and conveniently.

More benefits

I can bring you the service of friendly folk in a
store which has served Baton Rouge for generations,
folk who take a personal interest in your needs and
in giving you good service.

Action

Use me this month--attached is your current Rosenfields Credit Card, which enables you to charge your
purchases without delay.

With good judgment, sincerity, and imagination, you can develop a variety of
appealing miss-you letters. If you prefer, you can buy special-theme messages from
advertising specialists, with or without gadgets symbolic of various holidays, seasons,

[22] Courtesy of Rosenfields, Baton Rouge, Louisiana, and The Dartnell Corporation, *The Dartnell
File of Tested Sales Letters.*

products, and services. Be sure, however, that they relate closely to your company's business.

In summary, use the persuasive-request plan whenever you need to write a favor request, a nonroutine claim that requires persuasion, or an unsolicited sales letter. Begin with an attention-getting appropriate opening; arouse interest through physical description and/or reader benefits; create desire and conviction by developing your central selling point and benefits, by offering proof, and by handling price in a positive way; then ask for action. If appropriate, offer special inducements so that the reader will act within a certain time. The Capsule Checklists on pages 392–393 give a summary of the general plan and the three main kinds of persuasive requests.

EXERCISES

Requests for Favors

1. You are a senior in college and you are currently investigating the recruiting and employment practices in several medium-sized firms. You have an interest in seeking employment in these firms and need to have information to make some sound decisions as you seek your first job.

   Information you want should include such areas as: minimum experience required for the various job classifications for which you would qualify; whether grade point average is considered when employees are hired; if there is a strict dress code in the company; how many references are needed with an application; does the company administer tests as a prerequisite for employment; will there be an opportunity to seek additional education and training; does the company have a management training program and, if so, the nature of the training program; and any other information that you feel will be helpful to you.

   Write a letter that can be mailed to the personnel directors of several companies to solicit the information you will need to help you make your decision.

2. You are aware that any member of the United States Congress—senator or representative—can assist you in visiting the White House when in Washington, D.C. This assistance is commonly referred to as a Congressional White House Tour because you are given a special pass and a specific time to be at the entrance gate. Others who are not aware of this often stand in line for hours in order to make the visit, whereas those with the Congressional Tour tickets can walk in at the proper time.

   All that is needed is the proper identification.

   Assume that you are the state president of a group of professional people who are going to be meeting in Washington on March 20 and would like to go through the White House together. There will be about 40 at the meeting and you will be able to provide the names and an exact number of attendees by March 1.

   Write to a member of Congress (preferably the one who represents you) and ask if an afternoon tour at about 3:30 can be arranged. Explain the name and purpose of the association, at what hotel the group will be meeting, and any other pertinent information. Assume a reason why this request for March 20 requires persuasion, and include appropriate appeals. Ask for specific instructions about picking up the tour tickets prior to the date you will be using them.

3. The following form letter asks the reader to fill out a questionnaire. Criticize it constructively regarding you-attitude, tone, honesty, word choice, and the attention-getting and action paragraphs. What impression does the letter give you about the writer and the company? Would the letter persuade you to furnish the requested information? Why or why not? What improvements can you suggest? The letter was sent from a radio manufacturing company whose letterhead states "Offices: Tokyo, Japan, and Hong Kong; United States Offices (address) Los Angeles, CA (ZIP)." The envelope was postmarked in Los Angeles. The processed letter had no inside address. Notice the comments about enclosures, following the letter.

Greetings and Salutations.

We are sending this letter to a select group of people like yourself who have been recommended to us by an American research organization.

The courtesy we ask is that you read this letter and favor us with the answer to the enclosed questions. In appreciation for your co-operation, we shall do our utmost to reward you for your kind help. (Please read on.)

You can save us time and money in our marketing plans. We will be undertaking extensive advertising in the United States and are very anxious to place our advertising where it will best be seen by people like yourself--will you please help us by filling in and returning the enclosed questions in the free envelope--it is a two-minute service that will be greatly appreciated.

We are enclosing a brochure of the first selection of the (*year and name*) Portable Radio Models to appear on the American market. In return for your participating interest, we offer you a completely free gift of your choice of any nationally famous (*name*) watch.

Please fill in the questionnaire and mail to our Los Angeles office in the enclosed envelope. On the back of the questionnaire is the order form to choose your reward.

We beg you not to delay or put off your reply. Your immediate answers to our market questions are needed to complete our survey. Also, the initial supply of watches forces us to limit this free gift offer only to that quantity now in our Los Angeles warehouse.

Comments about enclosures: The printed questionnaire contained four questions (about the name and address of the reader's "favorite" newspaper, magazines, and local radio stores). Above the questions was this request: "Please fill out this questionnaire and mail it to our Los Angeles office with your radio order." On the reverse side of the questionnaire was an order form for radios and tape recorders, followed by this request: "Select one free watch for each radio or tape recorder you order. We regret we cannot send your free watch unless the questionnaire is completed." An enclosed leaflet pictured two radios, one tape recorder, and nine men's and ladies' watches. ("Completed" meant answering the questions and ordering a radio or tape recorder.)

4. Assume that you are program chairperson for your college chapter of a national organization composed of students whose major is the same as yours. For the past two years the members have repeatedly mentioned their desire to hear this organization's national vice president, Ms. L. F. Trenton. She is known to be an outstanding, dynamic speaker. Two of your members who heard her at the organization's national convention last June also have been enthusiastic about her. Because she lives 2,000 miles from your school and your chapter's treasury is small, everyone has just assumed that getting Ms. Trenton would be almost impossible. Fortunately, in yesterday's newspaper you happened to read that Ms. Trenton will be attending a one-day business conference in Somecity (you insert a city name), which is only 220 miles from you—just the day before your chapter's annual Founders' Day Banquet.

Now you want to persuade Ms. Trenton to accept your invitation to be principal banquet speaker. You cannot pay her any speaker's fee, but your budget enables you to pay traveling expenses equal to round-trip plane fare from (Somecity) to yours. Six planes daily fly between these cities; if she prefers a bus, buses run on an hourly schedule. A scenic ride by freeway takes about four hours, in case she prefers to drive a private car. Ms. Trenton will, of course, be your chapter's dinner guest. Maybe you can think of an inexpensive, courteous way to take care of her if she wishes to stay overnight after her talk? Assume any other necessary details that will make your letter complete—with you-attitude. Consider carefully the best appeal(s) to use.

5. (Memo) International Valve Corporation is the largest industrial employer in your city. Over the last five years, IVC has been the object of much unfavorable publicity, stemming from violation of water and air pollution regulations and controversy over discriminatory hiring practices. Its corporate image has suffered.

To increase its contributions as a responsible corporate citizen in the city's economic and social life, IVC has launched a drive to increase the participation of its employees in social service, civic, and cultural organizations. As a participant in one phase of this new direction, you have been delegated the responsibility of writing a form memo to all IVC executives to secure volunteers to serve as business advisors for Tomorrow's Managers. This is an organization which sends businesspeople into area high schools to assist students in forming and managing business enterprises to manufacture and market goods or services. The students thus obtain first-hand experience in how the free enterprise system functions.

IVC is sponsoring three advisors for Tomorrow's Managers. Each will devote two evenings a month to working with one of these groups at a city high school during the school year. There is no pay; the only benefits each volunteer receives come from working with young people, helping to develop their business skills and understanding of business enterprises. And, of course, International Valve will benefit from improved visibility in the community as an involved, public-spirited business organization.

Write a memo which will get at least three volunteers for this project. Select and develop appeals focusing on benefits to IVC, the executives, and the high school students they will be advising. Anticipate and overcome objections which your readers might have. Date the memo August 1—schools open in one month.

6. Point out the weaknesses, errors, and good points in the following letter. Then—as program chairperson—rewrite it, applying the principles you have learned, to make your request so appealing that the reader will want to accept. Address it to Mr. James Milliman, Director of Public Relations, KMRO Television, in a city about 80 miles from you. If your instructor approves, you may choose another topic instead of air pollution.

What are you plans for Saturday evening, March 20? The members of our (*city name*) Business Leaders' Club feel it would be a pleasure to us to have you as the principal speaker for our annual banquet that night.

Ways to fight air pollution is a topic that our members are concerned and realize the need of practical advice from experienced executives. Your many editorial comments on Channel 16 KMRO have shown us your sincere interest and extensive study on this subject. Our members and their spouses want to hear you in person. This banquet is our biggest function of the year, and we would be honored to have you and your spouse as our guests.

The banquet will be held in the Marlboro Room of the Plaza Hotel at 7 and will be informal. A varied entertainment program and an excellant dinner at $11.50 per person have been arranged.

Your traveling expenses would be provided, and I hope that you can take advantage of a visit to our city to settle any personal affairs you may have here. The Plaza Hotel is equipped with excellant facilities in the event you decide to extend your visit.

I shall appreciate your assent to this request so that I can welcome you on your arrival if feasible.

7. Assume you graduated from the university five years ago and you have become an active member of a certain professional (or business, social, or religious) group that owns the building in which meetings and activities take place.

You have just been elected treasurer of your organization for a two-year term. For about 14 years this organization has been saving money to build a much needed extension to its building. (Assume specific reasons why the addition is necessary and beneficial to members.) It has been planned that construction will begin next June 1—three months from today—and be completed by September 1. (Assume today is March 1.) The addition, as sketched by architects and approved by your executive board, will cost about $99,000. Your books show $43,000 cash in the building fund; your organization can get a $50,000 mortgage. You need to raise $6,000 cash between now and about April 5 or construction cannot begin.

Your task is to try to raise this money. After several meetings with the executive board, it is decided that, rather than asking your members to put on several fund-raising events (which are time-consuming), or assessing them a definite amount, you will urge them to make a donation. The board members want you to head this fund-raising campaign.

Write a letter, remembering that it is a form letter, to be sent to all members. Assume a mailing list of 650. Try to keep your letter to one typewritten page. Select the appeals (loyalty, pride, self-interest, and so forth) that you think will be most effective in moving your readers to take the requested action. Set April 1 as the deadline for donations, because adequate time must be allowed for making financial arrangements before construction begins. Make action easy and include any reasonable inducements for your readers to act now. Naturally, you'd rather have checks returned with each reply; however, for those members who would rather sign a pledge now and pay later—before completion of construction—plan an easy-action reply form you can depend on in your financial calculations.

8. As the new systems manager for the National Insurance Co., you have considered numerous ways to increase company efficiency and decrease costs. Your firm sends 1,800,000 letters and notices each year. Recently, after checking correspondence procedures, you were surprised to find several wasteful, unnecessarily time-consuming methods that you'd like to change. However, before authorizing any changes, you have decided to survey the preferences of the management staff in your home office and 60 branch offices. You have prepared an easy-to-answer two-page questionnaire asking for their reactions to eight money- and timesaving suggestions. Now write a persuasive, courteous memorandum urging these executives to fill out your enclosed form and return it to you by a certain date, so that you can complete a needed report on their replies. Promise anonymity to all respondents. Include appropriate appeals to urge their cooperation. Three of your money-saving suggestions may require a little explanation and "selling" before your readers approach the questionnaire.

   a. You advocate using window envelopes instead of individually addressed envelopes for the approximately 150,000 monthly messages your company sends to policyholders, prospective customers, suppliers, and stockholders. You think window envelopes could save thousands of hours of typing time annually, because the inside addresses on the letters or forms within the envelopes could serve for the envelopes too.

   b. You are considering adopting a standardized companywide letter format—blocked, open punctuation, with or without salutation and complimentary close. Such standardization, you feel, would give the company an image of uniformity and at the same time save stenographic time. (For examples, see Figures 6-4 and 6-5.)

   c. With each company letter that asks the recipient for a brief answer, you would like to enclose a courtesy carbon for reply. The recipient would then merely type the reply at the bottom of your letter, return to you the carbon copy (showing both your letter and the reply), and keep the original for his or her files. Such an enclosure would bring speedier answers to company requests and would cut down the need for second or third requests to get replies, thus saving postage and labor costs.

As you write your memo, remember that your readers are in management, just as you are, even if you do probably outrank many of them. Watch your tone and try to build pleasant relations and high morale.

9. You are vice president of the Greater Greenwood Community Council. (Greenwood is a residential area of a large city.) Your council members want you to write a letter to every taxpayer (about 12,000) in your community to raise money for a worthy cause.

   Fred More, your state senator from the 49th district, initiated and won a class action taxpayer's suit against the state in a precedent-setting case. Because he went well beyond the call of duty in taking this action in behalf of the community, he has personally incurred a financial burden of no small proportions. Senator More expended over three months of legal time on this case, having tried a six-day trial in superior court and having argued the matter twice in your state supreme court. He received no fee for his services and in addition personally incurred some $3,000 of out-of-pocket legal expenses. The Greater Greenwood Community Council has unanimously passed a resolution supporting a money-raising effort in behalf of the Senator. All residents (taxpayers) of this area in the city together saved over $6 million on their property taxes last year because of this one person's efforts in their behalf.

   Your council hopes to get at least small personal donations from most people in the entire Greenwood community, as an indication of their appreciation of Senator More's help. You all would rather have such donations than a few large contributions from business firms. Write an appealing, persuasive message that will get a large favorable response.

10. *(Memo)* As building manager of your company's three-story structure, you have just received an unusual report from your sanitation engineer. He has found that at least two rats have been attracted to the building recently. The employee practice of leaving food on bookshelves, desks, and other open locations will have to be discontinued or watched very carefully. Each office occupant must be made aware of the problem and the possibility that he or she is part of the cause. As rats will not bother to infest an area unless there is good reason to do so (food), the best way to maintain rat-free premises consists of denying them food, water, and safety. It would be economically unfeasible to make the needed structural changes for rat-proofing the entire building. (The cafeteria is, however, rat-proofed.) About four months ago you wrote a simple announcement (without appeals—merely a "direct request") to all employees. But apparently some (or most?) have forgotten about it. Now again two rats were seen, but many more, still unseen, could come into the building. Thus you must write a persuasive request in a memorandum to all employees, urging them to cooperate on preventive action. Instruct them to exercise utmost care with lunches or other food brought into the building. Instruct them not to leave any food in their offices overnight. Also request them to be alert for signs indicating rodent or insect activity: drop-

pings; gnawed food, odor; dark rub marks along wall, ceiling, under door, ventilator, which indicate a runway. Request that employees inform a certain office as soon as such evidence appears. Watch the tone of your memo, and be sure to consider the attitudes of your readers.

11. Assume you graduated from college two years ago and became an active member of a business, professional, social, or religious organization. You have just been elected vice president and have been asked by the executive board to see if you can increase attendance at meetings for next year. Assume that the organization has a potential membership of 200, but that during the past three or four years only 15 to 25 have been attending monthly meetings regularly. You would like to have at least 50 or 60.

Plan a letter to send to the 200 potential members, aiming to find out in a friendly, tactful way why so many have not been attending meetings and what types of programs, arrangements, or methods would get them to the meetings. Be careful to keep the tone positive and cheerful, filled with you-attitude. Suggestions: Perhaps more would come if they had transportation; if the meetings were held at a more central location, on different days, or during different hours; if the business portion were shorter and the programs more entertaining; or if someone would phone them shortly before meetings. In the past, written announcements have been sent to all members a week before a meeting. Devise some method which will make it easy for each member to answer your letter, giving you specific information about what is preferred in topics, speakers, activities, dates, times. Assume that your letter will be reproduced by Xerox or offset printing.

Nonroutine Requests for Adjustments, Credit, or Changes

1. Assume you have just received a credit turndown for a charge account with a local store. The reason stated for the refusal is correct. (Assume a legitimate reason such as under age 18, presently unemployed, or a similar one.) However, for various other reasons—perhaps a steady trust fund income you receive from a regular source, a verifiable record of integrity, or any other good reason(s) that might outweigh the shortcoming—you know that you will be a prompt-paying customer. You always take care of all obligations you have. Write to the store's credit manager an honest, persuasive request for credit. Make your reasoning logical and appealing, so that your reader will be convinced that she or he should make an exception for you and grant you a charge account.

2. You are manager of Vernie's Men's Wear in Sometown, South Dakota. You have two stores—one situated in the downtown area and one two blocks from a college campus. For years you have carried exclusively Van Doser shirts, which you buy direct from the manufacturer. On June 1, only four days after this firm's fall catalog came out, you again ordered a complete Van Doser line for your two stores. You asked for delivery by September 1. But today (September 8) you have noted with alarm the many changes the manufacturer made in your fall order.

Back-to-school goods scheduled by your sales staff for early delivery have been pushed to October and November. You haven't a plaid in stock and college opens next week. You've had to switch to other brands because you can't get all the Van Doser merchandise you'd like. You have faith in Van Doser merchandise; it's your preference of all brand shirts on the market. But this is the third time in four years that they have changed delivery time on your orders.

While you were in Minneapolis just a few days ago, you noted that the Custer Men's Store (a retail store for this shirt manufacturer) was stocked with everything in the Van Doser book, and Custer could not have ordered any sooner than you did. Just how does this manufacturer expect to keep good customers like you with that kind of treatment? Unless they can find some way to supply your stores adequately and promptly—by no later than September 20—you may have to find a replacement for Van Doser shirts. You feel you have helped considerably to build this manufacturer's business the past five years. (Your store's total Van Doser purchases were $200,000.) Right now you feel like giving your business to a competitor. Address your message to Mr. Thomas Hanson, sales manager of Van Doser Manufacturing Company, Chicago. Be tactful, firm, appropriately persuasive, and clear in your request.

3. You are a member of the National Association of _____ (supply a name appropriate to your major). In previous years your membership dues in this professional organization paid for a subscription to The National _____(supply the name of a magazine appropriate to your major). This year you received a notice from the organization that the magazine subscription was no longer paid as part of your membership dues. A few days later you received a letter from the magazine, offering a special subscription rate to members of the organization.

Because you think the magazine is an excellent source of current information in your field, you decided to take advantage of the special offer. The magazine normally costs $10 per year (for 12 monthly issues), but for members of your organization the magazine is offered at a special rate of $7.50 for a one-year subscription. Furthermore, you were offered the opportunity to subscribe for two full years at $15. Using the convenient order form provided, you indicated that you wanted the two-year subscription and that you had enclosed your payment. You attached your personal check #663 to the order form and mailed it in the envelope provided.

The order was mailed exactly three months ago today and your check cleared the bank the following month. You received your first issue of the magazine three weeks ago, along with an invoice for $15 for the subscription. The notice indicated that no further issues would be sent until payment was received. As you have your canceled check clearly showing that it was deposited by the American National Publishing Company (the publisher of the magazine), you realize that the company was in error. You wrote a letter to Ms. Jane Pierce (Circulation Manager, American National Publishing Company, 402 North Broad Street, Philadelphia, PA 19108), explaining the facts and asking her to see that your account (#0157392) was credited for the $15 and that the remaining 23 issues of the magazine would be sent promptly.

Today you received a second invoice, stating that you still owe $15. The computer-printed bill had the following message: "We have not heard from you." Obviously, they have heard from you: not once, but twice. Because your letter to Ms. Pierce seems not to have led to any action, you have decided to write a persuasive request for an adjustment directly to the party in power—the computer. Explain the situation again and ask for the appropriate action.

4. Your wholesale firm has a policy of granting a 2 percent discount for bills your dealers pay within 10 days of invoice date, and the full amount is due in 30 days. One of your customers paid a $560 invoice (dated October 11) with his check mailed on November 9. But he deducted $11.20 discount. Consequently, you wrote him a courteous direct-request letter, asking him to pay the $11.20. Today (November 20) you get an angry protest from the customer, stating that his cashier was in the hospital last month and so a number of bills accumulated that otherwise would have been paid within the 10-day period. He added, "Your company is the only one out of about fifty that has attempted to chisel us out of this discount. We can buy plenty of watches, equal in quality to yours, from folks who are willing to meet a customer halfway—and who realize there are always just exceptions to any business rule. Of course, if you insist, a check will be mailed; but it strikes me as a small amount to cause the severing of business relations between us."

To your company, a discount of $11.20 involves a long-standing company principle—that of impartial treatment of every customer. You maintain the "2/10 net 30" policy because it enables you to earn similar savings by paying your own bills promptly; then you pass the savings on to your customers in lower prices, as a reward for their promptness. When customers pay after the 10-day period, you make no savings. You do not want to grant special privileges to some concerns, because such inconsistencies involve much more than a small discount. Write a persuasive request to this customer (Mr. Harlan Burns, owner, Flatwood Jewelry Shop) urging him to pay this honest debt.

Unsolicited Sales Letters

1. Your company publishes sports books and how-to manuals for sales directly to consumers. Just off the presses is your newest book, *Everything You Always Wanted to Know about Running, but Couldn't Slow Down to Ask*. Because of the popularity of jogging and marathon running you feel that this book will be highly successful.

The book was coauthored by Mr. Jeff Long (an Olympic gold medal winner in the 10,000 meter run) and Dr. Gary C. Lane (an expert in the physiology of running and a consultant to the United States Olympic Team). Contained in the book are chapters on "The Beginning Runner," "The Physiology of Running," "Developing the Running Attitude," "Dietary Rules for Runners," and "Selecting Jogging and Running Shoes and Accessories." Other chapters cover the history of marathons, and Olympic track events, plans for developing speed and stamina, and information on avoiding injuries while running.

Because you think this book will be widely accepted you have, for the first time, arranged for its sale through selected book stores in several large cities. And, to promote the book, the authors will travel to each city to conduct running seminars and autograph copies of the book. You, as regional sales manager, have been asked to write a letter to a prospect list which your company has purchased for this purpose. Describe the book in detail and invite the prospects to attend the free seminars. Mention the time and location of the seminar and the name of the local stores where the books will be sold. If they take a copy of the book to the seminar, the authors will autograph it. The book will also be sold at the seminar. A runner's refreshment buffet (Perrier water, granola snacks) will be served.

2. Assume that last month you ran three advertisements in a local newspaper, announcing the opening or remodeling of your business. You sell a service—such as transportation, advertising, tax consulting, traveler's aid, or restaurant. Write an unsolicited letter selling your service to a select list of (imaginary but probable) prospects who you are sure can benefit from what you can do for them. The goal of each letter is to bring your prospect to your business for a first "purchase" or (if more appropriate) for a consultation. Select a central selling point and build your letter around it. For instance, if you write for a restaurant, perhaps you will want to emphasize a food specialty or a special plate for which your chef is famous. Perhaps you will also want to mention your speedy service, exotic decor, music, prices, extra-generous servings, or smaller servings for senior citizens and children. Your letter should contain strong reader-benefit appeals. If you want to offer some special inducement such as a free gift or a reduced rate for the first visit, that's fine. If yours is a service that customers use repeatedly (such as a restaurant or transportation facility), figure out an appropriate way to determine which customers are calling for the first time.

   With your sales letter submit to your instructor a complete "assumption sheet" that includes a brief statement on each of the following:
   a. The nature and location of your service
   b. Your reason for choosing this service
   c. Your central selling point
   d. The specific purpose of your message
   e. Any unique assumptions you have made (special letterhead, season)
   f. The kind of enclosure(s), if any, you would have

3. The cost of hospital room occupancy and care is extremely high and many families do not have adequate insurance coverage. If illness should strike such a family, the results could be disastrous—debt, loss of savings, emergency bank loans, mortgages, possible bankruptcy, and similar financial problems would have to be faced.

   As sales manager of the AAABB Insurance Company of Illinois, which is licensed to do business in your state and in 43 of 50 states, you have a special offer which you believe is attractive. No salesperson will call on prospective customers; no one who applies will be turned down if the application form is completely, accurately, and honestly filled out; the policy cannot be canceled for any reason if the premiums are paid on time; and the applicant can examine the policy in the home for a full 30 days and then cancel it if not satisfied. There are other features, too, which will be included in a brochure from AAABB if the prospective customer will just fill out the initial application-for-information blank.

Best of all, the policy will pay, IN CASH TO THE FAMILY, $40 per day for the period of hospitalization plus certain other fees which are listed in the policy. No matter what other coverage one might have, the $40 per day will still be paid for as long as one full year.

Write a letter which will be sent to the employees of the Acme Iron and Steel Company, in your city. You know that these employees have some health and hospitalization coverage, but the amount is insufficient for most serious illnesses. Although you will not mention this, you will also send a second letter four weeks later if the first one is not answered. After that—no more letters.

4. As sales manager for EXELL Manufacturing Company, Columbus, Ohio, you want to send—to retail store managers who have been your regular customers—a letter that ties in with your national advertising campaign. During November and December your company's all-purpose folding card tables with four matching folding chairs will be featured in two consumer magazines in full-page three-color ads. These ads will be read by 24 million people. You consider this the most powerful selling story you have ever put across. Now (October 1) you want to be sure that the 510 retail store managers that carry your products are sufficiently stocked with a variety of these table-chair sets to meet the expected consumer demand. Wholesale price of each five-piece set is $52.20. Retail price is $87; separate folding tables are $27 each and each chair is $17.50. Thus, by buying the combination set, consumers save $10. Each table is 36 inches square, with vinyl covered top and bronze-tone finish steel frame 28 inches high; shipping weight, 21 pounds. The matching folding chairs have padded vinyl seats, steel legs; shipping weight 12 pounds each. Colors for both tables and chairs, green or mushroom beige in plain or floral patterns. These beautiful, practical, and low-priced items are just what consumers will need for Christmas, and will find useful throughout the year for many years. In your sales letter, provide easy-action order blanks and promise prompt shipment; be as specific as possible. Orders you receive by October 18 can be filled and the sets shipped in time to be in stock by November 1.

5. You are a part-time employee for Mod Man, Inc., a men's clothing shop "For men who think young." Your employer, knowing you are a college senior and that you're studying business communications, has just offered you a challenging opportunity to try your skill on a sales letter. After you write it, she will pay all expenses for reproducing and mailing it—plus a 10 percent commission to you on the direct sales your letter brings in.

Here is her proposition: The store's men's formal wear rental department is sponsoring a special Senior Ball promotion. Your letter is to be mailed to all men in your college class. (If your college does not have a Senior Ball, assume you are writing to any other group of young people that do have an annual ball.) Assume at least 1,000 on your mailing list. Your employer has made arrangements with a local automobile dealer to have a brand new 198_ convertible on display right in the store starting this weekend until two days before the ball. Someone who registers will win the free use of this car for the night of the ball, courtesy of Tom Aime Auto Sales, Inc. In addition, there will be four other big winners, each of whom will get: Senior Ball tickets for two; a corsage of their choice; a $20 gift certificate for dinner for two at (name) restaurant (the best in your city); and their formal wear rental at no charge. All the readers have to do to get a chance to win is to register and choose their formal wear from your store. You have the largest and most fashionable collection in the city: everything from white dinner jackets to full-dress tails, with 23 styles in between including double-breasted coats, turtlenecks, and ruffled shirts, and all at Mod Man's low rental rates.

Your one-page letter will be processed in any way you choose—mimeographed, by computer, or printed—and will be on the store's letterhead. There is to be no enclosure. You may send the letter over your own signature, if you prefer. Design its layout in any way you choose. If you wish, you can give this promotion a special name (such as, "Your Prom Night on Us").

6. As manager of a large company that deals exclusively in mail-order clothes for executives, you have come up with a new idea to promote your product. You plan to let your customers sample your product before they decide to buy.

Sample clothes that you will offer include business suits for men and women, shirts, shoes, ties, belts, dresses, pantsuits, and top coats for men and women.

Since the high prices of clothes continue to rise rapidly, you have developed a plan to offer a variety of coordinated executive outfits to men and women at reduced prices. You can make this offer at such a low price because you deal in volume, and with low overhead.

For your plan, you have obtained several prepared lists of executives and have in your possession more than 1,500 names. Write a letter to the people on the lists. They should know that the plan is exclusively for executives; that the clothes can be worn for two weeks on a trial basis; that any outfit can be returned if the customer is not satisfied. Include brochures about your clothes with your letter. Also include samples of material used to make the clothes.

7. Assume you have been out of college almost 10 years. Recently a group of your former classmates persuaded you to be chairperson of the class Tenth Anniversary Reunion. The date chosen coincides with your college homecoming, at which the classes that graduated 10, 25, and 50 years ago are especially honored. You have rented the Horizon and Rainier Rooms of the Plaza Hotel for Saturday evening of homecoming weekend, and committees have been working on plans.

Now it is your job to write the "sales letter" to urge former classmates to buy reunion dinner-dance tickets and attend. It's to be a new-fashioned get-together of cocktails, dinner, dancing, and reminiscing. For an orchestra, you found three persons who play the kind of music that was popular when you were all in college. For those alums who also want tickets for the homecoming football game, against (assume name of a popular rival college team), you've managed to reserve a few ($8 each) for that Saturday afternoon. But they must get their requests and money in immediately. The seats aren't quite on the 50-yard line, but they're inside the stadium, which is pretty good, considering the limited supply.

Write a convincing letter that will urge—and get—an excellent turnout. Provide a good way for readers to make their reservations and make clear that $15 a person must accompany each reservation for the reunion dinner-dance (cocktails are extra) and $8 for each game ticket. Clearly state deadline dates for reservations. You already have a reservation from Fairbanks, Alaska, and you're hoping for many others from distant places. A prize will be given at the reunion dinner to the classmate traveling the longest distance.

8. You are general manager of the Uptown Auto Sales and Service. Your body shop department gets numerous opportunities to make repair estimates on automobiles damaged in accidents. Usually, prospective customers get estimates from three different repair shops. You have good reason to know that your shop's prices and bids are very similar to those of your closest competitors. Thus prospective customers who must choose one of three shops often have very little except price to guide them.

You want now to draft a form letter—on your company's letterhead—for your or your supervisor's signature. It is to be sent from time to time to each customer on whose car the shop makes an estimate. Typed on electronic typewriter, each letter will have a personalized inside address and salutation. Its purpose is to persuade each reader to bring his or her car to your shop because of the benefits offered in addition to the reasonable price. Your facilities are complete. Everything is done in your shop: paint, metal, mechanical, glasswork, frame straightening. Your personnel are hand-picked factory-trained specialists. They take pride in their work. You use only genuine factory parts, and you guarantee satisfaction. Your policy is service, quality, and integrity. You'll also consider a customer's credit for a budget account, so he or she can have the car repaired now and pay later. Write the sales letter that will help each prospective customer to decide that your company is the one to repair his or her car.

9. You are relocation director for a real estate firm in a large city (use your city or select a large city with which you are familiar). One of your primary activities is working with the management of companies, helping employees being transferred to your area find appropriate housing. Companies and other contacts provide you with the names of people who will be moving to your city within the next one to three months.

Write a personalized form letter in which you welcome the recipients as prospective residents of your city. Acquaint them with the many attractive qualities it boasts (comfortable climate, modern transportation facilities, renovated downtown area, quality schools, museums and orchestras, diversified recreational facilities, pleasant residential areas within easy commuting distance, etc.). Mention the special real estate services your company offers to individuals who are househunting in an unfamiliar city. One of your agents can pick up the prospect (and members of his or her family) at the airport, take them to their hotel or motel, escort them on a tour of the city, and show them homes in city and suburban residential areas which will satisfy their housing requirements.

Remember that other firms in your city will be offering similar services to relocating executives. Therefore, choose your appeals carefully and develop them imaginatively and concretely so as to set your relocation service apart from those of your competitors. Perhaps you can send prospective clients descriptive materials about the city and your real estate services. Indicate that you will call to discuss relocation plans within 10 days.

I Persuasive Requests—General Plan	II Persuasive Requests for Favors

1. ATTENTION (promise; star)
  a. Introduction of relevant reader-benefit or reader-interest theme—centered on reader, not on writer's organization
  b. Envelopes and letterheads sometimes specially designed for the message
	1. Attention
	  a. Sincere compliment
	  b. Questions
	  c. Agreeable comment or assertion
	  d. Basic problem
	  e. What has been done about a problem
	  f. Frank admission of a favor

2. INTEREST (picture; chain)
  a. Introduction of project or product's physical description, benefits, central selling point
  b. Appeals: appreciation, approval, beauty, cleanliness, comfort, convenience, cooperation, customer satisfaction, distinctiveness, efficiency, enjoyment, entertainment, extra earnings, fair treatment, friendships, good reputation, health, improvement, love of home and others, money and other valuables, peace of mind, pleasure, popularity, position, profits, recognition, safety, satisfaction of helping others, savings, self-preservation, and others
	2. Interest and
	3. Desire
	  a. Necessary physical description of project
	  b. Facts, figures, and reader benefits to convince reader that his or her contribution will be enjoyable, easy, important, beneficial—directly or indirectly
	    (1) In request for speaker: date, day, hour; place; function; topic; talk length; audience size, interests; honorarium; expenses; special attractions; appeals.
	    (2) In request for donation: problem; needs; past, present methods of meeting needs; costs; reader contribution: benefits; appeals.
	    (3) In request for cooperation: problem; facts, suggestions, committee, etc. to help meet goal; reader's part; benefits; appeals.
	  c. Positive handling of negatives and probable objections for favors that:
	    (1) Require time, knowledge, or effort
	    (2) Ask donations of money or other valuables
	    (3) Urge cooperation on goals and projects
	  d. Enclosures (brochures)

3. DESIRE (prove; chain)
  a. Desire: development of description, benefits, central selling point, appeals; perhaps with an enclosure
  b. Conviction:
    (1) "Outside" proof; perhaps with enclosures
    (2) Price and terms when needed and appropriate; perhaps in enclosure	

4. ACTION (push; hook)
  a. CSAD[1]
  b. EA[2]
  c. DA when desirable[3]
  d. Special inducement when desirable
  e. RB[4] (often tied in with opening statement)
	4. Action, same as I, 4

*Lists include possible content. For any one message, choose only pertinent and appropriate items.

[1] CSAD = clear statement of action desired.

[2] EA = easy action

[3] DA = dated action, if desirable

[4] RB = reader benefit

See also pages 108–109 for W's on complete action requests.

PERSUASIVE REQUESTS*

III **Other Persuasive Nonroutine Requests**	**IV** **Unsolicited Sales Letters**
1. Attention Same as II, 1; preferably an agreeable assertion or a principle which is used as a major premise	1. Attention a. Agreeable assertion b. Comparison or short story c. Event or fact in reader's life d. Problem reader may face e. Quotation f. Scare opening g. Significant fact about product h. Solution to a problem i. Special offer or gift j. Surprising or challenging statement k. Testimonials

2. Interest and
3. Desire
 a. All necessary facts and details pertaining to request for adjustment, credit, or changes in policy or performance—interwoven with reader benefits and appeals
 b. Description as needed by the reader to see that his or her firm is responsible (if applicable) and that the request is factual, logical, and reasonable
	2. Interest
	 a. Beginning development of physical description and product benefits, geared to prospect's needs; meaningful appeals
	3. Desire-Conviction
	 a. Full development of needed description, reader benefits, central selling point
	 b. Proof by users, laboratories and agencies, prospect:
	   (1) Facts about users' experiences with product
	   (2) Names of users (5) Performance tests
	   (3) Testimonials (6) Guarantee
	   (4) Free trial (7) Samples
	 c. Price presented in psychologically favorable way(s)
	 d. Enclosures to strengthen desire-conviction

4. Action
 a. Logical conclusion based on the major premise and the clearly stated facts; then same as I, 4
	4. Action
	 a. CSAD[1] c. DA[3]
	 b. EA[2] d. RB[4]
	 e. Inducements
	   (1) Credit cards
	   (2) Easy payments or no money down
	   (3) Free gift
	   (4) Free trial
	   (5) Last chance
	   (6) Limited quantity or time
	   (7) No obligation to buy
	   (8) Premium
	   (9) Special price for limited time

PART

THREE

SPECIALIZED MESSAGES

chapter 11

The Written Job Presentation

397

Sometime in your life—perhaps several times—you will probably seek a job through a written presentation. If you answer advertisements or choose companies that do not send recruiters to your campus, you will usually need to write and mail your application. Also, even if you interview a firm's representative on your campus, you may still be asked for additional, written information. Furthermore, several years after you graduate from college—if you desire to change jobs—the ability to write a good presentation of yourself will help you get a better, more satisfying job. Thousands of applicants have found that the best way to get interviews and desired jobs is through the direct-mail approach.

Actually, when you apply for a job you are selling a "product"—yourself. The research before you write, as well as the planning and writing of your "sales promotion" job presentation, should be as thorough as for selling any other product by direct mail. This chapter discusses the "product" analysis, market research, resume, and application letter.

"PRODUCT" ANALYSIS—EVALUATING YOURSELF

Whenever you are selling something, you want to be sure you are representing the product fairly. You need to analyze it to know *what* you are selling before you can start investigating *where* and *how* to sell it. The same is true when you are selling your services. For an adequate *self-appraisal*, take an *inventory* of your employment qualifications. Begin by listing—on several sheets of paper—your specific achievements, capabilities, interests, and characteristics. You might write them under various general headings and subheadings like the following:

1. *Work experience, skills, aptitudes*
   Your part-time and full-time jobs (paid and volunteer) since high school—dates, employer and supervisor names and addresses; your title(s), duties, responsibilities, successes, promotions.
   Your specific skills and aptitudes—speaking ability, report-writing ability, shorthand, etc.; also machines (office, industrial, craft) you can operate well.
   Military service—dates, responsibilities, achievements.

2. *Education*—Evidence of intelligence and knowledge
   Schools (colleges, technical, military, high, other) you attended—dates, names, locations; your degrees, major(s), scholastic standing in each.
   Courses—in major, core, and useful electives; grades; significant reports written.

3. *Activities, achievements, social development*
   Extracurricular and professional organizations—memberships, offices held, and noteworthy accomplishments in clubs related to your major, or in sports, church, social, community projects; coaching, student teaching, tutoring.
   Achievements, honors, awards—scholarships, honor rolls, and other recognitions.
   Travel, foreign language facilities, hobbies, personal business ventures, publications, attendance and responsibilities at conventions, and so forth.

4. *Interests, preferences, and attitudes*

Which courses in my schooling did I enjoy most? In which did I earn high grades?

Which duties and responsibilities did I like best? In which was I most successful or do I have a continuing interest?

Do I prefer to work with people, figures, machines, or ideas?

Would I rather sell, create, or design? Lead or follow?

Am I more comfortable in a large or a small organization?

What values do I consider most important in my career—salary, prestige, friends, family, material goods, leisure, travel, others?

In which locality do I prefer to live? Have I strong preferences?

How well do I work under pressure?

Am I a good listener? planner? leader? follower? (List evidence.)

What are my strongest skills?

Which hobbies do I enjoy most? Do they relate to the job I'd like?

What have I done to correct my shortcomings?

What responsibilities and salary do I aspire to in five years?

What are my goals and priorities?

What are my obligations to my community, family, employer?

5. *Personal Characteristics—Self-appraisal Checklist*

Rate yourself on the following characteristics considered important by employers who seek college graduates. Notice that "integrity" heads the list. (See also the discussion on Integrity, pages 47-50.)

	Excellent	Good	Fair	Poor
• Integrity, sincerity				
• Ability to think logically				
• Enthusiasm, initiative, drive				
• Dependability				
• Ability to communicate orally and in writing				
• Intelligence				
• Maturity				
• Analytical ability				
• Ability to get along and cooperate with others				
• Emotional stability				
• Evidence of good judgment				

	Excellent	Good	Fair	Poor
• Ability to make decisions				
• Health and energy				
• Physical appearance				
• Capacity for leadership				
• Self-confidence				
• Courtesy, tact, diplomacy				
• Adaptability				
• Sense of humor				
• Neatness of work				
• Determination				
• Bearing, poise				

An objective self-analysis like the foregoing inventory is strictly for your own use. It will not be mailed to anyone, but it helps you see patterns emerge regarding your capabilities, desires, interests, and achievements that are unique to you. Fortunately, no one else has exactly the same qualifications you have! Sort out your strengths (perhaps by double check marks) and try to determine your best salable qualifications.

MARKET RESEARCH—FINDING WHO CAN USE YOU AND WHAT THEY PREFER

The next phase of your job-getting campaign is to determine which jobs and employers require what you have to offer.

Perhaps you know right now the kind of career work you want and even the organization you will work for; if so, you are fortunate. More likely, however, you are one of the thousands of young people who are not sure which career they should pursue, where the job opportunities are, or what qualifications they must meet both personally and in their written job presentations. This section includes suggestions to help you in these phases of your job-market research, whether you are a recent or upcoming graduate or a person who has worked a number of years and now wants to change jobs or career.

Information Sources for Careers and Jobs

Various information sources can be helpful. Bear in mind, of course, that because supply and demand in the employment market change from year to year, it is best to get the most current information on both careers and job opportunities.

Publications Regarding Careers

To get ideas about various occupations and careers you will find useful printed materials such as the following in libraries and perhaps your campus career placement office:

Books   Among many books available, these six give a broad overview.

Career Planning Handbook; A Guide to Career Fields and Opportunities, U.S. Civil service Commission, U.S. Government Printing Office, Washington, D.C.

Dictionary of Occupational Titles, U.S. Department of Labor, U.S. Government Printing Office, Washington, D.C. Summarizes characteristics, abilities, and skills contributing to success in various occupations and careers. Includes 23,000 occupations.

Occupational Outlook Handbook, U.S. Bureau of Labor Statistics, U.S. Government Printing Office, Washington, D.C. Highlights employment opportunities in various fields.

Guide to Career Education, by Muriel Lederer, Quadrangle/The New York Times Book Co., N.Y., 1974.

What Color Is Your Parachute? A practical manual for job hunters and career changers, by Richard Bolles; Ten-Speed Press, Berkeley, Calif., 1977.

SRA Occupational Briefs, Science Research Associates, 259 East Erie Street, Chicago. Consists of 210 four-page briefs (of which 70 are revised each year) about major job areas.

Magazines and Newspapers

For lists of recent articles on careers you are considering, consult one or more of these periodical indexes: *Applied Science and Technology, Business Periodicals, Public Affairs Information Service, Readers' Guide, Standard and Poor's Industrial Index, Standard Register of Advertisers.* Among the magazines that occasionally devote a part or an entire issue to occupations are: *American Journal of Sociology, Fortune* magazine, *M.B.A. Magazine, Wall Street Journal,* and *Time.*

Publications and People Regarding Employers and Jobs

After deciding on the kind of career you want, you will need information about employers and various types of jobs available in your chosen field. Published materials and various people can inform you about openings, products, services, geographical locations, sizes, problems, and/or facts about the employers. Among them are the following:

College Placement Annual, College Placement Council, 35 East Elizabeth Street, Bethlehem, Pennsylvania. Contains an alphabetical list of United States and Canadian firms seeking college graduates; includes brief information on openings and the proper persons to contact; also includes alphabetical lists by majors and geographical locations.

Dun and Bradstreet Middle Market Directory. Names, addresses, telephone numbers, officers, products or services, number of employees, and alphabetical list of top management for about 33,000 firms whose net worth is $500,000 to $999,999.

Dun and Bradstreet Million Dollar Directory. Essentially similar coverage as for Middle Market, but focuses on firms with net worth over $1 million.

Fortune Magazine's Directory of Largest Corporations. Published annually in four parts. Includes industrials, financial services, retailing, transportation, and utilities.

Poor's Register of Directors and Executives; United States and Canada, published annually by Standard and Poor's Corporation, 345 Hudson Street, New York. Has an alphabetical list of over 27,000 leading business firms, their addresses, principal products, number of employees, directors, and key officers.

Thomas' Register of American Manufacturers, Thomas Publishing Co., 461 Eighth Avenue, New York.

Company annual reports, brochures, pamphlets, house organs, newsletters. (Get them in placement offices or by writing to the firms.)

Professional journals, business magazines, newspapers. Often periodicals have columns for both help wanted and position wanted. Sometimes special ads publicize openings. Also, occasional articles discuss companies' new ventures, expansions, additional products, and so forth. Such leads may suggest employment possibilities for you.

Besides these printed materials, you can get helpful advice and sometimes tips about good openings from persons familiar with work or firms in your chosen career. These may be useful sources of information:

Business librarians

Businesspeople in your chosen field or firm(s)

Chambers of commerce

Company representatives—traveling for book publishers, insurance companies, office supply firms, public relations departments

Counselors—in your school, business, sports, or activity programs

Employment agencies—including national, state, city, and private bureaus

Friends and relatives

Personnel departments—sometimes provide application forms and leads if you telephone or call in person

Professors and instructors

School placement offices

Desirable General Qualifications of the Applicant

Determining what the employers' (your buyers') needs and requirements are is an important part of your research about the job market. You will then be better able to focus on jobs that are in harmony with what you can contribute as an employee. Desirable general qualifications all employers look for usually include (in varying degrees, depending on the job) *the five broad areas listed in the self-appraisal*, pages 398–400. You will find detailed discussions on them later in this chapter.

In addition, employers also look for proper attitude toward employment. You will more likely make a favorable impression when your attitude shows a willingness to learn and work, sincere interest in the company as well as in the field, and reasonable attitude toward salary.

Willingness to Learn and Work

Especially if you are a recent college graduate, you should be willing to accept beginning or routine work within your chosen field. The many facts you've learned during perhaps 16 years of school before graduation, have been general enough to be useful for all types of businesses. On the job you will need to learn specific duties, procedures, and practices of the company that hires you. As newspaper correspondent Hal Boyle once wrote: "You have to learn how to saw wood before you can make a cabinet."

Yet employers receive many applications from recent (21-year-old) graduates for jobs that require years of service or training. These unrealistic requests indicate an unwillingness to learn or a naive idea of the work. They include applications to be personnel directors, store managers, editors, comptrollers, foreign correspondents, account executives, and so on. A college degree does open doors to employment, but you still have to prove your worth in your written application, interview, and actual performance on the job. You need to be genuinely willing to learn.

Try to show your self-confidence without being egotistic or timid. Overuse of the word *I* makes a negative impression. Some specific facts can help indicate that you have *determination, initiative, drive,* and *tenacity* to get work done. For example, if you had to drop out of school because of finances or poor grades, but managed to earn your degree by attending night school, you are certainly a determined person. Or if you quit school voluntarily and then returned to complete your degree—only through sacrifice—you have determination to succeed. This characteristic can be useful for learning the new job well and for carrying projects to successful completion for the company.

Sincere Interest in the Field and the Company

Employers expect you to know the type of work you prefer for a career and that you have chosen a career you will enjoy. Don't expect the employer to decide the type of work you are best suited for. You must reach your own conclusion about your estimated part in the world's work. Show that you have a *genuine interest in your chosen job or field.*

Your *interest in the company* should also be sincere. After you have studied the company, you can state why you feel it is the type of organization in which you feel you can do your most productive work. Employers appreciate the applicant with *you-attitude and integrity.* Be sincere. In your resume and letter try to *show how you can be helpful to the employer.*

Most personnel executives can detect when an applicant is insincerely praising a company or mechanically stating a desire to work only for that particular firm. Another type of insincerity—or even dishonesty—is exaggerating and padding qualifications. Sincerity doesn't mean, however, you need to expose your shortcomings. If you haven't had work experience or don't have a good grade point average, you need not mention these negative aspects at all in your written presentation. Instead, you should stress—honestly—other, positive qualifications that strengthen your presentation and show your sincere interest in being of help to the organization.

Reasonable Attitude toward Salary

Do not emphasize your own self-interest, such as what fringe benefits and salary the employer will offer *you*. Generally it is better to consider a challenging opportunity more important than a large beginning salary. Emphasis on salary—in the first written job presentation—creates an unfavorable impression. In general, especially if you are just beginning your career, it is best not to mention desired salary in the letter or resume. (This matter can be discussed during the interview.)

Desirable General Qualities for the Written Job Presentation

After you have evaluated your assets and researched job opportunities and employers' requirements, you are ready to prepare your written "sales promotion." The main purpose is to get an interview. You need to persuade the employer that you are the right candidate for the job. Many personnel directors have commented that only a small percentage of the hundreds of applications they receive each month are well written and appealing enough to warrant interviews. The rest must be discarded, for readers haven't time to figure out what the applicants have to offer. A sloppy, inaccurate message from an applicant supposedly trying to make a good impression causes the employer to wonder about that person's overall capability.

Your written job presentation—the letter and resume—will make a more favorable impression on the prospective buyers if it has the seven C qualities. The following desirable *general* suggestions apply to both the resume and the letter. Later in this chapter the separate sections on Resume and Letter of Application illustrate *specific* ways to include your various qualifications effectively.

1. *Present your message concisely, clearly, honestly, with consideration* for the reader. Desirable length is usually a one-page letter and a one- or two-page resume—unless you have many years of valuable experience pertinent to a top-level job. The employer is busy and unwilling to waste time on irrelevant details, minor points, or your life history. Focus on your credentials that show how you can help the employer in the job you seek.

2. *Include only positive specific information relative to the position.* Omit facts that may detract from your favorable qualifications. Such planned omissions are not considered unethical unless the excluded facts do definitely affect your ability to perform the job. Emphasize the areas of job-related responsibilities in which you have a past record of excellence. Such past records may strongly indicate future excellence with the employer's organization.

3. *Be yourself and don't use "canned" messages.* Your resume and letter should reveal your individuality. Personnel executives easily recognize and react negatively toward canned messages that sound as if they've been copied from a textbook or written by an employment agency.

4. *Use an appropriate businesslike approach.* You should sound serious, rather than smart alecky or "cute." Avoid slang and novelties like: a burnt corner (to show "a burning desire" to work), an upside-down letter (saying applicant is not afraid to start at the bottom), or reference to yourself as "a product originating only 21 years ago"! However, discreet originality is desirable for an applicant interested in a job—such as advertising—involving a high degree of creativity.

5. *Triple check for accuracy of facts and mechanics*—grammar, sentence and paragraph structure, organization, desirable headings, parallelism of items under each heading, punctuation, and spelling. Employers place heavy emphasis on spelling accuracy for these reasons:

   If you have *spelling* errors on the important job application, you'll probably continue having errors in letters to customers; and many customers judge the overall ability of a writer by spelling accuracy. Further, transposing letters within words—such as "teh" for "the"—shows carelessness in proofreading. Maybe (so the employer thinks) the writer is also careless in other aspects of work performance. Be especially careful about spelling names of persons, firms, and job areas. (Commonly misspelled words include "J. C. Penny" for "J. C. Penney," "Weyerhauser" for "Weyerhaeuser," and "personel" for "personnel.")

6. *Make appearance attractive and professional-looking.*

   a. Paper for the letter and resume should usually be 8½- by 11-inch bond, at least 16- to 20-pound weight, and 25 percent rag content. White is safest (but some readers consider beige or off-white desirably distinctive).

   b. Typing of both letter and resume should be with neat, black type (if desired, on an IBM Selectric machine with variations in type sizes and styles); margins, ample for easy reading of uncrowded data; erasures or corrections, unnoticeable. In the resume, to emphasize key words and headings, you can use underscoring, capital letters, italics, "frames" with rule-line drawings, and other devices.

   c. Duplicating—by offset (such as multilith), print, xerography, or other neat professional methods (costing only a few cents per page)—is permissible for resumes, but *not* for letters. Each application letter must be individually typewritten.

7. *Personalize your presentation as much as possible.* Tailoring a resume for a specific job or company is desirable. However, even if you are sending out numerous resumes (neatly reproduced), you should preferably address each accompanying *letter* to a specific person *by name* and use that name in your salutation. Address your letter to the person (chief accountant, sales manager, personnel director) who is in charge of employing applicants for the type of job you seek. Use the correct name and title of your addressee. (For applicants with many years of top-level experience for high managerial positions, some placement counselors recommend writing to the company president or vice president. When routed down to other officers such applications may get special attention.)

8. *Use good judgment in mailing your message.* Generally, be prompt. Sometimes it may be advisable to use special delivery to reach an executive at the best time, usually in the middle of a week. (However, some surveys show that letters answering a popular ad get better results if they arrive on about the eighth day rather than among the hundreds mailed the first seven days after the ad appears.) The only enclosure with your letter is the resume. You might *offer* to send samples of work, transcripts, or recommendations, but don't send them with the initial application.

RESUME

Though the prospective employer will read the letter first, you should prepare the resume first; for it includes facts on which the letter will be based.

The resume gives a general, concise picture of *you*—what you have accomplished in your education, experience, and activities that will benefit prospective employers. Contents and layouts vary widely; there is no one best type. However, an important rule is to place your most impressive qualifications first whenever possible and desirable. Present your information under headings in phrases instead of full sentences, and avoid using personal pronouns.

This section discusses the possible contents and ways of presenting a resume (also spelled "résumé" or "resumé"). From the following checklist you can select the parts that best fit your background and the job you seek. Then arrange them in any desirable order. "Accentuate the positive" honestly.

CHECKLIST FOR A RESUME

1. **Opening section:**
   Your name, address, telephone number
   Job title, career goal
   Summary of basic qualifications

2. **Education:**
   Advanced schooling and training—school names, locations; dates attended, degrees and certificates (include high school and military if significant)

Major, significant pertinent courses (required or elective), academic honors, grade point averages; special skills; speeches, research, reports

3. **Work experience:**
   Employer names, locations; dates (month year to month year); titles and positions held; duties; supervisors (or number supervised); accomplishments

   Volunteer work, research, tutoring, publications, etc.

4. **Activities, achievements, awards:**
   School and community memberships, offices held, honors, publications; travel, languages, self-support, other facts

5. **Personal data—optional:**
   Birthdate, health, height, weight, marital status, dependents, military service, hobbies, picture, date of availability

6. **Other relevant facts** (if not included under 1–5)

7. **References**

Opening Section

The information in the opening section (upper part of the resume) gives the reader a general picture of the applicant—who the person is, what she or he wants, and what he or she offers.

Title

The resume heading can range in content from your name alone—to your name and the title of the job you are applying for—to your name, address, and telephone number and/or the name of the firm receiving the job presentation. Also, you can choose other words besides *resume*, as in these examples:

1. Resume of Robert A. Fitchitt for Public Safety Position

2. Data Sheet of Deanna D. Bowman for Retail Management
                         4504 18th Avenue NE
                         Akron, Ohio 44304
                    Phone: (216) 543-1072

3. Qualifications of Betty Jo Anderson
   for a Position as Business Teacher
   in the North Shore School District

4. STATEMENT OF ASSETS
      FOR EMPLOYMENT IN AN ACCOUNTING CAREER
      LAURENCE H. FLINN
      13605 S. E. 171 Avenue
      Renton, Washington 98055
      Telephone: (206) 926-6031

Whatever title you choose, include your address and telephone number on your resume where *your prospective employer can see and use them easily.* A single person might have two addresses listed on the resume—permanent (parents') address and temporary school address. You can include both if they serve a good purpose. If you prefer to omit address and phone number in the opening, you can include them in the Personal Data section. Place them where the personnel representative can easily find them. Sometimes the resume becomes separated from the application letter; it must contain all needed contact information.

Job or Career Objective

One entry that interests every employer is the job (or professional) objective. This statement is sometimes in the heading (see examples 1–4 on page 407) or it is under a separate title. If you can do two quite different kinds of work—for instance, accounting and teaching—you should prepare two separate resumes, each with a specific objective and then feature different phases of your background in each.

Be careful to avoid inflexible titles or too narrow statements of objectives, because they decrease the scope of your availability. If a firm is seeking a sales representative, for example, the reader will discard a resume with a sales manager job objective (even though, unknown to the employer, the applicant might accept a sales job as a start). When your immediate goal is different from the ultimate goal, you should state both in your job objective, as in the following:

1. An accounting position with a reputable public accounting firm which is a leader in its field. The position should eventually lead to management advisory services. (*Notice the implied compliment to the firm.*)
2. To begin work in the comptroller's office of a small wholesale organization located in the Northeast, preferably in or near New York City, with goal of qualifying eventually for general management responsibilities. (*Mention your preferred locality only if you have strong geographical preferences.*)
3. A position in your management training program, with the goal of participating in some management phase of your overseas operations.
4. To work in your firm as an expeditor or coordinator with the eventual aim of a position in construction management.

Summary of Basic Qualifications

Immediately after—*or before*—stating your objectives (what you *want*), you can sometimes favorably impress the employer by emphasizing what you *offer.* Your heading can be: Significant Professional Achievements; Summary of Basic Qualifications; Capsule View of Public Relations Background; or others. Such a summary statement is effective if you have two or more *outstanding* qualifications that are basic or especially important for the job, like those below. (Notice they are concisely stated in phrases or partial sentences.)

1. Offering six years of progressively more responsible experience in office management and business administration, in addition to a master's degree in policy and organization. Record of accuracy, integrity, and ability to work with people.
2. Associate of Arts Degree in Business--major in transportation. 3½ years of full-time experience--specialization in in-bound cargo movement with steamship agency; and shipping department, order desk, and inside sales with manufacturing firm. (*For a community college graduate.*)
3. Bachelor of Arts degree with a major in personnel management and with emphasis in psychology, sociology, and business.
   Four years of part-time experience working with people.
   Student counselor in Alaska, summer of (*year*).
4. M.A. and B.A. degrees in Engineering.
   Six years' work in electronics.
5. A diligent worker with 10 years' successful job experience ranging from varied sales responsibilities to restaurant management. Proven ability to organize sales campaign and to supervise employees. (*This applicant had no college degree.*)

Education

The first major section following the resume opening should state *the most important qualification you can offer for the job (or the job area)*. If you are a recent graduate and education is your strongest selling point, cover this area first—in detail. The more years you are away from school, the less educational detail is required. But even applicants who have been away from school for a while should include (usually later in the resume) names and locations of schools as well as dates attended and degrees earned.

If education is your main qualification, you may want to include all the items shown on the Resume Checklist (page 406), provided this material strengthens your presentation. Include the name, location, dates attended, and degrees or certificates earned at all postsecondary schools you attended. (Even high school may be mentioned if its reputation or location or your achievements there somehow tie in with the job qualifications.) The number and kinds of courses to list vary with the type of work requested. Show that you have an acceptable background in the area of the requested work and also a broad understanding of the arts and sciences (if true). Also list useful elective courses related to your interest and the job. Good examples are courses in written communication, speech, and human relations; also others that helped you to reason objectively to a conclusion or to perform any skills needed for the job.

Grades are a controversial subject. To many employers, grades indicate how well the graduate has mastered program studies and met numerous requirements. As a result, applicants for some areas—such as accounting, teaching, and research—need high grades before they can be considered by the more desirable organizations. For other applicants, grades are weighed together with various factors: for example, a graduate who has had to work while in college, has dependents, and has participated in extracurricular activities isn't expected to have as high grades as a person who has not had to use time for such nonclass endeavors.

For positions that require the individual to work closely with customers and employers, personality is more important than grades; examples of such areas include selling, management training, and secretarial work. Furthermore, a graduate with a straight A cumulative grade point needs to prove he or she possesses more than intelligence, because the average employer is wary of an applicant who has little or nothing but high scholarship to offer.

Illustrated below are various ways to show pertinent facts about academic background. Rearrange your own educational material so it best presents *your* preparation for the job you seek. List your most recent education first, and choose meaningful titles.

1. **Concise listing of schools, with dates; then degrees, standing, major:**

            PROFESSIONAL TRAINING AND EDUCATION

University of Kansas   Lawrence, KS¹ Business Administration 1978-80
Everett Junior College Everett, WA   Liberal Arts   1976-78
U.S. Air Force School   Denver, CO   Electronics   1973-75
Martin High School   Martin, WV   College Preparatory   1969-73

  Degrees: Bachelor of Arts in Business Administration, U.K., 1980
             Associate of Arts and Sciences, E.J.C., 1978
  Standing: Top 5 percent of class at both E.J.C. and U.K.
             Valedictorian, high school
  Majors: Operations Management and Finance

2. **Listing of relevant courses as a subdivision** (under Education, center heading, and schools) when your strongest qualification is education:

                  Special Relevant Courses

In Major   Grade In Nonmajor   Grade
International Business Principles A   Written Business
Economics of Underdeveloped   Communications   A
  Countries   B   Speech Principles
International Marketing Research   A   (Group Discussion)   A
Overseas Operations Management   A   Principles of Operations
International Marketing   A   Management   B
Multinational Sales Forecasting   Scheduling and Inventory
  Models   B   Control   A

3. **Listing of courses functionally** (20-year-old community college graduate with no paid experience):

Associate of Arts Degree--Business Technology Accounting
Major, Metropolitan Community College, Syracuse, NY

Accounting   Accounting Principles 1-2-3, Advanced Account-
Techniques   ing, Federal Income Tax Accounting, Cost
              Accounting, Auditing, Governmental Accounting

¹ Abbreviations, if clear, are permissible on resumes.

<u>Business</u>	Business Organization and Management, Business Math, Business Law, Applied Economics, Business Statistics
<u>Communication Skills</u>	Written Communication, Speech
<u>Machine Operations</u>	Data Processing, Office Machines 1 and 2, Rotary and Electronic Calculators, Typing
<u>Working with People</u>	Introduction to Psychology, Office/Personnel Management, Public Relations, Psychology of Human Relations

4. **Inclusion of course information with the schools** instead of in a special subdivision (as in 2):

<u>Education</u>
University of Illinois, Urbana--Sept. '76-June '80
  Major: Accounting (42 quarter hours)
  Grades: Overall--3.01 (out of a possible 4.00)
             Accounting--3.51

<u>Accounting courses:</u>	<u>Other relevant courses:</u>
.Federal Income Tax	.Personnel Management
.Special Tax Problems	.Human Relations
.Auditing Standards and Principles	.Business Report Writing
.Case Studies in Auditing	.Principles of Economics
.Basic Accounting Principles	.Marketing Cases
	.Banking and Finance

Shoreline High School, Seattle--Sept. '71-June '76
  Major: General business and College preparatory
  Grades: 3.56 (out of a possible 4.00); top 5 percent of class

5. **Off-campus technical training** sponsored by a firm or branch of government or taken independently:

<u>840 Hours of Management and Technical Training</u>

Harbridge House, Inc.	Boston, Management Seminar	3/79-5/80
IBM Education Center	Chicago, Computer Programming	6/78-1/79
Military Service Schools	Radar Theory, Antisubmarine Warfare	'60-'66

6. **Emphasis on degrees and grades:** Put your best foot forward—and still be honest. If your overall average is just so-so because of poor grades during your freshman and/ or sophomore years, give the average for your major, for all business courses, or for your junior and senior years combined. If the overall grades were high, you might list as follows:

Master of Business Administration in Quantitative Methods, University of Michigan; Autumn 1978 through Winter 1980; Grade point, 3.7 (possible, 4.0)

Bachelor of Arts in Mathematics, University of Ohio; Autumn 1975 through Spring 1978; Grade point, 3.8 (possible, 4.0)

Work Experience

Any kind of work experience—related or unrelated—reveals information that helps the employer to evaluate the applicant. Work experience similar to that which you are applying for indicates you like the type of work in question and may shorten the training period. However, all types of work experience disclose pertinent facts about the applicant's work habits and personality, give a source for references, and perhaps show job preferences.

You need to be thorough in describing your work experience. If you are a recent graduate still in your twenties, you should account for all your jobs that are worth mentioning back to a certain age—perhaps 16 or earlier. If you are an older applicant with extensive experience, you will probably place Work Experience *before* Education. Also, you may prefer to include only the more recent jobs or those that best relate to the position you seek; the employer will appreciate conciseness, instead of a long list of irrelevant material.

Usually, for the standard "general" resume, list your jobs in chronological order with the present or most recent first. Try to include at least:

1. Type of work performed and your title (supervisor, bookkeeper, and so forth)[2]
2. Name and location of company[3]
3. Time worked (month year to month year)
4. Whether job was part-time (otherwise employer will interpret statement as full-time employment)

In addition, you should include the following if they strengthen your presentation:

5. Duties—work involving responsibilities, adaptability, similarity to what you're applying for, integrity, supervisory or budgetary functions, knowledge of products. Use *action words* like the following, and others that apply to your particular duties, whenever desirable:

advanced	coordinated	expanded	managed	reduced
analyzed	delivered	implemented	negotiated	researched
coached	demonstrated	increased	organized	sold
completed	developed	initiated	planned	supervised
conducted	directed	instituted	presented	trained
created	edited	instructed	produced	wrote

6. Name of immediate superior—if this person is still there and will be a good reference
7. Accomplishments—if they're important; unique or innovative projects

---

[2] Be honest. If you were a laborer, say "laborer." Don't try to put on airs by camouflaging the title. For example, don't say "sanitary engineer" if you were a garbage collector; say "garbage collector." [3] If you are currently employed and do not wish to disclose your employer on your resume, you can merely identify the firm by industry; for example, you might say "a medium-sized manufacturer of electronic equipment." That will give the reader some indication of your company without divulging its name and perhaps jeopardizing your job. If a firm's name is now different from what it was when you were employed there, state the present name and "formerly . . .)."

Arrange the facts for each job in the most "selling" order. You can begin with your job title, or employer's name, or dates you held each job, or the functions you performed on each job.[4]

1. Job title first:

<u>Office Manager</u> Fifth Investors Corporation, Norfolk, VA.; full time from September 1977 to August 1979. Duties: supervised 10 typists, checked typed material before printing, composed letters to publishers, and assisted with purchase orders.

<u>Service Representative</u> Pacific Northwest Bell, Seattle, WA.; full time from February 1976 to September 1977. Duties: gave service to telephone customers regarding telephone installations, questions on bills, complaints, selection of additional telephones.

<u>Assistant to Manager</u> of Accounts Payable, Associated Hardware, Tacoma, WA.; full time from June 1974 to February 1976. Duties: figured discounts on statements, filed, typed, posted accounts, wrote checks.

2. Employer first:

<u>California State Highway Department</u> 931 Ridgeway, Sacramento
    Draftsperson, March 1978 to December 1979**
        Duties: drawing roadway profiles and burrow sites
    Bookkeeper, May 1977 to March 1978**
        Duties: keeping time and equipment records for division
                and preparing vouchers
    Driller's Helper, January 1976 to May 1977*
        Duties: drilling test holes for proposed highway routes

<u>Washington State Highway Department</u> 1219 Capitol Way, Olympia,
    Engineering Technician, November 1972 to December 1975**
        Duties: processing traffic data and interviewing on truck
                surveys
    Saw Crewperson, July 15, 1972, to November 1972*
        Duties: sawing wood supports in highway construction

  *Full-time.
**Part-time during school, full-time summers.

3. Dates first:

June 1979 to October 1980	<u>Position:</u>	Legal Secretary Taking dictation, transcribing, typing, filing, receiving clients
	<u>Reference:</u>	Mr. William McGee, McGee, Strom, Burner, Attorneys 9988 Hightower Building Dearborn, Michigan 48121
School Year September 1978 to June 1979	<u>Position:</u>	Legal Stenographer Weekday mornings--writing shorthand, typing, filing

---

[4] Be sure to follow rules of parallelism—making two or more elements in a series similar in grammatical word structure. "Manager," "Representative," and "Bookkeeper" are all parallel to each other because each is a job title. "Managing"—which is a kind of work, not a title—would not be parallel to the other three titles. For duties: keeping, drilling, filing, typing are parallel; so are kept, drilled, filed, typed.

            Reference: Ms. Louise Jackson, Attorney
                          Barnes, Jayne, Jackson, Associates
                          Ridley Tower
                          Cincinnati, Ohio 45221

Other jobs   Worked as cashier in a restaurant Fridays and
before   Saturdays two months, typed business letters for
1978[5]   high school principal, picked strawberries,
                  helped with gardens.

4. Functions first:

The following example is from a general-purpose resume of a high-level executive who chose to omit dates of employment and names of employers. Usually these are included.

            FUNCTIONAL REVIEW OF WORK EXPERIENCE

General   As Vice President and General Manager of a highly
Management: diversified million-dollar company, was responsi-
                  ble for six operating divisions. Reduced personnel
                  turnover and increased profits by over 40%. In-
                  stituted methods and techniques of modern creative
                  management.

International   As Manager of International Operations of a company
Management: whose sales exceeded six million dollars annually,
                   was responsible for the overseas sales and distri-
                   bution of four producing divisions. Products
                   included plastics, pipeline coatings, and treated
                   wood products.

Management   Conducted seminars on a worldwide basis for . . .
Consulting:

If you have had little or no paid employment but have done volunteer work, tutoring, or research (perhaps even published a report) without pay, you may list such responsibilities under Work Experience or under Activities.

Activities, Achievements, Awards

Participation in extracurricular and cocurricular activities is usually a good indication of an applicant's personality—ability to work with others, leadership, and emotional stability. When listing your activities, mention any offices you held as well as projects on which cooperation, teamwork, and sincere interest in other people (or projects) were needed. Include athletics, writing (such as journalism), speaking (such as debate), professional fraternities, and student organizations that involve working with people. A leader or active participant in any worthy activity is far more valuable to an employer than a nonparticipant who is merely a "joiner" with numerous affiliations. Awards may be listed in this section or under Miscellaneous Relevant Facts.

You may want to list your activities in two or more divisions:

---

[5] To indicate industriousness previous to the earliest full job entry, "Other jobs before (year)" is acceptable for applicants in their early twenties but may be regarded as inappropriate for older (30 or older) applicants.

College and high school

College and (military) service

Community and other

Professional associations

Seminars, workshops, and speaking engagements

Identify (in parentheses) any activity the employer might not know the significance of. However, if you are or were active in a church or political party, you need not identify them (because of civil rights); but do mention your responsibilities if pertinent.

Beta Gamma Sigma (national scholastic business honorary)

Delta Sigma (national business fraternity)

Beta Alpha Psi (accounting honorary)

Alpha Sigma Phi (social fraternity)

Pilgrim Club (a church youth group)

Purple Shield (underclassmen's activities honorary)

Statements like the following indicate recognition, achievements, awards, and services:

1. Recognition, achievement, awards

    a. High school salutatorian
    b. Most valuable student--Elks Club Award
    c. Mistress of ceremonies at Olympic College Spring Awards
       Assembly
    d. Listed in the second annual edition of <u>Who's Who among
       Students in American Junior Colleges</u>
    e. Eagle Scout
    f. 4-year scholarship at Whitworth College
    g. Dean's list for high scholarship (*dates involved*)
    h. Two-year varsity basketball letterman
    i. Outstanding senior male at (*university*)

2. Service

    a. Assistant coach--Little League Football--Ballard Team (*city
       state*)

    b. Member of (*year*) World Deputation Team from my church. Sent
       to Yukon Territory, Alaska. Worked with high school, junior
       high, and primary age children--teaching and counseling

    c. Volunteer hospital work

```
d. Member (or chairperson?) Program Committee, (name) Club
   Vice President, Senior Class, Central College
```

Personal Data

The category of personal information is now entirely optional. Civil rights laws state that one may not discriminate in hiring on the basis of race, color, religion, sex, marital status, national origin. Exceptions include occupational qualifications that are reasonably necessary to the normal operation of particular businesses, enterprises, or occupations. For example, some jobs in modeling, sports, teaching, and professional entertainment (TV, movies, etc.) may reasonably require certain personal attributes.

Though no law forbids applicants from volunteering personal information, they must be careful not to include items that could possibly be used for discrimination and harm their chances for getting an interview and a job. Items that applicants usually include under Personal Data are birthdate, health, special interests and/or abilities, and hobbies. Many include also height, weight, and marital status, for various reasons. Some employers don't care whether or not they know this type of information, yet most won't react negatively if you include it. If you're in doubt, leave it out. Especially *omit any information that might be considered negatively and that is irrelevant to job requirements.*

Health

Good health is a prime requirement on most jobs because it determines both the physical and mental performance of the individual. You can indicate physical fitness in the Personal Data section or elsewhere by listing:

A statement that you have excellent health with no physical defects, if true.

The sports you participate in. An active swimmer, football or basketball player, or a contestant in intramural activities must be in good condition.

Your hobbies that require activity, endurance, strength, and stamina. Examples include hiking, fishing, mountain climbing, boating, and bowling.

If your health is unsatisfactory, or if you have a physical handicap or a disfiguring burn or birthmark, you need to weigh carefully what you include in your job presentation. If you feel the interview will probably eliminate you from further consideration because of your defect, perhaps you should not apply or you should state your disadvantage on the resume or in the application letter. But if you think you can sell the employer—once in the personal interview—on your overall qualifications, omit any statement about health or defects that could keep you from getting the interview.

Age

The same advice applies to age. If you think the employer may consider your age negatively (assuming that you are too inexperienced or overexperienced for the job you seek), but you feel you can sell her or him on your qualifications during an interview, omit age on the resume. Or you can indicate your birthdate *after* listing your other excellent qualifications, so the employer reads them before seeing your age. (A federal law protects applicants ages 40 through 64 against age discrimination.)

Here are two of many ways to list personal data:

```
Birthdate:    June 22, 1955   Marital status:   Married (1 child)
Height:       5'11"           Military          U.S. Army
Weight:       175               service:        (dates)
Health:       Excellent       Hobbies:          Reading, hiking

Born 8/19/53  Weight 125 lbs.  Height 5'7"  Health excellent  Single
```

Military Service

If significant for the job, military experience may be in a separate section or listed under Education, under Employment, or under Personal Data with more details than in example 1 above. Here are suggestions:

1. Received Air Force commission on (*month day, year*). Air Force pilot from (*month day, year, to month day, year*). Received honorable discharge as Captain on (*month day, year*).
2. Serving eight years (*year to year*) in the Coast Guard Reserve with meetings every Thursday night and two weeks' summer training each year. Satisfactorily completed five years of service. Six months of basic training: (*month day, year to month day, year*).
3. Six years in the Army Reserve (*month year to month year*). Active duty: (*month day, year, to month day, year*). Honorable Discharge.

Hobbies

Under Personal Data or elsewhere, hobbies may also be listed in detail if they relate to job qualifications; for example:

1. Requested work:
   a. Study the stock market.
   b. Tutored first-year accounting students during junior and senior years of college.
   c. Editor of school paper.
   d. An especially important report (oral or written) or article relating to your field of interest.
   e. Ability to write and/or speak foreign language(s).
2. Creativity—designing clothes, photography
3. Mental activity—playing chess, reading
4. Fine arts—music, painting, drama
5. Household tasks—cooking, sewing, knitting

Picture

Although including a picture on a resume was formerly considered almost "standard procedure," this practice has been rare since the early 1970s. The best suggestion now is to *omit* the personal photograph, for it may trigger all kinds of unfavorable, harmful subjective reactions by the personnel representatives. (Some firms even have a rule that all photographs must be removed before the resumes are considered by the personnel representatives.) Among the rare exceptions to omitting pictures are applications for theatrical or special photographic positions that require certain physical traits before an interview. Again, when in doubt it is better to *omit* the picture. But you can have a photograph ready if needed. For a favorable impression of you, the picture should be your best head-and-shoulders view (about 1¾ to 2 inches wide by 2 to 2¼ inches long) taken by a professional photographer.

Other Relevant Facts

If there are other relevant facts that you should include on your resume, but they don't fit comfortably in one of the sections described above, put them in this separate "catchall" section. Also, if you have a single entry for work experience or extracurricular activities—not enough to justify placing elsewhere—include it in this section. But beware of mentioning anything that might cause a negative reaction—for example, hobbies relating to gambling. Also, a salesperson should have hobbies that reveal physical fitness and ability to deal with people—not stamp or coin collecting. But for an accountant these last two hobbies are good—they show patience and attention to detail.

Given below are suggested entries that reveal some aspects of the desired qualifications discussed earlier in the chapter.

1. Expenses earned while you attended college

    a. `Completed college working full-time`
    b. `Worked full-time and supported family while attending college`
       `part-time from (month year, to month year) and full-time (month`
       `year, to month year)`
    c. `Earned 100 percent of my college expenses by working summers`
       `since (year)`

2. Indication of integrity

    a. `Secret classification security clearance—The Boeing Company--`
       `(year to year)`
    b. `Have taught Sunday School three years`
    c. `Bonded`

3. Personal data
    a. Parents' occupation (if work is closely related to the job you're applying for)
    b. Spouse's education (if he or she has college education)
    c. Results of personality test or interest test
4. Preferred location (for example "Prefer Pacific Northwest—will relocate")
5. Publications/Patents—any papers that have been presented at society meetings or published in trade journals; also patents awarded or under application
6. Skills—typing speed, shorthand speed, calculator use, use of office machines

7. Travel (to indicate knowledge of conditions and customs elsewhere)
8. Willingness to relocate (for example, "I will relocate to any city within the United States")
9. Willingness to travel (for sales work)

References

In general, if you are writing to one employer (or a few) for a position you know is available, to play it safe include references. However, if you are mailing your resume to a long list of employers, you'll be safer to merely state, "References will be sent upon request." (Then you won't risk having your references bothered by too many inquiries or being tired recommending you over and over again. Also, when you receive a request for references, you will know the specific kind the employer wants.)

Many employers don't want references until the interview. In fact, many employers question the use of references at all—especially the ones the applicant offers. The most worthless is the "to whom it may concern" message you carry with you, and next in line are the references of friends. You know the references you choose will say only nice things about you; otherwise you wouldn't give their names. The best references are those which employers dig out for themselves.

Nevertheless, sometimes it will be to your advantage to list references if the names you list are well known and respected by the employers. They may be more interested in you even before the interview when they see the name of a person they know and have confidence in or who is considered an expert in a particular field, or perhaps even an executive in or an important customer of the company to which you are applying.

If and when you give references, list about three to five. The most appropriate names include present or former employers and professors. Also acceptable is a character reference whose name or occupation is respected. State each individual's full name, title, organization (if any), complete business address and telephone number. Since you obviously should get permission to use the names you're listing you need not say "with permission." Relatives should not be used as references.

Summary, with Sample Resumes

In summary, the resume should contain selling facts about yourself in a neat, easy-to-read, well-organized format that best indicates your value to the employer. Accentuate the positive by focusing on your strengths and minimizing any job-getting handicaps. If you have little job-related full-time work experience, sell your part-time or volunteer work, your useful thorough educational foundation, your knowledge of the product or firm, and/or your working-with-people experience that can be adapted to the job. On the other hand, if your formal college education is irrelevant or limited, sell whatever other job-related training you do have, plus your work experience, significant activities, and your dependability as well as additional pertinent personal attributes—with specific facts for examples.

Whatever your real or imagined shortcomings may be, you can omit them if you are confident that you will be capable on the job. The foregoing discussions have included examples of various resume sections. Figures 11-1 through 11-4 illustrate a variety of resume contents and layouts—to help give you ideas of how you can arrange and sell your own qualifications.

Figure 11-1 is a personalized one-page resume containing both the job objective and the employer's name in the heading. It is especially useful when you know there is a job opening for the work you can and would like to do, and you want to type an individual resume to that employer. Notice it also lists references (though including them is a matter of personal choice).

```
                     QUALIFICATIONS OF CHRIS W. BENSON as
                STAFF ACCOUNTANT WITH JORGEN, BURGESS, AND ASSOCIATES

     EDUCATION      Bachelor of Business Administration Degree, June 1981
                       University of California, Los Angeles
                     Business Technology Accounting Major Degree, June 1979
                       Central Community College, Seattle, Washington

                     A thorough understanding of corporation, partnership,
                     and proprietorship accounting and financial analysis
                     developed through these courses:

                     Accounting (40 quarter hours, with 3.7 grade average--GPA
                     scale top, 4.0):  Auditing, Public and Internal; Cost;
                     Equity;  Consolidations;  Federal Income Tax;  Fiduciary

                     Related Courses (60 quarter hours, with 3.4 GPA):  Data
                     Processing, Business Communications, Business Law, Money
                     and Banking, Corporate Finance, Statistics

     EMPLOYMENT      June 1979-   Assistant Accountant, Purchasing and Personnel
                     Present      Depts.**  Doctors Hospital, Pasadena, CA

                     Dec. 1977-   Full-charge bookkeeper*
                     Dec. 1978    Marine Medical Clinic, Seattle, WA

                     June 1977-   Billing Clerk*
                     Dec. 1977    Cole Transfer and Storage, Los Angeles, CA

                     July 1973-   Bookkeeper and assistant to Secretary Treasurer**
                     Sept.1974    Hillside Hospital, Burbank, CA

                      *Full time
                     **Part time during school;  rest, full time

     ACTIVITIES      Member and Treasurer, Beta Alpha Psi, Accounting Honorary, UCLA
     AND HONORS      Chairperson, Student Association's Community Fund Drive, UCLA
                     Chairperson, Church Youth Activities Campaign
                     Award winner, Junior Scholarship Cup, Alpha Alpha Association
                     Dean's Honor Roll, UCLA School of Business Administration, 3 quarters

     PERSONAL        Home address:  2982 Norman Drive, Pasadena, CA 91115;  Phone 354-9876
                     Birthdate and place:  March 26, 1955, Pasadena, CA
                     Height:  5'9"  Weight:  139 lbs.  Health:  excellent
                     Earned 80% of college expenses.  Hobbies:  tennis, swimming, golf

     REFERENCES      Ms. Nancy Green      Mr. James Black       Dr. Fletcher Myran
                     Personnel Director   Manager               Prof. of Accounting
                     Doctors Hospital     Marine Medical Clinic School of Bus. Admin.
                     909 University St.   944 Terry Ave.        University of California
                     Pasadena, CA 91102   Seattle, WA 98104     Los Angeles, CA 90002
                     Phone (213)555-6666  (206)222-3333         (213)689-6666
```

Figure 11-1 *Personalized, one-page resume.* Job objective and employer name are included in the heading.

Figure 11-2 is a general-purpose resume typical of those that college graduates with limited working experience can send. Education—the strongest selling point—is listed first, in detail; and pertinent activities as well as other relevant facts are detailed to strengthen qualifications. An applicant with much work experience can, of course, also use the general-purpose resume; but work experience would come before education. This type of resume is easily processed for mass mailing to many prospective

```
                              Resume of
                           Jeanette H. Fulton

    8532 Lakeside Lane      Columbus, Ohio 43210      (614)726-8193

    Professional Objective:  A teaching position in the Business Education
                             Department of an Ohio Class-A secondary school

    Date of Availability:    September 1, 1980

                        Education for Business and Teaching

    Ohio State University, Columbus, Ohio, September 1976 to August 1980

              Major:  Business Education, secondary school emphasis
                      Courses in accounting;  business, government and
                      society;  business law;  secretarial procedures;
                      business communications;  marketing;  teaching of
                      typewriting, shorthand, and accounting
              Minor:  Economics
                      Courses in macroeconomics, microeconomics, international
                      economics, European and American economic history
              Grade Point Average:  3.82 (possible 4.0)
              Degree: Bachelor of Arts in Business Education

    Lincoln High School, Waukegan, Illinois, September 1973 to June 1976
              College preparatory curriculum with emphasis on business and French
              Grade Point Average:  3.84 (possible 4.0)

                           Helpful Job Experience

    Student Teacher--Broadway High, E. Columbus, Ohio, January to June 1980
      Supervisor:    Ms. Irene Grayson
      Courses taught: Typing 2, 4;  Shorthand 2;  Vocational Office Practice
      Responsibilities:  Supervised and planned three complete units for each
                         class, ranging from 20-30 students, with approval of
                         Ms. Grayson;  also worked with Mr. Ben Moor

    Title Clerk and--Larson Ford Motor, 5872 Raymond Avenue, Columbus, Ohio,
    Secretary        January 1978 to December 1979 (part time during school,
                     full time summers)
      Supervisor:    Mr. Charles Jones, Office Manager
      Responsibilities:  Varied over the two years.  Operated switchboard,
                         typed reports and letters, checked titles, recorded
                         accounts payable and cash receipts, assisted office
                         manager as secretary and mail clerk
```

Figure 11-2 *A general-purpose resume* (on two pages).

employers. References are omitted and "will be furnished upon request." If desirable to have only one page, this resume could be condensed by rearranging facts and omitting some details.

The third example, Figure 11-3, is useful for applicants with extensive work experience (listed before education). Though this example is a three-page resume, the applicant could mail only the first page, if necessary. However, pages 2 and 3 give a detailed "functional summary" of job duties.

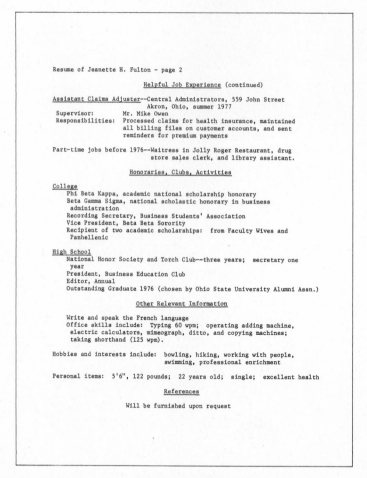

Figure 11-2 (Continued) Second page of *general-purpose resume.*

RESUME OF DAVID L. CHAPMAN—page 2

Functional Summary of Job Responsibilities

State Supervisor, Trade, Industrial and Technical Education (December 1977 to present)

STATE OF WASHINGTON - Department of Education (1977-present)
*Administered and supervised state and federal funded education programs.
*Performed administrative functions.
*Developed management controls for State Director to plan, schedule, and control educational programs in over 170 public institutions involving over 70,000 students.
*Worked with executive management from state and private industry representing Education, Labor, and industrial organizations.
*Organized and directed Washington State Association of a National Youth Organization.

General Supervisor, Production Engineering (June 1974 to December 1977)

THE BOEING COMPANY - Commercial Airplane Division (1974-1977)
*Directed Divisional Systems Development Committee designing production and inventory control affecting 5 Division branches.
*Developed management controls.
*Planned special projects, studies, and administrative functions for Production Engineer, with staffing of over 4,500 employees.
*Worked with senior and corporate executive management.

Senior Supervisor, Industrial Training (April 1976 to June 1977)

*Directed management and technical staff of six supervisors and four analysts, and the company support activities for statewide vocational education program, involving 41 public institutions and 3,000 students.
*Worked with senior and corporate executive management, Washington State Education and college officials, and school administrators.
*Performed local, state, and national recruiting of general and professional-technical personnel.

Supervisor, Industrial Training (June 1975 to April 1976)

*Supervised curriculum development and instruction of courses for Manufacturing Department training requirements.
*Coordinated special Company industry education program with U. S. Air Force.
*Instructed courses and developed training programs with department managers.

RESUME OF

DAVID L. CHAPMAN
13900 NE 32nd Place, Bellevue, WA 98005
Telephone: (206) 953-8111

FOR OPERATIONS MANAGEMENT POSITION LEADING TO
ULTIMATE GOAL OF CORPORATE MANAGEMENT

Summary of Basic Qualifications
Offering 10 years of progressively more responsible experience in Operations Management, in addition to a Bachelor of Arts degree with a major and continuing interest in this field.

Work Experience (See pages 2 and 3 for job descriptions.)
State of Washington—Department of Education—Olympia
  State Supervisor, Industrial & Technical Education—Dec.'77–present
The Boeing Company—Commercial Airplane Division—Renton, WA
  General Supervisor, Production Engineering—June '77 to Dec. '77
  Senior Supervisor, Industrial Training—   Apr. '76 to Apr. '77
  Supervisor, Industrial Training—   June '75 to Apr. '76
  Supervisor, Materiel Operations—   Feb. '74 to June '75
The Boeing Company—Aero-Space Division—Seattle, WA
  Supervisor, Production Control—   Dec. '71 to Feb. '74
  Methods Analyst, Industrial Engineering—   Jan. '71 to Dec. '71
  Lead Expeditor, Production Control—   Nov. '68 to Jan. '71
  Expeditor, Production Control—   June '67 to Nov. '68

Education
University of Washington—Seattle—Sept. '66 to Aug. '68
  Degree: Bachelor of Arts, Business Administration (Grade Average 3.4
  Major: Operations Management. Minor: Personnel) in major (4.0 scale)
Highline Community College—Midway, WA—Sept. '64 to June '66
  Degree: Associate of Arts, Business Administration
Technical Schools—700 additional hours of management and computer work
  Harbridge House, Inc.—Boston, MA—June '74 to Aug. '74
  IBM Education Center— Seattle, WA—Apr. '71 to May '71

Affiliations—Participating member of:
  American Management Association   National Vocational Association
  Boeing Management Association   American Production Control Society
  American Society of Training   Vocational Industrial Clubs of
  and Development   America (State Director)

Miscellaneous Activities, Awards, Interests
  Chairman of 3 state and 2 national education committees—May '75 to present
  Guest Lecturer—University of Washington—July to Aug. '78 and '79
  Awards: Management Cost Improvement, Boeing Co., Nov. '73
          Outstanding Service, Vocational Clubs of Amer. June '79
  Worked full-time and supported family while attending college part-time;
          personally financed total college education program.
  Secret classification security clearance, Boeing Co., 1967 to 1977

Personal Data: Born 7/6/48; 5'11" tall; 168 pounds; married; 3 children

References   Will be sent upon request.

Figure 11-3 (Left) General-purpose resume on three pages—for an "older" applicant (over 30). Concise summary on first page is attached to a functional summary on pages 2 and 3. (Right) Second page of general-purpose resume with two-page functional summary. Page 3 (not shown) continues like page 2 with functions David Chapman performed on the five additional jobs he listed under Work Experience, page 1.

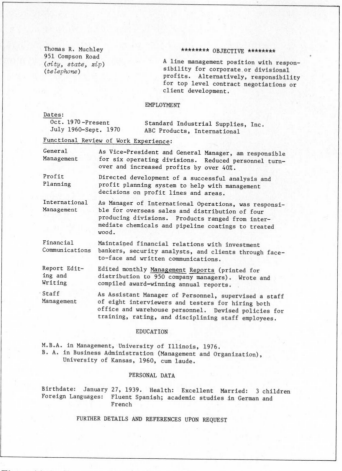

Thomas R. Muchley
951 Compson Road
(*city, state, zip*)
(*telephone*)

******** OBJECTIVE ********

A line management position with responsibility for corporate or divisional
profits. Alternatively, responsibility
for top level contract negotiations or
client development.

EMPLOYMENT

Dates:
  Oct. 1970 –Present   Standard Industrial Supplies, Inc.
  July 1960–Sept. 1970   ABC Products, International

Functional Review of Work Experience:

General   As Vice-President and General Manager, am responsible
Management   for six operating divisions. Reduced personnel turn-
                 over and increased profits by over 40%.

Profit   Directed development of a successful analysis and
Planning   profit planning system to help with management
                 decisions on profit lines and areas.

International   As Manager of International Operations, was responsi-
Management   ble for overseas sales and distribution of four
                  producing divisions. Products ranged from inter-
                  mediate chemicals and pipeline coatings to treated
                  wood.

Financial   Maintained financial relations with investment
Communications   bankers, security analysts, and clients through face-
                  to-face and written communications.

Report Edit-   Edited monthly Management Reports (printed for
ing and   distribution to 950 company managers). Wrote and
Writing   compiled award-winning annual reports.

Staff   As Assistant Manager of Personnel, supervised a staff
Management   of eight interviewers and testers for hiring both
                  office and warehouse personnel. Devised policies for
                  training, rating, and disciplining staff employees.

EDUCATION

M.B.A. in Management, University of Illinois, 1976.
B. A. in Business Administration (Management and Organization),
      University of Kansas, 1960, cum laude.

PERSONAL DATA

Birthdate: January 27, 1939. Health: Excellent Married: 3 children
Foreign Languages: Fluent Spanish; academic studies in German and
                    French

FURTHER DETAILS AND REFERENCES UPON REQUEST

Figure 11-4 *Functional resume* (one-page).

Figure 11-4 illustrates a one-page functional resume especially adaptable for the person who has had impressive work responsibilities related to the job sought. It is also useful for the applicant with long job stability and few employers. Notice that Mr. Muchley had only two employers in 20 years.

LETTER OF APPLICATION

The application letter is just as much a sales letter as any message selling a product or service[6]—and the resume is an enclosure. In your letter you tell the prospective employer *what you can do for her or him and why you feel you are qualified.* You inter-

---

[6] The application letter should, however, always be individually typewritten, although other sales letters may be processed for mass distribution.

pret only the important points in your resume as they *relate to the specific job requirements.* Try to focus on what you can contribute to the employer (your "buyer"), not how much he or she can offer you. In just a few paragraphs—probably five—you must "sell" readers to the point where they want to know more about you. The checklist below may be a helpful guide when you plan the content of your persuasive "sales" application letter—organized by the AIDA plan. Subsequent pages discuss ways to develop each item listed.

CHECKLIST FOR APPLICATION LETTER

A. Attention (1 paragraph)
  1. Businesslike beginning. Usually choose one or two:
      a. Summary—perhaps two or three outstanding qualifications
      b. Name—an individual or office the reader is familiar with or the publication in which the reader's ad appeared
      c. Question—for reader benefit
      d. News item—related to employer
      e. Other relevant reader-oriented statement
  2. Mention of specific job or field of interest

B. Interest, Desire, Conviction (2 or 3 paragraphs)
  1. Discussion of your qualifications from a reader-benefit or reader-interest viewpoint. Include your:
      a. Education and training—related to job requirements
      b. Work experience—related to job requirements
      c. Significant personal attitudes, interests, and/or qualities—related to job requirements
  2. Reference to resume (once)

C. Action (1 paragraph)
  1. Request for interview . . . at reader's convenience, with suggestions when you will be available
  2. Easy action
      a. Phone number
      b. Hours you can be reached
      c. Reply envelope or card enclosed only rarely. Consider reader!

Opening for Favorable Attention

The beginning of the letter should catch the reader's attention in a businesslike manner. It should also state definitely that you are applying for a job—not inquiring about one or studying this phase of personnel for a school project. Furthermore, you should identify the job (or job area) you're interested in.

Given below are examples of different kinds of first paragraphs for an application letter. You can adapt these suggestions to your needs whether you write a "prospecting" (unsolicited) letter to firms that have not announced an opening or a "solicited" letter about a known available position. Also, if appropriate, you may combine two of the kinds of openings into your one first paragraph, as shown in some of the examples.

Summary Opening

One of the most effective openings includes a summary of your two or three outstanding qualifications. Like the first paragraph of an article in a newspaper, the summary gives in capsule form the important points you'll expand in the message.

1. Retailing experience in a department store similar to yours, business knowledge gained academically, plus a sincere interest in these areas have helped me learn the basic requirements for running a department efficiently. I would like to contribute the practical skills I have acquired by becoming a part of your management training program.

2. If hundreds of effective retail calls, thorough knowledge of point-of-sale, and imaginative merchandising help make an appliance representative, then I've begun to learn the business. I would like to put this practical field experience to work for (*name*) Appliance Company.

3. It is my understanding that a continuity writer for your station must have an interest in and knowledge of classical music. She or he must have ambition and a desire to achieve. Above all, she or he must be able to write. I have these qualifications and should like to be considered for the job.

Name Opening

If someone—especially a person well known to the reader—has suggested you apply to a particular firm for a job, you can use that person's name in the opening—unless he or she has asked you to keep it confidential. Whether you identify this individual by title depends on how well the reader knows him or her.

If you are answering a job ad, refer to it and the name of the publication along with what you can offer. Avoid repeating requirements stated in the ad and don't include stupid statements or questions that have obvious answers. For example: "According to your ad, you are looking for an accountant who knows accounting theory and is accurate."

1. Dr. Horace Brann, professor of accounting and chairperson of the accounting department at (*university*), has informed me that your firm is looking for an accounting major who is interested in managerial accounting. I should like to be considered for the opening in your training program.

2. Your ad in the Sunday <u>Times</u> for an aggressive person to sell your
   graphic communication products and services calls for qualifications that match mine very closely. With three years' successful
   selling as well as servicing of duplicators and electronic systems,
   plus genuine enthusiasm for selling and ability to solve complex
   graphic communications problems, I would like to join your staff
   as a sales trainee.

Question Opening

Another way to catch the employer's attention at the beginning is with a properly
phrased question that shows understanding of a company problem or significant need
and the applicant's desire to help.

1. Do you need a reliable assistant store manager with a broad background of business training and experience who can speak French
   and German? If you do, please consider me for that position.
2. Can you use a salesperson with mechanical aptitude, a university
   education, four years of selling experience, and a strong desire
   to succeed? I will graduate from the University of (*state*) in
   December and believe I can help increase your company profits.

News-Item Opening

Sometimes you can mention a news event about a significant achievement of the employer or his or her company, or a contemplated change or new procedure—if it ties
in with your desire to work for a certain firm.

1. In a recent (*name of journal*) article I read with interest that your
   firm is planning to open a branch office in Mexico. Because my college background and work experience, plus facility with Spanish, fit
   your basic requirements for a research assistant, I would like to
   apply for that job in your branch office.
2. Your firm's consulting activities, and especially its work in "information systems," may attract you to an individual with my qualifications and aspirations. My academic concentration on "open systems theory," coupled with practical experience, would enable me to
   perform well as a member of your management consulting staff.

Other Beginnings

You should of course, design your own opening—the one most appropriate for you
and for the particular person to whom you are writing. As the following examples
illustrate, you can state an interest, previous experience with the same organization,
a belief or your present situation.

1. Swimming pool operation and maintenance have been of interest to me
   for the last few years. At the same time I have been studying business at the University of (*name*). I would like to combine these two

```
       interests by working for Pools as a salesperson and pool maintenance
       consultant.
    2. We both know that American Can Company prefers to pick its manage-
       ment trainees from the qualified employees in its lower echelons.
       After working six and one-half years in the various departments of
       Canco and attaining my college degree this June, I will be qualified
       to be of further benefit to our company as a future manager.
```

Middle Paragraphs for Interest, Desire, Conviction

After you have caught the reader's attention, you proceed to present your basic qualifications for the job you're applying for. In the short space you have (perhaps no more
than three paragraphs) you can't afford to repeat *unnecessarily* what is on the resume.
You need to select and emphasize key points, considering carefully every word in
every idea you include. The emphasis is on how you can be helpful to the employer!

As with most sales letters, *facts and figures* are more convincing than the writer's
opinions. But these facts *must relate to the buyer's needs.* When you write each paragraph, ask yourself, *"So what?" How do these facts relate to the requirements for* this
job and this *employer?* For example:

So what?	I am a recent graduate of City Community College.
Show how the facts relate to the job	The specialized textile training I received at City Community College will enable me to provide the expertise in fabrics your clients want.

In a solicited letter answering an ad, be sure to cover in a positive way every qualification the ad specifies. If you have a shortcoming (maybe you're too young or have
no work experience), emphasize other positive qualifications to strengthen the reader's
confidence in your capabilities.

The order in which you present these paragraphs is also important. If you use a
summary opening, you'll organize the paragraphs in the same order as the qualifications are listed in the opening—with the most important qualification first. If you
don't have a summary opening, you'll still organize by discussing the most important
qualification first. So that the reader doesn't divert attention to the resume before
finishing the letter, don't refer to the enclosure until the next-to-last or last paragraph.

Usually you'll devote one middle paragraph to selling your qualifications on education, one on work experience, and another on significant personal qualities—*pertinent
to the job requirements.*

Education

Most recent college graduates consider education their most important qualification;
if so, they should discuss it first—in the letter as well as in the resume. However, an
applicant must be careful not to imply that a college degree—even a master's degree—
is the only qualification for the job. Employers who hire college graduates *look beyond the degree, to determine what the applicant can do or what the degree indicates
about personality.* They appreciate such signs of intelligence as ability to think log-

ically, sound judgment, mental alertness, and good grades. In the paragraph on education you can:

1. Show that you have both a broad background in business (or arts and sciences) and also depth in a major or at least a certain area.
2. Highlight your overall education by showing how your college studies prepared you for the work (or area) you seek. Talk in terms of work and duties, *not* merely course titles.
3. Explain how and why you supplemented your major with important electives outside your major. Report writing, marketing research, and case courses should prepare you to gather facts. Sound judgment might be reflected in the reports you had to write for case courses, or perhaps in the results of a team project—especially if you headed your division or group. An important oral or written presentation in or outside of class shows ability to think clearly. Or perhaps you can mention the satisfactory outcome of a knotty problem you faced.

Examples

1. Training I received in production control and planning at (*name*) College enables me to analyze, study, and recommend methods of work simplification in factory projects. Concepts learned about time and motion studies will help me conduct a thorough investigation in any work area. Additional studies on person and machine output rates, personnel relations, and business communications provided knowledge to make job analyses and to write clear, concise reports.
2. The program I followed at the University of (*state*) included 40 credit hours of accounting courses--up-to-date procedures, principles, and theory--that afford a firm basis with which to grow in the auditing profession. Courses in data processing, in addition to my work experience at a computer installation, have led me to be especially interested in the auditing of such systems.

Work Experience

The jobs you've held—full- or part-time, related or unrelated to the position you're applying for—help strengthen your qualifications. Try to tell concisely how you performed some functions and what you accomplished. Through discussing responsibilities you had in one or more previous jobs, you can show:

1. You gained experience that will help you understand (or learn faster) the special techniques required for the new job.
2. You can adapt to people and to various assignments.
3. You like to work with people and help them.
4. You've supplemented your academic training with related work experience.
5. You can handle responsibilities.
6. You are familiar with and aware of the business world.
7. You can adjust to the new job with only a minimum of training.
8. You're a hard worker.

Examples

1. For the past four summers while working in your office as a shipping clerk and assisting in the accounting department, I have gained considerable knowledge of the techniques and terminology unique to the accountant in this industry. This previous work experience with your company will enable me to adjust to your program with only minimum training.
2. During my employment at (*name*) Food Centers, I have ordered merchandise for a store operating at a volume of $40,000 a week, formulated pricing policies, supervised merchandise allocation of the shelves as well as the activities of about 25 employees. This background has helped me develop a working knowledge of the food industry and also the capacity to help make policy decisions on retail food store operations.

Personal Attitudes, Interests, Qualities

In another paragraph or two you can highlight a few personal attitudes, interests, or qualities that relate specifically to the job requirements. You might discuss (1) your ability to work with people; (2) your attitude toward employment—your interest in the field, company, or geographic area; or (3) your personal qualities. If you are an applicant with little or no job experience (or perhaps irrelevant education), these qualifications may be your main selling points.

Ability to Work with People. If you genuinely like people and want to help them, you have a priceless quality to sell. You can convey to your prospective employer that you have this ability, as shown in the following examples:

1. As assistant manager of a Household Finance Corporation office and as a collection department supervisor for the National Bank of Commerce, I developed the ability to get along well with people. For both customer service and employee relationships it was necessary to exercise good judgment based on sometimes incomplete information, in varying situations or difficult circumstances. I enjoy opportunities to work constructively with people.
2. In several capacities I have been able to further develop my interest in communicating and working with people. Being the daughter of an Air Force officer, I have lived throughout the United States and in foreign countries and have spent most of my summers traveling. Furthermore, as hospitality chairperson of my sorority, I organized all affairs held at the house and acted as hostess for guests. As a result, I have learned to make friends quickly and to feel at ease with many types of people—attributes which will help me be beneficial in a retailing position.

Attitude toward Employment. Interest in the field, company, or area—should be substantiated by proof.

Examples

1. My interest in construction developed in high school, working summers and part-time in residential home building. Upon graduation,

I decided on a career in construction management, and consequently realized that a college background in business, combined with on-the-job experience, was essential preparation. As my interest and work experience indicate, I am very enthusiastic about a career in this field. Employment in construction completely financed my college education. Even in my spare time I am building a chalet, as the enclosed data sheet shows.

2. To supplement my marketing major, I sold men's clothing for three years part-time or full-time during school; this sales experience should give me a head start in your training program. I can sell, enjoy selling, and want to continue to sell. What's more, I proved my sales potential by winning the Arrow Shirt contest which I have mentioned on the enclosed data sheet. Selling stocks appears to be a challenge and I welcome that challenge.

Desirable Personal Qualities. By citing various parts of your background—schooling, jobs, and/or extracurricular activities, you can show you have personal qualities that are desirable for the job you seek. You may want to give evidence that you are adaptable, versatile, responsible, able to apportion time, recognized by peers, determined to succeed, and/or industrious.

Examples

1. As the enclosed data sheet shows, I found it necessary to work while completing my formal education. In fulfilling the roles of student, spouse, mother, and provider at the same time, I learned to be punctual and to apportion my time--requirements also confronted by an "audit team" in completing an audit within a time and fee limitation.

2. While attending the university, I worked part-time or full-time during the school year and up to 80 hours a week (on two or more jobs) each summer. I was entirely self-supporting throughout my college career, and feel I can offer your company qualities of adaptability, perseverance, and patience developed from working hard on many jobs with many kinds of people.

Toward the end of the message—usually in the next to the last paragraph but sometimes in the last paragraph—refer the reader to your resume. The best way to make this reference is by directing the reader's attention to some data on the resume (see example 1 above and the sample letters at the end of the chapter).

Last Paragraph

The last paragraph of your message usually asks for action—just as a sales letter does. Without begging or commanding, you ask for an interview and (if appropriate) say you will come to the employer's office when he or she suggests. Make action easy by giving your telephone number and hours to call if someone can't answer the phone throughout the day or evening.

Examples

1. As I will be in (*city*) from March 22 to March 27, I will appreciate the opportunity to see you during that time to discuss further my

desire to serve as one of your investigators. After you have reviewed my qualifications and examined the enclosed resume, will you
please name a convenient time in a letter to me at my Seattle address?

2. My class schedule allows me to come to your office any afternoon
except Tuesdays. May I have an interview to answer any questions
about myself that you might have? You can reach me by telephoning
997-1234 before 10 a.m. or after 4 p.m.

3. After you've had an opportunity to review some of the statements in
this letter and on the enclosed resume, will you please call me at
896-6622 after 3 p.m. or write me about the possibility of beginning a career with (*name of company*)? I'll be grateful for an interview to discuss my qualifications with you.

Even if you're sending your job application hundreds of miles away, you might
still ask for an interview if you think the company has a local representative who can
screen you in person. Here you must ask the employer to tell you the local representative's name, or ask the company to arrange the interview for you with the local representative. If you know it will be impossible for you to come to an interview at your
own expense, offer to send the employer additional information upon request. Between the lines of your persuasive sales letter, you're hoping the employer will understand that you can come to her or his office if your way is paid.

Examples

1. Although the resume and this letter give you some idea of my qualifications, I am eager to have a personal interview with you. Or
perhaps I could discuss my qualifications in greater detail with
your regional personnel representative. Please let me know how I
can get in touch with her or him.

2. If you wish additional information about my background, please let
me know. I'll be glad to send it to you promptly.

Sample Letters of Application

The following application letters apply suggestions discussed in this chapter.[7] Letter 1
illustrates both content and layout of an effective application letter that can accompany the resume shown in Figure 11-1. Notice how well this applicant relates highlights of each paragraph to the job he or she seeks—staff accountant in a CPA firm
which, the applicant knows, has an opening.

Letter 1

*Solicited application for a staff accountant position. This letter accompanies Figure
11-1, page 420, personalized one-page resume.*

---

[7] If you need additional discussion or examples, see books devoted entirely to job search and applications—for example, David Gootnick, *Getting a Better Job*, McGraw-Hill Book Company, New
York, 1978.

Name;
summary opening
(attention)

Training
(interest)

Useful bookkeeping
experience (desire;
conviction)

Personal qualities
(conviction)

Easy action

2982 Norman Drive
Pasadena, CA 91115
March 15, 198_

Mr. Ward Q. Jorgen
Jorgen, Burgess, and Associates
1820 Tower Building
Los Angeles, CA 90070

Dear Mr. Jorgen:

Professor Julius Barton has informed me that your firm is looking for a competent staff accountant. With thorough college training in accounting and related studies, varied bookkeeping experience, and proven ability to work efficiently, I feel I could be an asset to your staff.

To prepare adequately for a public accounting career, I have completed 40 quarter hours of accounting at the University of California, with a grade point average of 3.7 (on a 4-point scale). Two electronic data processing courses I studied, in addition to the accounting, provided information that will be useful in working with your clients who use computers. My studies in speech and business communication enable me to present clearly the financial data and reports for superiors or clients.

Since your firm specializes in medical accounts, I believe I could be of special benefit to you because of my interest and work in this area. At age 18 I was preparing weekly payrolls for 60 hospital maintenance employees. This position included keeping time and equipment records, calculating payroll deductions, writing monthly labor union benefit reports, and handling accounts payable. Later, as full-charge bookkeeper for a medical clinic and as assistant accountant in a hospital, accuracy and speed were necessary to meet deadlines at these fast-paced offices. My responsibilities included billing accounts receivable; monthly closing of general ledger; preparing financial statements, cost control data, and quarterly government tax reports. This experience will be useful in audits and analyses for cost control.

Serving as treasurer of the accounting honorary and chairperson of two charity drives required honesty, tact, and initiative. These qualities will be an important part of my code of ethics as a public accountant. By referring to the enclosed resume and contacting former employers, you will be able to form a more complete idea of my personality.

Will you call me at 354-9876 to name a time when I may come, at your convenience, to talk with you about being your staff accountant? I am usually home after 3 p.m. each weekday.

Sincerely,

Chris W. Benson

Chris W. Benson

Enclosure: Resume

Letter 2 shows the content of an application from a 21-year-old college graduate seeking a teaching position in a high school business department. It is a prospecting letter, because the applicant does not know whether an opening exists. Although the resume may be neatly processed for frequent use, the letter must be individually type-written and addressed to the superintendent or whoever is in charge of hiring business teachers in each city. Layout may be similar to that in letter 1 or any other appropriate letter style (as discussed on pages 136–138).

Letter 2

Prospecting application to a school superintendent for a high school teaching position. This letter accompanies Figure 11-2, pages 421–422, general-purpose resume.

Dear Mrs. Roberts:

Next September will one of your high schools need a business teacher who can make learning realistic and

Question; *summary opening* *(attention)*	interesting for the students? If so, please consider me for the position. My qualifications include a liberal business background, work experience, and enthusiasm for teaching.
Liberal business *background;* *specific courses* *(interest)*	In August this year I will graduate from Ohio State University in Business Education. Studies in business, education, and economics (my minor) have received special emphasis in my program. I am now prepared to teach any of these business courses that you offer on the secondary level: typing, shorthand (Gregg or Forkner), office machines, accounting, and business law or communications. If you are considering adding a course in economics to your curriculum, I will be happy to present to you my ideas about the advantages of teaching economics in high school.
Work experience *(desire; conviction)*	Two years of steady office employment and previous summer work have given me valuable insight into the growing needs of the business community for vocationally trained high school graduates. This practical experience expanded my knowledge of business education. I am better equipped to communicate to my students in an interesting manner the relationships between their goals and the requirements of the business community. The different positions I have held developed qualities of tact and adaptability, which I consider important when working with young people.
Personal attitudes *and qualities* *(desire)*	The past semester of student teaching--mentioned on the enclosed resume--convinced me that high school teaching is my chosen career. I will work with the same zeal that helped me earn an A- overall grade average throughout college and high school.
Easy-action request	An opportunity to discuss further your requirements and my qualifications will be appreciated. To arrange a meeting, will you please contact me at the above address?

The next example illustrates a prospecting letter from the 32-year-old experienced supervisor who wrote the three-page resume shown and discussed on pages 422–423.

Letter 3

Prospecting application to an airline executive for a position in operations management. This letter accompanies Figure 11-3, page 423, general-purpose resume with functional summary.

Dear Mr. Williams:

Summary opening *(attention)*	The extensive experience and academic background I have had in operations management would enable me to make a substantial contribution to your company. Please consider me for an assignment which will lead ultimately to corporate management.

Extensive experience; personal qualities (interest; conviction)

Previous jobs and a carefully selected education program have been pursued with this management goal in mind. Administering and supervising operational projects and personnel, in addition to chairing numerous committees developed my leadership qualities. The practical managing experience gives me a firm foundation for obtaining results with cost and schedule constraints under pressures of "produce or perish." My accomplishments in each job were acknowledged by substantial salary increases. In my present government position I have worked with senior and corporate executives in business, industrial, labor, education, and government organizations.

Relevant college education (desire; conviction)

A related college education has improved my ability to help develop the overall corporate objectives so important to your firm. The broad base provided through a business administration program increases one's scope to see the "big picture" and provides methods from which to proceed logically.

Easy-action request

The enclosed resume includes additional information. Page 1 summarizes my work experience, and pages 2 and 3 further detail specific jobs performed. After you have reviewed this information, will you please call me at (206) 953-8111 any time between 9 and 5 to state a time when I may discuss my qualifications with you? If you wish further information, I will be glad to send it to you promptly.

EXERCISES

1. This assignment helps you to know yourself better before you launch a job-getting selling campaign. Make a thorough self-appraisal by taking an inventory of all your employment qualifications. After rereading especially the suggestions on pages 398–400, list your accomplishments under these five main headings: (1) Work Experience, Skills, Aptitudes; (2) Education; (3) Activities, Achievements, Social Development; (4) Interests, Preferences, Attitudes; (5) Personal Characteristics. Add whatever subheadings are desirable. You might place check marks or asterisks by the qualifications you think are your strongest for the work you'd like to do. Support your personal qualifications with specific facts about your achievements.

   Type all your qualifications neatly under appropriate headings and subheadings; then insert them into a notebook. This information will help you to know what you have to sell. It is your "personal inventory" or "self-analysis."

2. Make a market survey to find what career opportunities and jobs are suitable for your qualifications. See suggestions on pages 400–403 regarding publications and people that can give you useful information.

3. The purpose of this assignment is to find out what qualifications the prospective employer looks for when screening you for your career job. Assume that in your market survey (Exercise 2) you discovered that sufficient existing publications are

not available locally. So you will write to an organization of your choice (but not the firm to which you plan to send your application letter and resume), asking for answers to your questions or arranging for an interview with the appropriate officer. Although you're not getting answers from the prospective employer, you *will* from a source that should reveal comparable information on the qualifications considered most important.

Prepare a list of 10 (or more) questions you must know the answers to before you can write your application. All your questions must relate to a particular job or job area. (You may use the answers later for a report writing assignment.)

Listed below are several questions that you should consider. They're possible springboards for the questions to which you must find answers.

a. What are the basic qualifications that you look for when you screen a recent college graduate for a job in (your career area)?

b. For this type of work what major do you think is best?

c. Outside the major what courses (business or nonbusiness) do you think will be helpful on the job?

d. What kind of previous experience do you look for in the applicant?

e. How do you evaluate personality from a written job presentation?

f. How important are grades?

g. To get into this type of work, what initial job should I apply for?

h. Do you prefer references in the initial written job presentation?

4. Prepare a letter of application with an accompanying resume for the career job you plan to get into after completion of your college education. Address it to the firm of your choice and to the individual who should receive it. [If you cannot find the name of a particular person, you might want to direct it to a particular department within the firm or to the title the receiver possesses (such as "personnel manager").]

To make this material as useful to you as possible, date the letter the month and year you actually plan to send it. For example, if you're graduating this year, the date of the letter should precede that of graduation by enough time (four to nine months) to have the job sewed up when you're ready to go to work. But if you're a sophomore and have at least two more years of college and then two years of graduate school, use the date you'll actually be sending the letter.

Use only facts, as far as possible, in both your letter and resume. If you are dating the letter in the future, assume the activities (especially schooling, work experience, government service) that will most likely take place between now and then. This timing permits you to update the written job presentation when you're ready to revise, type, and actually send it.

Try to make your message and data sheet so convincing and selling that they will stand out from many others that may be received the same day. Both should be neatly and accurately typed—100 percent correct in spelling and accurate in facts and figures.

5. On the day your application letter and resume (Exercise 4) are due to be handed in, bring them to class and exchange them (or copies) with a classmate—preferably

one you do not know very well. Each of you will then evaluate the other's written job presentation. Assume you are the addressee of the letter, a stranger to the applicant. Would the letter and resume convince you to invite the writer to your office for an interview? Why or why not? On a separate sheet write your answer to these questions. Also list (a) specific good qualities of the letter and resume and (b) specific suggestions for improvements. Sign the sheet and return it to the writer, together with the letter and resume. If your instructor wishes, each student will hand in these comments along with the letter and resume. (No changes should, however, be made on these messages before the instructor reads them.)

6. Below are four application letters. Explain orally in class which ones will most likely result in an interview. Which are totally unacceptable? Why?

Letter A

Application to a grocery chain for accounting position.

With my vast and diversified working experience in a (*town name*) Safeway store and my 5 years' college training in accounting and economics, I am well qualified to apply for an accounting position with Safeway Stores, Inc.

Having successfully completed studies in managerial and financial accounting while earning my degree at the University of (*state*), you will find that I can handle any accounting situation with ease and confidence.

While working in the many departments in Safeway in order to finance my college education, I became thoroughly familiar with every phase of operation of one of your stores. Because of my pleasing personality, my ability to get along well with others, and my excellent work record, I was chosen to supervise the night stock crew during the summers of (*year*) and (*year*).

My work experience with Safeway has been both valuable and enjoyable for me; therefore, I wish to continue working for your firm in my chosen field.

After you've had a chance to verify some of the things I've said about myself in this letter and on the enclosed data sheet, will you write me about the possibilities of working in one of your West Coast offices?

Letter B

Application to a firm for sales position.

Please consider my application for a position in your sales department. My qualifications are a bachelor of arts in General Business, a thorough and working knowledge of accounting and finance, and a sincere interest in selling.

I am seeking a position in your company in selling because I feel that I have the necessary qualifications to do a good job for the

company, while learning the basic components of your needs. I
selected your firm because it is the most rapidly expanding company
in this industry and a leader in research and development, which I
recognize as essential to maintain your present status. I feel that
I can contribute towards these goals. I have studied the basic background of the transportation industry, and am deeply interested in
furthering my knowledge, to the benefit of the company. I have
enclosed a resume of my personal background, complete with a transcript of my grades.

After you've had time to review my application and data sheet, will
you please call me or write. My address and telephone numbers are
on the enclosed data sheet. Thank you for your consideration.

Letter C

Application to home appliance firm as sales representative.

If hundreds of effective retail calls, thorough knowledge of
point-of-sale and imaginative merchandising help make a home appliance representative, then I've begun to learn the business. I
would like to put this practical field experience to work for Sack's
Home Appliance Company.

Field work as an assistant district sales manager for the ABC
Cleaning Products Company gave me an opportunity to plan and execute
sales promotions that sold cleaners. I have proven ability to open
nonbuying accounts, secure floor displays, sell additional packages
and achieve point-of-sale dominance.

In addition, I have conducted route analyses, set up key account systems, and conducted sales training meetings for wholesaler
personnel.

Frequent contact with retailers and consumers enabled me to
handle consumer complaints and utilize a good layman's knowledge of
various home appliances.

After you've had an opportunity to review some of the things
I've said in this letter and on the enclosed data sheet, will you
write me frankly about the possibility of beginning a career with
Sack's Home Appliance Company?

I would appreciate an opportunity to discuss my qualifications.

Letter D

Application to a newspaper for position as assistant music and drama editor.

In reference to your advertisement in <u>Editor & Publisher</u>
(3/14) for an assistant music and drama editor, the offer is worth
an inquiry because of my deep interest in theater. But, very frankly, I'm afraid it would have to be an exceptional salary offer to
lure me so far from the East Coast and what I'm convinced are its
greater professional opportunities.

However, you will find samples of my reviews and a brief resume attached. Should you desire to continue this correspondence further, I will send you references and other material customary to a job application.

My experience in motion picture-theater reviewing with the Sun has been limited to "filling-in" for the regular critic during his vacations or illnesses. Prior to that, I wrote a theater column in a weekly newspaper in Bath, Pa., a sideline to my daily reporting. I have engaged in all phases of amateur theater as an outside interest. I am not well versed in music—though I am confident in my critical capacities. Again, I have filled in at times for the Sun's music critic and, if need be, can also submit samples. I have handled general assignments and beats.

Your advertisement mentions "opportunity for advancement," without further elaboration. Your offer of the position of assistant music-drama editor would be considerably more attractive if coupled with a commitment to go to your Washington, D.C., bureau in two, or three, years or to whatever overseas bureaus the Daily Blat may sponsor, subject only to your complete dissatisfaction with the work produced for you.

The tendency, of course, of most newspapers is to fill the opening with the run-of-the-mill newsperson who is panting at the door and willing to accept chicken feed. Consequently, I have little reason to expect a favorable reaction to this letter. If I am mistaken, I hope you will advise me of the maximum salary you can pay for this position, the setup at the Blat and any arrangements that you would consider feasible. I hope we can discuss this matter further, but only with your understanding that I expect to drive a hard bargain.

My home address appears below and on the resume. Please address your reply accordingly.

Other Job Application Messages

The time you'll spend—and the number of messages you'll write—in getting your career job depends on economic conditions, need for graduates in your area, and your own qualifications and standards. If you're sending your job presentation when it's a seller's market and you have unusually good qualifications, you might land the job you want right away. But if the conditions are reversed, you can spend many weeks—even months—finding the right niche for yourself.

To be on the safe side, begin your job hunting at least four to nine months before graduation, and send your written job presentation with resume to more than one firm. But don't send out too many—say 50 or 100—at one time. Limit the number to 10 or fewer and then wait for replies before you mail more.

This chapter discusses the job interview, follow-up messages from applicant to employer, and follow-up messages from employer to applicant.

THE JOB INTERVIEW

As you know, the goal of your application letter and resume is to get an interview. Assume now that you achieved your purpose with your written "sales" presentation. The desired telephone call, letter, or telegram from the employer asks you to come for an interview on a certain day and time. That interview may be the most important step toward your getting the desired job. This section presents suggestions regarding preparation for the interview, conduct during the interview, questions frequently asked, and negative factors to avoid. (For *interviewer's* responsibilities see pages 690-697.)

Preparation for the Interview

Always prepare for an interview before you go to it. Remember that the interview is a two-way street. Your primary purpose is to get the best job suitable to your capabilities. The employer's goal is to get the best person available for the job. Take a look at yourself from the employer's point of view. In hiring you, the employer is making an investment that over a few years will mount to thousands of dollars considering salary, fringes, and taxes. Naturally the employer wants a quality product.

As the New York Life Insurance Company says so well in its booklet, *Making the Most of Your Job Interview:*

> The employment interview is one of the most important events in the average person's experience, for the obvious reason that the 20 or 30 minutes spent with the interviewer may determine the entire future course of one's life. Yet interviewers are constantly amazed at the number of applicants who drift into job interviews without any apparent preparation and only the vaguest idea of what they are going to say. Their manner says, "Well, here I am." And that's often the end of it, in more ways than one.

> Others, although they undoubtedly do not intend to do so, create an impression of indifference by acting too casual. At the other extreme, a few applicants work themselves into such a state of mind that when they arrive they seem to be in the last stages of nervous fright and are only able to answer in monosyllables.

These marks of inexperience can be avoided by knowing a little of what actually is expected of you and by making a few simple preparations before the interview.[1]

Adequate preparation includes:

- Know yourself.
- Do some research on the company.
- List questions you want to ask as well as answers to questions you'll probably encounter.
- Pay attention to your appearance.
- Check details about the meeting place and time for the interview.

Know Yourself

The most important preparation relates to knowing yourself. But, then, you have already looked critically at yourself before you wrote your resume and application letter. You should know the job or the job area you want to apply for, the requirements for the job, and how your qualifications (both your strengths and weaknesses) compare with the requirements. Take with you to the interview at least two copies of your resume. In case the interviewer doesn't have your resume handy, you can offer a copy.

Do Some Research on the Company

In addition to knowing yourself, you should bone up on the company. You can find excellent references in your library or school placement office and from employees or annual reports of the company itself. Among other facts you should know are the age of the company, location of its plants, types of products and services, its growth over the years (especially the last few years), and its prospects for the future. You'll make a favorable impression on the interviewer if you sincerely show interest in the company and show knowledge about it gained through your own initiative.

Prepare Questions and Answers

Another important step in preparing for the interview is to jot down questions you want to ask the interviewer if he or she doesn't first give you the answers. The questions you might ask relate to possible formal or informal training the company offers after employment, company policy about moving your family to a new location, what type of management system the firm uses, the average age of the executives, whether they are promoted from within, why the person you're replacing left the firm, and per-

---

[1] *Making the Most of Your Job Interview*, New York Life Insurance Company. Copies of this 22-page booklet may be obtained in reasonable quantity without cost or obligation from your New York Life Agent or the New York Life Office in your community.

haps also the company's profit picture (if you didn't find it in your research). The *last* questions may relate to fringe benefits and salary.

Also, you want to anticipate questions the interviewer will ask you. You can definitely expect to encounter revealing questions relating to what you have done; what you think about what you have done; your interests and hobbies; relationship to friends, school and work; your colleagues and family. Shown on pages 445–447 are questions frequently asked during the employment interview.

Be Careful of Your Appearance

The clothes you wear and your overall neatness affect your appearance. Wear conservative clothes appropriate for the office, clean your shoes, and use lotions or perfumes sparingly. Also see that accessories complement the suit or dress. Be sure your hair and fingernails are clean, your hairstyle is appropriate, and your breath is fresh. To project an image of quality and success, try to wear to the interview the best quality clothing you can afford.

Check Meeting Place and Time

Definitely know when and where the interview will be held—and be there 10 to 15 minutes early. Being late is almost always considered inexcusable. Also, know the full name and address of the company, the interviewer's name and current title, and how to pronounce his or her name. Put a working pen or pencil along with a small notebook in your coat pocket or purse. If the job requires creativity or high grades, you might take along samples of your work or your transcript of grades—perhaps in a neat briefcase.

Before you go into the room where the interviewer is, try to relax. If possible, sit quietly in the waiting room, and convince yourself that the interviewer is an individual who merely wants to find out whether you're the person for the job. In turn, you *want* to show the interviewer that you appreciate the opportunity you're being given and furthermore, that you're eager to tell about yourself.

Conduct during the Interview

From the time the interviewer first sees you until you leave, he or she will be observing you carefully and listening to everything you say and do. To make the best impression, you need to:

1. Show interest. You can do so by the way you sit and look alert, by eye contact, and by questions you ask.
2. Be courteous. Don't chew gum, and don't smoke unless the interviewer invites you to do so.

3. Be honest and sincere at all times. If you begin to exaggerate or fabricate details—and you're caught—the interviewer will be less likely to consider you as a favorable candidate for the job.

4. Be yourself. Don't try to put on airs. By being yourself, you'll be on more familiar ground, seem more comfortable, and be more at ease.

5. Be a good listener. By doing so, you will be ready to reply to a question the interviewer asks, seem interested, and also receive valuable clues from the interviewer's statements.

6. Avoid the negative attitudes or actions listed on pages 447–448 and also negative words such as *can't, won't, unable, hate, failure, incompetent.* Use positive expressions that indicate you are competent and dependable.

When you first see the interviewer, smile and greet him or her by name (if you know the name). From then to the end of the interview you should take your cues from the interviewer. If he or she offers to shake hands, do so. Be sure your grip is firm, not a bone-crusher or limp fish. Also remain standing until invited to sit down; the only exception is when you're in a small room and the interviewer remains seated or sits down immediately. Look at the interviewer and keep the proper eye contact throughout the interview. But don't stare!

Be on guard at all times for nervousness. If your hands want to wander or play with objects, put these hands in your lap.

After the warm-up period (exchange of pleasantries to develop rapport) be ready for the interviewer's first questions about your qualifications or interest. You might be asked, "Why are you interested in this company?" If so, merely give the answer you previously thought out. Or the interviewer might say, "I see from the company (or placement office) form that you're interested in making marketing research your career. Tell me how you prepared yourself for this area." Your answer may include excerpts from your education, work, and/or activities. Throughout the questioning, the interviewer tries to get information needed to evaluate you and what you can do for the company. Keep your replies positive and concise (but generally more than "yes" or "no").

Shown below are other suggestions to consider:

1. If you are strong in extracurricular organizations and the interviewer hasn't mentioned that area, watch for an opportunity to ask, "Are you interested in my extracurricular activities?" The interviewer is not likely to say "no." Highlight those that relate to the job requirements.

2. When desirable, explain why you could help the company in this job and why you like doing this kind of work. (If useful, pull out of your briefcase some examples of your past work.)

3. Be prepared to ask sincere questions about the company, because doing so shows interest and also helps you perceive key problems or needs of that company as well as the interviewer's likes and dislikes.

4. Never make a slighting reference about a former professor or employer. Assume part of the blame yourself. If you can't say something nice about a person, don't say anything.

5. Know the current beginning salary range for your type of work and experience.

6. Try to postpone salary questions, if any, until near the end of the first or second interview—after you and the interviewer have discussed the job responsibilities and your credentials that affect your bargaining power. When you are asked how much salary you want, you can indicate that you're more interested in a job to prove yourself than in a specific salary. Most reputable firms will offer the standard salary for the type of job in question.

7. Throughout the interview, smile at appropriate times—but don't maintain an artificial, plastered smile at any time; it's unnatural and insincere.

8. Even if you think the interview isn't going well and that you are rejected, don't let your discouragement show. Sometimes interviewers purposely appear disinterested just to test your reaction, self-confidence, and ability to respond.

9. Don't take notes during the interview, because this annoys some recruiters. Better jot notes immediately after the interview on points you want to remember.

10. Be alert for signs from the interviewer that the interview is about to end. And when you depart, be sure to thank the interviewer for seeing you.

11. Tactfully ask for some kind of commitment as to when the interviewer will let you know the decision.

12. If you are offered the job, you can accept immediately or ask for time to think it over.

Questions Which May Be Asked during the Interview

If you have prepared adequately, you should be able to answer questions honestly and intelligently. The plain truth—even if it may seem a little unfavorable to you—is always better than exaggerations that may entangle you in contradictory answers to other questions. The following are 59 employment interview questions as listed by Dr. Frank S. Endicott, director of placement (emeritus), Northwestern University, in a copyrighted report published by the Northwestern University Placement Center.[2] Try to answer these questions orally or in writing *before* you go to an interview.

1. What are your future vocational plans?

2. In what school activities have you participated? Why? Which did you enjoy the most?

3. In what type of position are you most interested?

4. Why do you think you might like to work for our company?

5. What jobs have you held? How were they obtained and why did you leave?

---

[2] You'll find these questions in the New York Life Insurance Company's booklet, *Making the Most of Your Job Interview.* For suggestions to employers regarding interviewing see Chapter 19, and for a list of fair and unfair preemployment inquiries see Appendix A.

6. What courses did you like best? Least? Why?
7. Why did you choose your particular field of work?
8. What percentage of your college expenses did you earn? How?
9. How did you spend your vacations while in school?
10. What do you know about our company?
11. Do you feel that you have received a good general training?
12. What qualifications do you have that make you feel you will be successful in your field?
13. What extracurricular offices have you held?
14. What are your ideas on salary?
15. If you were starting college all over again, what courses would you take?
16. How much money do you hope to earn at age 30? 35?
17. Do you think that your extracurricular activities were worth the time you devoted to them? Why?
18. What do you think determines a person's progress in a good company?
19. What personal characteristics are necessary for success in your chosen field?
20. Why do you think you would like this particular type of job?
21. Do you prefer working with others or by yourself?
22. What kind of boss do you prefer?
23. Are you primarily interested in making money or do you feel that service to humanity is your prime concern?
24. Can you take instructions without feeling upset?
25. Tell me a story!
26. How did previous employers treat you?
27. What have you learned from some of the jobs you have held?
28. Can you get recommendations from previous employers?
29. What interests you about our product or service?
30. Have you ever changed your major field of interest while in college? Why?
31. When did you choose your college major?
32. Do you feel you have done the best scholastic work of which you are capable?
33. How did you happen to go to college?
34. What do you know about opportunities in the field in which you are trained?
35. Which of your college years was the most difficult?
36. Did you enjoy your four years at this university?
37. Do you like routine work?
38. Do you like regular hours?
39. What size city do you prefer?
40. What is your major weakness?
41. Define cooperation!
42. Do you demand attention?
43. Do you have an analytical mind?
44. Are you eager to please?
45. What job in our company would you choose if you were entirely free to do so?
46. What types of books have you read?
47. Have you plans for graduate work?

48. What types of people seem to "rub you the wrong way"?
49. Have you ever tutored a freshman or sophomore?
50. What jobs have you enjoyed the most? The least? Why?
51. What are your own special abilities?
52. What job in our company do you want to work toward?
53. Would you prefer a large or a small company? Why?
54. Do you like to travel?
55. How about overtime work?
56. What kind of work interests you?
57. What are the disadvantages of your chosen field?
58. Are you interested in research?
59. What have you done which shows initiative and willingness to work?

Negative Factors to Avoid

Dr. Endicott, who compiled the questions that may be asked in interviews, also surveyed for negative factors evaluated during the employment interview.[3]

1. Poor personal appearance
2. Overbearing—overaggressive—conceited "superiority complex"—"know-it-all"
3. Inability to communicate clearly—poor voice, diction, grammar
4. Lack of planning for career—no purpose and goals
5. Lack of interest and enthusiasm—passive, indifferent
6. Lack of confidence and poise—nervous—ill-at-ease
7. Failure to participate in activities
8. Overemphasis on money—interest only in best dollar offer
9. Poor scholastic record—just got by
10. Unwillingness to start at the bottom—expects too much too soon
11. Excuses—evasiveness—hedges on unfavorable factors in record
12. Lack of tact
13. Lack of maturity
14. Lack of courtesy—ill mannered
15. Condemnation of past employers
16. Marked dislike for school work
17. Failure to look interviewer in the eye
18. Limp, fishy handshake
19. Sloppy application blank
20. Merely shopping around
21. Wants job only for short time
22. Little sense of humor
23. Lack of knowledge of field of specialization
24. No interest in company or in industry
25. Unwillingness to relocate

[3] *Making the Most of Your Job Interview.*

26. Cynical
27. Low moral standards
28. Lazy
29. Inability to take criticism
30. Lack of appreciation of the value of experience
31. Late to interview without good reason
32. Never heard of company
33. Failure to express appreciation for interviewer's time
34. Asks no questions about the job
35. High-pressure type
36. Indefinite response to questions

In summary, the interview involves at least two people—the interviewer and the interviewee. To find out if the applicant (interviewee) is the individual for the job, the interviewer will consider the interviewee's background, qualifications, personality, and attitudes. Then the interviewer will evaluate this information, along with facts from other sources (references, tests, and so forth), and decide whether or not to invite the applicant to join the company or to invite him or her to the home plant for further interviews with other officials. As the interviewee, you need to prepare well for the interview and then sell yourself (during the interview) by showing interest, being sincere and natural, stating your qualifications, and behaving like a person the company would want on its working force.

FOLLOW-UP MESSAGES FROM APPLICANT TO EMPLOYER

You strengthen your chances for the job you have applied for when you follow up your application letter and resume. Of the three ways to follow up—in person, by letter, or by phone—the written message is one of the most effective because employers can analyze the applicant's qualifications at their convenience. They can also more easily compare a large number of applicants at one time—either on the job or at home in the evening.

A written follow-up is effective for several good reasons:

1. Only a few applicants use a follow-up—probably fewer than 10 percent. Thus, the employer is favorably impressed by one.
2. A follow-up shows the applicant is genuinely interested in the job or the company.
3. This message indicates determination. Some firms won't reply to an applicant for a sales job until a follow-up arrives. Other firms intentionally mail the sales applicant a negative reply. The employer reasons that the applicant who follows up when applying for a sales job will follow up on prospects—even those who say no—when on the job in a sales territory.
4. A follow-up indicates courtesy (if it follows an interview), serves as a reminder to the employer, permits better understanding of the applicant (through submission of additional information), and shows sincerity.

This section first covers the two all-important and most frequently used types of initial follow-up messages and then presents other types involved in getting a job.

The Initial Follow-up

The first follow-up you'll use is either (1) a follow-up to the interview or (2) an inquiry about the application letter and resume when the employer doesn't reply.

Follow-up to the Interview

After you have had your interview, you should send the interviewer (or the appropriate company official) a written thank-you.[4] Remember, the interviewer spent some valuable time to talk with you; and for reasons of courtesy alone, you need to acknowledge this time, attention, and consideration. Only when you are told during the interview not to write will you refrain from sending this message.

In most instances this message is short—less than one page—and its organizational pattern is that of a good news or neutral letter:

1. In the opening paragraph, state the main idea—express thanks for the interview or say you're returning a completed form. (If you don't thank in the opening, do so in the last paragraph.) Also, identify the job and perhaps mention the time and place of the interview.
2. In the middle paragraph(s) you discuss one or more of the following ideas:
   a. Mention how you *now* feel about the firm or a job with the firm—now that you have visited the plant, listened to the interviewer talk, and toured the facility. Of course, you write only favorable responses.
   b. Add new material that might be helpful in determining your qualifications. For example, assume you've been considering continuing your education in the evenings after graduation. Then in the interview the employer says the company favors junior employees improving themselves by attending college at night. You go home, think over this idea, and decide to begin night classes. That's new material you can mention in the message. Other new material is reporting that you completed an assignment the interviewer gave you at the time of the interview (such as to read a brochure, see someone, or take a test).
   c. If you think the interviewer questioned one of your qualifications or you think you might have made a negative impression concerning one statement during the interview, include honest, positive facts to rebuild confidence. For example, if the interviewer seemed to want an older person, convince him or her that you are mature because you've dealt successfully with all types of people on your various jobs; or you have assumed responsibilities; or you have had to allocate your time as student, spouse, and breadwinner. Or if you think you treated one or more areas unsatisfactorily, try to reestablish your credentials.

[4] A Cincinnati executive, reviewing 35 different jobs in his company for which hundreds of applications were received, gives this tip: "In each instance the job went to the thoughtful applicant who followed up the interview with a sincere thank-you note." Numerous other executives as well as applicants have confirmed the effectiveness of these follow-up messages.

d. Other ideas which can occasionally strengthen your presentation are: (1) your favorable reaction to points covered by the interviewer and (2) highlights of qualifications discussed during the interview. (These two suggestions aren't as important as (a), (b), and (c) because they're a rehash of what the interviewer already knows.)

3. In the last paragraph you can use one or more of the following:
   a. Offer to send additional information upon request.
   b. Thank for the interview (if not done in the first paragraph).
   c. Say you can come in for another interview.
   d. Indicate hope (or confidence) that your qualifications fit the firm's requirements.
   e. Mention you're looking forward to a favorable decision.
   f. Ask for an opportunity to prove you can help the firm's sales, growth, and so on.

The best time to send the follow-up to an interview is a day or two after the meeting—at least within a week.

With this organizational plan in mind, study the following two examples of effective follow-up messages. Both applicants were successful in getting the job they sought. In each case the employer stated that the follow-up letter helped greatly.

Message 1 is from a 22-year-old applicant seeking his first career job as a sales representative after college graduation. Notice how convincingly he surmounts what appeared to be a shortcoming by showing that his responsibilities *during* college were equivalent to two years' business experience *after* college.

Message 1

A successful after-interview follow-up, to a national industrial firm.

Dear Mr. Simonson:

Your interview with me yesterday was both enjoyable and informative. Thank you for your courtesies and the interest you took in my qualifications as a sales representative for your firm.

During the conversation you mentioned that you were particularly looking for a person who had at least two years' business experience since finishing college. I agree with you that the knack of working with people and the mature outlook gained from practical experience are valuable for a prospective sales representative. These qualities were firmly developed in me <u>during</u> my college years.

As my resume shows, to obtain an Industrial Engineering degree I added an extra year of engineering and business courses to my studies. In various college activities my responsibilities were mainly with people. As Publicity Manager for <u>The College Engineer</u> magazine--after careful planning plus enthusiasm and drive--I increased sales 25% over the previous year. As president of our fraternity, I worked harmoniously with our 80 members and sold the alumni on the support we needed. My part-time and summer jobs during college ranged from clerking in a grocery store to tutoring first-year stu-

dents. I believe these activities, jobs, and additional studies
have given me a background of experience and judgment equivalent to
the two years' business experience your firm would like its sales
representatives to have.

You will find, I believe, that I can develop into one of your top
industrial sales representatives, Mr. Simonson. Will you give me
the opportunity to prove this statement?

Message 2 is from a 27-year-old recent accounting graduate applying for an accounting job in a community college. During the interview the college official was concerned whether the applicant—a quiet, soft-spoken individual—had adequate qualifications for leadership; she would have to supervise the work of six bookkeepers in the college office. This letter helped her get the job:

Message 2

A successful after-interview follow-up, to a college vice president and finance officer.

Dear Mr. Millard:

Thank you for taking time on April 4 to talk with me regarding my
application for the accounting position in your office. As you requested, I am enclosing the transcript of my grades from the University of (*name*).

During my five years at the (*name*) Company I worked in a lead capacity with many people. The experience I gained would be useful for
the job you outlined. For the first two of the five years I was
responsible for quality control in the Pensar Division. As one of
my duties I supervised 10 employees and trained new people to visually and dimensionally inspect vendor-made parts purchased for use
on the program. When I requested night-shift duty so I could carry
10 to 15 credit hours at Mason Junior College, I was given full responsibilities for the inspection duties on that shift, a position
I held three years.

Four years of college studies (with no financial help) while holding
full- and part-time jobs and raising a family indicate my perseverance. My school and work record of continuous four-year attendance
(except for a three-day virus illness last summer) will assure you
of my regularity and dependability on the job. We are buying a home
in Blanktown and will enter our daughter in the school system here
next fall; so my family is well established here.

I believe my education and 10 years of work experience will qualify
me to assume the accounting and office responsibilities you pointed
out to me. Please let me know your decision. You could depend on
me to be a hard-working, mature staff member.

Inquiry about Application Letter and Resume

If you haven't received a response to your written job application within three weeks, you are justified in sending an inquiry. Although it is unlikely your material was lost in the mail, it is possible the receiver misplaced or forgot about it. Anyway, a well-run organization should acknowledge—and if it does not, you certainly should inquire.

This type of follow-up is usually shorter than the one written after the interview. Since many firms keep the written job presentation for six months or longer, all you really need do is give enough identification so that the employer can locate your material. The inquiry should include: identification of job sought, date of application letter previously sent, and (if appropriate) a request for an interview. In addition, some employers suggest you also include one or more of the following:

1. Interest in job
2. Date of availability
3. New material about qualifications
4. Reasons for wanting to work for the company
5. Status of application
6. Highlights of major qualifications already given in the application letter
7. Offer to send additional information upon request
8. Telephone number

Don't repeat information the employer already possesses. Included in this category is the same resume because it takes up valuable file space. No personnel manager likes to receive an application letter—and then one or two follow-ups—each with another copy of the resume. Given below are two examples of acceptable inquiries.

Message 1

Emphasizes identification of applicant's file.

Dear Ms. Lindsell

On January 15, (*year*), I sent you my application letter and resume for an opening in your management training program. Because I'm interested in your firm and its future, I'm inquiring whether you received this material.

Please let me know what information you wish about my background. And, of course, I can come for an interview whenever you suggest.

Message 2

Includes highlights of the applicant.

Dear Mr. Huget:

Perhaps you will remember I sent you my application for a position in your grain department on February 8. I am primarily interested in cash grain purchasing and the use of the futures market to assist in the operations of your company.

The principal points in my letter were that:

1. A research project I conducted on the use of the commodity exchanges by members of the Iowa grain industry developed insights that I can use effectively for your company. I am now finishing the writing of the results for my master's thesis, also on aspects of the grain industry.
2. My college degree is in Business Administration, and I plan to receive a master of arts degree in June, (*year*), in marketing.
3. During 18 years on an Iowa farm, I became familiar with most of the grains in the grain industry.

I hope that you can use a person with my background. If you wish any further information, I will be glad to send it to you.

Other Follow-up Messages from Applicant to Employer

In addition to the follow-up messages just discussed, a job-hunting campaign can include quite a few other types. The following pages discuss and give examples of some of these.

Answer to a Noncommittal Letter

Assume that you have sent your application letter with resume—maybe even had the interview. Then you receive the following:

Dear Miss Randolph

We were pleased to receive your excellent application for employment.

We are very much interested in your capabilities but regret that at the present time, we cannot make use of them; with your permission, however, we will keep your name on file and if anything should develop in the future, get in touch with you.

Thank you for your interest in our organization.

What should you do? At first you might interpret this message as a routine refusal. However, the employer has said, "with your permission . . . keep on file," and you should assume that the message is sincere and you will definitely be considered when an opening occurs. A short message like the following is quite a satisfactory reply:

Dear Mr. Lewis

Thank you for your reviewing my qualifications for (*type of job*).

Will you please keep my name in your files so that you can consider me when a future opening in that field takes place? You can count on me to do a thorough, accurate job if I may join your staff.

I like what I read and hear about your organization--and hope some day to be part of such an organization.

If you receive a message that says essentially what Mr. Lewis wrote to Miss Randolph but does not ask your permission, a reply is optional.

Reply to Request for Additional Information

Occasionally an employer, interviewer, or school will request additional information about your background. If such a situation arises, think carefully about the topic(s) that have been asked about. As with the initial presentation, analyze your background thoroughly, so that you will include all the important details to back up and strengthen your presentation; then organize and write. You'll probably use an outline like the following:

First paragraph: Thank for interview and express eagerness to tell about whatever is asked for. Also identify the topic(s) you are discussing.

Middle paragraphs: If asked about two qualifications (say interest in field and interest in company), write separate paragraphs for each. The discussion will be persuasive—quite similar to the middle paragraphs that create desire in the application letter.

Last paragraph: In your last paragraph you might express:
1. Availability for another interview
2. Any other idea that rounds out and strengthens the message.

Given below is such a presentation. The admissions office of a law school asked the applicant to fill out the necessary form and, separately, to talk about her interest in law and give highlights of her background.

```
Admissions Council
University of (state) Law School
(city, state zip)


Gentlemen

As you requested, I am returning the completed Form A and a brief
discussion of two questions you asked for:  my interest in law and
highlights of my background.

Interest in Law
Before going into my background, I want to explain why I want a
degree in law.  The need has been there since childhood.  Unlike
most childhood fixations--teacher, doctor, and dancer--the desire
to be a lawyer has stuck with me since the age of twelve.  More than
a childhood dream is involved though.  I feel that a law degree and
the ability to use it embodies one of the most valuable assets a
person can own.

To me law pervades every aspect of our society.  Law is where the
action is.  It is one of the few professions that enable a person
to be actively involved in forming her culture while at the same
time enabling her to find a highly satisfactory role in life.
```

Specifically I plan to concentrate on corporate law with a later concentration on international legal business relationships. This area needs good lawyers, and I want to prepare myself to fill that need.

Background
Following is a brief sketch of my background that will help you in assessing my ability to study law. As the enclosed form shows, I was born in Germany. Though still a German citizen, I plan to go through naturalization during (*year*) to become a citizen of the United States. I was reared in South Africa from the age of three and am bilingual, speaking and writing both German and English without any accent or faults in composition.

I used my undergraduate years to gain as wide a knowledge of as many disciplines as I could. My program emphasized political science, social sciences, some humanities with a later concentration on general business courses. This was, in my mind, the most useful road toward my eventual goal.

My transcript that you should have received by now shows I spent five years on my bachelor's degree. The extra year was necessitated by a scarcity of funds in my family. Part- and full-time jobs have put me through school and have allowed me to save enough money to attend law school. Although outside work has detracted from study time, I feel that the work discipline and the ability to communicate and work with all types of people more than offset any loss in academic learning.

If you should need any additional information to aid you in your decision, please let me know.

Acceptance of Invitation for Interview

This type of good-news message has as its main purpose acceptance, which should appear in the first paragraph. Usually the employer leaves it up to you—at least within a limited time span—to decide when to make the trip. In turn, you must be considerate of the working days and hours of the employer. Give a choice of several times within a certain week so that the employer can choose the most convenient date and hour. The last paragraph should express sincere interest in the forthcoming interview. Message 2 on pages 463–464 is a good example of an applicant's acceptance of an invitation for a plant interview.

Follow-up after Interview

If you receive no reply by the promised date, remember it takes time for the employer to interview all applicants, route the qualifications to interested officers in the organization, and make a final choice. However, if you have waited what you consider ample time and also *beyond* the promised date of notification—especially if another firm is waiting for your reply—you might want to write a nonpersuasive inquiry similar to the one below.

Dear Mrs. Johnson

Four weeks have passed since I had the opportunity to talk with you about an opening in (*field*). At that time you said you'd notify me of your decision by (*date*).

Meanwhile, another firm has offered me a position and has requested a reply within the next 10 days. Before answering them, I would like to know whether you have reached a favorable decision as to my working for your company.

I sincerely prefer your firm, and will very much appreciate your reply before (*date*).

Request for More Time to Decide

Sometimes the situation arises in which you receive an offer while you still have several interviews to complete, and you need more time before making a decision. Although you're taking a chance by asking the offering firm to give you more time to decide, usually the employer understands and wants you to be satisfied in your final selection. You usually preface the request with a buffer paragraph; then you explain and add a paragraph on your particular interest in the firm. The last paragraph should keep the door open for you to make a hurried decision if the employer decides not to grant the extension. Also, ask for a confirmation of the extension if the employer decides in your favor. (Message 5 on page 465 is a good example of a request for more time for the final decision.)

Acceptance of Offer

When you receive an offer you want to accept, reply soon—perhaps within a week. Begin with the good news—that you accept with pleasure. In this first paragraph identify the job you're accepting; the next paragraph might give details about moving (if distance is involved) and reporting for work. Naturally what you say in this explanation depends on what the employer has already told you during the interview or in the job-offer letter. End with a rounding-out paragraph indicating you're looking forward to working for the firm. (See message 7, page 466, which is a good example of an applicant's acceptance.)

Rejection of Offer

Occasionally an applicant will need to turn down a job offer. When you refuse an offer, you're writing a bad-news message. The organizational pattern is: buffer; explanation; refusal (implied or expressed); and a friendly, positive closing. Even more important than the outline, however, is the attitude you have toward the company. Remember this firm seriously considered your qualifications and spent its time and money to bring you to the plant for an interview. If your refusal is discourteous and abrupt, you leave a bad impression and perhaps cause an unfavorable attitude toward *all* college applicants.

Shown below are two examples of well-written job refusals. Notice the outline, tone, sincerity, and positive approach.

Message 1

From a business administration graduate to a personnel director.

Dear Mrs. Adamsen

Thank you for offering me a position in your management training program.

During my job hunting these last few months, I've sent applications to several firms that I regard highly--only those I could be happy working for. Fortunately for me, both you and another firm offered me a job. Because my qualifications, interest, and background fit in more closely with the other job, I have already mailed in my acceptance.

I do thank you for your consideration of my qualifications, the thorough one-day interview at the plant, and the opportunity to meet all department heads in production. I'll always think of your organization as one in which management treats the employees as a highly prized commodity.

Again, thank you for your consideration. I will always remember it.

This refusal is effective because it is simple and sincere from beginning to end. In a tactful way it explains first, then refuses the offer, and finally follows up with a paragraph that genuinely compliments the firm.

Message 2

From a graduate in education to a superintendent of a school district.

Dear Mr. Selby

I appreciate your offer to teach business education in one of Winchester's high schools.

As I explained in our interview on April 21, my wife and I must find jobs in the same locality. Since the interview, we have received an offer for both of us from Mrs. Jackson of the Logan school system.

I hesitate to decline your offer since the experience in the Winchester system would be both profitable and enjoyable. However, under the present certification requirements, my wife must teach one year before completing her education. Since it is unlikely that she will be able to teach in this area, we find it necessary to accept the Logan positions.

Please keep my qualifications as a business education teacher in mind when openings develop in the future.

This message, like the previous one, is straightforward, sincere, and positive. Furthermore, the applicant doesn't burn his bridges behind him; the reader will probably consider him when an opening occurs.

FOLLOW-UP MESSAGES WRITTEN BY EMPLOYER TO APPLICANT

Not only should you be able to write messages the applicant must send, but also—since you will be in business someday—you need to dictate effective messages that will go to the applicant.

Invitations to Interviews

Depending upon circumstances, there are times when the employer writes direct to applicants to arrange interviews either at the company offices or plant or on a college campus near the applicants.

Applicant Invited to the Company for Interview

As the employer writing this letter, you must realize that this message is second in importance only to the offer itself. Thus you must make the reader feel that you genuinely want a personal interview. Also clearly get across that you'll help in every way possible—for example, you'll send a round-trip ticket, reserve a hotel room during the stay if necessary, and reimburse all incidental expenses. In addition ask which dates will be convenient for a visit. Maybe you will make responding easier by enclosing a card (see message 1, page 463).

After you receive the applicant's acceptance of the invitation, you'll send a reply similar to message 3 on page 464. You not only enclose a check for travel expenses, but give all necessary details and indicate interest in the forthcoming visit.

Employer Announces Impending Visit on Campus

Instead of asking applicants to come to the plant, you might notify them that you will come (or return) to the campus (or elsewhere) to interview. You're writing to the applicant because he or she is one of the graduates you particularly want to talk to. Qualifications on the application letter and resume interest you. Messages 1 and 2 below are notifications of an impending visit. In addition to giving the details about the visit, you have the opportunity to "sell" the applicant on something ("selling" in message 1 and "your interest" in the applicant in message 2).

Message 1

Sells the applicant on being a sales representative.

Dear Mr. McTaggart:

Last fall I wrote you concerning job opportunities with (*name of firm*). I will again be on campus this winter and would like very much to see you.

As I told you earlier, we have many openings for graduates--openings which include the functions of development, design, headquarters marketing, technical sales, manufacturing, and others.

Before our get-together I want to describe briefly now (*firm's*) position of sales engineer. The word <u>salesperson</u> in this country is tainted. Many people picture her or him as a used car dealer-- public beware; door-to-door salesperson; loud-mouthed extrovert; or an order taker with catalog, order blank, and poised pencil.[5]

The industrial sales engineers are anything but these. They are technically competent. These engineers solve engineering problems for customers. They are innovators and thoroughly enjoy being with many types of people. They possess empathy, the capacity to under- stand another person's feelings or ideas. They are principally interested in the large conceptional problems of engineering. And, with experience and further study, they become competent in several engineering disciplines, because in industry the several branches of engineering cannot be separated.

One other thought. In American industry today you'll find most of the jobs for engineers in technical sales. Also, here's where the money is, and this job is the route to higher management.

I will be at the University of (*state*) on February 16, (*year*), for interviews. Please arrange to see me by contacting your placement director.

Message 2

Sincerely compliments the applicant on her qualifications.

Dear Ms. Webster

Thank you very much for coming to the placement office at the University of (*state*) for an interview with (*name of firm*). Since you and I had our visit, I have interviewed on approximately 20 other college campuses and talked to approximately 200 students.

This has been my first opportunity to review the resumes of these students from which I have selected approximately 15% suggesting further interviews. Mary, you are included in this group of stu- dents whose scholastic ability, personality, grooming, motivation, and overall personality place you in the upper 15% of those I have talked to.

Our spring interview date at the university has not been definitely established at this time, but as soon as it has been, I will drop you a note; if you are interested, arrange to be placed on our spring interview schedule in the placement office. You may recall that we select somewhere between 10 and 15 young men and women each year to go through our Management and Underwriter Training Program, which runs from the third week in June until the middle or end of September.

---

[5] The third paragraph might seem negative, but it is directed to an applicant who exhibited an un- favorable attitude toward selling, and who needs to be convinced of the true picture.

```
Again we commend you for your fine scholastic record you have been
able to maintain and at the same time be responsible for 100% of
your college expenses.  We look forward to visiting with you again
in the spring, for I feel certain we both have much to offer each
other by way of ability and opportunity for growth.
```

Follow-up Messages from Employer after Interview(s)

As a personnel representative or officer concerned with employing applicants, you will have a variety of other letters to write after interviews with applicants. The following pages include suggestions for such messages.

Request for Further Information

During the interview you may have questions about the applicant's enthusiasm or sincerity toward the company or toward his or her chosen field. To check on your hunch you might ask for a written statement of why the applicant wants to work for your firm or get into this type of occupation. Or you might ask the applicant to show why he or she is the individual you should hire for the opening. Or you might simply need additional information, as the letter below illustrates:

```
Dear Mr. Juntwait:

Recently we had the pleasure of talking with you in connection with
our college recruiting activity.  Thank you for the time you gave us.

Our staff has had the opportunity to review your qualifications and
we are interested in learning more about you.  Accordingly, will you
please complete the enclosed application and return it to me by
(date)?  Also explain in an attached letter your interest in (name
of field).  After this information reaches us, we will get in touch
with you on a more specific basis.

Thank you for your interest in (name of firm); we look forward to
hearing from you in the near future.
```

Another type of "request for information" is the letter that asks the applicant to do something—perhaps to read a brochure, have an interview with a local representative of the firm, or take a test. The purpose of such requests is to make sure the applicant is getting into the right field, as the letter below illustrates:

```
Dear Steve:

Thank you for taking the time to learn more about (firm).  You have
the attitude and appearance that make a good sales representative.

During the next few months I suggest that you find out all you can
about the practical area of industrial sales.

Since you do not graduate until June of (year), if you still feel
that this is the type of career you would like to pursue, please
```

contact our local (*city*) district manager for a more detailed interview. Her name is Mrs. A. I. Theriot, and she can be reached at:

(*name of firm*)
6536 - 6th Avenue, South
(*city, state ZIP*)
Phone: (*number*)

It was a pleasure talking with you. And the best of success in
your studies.

Offer of a Job

When you send a job offer, begin by telling the good news in a friendly manner. In the
first paragraph also identify the job and state the salary (usually on a monthly basis).
In the following paragraph(s), try to anticipate any questions the applicant might
have—such as what moving expenses the firm will pay—and answer them. (Naturally
you won't go into detail about expenses until she or he accepts.) Also, leave the door
open for the applicant to ask questions before making a decision. Be sure your tone is
appropriate—convey that you're interested in the applicant and sincerely want him or
her to join your organization (see message 4, pages 464–465).

Grant of a Time Extension

If you believe an applicant has a sound reason for requesting more time to consider an
offer, you may decide to grant the extension. Grant the request in the first paragraph,
explain (and in general terms set the cutoff date), express interest in the applicant, and
end on a friendly and positive note. (See message 6, pages 465–466.)

Reply to Applicant's Acceptance

Even when the applicant has accepted your job offer, you still need to remember the
value of public relations. The applicant doesn't expect a long letter, but abrupt messages can be disappointing. For example, after receiving message 8 (see page 466), the
applicant felt let down because the employer didn't show any interest—*enthusiasm* is
perhaps a better word. The you-attitude of this message could be improved by a few
small changes. For example, the second paragraph could begin with, "You will receive . . ." instead of, "We will forward . . . ." And, *if true*, an encouraging sentence
would be appreciated—perhaps regarding the applicant's potential for broader responsibilities in line with the company's expected future growth.

Refusal of Job

A refusal—even a tactful one—is a blow to the applicant, and the tone of your refusal
is very important. At all costs you want to avoid leaving the applicant with a lasting
negative reaction to your firm.

The individuals being turned down don't want limp excuses or outright false statements. They want honesty—but not discourteous bluntness or crudeness of expression. They will appreciate sincere, complimentary remarks about qualifications; proper consideration of background; and proper personal attitude. Give applicants the feeling you realize that you're talking to intelligent human beings.

In the first paragraph, give a buffer—appreciate their interest in the firm or the opportunity to talk with them, or thank them for coming in for interviews. In the second paragraph, explain. You should first say something neutral (for example, that you have reviewed the qualifications) and then refuse in as positive a way as possible. One of the best explanations seems to be, "There are several other candidates whose overall qualifications are more in line with our requirements."

Be sure your last paragraph is positive and friendly. Wish the applicants success, tell them you enjoyed the opportunity to talk with them, thank them for the interest in the firm. Obviously you won't repeat in this paragraph what you said in the first.

Below is an unusually effective refusal which follows the outline just discussed.

Dear Ms. Cotter:

Thank you very much for taking your time to be interviewed and tested for the position of systems engineering representative with (*firm*).

We have reviewed your educational background, work experience, and aptitude tests, along with others we are considering for employment. Our analysis indicates that there are several other candidates whose overall qualifications are more in line with our requirements.

We enjoyed having the opportunity to interview you and sincerely appreciate your interest in (*firm*). Please accept our best wishes for success in your chosen career.

Some taboos to be avoided in writing your refusal are given here.

1. Refusal in opening

   We have considered your qualifications; however, we do not have a position available for you.

2. Abrupt refusal in the first sentence of the second paragraph

   Unfortunately we have no opening for you.

3. No reason for refusal

   A review of your qualifications indicates that you have a background which is commendable in many respects; however, we are not in a position to further pursue the matter of your employment with (*firm*) at this time.

4. Negative attitude ("sorry," "unable," "regret," "cannot," "not suited," "do not feel," "do not have," "delay")

In view of our needs, however, we regret we do not feel additional interviews would be mutually beneficial or advisable.

5. Vagueness

I hope that we shall have an opportunity to review our mutual interests again at some future date.

Based on your recent interview and your qualifications, we cannot encourage you about employment with (*firm*) at the present time.

SITUATION

Now that you have studied separately different types of messages that the employer and applicant use in securing a job, study the letters below, which were written over a period of time by an applicant for an operations management position with a national firm and the representatives of the firm.

Message 1

Mr. Hanson, Supervisor of Employment Personnel Services, invites applicant for plant interview. The plant is about 1,000 miles from the campus.

October 28, (*year*)

Dear Mr. Webb:

Following our recent interview on campus, we wish to invite you to visit (*name of firm*) for plant interviews; you will receive the necessary expenses for air travel to (*city*), and return, as well as incidental expenses.

If a plant visit is agreeable to you, please let us know when you can make the visit and we will confirm a mutually agreeable date. A card is enclosed so that you can notify us of your plant visit decision. If possible, plan to spend one full day at the plant.

Thank you for the interest you have expressed in (*name of firm*). Upon confirming an interview date, we will forward a check covering your travel expenses, details for getting to the plant, and we will also reserve hotel accommodations in (*city*) if you so desire.

Message 2

Applicant's reply to message 1; acceptance of invitation.

November 4, (*year*)

Dear Mr. Hanson

Thank you for inviting me to visit your plant. I very much want to study your organization and operation.

Because of class schedules and previous commitments, the best dates are November 15-19, inclusive. Any one or more of these days permits ideal timing for the trip.

I'm looking forward to visiting your plant and talking with both management members and workers in production.

Message 3

Reply by certified mail to message 2; Mrs. Benson, assistant supervisor of employment personnel services, gives details for visit and encloses check.

November 7, (*year*)

Dear Mr. Webb

Thank you for informing us of your intended visit to (*firm*) for interviews. We have set the date on November 18 and are enclosing a check to cover your plane fare, meals, and miscellaneous expenses. Please retain any receipts for air travel and lodging for our expense account purposes.

We have arranged prepaid hotel accommodations for you for Monday, November 17, at the Sheraton-Palace Hotel, (*city*). You can come to the plant Tuesday morning in a company car which leaves our (*city*) office every morning at 6:45 a.m.

To get this car you should report by 6:30 a.m. to the mail room, twelfth floor, Equitable Life Building, 120 Berkeman Street, (*city*). Because of the early hour, you can plan on having breakfast when you reach the plant. You will be able to return to (*city*) from the plant in the same manner, leaving here at 4:40 p.m. and arriving in (*city*) at about 6:30 p.m.

The interest you have expressed in (*name of firm*) is appreciated, and we look forward to your visit on the 18th.

Message 4

Job offer by Mr. Dorman, general superintendent, following plant interview.

November 22, (*year*)

Dear Mr. Webb:

We are pleased to offer you employment as a management trainee, assigned to our industrial engineering department. Your starting salary on this position would be $--- a month.

Should you decide to join our organization, we will provide the cost of travel for you and your wife and move your household effects.

Thank you for the interest which you expressed when you visited the plant; I am sorry that circumstances did not permit me to meet you then. We hope that you will decide to make your career with us. If you have any question concerning our offer or employment in general, please call Mrs. R. A. Benson in the personnel office. Her telephone number is 543-4889 (area code 123).

Message 5

Applicant requests more time for final decision.

December 2, (*year*)

Dear Mrs. Benson:

Mr. Dorman just sent me a job offer as a management trainee in the industrial engineering department and said for me to get in touch with you if I had any questions concerning the offer.

Before making a final decision concerning this offer, I will appreciate your allowing me until January (*year*) for my reply. My reason for requesting this extra time is to permit me to complete my interviews with several other companies--especially those that have already invited me to visit their plants.

At the moment, even with these other opportunities, I am more interested in (*reader's firm*) than all the others because there are many aspects of your company which appeal to me. I was particularly impressed by the speed, efficiency, and precision of the manufacturing plant.

If you need my decision before the end of this month, please let me know as soon as possible so that I will have the opportunity to make my final decision. Also, if you are giving me this extended time, please notify me to that effect.

Message 6

Mrs. Benson gives applicant extension of time to accept offer.

December 11, (*year*)

Dear Mr. Webb

As you requested, we will be glad to allow you additional time to decide whether you want to accept our previous offer to work for (*firm*).

We realize that you have many things to consider to reach a final decision regarding employment; therefore, we want to allow you as

much time as possible for your evaluation of all opportunities. In
order for us to establish the proper control on our recruiting activities and to make plans for the coming year, I will appreciate
knowing your decision as soon as possible. However, inasmuch as you
will not be available until June (*year*), your advising us a couple
of months from now will be quite acceptable.

We feel that you are well qualified for the career employment opportunities available within (*firm*) and hope that you will decide to
make your career with us.

I wish you and your wife the best of health and cheer during the
coming holidays; and if I can be of any further assistance to you,
please write or telephone me. My number is 543-4889 (area code 123).

Message 7

Applicant's acceptance.

January 5, (year)

Dear Mrs. Benson:

I am glad to accept your offer of $--- a month as a management
trainee in your industrial engineering department.

Since graduation is Saturday, June 13, (*year*), my wife and I plan
to leave (*city*) the following Monday, June 15. We should arrive in
the (*city*) area the following day--Tuesday, June 16. Allowing a few
days to locate living accommodations and to get settled, I should be
ready to start work on Monday, June 22. Please let me know if this
schedule is satisfactory with you.

I am very pleased in becoming a member of your organization; it is
with great appreciation that I look forward to what I am sure will
be a challenging future with (*name of organization*).

Message 8

Benson's reply to applicant's acceptance.

January 13, (year)

Dear Mr. Webb:

We are very pleased that you are coming with us, and we look forward
to seeing you on June 22.

We will forward travel expenses in May and will contact you at that
time regarding moving arrangements.

Please contact us if we can be of any assistance before that time.

EXERCISES

1. Below are four refusals to applicants by outstanding national companies. Evaluate by telling what you like and dislike about each message. Be specific in your discussion. Which one does the most satisfactory job?

   a.
   Thank you for coming in to discuss employment possibilities during our recent visit to your campus.

   As you can appreciate, there is considerable competition for our limited openings. It is always a difficult task to select a few people from the many fine candidates we are given the opportunity to consider. After careful consideration of your qualifications with regards to our specific job requirements, we will be unable to offer you further encouragement.

   We do, however, appreciate your interest in (*firm*) and extend our best wishes for success in your business career.

   b.
   In reply to your letter of application dated January 5, (*year*), we do not have an opening on our staff. However, we shall be pleased to keep your application on file for future vacancies.

   Thank you for writing us.

   c.
   The delay in advising you regarding employment possibilities with (*firm*), following your interview with our recruiter, has been due to your application and file being forwarded to departments dispersed over a wide geographic area.

   Your background and qualifications have now been carefully reviewed by these various departments; but, we regret we are presently unable to offer you a position that would be of mutual advantage.

   We appreciate your interest in (*firm*) and wish you every success in the future.

   d.
   Thank you for scheduling an interview with (*firm*), giving our recruiter, Mr. C. W. Lindenmeier, the opportunity to talk with you during our recent visit to your campus. He commented favorably about his conversation with you.

   We have carefully reviewed all openings anticipated near your availability date which we believed might be of interest to you. I am sorry to inform you that we were unable to locate a position matching your background, training, and interests. We are, however, taking the liberty of holding your application on file should any appropriate openings develop in the near future.

I do regret that we cannot offer you more encouragement at this time. We appreciate your interest in our activities and wish you every success in beginning your professional career.

2. Evaluate the three messages below. The applicant is a graduating senior who sent her application letter with resume to a large department store chain in a large city 1,000 miles from the campus. In the letter she mentioned she'd be in the city between winter and spring quarters (usually the latter part of March) and requested an interview, which she received.

Message 1

Applicant receives this offer after she returns to the campus.

As a result of our conversation with you, we are pleased to offer you the opportunity to join the (*firm*) Executive Training Program at a starting salary of $--- a month. Employment is contingent upon your passing a medical examination which will be given when you start work here in (*city*).

Enclosed for your perusal is a copy of our Annual Report, which we trust you will find of interest.

We look forward to receiving your favorable consideration of this offer, and I am sure you will find this a most stimulating opportunity.

Message 2

Applicant accepts job offer.

April 17, (*year*)

It is with pleasure and excitement that I accept your offer to join the (*firm*) Executive Training Program. I have been reading the Annual Report you enclosed and am looking forward to working for as fine a company as (*firm's*).

Will you please tell me when you want me to report after graduation, where, to whom, and at what time? I can be in (*city*) within two weeks after University of (*state*) commencement exercises June 13.

If you need any further information before giving me the details of my assignment, please write to me at my (*city*) address before June 9 and at my home address after that date.

Message 3

Reply to applicant's job acceptance and inquiry.

April 21, (*year*)

Thank you for your letter of April 17. We are pleased to know that you will be joining our Executive Training Squad this summer.

You may report for work any Monday convenient to you. You indicate that June 29 would be a convenient date. This is most acceptable, and we will look forward to your reporting at 8:55 a.m. to the personnel department, which is on the eighth floor. You may enter the building through the company entrance (on Westfall near Donson Street) and the guard at the door will direct you to the personnel department.

Enclosed is a booklet, which is given to all new Training Squad executives when they report for work, which may answer many of your questions. We are also enclosing a booklet given to every new employee, which will give you information as to dress regulations, etc.

Congratulations on your coming graduation. We look forward to seeing you again on June 29.

3. Assume you have written to a large corporation the application letter assigned in Exercise 4, page 436. Today you received an invitation for an interview next Friday (in your city). To prepare well for this interview study a copy of the firm's recent Annual Report. List information about its products, personnel, and other items of interest to help you answer pertinent questions. (See questions on pages 445–447.)

4. Assume you sent your application letter and resume to the personnel manager of a particular firm; shortly afterward you received an invitation to come to his office for an interview. He is located in your city. During the 30-minute interview, he asked you questions about your qualifications and explained company policy, beginning salary, and other pertinent information. Write a follow-up for one (or each) of the possible outcomes below:
   a. At the end of the interview he told you he'd notify you of his decision.
   b. At the end of the interview he asked you to write him why you want to get into the type of work you're applying for.
   c. At the end of the interview he asked you to visit the manager in one of the organization's several local retail stores; while there you should interview the manager and other employees to find out whether you want to make a career in this type of work. Then you're to write the personnel manager if you're still interested. Assume you are favorably impressed.

5. Assume you mailed your application letter three weeks ago but have received no reply. Send an inquiry to the firm.

6. Assume you received two offers for career jobs.
   a. Write the acceptance message.

b. Write the refusal message.

7. As the employer, you must refuse a graduating senior the job she applied for because her qualifications aren't as good as those of the others you interviewed. Furthermore, one reference indicated this person is a troublemaker. Write the refusal message.

8. As a graduating senior, you received the following letter from Mrs. Alexander, recruiting coordinator. Unfortunately you can't see the representative on January 30. However, you're very much interested in working for this company. Write the appropriate message to the coordinator, assuming any facts you wish as long as you don't alter the assignment.

Dear (*your name*):

Please forgive my resorting to a form letter to reach you--but time is getting short and I want to let you know that one of our executives plans to visit your campus soon.

Her primary purpose will be to interview (*year*) graduates for career employment with our newly merged organization. As you might imagine, we have an even greater horizon now to present to promising young people like yourself. Moreover, we have a number of good summer job opportunities for undergraduates this year.

In any case, I have been alerted to your fine summer employment record with us and assure you our interest in you continues strong. Accordingly, if you want to explore a position with us, I urge that you sign up to see our corporate recruiting representative when she visits your placement office on January 30.

If you cannot make that date, please drop me a line and let's try to arrange for you to visit some nearby branch office. I am enclosing a return envelope for that purpose, together with a copy of our Annual Report and some other literature for your reference.

Meanwhile, accept our sincere best wishes to your forthcoming graduation.

9. What kind of an impression do you think the following applicant made on the firm considering him for a management job? Given below are the details.

The applicant was invited in for an interview at company expense. He lived in Madison, Wisconsin, and the company was located in St. Louis, Missouri. Although it was only normal to use plane, train, or bus for transportation, he felt he could get "in" with the company by saving them money—by hitchhiking.

Here's the expense account he submitted to the company for reimbursement:

Bus fare in Madison, Wisconsin	$ .35
Bus fare in Janesville, Wisconsin	.35
Dinner in St. Louis, Missouri	4.95

Hotel room and tip in St. Louis, Missouri	15.50
Movie	2.00
3 cokes	.60
12 cigarettes (2 of the fellows I hitchhiked with borrowed these from me)	.60
Hamburger and coke for lunch in Moline, Illinois	.95
Hotel room and tip in Moline, Illinois	12.50
Shoe shine	.70
1 suit cleaned (1 of the fellows I caught a ride with had been drinking and spilled a bottle of beer on me)	4.95
	$43.45

10. Assume that three weeks ago you had an interview on campus with a representative of a national company whose head offices are 1,000 miles from you. Before parting, the interviewer asked if you would be willing to come to the head offices some day for further interviews, and you had replied that you would be glad to. Today you receive the following letter, dated February 2, from the personnel manager:

Dear (*your name*):

It is with a great deal of pleasure that I confirm our invitation to visit us in (*city*) in order to pursue further the possibility of your joining (*firm name*). We have arranged a schedule for which we would like to have you arrive at our executive offices at (*address*) at 1:30 p.m. on Monday, April 10; be prepared to stay with us through the following day.

As I pointed out during our brief meeting, at (*firm name*) we feel strongly that the matter of selection is a "two-way street," and we look forward to this chance of making you better acquainted with us and the opportunity we offer. Also, of course, we would like to review your qualifications more fully.

I know you have already accepted our invitation for further interviews, but we would appreciate a letter indicating that you still plan to come. It might be a good idea if you were to make airline reservations right away and let me know the flight numbers. I will then reciprocate by sending you an open ticket drawn on the airline you designate.

We will make a hotel reservation for you for the night of April 10, and for the night of the 9th too if schedules require you to come the night before. As a last point, please keep track of the incidental expenses incurred by your trip so that we may reimburse you for them.

```
That would seem to cover it, (your name), but please let me know if
you have any questions.  I'll be looking forward to seeing you again.
```

Write the complete, thoughtful, friendly letter this invitation calls for. Before you do so, however, consider the kind of airline passage you should reserve. Should it be first-class? Coach? Economy? Why? Why do you think the employer leaves the choice up to you? (You might also discuss in class the kinds of incidental expenses that will be appropriate for you to include in your later request for reimbursement—after this second interview. See, for example, the list in Exercise 9.)

11. If you and your classmates would like practice interviews, try this assignment. For one interview half the class members will volunteer to be job applicants and the other half will be employers' personnel representatives. For a second interview all students will switch roles.

    Each interview will be based on an application letter and resume the applicant has written (as, for example, Exercise 4, page 436) and, presumably, mailed. In class students will merely exchange these papers.

    Each interview should preferably be about 20 to 30 minutes in length between students who do not know each other well. Both the applicant and the assumed personnel representative (or higher executive, if appropriate) should make all necessary preparations before the interviews. The applicant (interviewee) should review pages 441–448. The employer's representative (interviewer) will find helpful suggestions in Chapter 18, pages 690–697, regarding how to conduct an interview. He or she will, of course, also study the applicant's resume before conducting the interview and know something about the company the interviewer represents.

chapter 13

Collection Messages—Written and Oral

Collection of past-due accounts is an important part of any business. After a borrower gets a loan or a customer purchases something on credit, payment should be made within a specified period—according to the terms of the agreement. When obligations are not paid on time, collection messages become necessary. Customer reasons for not paying are usually one or more of the following: they've overlooked the invoice or statement; they're dissatisfied with the merchandise, delivery, billing, or handling of a complaint; they're temporarily short of funds; they're chronic debtors.

Collection messages have an important, twofold purpose: to *get the money* and to *keep customer goodwill.* These messages may be delivered by mail, phone, personal visit, telegram, or Mailgram. To carry out the twofold function requires an understanding attitude and effective messages appropriately planned and timed throughout the collection stages. Most collection procedures have similar basic characteristics whether the messages concern retail credit (to customers) or mercantile credit (to business firms), and whether they are for open account or installment credit. For various reasons, they also have differences. This chapter discusses:

1. Right attitude for effective collections
2. Collection stages
3. Variations in collection series
4. Telephone collection procedure

RIGHT ATTITUDE FOR EFFECTIVE COLLECTIONS

A debtor may be touchy about how and when the creditor asks for payment even though it is for a legitimate debt. The longer past-due the payment is, the more difficult the situation becomes. The right collection attitude for a creditor requires an understanding of human nature, careful choice of collection appeals, knowledge of the debtor's past credit record, as well as regulations affecting collection policies.

Understanding of Human Nature

When you send a collection message, remember you are communicating with a person, not with an account number. Each person has a different mental filter, with attitudes, prejudices, perceptions, and problems. All human beings have feelings and react negatively to offensive expressions, sarcasm, anger, and insults just as quickly as you do.

The fairest assumption to make is that your customers honestly want to pay as agreed. The majority of customers will pay when reminded. However, conditions change and with them the customers' ability and willingness to pay may also change. Some debtors conscientiously promptly write or telephone their reasons for lateness and explain when they will make their next payments. Some remain silent, and a few are repeatedly uncooperative.

A tactful, courteous attitude coupled with firmness and patience always collects more money in the long run than impolitely worded demands. As a collection manager you are on a tightrope regarding messages to customers with past-due accounts. If you're too lenient, some individuals may pay other bills that seem more pressing, and you won't get the money coming to you. On the other hand, if you threaten or bully customers, they may not pay either.

How and *when* to probe for the reason a debtor hasn't paid is important. (Whenever possible, you want to avoid turning an account over to a collection agency because everyone loses except the agency.) Some people just don't know how to manage their financial affairs. Merely putting pressure upon them to pay is not enough. The understanding creditor may show them how to pay, perhaps help them plan their budgets (if appropriate) and arrange terms of payment so they can pay their debts and regain their self-respect. The unhappy person who has suffered temporary financial embarrassment because of family illness or business reverses appreciates collection messages that are considerate and helpful. Such individuals are more likely to do their best to cooperate.

In result-getting collection letters, expressions like "you are delinquent" should not be used; phrases such as "two payments are delinquent" or "the delinquency of this account" are less offensive because they are impersonal. "Past due" has a better connotation and is preferred.

All you have learned about consideration, concreteness, and courtesy for the customer (Chapters 3 and 4) is important for effective collection messages. Also, the suggestions for proper attitude in bad-news letters (pages 262–263) apply to collections.

Choice of Collection Appeals

As you will read later in the discussion on Collection Stages, those collection messages which must be *persuasive* should include well-chosen appeals. These choices relate closely to the attitude you have toward the debtor. The following positive and negative appeals are effective in persuasive collection messages:

Positive appeals focus on cooperation, fair play, pride

Cooperation, the mildest appeal, caters to one's desire to be considerate of others—in this case, loyal to the creditor who has been courteous and friendly in asking for what is rightly due. (This should not, however, be a whining "poor me" appeal.)

The **fair-play** appeal is usually developed by reviewing the facts—how long a payment has been pastdue—and showing that since the creditor has carried out his or her part of an agreement, the debtor (customer)—to be fair and honest—should keep his or her promise and pay. Resale on items bought is also effective.

The **pride appeal** should be subtle, not a high-pressure tactic. You can develop this appeal in various ways by referring to what you know the customer is proud of—a good credit record, (sometimes) the items bought, or the respect and good reputation enjoyed in the community.

Negative appeals arouse debtor's emotions of self-interest and fear

Individuals who care little about cooperation or fair play may be motivated to pay when you show what they will gain by doing so and will lose by further delay.

The **self-interest** appeal usually has two objectives—to show the value of the present advantages the customers have and to convince them that further delay may cause them to lose the advantages.

Fear appeal, instead of stressing the value of keeping various benefits, stresses the loss of such benefits (good credit standing or possessions). The past-due account will be reported to the credit bureau and turned over to an attorney or collection agency, or be taken to court as a lawsuit, which will be extra expense for the debtor.

You can use effectively one or a combination of these appeals in a persuasive message. Your choice of appeals is influenced by your attitude regarding the type of debtor, knowledge of collection policies, and the place of the message in the collection stage.

Types of Debtors

Various circumstances affect the paying habits of customers, and thus their promptness may change from time to time. According to their paying records debtors can be grouped broadly into three types: good-pay, fair-pay, and poor-pay.

Good-pay customers pay on time and need little or no reminding. For those few times when a reminder is necessary, you can usually collect payments after pleasant reminder messages using the direct-request pattern—without appeals. On the rare occasion when accounts become past due, you will persuade these customers through a positive appeal to cooperation or fair play.

Fair-pay customers always pay, but slowly, and often need reminders and persuasion. Your attitude toward payment should be firmer and your reminders are more frequent. These customers may be very respected, honest persons in your community, but perhaps absentminded or just disorganized in paying and business habits. Like the good-pay customer, the fair-pay customer will respond to positive appeals; but instead of motivating by appeals to cooperation and fair play, you may have to use pride and self-interest appeals. Because of procrastination sometimes two or more payments are past due, and you may have to caution about the risks involved —and occasionally bring in a mild negative appeal.

Poor-pay customers are repeatedly late in payments. These customers have probably received numerous collection notices before, not only from your firm, but from other creditors. They ignore the pleasant, mild reminders because they know there is still time to delay before creditors get tough. Sermons and scolding bore them. For this type of individual you include a few surprises and shocks—and more negative than positive appeals. You must persuade them to pay because not doing so will be detrimental.

You will see how to use the various appeals in collection messages when you read about collection stages, which are directly concerned with the debtor's payment record.

Knowledge of Collection Policies and Laws

Besides understanding human nature and choosing collection appeals carefully after considering the debtor's past credit record, you and your assistants need also to know your firm's collection policies and government regulations. They may relate to various time limits on installment or mortgage late payments, foreclosures, and procedures regarding consumer credit and collections.

An effective collection policy necessitates bringing the debt to the debtor's attention *promptly* and *regularly*, with *increasing firmness* as the past-due period lengthens. Just how soon after payment due date the messages should be sent, and what you say in these messages, varies also according to the type of credit account, the particular debtor's situation, your firm's collection policies, and various legal aspects. (See Appendix A.) These factors also influence the time interval between collection messages and overall length of the collection process, as is discussed later in this chapter.

To summarize, the right attitude for collection messages requires tact, courtesy, consideration, fairness, firmness, and a positive viewpoint. It requires understanding of human nature, knowledge of collection appeals and the customer's past payment record, plus adherence to your firm's collection policies and government regulations.

COLLECTION STAGES

The first notification the customer receives after purchasing on credit or borrowing money on a loan is a statement (bill) or invoice showing the amount owed. This notification usually lists the transactions for the time period involved and states the terms and date of payment.

If the customer does not pay by the due date, you begin to send a series of messages called a *collection series*. Though the length, content, and collection methods of a collection series may vary according to circumstances, a well-planned series usually has three stages. The messages in each stage vary in number but usually follow a somewhat typical organizational plan and general assumption.

1. **Reminder** Stage	Plan:	Routine request
	Assumption:	Oversight
	Number:	Varies from 1 to 6 or 7
2. **Discussion** Stage	Plan:	Persuasive request (modified)
	Assumption:	Something unusual happened
	Number:	Varies from 2 to 5 or more
3. **Urgency** Stage	Plan:	Persuasive request (modified)
	Assumption:	Debtor may need to be scared into paying
	Number:	Usually 1 or 2

Regardless of stage in the collection procedure or other differences, all collection messages should make clear two facts—the amount due and the account number. Also, an easy-action envelope, perhaps postpaid, is appreciated and often speeds the reply.

Reminder Stage

Messages in the reminder stage are routine, direct requests. They range in number from one to several. In this stage, all you want to do is to jog the customer's memory. You first present the *main question or subject,* then *explain* (when necessary), and end the message by *requesting action.* You don't attempt to persuade by using any of the five appeals. Although some reminders—especially those sent to installment credit and slow-pay customers—might have a personalized inside address, generally they are obvious processed forms to avoid any suggestion that you are questioning the customer's integrity or ability to pay. They usually range from one or more standard statements (usually not itemized), to computerized card-size messages, to an obvious form letter on company letterhead stationery.

The statement(s) following the first one might include rubber-stamped or hand-written messages that say "Please" or "Perhaps you have forgotten" or colorful stickers like the four shown here (which can be purchased in quantities from a printer).

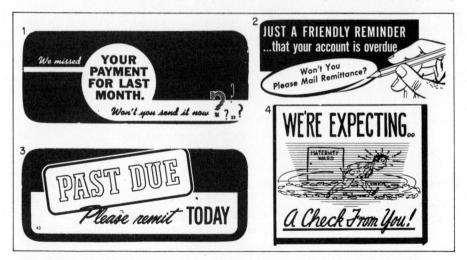

Shown below are examples of a computerized message and two short letter reminders which are obviously processed forms on the firms' letterheads:

Reminder 1

A computerized form 3¾ by 6½ inches in size on green pastel paper. A large department store sends it to a customer along with a second statement (and sometimes a leaflet advertising new merchandise items—for sales promotion).

Customers say they appreciate being reminded when their accounts are a little overdue.

So, we hope you will accept this reminder in the friendly spirit with which it is intended.

If our letters happen to cross and your check arrives in the next mail, please disregard this notice and accept our thanks for your payment.

Reminder 2

A short form-letter request from an oil company to a credit-card customer who had previously received a statement and a form-notice reminder.

Dear Customer

Main idea and amount due

It's easy to misplace statements and overlook form notices. That's why we're sending this letter to remind you of your balance amounting to $___.

Action

The account is somewhat past due and we would appreciate your sending us a check in the next few days.

Reminder 3

A processed form-letter reminder on savings and loan association letterhead—for one overdue installment.

Dear Mrs. Grown:

Main question

Have you overlooked the first payment on your account?

Explanation, with amount and date

As shown in your mortgage, your monthly installments of $___ are due on the ___ of each month. The first payment is now past due.

Action

Please send your remittance today and make future payments promptly so they will reach this office on time. If you have already mailed payment, please accept our thanks and disregard this notice.

Humor, witty short poems, anecdotes, and pictures that relate to the creditor's business or products can be quite effective—if they are used in the reminder stage—for small amounts. For example, some magazines use humor for subscribers who haven't paid. One method is to send only the front cover of their current issue, with a statement on the back: "Sorry, this is all we could send you this week." Then it includes brief resale on the magazine and a request for payment. Originality and good judgment are necessary, of course, for appropriate humorous reminders. Think seriously how the customer might react to humor. There's nothing funny about owing money or trying to collect money. Furthermore, what is funny to you might not be funny to another person.[1]

---

[1] For three other examples of unusual collection messages, see Exercise 2, pages 496–497.

Discussion Stage

If you receive no response after the routine-request reminders you sent to the customer, you progress into discussion stage messages that are *persuasive* requests. In this stage you usually personalize your messages by using an inside address and a salutation with the customer's name. You assume that something unusual has happened. For some reason unknown to you the customer cannot or doesn't want to pay. (Do *not* revert again to the "oversight" assumption used in the reminder stage.) *Your purpose now is to get the debtor to send the payment or at least an explanation*—if there is a reason for not paying.[2] Then you may be able to make mutually satisfactory alternate payment arrangements.

Depending upon the type of debtor and account, discussion messages range in number from two to five or more. To get the customer to read your messages, you will need to *attract attention* in the first paragraph. You try now to begin with a reader-interest theme—something beneficial, pleasant, interesting, and/or important to the reader. Your *desire-conviction-proof* paragraphs may include facts, figures, and reasons why the debtor will benefit by doing as requested. Well-chosen *appeals* (see pages 475–476) will help convince the customer and stimulate a desire to do what is right. Usually your first message is an inquiry, asking if something is wrong and inviting the customer to send either an explanation or a check; the positive "cooperation" appeal may be effective. Successive messages become progressively stronger, ending with a hint of negative appeal in the last discussion message. You may also include more than one appeal in any message.

Some small business and professional firms that have no collection department continue their collection efforts by merely attaching colorful discussion-stage stickers on their monthly statements showing amount due and the account number. Stickers like the following can be useful in the early part of the discussion stage.

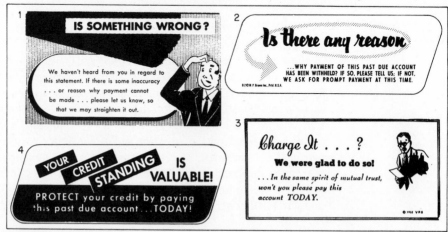

[2] Twice a year, according to the Federal Truth in Lending Act, creditors must mail to all credit customers a printed form titled, "In Case of Errors or Inquiries about Your Bill." (Creditors decide what months these will be sent; in large stores the mailing is automatically computerized along with two monthly statements a year.) This form explains rules about customers' rights and obligations if they question the accuracy of a bill. (See Appendix A.)

Some nonprofit organizations and other firms that must collect small amounts have used the cooperation appeal effectively with a simple short note like the following:

```
PLEASE HELP US KEEP COSTS DOWN.  By sending your check
with the enclosed bill now, you help us avoid the ex-
pense of sending additional reminders and letters.
That saves both postage and clerical expense . . . sav-
ings we can pass on to you our customers.

If possible, please mail your check or money order
promptly.  Thank you for your cooperation.
```

For more persuasive requests it is better to write personalized letters. If necessary, they can be essentially form messages—individually typed by computer or automatic or magnetic card typewriters—identical for many customers but personalized by insertions of the date and other variable information, as in letter 1. Notice how skillfully this letter avoids suggesting a negative idea about the reason for nonpayment. It does *not* ask if something is wrong with the store's merchandise or service or billing; yet if any of these should happen to be problems, the customer is free to mention them and thus help "to expedite any possible adjustment." Easy action is provided by lines at the bottom for the customer's reply and by an enclosed envelope.

Letter 1

A tactful, persuasive, personalized form letter from a department store to a good-pay customer.

```
                          Dear (Mr., Mrs., Miss, Ms. name):
```

Attention (compliment)	The privilege of serving you is certainly our pleasure. For this, we extend our sincere thanks.
Appeal (cooperation)	You have always been cooperative in the past by keeping your account paid on time according to your credit agreement. As we have received no remittance from you for over three months, we wonder if you have a question concerning the balance.
Request for reason or check	Whatever information you request will receive our prompt attention, as we want to expedite any possible adjustment. A note at the bottom of this letter will do. Then just mail it--or your check for $--in the enclosed envelope.
Easy action	
Goodwill	Your cooperation will be greatly appreciated.

Another popular way to attract attention and also make action easy is by a message that begins with this statement: "There Are Two Sides to Every Story." The rest of the message may be in the shape of an open book. The left side is marked "This Is Ours"; the right side, "This Is Yours." The creditor's "story" may be introduced by sentences like these: "Won't you give us *your* side of the story? If there is no question, how about sending your remittance right away . . . for the amount shown on the attached statement. YOU NOW HAVE THE FLOOR!"

In letter 2 a wholesaler includes several appeals to the mercantile customer. By reviewing the facts about the overdue account and mentioning the high-quality merchandise plus a willingness to help, the writer makes a fair-play appeal. In addition, the compliments on the dealer's good-pay record and the reiteration of the value of a favorable credit rating develop both pride and self-interest appeals.

Letter 2

An effective personalized letter from a wholesaler to a mercantile customer.

Attention (agreeable comment)	It would be nice if we could get together in person to talk over your overdue account with us, but the demands of our businesses and the distance make this impossible.
Facts; compliment	Your account is 80 days past the final due date on our terms of 2/10, net 30. This is exceptional, considering your past prompt payment record with us; and we would like to know what is wrong.
Pride; self-interest appeals	You have worked many years to establish your favorable credit rating, Mr. Jones. It allows you to stock high-quality furniture such as the Allwood chairs when you need them and even take advantage of a discount if payment is made within 10 days. You can have an adequate supply of merchandise on hand at all times, without maintaining a large amount of cash for working capital. Your credit rating not only makes conducting of your business easier but also allows you to establish yourself with new suppliers quickly and easily.
Fairness appeal	Is there anything we can do to help you overcome a difficulty? We want to be fair with you. I'm sure we can work some kind of a plan for payment that will be compatible with your situation. Of course, the most satisfactory solution would be a full payment of the $629.57 in the return mail. If you cannot manage this, then send us a frank explanation of the problem you are facing and we will see what plan we can come up with to clear your account.
Easy action, with suggested time	The enclosed envelope is addressed to come directly to my desk unopened, Mr. Jones. I hope to see it again next week with your check for the full $629.57 inside. If this is not possible, then use the envelope to send me a full explanation of your situation so that we can help you find a solution.

The writer of the next letter uses the positive pride and self-interest appeals plus the negative loss-of-comforts-and-advantages appeal. Even though this borrower owes three payments, the letter (from a bank's lending officer) avoids a scolding tone and tries to keep the customer sold on the values of home ownership.

Letter 3

A bank lending officer's helpful, persuasive request to a borrower for a home loan.

Attention *(pride appeal)*	You have probably often heard the statement, "There's no place like home."
Appeals to self- *and family interests*	You and your spouse made a wise decision when you invested in your present four-bedroom home. Close to schools, your church, and stores, it has the ideal location for your growing family. Your loan department personnel here at (*name of bank*) were glad to help you with financing by extending you the loan you needed three years ago.
Comfort, security	So that you can continue to enjoy the comfort and security of owning this home, it is important that you keep up your payments on your loan. Four messages have been mailed to you about the three payments that are now past due:

May 10	$252.00
June 10	252.00
July 10	252.00
Late charges	30.24
Total	$786.24

Easy-to-read facts

Economic self- *interest and* *risk-of-loss appeals*	It is easy to become so accustomed to a privilege that we take it for granted. You were fortunate to buy when you did, for today the same kind of home--even without the playroom and patio you have--would cost you at least $9,000 more, at a higher interest rate. You'll agree you can't afford to risk losing the comforts and advantages you now enjoy.
Action	So please send your check for $786.24 today or call me at (*number*) so we can discuss a satisfactory solution.

In any business you may find some customers who are repeatedly late in paying their bills. To such persons—who have in previous delinquencies received a variety of detailed letters from you (with inquiries and positive appeals), you may wish to concentrate on a negative appeal. The following letter emphasizes what the customer with a poor credit rating will experience.

Letter 4

A persuasive request with a strong fear appeal to the repeatedly late payer.

Attention	Just how valuable is your credit rating to you? If you possess a good rating, you are able to buy on a charge basis whenever necessary. You can buy ex-

Self-interest
appeal–positive

pensive items without paying the entire cost in cash
at time of purchase. Also, if an emergency arises,
your credit will be helpful.

Self-interest–
negative appeal

However, if your record in various places shows you
are a poor credit risk, this valuable possession of
credit will be lost. You are likely to be subjected
to the unpleasantness of drastic collection measures.
In addition, your credit reputation will follow you
wherever you go. It will take years to restore a
good rating. You may be deprived of items you would
like to purchase, because of the necessity for paying
cash.

These are facts. We mention them only so that you
will not take lightly the possible loss of your credit
which may follow unless your account with us is paid.

Action

It is still possible to salvage your credit reputation. Please use the enclosed envelope to mail your
check for $ (*amount*) today in payment of this account
which has been overdue since (*date*). If you cannot
pay it all immediately, you will find us willing to
discuss a definite arrangement to take care of it.
Please call me at (*number*).

For chronic "delinquents" you might omit the offer (in the last paragraph) to discuss a
payment arrangement and simply ask for full payment.

To customers who send only a partial, inadequate payment in answer to previous
collection requests, a department store sends messages similar to letter 5, with only a
mild fair-play appeal.

Letter 5

Acknowledgment of partial payment, and request for remainder.

Thank you for your recent partial payment; however, your account
still remains in a past-due condition.

This is not acceptable, unless prior arrangements have been made
with our collection department. You realize, we believe, that it
is only fair for you to pay in accordance with the payment agreement you signed.

Please send us the remaining amount due of $ today or contact me
immediately (206-333-9999).

Urgency Stage

During the reminder and discussion stages most messages may have been signed by
someone in the credit or collection department. In the urgency stage—for greater impact on the past-due customer—messages may be signed by a higher executive, such as
a vice president or even the president, in some firms.

Even in this last stage the messages still aim to keep the customer's goodwill. (Even when credit is no longer available, the customer may still purchase with cash.) These messages follow the persuasive-request plan and use the strongest appeal—fear. They mention the unfortunate consequences of collection enforcement if you must resort to drastic action, such as turning the account over to a collection agency or lawyer or repossessing the merchandise. You will usually tell the customer that you don't *want* to take this drastic action, but (because of your obligations to credit reporting agencies and company procedures) you must do so unless the debtor pays or explains.

Although you might feel exasperated and annoyed with the individual, you won't help your cause by showing anger, preaching, harassing, or using insulting remarks. In fact, you could get into a libel suit (see Appendix A). To protect yourself from legal problems, be sure to *get your facts correct, make no malicious or defamatory accusations, and see that your messages are in sealed envelopes addressed to the debtor personally.*

To offset the negativeness of the appeal to fear, it is often desirable to include at least one positive appeal—to give the debtor a chance to avoid the drastic action and extra costs. The action request is firm and definite about the amount the borrower must send and the office to which it should be sent.

As the following examples illustrate, you can use one or two messages in the urgency stage. If two, the first one doesn't set a date for the drastic action, but the final message *always* sets the date.

Example 1

First of two messages in the urgency stage.

Fairness; review of facts	The time has come when we must write the kind of letter we dislike very much. In previous letters we said about everything we could think of in urging you to pay your long-overdue bill, which is now $355.70. But we have received no replies to any of our requests.
Fear; self-interest; fairness	Must we now turn your account over to our attorney for collection? A lawsuit would require you to pay not only the bill but also the court costs. We don't want to do this without giving you one last chance to write and let us know your side of the story.
Self-interest; reader benefit	We have been good business friends for many years, (*name*). Please don't make it necessary for us to end our friendship in such an unpleasant way. Write us immediately--or better still, send us your check to pay this debt, now 115 days past due. But do it today, please!

If you are using only one letter in this collection stage, you can still use example 1, adding the following paragraph before the final one:

For that reason we will delay action for five days--until July 22--before turning your account over to Smith, Smythe, and Smothers.

If you feel that in the discussion stage messages you have given the debtor sufficient time to "discuss or pay" (especially when dealing with chronic late-payers), you might use a telegram or Mailgram as the first message in the urgency stage. According to Western Union, companies using Mailgrams report collection efficiency improvement of up to 70 percent.[3] You can, of course, send any length of message you wish. Here are two short messages that have shock value:

Example 2

Mailgrams as the first of two messages in the urgency stage—especially for chronic late-payers.

   a. YOUR ACCOUNT #____ WILL BE REFERRED TO AN OUTSIDE COLLECTION AGENCY. ONLY YOUR REMITTANCE FOR $____ WILL STOP FORMAL CREDIT ACTION. SEND IT TODAY.

   b. IMPORTANT YOU CALL COLLECT IMMEDIATELY (*TEL. NUMBER*) BETWEEN 8AM AND 4PM CENTRAL STANDARD TIME CONCERNING YOUR CREDIT CARD ACCOUNT NUMBER (____). PLEASE TELL THE OPERATOR YOU RECEIVED THIS MESSAGE.

Example 3

Final letter that sets a date. (Letter is signed by the collection manager or a vice president.)

Your account has just been referred to me, marked for "final action."

Because it is the policy of this company that every contact with our customers shall be one of courteous interest in their behalf, I am writing you this letter as a last appeal that you mail us your check for $623.02, or call personally to see us. I have withheld any action on your account and feel sure we can work out some mutually satisfactory arrangement for settlement.

I shall hold your account on my desk for 10 days, hoping that you will attend to it at once. Unless I hear from you by June 25, I shall have no alternative but to assign your account for collection. I anticipate you will not force me to take a step that would have such a serious effect upon your credit reputation.

Some firms collect almost entirely by Mailgrams, using discussion-stage as well as urgency-stage messages. If you wish, you can store your collection-letter formats on a Western Union computer and file with that company the names and addresses of customers. Then you simply direct Western Union to send, for example, "format 31" to customers 10 through 50 and indicate amounts due. Each debtor gets a personally

[3] *How to Excel in the Art of Friendly Persuasion,* The Western Union Telegraph Company.

addressed Mailgram. A lending officer, for instance, might send a message similar to the following, which includes her or his name and "Assistant Cashier" at the end.[4]

Example 4

Mailgram that sets a final date for payment of overdue installments.

> REPEATED REQUESTS HAVE BEEN MADE FOR PAST-DUE PAYMENTS ON YOUR LOAN AT OUR OFFICE. YOUR MANNER OF REPAYMENT IS UNSATISFACTORY AND WILL NO LONGER BE TOLERATED.
>
> WE MUST RECEIVE YOUR OCTOBER AND NOVEMBER INSTALLMENTS INCLUDING LATE CHARGES AND SERVICE FEES NO LATER THAN NOVEMBER 25. FAILURE TO MEET THIS REQUEST WILL FORCE US TO TAKE WHATEVER STEPS ARE NECESSARY TO PROTECT THE BANK'S INTEREST.
>
> PLEASE MAIL YOUR REMITTANCE FOR $_____ TO (*bank name*), P.O. BOX (*number, city, state, ZIP*).

Example 5

Final message that sets a date. This printed form goes to customers who live within the city which is within the jurisdiction of the specific credit bureau.

```
                                                    No. 1982
              Please Read This Carefully
                           _____ 19 __ ____
  To: _____

  _____
         Address              City              State
                It is the purpose of this notice to inform you, as a matter of courtesy, of our
  intention to assign your account to the  COLLECTION DEPT.,   (NAME) CREDIT SERVICES, INC.
         for collection unless your remittance is in our hands on or before _____ 19 ____
  This can be avoided if PAYMENT IN FULL is made on or before the above date, but you must ACT WITHOUT DELAY.
                             The amount is $_____
  (GUARD YOUR CREDIT        _____ (CREDITOR)
   AS A SACRED TRUST)       _____ (ADDRESS)
                             By_____

      Pay your bills in full TODAY So that your Credit will be good TOMORROW
```

---

[4] Courtesy of Tom Hardeman, sales representative, Western Union, Seattle, Wash., 1979. All employees handling telegrams and Mailgrams are (under the Communications Secrecy Act) bound to secrecy. They may not divulge content of any message or even that a communication was made between any two people. (For Methods of Sending Mailgrams, see page 149.)

VARIATIONS IN COLLECTION SERIES

As previously stated, the basic psychology and characteristics of collections are similar for all types of business. However, the number and frequency of messages and the degree of insistence within each collection series vary because of debtor's paying habits, type of account, and creditor's business situation. This section discusses variations and describes collection practices in three businesses.

Debtor's Paying Habits

Competent credit and collection departments adapt their procedures somewhat to debtors' paying habits.

The collection procedure must be flexible to take care of unusual circumstances relating to the debtor. The time intervals between messages are usually longer in the beginning of a series (reminder stage) than near the end (urgency stage). Whenever the customer explains the reason for lateness (and perhaps agrees to a new payment plan), your collection department should of course cease sending the usual messages at the former time intervals. Customers become justifiably irked if they continually receive duns after they have paid or made special arrangements for payment. Also, whenever the firm adjusts an account balance because of a customer's complaint about goods or service, *some* department (adjustment, accounting, credit, or collection) should inform the customer of the new balance and see that the "late-payment charge" is removed from future messages.

Debtors also affect the number of collection series a firm has. Because some customers are late with payments several times a year, the firm needs more than one collection series. It is desirable that debtors do not get the same messages twice.

Types of Accounts and Creditor's Business Situation

The collection policy for *installment* accounts is basically similar to that of *open credit* accounts, but there are differences. In general, with monthly installments, creditors tend to be somewhat stricter, because installments pile up quickly. As you know, some stores have installment accounts for large purchases which go over the customer's established charge account limits or for customers who do not have charge accounts.

If the goods are sold on a conditional sales contract, the seller retains the title to installment-purchased goods until the last payment has been made and may repossess if the debtor defaults. This fact can be an effective fear appeal. However, if market conditions are unfavorable for disposing of used merchandise, the creditor will prefer not to repossess, but will give the debtor a time extension that will ensure full payment on the purchased item. This arrangement will of course affect the collection procedure and messages sent.

In *mortgage lending*, because of various laws requiring foreclosure within certain periods of nonpayment (perhaps three months), the collection procedure is stricter than for charge account selling.

For *utility companies*—those providing telephone, gas, water, electricity services—the collection policies are likely to be stricter because each month's usage adds new charges. The fear appeal in these firms' urgency-stage collection messages is that the service will be disconnected after a certain late period.

Different business situations also affect collection procedures. The department store's relation to its thousands of retail consumer customers is different from the manufacturer's or wholesaler's relation to the retailer. Because the manufacturer or wholesaler typically has a relatively large volume of business with a relatively small number of customers, each credit situation is investigated individually and collection messages are likely to be individually geared to each dealer's problem. Letters may be fewer—and perhaps longer—than those of the department store collection department. For the latter, the volume of business with each customer is relatively small, but the total is important. Large department stores have elaborate series of collection notices, letters, and telephone messages. Some have 50 or more form letters to choose from. Yet, for the more important or complex situation the credit or collection manager will compose original, personalized letters.

Collection Practices of Three Diverse Businesses

To illustrate differences and similarities among collection series, brief descriptions of the actual collection practices of three diverse businesses—a large department store, a savings and loan association, and a large utility company—are given below.

Department Store

This organization for the first four months uses only computerized statements and duns.[5] A statement is prepared once each month for every account as of its billing date as long as a balance exists. All financial transactions which have occurred since the last billing date through the current closing date are identified.

The computer not only analyzes and evaluates many different conditions for each customer's account; with the information digested, the computer also automatically chooses the appropriate text from a selection of messages and automatically prints the customer's name, address, account number, and the chosen letter, incorporating into the body of the letter the exact amount owed (so current that it reflects payment received the day before). This entire procedure takes about two seconds.

[5] The facts for the department store come from a master's thesis by Richard Craig Anderson, for the Graduate School of Business Administration, University of Washington, Seattle, Wash., 1970, entitled "Collection of Past-due Accounts: A Study of the System Used by a Large Retail Store in a City of 500,000." Mr. Anderson has given permission to quote liberally from his material.

The schedule here refers only to the regular account—not to the flexible account, deferred account, or the 90-day account, each of which differs in length of the series but all of which follow the same format in the dunning sequence schedules. The collection department for this department store maintains twelve in-state and out-of-state offices. The number of credit or charge accounts at any one time varies somewhere between 250,000 and 305,000 accounts. In addition, there are another 100,000 to 125,000 dormant accounts. About 3.5 percent of the accounts that are opened at any given time are written off as bad debts. The number of accounts that are three or more months delinquent at any one time varies from 4,000 to 6,500.

After the first four months, the department store switches to manual communications (telephone, letter, and wire) to break the cycle of "no pays" that have built up; and a particular collector in the office becomes responsible to certain delinquent accounts. The telephone call is used throughout the collection effort that follows. After the initial telephone call, the collection effort follows no definite sequence. The collector uses extensively the telephone with personal letters and wires sandwiched in throughout the discussion and urgency stages.

The collector also uses personal, dictated letters either to confirm in writing what customers agreed to over the telephone or to remind them that they agreed to a payment plan and to ask why they have broken their promises. If the collector cannot reach customers by phone, one or more of five form letters is then used. Form letter 4 is sent on the store's attorney's stationery. Form letter 5 informs customers that they can still deal with the store; but if they do not, the next collection effort will come from the store's collection agency. (The average delinquency of accounts turned over for collection is eight months.)

In summary, the collection series for this department store consists of:

1. Computerized statements and duns that include the first statement, plus four monthly statements, three reminders, and two letters in the discussion stage.
2. Manual communications that complete the discussion and urgency stages. The store covers the urgency stage by telephone unless the past-due customer doesn't have a telephone; then it uses two form letters or wires.

Savings and Loan Association

The collection procedures of this particular savings and loan association are notable for the lack of any firm policy.[6] Even though the association services over 4,500 loans, it doesn't have a formal collection department. The responsibility for collections is shared between the accounting and the loan departments.

The first step toward the collection of a delinquent account is taken by the accounting department. Within 10 to 15 days after the due date of a loan, a first reminder is sent. A second, more strongly worded notice is sent if the account is still delinquent after 20 to 25 days.

When an account becomes one month delinquent, it is turned over to the loan department. An attempt at telephone contact is made by one of the two members of the loan department. If the individual involved cannot be reached by telephone, a brief letter is written. Both the telephone call and the letter are in the form of reminders, with emphasis on the importance of keeping the account current.

Each delinquent account two or more months past due is handled on an individual basis by the loan department. The action taken is generally determined by the association's past experience with an account.

---

[6] This association has assets of $72 million, one home office, and six branches.

Charges for late payments are 4 percent of total monthly payment on home mortgage loans, and 5 percent on consumer loans such as for autos, mobile homes, students, recreational vehicles.

Accounts three or more months past due are generally given a specific date by which the account must be current. Notice is given that if the account is not current by the specified date, it will be turned over to the association's attorney for foreclosure action.

As mentioned earlier, each of the more serious delinquent accounts is handled on an individual basis. As long as the association is able to maintain communication with the persons involved, it attempts to help them create a workable solution to the problems causing their delinquency. The association is very lenient and flexible in working with these accounts and will go to great lengths to avoid taking foreclosure action.

Utility Company (in a City with Population over 1 Million)

Practically all gas meters in this city are read on a bimonthly basis. The customer is billed within 10 days, and a 10-day net payment period is shown on the bill.

Fourteen days after the net payment period has expired, the credit and collection department is notified of all unpaid accounts totaling $10 or more by receiving gas collection statements together with two notices. The first or reminder notice is mailed immediately.

In most cases the second or final notice follows seven days later. The final notice bears a seven-day expiration date after which a collector may call and discontinue the service. If an account shows a good payment record, the final notice may be preceded by a special reminder letter. Or the final notice may be followed by a letter. These exceptions are made at the discretion of the collection reviewer, who directs the general collection activity.

TELEPHONE COLLECTION PROCEDURE

As the preceding discussions indicated, both written and oral messages can be effective for collecting past-due payments. Basically, the goals, attitudes, and procedures are similar whether you collect by written communication or through oral contacts—face to face or by telephone. You need also to be aware of prohibited collection practices.

The following quotation expresses some advantages of the telephone method:

Increasing use is being made of the telephone in collecting, both in early and late stages of the collection process, for this method, because of its directness, often succeeds where other methods fail. One of the chief advantages of this method is that it is somewhat surprising to the debtor and may, therefore, catch him unguarded with small alibis and grievances with which to excuse his delinquency. It furnishes the collector a good opportunity to impress him emphatically with the urgency of payment, varying the appeals as the need arises. Frequently, when the reason for nonpayment is understandable, although the failure of the debtor to communicate it is not, a plan of payment may be worked out, usually with a partial payment to be made immediately. Thus, by telephoning nearly all can be accomplished that could be gained by a personal solicitation. Telephoning, however, is often the speedier method, the more flexible, particularly in tracing skips, the less costly, even in the use of long-distance service, as long as it is used with efficiency and discretion.[7]

Because of the growing importance of the telephone in all three collection stages, this section focuses briefly on two special phases of telephone collection techniques: precall planning and the actual collection conversation.

Precall Planning

The steps a collector takes before an important telephone call—or a personal conversation—are similar to the first five planning steps before writing (see pages 96-101).

1. Determine Your Purpose
Besides the general goal of collecting the money and keeping goodwill, you probably have a specific purpose too. Be sure to check all previous letters, calls, and any response to them. Is your purpose now to work out a special payment arrangement? Or to remind the debtor of a promise made recently but not kept? Or to urge the debtor to pay by a certain date? Or to present an important decision?

2. Visualize Your Customer
First determine the right person to talk to. He or she should be the *only* one who is responsible for paying the bills. Try to judge whether the customer would respond better to a hard or a soft line. If the customer has just received the first overdue notice, your approach should of course be different from the approach to the customer who has ignored several previous contacts. Is the customer likely to be angry? Friendly? Cooperative? Hostile? The payment history is a good clue as to the way the customer will respond to your call.

3. Collect All Necessary Facts
(a) Determine if your own company is at fault. Were shipments and billings correct? Were all payments recorded? If you find errors, take time to have them corrected before calling the customer to bring the account up to date. *(b) Check the past payment record.* How often were the customer's payments delinquent in the past? How long past due is the account now? If the customer has been late only once in the last year, he or she will probably more readily accept a payment plan than the customer who has been delinquent most of the year.

4. Consider the Ideas to Cover
(a) Prepare the questions you'll ask the debtor to determine reasons for not paying bills on time. You'll want to make the customer feel that you are both on the same

[7]Theodore N. Beckman and Ronald S. Foster, *Credits and Collections,* 8th ed., McGraw-Hill Book Company, New York, 1969, p. 533.

side. Plan open-ended questions that allow the customer to do the talking rather than merely answering "yes" or "no." Good questions begin with the five W's—who, what, when, where, why, and the H—how. *(b) Be ready to present a payment plan.* This is the heart of precall planning. The payment plan must account for all the overdue payments, not just one or two; and it must include a *specific* schedule that will bring the overdue account to current status. Prepare to sell the plan to the customer in a positive way, without insulting or harassing statements.

5. Plan and Organize

Prepare an opening statement and—at least in general—the order in which you'll present the material you want to cover.

Analysis of the Collection Call

Like the well-written collection letter, the collection call should likewise be tactfully persuasive.[8] The conversation contains the following parts:

1. Opening Statement

After identifying yourself and your firm, state the reason for calling. Then use a strategic pause—about six seconds. It is important that the pause be used in every call. Experience shows that if the customer is sincere in the desire to pay overdue bills, he or she will offer to pay or give a reason for not paying as soon as the reason for the phone call is given. Many collection calls are completed successfully immediately after this strategic pause.

2. Fact-finding Questions

As you hear the customer's answers to your preplanned questions, try to determine whether the payment plan you designed is realistic. Be ready to adapt it to meet the customer's situation. When you can say to yourself—using either your original plan or a newly devised one—"This payment plan will get the account current, and it meets my company policy," go on to the next step.

3. Presentation of Payment Plan

You might begin to focus the customer's attention on your plan by statements like these: "Well, I've been thinking seriously about your account, (name), and have come up with a plan of action that will get your account right back on a steady course. . ."; or, "(name), I'm glad you mentioned that you wish there were a way you could get your account back up there without having to do it today. I believe there is. How does this plan sound to you?" At this point you have focused the customer's attention on the payment plan. Regardless of who proposes the plan or how it is altered, if the final plan is a schedule of payments that will result in an up-to-date account, it is a satisfactory arrangement.

If the customer agrees to a plan, you have been successful and can move directly to closing the call. However, if the customer does not agree to all or part of the payment plan, you must take further action—namely, overcoming objections.

---

[8] This section on telephone collection procedure is based on findings from the previously cited master's thesis by Richard Craig Anderson.

4. Overcoming of Objections

Almost always, objections are postponements—reasons for not agreeing to the payment plan now. Three basic steps you can take in overcoming objections are:

a. Determine specifically what the customer is objecting to. You can't overcome an objection until you know what it is.

b. Get agreement on those parts the customer is not objecting to. It may be that the customer's objection only concerns one of the payment dates in the plan. If so, get agreement on all the rest.

c. Work out the parts the customer objects to. If the objections are minor, you can compromise as long as the plan is specific and it gets the account current. However, if the customer's objections are serious, you should be sure that the reasons are valid. Then stress the benefits to the customer of paying and keeping the account current.

5. Closing Statement

Summarize the payment plan and thank the customer. The following is an example of a good close. "Fine, Mr. Dawes. Now let me summarize to make sure that I have everything straight. You are going to send me a payment of $41.20 on Friday, the 16th. I should have that on the following Monday. Then you will send another payment of $41.20 on Friday, the 23d, which I should receive on the 26th. That will bring your account up to date. Thank you very much, Mr. Dawes. Good-bye now."

After the call is finished, write down for future reference everything that was said. Note the pertinent information on a card and file it with any other information on the account. (Of course, if the customer does not abide by the terms of the agreement, you or another collector must take further action.)

Prohibited Collection Practices

During the entire collection procedure—written and oral—creditors have, of course, the right to demand payment from debtors. However, they must be careful not to do anything illegal. The Federal Communications Commission released a public notice (70-609) reminding creditors that it is a violation of the telephone company's tariff to use the telephone to frighten, torment, or harass a person. The following practices are prohibited:

1. Calling debtors at odd hours of the day or night
2. Repeated calls
3. Calls to friends, neighbors, relatives and children, making threats
4. Calls asserting falsely that credit rates will be hurt
5. Calls stating that legal process is about to be served
6. Calls demanding payment for amounts not owed
7. Calls to place of employment

In addition, it is a crime under federal law when collecting private debts to use in any communication the words *national, federal,* or *United States (U.S.)* to convey a false impression that such communication is from a government-related department, agency, or bureau or in any manner represents the United States. Furthermore, various state laws condemn threats of violence to a debtor's person, property, or reputation; false accusation of fraud; threats of arrest; anonymous calls; deceptive or misleading representations regarding claims; and other unfair practices.[9]

SUMMARY

A customer does not settle an account for one or more of the following reasons: overlooked paying, is temporarily short of funds, forgot to pay, dissatisfied with something, is a chronic debtor. When an account becomes past due, the creditor begins a collection series. Its goal is to collect the money and maintain goodwill.

A good collector must treat the customer with consideration, remembering the customer is also a human being and should be treated like one always. Furthermore, the collector must realize there are bound to be some customers who will not always pay when they should. And finally, the collector should try in every way possible to help a defaulting customer arrange to pay an account. The creditor does not want to sue, because everyone but the collection agency or attorney loses.

The collection series is a preplanned but still flexible procedure to collect from the past-due customer. It consists of three stages and five kinds of appeals. As the series progresses, each message makes greater pressure on the customer to pay. The length of the series and the insistence to pay depend on the credit record of the individual. Contacts with the customer can be by mail, telephone, wire, or personal visit. Messages by mail consist of statements, reminders, letters, and wires. A collector who uses the telephone or makes a personal visit, should be versed in the proper procedure, which includes precall planning and detailed analysis of the call (or visit). In all collection procedures—both written and oral—creditors must be scrupulously careful that their practices are within both federal and their state laws, and in keeping with company policies (if legal).

EXERCISES

1. Evaluate the effectiveness of the following early reminders that follow the statement(s). Which ones do you consider appropriate? Which ones do you consider inappropriate? Why?

Reminder 1

Obvious form letter on letterhead stationery from an oil company (added are the personalized inside address and salutation).

```
We know it is easy to lose a statement or forget to pay a bill,
particularly if it is a small one.
```

[9] Adapted from "Legal Phrases of Collections," *Credit Manual of Commercial Laws,* National Association of Credit Management, January 1979, pages 543–545.

In case one or the other happened in connection with your account for $\_\_\_$, will you consider this as a reminder to drop a check in the mail today?

Reminder 2

Personalized inside address and salutation with a typewritten body, on letterhead stationery from a bookstore.

We want you to know that we appreciate your patronage and we hope therefore that we will not offend you when we mention that we haven't received anything on your account since we sent you your statement.

We would appreciate it if you could send us something this month.

Reminder 3

Printed message on a 3¾- by 7-inch piece of paper from a department store. There is no salutation, and the inside address below the message also serves as the address for a window envelope.

It's such a small amount that you probably haven't bothered with it—only $\$\_\_\_$; nevertheless, we would appreciate receiving payment so that we may balance our books.

Reminder 4

Obvious printed message on a 5½- by 7-inch paper from a weekly newsmagazine. There is no inside address or salutation.

Just a brief note to repeat our thanks to you for your interest in (*name of magazine*) and for your order that will bring you its quick, complete, and competent news briefing in the many eventful weeks ahead. I feel sure you'll find both pleasure and profit in its pages!

And may I add another thanks—in advance—to you for taking care of the enclosed bill promptly. I've sent this copy in case our previous invoice was mislaid or overlooked.

And from all of us at (*name of magazine*)—sincere wishes that your (*name of magazine*) subscription will mean the best of good news to you!

2. Below are unusual collection messages. Which do you consider appropriate to send as reminders? Which would you not send? Give reason(s) for your decision.

Message 1

Below the personalized salutation appears the picture of a sad-looking man in old, patched clothes.

You have received some of my letters in the past which were epitomes of that stateliness befitting the true nobility of executive correspondence. That was when I was a dignified credit manager.

Time, circumstance, and necessity force me to be candid and tactless. Yes--I am the miserable wretch whose portrait appears upon this page.

I was reduced to this plebian state by being a virtuous paragon standing high on a pinnacle of patience, turning a kind ear and an open heart to all who owed past-due accounts. Then, one day not so long ago, those hounds of the apocalypse, my creditors, began gnashing and clawing until finally the pinnacle was torn asunder and I came crashing down into an ignoble plight.

I stand before you in my darkest hour. In this, my most perilous moment, I beseech you . . .

PAY YOUR COTTONPICKIN' ACCOUNT AND GET ME OUT OF THIS MESS ! ! ! !

Message 2

Obvious form letter with no inside address. Attached is a real paper clip.

No! That little paper clip in the upper left-hand corner hasn't been left there by a careless stenographer. That's Elmer, our pet paper clip.

His sole purpose in life, as you know, is to hold two pieces of paper together. But our Elmer has enlarged his scope of usefulness and has accepted two very definite tasks which we have asked him to do:

1. To securely hold your check for $4,286.61 to this note, which will clear up that little account we've talked about, and . . .

2. by doing so, to bind the amicable relationship which exists between our two companies.

Let's get this little matter under the bridge. What do you say?

Message 3

Obvious form letter.

Dear Customer

Cordially yours,
(*signature, etc*)

P.S. I'm practically speechless, but could whisper a hearty "thank you" for your check for $131.32 to clean up that balance on your June purchases.

3. Evaluate the following four collection messages. What improvements can you suggest in each for the discussion stage?

Message 1

Personalized letter throughout.

Dear Mrs. Kuper

This is not a dunning letter.

Neither is it an attempt to gloss over a serious situation with fancy language concealing a strong-arm attempt to pry money out of you.

Time and distance make it impossible for me to come to you for a friendly chat, so I must ask you to accept this letter as the next best thing. You owe us $84.25, long past due. You have always paid your commitments promptly. Therefore, there must be some special reason for your delay in this case.

I am not so much interested in the cause of this delay as I am in how we can help you over the rough spot. If one can't look to friends for help in times of stress, who on earth can one look to-- and I hope our past relationship entitles us to be classed among your friends.

We want our money, of course. But we also want to keep your friendship. I am sure we can accomplish both ends by being entirely frank with each other.

What is wrong? What can we do to help you?

I suggest you write me in full, in confidence. Perhaps between us we can work out some plan whereby you can take care of the past-due balance without crowding yourself too much and, at the same time, we can continue to make shipments to take care of your immediate needs.

Message 2

Obvious form letter with inside address and salutation typed in.

You must have a good reason for not having paid anything on your account after our recent letter--we are sure of that. But you do not tell us what the reason is.

If we only knew what the situation is, no doubt some arrangement could be made that would relieve your mind of the worry of an overdue debt, and satisfy us, too.

If you can, send in a part payment with your answer. Whether you can do that or not, at least tell us just what is wrong. Give us a chance to help. What do you say?

Message 3

Form letter with inside address, salutation, amounts, and account number typed in; signed by someone in "Collection Department."

Your payment history indicates that our Flexible account is more suitable to your needs. The Flexible account requires a monthly payment of approximately 10% of the balance and assesses a finance charge of 1% per month (12% per annum) of the previous month's balance. Finance charges may be avoided by paying in full each month.

The Regular account, which you now have, requires that the full balance be paid each month to avoid delinquency. If you wish to retain this type of account please remit the balance of $____ in the enclosed envelope.

If you wish to convert your account to a Flexible, please fill out and sign the enclosed application and return it along with your first monthly payment of $____ and the change will be made.

Message 4

Personalized inside address and salutation, typewritten body. Dated May 31.

Over a hundred and fifty years ago Sir Walter Scott said, "Credit is like a looking glass, which, when once sullied by a breath, may be wiped clear again; but if once cracked can never be repaired." The importance of a good credit rating has not changed today.

The barbecue you bought at Wardman's in January will continue to give many hours of enjoyment as you use it in your backyard this summer. We, however, have become concerned about your account listing that purchase. It is past due almost four months. Because of our satisfactory past dealings with you, we feel there must be something wrong, but you have not indicated this by a response to the other letters sent to you.

Because of your very active participation in community affairs, you can realize the importance of having a high credit rating in order to keep in good standing with the other merchants about town. Your good rating was given to us originally by the Lakeview Merchants' Credit Association, of which we are a member. Our agreement with these people requires that we report all those accounts that are seriously past due. Because this is such a serious action, we always wait with our better customers like you hoping for an explanation or, preferably, payment of the past-due account. In keeping with the Credit Association's requirements, we, however, will have to refer your name to them by June 5.

To keep your credit "glass" from being broken, just mail your check for $71.60 to us in the enclosed prepaid envelope. Then come to the store and see the new attachments and utensils for outdoor cooking, which you will continue to enjoy this summer.

4. The following letters are from different firms to customers who have either monthly *installment* accounts or who receive *utility services* monthly. Compare and evaluate them regarding: considerate tone, appeals, and strictness in collection policies. Which one(s) do you prefer? Why? Can you find any serious errors?

Letter 1

Personalized form letter signed by the manager of a credit corporation, to a borrower when the first monthly payment was six weeks overdue.

Your account was referred to me this morning as SERIOUSLY DELINQUENT. Upon reviewing it, I am indeed surprised that it is not up to date in payments. You have been extended every courtesy both by notice and letter, but there has been no response.

We go through the above-mentioned courtesies when an account becomes delinquent for a few days. Almost 100 percent of our customers APPRECIATE A COURTEOUS NOTICE AND MAKE PAYMENT PROMPTLY. Your FAIL- URE to do so, therefore, AMAZES us.

Your account is seriously past due. IS IT NECESSARY FOR US TO TAKE ANY FURTHER ACTION OTHER THAN WRITE THIS LETTER IN ORDER TO HAVE YOU SEND THIS AMOUNT BY RETURN MAIL?

Letter 2

Personalized inside address and salutation added to an obvious printed message on letterhead stationery from an electric power company.

Since you are one of our new customers and we have been unable to reach you by telephone, we are taking this opportunity to write to you to discuss your electric light account.

We would like to explain briefly our billing practices so that you will have a better understanding as to how our bills are rendered and when they are considered due. Bills are mailed to you five or six days after the date appearing on the bill and are due and payable upon receipt and become delinquent in fifteen days. However, if there is some particular time during the current month which is more convenient for you to pay your bill, will you please notify us so that we can note our records and in this way eliminate any unneces- sary treatment in the handling of your account?

According to our records the statement recently mailed has not been paid. If there is some question regarding your bill, please call our business office at (*telephone number*) or come to our office at (*address*). Unless you wish to make other arrangements, we will appreciate receiving your payment within the next five days.

We welcome the opportunity of furnishing you with the electricity service and hope that we may continue to be of service to you.

Amount due: $_____ .

Letter 3

Personalized letter (dated February 28) from a real estate loan department to a borrower for a home loan.

Re: Loan No. 8-888888

Dear Mr. and Mrs. Green:

It has come to our attention that your account is presently delinquent for your February 1 payment plus late fee of $5.90, for a total
of $171.90. In addition, your March installment of $167.00 will be
due and payable tomorrow, at which time your full arrearage will
amount to $338.90.

This is to advise you that unless the full sum of $338.90 is re-
ceived in this office on or before March 6, your account will be
placed before our board of directors for review, with a recommendation of immediate referral to counsel for legal action.

Sincerely yours,

5. The following collection messages fall within the urgency stage. Your job is to
   determine whether each message is effective. In your evaluation, ask yourself
   whether the wording is too strong or not strong enough, whether the writer is
   still trying to help the individual, and whether the message accomplishes the
   twofold job of collecting the money and retaining the goodwill of the customer.

Message 1

Personalized inside address and salutation, typewritten body. Dated March 8.

It seldom becomes necessary for us to turn an account over to an
attorney for collection. And on those few occasions when circumstances leave us no other alternative, we consider it only fair to
tell the customer exactly what we intend to do.

Certainly, you must realize that we have made every effort to be
fair and patient in requesting that you settle your January account
of $205.40. We have written to you several times, asking that you
let us know how we could cooperate with you in getting this indebtedness straightened out.

Your continued silence leaves us no other alternative than to refer
your account to our attorney for collection--a step that we sincerely
regret. So won't you respond to this final appeal for your cooperation and thereby avoid a procedure that can only mean embarrassment,
inconvenience, and additional expense to you?

Unless we hear from you by March 22, we shall be compelled to transfer your account to the office of our attorney. Please use the enclosed reply envelope to let us hear from you.

Message 2

Personalized inside address and salutation, typewritten body. Dated October 16.

A short time ago you and Ed Taylor registered in our hotel on September 18 and stayed two days, checking out the 20th. The rate on this room is $20 per day. Our clerk, Mr. Newcomer, was on duty (his first day) when you checked out and he made an error and collected for only one day. You still owe us for that, and while Mr. Newcomer wrote you he would have to stand good for the $20 we thot you would send it to us. However you probably didn't give it much thot and perhaps have forgotten it. So we will appreciate your sending this to us at once.

For we are sure you would not intentially dismiss the subject and refuse to pay.

However, if this is not paid by November 1st, we are forced to turn the account over to the American Hotel Association and they would print your name in all the hotel magazines as one not paying hotel bill which would go to every hotel in the U.S.

I know you are a fine fellow and will take care of this. For we do appreciate the visit you made us and we want you to come back next time you are in (*city*). American (*name*) Show is now on. It's a wonderful show. Why don't you come see it.

Message 3

Obvious form message without an inside address. This message appears printed on the inside of an envelope that the customer puts together and uses to send in the money owed.

You have disregarded the several reminders sent to you regarding the amount overdue on your account and I am wondering whether you realize the importance of making payments as agreed. You have even ignored my requests to call at the office so that this matter might be discussed. Now, two payments are past due.

The agreement that you signed provides that the merchandise is our property until fully paid for. I have not made any attempt to exercise our rights because I believed it unnecessary in your case. However, if you continue to disregard my letters, I shall be forced to proceed with more drastic measures.

I am, therefore, giving you seven days to pay the amount shown below. Our future action depends entirely upon you.

6. The Denison Tire and Battery Company was established in your town for the purpose of providing service stations and small garages with resale merchandise at low prices. You stock first-line merchandise at reduced prices so that your customers can more effectively compete with the large chain stores and discount houses. At the low prices you charge the service stations and garages, all understand that any

purchases from you must be paid within 10 days of the delivery date. (Otherwise, you could not afford to keep the prices so low because of the high cost of doing credit business.)

The C, M, and T United Oil Company Service Station at 1001 Broadway ordered $271.89 worth of tires, batteries, and fan belts on July 14. Your truck delivered them on July 16 and you expected payment no later than July 26. It is now August 1 and the bill has not yet been paid.

Write to C, M, and T United Oil Company Service Station and remind the owners of the overdue account. Be strict, but remember that this is the first time that C, M, and T has been late in payments; perhaps a mere oversight is involved. Ask for payment by return mail; enclose a stamped, addressed return envelope; and try to keep the goodwill of the station management.

7. You are the manager of a swimming school that offers swim lessons as its main service. Nine sessions cost $27. Each class is small, no more than five children. Your office requires parents who sign their children up for lessons to pay a $5 registration fee and the balance—$22—on the first day of the lessons.

Just recently Mrs. Richards signed three of her youngsters up for lessons. You had a terrible time getting her to pay the registration fee. Although you tell your customers that if they don't pay a registration fee, you cannot hold a space for them, you do not often follow through with the threat, since people usually pay the fee. Mrs. Richards finally did come through with the registration fee, but when the lessons began, she asked if she could wait to pay the $66 balance.

It is now the third lesson and she still hasn't paid. Furthermore, you learn that she placed a fourth child in a class on the second lesson, without paying the registration fee or balance. You checked with the instructor to find out how this happened, and he explained Mrs. Richards said that the office had told the child to be in the class. The instructor was new and didn't realize that such an action was highly irregular.

You must explain to Mrs. Richards that if she wants her fourth child in class, she will have to register and pay the balance. Also, you want to remind her of the outstanding balance. You have tried to telephone her, but no one ever answers. She didn't accompany the children for their last lesson, either. She owes you $93, including the fees for the fourth child, and you want to collect. Write a letter that will get the money and at the same time keep the goodwill of Mrs. Richards. You feel she has plenty of money because she lives in a very exclusive residential area and you notice her name often on the society page of the local newspaper.

8. As controller for Apex Corporation, manufacturers of plastic toys and specialties, you need today to write a personalized collection letter. You have just received today (July 25), from the U&I Distributors, a check for $182.37 in payment of your May 5 invoice of $213.16. You note they have deducted $4.26 cash discount, which you can't allow because of late payment. With terms of 2-10 E.O.M., this invoice should have been paid by June 10; but this customer's check was dated and mailed more than a month later. Also you need to know why they

deducted the $26.53; so far as your records show, there is no such amount anywhere. Write them an appropriate inquiry and request for their payment in full.

9. You are a "collector" in the department store described on pages 489–490. The delinquent account of Mr. Joseph A. Burns (628 Park Dr., Woodbury, NY 11797) was turned over to you two months ago. At that time, Mr. Burns's account (#567-555-7601) was four months overdue and he owed the store $433.02 for purchases made five to six months ago.

Your first step was to call Mr. Burns for an explanation of why he had not made payment. Mr. Burns was apologetic and sounded somewhat embarrassed, as his account had never been delinquent before. He explained that his family had some unexpected medical bills and that he had been laid off his job in a manufacturing firm for two months because of a labor strike against a supplier. As a result, he had gotten behind in his payments to all his creditors.

As skillfully as you could, you tried to reassure Mr. Burns that your store wanted to be fair and could appreciate his problem. You offered to work out a repayment plan which would stop the collection messages and help him recover slowly. Mr. Burns agreed to pay $70 per month on the account until it was paid off. You confirmed the agreement in a letter and, the following week, you received a check from Mr. Burns for $70. However, you did not receive his check this month and your efforts to talk to him by phone have failed. (Either no one answers the phone or, when someone does answer, you are told that Mr. Burns is not available.)

Now you must write a letter to Mr. Burns to ask why he has broken his promise. Because you believe that Mr. Burns sincerely wants to take care of his account, you will offer to keep the agreed-upon repayment plan in effect if he sends you a check for $70 or more within a week and if he continues to send monthly checks until the account has been cleared. Write the letter, using the appropriate appeals.

10. You are credit and collection manager of the Midtown TV and Electronics Sales Company. Yours is one of the three major such stores in the city. Mr. James Johnson, a resident of your city, has been a credit customer of yours for six years, and his record is "good."

On February 10 this year Mr. Johnson bought a portable tape recorder for $72.90 and charged it to his account. March 1 you sent him a bill for this amount, due March 10. April 1, since you had not heard from him, you sent a second bill. May 1 you sent a third bill, with a sticker at the bottom saying, "You Forgot, Didn't You? Please mail us a check now—while you have it in mind." On June 10 the account is considered 90 days overdue. Address a discussion letter to Mr. Johnson, offering to help any way you can. Make the basic purpose of your letter a reply from him—either a remittance, a letter, a phone call, or a personal visit. Prepare the letter as a form message with a personal inside address and salutation. Make it sound personal, but write it so that the body is applicable to any "good" customer with an account 90 days overdue.

11. Prepare a second urgency-stage collection letter for Mrs. Marion Esterwood, 657 West College Avenue, Fort Washington, PA 19034. (You are assistant credit and collection manager for Millstream Contemporary Furniture Showcase of Allentown, Pennsylvania.) Millstream's policy is to repossess furniture after the fifth payment is missed unless the customer and you can agree on and implement a reasonable alternative payment plan.

   Four weeks ago, you notified Mrs. Esterwood that repossession of her dining room suite, according to the terms of her conditional sales agreement, would be the logical action to take if she did not bring her account up to date or make some other payment arrangements. She had missed four monthly payments of $110 each and since then has made repeated promises to make payments, but so far she has paid nothing. Now she is five months behind in her payments.

   Your letter will be the last letter in the collection series. State clearly (but with an air of reluctance) that her dining room suite will be repossessed two weeks from today unless full payment of $550 is made, or another course of action is mutually agreed upon. For greater impact, this letter will be sent by certified mail and signed by one of the partners in the business. Although you must use the strong fear appeal and develop the unpleasant consequences of your drastic action, you still want to maintain Mrs. Esterwood's goodwill as a potential cash customer. Therefore, incorporate one positive appeal.

12. Assume you are assistant manager of Quality Hardware, a neighborhood store carrying a complete line of hardware and electrical supplies. The store is located in a fast-growing, attractive residential section of your city; and there is only one other, but very small, hardware and variety store in the same shopping district. Most of your credit customers are homeowners, living within two miles of the store, and you are at least casually acquainted with most of them. Being active participants in the social life of the community, they are mentioned frequently in the society columns of the local newspapers.

   You have made a list of those customers whose accounts are more than three months overdue—with balances of between $30 and $150—and who have not used their accounts since they became past due. Assume you are including on this list only those customers who have never before been seriously delinquent on payments to you, though they have all been trading with your store for two to five years. You are not worried about their eventual payment, but you would like to collect these accounts now to reinvest the money tied up in them. The following reminders have already been mailed to these customers:

   An itemized statement

   A second, un-itemized statement with a sticker, "Your prompt attention to this account will be appreciated."

   A mild letter of reminder, suggesting that payment of the account has been overlooked

   A stronger reminder, appealing to cooperation in paying up

A third letter based on the fair-play appeal, indicating that you have supplied quality merchandise at moderate prices, have waited patiently for payment, and feel sure the customer will show fairness by paying the amount due

Today is November 20. You decide to write a friendly, informal "discussion" letter with a definite request for an answer or preferably a check. It is to be essentially a form letter, but as it will be personally typed for each customer, you may have some variable paragraphs. (Indicate the variables by parentheses.) Probably the most effective appeals will be to pride, self-interest, or loyalty to your store. Each of these customers will naturally wish to protect his or her credit standing in the community and maintain a record of reliability as your charge customer. As you are a member of the local Retail Hardware Merchants Credit Association, your collection department automatically reports to the association the names of customers whose payments are seriously past due. If you mention this, do so not as a threat, which might offend the customer, but as an indication of your honest desire to protect the customer's credit reputation. Try to induce each customer to pay the past-due account immediately, or at least to make definite arrangements for payment. Be so courteous and tactful that you will retain the customer's goodwill and patronage.

13. Assume that you are the credit collection manager for the Skyway Airlines, whose air routes extend throughout the United States and overseas. The extensive routes that your planes travel make your airline very popular. In addition to the popularity that your airline already enjoys, your company has attempted to increase its passengers even further by offering a variety of credit plans to encourage travel.

    One plan that your company offers is a credit card that will allow a passenger to charge up to a limit of $800 for trips. The terms of the air travel credit card account are payable in full upon receipt of the bill.

    During the month of September, Ms. Cheryl Farmer, one of your credit card customers, charged several trips to her air travel credit card. The total amount of charges was $500. When Ms. Farmer mailed in her payment for September, she sent only $200 with a note that she would pay the remaining $300 in $100 installments.

    As credit collection manager, write Ms. Farmer a personal letter and request the full balance to be paid within 10 days. She has been a good-pay customer in the past, but you must reluctantly tell her that credit privileges will be withdrawn until full payment is made. After full payment has been received by your office, full credit privileges will be restored. In your letter, reexplain the terms of the credit card account, but try to keep her as a customer. Prepare this letter for the signature of the president of Skyway Airlines.

14. You are the credit manager of High Fashion Apparel, Inc., of Dallas, Texas. Your stylish women's apparel is expensive and the style itself is often short-lived. Buyers who order your merchandise for their stores are aware that you allow no returns. You have few collection problems—and those few you do have are either with new accounts or with small business operations.

In today's mail was an order from the Fan Fair Boutique, which is located in the Northwoods Mall in Pontiac, Michigan. This is the first time that Fan Fair Boutique has ordered any merchandise from you, and none of your salespersons has ever called on that store. In the order letter Mrs. Levand Royal, the buyer from Fan Fair, stated that one credit reference which could be used was the Upright Leather and Suede Company of Detroit. She also stated that her store was rated by Dun and Bradstreet.

Your first act was to call Dun and Bradstreet to inquire about the credit rating of Fan Fair Boutique. The information you received was not exactly negative, but it did raise some doubts in your mind. Your next action was to call the credit manager of Upright Leather and Suede Company in Detroit to ask about the experience of that firm with Fan Fair. That answer was somewhat similar to the Dun and Bradstreet report—not conclusive: sometimes slow pay; a few returns; questionable (mostly from inexperience) business practices.

Write to Mrs. Royal at Fan Fair Boutique and suggest that her order can be filled in the following manner. The total amount of her order ($365.80) should be paid, in advance, as this is her first transaction with High Fashion Apparel. Remind her of the stylishness of the clothing and customer recognition of your label (resale), that it will take about three weeks for her ordered apparel to be custom made and delivered, and that the processing cannot begin before her check for $358.48 arrives. She gets the 2% discount which is given to those who pay for an order within 10 days (the commonly used 2/10, net 30 terms) and this makes her net cost $358.48 plus freight. You will bill Fan Fair for the delivery charges, after shipment, on a separate invoice on which you expect immediate payment.

Remember that this is a first order and you hope to receive future business, so keep goodwill in mind while writing. Remind her that your salesperson in the Midwest area, Jane Mason, will visit Fan Fair on her next trip to Michigan. Tell her, too, that High Fashion Apparel, Inc., will have a booth at the national fashion show which will be held in the Chicago Merchandise Mart during April, and that you hope she will stop by and introduce herself.

Because this exercise is for a mercantile credit refusal, you may wish to review the suggestions on pages 284–285 before writing your refusal letter.

Goodwill Messages

So far, the messages you have studied are necessary in the usual course of business. Their chief purpose is to take care of day-to-day problems through requests, replies, and announcements. In contrast, the letters and memos covered in this chapter are not absolutely essential or required for the operation of a business. Their main purpose is to convey a friendly, usually unexpected, message that builds goodwill.

Besides being friendly, unexpected, and outside the usual course of business, goodwill messages have several other characteristics in common. Their organizational plan resembles *a good-news or neutral message*—most important idea first, then brief comments and details (if any), and a final cordial ending (if needed). Like all letters, goodwill messages should be honest and sincere and avoid gushiness or wordiness. They can be sent to the reader's home or office. Depending upon their content, destination, and quantity, goodwill messages may be typewritten, handwritten (for an extra, personal touch), or printed, perhaps on special paper appropriate for the occasion or season. Unlike most business letters, however, genuine goodwill messages should not contain statements that try to sell the reader on buying additional products or services. Most people dislike messages that pose as "goodwill only" letters but that actually have strings attached.

A genuine goodwill letter is almost always favorably received, for at least two reasons:

1. The writer presumably is not sending the message because of some business scheme.
2. The message comes as a pleasant surprise, for the recipient doesn't expect it. Bills will come if money is owed, but a thank-you from the seller for paying promptly or congratulations for winning an honor or celebrating a special anniversary isn't expected.

An important value of goodwill messages is that their effects sometimes develop months, even years, later. Because these messages reach out in a pleasant, friendly way to readers, they are remembered when the recipients want to buy products or services. Especially when competing firms sell goods of almost identical quality and prices, customers tend to buy where they get that extra ingredient—service with friendly, personal consideration and appreciation. Thus, although goodwill messages omit sales talk, they are actually an excellent way to promote business, as the following discussion and examples illustrate.

Thoughtful persons—especially executives—often write messages designed to foster friendly relations with customers, suppliers, and others by:

1. Congratulating or giving deserved praise
2. Expressing appreciation
3. Extending seasonal greetings
4. Conveying sympathy
5. Welcoming and/or offering favors
6. Showing continuing special concern

CONGRATULATING OR GIVING DESERVED PRAISE

A sincere, enthusiastic note of congratulations or deserved praise—sent promptly—can have an unforgettable impact on the recipient, especially because not many people take the initiative to send such messages.

Congratulatory Messages

The opportunities for congratulating are numerous, for congratulations may relate to any significant news about an individual's business, family, or personal achievements. For instance, you might congratulate a business executive when her firm has opened a new branch, reached its twenty-fifth or fiftieth anniversary, moved to larger quarters, attained a publicized milestone in total volume of sales, received a well-known award for distinguished service to the industry or community, or achieved special favorable publicity. You might congratulate an individual when he or someone in his family has made a significant achievement or won an honor. Among the events and activities that merit congratulations to an individual are: election to an office; promotion; graduation; birth of a child; winning a competitive contest, scholarship, prize; making an outstanding speech; writing a good magazine article or book; performing well in a theater, debate, or other public gathering.

When you write a congratulation, "talk" informally and enthusiastically—without flattery—as you would in a personal contact with the recipient. Focus on your reader instead of on yourself. And write promptly—as soon as possible after you learn the good news. The letters below are examples of various congratulatory messages. Letters 2 through 6 are well written. Letter 7, though it begins with congratulations, is really a sales letter, not a genuine goodwill message.

Letter 1

A stilted, writer-centered congratulatory note about a promotion.

I have just read that you have been promoted to vice president of your company.

I am sure your attainment unequivocally substantiates the exemplary service you are giving your employer. I believe you can be justifiably proud of your outstanding performance in the industry.

I forward my heartiest congratulations and wishes for your continued success in your endeavors.

Letter 2

A revision of letter 1, with improved tone and word choice.

Your promotion to vice president of General Construction Company was great news. I was happy to read about you in this week's Trade Press.

If ever a person deserved company recognition, you do. Your courage and hard work in developing new ways to promote the services of your firm have won the admiration of many, including your competitors.

Congratulations to you--and best wishes for your continued success!

Letter 3

A banker congratulates a businessperson on an election. (A similar note brought the banker who wrote it millions of dollars of business in installment loans.)

Congratulations, (*name*)

. . . upon being elected president of the Westside Lumber Dealers Association, as announced in yesterday's Times.

Under your capable leadership, this organization will reach a new high in activity and service.

Letter 4

A manager congratulates a customer for favorable publicity about the customer's business.

Heartiest congratulations to you on the splendid progress you have made with your poultry plant! It was a real pleasure for me to see your picture and read the feature article about your new cage house in the May issue of American Poultry Journal.

Verna Barns has spoken enthusiastically of your model operation and the excellent job you are doing. This article and its labor-saving suggestions have already been filed for future reference in our "idea" folder.

On my next field trip to Minnesota I want to meet you personally and visit your place. My very best wishes to you for your continued outstanding results with Erving's Chicks.

Letter 5

A vice president congratulates a scholarship winner.

Dear (*first name*):

We extend to you hearty congratulations upon your selection as the winner of the Beakins & Worth Foundation's scholastic award for excellence in accounting for 198_ at the University of (*state*).

Your achievement should be a source of pride to you, to your professors, and to your university. It is to young people like yourself that the accounting profession and the business and civic community look with confidence for their leaders of the future.

The best of success to you!

Sometimes, in addition to congratulating a person, you may want to send along a clipping of a picture or article published concerning the event. Some firms have specially designed folders to which such clippings may be attached with scotch tape or clips. Printed on the outside cover may be a message like "Congratulations," or "You're in the News," together with the company's trademark. For instance, the Carnation Company (dairy products) used a folder that pictured on the outside three carnations under the words, "Carnations to You!" On the inside is an attractive design and this message:

```
We Read With Interest . . . The attached clipping about you and
                              thought you would be interested in
                              receiving our copy.

At Carnation we are always pleased to read about those people who
help make the Northwest such a wonderful place in which to live.
```

Sending an invitation or an inexpensive gift along with the congratulations, as in letter 6, can be an effective way to build goodwill. However, many other letters that begin with congratulations are actually not true goodwill messages, but disguised or obvious sales messages, like letter 7.

Letter 6

A retail store sends layettes with congratulations to parents of twins. [Letterhead states: "Headquarters for clothes from crib to college." Salutation is "Dear Mr. and Mrs. (name)."]

```
May Barons add their congratulations to the many you have already
received.  It is a pleasure to send two layettes for your twin
arrivals on April 23, 198_.

Your babies will no doubt model all garments beautifully.  We are
happy to send you these "double congratulations" for your doubly
happy event--with compliments of Barons.

You can expect the layettes by mail within a few days.  May you
have many happy days and years ahead.
```

Letter 7

An obvious processed form message on a special letterhead picturing a baby and many toys. (This is a sales letter. Salutation is "Dear Parents.")

```
     Congratulations! . . . for this is a proud time for you.  And
your new baby is going to give you reason for pride for many years
to come!

     To help you during this period of extra expenses . . . WE EXTEND
THIS SPECIAL INVITATION TO YOU TO SEE US FOR THE CASH YOU NEED.
```

You are invited to come in with the enclosed MANAGER'S INVITATION at your earliest convenience. You can get a Cash Loan, up to the amount shown, to pay doctor and hospital bills, buy things for the new baby, pay old bills, or for any other purpose.

Come in today. Bring the special INVITATION with you. Choose from our several popular plans. Receive the MONEY promptly!

Messages with Deserved Praise

In addition to congratulating people for various achievements that are in the news, you may also find reason to give deserved praise for good service that has not been publicized.

For instance, you might compliment your employee(s) on exceptionally fine work —perhaps for achieving a new high record of sales or accuracy or attendance or other performance. Also, as a customer, you might write to a company executive to tell about unusually good service you received from his or her employee(s). Such sincere praise, judiciously given, is appreciated by both the executive and the employees; often the sincere compliments stimulate recipients to do even higher-quality work.

Sometimes your praise of employee service must be general, as in letter 8, because you do not know who performed the work for you.

Letter 8

A bank director praises a laundry's service by writing to its general manager.

You may be glad to know how much I like your Troy Laundry service on my shirts. Every morning I have a pleased grin as I pull one of your immaculately laundered shirts out of the smooth plastic case. Exactly the way I like it!

For the past dozen years or so I've tried several different laundries. But so far Troy has topped them all. I like the way your employees and machines roll my shirt collars neatly, press the shoulders without a wrinkle, AND sew on buttons whenever they're missing.

Your TV commercials first attracted Troy to me. I'm glad to tell you that I found everything those commercials say is true. Congratulations--and thanks!

Whenever possible, the person(s) you want to praise should be mentioned by their name(s) or identifying number(s). Military personnel appreciate words of praise, as shown in the following example. A retired *Army* sergeant, after being treated in an overseas *Navy* hospital, wrote to the commanding officer of the overseas U.S. Naval Regional Medical Center, expressing grateful praise for the "highly qualified and dedicated" medical personnel. He included names of two doctors and three assistants and then praised also "the unseen and unsung people in the laboratories, supply, kitchen, and other departments who help make things run smoothly." A few days later he received from the commanding officer the following pleasant reply, typewritten on official stationery in memo format:

Letter 9

(Memo) *A Navy commanding officer's reply to a letter of praise.*

> Your letter in appreciation for the care you received has been for-
> warded to all personnel concerned. A copy will be available in the
> appropriate records of those whom you named for commendation.
> It is gratifying to know that there are recipients of our health
> care delivery efforts who are not only appreciative of our endeavors
> but also willing to express that appreciation in a letter.
> You can be assured that your expression of satisfaction will enhance
> the motivation of the involved staff members not only to continue
> their good work but also to strive for improvement.

The results of the commanding officer's memo were partly indicated by the appreciative comments the sergeant received later from various staff members and the fact that more people at the dispensary addressed him by name.

From time to time you will encounter employees—salespeople, bus drivers, police officers, teachers, clerks, and many others—whose service to you is far beyond the call of duty. A sincere note of praise written to the employee's superior has sometimes brought unexpected benefits to an otherwise unnoticed employee. One of many true stories with a happy ending began when an airline passenger wrote a letter to the company president praising an employee (Paula) who had traveled 26 miles in her own car and at her own expense to get medical care for a traveler sick in a Hawaiian town. The president showed the letter to the vice president, who wrote the employee a message of praise (letter 10); and less than four months later Paula received a long-hoped-for promotion. Though her advancement was no doubt earned through years of good work, Paula felt that a letter such as the one the passenger wrote first brought her to the attention of management.

Letter 10

Letter of praise from an airline executive vice president to an employee.

> Attached is a copy of a letter President Jack Doe has just received
> which is indicative of the unusually fine job you are doing for us
> in (*name of town*). There is no question but that you made a life-
> long friend for Hawaiian Airlines.
>
> Congratulations, Paula, on a job well done!
>
> I am requesting Bob Cann to make this letter a part of your perma-
> nent personnel file.

EXPRESSING APPRECIATION

Everyone likes to know that his or her efforts are appreciated. Throughout your life you will have numerous occasions to express appreciation and thanks. As a business executive, you can express appreciation to customers, suppliers, employees, stockholders, and to many others whose activities relate to your business. Likewise, away from the office, you will have many opportunities to send such personal goodwill messages. Some of these messages will pertain to favors extended repeatedly over a period of time; others will thank for one-time kindnesses.

Appreciation for Favors Extended over a Period of Time

When you write to established customers, you can express appreciation for their patronage, for prompt payment of bills, for recommending your firm to friends, or for other courtesies. Some of these messages may become part of your regular company policy; others will be written individually as the occasions arise. Often these thank-you letters contain words of praise, as in letter 1 below; sometimes they also include a small gift or a special privilege, as in letter 2.

Letter 1

Personalized form letter, individually typed, expressing appreciation for a prompt-pay record (sent once to each customer after a three-year good record).

Thank you, Miss Albrecht,

for the fine manner in which you have paid your bills year after year.

Such a customer as you, because of your spotless paying record, seldom hears from our credit department. But the manner in which you have handled your MacDougall account has often been noticed and appreciated. It has also established for you a credit record of which you may be justly proud.

We are pleased to have you as a MacDougall customer, and thank you sincerely for your splendid cooperation.

Letter 2

A computerized, personalized form letter sending appreciation and a lifetime privilege to a preferred credit customer.

We sincerely appreciate how promptly you have paid your (*company name*) account each month. Most certainly you can be proud of the excellent credit record you have established, Mr. Juntwait.

In appreciation to a preferred customer, your new credit card is now good for life!! Your card will be replaced about every two years. This will enable us to update the number of years shown on your card. Also, it will assure that your card remains clean, fresh, and attractive.

I hope you like your new card and that we may have the privilege of serving you for a lifetime.

Though messages such as letters 1 and 2 are usually personalized form letters—with matching insertion of the customer's name and address—some large companies have found it desirable to send printed thanks, as in letter 3. Customers usually appreciate even a printed message—unless the same message arrives every month for six months, tucked in with the monthly statement (as it did for customers of one firm).

Letter 3

A manufacturer's thanks for patronage—printed on special letterhead showing two hands clasped and the word THANKS at the top in red.

Too often in the rush of business life, we forget to say "THANK YOU" so that you can hear it, but you can be sure we always appreciate your patronage. It is our constant aim to please and satisfy you more each time.

Serving you is a real privilege and we are grateful for your confidence in us. Anytime we can be of service to you in any way, just pick up the phone and call us collect at (209) 887-6499.

Some favors require special notes planned for the situation, as letter 4 illustrates:

Letter 4

A shop owner's personal thank-you to a customer who has recommended the shop to friends.

Yesterday, when Mrs. A. R. Wright visited us upon your recommendation, I was very much pleased--both because she had come in and because you like our shop well enough to recommend it to your friends.

You will be interested in knowing that so far nine members of your Art Guild have become our steady customers. All of them mentioned that you had recommended us and they respect your judgment.

Thank you, Mrs. Gunnerson, for your confidence in The Boutique and its services. We will always try to do our best to give you the service you expect.

Also, it is good for every successful person to express gratitude to the individuals—perhaps a relative, coach, scout leader, teacher, or former employer—who have contributed something memorable to his or her life—especially if (as in letter 5) years have passed since they met.

Letter 5

A professional person thanks a former Army officer.

Eight years ago, a young 1st lieutenant at Fort Ord, California, went out of his way to arrange transportation for a young staff sergeant who worked in his section. The transportation was for a

unique purpose--not for a pleasure trip or for official duty, but
for an education.

Mr. Watters, I want you to know that the favors you did for me have
had a great influence on my life. At the time you arranged for a
jeep for my use in attending high school classes at Palo Alto, I
thought it just another ordinary event in my life. Never did I
dream that those twice weekly rides would become my first route on
the road to higher education. The diploma I received was the ticket
I needed for admission to college. However, I needed more than that.
I needed someone to encourage me and show me the benefits that a
college education would give to me. You were persistently trying to
convince me of this value during my last days of duty. And though
your work was filled with pressure and tension, you always managed
to remain calm and ready to cheer me on.

You helped me in so many ways; I'm deeply grateful to you. You'll
be glad to know that your wise words didn't go unheeded. I graduated
from the University of (*state*) last June and am now in my first year
of medical school. Thank you for starting me on the road to a better
education. I hope some day to help other youngsters the way you
helped me.

Such thank-you messages are an appreciated surprise to their recipients, as the following typically sentimental excerpts from replies indicate:

From the president of a publishing company

. . . I am most grateful to you for your delightful, thoroughly human letter. . . . It really brightened a rainy and overcast day!

From a retired teacher

. . . I can't tell you how much your letter meant to me. I'm in
my 80s now, lonely, living alone in a small apartment, cooking my
own meals. Though I taught school for 47 years, yours is the first
note of appreciation I ever received. It came on a blue cold morning and it cheered me as nothing has in many years.

From a former employer

. . . Your letter was so touching that as I read it tears of gratitude fell from my eyes . . . . You could not guess how much your
words have warmed my spirit. I have been walking around in the glow
of them all day long.

Letters of appreciation are also due to people who have spent many hours on a worthy cause—like serving on committees, soliciting funds, or helping with an election campaign. To save expenses, a form letter similar to letter 6 is acceptable.

Letter 6

A successful candidate thanks volunteer assistants. [Instead of a personalized saluta-tion, a general salutation such as "Dear (committee name) Member" could be used to further save time and expense.]

Dear Ms. Tomkins:

During the city campaign just closed, several hundred public-spirited citizens gave of their time and personal service to do the necessary mailing, telephoning, and campaigning which played so vital a part in the election. It is to you, one of these loyal workers, I want to express my sincere appreciation.

The fine work accomplished and the effort which no money can buy, come only from those who feel, as I do, a sense of responsibility for decent city government. I honestly believe that without the many tasks carried out by your committee the result would have been different.

Again I thank you for your part in the campaign and give you my sincere promise that I will do everything in my power to carry on in this city the kind of government for which you worked so diligently.

Thanks for One-Time Favors and Kindnesses

Thanking people promptly for any significant one-time courtesy is desirable for a successful business or professional person, as well as for everyone else with good manners. Whenever possible, a thank-you message should go to the person who: gives a speech without honorarium; writes a letter of recommendation for you; helps you win an honor or award; grants an informative, lengthy interview; sends you a letter of praise or criticism about you, your business, employees, or others in whom you are interested; donates money, gifts, or awards. Some firms even thank new customers for a first purchase or first use of a new charge account.

Of course, circumstances will govern the length and content of these thank-you notes, which may range from a few sentences to several paragraphs. Letters 7 through 11 are thank-you messages which thoughtful, courteous businesspersons have written on various occasions.

Letter 7

A program chairperson thanks a popular speaker—in an unusual, but gracious and sincere, letter.

At the risk of contradicting the general theme of your talk on "The Freedom of Movement" at the Uptown Business Luncheon meeting last Thursday, may I say that you made captives of all of us.

Believe me, I did not--after noting what was a record attendance for our meeting--speak lightly when I told you that your reputation as a speaker, a scholar, and, above all, a charming guest of honor had preceded you.

I cannot resist adding, with all due apologies to Shaw--"What really flatters a man is that you think him worth flattering." On this point, certainly--and I speak with confidence for the club members and our guests--there is not the shadow of a doubt.

We hope that your future will provide some respite from hard work and that you will be free to join us again. Thank you so very much.

When a customer compliments your firm or employees by letter, you should acknowledge the praise by writing a note similar to letter 8. [See also the commanding officer's memo (letter 9), page 514.]

Letter 8

A company president thanks a customer for her complimentary letter about an employee.

> Thank you very much for your warm and cordial letter of August 29. It is really a pleasure, upon opening the morning mail, to find a letter like yours.
>
> Nothing gratifies me more than to learn that the efforts of our employees are so thoroughly appreciated. Many people are quick to write criticisms, but seldom does anyone take the time to say something nice. So it is always pleasing to hear from the many, many people who are satisfied.
>
> We will do our best to continue to provide you with the service you like.

Criticisms should also be acknowledged courteously. A large, nationally known publishing firm, for instance, sends a card labeled "Post-o-gram" with this mimeographed message: "We appreciate your comments on (name of book) and the interest which prompted you to write. If we may serve you any time in the future, please let us know." Letter 9 includes in addition to thanks an apology and brief resale.

Letter 9

A passenger traffic manager thanks a passenger for a criticism.

> Thank you for taking a few moments of your valuable time to fill out the comment card while a recent coach passenger on our (*name of carrier*), December 18.
>
> We are sorry to learn of your disappointment in your recent trip. In this connection, we have referred your comments to the supervisory officer for her information, investigation, and correction.
>
> Giving you prompt, courteous service on every trip is our constant aim. We look forward to serving you many times in the future.

For thank-you messages that acknowledge money donations, the explanation section usually should include a few details telling the success of the campaign or how the funds are being used, so that the donors will feel good about having contributed. If you are an officer in an organization that must solicit donations year after year, appreciative messages similar to letters 10 and 11 may well serve as incentives for future donations.

Letter 10

(Memo) *A plant manager thanks employees for generous contributions.*

TO: All employees
FROM: John Mains, Manager, Plant 2
SUBJECT: <u>Plant 2 UGN Contributions 198</u>

On behalf of the United Good Neighbor Fund I thank all of you who so generously contributed to our UGN campaign.

This year, our plant had approximately the same number of contributors as last year, but a <u>21%</u> increase in contributions! Our company goal was a 9% increase. Obviously we have substantially exceeded that amount.

Thanks again for your strong support at a time when it is needed more than ever.

Letter 11

The president of a civic charity board thanks donors.

THANK YOU!   THANK YOU!   THANK YOU!

Words cannot adequately express our deep appreciation for the gift you sent in response to our Christmas letter for the poor. Because of kindhearted friends like you . . .

> Many hungry fathers, mothers, little children have enjoyed a special Christmas dinner--surely they are thinking, "THANK YOU."

> And the shabbily dressed--as they left with a "change of clothing" bundle under arm--are surely thinking, "THANK YOU."

> And the children--if you could have heard their cheers of joy as they opened their packages--are surely thinking, "THANK YOU."

They are all grateful there are "people who care." Thank you for your generosity and thoughtfulness. You can take satisfaction in knowing that your contributions have helped bring happiness to these deserving people.

EXTENDING SEASONAL GREETINGS

If appropriate, you can send a seasonal message to customers (or others) near any special holiday—New Year, Valentine's Day, St. Patrick's Day, Easter, Memorial Day, Independence Day, Thanksgiving, Christmas—or any season that may be meaningful to your recipients. The main purpose of these messages is to extend season's greetings and good wishes, although they often also express appreciation. Sometimes a small gift—calendar, ornament, picture—accompanies them. In any case, the message should preferably be unique for your type of business as well as the season, and appropriately different from others the reader may receive during that season.

Because most companies choose the Christmas and New Year holidays for their seasonal greetings, this section focuses on these messages. Of course, if the type of product or service your firm sells can be appropriately linked with any other special day, greetings sent then will have less competition and probably receive more attention.

Often, originality in special letterhead designs—symbolic of both the firm's business and the season—adds to the effectiveness of the message. For example, the president of a popular firm that sells heating products has his firm's greetings multilithed on a folding card which pictures on the front an attractive etching of a historical fireplace (different each year and suitable for framing). The greetings also include a brief story about that particular fireplace; his complimentary closing is "Warmly."

If a firm operates internationally, a different nation's Christmas custom could be featured each year in the season's greetings. Or if a firm's customers are concentrated in a geographic area where a certain nationality predominates, the greeting might be tied in with an appropriate national tradition. For instance, a bank's public relations manager sent the following message (individually typewritten in green) on a Christmas letterhead picturing a lighted candle in a holder.

Message 1

A Christmas greeting and gift linked to a pleasant custom.

> Lighting candles on Christmas Eve is another of those old Scandinavian customs like smorgasbord dinners. The legend says that these candles must not be made or purchased for the occasion, but that they must be a gift from friends--or the flame will not burn brightly.
>
> In tomorrow's mail you will receive a candle from us--to carry on that friendly tradition. Along with it go our best wishes.
>
> All of us here--your staff and directors in the (*name*) bank--say "thank you" for your continued patronage. It adds to our Christmas cheer to know that we have loyal friends like you.
>
> We all wish you a warm and happy Christmas and an interesting New Year in 198_.

Though individually addressed and personally signed messages are ideal, most business firms find it necessary—because of volume and expense—to send undisguised form messages. Many send conventional Christmas or New Year greeting cards signed by a facsimile of an officer's handwriting. Some have the entire message written (and processed) in an executive's handwriting on specially designed colorful Christmas letterheads. If space allows, you can have all officers—sometimes even all employees—personally sign your organization's greetings, as in message 2. Another interesting alternative is to include individual pictures of all employees, as in message 3, which can help customers become acquainted with the employees.

Message 2

A form-letter Christmas greeting signed by all 21 employees (message is typewritten on green and gold paper bordered with colorful holly, bells, and ornaments).

```
TO OUR FRIENDS:


                    SEASON'S GREETINGS

            There are days for sending merchandise
                 And days to send a bill
               But this one day of all the year
                 We send you just GOODWILL!


        Yes, it is Christmastime again.  We want to take this
    opportunity to say "Thank You" for all the favors you have shown
    us . . . and wish you a Very Merry Christmas and a Prosperous
    New Year.

        We've sincerely appreciated the business you have given us
    in the past, and we'll try mighty hard to merit your continued
    goodwill in the future.

        May you and your family have a wonderful Holiday Season and
    may the coming year be the happiest of your life.  That is our
    Christmas wish for you.
```

Message 3

A Christmas form letter surrounded by 1-inch facial pictures and names of 40 employees. [Message is printed on white paper edged with a star and sketches of the three wise men bearing gifts; at the bottom are the words, "Serving (city name) since 1919."]

```
    One of the real joys of the Holiday Season is the opportunity for
    the expression of goodwill and the exchange of friendly greetings.

    In this spirit of friendship and with sincere appreciation for the
    pleasant relations we have enjoyed with you, we extend the Season's
    Greetings and wish you Health and Happiness every day of the New
    Year . . .
```

CONVEYING SYMPATHY

When people suffer a serious misfortune, they may be encouraged by messages of sympathy from business associates as well as from personal friends. Because they pertain to sad or unpleasant circumstances, goodwill letters of this type are much harder to write than those already discussed. However, in times of distress, the recipient may value these messages even more highly than expressions of congratulation or thanks.

You can express condolence to a customer, competitor, colleague, business friend, or employee. The occasion may involve a death, accident, loss of material possessions (such as a business wiped out by fire or flood), sickness, major operation, or other misfortunes that can happen to an individual. Expressions of sympathy can be shown by cards, flowers, attendance at a funeral, offers of tangible help, visits, written messages, or a combination of several. This section concentrates on the individual messages you can write expressing sympathy.

If you are writing for your company and the relationship is purely a business one, your secretary can type the message on letterhead stationery. Otherwise, use your own stationery and write (preferably not type) what you want to convey.

Although you cannot mechanically follow a set outline for expression of sympathy, here are suggestions to consider:

1. Begin with the main idea—sympathy and identification of the problem (such as accident, death, or loss of business).
2. Add only those details, if any, that are desirable for the circumstances. (For example, when writing to a survivor, you might express how much the survivor meant to the deceased.) Make all statements restrained and sincere.
3. Stress the positive—the good characteristics and best contributions of the deceased or ill person (if you knew him or her)—rather than the negative (pain, suffering, distress).
4. Offer assistance, if appropriate, but don't dwell on details. Perhaps you will offer to lighten a customer's monthly payments, move a due date forward, or make your warehouse available to a friend whose factory burned down. Omit such business matters as the amount the customer owes you, how long a debt is past due, or similar subjects which can and should be taken care of in another letter.
5. End on a pleasant, positive, reassuring idea, perhaps looking to the future. Below are acceptable messages of condolence.

Message 1

Memo telling employees about the sudden death of a coworker.

```
TO ALL EMPLOYEES:

We are saddened by the death of Thor Bjornsen.  Thor was killed in a
private-plane accident last Friday en route to a conference.  Funeral
services will be held tomorrow at (name) funeral home, 1111 Broadway
Avenue, at 1:00 p.m.

Thor was one of the finest chaps in the company--always helping
others, especially newcomers.  He was tops in his field and was gen-
erous and kind.  We will all miss him.

Thor's family does not want flowers for him; so arrangements have
been made with the Children's Orthopedic Hospital of (city name) to
receive sums for a memorial fund.  Checks are to be made payable to
that hospital.  Address contributions to Thor Bjornsen Memorial,
333 Ridgeway Road, attention of Mrs. Jackson.
```

Message 2

A personnel director's condolence to a widowed customer (whose wife he had never met personally).

> With profound sorrow we have just learned of the death of your wife.
>
> Though there is little one can say or do to lessen the grief that must be yours, we want you to know the heartfelt sympathy of all your friends at Boardson's is with you.
>
> We hope that the cherished memories you have of your many years together will comfort you in the months ahead.

Message 3

Sympathy letter to a business friend whose store burned to the ground.

> Dear Joan
>
> The announcement on television yesterday about the widespread fire in your buildings distressed us greatly. I want to convey our sympathy to you and your employees.
>
> If there's anything that I as an individual can do to help you at this time, please call me (here at the office: 894-6666, Ext. 562, or at home: 445-2323 evenings). Also you're welcome to use (at no charge, of course), our company's Lander Street warehouse (about 500 sq. feet) to store any materials during your reconstruction period, and our conference rooms for offices and meeting places as long as you need them.
>
> All the employees at the (*name*) Company join me in wishing you a fast recovery.

If Joan were an out-of-town customer with an outstanding balance on her account, the sympathy message might have included an offer like the following to replace part of the second paragraph:

> If we can help you by extending your credit terms and the payment date on your account, just let me know. I'll consider it a privilege to come to your aid to show—even in a small way—how much we have appreciated your friendship and business through the years.

WELCOMING AND/OR OFFERING FAVORS

Some of the good-news messages discussed in Chapter 7—for instance, those granting credit or acknowledging first orders—include a welcome to the customer and some grant favors that the customer asked for.[1] Also, many sales letters offer a favor or gift. All those messages are necessary in the daily course of business operations.

---

[1] For favorable credit and order acknowledgments, pages 226-234; favor grants, pages 234-235.

In contrast, the welcome and favor-offering letters discussed in this chapter are those "extra" messages that are not absolutely essential but are written mainly to build goodwill. The favors are freely offered, not written in answer to a request or to sell.

Sometimes these welcome messages go to persons who have not yet dealt directly with your firm or perhaps not with your department. Among them are messages you may send to newcomers in a city or state, to new employees in your firm, or to new "customers" of an organization whose work is related to that of your firm. Notice how letters 1 and 2 focus on the welcome and service, and do not try to sell the reader anything.

Letter 1

A secretary of state welcomes a new incorporator in the state.

> Your name has been listed as one of the incorporators in a filing
> just made in my office, and I am pleased to extend a warm welcome
> to you.
>
> It is a real pleasure to have been of service to you and your fellow
> incorporators in a matter which reflects your confidence in the con-
> tinued growth and prosperity of our state.
>
> You have our sincere good wishes that you will find this confidence
> amply rewarded in the success of your venture.

Letter 2

A hospital pharmacist welcomes each newly admitted patient. (This letter or card could bear the pharmacist's picture. Salutation is personalized.)

> Welcome to (*name*) Hospital. Although you probably will not see me
> while you are here, I will be working for you. My function is to
> cooperate with your physician and nurses to assure you the best in
> drugs and pharmaceutical service. Here at (*name*) Hospital we take
> a personal interest in every patient. We want you to know that we
> are here to help ensure your speedy recovery.

A letter from an officer of any business firm, welcoming a distinguished newcomer to the area and offering assistance is usually a low-pressure *sales* message. Besides the welcome, it may include a city map, real estate guides, and a pamphlet or paragraph about the institution's services or products. Though such letters are useful for business, they are *not strictly goodwill* messages.

However, a welcoming message like letter 3 to a new customer can be considered strictly goodwill; it does not try to sell the reader on additional services but merely contains *resale* material (as in paragraph 2). Also, letter 4 is a goodwill message—to let a once "lost" customer know that renewed patronage is appreciated.

Letter 3

A savings and loan officer welcomes a new savings account customer.

It is a pleasure to welcome you to membership in our organization. Many thanks for opening a savings account with First Federal.

Here your savings are safeguarded by careful management, investment in sound home loans, and insurance of accounts by the Federal Savings and Loan Insurance Corporation, an agency of the United States government. At the same time, we maintain ample reserves for the purpose of meeting withdrawals, should you need all or any part of your savings; and in addition you earn an above-average dividend on your savings, compounded semiannually at the regular rate.

You receive the same personalized services at either of our offices-- the Mountview Savings in the Southside Shopping Center or the down town office.

Please call on me or any member of our staff when we can be of service to you. Our telephone number is 543-4444.

Letter 4

A credit manager welcomes back a long-absent customer.

The return of a good friend is as happy an occasion in the business world as it is in one's private life. Your recent purchase here at Baylor's was the first to be charged to your account for a considerable time . . .

and we take this opportunity to welcome you again to the Baylor Store. Thank you for your patronage.

You can be sure that it is our sincere wish to serve you to your complete satisfaction.

The last example, letter 5, is an offer of a favor at "no charge or obligation" to noncustomers and customers. This message contains no direct sales plug for the writer's organization and does not ask the reader to buy or sell stock through the writer's firm. Thus, although the reason for the letter is probably to promote sales eventually, here it is mainly a goodwill message.

Letter 5

A stock brokerage firm's vice president offers a free current report. (A small, printed fill-in form is at the top of the letter; salutation is personalized.)

I'd like to offer you a Thompson Fynch service that many of the investors in (*city name*) have come to value highly: the opinion of our research department about any stock listed on the New York Stock Exchange. If you'll just write the name of the stock on the form above and mail it to our Central Information Bureau, I'll get an up-to-date report from our research department back to you just as promptly as I can.

Then, if you have any questions about the report, please call me at
(206) 549-2222. I'll be glad to make an appointment at your convenience.

We are pleased to do this, (*name*), whether you have an account with
us or not. There is no charge or obligation for this service. In
fact, the only charge you ever pay at Thompson Fynch is the minimum
commission when you buy or sell securities.

SHOWING CONTINUING SPECIAL CONCERN

Another type of goodwill message shows that you are sincerely interested in maintaining confidence in your firm's goods and services. To demonstrate your concern, you
can write various follow-up requests and announcements to customers, stockholders,
suppliers, or employees. The purpose of these goodwill messages is to get feedback on
products used or returned, to maintain the firm's good image, or to help the customer
get the best use from your products which she or he has already bought.

For example, some firms systematically send messages similar to letter 1 to solicit
comments from their product users and maintain quality control.

Letter 1

*A manufacturer of outboard motors strengthens goodwill by inviting purchasers' com-
ments.*[2]

HOW DO YOU LIKE YOUR EVINRUDE?

A good part of the boating season has slipped past since you bought
your motor.

We hope you've had the opportunity to log a lot of pleasant hours
with it. We're going to ask a favor of you--a report from you on
the "good conduct" of your motor. (Or your frank criticism, if you
have any you wish to make.)

For over 65 years our steady aim has been to make the most perfect
outboard motors that can be built. We've spent millions on engineering, fine production facilities, and the most rigorous testing
any manufacturer can give his products.

But there is one test that really tells how successful we have been.
And that is your complete satisfaction, as the owner and user of our
product.

Will you please send us your comments? For your convenience, a blue
"stamped" envelope is enclosed--and if you like, simply jot your
reply on the back of this letter.

Thank you--here's wishing you many seasons of happy boating.

---

[2] Courtesy of Evinrude Motors, Milwaukee, Wisconsin.

Besides getting comments from present owners of a product, some firms seek to find out—through messages like letter 2—why former owners returned various items.

Letter 2

A department store shows concern for customer desires by inviting comments and reasons for return of merchandise.

Recently you had occasion to return, for a $48.30 refund, an item purchased from (*store name*). Your opinions regarding that item and our service are valued highly.

We desire to provide an adequate selection of quality merchandise and to see that our sales force is courteous at all times. In this instance we are sorry the product did not fulfill your desires, and we want to be sure that in returning the item you received the same courtesy as when it was purchased.

Will you please jot your comments and suggestions for improvement on the back of this sheet and mail it to us in the enclosed stamped envelope? We will very much appreciate your assistance, for it will enable us to provide the kind of service you like.

If your corporation has a widely dispersed management group and a large number of stockholders, many of whom cannot attend the annual meetings, and you want to exchange viewpoints with these stockholders, you might consider writing a goodwill-building message similar to letter 3. (Each has a personalized salutation.)

Letter 3

The senior officer of a nationwide public utility invites stockholders to have an individual visit with a management representative.[3]

Across the nation in recent years, Bell System management men and women have met with over half a million AT&T share owners like you in their homes and offices for face-to-face discussions of the telephone business. Viewpoints have been exchanged, questions cleared up and in many instances assistance provided on matters of mutual interest.

These informal discussions have benefited our owners and your Company to such an extent that visits with share owners have been made a part of management's responsibility in Bell System Companies.

With over three million share owners we cannot hope to visit them all at once or in a short period of time. So, from month to month and on a random basis, we select a number of share owners to be visited.

---

[3] Courtesy of Mr. Charles E. Wampler, formerly vice president and secretary of American Telephone and Telegraph Company, New York.

We would like very much to visit you. I am arranging, therefore, to have one of our Bell System management representatives in
your area get in touch with you in the near future for this purpose.

If your company is planning to expand, a letter similar to letter 4 builds goodwill
by letting your customers know you have a continuing concern for their needs and
preferences.

Letter 4

A department store invites customers to send suggestions before a planned expansion.
(Letter is dated January 2; salutation is "Dear Customer.")

This letter has a double significance. First, of course, we wish
to send you and your family our very best wishes for a happy and
prosperous New Year. We also want to tell you that we appreciate
having you as a customer of (*name of store*) and we thank you for
your patronage.

The second reason for our writing you has to do with our planned
expansion of five floors on the present building. Inasmuch as our
whole aim in this expansion will be to improve our service and our
merchandise, we thought we might ask your advice.

If you have any thoughts regarding the improvement of our business,
we would be very grateful if you would pass those thoughts along to
us. For instance, there may be some new departments that you would
like to see us have or there may be some new types of merchandise
that you would like to have us carry. Or again, you may have some
thoughts on the improvements of our physical layout, lighting, or
customer facilities of any kind.

We are sure that you do have some ideas in this respect; so if you
would jot down anything you might think of on the back of this letter and return it at your convenience (in the enclosed envelope),
we would appreciate it. After all, we want the new (*name*) to be
your store from top to bottom.

Any comments you send will be welcome and appreciated.

Still another excellent way to show concern for your customers (and others) is by
anticipating (hopefully forestalling) complaints. If you discover that your company
(or a supplier) has made an error which directly affects customers, you have the opportunity to admit the mistake to everyone who may be affected by it—before any customer finds it necessary to ask for an adjustment. Those who have done this (rather
than staying silent, hoping only a few people will discover the error) have usually been
pleasantly surprised at the loyalty, appreciation, and fairness of their customers.

Among the many examples of the goodwill-building power of announcements made
to forestall complaints, two are mentioned below:

1. Following a serious storm a subsidiary of Bell Telephone Company sent an inquiry
   to customers asking them to name, on an enclosed reply card, the period for which

they had no service and to state how many days they wanted the company to deduct from their phone bill. Most customers complimented the firm for its forthright message (and its "excellent emergency action"), and they appreciated but rejected the firm's offer to reduce the phone bill.

2. A candy department manager, upon discovering after Christmas that about 50 out of 200 charge-customer orders for a certain quality gift-box candy had been incorrectly filled with slightly lower-quality candy than ordered and sent to the customers' friends, wrote to all 200 customers offering to send a free replacement. As the store did not know which of the 200 customers had been incorrectly served, the manager invited everyone whose friend had received a gift box with a certain code number at the bottom to ask, on an enclosed reply card, for a free box of the ordered candy; she or he need not return the original. Although obviously at least 25 percent of the customers could have honestly asked for a replacement, less than 5 percent did so. All others who replied—including those whose friends had received the "wrong" candy—thanked the store, commented on the good-quality candy their friend enjoyed, and declined the free offer.

The managers who sent these messages were sure that the small cost of their letter was far outweighed by the resulting goodwill.

In the first paragraph of this type of announcement you frankly admit the mistake and sometimes announce the "good news" adjustment that you will make. The explanation section contains an apology (if it isn't in the opening) plus whatever details are desirable for showing how the error occurred. Like other adjustment-granting letters, this announcement should emphasize positive aspects and convey a sincere desire to serve the customer, as in letter 5.[4]

Letter 5

The customer service manager of a national oil company announces credit to customers' accounts for an error made by a supplier (completely processed form).

Dear (*firm name*) Credit Card Customer:

We owe you an apology . . . and have credited your account for $9.83.

The hot tray that was shipped to you in response to your recent order was not the model pictured in the advertising brochure. This error on the part of the supplier of the hot tray has just recently been called to our attention.

Since you did not receive the correct merchandise, we are crediting your account with the total cost of the tray you purchased as a meaningful way of correcting this error. Please keep your hot tray as a small gift from (*firm name*).

If you would still like to receive the advertised hot tray, simply check the box and sign and mail the enclosed order card.

---

[4] See also the example in Chapter 5, page 74.

We will be glad to send the tray to you as soon as possible and
bill you accordingly.

You can always depend on (*firm name*) for top quality.

In summary, a goodwill letter is one that you don't *have* to send and that doesn't
include a sales pitch or have strings attached. These messages congratulate, praise,
thank, greet, sympathize, welcome, offer favors, or show special concern for the reader
—without including any obvious sales material. The message plan is direct—main idea,
details, courteous close.

EXERCISES

1. Below are two messages about free gifts the companies offer. Is each one truly a
   goodwill message? If not, why not? What do you like or dislike about each one?

   a.
   The Next Issue of (*name of free booklet*)

   will be mailed on Monday, October 25. The (*name of booklet*) is sent
   free each month to business firms employing three or more department
   heads.

   Before we address the envelopes for this issue, we want to make sure
   that our mailing list is complete and accurate. On the sheet that
   comes with this letter, you will find reproductions of <u>all</u> the Add-
   ressograph plates we have for members of your staff.

   Please take just a minute to go over the list. Make any corrections
   called for. Cross out the names of people who are no longer there.
   Add the names of members of your staff for whom we don't have plates.

   The (*name of booklet*) is "different." Each issue is of direct interest to supervisors and managers working with people daily.

   Please correct and mail the sheet today--in the enclosed envelope.
   No stamp is needed. You and your associates will then be sure of
   getting (*booklet*) free throughout the year.

   b.
   We know you will enjoy having this special edition of our 198_
   color calendar, compliments of (*name*) Travel Service. We hope
   that it proves to be both useful and convenient in your office.

   This affords us the opportunity to let you know that we appreciate
   the privilege of serving as your travel agent. We thank you for
   your past business and we look forward to hearing from you whenever
   we can assist you with future travel plans in connection with business or pleasure.

   We handle all forms of transportation - air, rail, steamship, bus,
   as well as reservations for hotels, motels and U-drive service. Our
   daily delivery service to any downtown business office is a time-

saver for you and your staff, and we want you to feel free to make use of it.

ONE CALL DOES IT ALL! - 333-0020

2. As assistant customer service manager of a national airline, you need to write a letter to accompany a lost sorority pin which you are returning to its owner. The pin had fallen under one of the coach seats on Flight #742 to Chicago, June 29. No one wrote to report this lost pin; thus there has been considerable delay in establishing ownership. You first had to identify the sorority and then the chapter and where it was located, all of which was time-consuming. However, you were eventually successful in learning this traveler's identity through Joanne Jones, president, Alpha Chapter at Texas State College.

Ask the recipient of your letter to sign an attached lost property card and return it to you. Will your reply be a goodwill letter with no strings attached? Or will you include some sales talk and a look forward to future business?

3. The following message was sent by the general manager of a hotel to all business executives who had attended a national convention there seven months earlier. Is this letter a goodwill builder? Why or why not? What improvements can you suggest? (Each letter has a personalized salutation.)

May I take this opportunity to thank you for your patronage to (*name*) Hotel, and all of us here sincerely hope that you enjoyed your visit to (*city*).

Have you any friends or business associates that might be coming to (*state*)? I would appreciate it very much if you would give me their names and addresses on the enclosed card so that I may send them a brochure of our hotel and invite them to stay with us while they are in (*state*).

The staff of the (*hotel name*) joins me in looking forward to your future visits with us.

4. Assume that one day six years from now you happen to read, in a professional or business journal, about a former college classmate of yours. She has been chosen to deliver the main address at the next regional convention of a national organization you belong to. You're pleased that she has gained a distinguished reputation as a technical expert in the field—all in the few years since her graduation. Write her an appropriate note of congratulation.

5. As manager of a wholesale hardware firm with customers in three states, you have just heard that Mr. Archie Oltimer will retire next month, after being in business for 45 years and your customer for 15. Mr. Oltimer's store is over 500 miles from your office—in a town not served by an airline—and you have never met him personally. However, his orders have come regularly through the years and his payments have been prompt. Now he has sold his store to a younger man. Write him a sincere message of appreciation.

6. Evaluate the following letter; is it candid, sincere, and businesslike, yet also a goodwill builder? Assume the firm is a national manufacturer of calculating machines. Salutation is "Good morning, Mrs. Mardon."

   ```
   We got to thinking about you the other day, and we realized, though
   it hardly seems believable, that a whole year has whizzed by since
   we shipped you the two Model XX Comptometers!  But the calendar says
   so, all right, and we are impressed with how time flies.

   Now, on this first anniversary of your ownership of the two comptom-
   eters, let's just check to make sure they are giving you the service
   you had expected and paid for.  We want you to know we think of you.

   Are these machines doing their job, Mrs. Mardon?  Do your operators
   like them?  Have any problems with them?  Any questions you want
   answered?  Do the machines need a year's checkup?

   Just jot down any remarks from your operators or yourself on the
   enclosed, self-addressed card and shoot it right back to us.  We'll
   gladly help you promptly.  And you'll be helping us to maintain the
   quality you expected when you decided to buy your two Model XX's.
   ```

7. This assignment can be a message you will actually mail. (If your instructor approves, you can hand in your carbon copy and mail the original.) Write a sincere letter of appreciation to one person who has had a profound and lasting good effect on your life. Perhaps he or she encouraged you to stick with a job when you almost quit, helped pay your college expenses, or contributed in any other special way(s) to your well-being and achievements.

8. As manager of the foreign department of Your City Bank, write a congratulatory letter to Mr. Paul Mifford, recently elected president of Pan Xenia, international business honorary at his college chapter. Assume any other pertinent facts.

9. In the evening paper you read that Ms. Adelle Adamson of the Harbor Products Company has been promoted to public relations director of the company. During the past 10 years you have had many business transactions with Harbor Products and most have been through the excellent, courteous service Ms. Adamson gave your firm. You consider her one of those career people who has all the qualities needed for management, as well as personal charm. Yet she has been held back; this is the first time Harbor Products has appointed a woman to an executive position. You personally know of several situations involving thousands of dollars, necessitating delicate yet efficient human relations, that Ms. Adamson handled entirely herself, but in each case her "superiors" got the credit and praise. Write your sincere letter of congratulations to her now.

10. You are business manager of the Friedman Jewelry firm, registered jewelers in the American Gem Society. The largest bank in your city has just bought from you 35 of your $150 watches, which the bank will present to its employees who become members of the Quarter Century Club (25-year employees of the bank). The

watches will be presented at a banquet two weeks from today. Your jewelry store has agreed to take care of all the service on these watches for one year free of charge. Write a letter of congratulation to be addressed individually to each new Quarter Century Club member, and include whatever goodwill-building material about your store is desirable. Make these people feel welcome to use your services.

11. Assume you graduated from college 10 years ago and have been successfully employed in work you like. You have also been active in a volunteer organization that helps a clinic for handicapped people in your community. Recently you were appointed chairperson of a fund raising committee which decided to send persuasive letters to three groups of people asking for donations. Because you felt you needed some (free) expert advice on your three rough drafts, you phoned your former business communication instructor. Though that particular week happened to be a time when this professor was heavily involved with responsibilities and deadlines on previous professional commitments, he or she willingly devoted an entire evening to your drafts and rewrote one of them almost completely.

   During the past three weeks since these letters were mailed they have already raised $2,400 in donations, and the committee plans to use them again and again for future fund raising campaigns. Write a letter of appreciation to your former professor for time and help given. Perhaps you can assume some definite equipment or services that the $2,400 have already purchased, and invite this professor to come visit the facilities at the clinic. Be sincere in your thanks and comments.

12. Assume that you are customer service director for Prescott, Inc., a large manufacturer of silver hollowware and flatware. Four times a year the major department stores send your company the names of all the brides who have registered your silver patterns in the stores' bridal registries. The stores also send a copy of the purchases made for each bride. You would now like to send to each bride who has received some of your silver a goodwill letter giving her helpful hints on caring for her silver. You sincerely hope she will get maximum satisfaction from your silver. Go to a nearby jewelry firm or department store and collect the data necessary for giving her helpful hints on cleaning and caring for silver. Remember, your goal is not to sell any more silver. You are just writing a goodwill letter to young brides.

13. You are the public relations officer for the light company in your city. Every four months you receive the names and addresses of people moving into your community. This list specifies whether they are building a house, buying, or renting. In any case you would like them to know that if they have any electrical equipment in their home, you have repairers who will come to service these appliances free of charge for labor. The only charge is for parts. You also want to tell them about your home economist, who will make house calls to help the homemaker learn to use electrical appliances in the most efficient manner. This home economist comes equipped with recipes and helpful hints for household management and will answer any questions the homemaker may have. Write a letter explaining your services and the fact that they are complimentary. If you need more information for this letter, check with your city light company for additional details to include.

14. You are manager of a large sporting goods store located in a wealthy suburb of a large city. Many avid weekend hunters come into your shop. Every year you compile a record of names and addresses of customers who purchased shells and hunting equipment during that year. In the past the state game department has published annually a brochure listing the hunting season dates for the coming year. This year, to cut down on expenses, the state has eliminated these brochures, but has sent a complete brochure to all sporting goods stores explaining the regulations and the season dates. You would like to write a letter telling your customers the season dates and explaining to them that you have a complete listing of the regulations posted in your shop if they would like more information.

15. Write (or revise) a goodwill message that relates to one of the following situations.
    a. A Christmas or other seasonal greeting for your company. (Choose a line of business you are familiar with.)
    b. Condolence to the wife or husband of a long-time employee who died.
    c. Message to someone in the hospital because of an automobile accident.
    d. Thanks to a customer for being prompt in making loan payments the last three years. (Assume a bank or savings and loan association.)
    e. A message to accompany a clipping you're sending to a business friend.

16. As customer relations manager of the National Products Company, write a checkup letter to all business executives who have bought one of your machines to be used in their offices. (Assume any machine with which you are familiar.) Your letter is to be mailed one month after a machine is sold—to check on performance and to catch minor annoyances before they become major grievances. You want to make sure the machine is doing a good job for the reader, or you might want to know if the operators have any questions you can help answer. Will you enclose something for easy answering? Make sure your readers understand that your purpose is to help maintain the high standards for which your products have been famous, not to sell more machines.

17. The following letter from an auditor to the office manager of business firms he visited uses a play on words. Do you think the tone is appropriate and the message pleasingly unique? What do you like or dislike about the letter? It is dated December 18 and addressed individually, "Dear Mr. (name)."

    I enjoyed the friendly atmosphere of your office during the brief time I was with you this year. Then your financial statements were done and I was on my way--to another office and another short story.

    With 198_ almost gone it's time again for a statement--this time a personal one in which friendship and goodwill rank high.

    As I look back over my own accounts I know that many things have been left undone. With the end of the calendar period coming near, it's time to stop and credit them to your account.

I wish to enter my appreciation for the courtesies you and your staff
showed me, the pleasure I felt in working with all of you, and the
"thank you" I thought of but might have left unsaid.

Let me record all these, so my thoughts will be clear, while I send
you BEST WISHES for a HAPPY NEW YEAR.

18. You are public relations manager of a firm that manufactures lighting fixtures.
Yesterday you read in *Illuminating News*, a trade journal, that one of your good
customers—Patrice O'Leary—has just opened her fifth lighting goods store in
Florida this month. The article states that the store is considered the largest and
most modern store of its kind in the Southeast, in keeping with the tremendous
growth of the area. You recall that eight years ago, when you were credit manager, you first opened Ms. O'Leary's charge account with your factory; she then
had only one store. Through the years she has placed increasingly larger orders
with your firm and has paid them all promptly. Though your lighting fixtures
have had a part in her success, resist the temptation to claim credit yourself or to
dwell on the merits of your products. Write Ms. O'Leary a letter of congratulations.

19. You are the public relations director for a company that sells electric food chop-
pers and blenders for home use. Each person who buys one of your blenders is
asked to fill out a card telling the serial number of the machine purchased and
other pertinent information—address, date, and place of purchase. The computer
that you put these cards into sends you back a complete list of people who have
taken the time to fill out the card and send it in. You would like to send these
people a letter thanking them for registering their blenders. In addition you want
to give them a free booklet that includes 10 prize-winning recipes for use with the
blender. (The recipes were submitted by other customers to a national contest
your firm sponsored recently.) They are not in the booklet each owner receives
with the blender.

PART

FOUR

REPORTS

The What and How of Business Reports

Thousands of modern businesses need various reports to carry on efficient operations. In almost any kind of responsible business job—whether you are a management trainee, a salesperson, an accountant, a junior executive, or a vice president, you may have to write reports. Your communication effectiveness and, often, your promotion are affected by the quality of reports you write.

Three chapters in this text are devoted exclusively to written reports and a fourth chapter includes oral reporting. In addition, as you proceed in your study of reports, you will see how some parts of Chapters 1 through 6 and Appendix B also apply to reports. You may occasionally find a brief review of them helpful, because a sound understanding of the communication process, business writing principles, planning steps, and formats of related business messages is desirable for effective report writing.

This chapter provides a general overview of business reports. It includes: what reports are and how they are classified; how to plan, prepare, organize, outline, and illustrate the report body; and how to achieve the C qualities in written reports.

Chapter 16 illustrates short, informal reports; and Chapter 17, long, "formal" reports. Chapter 18 suggests ways to plan and present oral reports.

MEANING AND CLASSIFICATION OF BUSINESS REPORTS

Because of the wide variety of reports, they can be and have been defined and classified in a variety of ways.

What Is a Business Report?

Although the following statement is only one of many good ways to define a report, it covers adequately the types of reports presented in this book: A business report is an impartial, objective, planned presentation of facts to one or more persons for a specific, significant business purpose. Usually a report pertains to a more complex topic than is covered by the typical one-page factual business letter or memorandum. It requires more attention to organization, visual aids, and other techniques for improving readability. Also, to be impartial and objective a report presents accurate, reliable information logically, without emotional appeals.

Reports travel upward to supervisors and management policymakers; downward and horizontally to those who carry out the work and policies; and outward (outside the firm) to stockholders, customers, the general public, and perhaps to government officials. A report may be written or oral, but most significant reports are written. The report facts may pertain to events, conditions, qualities, progress, results, investigations, or interpretations. They may help the receiver(s) understand a significant business situation; carry out operational or technical assignments; and/or plan procedures, solve problems, and make executive decisions.

How Are Business Reports Classified?

You can classify business reports in at least six different ways—according to:

1. *Frequency of Issue:* . . . whether periodic or special. The periodic report comes out at regular intervals, such as daily, weekly, monthly, or yearly. The special report involves a single occasion or unique situation.
2. *Origin:* . . . whether authorized or voluntary; also whether private or public. You write authorized reports when requested or authorized to do so by another person. The voluntary report you write on your own initiative. The private report originates in a private business firm; the public report originates in a government, school, or other publicly financed office.
3. *Function:* . . . whether to inform or to analyze. The informational report merely presents the facts and a summary—without analyzing, interpreting, drawing conclusions, or making recommendations. Among the informational reports that have special names are "progress reports."

   The analytical report presents facts, analyzes and interprets them, and makes conclusions as well as recommendations if needed. Some analytical reports have special labels—such as "recommendation report," "proposal," and "justification report."
4. *Subject Matter:* . . . usually in keeping with the department from which the report originates. Examples include: accounting, advertising, collection, credit, engineering, finance, insurance, marketing, operations, personnel, production, statistical, and technical reports.
5. *Formality:* . . . whether formal or informal. Formal reports are generally long and about complex problems. Informal reports are generally short. However, meanings of the terms "long" and "short" vary depending upon circumstances as illustrated in Chapters 16 and 17. General differences in the main parts of formal and informal reports are noteworthy here.

   Formal reports always include—in addition to the body—some or all of these prefatory and supplemental parts:

   Prefatory parts—cover; title fly; title page; letters of authorization, acceptance, approval, transmittal; acknowledgments; table of contents; table of tables; synopsis, abstract, or summary

   Body—introduction, text, terminal section

   Supplemental parts—appendix, bibliography, index

   Informal reports usually include only the body. Some informal reports, however, may have a title page, transmittal, and appendix.
6. *Type or Appearance:* . . . mainly influenced by report length and formality. Reports (a), (b), (c), below, are popular types of informal, short reports; (d) is the formal, long report.
   a. *Memorandum report* uses memo format with TO, FROM, SUBJECT, DATE heading; is usually single-spaced, and used within the organization.
   b. *Letter report* uses letter format with letterhead, inside address, salutation, complimentary close, signature area, and reference section; is usually single-spaced; and goes outside the organization.

c. *Printed report* has printed blank lines and spaces left for the writer to fill in pertinent specific facts and figures. It is used both inside and outside the firm.

d. *Formal report* is usually longer than the **a**, **b**, **c** reports, above, and includes parts other reports don't have. It is used both inside and outside the organization.

In addition to these types, there is one called the *standardized form report*. It is called "standardized" because the department or company dictates the wording and order of the headings for the purpose of uniformity. Actually this report isn't a type, because policy can decree standardization of headings in all types of reports.

You have probably noticed that the various classifications do not place reports into mutually exclusive categories. In fact, one report may be part of all the categories—as, for example: a monthly authorized analytical memo report from the marketing department, written in a standardized form.

PREPARATION BEFORE WRITING REPORTS

As with letters and memos, you want to consider the planning steps (first discussed in Chapter 5) before you begin to write a report. This planning process is, of course, much more detailed for long, formal reports than for shorter presentations. Nevertheless, for all reports adequate preparation *before* writing involves *six important steps* regarding purpose, reader, ideas to include, facts to collect, interpretation, and organization.

Define the Problem and Purpose

The first planning step is to analyze the problem involved and know the purpose of your report. Ask questions like *"What* is wanted?" *"How much?" "Why?" "When?"* The answers will help you determine your problem, purpose, scope, limitations (in time and perhaps funds), and title of the report. Then try to write your purpose in one concise, clear sentence.

The central purpose of many business reports often is to help the receiver solve a problem and/or make a decision. For example, if your firm is experiencing too great a turnover of employees, that's a problem. The purpose of the report may be to find out what causes the high turnover and—better yet—how to keep the employees after they have been hired. Your scope might include surveying all employees or a random sample; you might also need to find out how other firms have solved similar problems. Or, in other reports, your problem may be concerned with an investment and a choice between two or more methods, machines, or policies. Your question might be: "Which proposal is better?" "Should we buy, rent, or lease?" "Should we choose *x, y,* or *z* machines?" and so on.

Consider Who Will Receive the Report

Visualizing your reader and his or her needs is an extremely important step in business report writing. Who wants (or needs) this report? Who will read it? How much detail do they prefer? What is the reader's point of view? Experience? Knowledge? Prejudice? Responsibility? Is the recipient an officer of your firm? Stockholder? Customer? Government official? Will the report be sent to several—or perhaps hundreds—of persons at the same time? Will it be passed on from the primary reader(s) to secondary readers? What are their needs and interests?

If your report goes to, say, your department supervisor, you can use technical terms and abbreviations used in your area. But if it is routed to other departments within your firm—or if it goes to someone outside the firm, or to your stockholders—your language may have to be nontechnical, with intricate explanations. Also, department heads may want and need a substantial number of facts, figures, and details. On the other hand, top management members may prefer few details and perhaps a one-page summary.

Determine Ideas to Include

In short reports this third step may involve merely writing down the general ideas and main topics you'll need to develop in order to accomplish the report's purpose. For some reports, formulating hypotheses is desirable (even essential) as a basis for determining what information you'll need; and then you will jot down the tentative topic headings in a preliminary, tentative outline.

For instance, if your purpose is to find out what causes the high turnover within the company, you might first jot ideas like these: working conditions, supervision, salaries, promotion policies, fringe benefits. Then you might consider subdivision of these topics. Working conditions might involve ideas about physical environment (location of offices or factory, conveniences such as desks, chairs, temperatures, lighting, employee lounge, cafeteria), and intangible factors (such as noise, odors, and transportation). This step helps guide you to kinds of facts you'll need to gather. In long reports you should formulate a working plan—as discussed in Chapter 17.

Collect Needed Material

From what sources will you get the needed facts and figures? For some reports you may have all the data in your head or nearby records. For others you may have to do extensive secondary and/or primary research involving "legwork" in addition to brain work.

Secondary Research

Research through published material is *secondary research*. Publications already in print—books, magazines, newspapers, pamphlets, government documents, atlases, encyclopedias—are known as *secondary data*. A good start for your research may be in company, city, or college libraries, to find relevant materials that have been gathered and reported by other persons. Some researchers have saved their company hundreds of hours—and dollars—by avoiding unnecessary duplication of research and reporting because they first consulted already printed materials. *Caution:* Check your sources' reliability carefully; not everything is true just because it is in print! Are the facts unbiased and accurate? Slanted, prejudiced, or incorrect? What is the reputation of the author and of the publisher? (Check *Who's Who* volumes in various fields and perhaps statistical source books like *Statistical Abstract of the United States, Survey of Current Business,* and others.)

Primary Research

To collect *primary data* (that which you "dig up" firsthand from unpublished information), you may use—with permission:

1. Records from your organization's files
2. Original letters, diaries, minutes
3. Questionnaires—mailed, telephone, or taken in person (For suggestions on wording questionnaires, see pages 163–164.)
4. Interviews
5. Personal observations—such as counting cars in a parking lot at different hours of the day, observing mannerisms of individuals as they approach a cashier to pay their bills, or witnessing car accidents
6. Experiments—such as comparing two groups in which all factors, except for one variable factor with which you are "experimenting," are the same. This method is common in measuring effectiveness of advertising and communication media.

Words of advice from experienced researchers and report writers are: Collect all possible data that might be needed. Record your notes on cards or sheets of paper any size you prefer, usually with only one fact or idea on each.

Perhaps you already have your own good system of preparing note cards; that's fine! If you need suggestions, you might find these helpful:[1]

1. At the top of the sheet (or card) place the heading under which the information will be filed. (See your preliminary outline, made in step 3, page 543.)
2. Next, write the data source—author, book name, or title of article and magazine name; edition, publisher, city, state, date, page numbers. (In long reports you'll need this information for your bibliography.)
3. Record (with any of your own abbreviations) the facts you need. Decide whether you should quote verbatim, paraphrase, or merely record the gist in your own summary words. When in doubt, write a little more than you'll need—rather than statements so inadequate or vague that you must discard them later.

Sort and Interpret Data

The amount of brain work in this fifth step depends of course on the complexity of your research as determined by purpose and reader needs. In a short, informational

---

[1] If you need additional details on research methods, see books such as the following which specialize on report writing: Leland Brown, *Effective Business Report Writing,* Prentice-Hall, Inc., Englewood Cliffs, N.J., 1973; Raymond V. Lesikar, *Report Writing for Business,* 5th edition, Richard D. Irwin, Inc., Homewood, Ill., 1977. Brown also includes bibliographies for further study on business reports and communication. Another extensive bibliography on business and technical writing is in *The Journal of Business Communication,* published by the American Business Communication Association, University of Illinois, Urbana, Winter 1975, pp. 33–67.

report this step may take only a few minutes. In a long, analytical report based on masses of detailed data from many sources, this step may require weeks of study, re-arranging, and analysis between the first sorting and the final interpreting of data. Your analysis and interpretations should of course be objective, free from your own personal bias (if you have any).

If some (or all) of your facts came from questionnaires, you will need to rearrange and analyze the data after you have tabulated the answers. Column after column of figures, perhaps on computer printouts, are meaningful only after they are carefully analyzed so they can be grouped under appropriate headings. *Always* consider what information is most important to the reader and what is not applicable.

Prepare any desirable charts, graphs, and tables (in rough draft) before beginning to write the report (see pages 555-561 for suggestions on graphic aids).

Now is also the time to reconsider the logic of your hypotheses and whether any main ideas in your original, tentative outline (in step 3) should be revised. Occasion-ally, after investigating your primary and secondary sources, you may find that some points in your tentative outline are not logical or possible to complete. Conversely, some areas which should have been included in the outline were omitted. And so you now revise, add, and delete topics where necessary.

Organize Data and Prepare Final Outline

After careful analysis and interpretation, you will organize the findings and make the final outline. But before preparing this important outline, you need to know what con-stitutes the report body and consider methods of organizing and outlining. These areas are discussed in the next two sections of this chapter.

PARTS OF THE REPORT BODY

One part that every report has is the body. This part includes (or implies) three sec-tions—introduction, text, and terminal section.

Introduction—Eleven Elements

The purpose of the introduction is to orient the reader toward better understanding the rest of the report. You can include in the introduction any of the following ele-ments if they are helpful to the reader(s) and apply to your report:

Authorization	Sources
Problem	Background
Purpose	Definition of terms
Scope	Brief statement of the results
Limitations	Plan of presentation
Methodology	

A brief explanation of the 11 elements follows:

1. *Authorization* tells the name of the person (if any) who asked the writer to tackle the report. If no one did (as in a voluntary report), then this introductory element doesn't appear. But when you do include the authorization, present it in conversational language—such as, "as you requested" or, "as (name), (title) authorized" rather than stiff language—such as, "pursuant to your request."

2. *Problem* is usually defined in the early portion of the introduction. In fact, many introductions begin with the problem and then proceed with the purpose—which is often determined by the problem (see step 1, page 542).

3. *Purpose* is the one element that must appear in every introduction. Furthermore, it is the most important single element because it determines what the writer includes in the report. You must clearly get across to the reader what the purpose is, by a statement like, "The purpose of this report is. . . ." Among other names for purpose are: "objective," "aim," "goal," "mission," "object."

4. *Scope* relates to the boundary of the investigation and hence of the report. If you are finding out by questionnaire what married women customers between 22 and 30 years of age with three or more children think about something—that's your scope or boundary. You don't consider anyone else.

5. *Limitations* refers to limitations such as time, money, research assistance, or available data. Without sounding negative, the writer should mention those factors that precluded further investigation.

6. *Methodology* means the method(s) of collecting information. You might get data by reading library materials, by interviews, by survey, by observation, or by experiment. In production reports, you may need to describe apparatus and materials used for experiments.

7. *Sources*—primary and/or secondary—are all those that furnished information for your report. You may include publications, company records, letters, minutes, documents, interviewees, employees, homeowners, and so forth.

   If you are writing an informational report of your own experience, you are your own source relied on for the statements made in the report. But if you "leaned on" other sources, you state them. You well know that a fact, figure, or statement is only as good as its source. For this year's population of your city, you don't rely on a 1950 or 1960 census when more recent figures are available. Mrs. X, an authority in the field, is a much more reliable source than Mr. Y, who is a novice in the field.

8. *Background* (or history) of the situation being investigated is sometimes included if the reader needs the information to grasp the overall picture. But include only enough of the past so the reader clearly understands the present discussion; emphasis throughout the report should be on the findings or results.

9. *Definition of terms* is sometimes vital. If you use any term that has several possible interpretations, you need to tell the reader the exact meaning you have in mind.

   Actually, you can define terms three different places within a report—in the introduction, in a glossary at the end of the report, or within the text of the report. The introduction is the best place when you have only a few (say, one to three) terms to define and the meaning dominates throughout the entire report. If you have many definitions, a glossary is the best. Defining each word as you develop the text is also quite acceptable—especially when the words don't carry the impact of those defined in the introduction—when the discussion of each word being defined doesn't prevail throughout the report.

10. *Statement of the results* in the introduction tells the reader at the beginning the decision—whether or not to buy, which machine is the best, who is your choice of applicant. Then as the reader reads the details in the text, he or she knows how the ideas fit together. This element is appropriate only when the terminal section comes at the end of the body and when revealing the decision before the discussion is psychologically sound.

11. *Plan of presentation* tells the reader in what broad areas (major divisions) the text is developed and in what order the topics will be presented. This preview is usually at the end of the introduction; in a one-page report it may be omitted because the reader can see at a glance what the report covers.

Try to include in your introduction all elements that are desirable for giving your reader the orientation needed, but omit all unnecessary elements. If one or more lengthy elements tend to make the introduction disproportionately long, you can take them out of the introduction and place them separately under specific headings or as part of the appendix.

In short reports the few needed elements may be combined into one or two paragraphs with or without the title Introduction. In some short, periodic reports (especially those covering the same topics every period) you might even omit the introduction if its contents are the same each period and your reader knows them.

For long formal reports the introduction may occupy a full page or several pages, but usually less than one-tenth of the entire report. In these long reports the title Introduction—or a meaningful substitute—always precedes this section. Also, subheadings (for example: Purpose, Scope and Need, Background, Methodology, or Plan of Organization) should always be used whenever such guides would be helpful to the reader.

Text—All Necessary Explanation

The longest portion of any report body is the text. In fact, sometimes (in short, routine, periodic reports) the text may be the whole report—if introduction and terminal section are omitted. In this section you discuss and develop the necessary details that help you fulfill the report's purpose. As with all good business writing, include pertinent facts and trim away nonessentials. Anything you think your reader will want to see immediately while reading the text should be in this section. Other materials—such as copies of questionnaires, supporting documents, long lists of figures (except for statistical reports), should be in the appendix.

The text is never labeled Text. Its title may be Discussion, Findings, Data, or other meaningful words. Or, instead of one main title for this section, you may use a series of headings throughout the text, corresponding to the main topics discussed in it. Both Chapters 16 and 17 illustrate various headings for the text portion.

The content, organization, language style, and visual aids of every report should be adapted to the reader's needs. The *longer and more complex the content, the greater the need for careful organization, headings, transitional devices, and other qualities that aid in readability.* Because these aspects are so important for the entire report as well as for its longest section, the text, they are discussed separately later in this chapter and illustrated in Chapters 16 and 17.

Terminal Section—Summary, Conclusions, Recommendations

Whether the terminal section appears before or after the text, it should be an integral part of the entire report and definitely add to its value. Its functions are to point up the whole report and make its final meaning clear and distinct. This terminal section should be based on the text and should not include new information. This closing merely summarizes, concludes, or recommends.

The terminal section for an informational report is usually called Summary. For an analytical report, it is usually called Conclusions, or Recommendations (or a combination—such as Conclusions and Recommendations). The terminal section is never labeled merely Terminal Section.

1. *A summary* condenses the text discussion. But it doesn't have to condense the entire text—perhaps only the main points, strong and weak points, or benefits and disadvantages.
2. *The conclusions* section evaluates facts discussed, without including the writer's personal opinion. (Actually it's impossible to completely filter out personal opinion, but you should be careful to make your evaluation only from data in your text. Disregard your own biases or desire for a particular outcome. Regarding the influence of attitudes, opinions, and emotions, see pages 24-26.) A variation of this type could be a forecast, such as an economist might make.
3. *Recommendations* go further and suggest a program of action based on the conclusions. If you make recommendations throughout the report, you will probably summarize them here. (The same is true for conclusions.)

Sometimes an unusual title such as Benefits or Suggested Course of Action is appropriate for the terminal section. Among other possible titles are: Probable Developments, Pertinent Suggestions, Merits of the Plan, Final Decision, Forecast, and Important Precautions.

ORGANIZATION AND OUTLINE OF REPORT BODY

The way a report is organized has a distinct bearing on the manner in which it will be received and acted upon. The report's reader(s), purpose, and subject matter must be considered when you choose the organizational plan for the entire report body and the text section. Then you will need to outline the topics correctly.

Plans for Organizing Report Body

The two main ways to organize the three sections of the report body are: inductive and deductive.

Inductive Arrangement

The words *indirect, logical* and *known-to-unknown* highlight the inductive organizational plan. It is basically the same indirect plan you have used for bad-news and persuasive-request messages (as outlined in Chapter 5, pages 103–104). You present *explanation before* the *main idea(s)*. For reports, the three sections are arranged in this order:

Introduction

Text (discussion and explanation)

Terminal section

When should you choose inductive arrangement for a report? In general, you may use this plan if you estimate that your reader:

1. Must have a detailed explanation in order to understand the conclusions and/or recommendations; for example, in scientific and technical reports
2. Is the type who will fight your decision unless he or she is first given complete details and becomes convinced by logical development of facts
3. Will consider your conclusions bad news, because they are contrary to the expected outcome of the study
4. Might feel less bias toward conclusions and be more likely to accept them if first given an analysis of important factors
5. Needs to be encouraged to read the entire report, not just the terminal section . . . and/or
6. Prefers that this report (or all reports) be organized in this order

Deductive Arrangement

The words *deductive* and *direct* briefly describe the psychological organizational plan. It is comparable to the direct plan you used for direct requests and good-news messages. (See Chapter 5, pages 101–103.) You state the *main idea(s) before presenting the explanation.* For reports, the three sections may be arranged in one of these two ways:

Terminal section		Introduction
Introduction	or	Terminal section
Text (discussion and explanation)		Text (discussion and explanation)

In a lengthy report readers usually prefer the deductive arrangement because it gives them an overall picture before they delve into the mass of details. If the terminal section *isn't* at the beginning, some readers skip to the end of the report, read the terminal section, and then return to the beginning. Even in the one- or two-page memo report, many business executives prefer the deductive to the inductive order. In general, you may (or should) use this plan if your reader:

1. Is a busy executive who wishes to know only what the conclusions are or what action is to be taken, where, and who has the responsibility
2. Prefers to determine quickly whether to scan the text for confirmation of conclusions or recommendations and whether the rest of the report is worth reading
3. Will consider your conclusions good news or neutral information
4. Can better analyze data if conclusions or recommendations are given first
5. Wants the writer's point of view promptly
6. Dislikes suspense and prefers to see the recommended action first so that the discussion then substantiates it . . . and/or
7. Prefers that the report (or all reports) be organized in this order

Ways to Organize Report Text Section

One of the most challenging tasks in report writing is to decide upon the best way to organize the mass of details in the text section. You must make this decision before you prepare the final outline (step 6, page 545) and, of course, before you begin writing the report. You can develop the text in one of the following ways:

1. *By Criteria.* Your main topic headings may be the standards, factors, or characteristics—criteria—on which a decision rests. For example, if your report's purpose is to determine whether the firm should buy, rent, or lease trucks; or whether to open a new branch in City X or Y; or which applicant to hire for a management job, and so on, you first decide which criteria are important for the decision. You use them as headings; also, you try to determine subtopics (subheadings) which relate to them.
2. *By Order of Time.* Programs, agenda, minutes of a meeting or convention, and progress reports or write-ups of an event or a procedure may follow this chronological arrangement.
3. *By Order of Location.* Real estate description of a house, for example, follows this plan. The realtor first describes the outside, then the inside; for the interior, first the living room, then the dining room, and so on. This organization is useful for any orderly description focusing on space locations of units—whether they are in a house, factory, office building, shopping center, or international firm with branches widely distributed geographically.
4. *By Order of Importance.* First you present the most important ideas, events, or topics and proceed to the less important points. If all items are of almost equal importance, arrange them by some reasonable plan. Also, when you organize your text by criteria, you can arrange them by order of importance, if desirable.

5. *By Order of Familiarity.* Always go from the simple or familiar to the complex or unfamiliar, because the reader can comprehend better what is known than what is not known. Going from the present situation to the proposed also fits into this category.
6. *By Sources.* This method is less desirable unless you are sure your reader is most interested in what each source revealed rather than in the criteria or other important ideas. You can use this way if, for example, you are reporting on prominent experts who spoke at the convention your firm asked you to attend (at company expense). (See for example, pages 588–589, Memo Report 6.)

Methods of Outlining

After you have decided how to organize the body and the text, you will arrange the headings and subheadings in an outline. A good outline, especially for reports two or more pages long, is an essential tool and a real time-saver. It will become your guide for writing the report. In a long formal report, it also becomes your table of contents.

The outline helps you—before you write the report—to see the relationship between topics, compare proportions and headings, check for loopholes in logical order, and eliminate overlapping. Before you word and set up the headings in your outline, you need to consider types of headings, formats of outlines, and parallelism in headings.

Types of Headings

For the wording of headings, you can choose from three heading types: topic, sentence, or variant. Topic headings are the most common. They consist of single words, a few words, or short phrases. Sentence outlines use complete sentences for the headings. A variant of the complete sentence drops the subject and begins with a verb form. Compare these examples of different ways to write one heading:

Topic Headings

Preparation   *or*   Preparation before Writing

Sentence Headings

Preparation Is Essential   *or*   A Writer Should Prepare before
before Writing Reports   Writing Reports

Variant Headings

Prepare before Writing   *or*   Preparing before Writing

A good heading should clearly indicate the subject matter below it, preferably using no more than seven words. If you choose a one-word topic heading, be sure it doesn't indicate broader discussion than actually is included under it. For instance, the heading Students would be far too broad for a report on the living expenses of college seniors at a particular college.

Formats of Outlines

Having chosen your organizational plan and the wording of your main headings, you next choose a way to show levels (degrees) for the various items in your outline. For short outlines (of only three or four headings and subheadings), you may prefer a format of simple indentations. Longer outlines will be clearer if you use either the traditional popular numeral-letter combination or a decimal system (favored in scientific and some business reports). Compare the formats in the following table for numbering up to five degrees of headings. The numeral-letter system shows five heading degrees by alternating a specific style of numeral and letter: I, A, 1, a. (1). The decimal system shows five heading degrees entirely by numerals—1, 1.1, 1.11, 1.111, 1.1111; an additional digit to the right of the decimal indicates a degree subdivision. (Only rarely do reports require five degrees of headings.)

Degree of heading	Numeral-letter combination			Decimal system	
1st	I.			1.0	
2d		A.		1.1	
3d			1.	1.11	
3d			2.	1.12	
3d			3.	1.13	
2d		B.		1.2	
3d			1.	1.21	
3d			2.	1.22	
4th			a.	1.221	
4th			b.	1.222	
5th			(1)		1.2221
5th			(2)		1.2222
1st	II.			2.0	
		A.		2.1	
			1.	2.11	
			2.	2.12	
		B.		2.2	
		etc.		etc.	

When arranging your headings and subheadings in the report outline, remember these five *important cautions:*

1. Place most important ideas (for instance, your criteria) in the highest degrees of headings possible, considering report length, subject matter, and reader.
2. Try to balance the sections as well as possible. For example, if Section I-A, illustrated above, had 12 subheadings and section I-B had no subheadings, the proportion would be lopsided. You might then try to narrow the scope of heading I-A (by rewording it and by rearranging facts) and broaden I-B.
3. Have at least two subheadings if you divide any topic; for example, A-1 and A-2; *never* merely A-1.

4. Use good judgment in the number of section headings for readability—neither too many (which could be annoying) nor too few. (Usually three to seven main sections are considered desirable.)

5. Never use the report title as a section heading.

Parallelism in Headings

For parallel construction, all headings of the same degree within any part of an outline should be parallel to each other. This means they should have the same grammatical form—all nouns, all phrases, or all clauses or sentences. For example, in the numeral-letter outline above, the following headings should be parallel to each other: I and II; A and B; 1, 2, and 3 under I-A; 1 and 2 under I-B; and so on. However, note that sub-headings 1, 2, 3 under I-A need not necessarily be parallel with subheadings 1 and 2 under I-B, even though they are all the same (3d) degree. Compare these headings for parallelism:

Parallel	*Parallel*	*Not Parallel* (topic, variant, and
(topic headings—phrases)	(sentence headings)	sentence headings)
Types of Headings	Select Heading Types	Types of Headings
Formats of Outlines	Choose Outline Formats	Choosing Outline Format
Parallelism of Headings	Make Headings Parallel	Make Headings Parallel

VISUAL AIDS

To help improve both readability and appearance of a report, good writers use headings and—when desirable—also graphic materials. Because of their importance, these visual aids deserve special attention both before and during the actual writing of the report.

Headings as Directional Signs

The headings you have selected for your final outline will be directional signs for the reader of the finished report. Use headings within any report if they will help direct the reader(s) through the entire presentation. Whenever a heading has subheadings, always first tell your reader what subheadings are included under that heading *before* you discuss them. See, for example, the various transitional introductory sentences and paragraphs in this chapter (and throughout the text) after all headings that have subheadings. Notice the transitions come before the subheadings are used.

The boxed material below, on pages 554–555, shows one popular system of placing the degrees of headings you may need for various lengths of reports. Other styles of placement and typing (or printing) of headings may be acceptable too, but the chosen style must be used consistently throughout the report. If your typewriter has variable type, you may of course choose different type sizes and styles (including italics— with or without underscoring) as printers do. (See also variations on pages 591–593.)

FIRST-DEGREE HEADINGS

For the title of your report or article that requires four or five degrees of headings you can use a first-degree heading as shown above. It is centered and typed in all capitals with or without underscoring, a triple space above the first line of the body. No other heading in the report or article should be typed in this form.

However, if you are writing a long report or a book with chapters--each of which may require three to five levels of subheadings, you will need a higher-level heading for not only the main title of your manuscript, but also the chapter titles. For the latter, you may use $S\ P\ A\ C\ E\ D\quad C\ A\ P\ I\ T\ A\ L\ S$; for the main title, still another distinctive title. Then for all main sections in each chapter you can use the first-degree heading shown above, and all subheadings within the sections will move up one level.

If your typewriter has variable type, you may of course choose different type sizes and styles as printers do. For example, notice the type for the main title of this book (on the title page), the type for chapter titles, and the first-degree headings for all main sections within the chapters.[2] Consistency is important for whatever headings you choose.

Second-Degree Headings

If your report's title is the all-capitals first-degree heading, you may use second-degree headings for main sections-- introduction, text main divisions, and terminal section. These headings are centered and typed with or without underscoring.[2] You capitalize the first word and all others except prepositions with less than five letters (such as *to, of, with, on*), conjunctions (for example, *and, but, as, when*), and articles (*the, a, an, this*). Double spacing before and after them is desirable.

If in a long report you use first-degree headings for the main sections, then the highest-level subheadings within those sections will have these second-degree headings.

In a report that has only two or three degrees of subheadings, you may if you wish use a second-degree heading for its title.

Third-Degree Headings

Placed flush with the left margin, third-degree headings are underscored (in typing). Leave a blank line before them and (usually) a blank line after them. Capitalization can be the same as for the second degree (as in this example), or only the first word need be capitalized. (Then *D* in *Degree* and *H* in *Heading* would be in lower case).

---

[2] Because of the extra wide left margin in this book, the editors decided to have first- and second-degree headings printed in that margin, instead of in the center.

<u>Fourth-degree headings</u>.--When you need a fourth level for subheadings, you can type them just like the third-degree headings except that they are indented, usually five spaces, from the left margin and followed by a period. (Adding a dash is optional.) These headings are always underscored if regular type is used. The paragraph begins on the same line as the heading.

<u>Fifth-degree headings</u> consist of merely the underscored (or italicized) first key word or words of the first sentence in the paragraph. Use this degree of heading when the report requires all five degrees or when you started with third-degree and are using third-, fourth-, and fifth-degree headings.

Graphic Materials for Quantitative and Other Data

Whenever you must present numerous figures (quantitative data) or describe a technical process or a procedure, well-planned graphic materials can help give your reader the picture more quickly—and interestingly. Graphic aids (also called visual aids) include *tables, charts, graphs, pictograms, maps, pictures, and other display materials.* They help you avoid cluttering your paragraphs with masses of figures. They also improve the physical appearance of the report, making it more interesting and inviting. This section suggests ways to correctly present visual aids for quantitative data and then illustrates several popular types.

Essentials for Correct Presentation

The following brief suggestions give you a general overview of essentials for correct presentation of graphic materials in your reports:

1. *Placement.* Usually the best place for each illustration is within the text discussion if it is directly relevant and the reader will need to refer to it while reading the report. Place it as close to the discussion as possible—preferably in the same paragraph or page (or, if it is long, on the immediately following page).

   Two other possible placements are: (a) in the appendix—if the information is only supplemental to the discussion and/or extremely lengthy (as, for instance, a five-page table); (b) in a footnote—if the illustration is small and concerned with the discussion but is not vital to it. This placement is generally not recommended, but it is useful if you feel your reader would rather refer to a small visual aid on the same page than turn to the appendix.

2. *Introduction and Interpretation.* Always introduce the reader to the illustration *before* you show it. Emphasize the highlights, averages, extremes, or other significant aspects of the illustration—whatever is most important for the report you are developing. But don't detail all the minute data, for such unnecessary repetition will be boring and wasteful of space and reading time. Also, if the graphic is so simple that its meaning is obvious, omit interpretations because they may be insulting to the reader's intelligence.

3. *Lead-in Sentence.* The sentence just before the visual aid may end with words like, "as the following table (chart, picture, graph) shows (or illustrates)." If the visual aid is in the appendix, refer to it in the introduction and/or in the text.

4. *Numbers.* Normally, do not number small spot tables, charts, graphs, and so forth when they are placed within a paragraph. However, in longer reports if you have several formal illustrations with a large amount of data, these should be numbered— Figures 1, 2, 3; Charts 1, 2, 3, 4; Tables 1 and 2; Maps 1, 2, and so on. If you have several graphics but only one or two of each kind (figures, charts, tables), you may number them all in one series, naming each a "Figure." All illustrations should have meaningful titles. If desirable, the titles can then be included in separate lists of tables and/or charts after the table of contents, for easy reference.

5. *Expression of Figures.* Express important figures as simply and meaningfully as possible—perhaps in percentages, ranks, or rounded-off numbers. For example, your reader can more easily compare 3 percent with 75 percent (or $8,000 with $200,000) than $8,243.21 with $206,080.25. (If you are multiplying figures, do *not* round off *before* multiplying, for the results may be distorted.)

Following are illustrations and brief explanations of these popular graphic aids: tables, bar graphs, pie charts, line graphs, and pictograms.[3]

Tables

When you need to present quantitative information systematically in rows and columns, use a table. Titles of the rows are usually called "stubs" and titles of the columns are "captions," as marked in the following illustration:

	Captions			
MORTGAGOR'S NET EFFECTIVE MONTHLY INCOME	1978		1979	
	PROPERTIES ACQUIRED %	TOTAL INSURED %	PROPERTIES ACQUIRED %	TOTAL INSURED %
LESS THAN $300	2.7	2.4	1.3	1.8
$300 TO 399	25.8	19.2	23.7	16.9
400 TO 499	33.3	28.8	34.5	21.9
500 TO 599	20.5	21.8	21.4	25.3
600 TO 699	10.5	13.5	10.8	16.2
700 TO 799	2.5	7.4	4.3	9.4
800 TO 899	3.7	3.6	2.0	4.5
900 TO 999	.2	1.5	1.5	1.9
1,000 TO 1,199	.4	1.2	.5	1.4
1,200 OR MORE	.4	.6	--	.7
TOTAL	100.0	100.0	100.0	100.0

Stubs {

Table 3.   PERCENTAGES OF PROPERTIES ACQUIRED AND INSURED 1978 and 1979

Figure 15-1 Illustration of a numbered table.

[3] The emphasis in this book is on presentation. If you need help in constructing tables, charts, and graphs, you can find detailed chapters in texts devoted entirely to statistics or report writing.

Bar Graphs

Easy to construct and understand, the bar graph is one of the most common and adaptable types of graphic presentation. The bars of equal width but varying lengths help to show changes and comparisons in certain areas. Careful labeling is necessary for the bars and the units in which the values are measured. Though there are several other variations of bar graphs, three types you will probably use most often in your reports are the vertical, horizontal, and subdivided bar graphs—illustrated here.

Vertical Bars. When a time factor is considered, vertical bars are especially useful. Notice that in Figure 15-2 the dates are placed across the bottom scale. Millions of dollars beginning with zero at the bottom are listed upward at the left, to help determine the height of each bar.

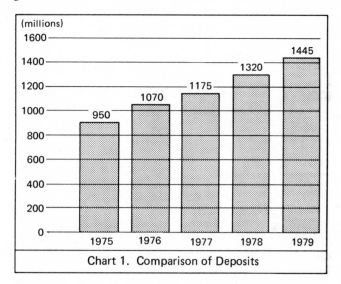

Figure 15-2   Example of a vertical bar graph.

Horizontal Bars. Many uses and variations are possible with horizontal bar charts. They may include single bars (as in Figure 15-3) or multiple bars (Figure 15-4), which compare two or three variables within each single bar. The scale at the bottom line may list percentages (as in both figures below), dollars, tons, barrels, miles, or whatever is the basis for comparison. Each horizontal bar begins on the vertical line at the left and each has a name. For example, if the report compares total exports of five states in millions of dollars, each bar represents a state, named at the left. In Figure 15-3 each bar names an area of energy use. In Figure 15-4 each double bar represents a use of plastic cards—compared for the years 1977 and 1979.

For extra clarity, you can have both a bottom scale and figures within the bars. With or without a bottom scale, every bar must be in exact, correct proportion according to a specific scale. Among other variations are showing totals and/or percentages at bar ends or listing these figures in nearby columns, as in Figure 15-5.

The number at the end of each bar helps readers to see easily the exact percent for each area. A lead-in sentence in the report states that the graph "helps to identify the areas of energy use where conservation measures can accomplish the most significant savings: Transportation, heating, and industrial processes." As this is a spot graph within the report, it is not numbered.

Source: U.S. Energy Prospects: An Engineering Viewpoint, National Academy of Engineering, Washington, D.C., 1974, p. 26.

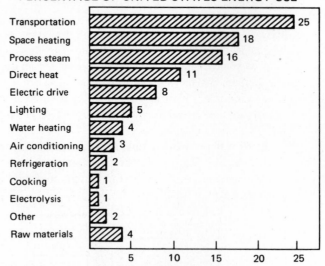

Figure 15-3   A horizontal bar graph.

To distinguish the years in each double bar, crosshatcing, shading, or colors may be used. The key to the years (or whatever the variables are) is placed wherever space is available.

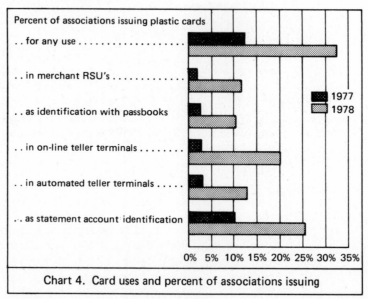

Figure 15-4   A horizontal multiple-bar graph.

Subdivided Bar Graphs. To show the constituent elements or parts of a whole area or subject which is being compared with other subjects, a subdivided (component) bar graph is helpful. Each part of a bar has a certain color, shading, or cross-hatching—as in Figure 15-5—to distinguish it from the other components. A legend explains the markings on all parts. Notice that in Figure 15-5 the dates are across the bottom. All bars except two contain figures within the segments (components); for the two smallest the figures are outside at the right.

Figure 15-5 A subdivided bar graph.

Pie Charts

When you want to show relative sizes of parts in a whole or group, pie charts are effective. To make a comparison of facts easier, the pie segments (pieces) should be shown in percentages, as in Figure 15-6—and perhaps also total figures, if useful. With this pie chart the total dollars for each segment were listed in a separate column below the pie. Notice that each piece of the dollar (pie) is clearly labeled, with labels inside the larger pieces (starting at the 12 o'clock position) and labels outside the smaller pieces.

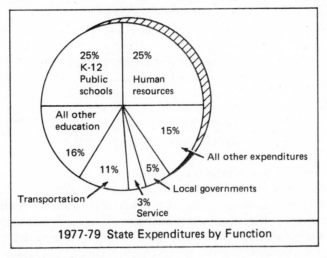

Figure 15-6 Example of a pie chart.

Line Graphs

When you want to portray a trend or series of figures covering a large number of time periods, the line graph is useful and fairly easy to construct. In a line graph, the time scale is usually across the bottom and the magnitudes are placed near a left-hand vertical line, as in Figure 15-7. One extra feature of this graph is that the peaks are clearly marked with figures.

Figure 15-7 Example of a line graph.

Pictograms

You can present the same types of data in pictograms as in horizontal or vertical bar graphs. The main difference is that in the pictogram—instead of using lines to outline the bar rectangles, you insert simple small pictures that represent the data. Depending upon your subject matter, the pictures might be people (👥) or moneybags (💰) or houses (🏠) or any other simple, pertinent sketches. As in the pictogram shown in Figure 15-8, all units should be identical. Notice that each car represents the same number of units, 1 million vehicles. Pictograms are often used—because they are interesting and attractive—in reports to the general public, annual reports to stockholders, company advertising booklets, and magazine articles.

Maps and Other Visual Aids

Maps help reveal geographic facts and comparisons. They can show locations of natural resources (as in Figure 15-9), company offices, transportation routes, environmental or weather patterns, quantities of products sold in certain areas, and various other data.

Figure 15-8 Example of a pictogram.

The following map uses crosses and triangles to mark locations of two products. Other ways to show facts on a map are by use of different colors, shading lines, cross-hatching, dots, numbers, or various sketches or pictures.

Among other visual aids that help enliven a report are cutaway drawings (like those showing parts of a machine), organizational charts, flowcharts, and photographs.

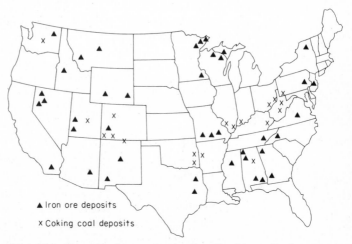

Figure 15-9 Example of a map showing deposits of two natural resources.

QUALITIES OF WELL-WRITTEN REPORTS

After you have completed your outline and any needed visual aids (in rough draft), you are ready to write the report. And then—before you transmit it—you'll revise wherever necessary. The way you write the report often determines whether it will be accepted by the management people involved.

Actually, all the business writing principles you studied in Chapters 3 and 4 also apply to reports. Because reports must be objective as well as interesting and because they are generally longer and more complex than letters or memorandums, they require special attention to all areas.

The following checklist summarizes ways to achieve the seven C qualities for good report writing. In addition, you will benefit by reviewing the writing principles (at least the Checklist of Business Writing Principles, in Chapter 4, and reading Checkpoints When You Edit Writing for Business, in Appendix B, pages 720–723. Chapters 16 and 17 provide additional details and examples about the various parts, procedures, and requirements referred to in this checklist.

CHECKLIST OF C QUALITIES IN WELL-WRITTEN REPORTS

A. Completeness and Conciseness

1. *Include—in the body (introduction, text, terminal section) all facts needed to answer both primary and secondary readers' questions relevant to report's purpose.* Use an appendix for relevant facts too detailed to be in the body.
2. *Cover the what, why, when, where, who, and how* whenever appropriate for purpose and reader(s).
3. *Give the person who requested the report what he or she wants*—detailed descriptions and figures or mainly highlights with minimum supporting data. (If this person didn't specify, use your good judgment and creative ability to design an effective, complete report.)
4. *Trim the report to essentials that fit purpose and reader requirements. Omit all irrelevant material* even if you devoted many hours (perhaps days) to gathering and preparing it. The busy executive needs a concise story on which to act.
5. *Avoid wordy, trite expressions, unnecessary repetitions, and overuse of articles and prepositional phrases.* Instead of "Analysis *of the* data shows," write "Data analysis shows." Good business writing averages only one prepositional phrase to every 11 words.
6. *Present both favorable and unfavorable factors* that affect the situation your report covers.
7. *Include whatever prefatory and supplemental parts are desirable,* depending upon the report's complexity, length, and "formality." Avoid unnecessary overlapping with the report body (as, for instance, in the transmittal letter and the introduction).

B. Concreteness, Conviction, Objectivity

1. *Use specific words and figures* ("52 percent" or "8,100 employees" instead of "many" employees), because they are essential for fair and convincing reports.
2. *Identify information sources* within the introduction, text, and/or appendix. For long, formal reports include documentation. (See pages 639–648.)

3. *Substantiate a source's reliability (if necessary for reader conviction),* by stating truthfully (briefly) whether the source is a recognized authority; where, when, how, and under what conditions the person made the quoted statements; and whether they are likely to be biased.

4. *Be sure you yourself are objective in your quotations, paraphrasing, and abstracting.* Do not quote a source out of context or slant statements with your own intentional bias or opinion. Try to make the abstracted material a fair representation of the whole situation or area from which you abstracted. (See also Chapter 2, pages 19–24 on Perceptions of Reality.)

5. *Consider carefully the bases for your inferences.* Inform your readers as to what portions of your statements are mere assumptions. Distinguish between verifiable facts, inferences based on facts, and your own assumptions. (See also Chapter 2, pages 21–22, on Inferring.)

6. *Avoid emotional writing,* with glowing adjectives and adverbs based on your opinions.

7. *Present facts impartially, showing both sides whenever necessary. Don't discolor facts with your personal feelings and prejudices.*

8. *Use concrete nouns as subjects of sentences.* Whenever possible, avoid beginning sentences with abstract, intangible nouns or with expletives (*it* is, *there* are, etc.).

9. *Use mostly active—not passive—verbs.* (Read again the examples on pages 51–53.) Instead of the passive verbs in "An observer *was sent* around the plant to . . . , and it *was found* that . . . ," use active verbs: "Management *dispatched* an impartial observer to officially record incidents of . . . . He (or she) *discovered* that . . . ."

10. *Avoid the subjunctive as much as possible,* because it conveys contrary-to-fact ideas in the reader's mind. Instead of *would, could,* and *might* (all subjunctive), use *will* (future) or *can* and *may* (present tense). For example, instead of: "For better product distribution your firm *would need* three branch stores; each *would have* a manager who *would* . . .," write: "For better . . . , your firm *needs* three branch stores; each *will* (or *can*) *have* a manager who *can* . . . ."

11. *Write in present tense whenever possible.* Besides using present tense when you refer to the present, use it also when stating a fact that was true in the past and is still true: "The manager informed the trainee that promptness *is* (not *was*) expected." Furthermore, use present—not future —tense when referring to something that seems to be happening in the future but actually exists now:

    a. In the introduction write, "This report *shows* . . ." (not "will show"), because the reader has the completed report before him or her and whatever you're referring to is present now.

    b. Instead of future tense: "Two years of challenging work *will be* ahead for those who *will enter* this program. They *will spend* six months in each area . . . ," write in the present tense: "Two years of challenging work *are* ahead for those who *enter* the program. They *spend* six months in . . . ."

12. *Base your conclusions (if any) or your summary statements on adequate facts and be sure your written presentation is logical.* Avoid unwarranted, hasty generalizations.

C. Consideration and Courtesy

1. *Apply integrity in your research, analysis, interpretation, organization, and presentation of all facts, figures, comments.*

2. *Choose your organizational plan (inductive or deductive) for the most effective reader reaction.*

3. *Organize text topics after considering what will be most meaningful for the reader.* If possible, place favorable aspects before the unfavorable and the simpler ideas before the complex.

4. *Adapt writing style and formality to the reader* by using one of these choices:

   a. *In all memo and letter reports and* in other *informal* reports use the same informal style as in letters and memos—personal pronouns (I, we, you).

   b. *In longer, formal reports*—for instance to top company, public, or government officials or to the general public (and sometimes also in reports with controversial subject matter) you can use impersonal style in which you never refer to yourself at all. (But try to avoid overuse of passive verbs and expletives with this style.)

   c. *In a more formal report style*—seldom necessary or desirable in business reports—you might refer to yourself as "the author" and your assistants as "the research staff," "committee," or a similar title.

5. *Handle disagreeable material tactfully and courteously.* If you know your findings are contrary to the reader's opinions or expectations, you might precede your unfavorable statements by a tactful statement like, "Although one might have expected a different outcome, nevertheless . . . ," or, "Considering your previous experience, a study of these data leads to an unexpected conclusion. . . ."

6. *Watch your tone and logic,* to establish or reinforce the reader's confidence in you, the writer.

7. *Base your recommendations, if any, on logical conclusions resulting from the facts presented—and not on emotional appeals. Omit "sales talk"; depend upon objective presentation* of facts.

8. *Omit your own opinions unless the reader asked for them and you clearly label them.*

9. *Make your report interesting as well as readable* by using topic sentences; headings; and tables, graphs, charts, pictures, or other graphic aids if they will be helpful. Also, occasional questions, pertinent stories, and examples spark interest—if appropriately related to the report's purpose.

10. *When a decision is close, present in the terminal section both the pros and cons;* list favorable aspects (advantages) before the unfavorable (disadvantages), usually in the same order as in the text discussion.

D. Clarity

1. *Phrase all statements so the reader can easily understand them.* Keep sentences within 17 to 20 words; paragraphs, 15 typewritten lines maximum. Include a topic sentence for each paragraph.

2. *Include definitions of any technical terms*—in the introduction, text, and/or appendix.

3. *In comparing figures, use percentages, ranks, ratios, or rounded-off figures for easier reader comprehension.* But show exact figures somewhere in the report, perhaps in a table right in the text or the appendix.

4. *Use graphic aids*—charts, graphs, pictures, etc.—whenever they help clarify your presentation of quantitative data.

5. *Discuss a graphic aid briefly (highlights) before you present it.*

6. *Use headings to guide the reader, but be sure your writing is clear and coherent without them.* In the sentence immediately following a heading, do *not* refer to the heading by the word *this* or another pronoun.

7. *Use transitional words and phrases* (such as "also," "on the other hand," "similarly," "for example,") *to link sentences* and tie ideas together. (For a list of transitional words and phrases see pages 738–739.)

8. *Use transitional sentences with forward or backward references to link paragraphs or sections.*

   a. A *forward* reference is placed at the end of a paragraph. For example, the last sentence in a paragraph about education might lead to the next paragraph this way: "Thus education of the recent college graduate is important, but so is attitude toward employment."

   b. A *backward* reference sentence can effectively begin a paragraph and serve as both a transition and a topic sentence of that paragraph. In the previous situation, the attitude-toward-employment paragraph could begin with a topic sentence that ties the two paragraphs together, like this: "Not only is education an important job qualification for a recent college graduate, but so is attitude. . . ." (Do not use both (a) and (b) in consecutive paragraphs.)

9. *Use introductory, summary or concluding, and transitional paragraphs to tie together sections of a report.*

   a. The *introductory* paragraph of a section serves a section the same way a topic sentence serves a paragraph. If a section has two or more subdivisions, always introduce them to the reader before you discuss them.

   b. A *summary or concluding* paragraph can be effective if a section is quite long—say, three or more typewritten pages—but this final paragraph must definitely be helpful to the reader.

   c. A *transitional* paragraph is especially helpful in a very long report—perhaps with 30 or more typewritten pages. You add this paragraph somewhere in the middle of the report body to tell the reader where she or he is; it tells what has been covered and what is yet to come.

10. *List and number conclusions or recommendations* if you have more than one.

D. Correctness

1. *Double-check accuracy of all facts, grammar, spelling, parallelism of headings;* relationship of prefatory and supplemental parts (if any) to the text; sentence structures; typing; and mechanics.

2. *Distinguish clearly between facts, opinion, inferences* throughout the text and in the terminal section.

3. *Observe the five important cautions* (pages 552–553) regarding arrangement of headings and subheadings.

4. *Word your conclusions accurately,* with conservative, unexaggerated statements. If they are based on an estimate, clarify the basis.

5. *Check to see that your report has all the other good qualities* of report language, readability, and objectivity already mentioned in this checklist, and that important ideas are correctly emphasized (by adequate details, placement, headings, and other visual aids).

6. *See that report layout is attractive and uncrowded,* with pleasing margins and white space.

7. *In a long report, check for accuracy of all prefatory and supplemental parts* (Chapter 17) as well as of the body, and see that all parts are placed in correct order.

8. *Include no new material in the terminal section.* It must be based on facts in the discussion section.

EXERCISES

1. Below is a message with a TO, FROM, SUBJECT, DATE heading. Is it a memo or a memo report? Why? Which organizational plan does this message follow? Evaluate the message as to its organization, tone, and probable effectiveness.

```
                                          Date: May 10, 19_
TO:             All departments, Aloha Street Office
FROM:           Sally Rand
SUBJECT:        New Procedures for Checking out Collection Folders
```

A check of the collection file shows that many folders are missing and aren't checked out to anyone; neither are they in the closed file. As a result, we ask your cooperation in solving this problem by following the new procedure outlined below.

Effective this date, all collection folders at the Aloha Street Office will be filed on the first floor in the safe deposit area. Patricia Wallace will assume the responsibility for checking the folders in and out. You can reach her at Ext. 222. If you receive no answer on this extension, call any New Accounts person to check out a folder.

Under no circumstances is any folder to be removed from the file unless Patricia or someone in New Accounts checks it out. If you check out a file and then give it to someone else, it is your responsibility to notify the file clerk that you no longer have the folder. Otherwise, you will be held responsible for returning it to the file.

Please check your department and return any collection folders you are not using. We will appreciate your assistance.

2. Revise the following sentences and paragraphs to make them conform with the suggestions in this text. What principles does each violate?

   a. To have proper accounting control, your organization would need a central receiving department under the direct supervision of the chief accountant. His assistant, a receiving clerk, would be responsible for all incoming and outgoing merchandise. At the time of purchase or withdrawal, all purchase orders and warehouse withdrawals would go to the receiving department, so that the clerk could make the proper entry in his ledger. In turn, the clerk would count all incoming and outgoing merchandise and would record it on proper sheets. Only then would he permit delivery to the department intended. By doing so, you would have an up-to-date record of your inventory.
   b. According to Mr. Metz, "two years of interesting work will be ahead for those who will enter the program." Six months will be spent in each of the four areas—plant, traffic, administration, and accounting. In each area, the trainee will become acquainted with the operations by working with an experienced craftsman. Sometime before the six months will be up, the trainee will take over the responsibilities of a line supervisor in that department.
   c. An observer was sent around the plant to investigate possibilities of employee carelessness as the cause for rising utilities. It was observed that many of the drinking fountains were left running continuously. It was also noted that lights were left on by many

of the supervisors in offices while they were in the shop. And
although not as prevalent, many of the lights are left burning
throughout the noon hour. Finally it was observed that even on
cold days many of the outside windows in the various departments
were left open. Since most of the rooms have thermostats, the
heating system is overloaded in trying to maintain constant temperatures.

d. This corporation adheres to a policy of nonacceptance of gratui-
ties from firms or their representatives with which the company
has, has had, or may have business agreements, contractual or
otherwise.

e. The calculation of savings accomplished through absorption of volume is based on converting the increase in realization since the
reference period to equivalent personnel.

f. Production increased during the last quarter because there was
less absenteeism, improved working conditions in the laboratory,
metal shop, and factory, and equipment was maintained better; also we had more effective quality control procedures.

g. It was found that greater tensile strength was developed under
high temperatures.

h. Following the approach outlined in your memo of April 5, the warehouse was surveyed for the availability of space for storage.

i. If you paint the shop in light colors, you can expect the following advantages: (1) reduced lighting costs, (2) increase the productivity, (3) the shop will appear larger.

3. Assume the paragraph just before the one below discusses the firm's tax difficulties.
In each blank space insert a transitional word or phrase from the list on pages 738–
739 (or any other source). The words in parentheses guide you toward the intended
meanings.

> Wages. Labor relations present an even more pressing problem. The
> cost-of-living index is rising; (*result*), the company's wage policy
> may have to be reexamined. It is true that the ABC Amendment per-
> mits wage raises to be passed on to the consumer. (*contrast*), many
> branches of the company will not recover the increased costs. The
> appliance division (*instances*) would encounter heavy sales resis-
> tance. (*addition*), management will have to consider the effects of
> price increases or labor difficulties in an election year. (*sum-
> mary*), negotiations with labor will have to be taken with caution.

4. Evaluate the following report by answering these questions:
   a. What improvement can you make in the subject line?
   b. Does the introduction orient the reader to the material that follows? Why or
   why not? What elements do you find in the introduction? Should it have a heading?
   c. What is the purpose of the introductory paragraph immediately following the
   Discussion heading? Can you suggest a way to improve it?
   d. If the writer had chosen to omit the heading Discussion and instead had placed
   the titles of the three reports as second-degree headings, what change would this
   choice have required in the introduction? Which setup do you prefer?
   e. What degrees of headings does this report have? What degrees would it have if
   the change suggested in (d) were made?

f. Is the text organized logically or psychologically?

g. Underline all passive verbs. How many do you find?

h. Circle the active verbs. Does the report have more active than passive verbs?

i. Does each paragraph have a topic sentence?

j. Is the terminal section correctly labeled? Does it satisfactorily carry out its function? Why or why not?

k. Can you suggest any other corrections or improvements?

TO: Malcolm Greene   November 10, 19--
FROM: Thomas Jones
SUBJECT: Installment Credit Department Reports

Here is the report you requested concerning reports written by one commercial bank here in (*city*). I interviewed Diana Anderson, assistant cashier at State National Bank, concerning business reports used in her organization. Since you are especially interested in installment credit, I have limited my discussion to reports prepared and used by the Installment Credit Department.

Discussion

The three types of reports used in this department and discussed in this report are the Interoffice Memorandum Report, Statistical Report, and Memorandum Report for the Credit File.

Statistical Report

The statistical report is compiled monthly by employees of the installment credit department, under Miss Anderson's supervision. The report is a statistical presentation of the total loan balance of each of the department's individual accounts. These individual accounts are then divided between punctual and delinquent accounts.

The purpose of a statistical report is to inform the department manager and the branch manager of the quantitative and qualitative aspects of the department's operations. The branch manager consolidates this report into a branch report, which she or he then sends to the divisional manager and ultimately the executive vice president in charge of operations.

The report is presented in table form to provide quick evaluation of the department's performance. This presentation points up delinquent accounts, which are given closer examination in the interoffice type discussed next. Since statistics are emphasized, little or no discussion is included.

Interoffice Memorandum Report

Miss Anderson or employees in her department write the interoffice memorandum to supply credit information to upper management and any other bank officer, concerning any of their installment credit accounts. The upper-management reports are the most important and are concerned with delinquent accounts.

Report writing training that all bank officers receive provides standard guidelines for credit appraising. Upper management evaluates the delinquent account credit reports on the basis of the thorough application of these guidelines and the validity of corrective action taken. The standard length is usually one page or less.

Credit File Memorandum Report

The credit file memorandum report is written by any bank officer. Each time a bank officer comes in contact with an installment credit account, he or she makes a report of any new information that has been learned. This report is then included in the account credit file and provides the bank with a more detailed picture of the account. This procedure guards against the possibility of one officer being the sole contact with an account and also enables any other officer to become familiar with that account quickly and easily by reading the credit file.

Although the credit file memorandum becomes part of an account's file, copies of these reports are sometimes sent to other interested bank officers; an example is a person who mentions over lunch that she or he wishes to organize an employee trust fund. The officer, upon learning this information, then makes a comment on a memorandum-for-credit-file form. A subject line is provided for the account name, and a colume is provided for the date and origin of the report. In the column the bank officer places the date and his or her name, and any persons to recieve copies, in this case the Trust Department. The comment is entered opposite the date and is usually no longer than one or two lines.

Summary

The three types of reports used in the Installment Credit Department of State National Bank are statistical report, inter-office memorandum report, and memorandum report for the credit file. The statistical report is an operating report to upper management for the department with little or no discussion, while the other two are written reports concerned with individual accounts. The inter-office memorandum is used mostly for delinquent account evaluation for upper management, while the credit file memorandum contains any pertinent information about an account. All three go outside the department, but a copy of the credit file memorandum is retained in the account credit file to build a more complete file.

5. When you evaluate the report below, answer the following questions:
   a. Does the subject line clearly identify the subject of this memo report? If not, how can you improve it?
   b. Why should a writer initial the report?
   c. Does the introduction orient the reader to the material that follows? Why or why not? What elements do you find in this introduction? What improvements can you suggest?
   d. Do you like the three major divisions of the text or would you prefer only two? If two, and they were Skills Needed and Training Needed—what would be the two subdivisions under Skills Needed?
   e. What improvements can you suggest for the format and spacing of the TO-FROM-SUBJECT lines, numbered items, and headings?
   f. Is the terminal section correctly labeled? If not, what better heading can you suggest?

Date: October 19, 19--

TO: Superintendent Frances Lasson
FROM: Robert Cummins, R.C. High School Placement Counselor
SUBJECT: Communication Skills Audio-Visual Center Needs

On October 10, as you requested, I asked Mrs. Ethyl Holmes, management representative of the Audio-Visual Center in (*city*), what communication skills high school people need to work for her company. This report will give the results.

According to Mrs. Holmes, students need training in both oral and written communication. Even though new workers may not be responsible immediately for writing, their writing skills are considered at the time of employment and during their early days on the job. This is because the Audio-Visual Center generally advances personnel from within the company.

Oral Skills Needed

Since the Audio-Visual Center hires most beginning workers in clerical positions, they must be able to communicate orally in the following ways. (1) Talking and listening on the telephone, (2) Receiving and introducing callers, (3) Working well with many other people.

Even though these are beginning jobs, the employee is responsible for the image of the company and must be able to communicate clearly and tactfully with customers and other employees.

Written Skills Needed

As the beginning worker advances, he or she needs to write more and more. However, even a beginner's duties could include the following. (1) Taking telephone messages, (2) Filling in office forms, (3) Writing routine letters, (4) Addressing envelopes.

If a worker advances to a supervisory position, he or she needs to write periodic evaluation reports on the people in the unit.

Training Needed

The Audio-Visual Center does not have any in-service training or company manual. Therefore, applicants must get their training in school. There are several specific areas that Mrs. Holmes thinks the schools should be teaching.

1. Students should learn correct telephone techniques
2. Everyone, including young men, should learn to type
3. Students must learn to write legibly
4. All future employees should learn to spell correctly and use a dictionary
5. Schools must teach correct business attitudes

The last item is perhaps most important. Students must know that regular attendance, punctuality, appropriate dress, and getting along with others are every bit as necessary as their skills.

Conclusions

Teachers cannot assume that students can communicate well; they must teach them to speak, listen, and write. The Audio-Visual Center feels that these are qualifications for even the most basic job.

chapter 16

Short Reports

What business executives look for in a report is concise, accurate, unbiased material with appropriate supporting evidence to help them make needed decisions. The preceding chapter can serve as your general guide for good work in planning, organizing, and writing the body of any report, regardless of its length. However, short, informal reports require fewer elements in their introductions, fewer transitional devices for continuity, fewer headings, and a more personal writing style than do long, formal reports.

This chapter begins with a checklist of suggestions for writing short business reports, and then it illustrates those which are most frequently written in business—memorandum reports, both analytical and informational; printed and standardized reports; letter reports; and other short reports.

CHECKLIST FOR SHORT REPORTS

1. **Subject line**. In a memo report or letter report, identify the subject on the subject line.
2. **Introduction**. Explain the problem (if there is a problem), and clearly state the purpose. Also include other introductory elements (see pages 545-547) that are necessary to orient the reader to the material that follows.
3. **Text**.
   a. *Present all relevant facts accurately and impartially,* for both sides of a situation. Do not allow your personal feelings and prejudices to affect the facts. If you express an opinion, be sure the reader knows it's an opinion and not a fact.
   b. *Organize* your report by the inductive, logical plan or the deductive, psychological plan. (These are similar to the bad-news and good-news plans, respectively.)
   c. *Emphasize important ideas* by showing more details; placing them in prominent positions; and/or using mechanical means such as amount of white space, capitalization, underscoring, visual aids, and repetition.
   d. *Use headings* to guide the reader through the report, but write your sentences and paragraphs so they can stand alone—as if the headings didn't exist. Usually headings range from second- to fifth-degree, with not more than two or three degrees of headings in any one short report.
   e. *Use topic sentences* for your paragraphs, *and* use *an introductory paragraph at the beginning of a major section that contains two or more subdivisions.*
   f. *Apply the seven C writing principles.* (For details, see pages 561-565.) Throughout, make your writing easy to read; use understandable words, sentences averaging 17 to 20 words, concrete nouns, few adverbs, few adjectives, and paragraphs whose maximum length doesn't exceed 15 typewritten lines.

4. **Terminal section.**
   a. Make certain that your terminal section is an integral part of the report and *results logically from the facts already presented in the text.*
   b. *Remember that a summary condenses the text, conclusions evaluate the text, and recommendations offer specific courses of action.*
   c. Don't include any new material in this section of the report.
   d. Usually list summary points in the same order as topics are discussed in the text.
   e. If you have more than one conclusion or recommendation, list and number them. You might do the same in a summary, if desirable.
   f. Support your conclusions or recommendations with ample appropriate facts that are up-to-date and accurate.
5. **Appendix.** Put material in the appendix that would clutter up the text. Use material that belongs in the report but isn't vital to the development or presentation of the text.

ANALYTICAL MEMORANDUM REPORTS

To show you one way of planning, organizing, and writing an analytical memo report, the following discussion presents first a step-by-step analysis of a specific situation. Thereafter it includes three ways to organize justification reports and illustrates two periodic reports with figures.

Steps in Preparing an Analytical Personnel Report

Assume that Gene Mohr, manager of your bank's head office savings department has asked you (assistant manager of the personnel department) to help find a replacement for a teller who is quitting work and moving to another city. You advertised and 15 people applied for the job. After carefully checking their application forms, test scores, and your own interview notes, you narrowed your choice to the five best candidates. Then you wrote to their references for recommendations. After receiving the replies, you have chosen the three best candidates. Your task now is to evaluate each of the three in a memo report to Mr. Mohr. He likes you to analyze the facts for him—even rank the applicants—but he wants to make his own recommendations and decision.

Here are facts about the three applicants:

Helen True:
1 year business college; high school graduate with a 2.9 (out of a possible 4.0) gradepoint average; completed in high school an office machines course with a grade of B; typing, 60 words per minute; arithmetic aptitude, excellent; neatly groomed for business appearance; excellent references—"highly dependable, cour-

teous, and honest"; excellent health; 11 years of business experience—all with one company.

James Mace:
High school graduate with a 2.5 GPA; completed in high school an office machines course with a grade of C; typing, 50 wpm; arithmetic aptitude, good; fairly neat and well groomed; good references—"Dependable, tactful"; good health; 6 years of business experience with two different firms; 2 years' military service.

Beth Astor:
1 year at the local four-year university, with a 3.0 GPA; high school graduate with a 3.3 GPA; completed in high school an office machines course with grade of A; typing, 65 wpm; arithmetic aptitude, excellent; very neat, well groomed; references —"good worker but has difficulty getting along with others"; fair health; three years' business experience with three different firms; attendance irregular in two.

With all these figures facing you, where do you begin? One way is to group these facts under headings representing *criteria* (see item 1, p. 550) you will be using to measure the three people's qualifications. Notice that if you merely group them by their names as in the above list, comparisons are difficult. After some juggling, you decide that all the data fall under the headings of Education and Skills, Personal Qualifications, or Probable Permanency with Firm. (Many times when organizing you have material that doesn't fit exactly anywhere. Health is an example of such material. So you organize such material the best way you can; in this report it can fit under Personal Qualifications or Probable Permanency with Firm.) You can now arrange the backgrounds of the three applicants in working tables like the following:

Education and Skills

	True	Mace	Astor
Education	H.S. graduate 1 year business col.	H.S. graduate	H.S. graduate 1 year at university
Grade point	2.9	2.5	3.3 in H.S. 3.0 at university
Arithmetic aptitude	Excellent	Good	Excellent
Typing	60 wpm	50 wpm	65 wpm
High school grade in machines	Grade B	Grade C	Grade A

Personal Qualifications

	True	Mace	Astor
Appearance	Neat and well groomed	Fairly neat; well groomed	Very neat and well groomed
Dependability	Excellent	Good	Fair; but good worker
Compatibility	Excellent	Good	Fair; difficulty working with others

Probable Permanency with Firm

Number of jobs	1	2	3
Years of work	11	6 plus 2 military	3
Health	Excellent	Good	Fair
Attendance record	Excellent	Good	Fair (irregular in two firms)

Now you can begin to analyze and interpret the material. Suppose your interpretation results in the following ranks and points for these candidates (assuming you decide to assign 6 points for first place, 4 points for second place, and 2 points for third place):

Criteria	True Rank	Points	Mace Rank	Points	Astor Rank	Points
Education and skills	2d	4	3d	2	1st	6
Personal qualifications	1st	6	2d	4	3d	2
Probable permanency	1st	6	2d	4	3d	2
Total scores		16		10		10

From this analysis Helen True wins first place; and although Mace and Astor are tied for second place in scores, it is obvious that Mace is ahead of Astor in two of three criteria. Thus he wins second place; and Astor, third.

Your next step is to write the report, in rough draft. You know you'll be sending a memo report because that's the form you use between individuals within an organization. And you'll use the logical organizational plan because Mr. Mohr told you once he preferred that plan for all memo reports.

The following discussion assumes you have already studied and interpreted the data in the tables shown above. You decide to leave the first table as it is and to place Appearance as the third item in the second table. In the Probable Permanency table you decide on these new criteria titles and arrangement order: Experience (instead of Years of work); Previous jobs (instead of Number of jobs). You have omitted such items as marital status and ages because the hiring decision is based on other criteria.[1] With that groundwork completed, you begin to write—first the *subject line*, which should contain no more than five to seven words, preferably. You decide on "Evaluation of three teller applicants." Then you write the introduction, next the major divisions in the text, and finally the terminal section.

---

[1] Although Title VII of the Civil Rights Act does not specifically mention marital status, this topic is closely related to and often interpreted under sex discrimination. Furthermore, many states have laws that employers may not discriminate against applicants on the basis of marital status, age, or sex preferences.

Introduction

The following list shows which of the 11 introductory elements (pages 545-547) you should include in this particular report. (The others are irrelevant.)

Element	*Comment*
Authorization	Mr. Mohr asked you to assume the assignment.
Purpose	To evaluate the three applicants' qualifications for one opening as teller.
Background	You narrowed the applicants from 15 to 3.
Methodology/sources	You used application blanks, test scores, your own interview notes, and recommendations from references.
Plan of presentation	You will develop the text according to the three criteria for a teller.
Brief statement of your decision	Optional. You may tell Mr. Mohr that Mrs. True ranks highest of the three candidates; or wait to tell this only in the terminal sections. Your choice will depend upon what you think Mr. Mohr prefers.

When you put these six or seven elements into words and sentences, you might have an introductory paragraph like one of the following:

```
Here is the report you requested concerning evaluation of candidates
for a suitable replacement for your retiring teller.  On the basis of
company test scores, screening initial applications, my personal in-
terview with each applicant, and recommendations from references, 3
final candidates have been chosen from 15 who applied.²  In evaluat-
ing the candidates, primary importance has been placed on (1) educa-
tion and skills, (2) personal qualifications, (3) probable permanency.
On the basis of these considerations, Mrs. True rates the highest of
the 3 candidates.
```

or (for the reader who fights your decision before reading the text):

```
As you requested, here is the report concerning the evaluation of
candidates for a teller as a replacement for the employee who is re-
signing.  Through careful screening of application forms, test scores,
my own interview notes and recommendations from references, I have
selected 3 out of 15 applicants for final consideration.  Mrs. Helen
True, Mr. Thomas Mace, and Miss Beth Astor were chosen on the basis of
their teller proficiency, personal qualifications, and probable perma-
nency of their employment with our bank.
```

---

[2] Previous chapters in this text have adhered to the Rule of 10 regarding numbers. As discussed in Appendix B, page 725, you should write out (with exceptions) numbers one through nine; but beginning with 10 you use the figure. Departing from the Rule of 10, this chapter uses—in informal reports and messages—figures for all numbers—except one. Because of a trend in business toward writing figures for all numbers (unless the number begins the sentence), you can decide for yourself what you prefer and act accordingly—in *in*formal reports and messages.

Main Divisions of the Text

You will use three main sections for your text—one for each criterion. You will study each table (which you prepared in rough draft) and analyze the facts. If your reader wants all the details, you will include each exact table or a variation of it within the text. The discussion which follows concentrates on the section labeled Probable Permanency . . . . Your procedure for the other two sections will, of course, be similar. What are the most important facts you can pull from the table? Avoid saying in sentence form before or after a table everything that's in the table; that wastes time and is monotonous. After careful thought you might write a paragraph like this to place before the table:

> Mrs. Helen True's experience and her previous job responsibilities show a background and future potential for a greater degree of permanence with our organization than either Mr. Mace or Miss Astor. The following table shows that both Mr. Mace and Miss Astor might have a greater tendency to leave since they have less stable past employment records and they do not possess the excellent health that is preferable for the teller work.

After the table you might include comments like these:

> Mr. Mace rates as a second choice. His two jobs in 6 years and good health are a better record than that for Miss Astor. Also in his favor is the fact that he plans to make a career of working with people.

Terminal Section

You have the choice of a summary or conclusions, because Mr. Mohr doesn't want recommendations. Which would he prefer? If you decide on conclusions, you should state an overall evaluation of your preference and number the conclusions.

The following illustration (memo report 1) is one of several ways this completed report may be worded. It is typewritten on your bank's memo stationery, addressed to Mr. Gene Mohr, without his title as manager of the head office savings department. This title could, however, be included if company policy so dictates or when the organization is large enough to justify a title for clarification. (Usually memos and memo reports don't include the title of the individuals because the people involved know one another and don't need any identification other than the name itself.) When you're writing to a superior, it may be wise to include the courtesy title ("Mr.", here). Notice that the introduction for this memo report doesn't require a heading, but the main sections within the text and the terminal section have headings—parallel grammatically. Also, all headings and the subject line should be underlined for emphasis.

Memo Report 1

A personnel department officer's analytical report to a savings department director.

M E M O R A N D U M   (*bank name*)

TO: Mr. Gene Mohr   DATE: March 15, 19--
FROM: (*your name*)
SUBJECT: <u>Evaluation of Three Teller Applicants</u>

Here is the report you requested concerning the choice of a replacement for your teller who is resigning. On the basis of information obtained from applications, test scores, personal interviews, and recommendations from references, I have selected
3 out of 15 applicants for final consideration. Of these 3, I
feel that Mrs. Helen True best meets the job requirements of
permanency, education and skills, and basic personal qualifications, as discussed below.

Probable Permanency

Mrs. Helen True's experience and her previous job responsibilities show a background and future potential for a greater degree of permanence with our organization than either Mr. Mace or
Miss Astor. The following table shows that both Mr. Mace and
Miss Astor might have a greater tendency to leave since they
have less stable past employment records and they do not possess
the excellent health that is preferable for the teller work.

Criteria	Helen True	James Mace	Beth Astor
Experience	11 years	6 years	3 years
Previous jobs	1 firm	2 firms	3 firms
Health	Excellent	Good	Fair
Attendance record	Excellent	Good	Fair (irreg-ular in 2 firms)

Mr. Mace rates as second choice. His 2 jobs in 6 years and good
health are a much better record than that for Miss Astor. Also
in his favor is the fact that he plans to make a career of working with people.

Education and Skills

On the basis of education and skills, Miss Astor is an outstanding applicant. The table below provides facts in which Miss Astor ranks consistently higher than the other 2 in everything--
education, aptitude, grades, and skills.

Criteria	Helen True	James Mace	Beth Astor
Education	H.S. graduate 1 year busi-ness col.	H.S. graduate	H.S. graduate 1 year at university

Grade point	2.9	2.5	3.3 in H.S. 3.0 at uni- versity
Arithmetic aptitude	Excellent	Good	Excellent
Typing	60 wpm	50 wpm	65 wpm
H.S. grade in machines	Grade B	Grade C	Grade A

Although Mrs. True's results are not as high as those of Miss Astor, she shows a more than adequate proficiency in her skills.
She should prove just as efficient and capable as Miss Astor in a
teller's position.

Personal Qualifications

Primarily on the basis of references from past employers, Mrs.
True possesses the personality that best fits the performance
and image of the position. As the following table shows, she is
the only applicant of the 3 who has excellent references with no
additional qualifying statements by those references.

Criteria	Helen True	James Mace	Beth Astor
Dependability	Excellent	Good	Fair; but good worker
Compatibility	Excellent	Good	Fair; dif- ficulty working with others
Appearance	Neat and well groomed	Fairly neat; well groomed	Very neat and well groomed

I am concerned about the references of Miss Astor because of comments of former employers about her ability to get along with her
fellow workers.

Conclusions

1. Mrs. Helen True is the best suited to fill your teller vacancy.
    She rates highest in degree of expected permanence and in per-
    sonal qualifications for the job. Although her professional
    ability does not rate highest of the 3 applicants, she ranks
    second and shows a more than adequate proficiency.

2. Mr. Thomas Mace rates as a good second choice, mainly on the
    basis of his expected permanence. He also rates second on
    compatibility. Although he does not rank as high on skills
    and grades as either of the other 2 applicants, his education
    and scores indicate he can perform the job adequately.

3. Because of the questions raised in her references, I feel
    Miss Beth Astor is definitely in third place among these 3
    candidates for this position. Another less desirable fac-

> tor is her "fair" health and the uncertainty of her per-
> manency with our organization. Her outstanding profession-
> al ability is too greatly outweighed by these 2 factors.

With this memorandum report, Mr. Mohr can quickly glance through the facts and decide whom he should hire.

Justification Reports

Many analytical memorandum reports in business have a special purpose—to justify an expenditure or a change in procedures. Among various reasons for such reports are specific suggestions to help the organization increase profits, save time and money, reduce accidents, reduce employee turnover, and improve customer goodwill. Often these reports are voluntary—written by the suggestion maker; but sometimes they are authorized (requested)—for a thorough study to be made of a suggestion an employee left in a company suggestion box.

Reports 2 a, b, and c show three ways to organize such a report; plans 1 and 2 are preferred because they give the busy executive the main ideas (conclusions) first.

1. *Psychological plan:*
   Conclusions before or after the introduction but always before the discussion
2. *Variation of psychological plan—*
   Commonly called "Justification Report"—for top management: Purpose, cost and savings (sometimes also method of installation—if an intricate system), conclusions, discussion
3. *Logical plan:*
   Introduction, discussion, conclusions

The discussion section in any of these reports usually is 50 percent to 75 percent of the entire body.

Memo Report 2a

Organized by psychological plan.

                                                    DATE: May 3, 19__
TO: William David, Director, Purchasing
FROM: Joan Swanson, Assistant Manager, Electrical
SUBJECT: Justifying Purchase of Wire-measuring Machine

                         Conclusions

1. A capital outlay of $200 for a wire-measuring machine will save
   us $452 gross or $252 net the first year and $2,060 net for the
   5-year guarantee period.
2. The machine will save the clerk the cumbersome job of coiling
   up the wire and also free the customer's time by 10 minutes for
   each wire purchase.

Introduction [3]

Recently I became aware of a costly procedure in the electrical department—a procedure of hand measuring wire which we should change because it is costing us about $450 of unnecessary expense each year. In addition to possible dollar savings, this report shows a convenience to both the clerks and the customers with the purchase of a wire-measuring machine manufactured by the Pacific Tool Company.

Possible Savings [4]

In our downtown hardware store we can expect savings in wages and in elimination of losses due to measurement errors after we change from the present hand measurement system to machine measurement of wire. (Similar benefits may be expected for our branch stores, but this report covers only the downtown store.)

Possible Savings on Wages

Presently we are hand measuring the electrical (copper) wire on a yardstick that is permanently affixed to the counter. I made a random check of 100 purchases and found it takes an average of 15 minutes for one clerk to measure, coil, and price 50 yards of wire. The measuring machine can perform the same job in 5 minutes—a savings of 10 minutes or 1/6 of an hour for every 50 yards of wire.

Since business is booming so much that we always have to hire extra help throughout the year, time saved in measuring means money saved in wages. We sell an average of 2,000 yards of wire a month or 24,000 yards yearly and clerks' rate of pay is $4 an hour. With a measuring machine there is a possible savings of $320 in wages, as shown below:

$$\text{Estimated time saved: } \frac{24{,}000}{50} \times \frac{1}{6} \qquad 80 \text{ hours}$$

Estimated savings in wages: 80 x $4 $320 yearly

Possible Savings on Measurements

During the past 6 months, in my quarterly inventory checkups, I have found that an average of 50 yards had left the store but was not accounted for over each 3-month period. This 50-yard loss was attributed to errors in measurement, although we have had no complaints of short measurement nor reports of excessive measurements.

At 22 cents a foot (or 66 cents a yard) for the wire, we can save an additional $132, as the following figures show:

50 x 4 (quarters) x .66 = $132 savings realized if we
                                           eliminate shortage loss
                                           by hand measuring

We can realize a total gross savings of $452 ($320 and $132) yearly with the measuring machine. And because the machine sells for $200 and carries a 5-year guarantee, we can save $252 net the first year or $2,060 within 5 years ($452 x 5 - $200).

---

[3] Introduction could also come before the Conclusions. The heading Introduction may then be omitted if the introduction is only a paragraph or two.
[4] This section could also be organized without the subheadings.

Convenience Factor

In addition to the dollar savings, both the clerks and the customers will appreciate the convenience factor of the machine. Because the wire comes in spools of 1,000 yards, the clerks now have difficulty in hand measuring less than a whole spool--but a large quantity, say, 150 yards--of wire. They must measure off 150 yards and then coil it in some fashion so that it won't tangle and will be easy to carry.

As a contrast, the machine measures wire of all diameters, meters up to 1,000 yards, and includes 3 parts:

1. A spindle to hold the spool of wire to be measured
2. A meter that measures and prices the wire
3. A spindle to receive and coil the wire that has been measured

Thus, this machine will not only eliminate mistakes in measurement and pricing; it will also save the clerk the cumbersome job of coiling up the wire and also free the customer's time by 10 minutes for each wire purchase.

Memo Report 2b

Variation of psychological plan.

TO: *Same as 4a*   May 3, 19__
FROM: *Same as 4a*
SUBJECT: *Same as 4a*

Purpose

To show the dollar savings and convenience factor with the purchase of a wire-measuring machine for the electrical department.

Cost and Savings

For a capital outlay of $200 for a wire-measuring machine, we can save an estimated $2,060 in 5 years.

Conclusions

1. Possible savings: $2,060 net for the 5-year guarantee period
2. Convenience factor: For both clerks and customers

Discussion

Recently I became aware of a costly procedure in the electrical department. By purchasing a wire-measuring machine manufactured by the Pacific Tool Company, we can save money and at the same time assure convenience to both the clerks and customers.

Possible Savings
(Same as that section in the psychological plan. If two subheadings are used, they will be 4th-degree headings.)

Convenience Factor
(Same as that section in the psychological plan.)

Memo Report 2c

Organized by logical plan.

```
TO:        Same as 4a                              May 3, 198_
FROM:      Same as 4a
SUBJECT:   Same as 4a or change to noncommittal
              (See number 1 below)
```

Recently I became aware of a . . . (*same introduction as for psycho-logical plan, but the title "Introduction" is omitted because this section is the first part of the report body.*)

<u>Possible Savings</u>
(*Same as that section in psychological plan.*)

<u>Convenience Factor</u>
(*Same as that section in psychological plan.*)

<u>Conclusions</u>
(*Same as those shown in psychological plan.*)

In the introduction for report 2a you let the president know your results—that a wire-measuring machine will save both money and convenience. But suppose you are a management trainee and you're writing to a 65-year-old penny-pinching owner whose usual reply when someone suggests a change that costs money is, "We've been doing all right so far; why should I spend more money to buy something new?" When you write to this person (or to anyone else who will begin to fight you if the decision is given before the facts), you'll need to change the report in the following ways.

1. You'll need a *noncommittal* subject line:

   <u>Cost Comparison of Hand and Machine Wire-measuring Methods</u>

2. You'll need a noncommittal introduction:

   Recently I became aware of a costly procedure in the electrical de-partment--a procedure of hand measuring wire. This report compares cost and convenience factors of two alternatives--continuing with the present hand method or buying a wire-measuring machine manufac-tured by the Pacific Tool Company.

3. Text (same as above)
4. Conclusions (same as above)

With this presentation, you don't indicate the conclusion until the terminal section —until you have given all the facts to the reader.

Two Periodic Reports with Figures

Reports with many figures in the text require special attention for clarity, as the next two examples illustrate.

Memo Report 3

Hard-to-read report with many figures.

TO: Sarah Spade, Vice President   DATE: November 3, 19__
FROM: Loren Monee, Treasurer
SUBJECT: Treasurer's Savings Analysis Report

The following schedules provide an analysis of the number and balances of the association's savings accounts in groupings of $1,000 for
the month of October, 19__. These schedules were obtained as a supplement report of our regular monthly trial balancing of savings accounts. The accounts were processed October 23 and 24 and reflect
balances at those dates.

Total savings accounts were 5,098 with balances of approximately
$20,900,000. The average account balance for all classes of savings
accounts is $4,100.

A gain of 504 accounts has been registered since the October 19__
analysis, for an increase of 10.97%. Account holders with balances
of $5,000 or more make up 35.79% of our savers. These savers hold
81.58% of the association's total savings dollars. Savers with balances of $10,000 and over make up 17.65% of our total account hold-
ers and they hold 52.21% of the total dollar value. This compares
to 48.78% of one year ago, for an increase of 3.43%.

Savings balances have increased $2,341,334 (including the crediting
of $568,850 in dividends) for the 12-month period October 19__
through September 19__. This represents an actual gain of
$1,772,484 or 9.55%. Accounts with balances of $1 through $4,999
increased $53,110 while accounts with balances of $5,000 or more increased $2,288,224. Accounts in the $5,000 to $5,999 grouping
showed an increase of approximately $500,000 and in the $15,000 to
$15,999 category gained $620,679. Savings certificates which have
been issued since January 2, 19__, totaled $4,005,000 or 19.16% of
total savings. New money invested in savings certificates was
$1,347,572 (gross $1,414,572 less withdrawals of $67,000) while
transfers from existing accounts equaled $2,657,428.

As a welcome contrast to report 3, the following revision not only organizes the
many figures in table format but shows two comparisons—first by number of accounts
and percentages, then by dollar balances. This revision permits the reader to grasp the
data more quickly and more thoroughly. Notice that this monthly analytical report
includes "A Few Highlights" for a brief terminal section before showing comparisons
and analyses of various totals.

Memo Report 4

Revision of report 3 illustrates effective organization of many figures.

TO: Sarah Spade, Vice President   DATE: November 3, 19__
FROM: Loren Monee, Treasurer
SUBJECT: Treasurer's Savings Analysis Report--October 19__

The following schedules provide an analysis of the number, percentages, and balances of the association's savings accounts in groupings of $1,000 for October 19__. These schedules were obtained as a supplement report of our regular monthly trial balancing of savings accounts. The accounts reflect balances on October 23 and 24.

A Few Highlights
Our 5,098 savings accounts totaling $20,900,000 as of October 24 include 504 new accounts opened since October last year. Four-fifths of our association's total savings dollars are held by savers with account balances of $5,000 or more.

Comparisons by number of accounts and percentages
Total number of savings accounts   5,098
Gain of accounts since October 19__ (previous year).   504
% of increase in number of accounts 10.97%
% of savers with account balance $5,000 or more 35.79%
% of our association's total savings dollars that
    these savers hold 81.58%
% of savers with account balances $10,000 or more 17.65%
% of our association's total savings dollars that
    these savers hold 52.21%
% of increase over last year 3.43%
% that savings certificates are of total savings 19.16%
% that savings balances increased (actual gain) 9.55%

Comparisons by dollar balances
Total balances of all 5,098 savings accounts $20,900,000
Average account balance for all classes of savings
    accounts $4,100
Increase in savings balances Oct. 19__
    through Sept. 19__ $2,341,334
Dividends included $568,850

Actual gain (9.55% minus
    dividends). $1,772,484

Increase for savings account holders with balance of:
    $1 - $4,999 . . . . $ 53,110
    $5,000 or more   2,288,224
    $5,000 - $5,999 . . . . (approximately)   500,000
    $15,000 - $15,999   620,679
Total of savings certificates issued since
    Jan. 2, 19__ $4,005,000
New money invested in savings
    certificates (gross) $1,414,572
    Less withdrawals   67,000

    Net new money invested in savings
    certificates $1,347,572

    Transfers from existing accounts $2,657,428

If you wish to discuss any part of this report with me, please let me know. I'll come to your office at your convenience.

Numerous other analytical periodic reports are written in business. They of course vary widely—in periods covered (daily, weekly, monthly, yearly) as well as in subject matter and purpose.

INFORMATIONAL MEMORANDUM REPORTS

In contrast to analytical reports, which give conclusions and/or recommendations, informational reports merely present and summarize facts. Obviously, information reports vary widely in content, depending upon the type of business, purpose, topics discussed, and readers' needs. The following examples illustrate three kinds of often-used informational reports: conference reports, progress reports, and monthly reports.

Conference Reports

The subject matter of conference reports ranges from summaries of personal conferences to write-ups of meetings attended by hundreds of persons.

For example, an advertising account executive may write a conference report after every meeting between the agent and a client. Its purpose is to record all decisions made concerning a campaign. A credit or collection manager may make similar reports after conferences with customers. Likewise, many other employees as well as executives may be responsible for writing reports after any significant conferences with individuals or committees. *The text of such reports is usually organized by topics discussed.* Some firms have standardized headings for the often-written reports to assure that the same information or main topics are recorded in all of them.

In a different situation, a company's delegate to an important convention may be asked to present a report to superiors. Its purpose is to inform other management personnel of significant happenings, decisions, or topics discussed. How would you organize the text of such a report? According to the list on pages 550–551, you might choose to *organize by order of time, topics (criteria), importance, or sources.* In report 5 the sales manager (who attended the firm's regional conference of sales managers) used *a combination of the first three choices.* The three main topics and their subtopics serve as *guides (or criteria)* for planning this particular sales campaign. Headings 1, 2, and 3 are the *main topics in order of importance.* Under the Open Houses heading, items (a), (b), (c) are *arranged by order of time.* This report uses third- and fourth-degree headings.

Memo Report 5

A sales manager's report on a regional conference.

```
TO:     Martha Gerbman          DATE:    June 5, 19___
FROM:   Matt Deaning            SUBJECT: Open Houses and Promotion

cc:   Frieda Dinson      Bill Campbell      Pete Mallon
      Terry Moran        Lana Jarvis        Tyna Green
      June Donaldson     Erick Brown        John Raney
```

The following is a report on the items we discussed during our recent meeting in (*city*) regarding our XL product. They pertain to the

scheduled open houses, our promotional programs, and the signs and
identification of our products. The names of those who were asked to
be responsible for the various parts of these plans are listed in the
right-hand column below.

1. <u>Open Houses</u>
    Here is the tentative schedule that was established, subject pri-
    marily to availability of dignitaries at the ribbon-cutting cere-
    mony.

    a. <u>Employees' Meeting</u> - Thursday, July 20   Terry Moran
        (1) Families will be invited, and sand-
             wiches and refreshments provided.
        (2) This will provide an opportunity to dry
             run the tours being conducted on suc-
             cessive days.

    b. <u>Ribbon-cutting Ceremony</u> - Friday, July 31   June Donaldson
        (1) Dignitaries to be invited need to be
             agreed upon. We generally agreed that,
             as this occasion presents an exception-
             al opportunity to publicize the growth
             of new and nonpolluting industry in our
             state, as well as an opportunity to gain
             state and regional publicity for the
             expanding capabilities of our company
             in the XL product business, an effort
             should be made to include those state
             officials most capable of gaining this
             type of publicity.
        (2) Additionally, press invitations need to
             be extended to press releases developed.

    c. <u>Distributor Event</u> - Saturday, August 1   Martha Gerbman
        (1) Begin tour at 10 a.m. followed by lunch
             at Ritz Plaza Hotel.
        (2) Develop a program to impress upon the
             distributors our program for XL Product
             Division.

2. <u>Promotional Programs</u>

    a. The XL product brochure was reviewed and   Frieda Dinson
        relatively minor changes agreed upon.
        Another draft will be sent to Bill Campbell
        for approval prior to setting type. Bill
        Campbell will prepare and forward guarantee
        copy to agency. This project is to proceed
        as rapidly as possible. The agency will
        prepare a list of names for the prefinished
        RM product line.

    b. <u>Introduction Brochure</u>
        (1) We agreed that a brochure to familiarize   Erick Brown
             our customers with the operation of the
             XL will be desirable.

> (2) We agreed that the procedure used for-
> merly in materials showing photographs
> of the various personnel will be a good
> approach. Agency will develop layout.
> (3) Those to be included in this brochure
> will be Tyna Green, Martha Gerbman, Bill
> Campbell, Frieda Dinson, Pete Mallon,
> Erick Brown, and John Raney, the sales
> secretary.

    c. <u>Advertising and Direct Mail</u>

> (1) A direct mail program directed to build-   Frieda Dinson
> ers needs to be developed, perhaps in   and
> conjunction with local distributors.   Matt Deaning
> (2) We agreed that advertising regions should
> be expanded to cover the entire region.
> This project will be further developed.

3. <u>Signing and Identification</u>   Matt Deaning

    a. <u>Unit Signs</u>
> White cardboard unit signs which will
> fold over the top edges of XL products
> displayed will be printed at the Print
> Shop. Design approved was forwarded to
> the Print Shop for production and de-
> livery to the plant by June 23.

    b. <u>Property Signs</u>
> Building and property signs were agreed
> on and covered in a separate memo.

In report 6 the assistant manager organized the conference report by *sources*, because the division manager was mainly interested in the presentations of the three
national experts in the field. Second-degree (centered) headings are used. (Perhaps to
save space, no blank lines were left after these headings.)

Memo Report 6

An assistant manager's conference report (organized by sources, logically).

TO: Anthony Bloome   DATE: October 2, 19__
FROM: Verna Bennett
SUBJECT: <u>Summary of St. Louis Regional Conference</u>

Here is a brief summary of the St. Louis meeting that I attended September 30 on coin service at military installations. Because you are
mainly interested in the presentations of John Klinest, Wardman Jones,
and Kathy Cummings, I am focusing this report on their contributions
to this conference.

John Klinest's Presentation

John Klinest conducted our meeting and introduced the subject. Because of the current situation at military posts, coin service at
these posts will be a problem for years to come. It's important to
improve our service because:

1. The need is there. The present military situation requires more coin service.
2. Many of the young men and women on these posts are making their first real acquaintance with public telephone service. Their opinions of our service now are likely to be lasting.

A series of slides shown by Klinest pointed out that coin conditions around the country vary from very bad (standing in mud puddles to use coin kiosks) to very good. The coin center at (*name*) is so plush it is used as a reception center for guests.

<u>Wardman Jones's Presentation</u>

Wardman Jones talked about some of the revenue characteristics of military coin service . . . .

(Three paragraphs follow, including itemized facts and figures.)

<u>Kathy Cummings's Presentation</u>

Regarding the traffic considerations, these were enumerated by Kathy Cummings. She emphasized that . . . .

(Two paragraphs follow, highlighting her suggestions.)

<u>Plan of Action</u>

John Klinest recommends the formation of an interdepartmental district team to evaluate our coin service at (*names*) and report its findings to higher management. The team will use the attached checklist.

Progress Reports

As the name implies, progress reports show "progress," accomplishments, or activity for a certain period or stage of a major assignment.[5] The organizational plan is usually the logical, including topics similar to these:

Introduction (purpose, nature of project)

Description of accomplishments during the reporting period

Unanticipated problems (if any)

Plans for the next reporting period

Summary (overall appraisal of progress to date)

The example below is a general chairperson's progress report to the executive vice president of the company, which is hosting the first purchasing managers' regional convention in that city. It uses the logical organization plan, with third- and fourth-degree headings.

---

[5] Progress reports may also be in letter-report format; see pages 598–602.

Memo Report 7

A general chairperson's progress report on convention plans (logical).

TO: Bruce Boyne, Vice President   DATE: November 9, 19__
FROM: Vivian Porte, Convention Chairperson
SUBJECT: Progress Report on Purchasing Managers' Convention,
         January 26, 198_

To keep you informed about the activities of our planning committee
for the first regional purchasing managers' convention to be held in
our city, here is a brief report of our progress so far. Because
some plans from now on will depend upon funds available and your
preferences, you will also find a few questions on which we will appreciate your suggestions and approval.

Date, Time, and Place

The Tower Oaks Hotel offices are holding the following reservations
for us:
Date: Tuesday, January 26, 198_
Informal luncheon: 12:15 - 1:30 Regency Room--for up to 100 persons
Conference rooms: 9:00 - 4:30 Mezzanine rooms 202, 203, 204--each
                               accommodating up to 40 persons plus
                               exhibit tables.

Tentative Program

So that the convention will have an appropriate official opening,
the committee members are delighted that you have agreed to express
the opening welcome--as executive vice president of the company that
is sponsoring the convention.

    Keynote Speaker.--You will probably be glad to hear that for key-
noter we can count on having Jonathan Harrison, vice president and
general manager of National Products Company. The topic he has chosen is "The Challenge Ahead for Purchasing Shortage Items."

    Other Participants.--As the attached tentative program (Exhibit
A) shows, we will have 10 outstanding business leaders on panel discussions in the morning and afternoon sessions. A 15-minute coffee
break is planned for 10:30 a.m. and 3 p.m.

Publicity

Our first announcement in newspapers (local and in three states) will
be early in December. One or two other news stories should appear
during January.

If funds allow, we would like to mail two letters to all purchasing
managers in this region, along with a colorful brochure of the conference program, exhibits, film specials, and evening entertainment
for those staying in the city overnight. Exhibit B shows the planned
layout. The ABC Printer has quoted a price of $ for 200 copies
and $ for 150 copies.

Estimated Financial Requirements

Exhibit C, attached, is a suggested tentative budget. The estimated
total of $ excludes the cost of stationery, typing master copies,

and mailing services. Norma Haney has assured me that these expenses
can be taken care of through our company's usual supplies and postage
budget and need not be itemized here.

We will appreciate any suggestions you may have about our estimated
expenses and your approval of the needed funds. Then we can proceed
to make the necessary arrangements.

Summary

To date many persons have already assisted our committee with their
expressions of preferences and suggestions. We have hotel reservations, firm acceptances from keynote speaker and panelists, price
quotations on a brochure for mailing, and tentative publicity plans.

You will receive from us a definite program soon after plans are
completed and another progress report on December 10. We expect to
devote many more hours to planning and writing. After that we can
all look forward to an interesting and successful convention.

In the meantime, your preferences regarding publicity brochure,
estimated financial needs, and any other suggestions you may have
will be sincerely appreciated.

VP:wh
Attachments: Exhibits A, B, C

cc: Susan Rader
    Timothy Blythe

The next progress report example is organized psychologically—with summary first.
Notice its unusual typing and placement of headings.

Memo Report 8

A manager's progress report on storage space improvements (psychological).

                                                  DATE: April 19, 19__
TO: Annette Smith, Chicago Factory Representative
FROM: Nicolas Lamonter
SUBJECT: Progress Report--First Floor Drug Produce Capacity
           Increased by 30% since January 1

SUMMARY: During the past three months the first-floor storage
             space for drug products at South Warehouse has been
             reorganized to provide storage space for 14,000 (Full
             Box value) additional cases of drug products. This
             addition provides maximum storage with a minimum of
             brand blocking.

ACTION   1) The average daily shipment of each brand and
TAKEN: size of drug products was determined.
             2) First-floor storage areas were rearranged to
                 conform with the average daily shipments.
             3) All drug product pallet patterns were reviewed
                 and increased in size where possible.

DISCUSSION: A 30-day supply of drug products is consigned to the Chicago Factory and is stored at South Warehouse. It is desirable to maintain a maximum inventory on the first floor to eliminate the double-handling of stock to the upper floors. In the past, no definite formula was used to determine the amount of each brand which should be stored on the first floor. Unnecessary movement of stock was taking place. Brand blocking made inventory control difficult and sacrificed storage space.

    By means of storing a 25-day supply of each brand on designated areas on the first floor, maximum storage has now been obtained with a minimum of "brand blocking." First-floor capacity has been increased from 48,000 to 62,000 (Full Box value) cases. Less stock movement is necessary. Inventory control has been simplified. Maximum warehouse height has been utilized.

Monthly Reports

Included in this section are only those informational reports that are written monthly in memorandum report format. (As you know, there are numerous other monthly reports; many are analytical—mentioned in the preceding section; many others are presented on special printed forms—discussed later in this chapter.) When a memorandum report is written each month about the same department and to the same reader(s), an introduction and terminal section are unnecessary. Report 9 keeps the home office informed about certain activities at the branches. The text headings help the reader grasp the main topics quickly and easily. Instead of the signature and typewritten title after the report's last paragraph, Mr. Kay could have initialed or signed his name near his typewritten name after FROM. Also, a blank line after each heading and paragraph would improve the report's appearance.

Memo Report 9

This monthly memo report—from a branch manager to an official at the bank's home office—does not include an introduction or terminal section.

TO: A. B. Sea   DATE: November 2, 19__
FROM: U. R. Kay
SUBJECT: <u>Branch Activities - October 19__</u>

<u>Personnel Training</u>
1. October 31 marked the midway point of the second phase of the National Bank Offices' training program. Training is progressing satisfactorily and on schedule. With the termination of Pat Harris (Smith), we need to make a slight alteration in the program, but don't expect any delay or postponement of any training. In fact, this termination will advance the training of Mary Jackson and Jean Miller.

Business Development Activity

1. I again contacted Ann Kast, dentist, regarding transfer of funds from National Association of Orthodontists, of which she is national treasurer. She says she has received permission to transfer about $40,000 more to National Bank after January 1. This additional amount brings the total to about $75,000.

2. Although 3 employee vacations and one prolonged illness have disrupted my outside business-call activity, I have made it a habit to attempt to converse with every broker, real estate agent, insurance agent, and attorney that comes into the office. Although it is difficult to assess results from the little additional time and effort spent on this form of intraoffice business development, numerous phone calls for loan information and a couple of loan commitments were a direct result of this activity.

Customer Comments and Action Taken

1. An unusually high number of customers in October complimented us on the friendly and courteous service of our personnel.

2. We had a complaint from a large checking account depositor regarding a check on which he had stopped payment too late (his creditor had already cashed the check). Meanwhile our depositor had mailed to his creditor a second check (with a slightly different amount), which was also cashed. Both were paid by our bank. He blamed us for allowing this situation to happen and condemned our system for not catching the stop-payment in time. He quizzed Helen Hunt unmercifully until I interfered. When he started swearing, I invited him to leave the office. Finally he calmed down, listened to my review of the entire matter, apologized for his error, and left, still a friend of the bank.

Building, Equipment, and Parking Lot Comments

1. We encountered the usual winter heating problem at Riverview Office—hot in the morning and cold in the afternoon. Blower fans are turned off at noon each day. We have told Lewis Company of this circumstance many times, but they cannot rectify the situation.

2. Interior clock does not keep correct time. Maintenance department knows about the trouble with this clock and will take care of it.

(signature and title of branch manager)

In summary, although one of the distinguishing features of memo reports is the three-part body (introduction, text, and terminal section), sometimes the introduction and/or terminal section may be omitted. When you understand the three basic plans for memo reports, however, you can adapt to the special formats and headings you'll encounter on the job.

PRINTED FORM AND STANDARDIZED REPORTS

To save time in writing often-used reports, business firms develop printed forms and/or standardized headings for reports.

Printed Form Reports

The printed form report should be used when a company follows or uses the same format often enough to justify the "jelling" of the report body, headings, and instructions into a printed form. The individual filling out the form merely adds the necessary figures, sentences, and identifications.

Although filling out this form is quick and easy, preparing it is more difficult. It should be clear and simple, to provide the needed information in the quickest and easiest manner. Those who will be filling out the form and using the information should be consulted. They can make suggestions before and after the form is drawn up

SALESMAN'S EXPENSE VOUCHER

IMPORTANT   ENTER ALL EXPENSES OF THE TRIP.   ATTACH ALL HOTEL BILLS, ALSO RECEIPTED BILLS FOR OTHER EXPENDITURES OF $25.00 OR MORE EACH.   ENTER COMPANY CREDIT CARD ITEMS   IF ANY, INDICATE SUCH BY *; DO NOT INCLUDE IN TOTAL.   SEE REVERSE SIDE FOR INSTRUCTIONS

NAME _____ FOR WEEK ENDED _____

DAY DATE	CITY	HOTEL	MEALS	ENTERTAIN- MENT (SEE BELOW)	FARE	TIPS	PARKING & TOLLS	STAMPS TEL. & TEL.	OTHER (SEE BELOW)	TOTAL	MILEAGE
SUNDAY											
MONDAY											
TUESDAY											
WEDNESDAY											
THURSDAY											
FRIDAY											
SATURDAY											
TOTAL											

MAIL CHECK TO:

AUTO AT 8¢ PER MILE

TOTAL EXPENSE

CHECK NO. _____

SIGNED _____

APPROVED _____

I. EXPLANATION OF ENTERTAINMENT:
    AMOUNT, DATE, PLACE, TYPE (LUNCH, DINNER, THEATRE, ETC.) BUSINESS PURPOSE; LIST NAMES, TITLES AND BUSINESS AFFILI- ATION OF EACH INDIVIDUAL PRESENT (IF THE ENTERTAINMENT DI- RECTLY PRECEDES OR FOLLOWS A SUBSTANTIAL BUSINESS DISCUS- SION, IN ADDITION TO THE FOREGOING, SHOW DATE, DURATION, NATURE AND PLACE OF BUSINESS DISCUSSION)

II. OTHER (EXPLAIN EACH ITEM)

    (ATTACH ANOTHER SHEET, IF NECESSARY)

Figure 16-1 Weekly expense voucher. When filled out, this report reveals each day's expenses and entertainment. It is approved by the district sales manager and reported to the regional office for reimbursement. Detailed instructions on the reverse side of the voucher explain what the sales personnel should include under each heading.

in rough draft. Figures 16-1 and 16-2 are printed form reports that business firms use. Among others are the company job application form, police officer's graphic location of a collision of cars at an intersection, Internal Revenue Form 1040 for reporting year's income, automobile accident report, claim for damages suffered, and the form the personnel worker fills out after interviewing an applicant. In all examples, the form consists mainly of the text portion of the body. No introduction, terminal section, or even TO, FROM, SUBJECT are included, because the reader is sufficiently oriented by frequent usage, report title, columnar headings, date and/or other information.

Figure 16-2 Example of an evaluation form that a supervisor fills out for each employee twice a year and files in the employee's personnel folder.

Standardized Reports

Though printed forms are adaptable for a tremendous variety of uses, there are situations that require another method of saving time. When the reader needs the same type of information in every report but the requested facts under each heading are likely to vary significantly in length depending upon the situation, standardized headings may be desirable. Such reports are called "standardized reports." The same headings are used repeatedly for any one type of report, but the report writer begins with a blank sheet of paper *not* with a printed form on which the facts are filled in (either in handwriting on lined forms, or in typewriting).

Standardized headings for a company's reports assure uniformity and completeness of coverage and permit the receiving officer to know what to expect so he or she can compare it by periods. Also, the suggested format makes it easy for the report writer to include the data the receiver wants. The writer merely adds the needed information under each heading, without worrying about what headings should be used.

Among well-known examples of reports with standardized headings are the Balance Sheet and the Statement of Earnings and Expenses. Within any one firm the headings used for these reports are usually the same month after month. Here are three other examples:

Example 1

Standardized headings used by report writers for the Federal Aviation Agency.

a. Problem
b. Facts Bearing on the Problem
c. Discussion
d. Conclusions

e. Alternative Courses of Action
f. Recommendations
g. Coordination
h. Attachments

Example 2

Standardized headings used by a real estate appraisal firm.

a. Location and legal description
b. Description of improvements

Roof	Interior Walls	Electrical
Exterior Walls	Millwork	Plumbing
Floors	Appliances	Heating

c. Valuation (with Physical Value Table and Comments)

Example 3

Standardized headings used by Dun & Bradstreet credit reporting service (Figure 16-3).

a. Data Universal Numbering System (DUNS)—a nine-digit code that identifies a specific business name and location. It is also the "address" of the detailed marketing and credit facts for each business listed in the Reference Book and in the **Dun &** **Bradstreet Data Bank**, or files.

b. Summary—overall highlights: buying name, ownership, line of business, date started, D&B rating, salient credit data facts.

c. Payments—how the business pays its bills.

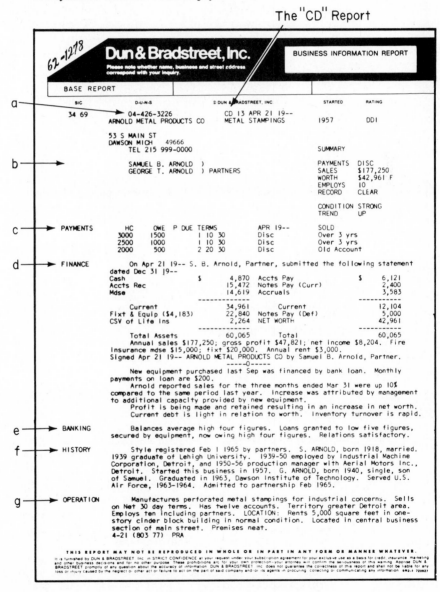

Figure 16-3 Dun & Bradstreet report using standardized headings.

    d. Finance—financial condition and business trend, etc.

    e. Banking—relations with principal depositories.

    f. History—background and experience of principals and the business.

    g. Operation—What the business does, how, under what conditions, etc.

Figure 16-3 illustrates a sample Dun & Bradstreet report. The initials CD near the top indicate the report is a complete revision or "condensation" of all previous reports on the same name.

LETTER REPORTS

As the title indicates, a letter report uses the format of a letter—with date, inside address, salutation, body (different from a letter), complimentary close, signature, reference section (see Chapter 6). Often it has a subject line typewritten a line or two below the salutation. Since this report goes outside the company, it is typed on the firm's letterhead. Its length may range from two to five (seldom more) pages. Pages beyond the first have the same heading (reader's name, page number, date) as for a letter.

Though the general format of the letter report is like that of a letter, its body requires some of the special qualities of short reports, as discussed below.

1. *The first paragraph* usually includes the following elements found in an introduction:

    Authorization (if one exists)

    Purpose (always)

    Problem (if one exists)

    Statement of the results (optional)

    Plan of presentation (depends on length of report)

Examples:

    a. As you requested, I am glad to tell you our experience with the XYZ machine. Overall, we're quite pleased with its performance and dependability.

    b. It is a pleasure to report to you our progress in the year just completed and look ahead with you for this year just started.

    c. I have made an investigation of the delivery service department, as requested in your January 7 letter, with regard to reducing the operating cost of the department.

    d. While auditing your books last month, I noticed your firm does not have a centralized receiving department. The purpose of this report is to explain the present setup and then show how a receiving department will benefit your organization.

2. *The middle paragraphs* comprising the text should present *objectively, without emotional appeals, all pertinent facts—both favorable and unfavorable.* Sources and methods should be mentioned along with emphasis on findings or results. Headings, visual aids, and transitional sentences are also included wherever desirable and feasible.

3. *The last paragraph* brings the letter report to a pleasant, friendly close, as for letters (pages 108–111). If you need to conclude or recommend, do so just before the last paragraph. If appropriate, offer to discuss further or to come to the reader's office.

In letter report 1, Mr. Jones, a business manager in New Orleans, informs an inquirer (Mrs. Davis, manager of another company in Tennessee) about his firm's one-year experience with a Ditto-Print machine. Mrs. Davis wrote that the Ditto-Print Company gave her Mr. Jones's name as an example of a new (one-year) customer. She said she is especially interested in hearing Mr. Jones's comments on performance and dependability of the machine.

Letter Report 1

A manager's report on his firm's use of a machine.

Dear Mrs. Davis

I am glad to answer your request concerning our experience with the Ditto-Print machine. On the basis of our use and plans for this machine, I can assure you that we have been pleased with its dependability and performance.

Our present and expected use of this machine
As you know, we have had a Ditto-Print machine for about a year. Because of our success with the machine, we plan to install another one in another department in 6 months. Also, future plans include supplying each of our 9 departments with a machine.

Dependability
The machine worked up to expectations during the first 2 months and needed only one minor repair; the repairman was prompt and completed his work in one day. Since then, the machine required no major repair except for the scheduled 6-month checkup.

Performance
In addition to good dependability, our Ditto-Print machine has performed well. We have realized considerable dollar savings because the secretaries can copy and distribute correspondence from suppliers in a fraction of the time formerly required. Also the machine turns out good, clean copies.

Although we have noticed poor copies when more than 100 were run off the same master, this is no problem for us because we seldom need to run more than 50 copies off a master. Also, when we need copies be-

```
yond 100, the secretary can make a new master in 5 seconds.  We have
also noticed that high-rag-content paper results in poor copies; but
once again there is no real problem since we seldom use this type of
paper for masters.

It has been a pleasure to help you, Mrs. Davis.  Please let me know
when I can be of future assistance.
```

Like all other unbiased reports, this one shows both the good and bad features of the machine. Mr. Jones's report also states (in the first paragraph) his overall favorable impression.

Perhaps you have already noticed that a letter report like the one above about a machine is organized the same way as a letter of recommendation you might write about a person—his or her work for you or credit record with your firm. In fact, as mentioned in Chapter 8 (page 213), basically "a recommendation is a confidential report."[6] If the inquirer asks you several (say, five or more) questions about broad areas and doesn't furnish a printed report form for your answers, you will need to write a long, factual, objective message that is really a letter report. If your answers require more than one paragraph under each question, you should of course number the questions and/or use headings to help improve readability. Your own good judgment should guide you in choice of headings and format.

Besides writing letter reports to answer inquiries about persons or about products you don't sell, you may also need to write letter reports about the products (or services) your firm does sell. In general, the same care and techniques you use for planning and writing any other objective report should be used for these letter reports, whether they go to a government agency or a customer.

Another popular use of letter reports is the annual message the company president sends to stockholders. In many firms—especially the larger ones—this letter report is part of the printed annual report. However, in other firms the president's letter report is mailed on company letterhead stationery along with enclosed financial statements, as in the following example. Headings for this letter report are unique in placement and color (light blue).

Letter Report 2

A savings association president's annual letter report to shareholders.

```
                                               January 30, 19__
Dear Shareholder:

The year 19__ was one of change and adjustment for our state and, to
a lesser extent, for your association.  In reviewing our activities
it is a pleasure to report to you that the year was one of our most
productive.  Here are highlights of our accomplishments.
```

---

[6] Recommendation letters were included with good-news replies because they are important good-news or neutral replies to nonsales-related inquiries. See pages 212–217. For examples of answers to nonsales-related inquiries when information is unfavorable, see pages 269–271.

Growth

Assets reached $9½ million by December 31, an increase of 10% during the year, as the enclosed comparative statements show.

Deposits increased 9% to a new high of $7 million. Both branches contributed to this growth.

Loans rose by $½ million, or 8.4%.

Capital structure by the year's end had increased over 25% (from $ to $). Also, that growth was reflected in the increased book value of the permanent reserve shares from $1.95 to $2.25 a share during the year.

Operations

During the year, your association implemented the recommendations for improving operation procedures proposed by management consultants late in (*year*). This action has resulted in visible direct savings in excess of $2,000 on an annualized basis, and it is expected that considerable additional amounts will be saved as the program continues.

Your association's electronic data processing, communications, and record-keeping system was expanded during the year. A savings customer now may make deposits or withdrawals at either branch tied in with the computer, and the transaction is promptly recorded in the customer's deposit book.

Personnel changes

Trustees. With a deep sense of loss and regret we report the passing of our esteemed trustee (*name - and two sentences about that person*).

Fortunately, the Association has elected an outstanding business leader (*name*) to the board to fill the vacancy. (*Two sentences about the new trustee*).

Officers. The growth of your association and the retirement of two officers provided openings for advancement of qualified people. Three officers were advanced in rank and four employees were elevated to official positions. (*Names and titles*)

Staff. Two college graduates were hired as management trainees. These young people and others of the staff are being prepared for positions of responsibility and leadership.

A look at what lies ahead

The present year will be another year of adjustment and change. We anticipate some pickup in the economy on the national scene and in this area the last half of the year. Thus, insofar as your association is concerned, we would expect that savings for the year will perhaps equal or possibly exceed the splendid results of last year, with a fairly even growth over the 12-month period.

Perhaps the greatest challenge (and this we expect to meet successfully) will be that of investing the inflow of funds promptly and safely at a satisfactory rate in a period when the local mortgage demand will not be as great as in recent years.

We at First Federal continue to be optimistic with regard to the future of our great nation, our state, and your association. Our long-
range plans call for expanded activities, to continue providing more
and better service to an ever increasing number of our citizens.

(signature)
(Typed name), President

In addition to the various kinds of letter reports already discussed or shown, one
more deserves special mention here. It is the *progress report*. If you are a management
consultant, an independent researcher, or a representative of a firm doing work under
contract on a long-term (perhaps yearly) project for another company, you should report your progress periodically—in letter-report form. Under some agreements such
reports must be made monthly, quarterly, semiannually, or annually.

Basically, the general topics discussed in a progress report in letter form are similar
to those outlined for a progress report in memorandum format. (See page 589.) Instead of having memo format, however, these reports will be typed on your firm's
letterhead stationery and have the usual letter parts plus your signature and title at
the end. Often they have attachments too. And of course if you have a staff of assistants and expenses that the contracting firm is to pay, you will need to attach an
adequate accounting sheet of your payments and budget.

OTHER SHORT REPORTS

You will also see—and write—in business other short reports besides the memo report,
letter report, and printed or standardized reports. The three most significant are annual reports, "dressed-up" short reports, and proposals.

Annual Reports

Every organization—business, government, religious, athletic, and so forth—has annual
reports that summarize activities and financial affairs. For some small concerns the
report is exceptionally "short"—consisting of perhaps a brief transmittal letter with
one or two pages of financial statements. For other organizations—especially corporations which must report to their stockholders—the annual report may begin with a top
official's summary similar to letter report 2 illustrated on pages 600–601. Sometimes
the letter is the entire report (perhaps eight or more pages). If not, then the report
body discusses operations and activities; and of course every annual report should
have a balance sheet and statement of earnings and expenses.

Some reports also include pictures of officers, employees, products, machines,
operations—plus charts or graphs and easy-to-understand explanations in nontechnical
terms.[7] Financial statements also may have simplified discussions understandable by

---

[7] For some large national and international corporations annual reports are often elaborate, colorful brochures printed on glossy paper with 40 or more pages. As such, they are outside the scope
of this chapter, for they are not "short." Actually, they are impressive advertising brochures for
the public as well as stockholders. They also are informative for college graduates and others seeking jobs with reputable firms.

any stockholder with little knowledge of accounting. To see examples of various annual reports, you might write to selected corporations or consult your business or general library—or your campus placement office.

"Dressed-up" Short Reports

In some situations a comprehensive, important memo report or letter report would be more impressive if it had some of the "dress-up" features of a long report. If your report is, for example, four or five single-space typewritten pages long and has several attachments, you might consider using: a title page, transmittal letter or memo, the report body (typed in single- or double-space), plus an appendix for the attachments. (For discussion and illustrations of these prefatory and supplemental parts, see Chapter 17.)

To give you an idea of how one of the short reports already discussed in this chapter might be dressed up, let's look again at memo report 1 on pages 578–580. Suppose you were also required to attach to this report confidential copies of recommendation letters and test scores for each of the three tellers. Your report would then have 10 pages of attachments plus three single-spaced or five double-spaced pages of body (tables would remain single-spaced). If you decide to add a title page, it will include the TO, FROM, SUBJECT, DATE information attractively set up in these three parts: (1) Evaluation of Three Teller Applicants, (2) Prepared for Mr. Gene Mohr, Manager, Savings Department; and (3) By (your name), Assistant Manager, Personnel Department, March 15, 19___. You will then omit this information from the first page of the report. If you use a transmittal memo, you'll also make a few changes in the first paragraph of the report introduction (as discussed on pages 634–636, in Chapter 17). Your 10 pages of attachments can become the appendix; pages will be numbered consecutively after the last page of your report. For example, if your report body (double-spaced) ends on page 5, the appendix first page will be page 6, and so on through page 15.

Short Proposal Reports

A special type of report that has become increasingly important in business and industry as well as in government and education is the proposal. In a survey of the chief executives for nearly 50 randomly selected manufacturing firms with $1 million minimum annual sales volume, 65 percent reported that proposals play an important part in the operations of their firms. Of these, over 50 percent said the part is "great" or "crucial."[8]

Like other reports, some proposals are short and informal; others are long and formal. In Chapter 17 you will read about "formal" proposals. The present section discusses an informal short report proposal. Usually it is in letter-report form, with attachments. Its purpose is (a) to get a project accepted and/or (b) to get your company—or you—accepted for work on a project. The proposal illustrated here is a sales

[8] Bill G. Rainey, "Proposal Writing—A Neglected Area of Instruction," *The Journal of Business Communication,* vol. 11, no. 4, Summer 1974.

presentation a firm makes to a prospective buyer. (Do not consider it a model of perfection; it is, however, an example of a fairly typical informal proposal to sell an installation product. You can probably suggest ways to improve it.) Before sending the proposal, the seller has visited the company's place of business, studied its present setup, and discussed its needs.

The proposal consists of:

Covering letter

Attached report on: Explanation of Spacefinder Filing System
Advantages of Spacefinder System
Present System Now in Operation
Proposed System
Cost of Proposed Equipment

This letter and the attachment are comparable to the application letter and resume; the letter sells, while the enclosure or attachment presents pertinent facts effectively. Notice that the letter follows the AIDA formula for sales letters. The first paragraph catches the reader's attention; the second and third paragraphs create desire by referring to facts and figures in the attached report (about present system and benefits of the Spacefinder System); the last paragraph asks for action.

The attached report permits the writer to streamline the letter without cluttering it with details. As with any good sales pitch, the report leads the reader through explanation and advantages of Spacefinder, details of the present system, and proposed system before it mentions cost. The letter and the report together constitute the proposal which is to convince the reader to convert to the new system.

Dear Mr. Jaysen

The attached proposal is for a conversion by your firm from drawer files to TAB PRODUCTS' Spacefinder Filing System. This conversion will result in significantly increased filing efficiency and a saving of floor space.

In addition to quoting facts and figures, we have laid out on quarter-inch grid paper the system you now use in the vault on the third floor. The vault is drawn to exact scale and the drawer files now being used are placed in their present position. Using an overlay we are able to illustrate how much space you can save in this vault and yet increase efficiency in locating records and returning them to the file. Also you can use this floor plan in the future to expand storage in the same area.

It is a proven fact that the Unit Spacefinder Filing System does increase filing efficiency up to 50%. You are welcome to see time studies made by firms other than TAB PRODUCTS which indicate this increase.

On the attached pages I have indicated floor space savings and efficiency factors using the Unit Spacefinder System. If you need further information, please call upon me for assistance. My telephone number is 111-2222. Thank you for this opportunity to quote on TAB PRODUCTS Unit Spacefinder Filing System.

PROPOSAL
to (*name of receiver's firm*)
for conversion to TAB PRODUCTS' Unit Spacefinder
Filing System

Explanation of Spacefinder Filing System

The Unit Spacefinder Filing System differs from shelf and drawer filing in many respects. Listed below are the efficiency factors of Unit Spacefinder:

1. You file in a container, not in a drawer, on a shelf, or in a cabinet. The unit box is 4" wide. This means that the documents have support every 4". This need is one of the most important required in lateral filing. The more support, the easier it is to "in-file" and pull records. (See sketches attached.)

2. The unique "stair-step" effect, caused by the angle in which unit boxes are hung, gives you easier accessibility never before possible. This accessibility is an exclusive feature of Unit Spacefinder. Every folder is easy to reach and easy to see.

3. You get flexibility. You can rearrange and expand without a lot of time-consuming bother, such as in the case of drawer files or shelf files. You create space where you need it simply by sliding boxes easily along rails. There is no need to transfer records handful by handful.

Advantages of Unit Spacefinder Lateral Filing System   2

1. The "stair-step" effect allows folders to be readily identified, removed, and replaced with the least effort.

2. The unit boxes can be removed from the racks, a feature which allows:
    a. Work with the records at a desk for purging or for checking, etc.
    b. Fast fleeting of records by rearrangement of the unit boxes.

3. Visibility is a definite advantage. All folders are exposed to the file clerks and with proper indexing can be located at least 50% faster than when the folders are used in drawer files.

4. A 50% increased efficiency by record staffs handling their work load has been proven in many filing areas, both large and small. Efficiency means saved person-hours, which in turn, means saved dollars.

5. Flexibility of the Unit enables us to assure you we can tailor the Unit Spacefinder framework to fit your needs. It is freestanding and does not have to be anchored to the walls or floor; therefore, if you need a different configuration to fit a particular location, we can easily meet your desires.

6. You get more filing space in less than half the floor space.

3

Present System Now in Operation

12 ea. 5-Drawer legal-size files
8 ea. 4-Drawer legal-size files
Total filing inches   2,300"
Total floor space   122.11 sq.ft.
  (including drawer pull)

Folders used are 3d cut, top position right-hand side, legal. Filed in numerical sequence.
  a. Conversion factor - use same folders
  b. Use Colorvue Guide Cards, which reveal inserted number on both sides.

Proposed System

Use combination of 42" and 30" Single Face Sections of Unit Spacefinder against wall and double-face Unit Spacefinder spaced 42" to provide ample aisle space.

Total filing inches   2,380"
Total floor space   47.02 sq.ft.

4

Conversion
Present folders can be used. Right-hand tab allows easy identification of numbers.
Guide Cards should be inserted in file every two to three feet.

Summary
1. Increase in filing inches - 80"
2. Floor space released for expansion or other purposes-- 75.09 square feet
3. Efficiency increase - minimum 35%

Cost of Proposed Equipment

1 ea. 5422	Initial 45" legal-size single	$---.--	$---.--
2 ea. 5334	Additional 42" legal-size with worksfelf, single	---.--	---.--
3 ea. 5404	Additional 30" legal-size single	--.--	---.--
1 ea. 5430	Initial 45" legal-size double with two worksfelves	---.--	---.--

```
   1 ea. 5408   Additional 30" legal-size
                double                              ---.--    ---.--
                                                   ─────────────────
                                                             $-,---.--
 100 ea.   C4345-2   Colorvue Short Guides          $    --.--

 Trim color standard -
    desert tan - mist green - tab gray
 Colors on color-sheet 3%

 Delivery schedule:  21 days
    Terms:  Net 30 days
      FOB:  Factory
```

The preceding illustrations and discussions have indicated the wide variety of subject matter, uses, and formats for memorandum reports, printed and standardized reports, letter reports, and other special reports. Yet, basically, all short reports have various characteristics in common. If you think logically and objectively, consider your reader(s), use good judgment with facts, plan and organize carefully, and achieve the qualities of well-written reports as suggested in both Chapters 15 and 16, you will turn out commendable short reports on the job.

EXERCISES

Situation That Requires Discussion but No Writing

1. Evaluate the memo report below by discussing:
   a. Clarity of the subject line
   b. Reason for omission of an introduction
   c. Appropriateness of headings
   d. Reasons for omission of a terminal section
   e. Quality of content and wording
   f. Consistency of paragraph openings and spacing

```
TO:        H. H. Helium               DATE:  May 2, 19__
FROM:      R. R. Ralston
REGARDING: Office Activities Report for September, 19__

PERSONNEL
The employees are all taking A.S.L.I. courses.  The manager signed up
for Insurance; but since there were insufficient registrants, the
course was not offered.

    Ms. Lee was on vacation for 2 weeks and one day.  During this
time, Mrs. Santa Marie attended Orientation at our main office.
    I hope to begin training Mrs. Mueller on insurance within 4
weeks.  This is later than I had originally planned, but I ordinarily
have taxes paid by this time.
```

BUSINESS DEVELOPMENT SITUATION
I made 8 completed calls on realtors to discuss our restricted sale
clause. I was invited to attend a sales meeting. This resulted in
my addressing 8 salespeople and answering their questions.

UNUSUAL OCCURRENCES
I was subpoenaed to appear in court on September 17 as a witness on
one of our escrows.

POLICY OR PROCEDURAL PROBLEMS
We were notified on 3 separate occasions, by the U.S. Postal Service,
that our metered mail was being deposited with wrong dates or illegi-
ble dates. This led to our inquiring about the postal service and
what is expected of us and why. As a result, we have a better understanding of the system and what we can do to give our customers better mail service.
     Also, the time for last mail pickup on various mail boxes
throughout the city were obtained.
     One of our Series 05 SAC customers came into the office to
change the name on his account. We discovered that we had sent all
05 SACs to the main office shortly after July 10, 19__, and did not
keep any on hand. This has now been rectified and we have a couple
on hand to serve our customers without inconveniencing them.

Rewrites

1. The following letter report (also an acknowledgment to an inquiry) is quite good.
   Your job is to make it even better. Assume the customer asked about all the
   topics mentioned; thus, keep all the ideas but improve the letter report in these
   ways:
   a. Insert headings—second- and third-degree or third- and fourth-degree headings.
   b. Show more you-attitude.
   c. Change at least five passive verbs to active voice (and of course make whatever
      subject changes are necessary).
   d. Tabulate some listed details—for easier reading.
   e. Make any other minor changes desirable for good business writing.

Thank you for your request for information relating to INSURED savings accounts in this association. This reply includes facts concerning types of savings plans, security of savings, withdrawal of
funds, and necessary forms for opening an account. I am also enclosing a copy of our latest financial statement and several pamphlets of
general information which give you essential facts you desire about
us and the savings accounts we issue.

We have two types of savings plans available--a passbook savings account and a 6-month savings certificate.

Briefly, an insured passbook savings account may be opened for any
amount at any time. Upon receipt of your remittance, we issue to you
our savings passbook with the amount credited inside. Additional
sums may be added in any amount and at any time you desire. Savings
received on or before the 15th of any month are credited with earn-

ings as if received on the 1st of the month. Savings received after
the 15th receive earnings from the beginning of the next following
month. When the 15th falls on a Saturday or Sunday, on which days we
are closed, the time for receiving earnings from the 1st of the month
is extended to the 16th or 17th as the case may be. Dividends (earnings) are credited to passbook savings accounts on March 31, June 30,
September 30, and December 31 of each year. This is done automatically on these dates whether you send in your passbook or not. Gold
Bond stamps are given as an extra bonus to passbook savers, as outlined on the enclosed card. The current rate of dividend on passbook
savings is $5\frac{1}{2}\%$ per year, compounded quarterly.

In addition to our savings passbooks, we also issue insured 6-month
savings certificates. Designed to offer larger, longer-term investors the maximum rate for insured savings, these certificates are issued for a minimum of $1,000, with larger amounts in multiples of
$100. They differ from passbook accounts in several respects. Earn-
ings on certificates begin on the day of purchase and are paid at the
end of each 6 months on maturity dates. The certificates are in certificate form, and dividend checks are mailed to the certificate
holders every 6 months from the date of issue, instead of being automatically credited to the account as is done on passbook accounts.
Of course, if you have a passbook savings account with State Federal,
the dividends on your savings certificate may be automatically credited to your passbook account upon your request. For your convenience, savings certificates are automatically renewed on the maturity
dates for an additional 6 months unless you are notified at least 30
days prior to a maturity date. The current rate of dividend on six-
month savings certificates is $6\frac{1}{4}\%$ per year.

Savings in this association are INSURED up to $40,000 by the Federal
Savings and Loan Insurance Corporation, Washington, D.C. We are also
members of the Federal Home Loan Bank System, a reserve credit system
for associations. We lend our funds upon the security of selected
monthly reducing first mortgages on homes. So, you will see, there
is really exceptional security for savings placed with us.

You will probably wish some information concerning withdrawal of your
funds. It has always been the policy of this association to pay
withdrawals in PART OR IN FULL without notice. We have followed this
policy ever since organization in 1926. However, a savings and loan
association may require notice of withdrawal if necessary. If the
country should again experience an economic emergency such as pre-
vailed in 1932-33, it is possible that we would require notice. Under such circumstances it is quite likely that every financial institution would necessarily restrict withdrawals. This provision in the
savings and loan laws is a wise one for the protection of the customers.

For your convenience I am enclosing a signature card which may be
used either for an individual or a joint account. If you desire to
open an account in your own name alone, you should use Form 100. If,
however, you wish to open an account in your name jointly with some
other person, probably another member of your family, you should use
Form 200, on the reverse side of the card. If you desire a six-month
savings certificate, the same signature card may be used.

We also have trust accounts, frequently used by parents in carrying savings accounts for children, or by persons who desire to hold funds in trusts for another. Signature card forms for this type of account will be mailed to you upon request.

I thank you kindly for your inquiry and extend to you a cordial invitation to use the facilities of this association.

2. Given below is a report to shareholders. Assume this message appears on one side of an 8½- by 11-inch sheet and the annual statement of condition appears on the opposite side. Rewrite so that the information is easier to read. For example, can you put in table form some or all of the figures and dates given in the first three paragraphs? And can you list the names and titles in the last two paragraphs? Also, add an appropriate rounding-out last paragraph.

Report to the Shareholders
We ended our 61st year May 3, 19__, which proved to be a very good year. Our assets totaled almost $12,000,000 being $11,997,728.90, representing an increase of $430,315.75 which was due principally to the increase in home loans of $538,622.30.

Savings accounts reflected a total of $11,013,074.26, representing a gain for the year of $385,321.70, which was substantially greater than the gain in the previous year. During the year the association repaid $265,000 to the Federal Home Loan Bank and had no notes payable May 3, 198_. Net operating income, after expenses, amounted to $558,293.40, reflecting an increase of $32,423.01 over the prior year. The operating ratio of the association for the fiscal year was 17.87% of gross operating income, which was substantially lower than the national average, which is in excess of 27%.

During the year, $42,000 was added to reserves, $495,810.52 was distributed as earning on savings accounts, and $20,482.88 was added to undivided profit. Total reserves were $514,000 and undivided profit $87,505.03, making a total of $601,505.03, representing over 5% of total liabilities. Our reserves and undivided profit places us in a rather enviable position and leaves no question, in my opinion, of our ability to continue at our present rate of return to our savings accounts.

At our Shareholders Meeting held Monday, April 5, the following were elected to serve as directors for the ensuing year: William E. Brady, Robert E. Becker, Stephen G. Mills, Mary A. Aitken, Daniel A. Roberts, Lisa L. Gifford, and Louise G. Hulett.

At the Directors Reorganization Meeting, immediately following the Shareholders Meeting, the following officers were elected: Chairperson of the Board of Directors and President, Judy E. Brady; Vice Chairperson, Robert E. Becker; Executive Vice President, Secretary and Treasurer, Stephen G. Mills; Vice President and Assistant Secretary and Treasurer, Louise G. Hulett; and Assistant Secretary, William A. Dugger. Sylvia Reddie was reappointed Savings Officer and Bonnie Whittemore was appointed Head Bookkeeper. Fred L. Sharp was reappointed attorney.

Problems

1. Your employer is interested in expanding her business and asks you to prepare some information about these cities: Jacksonville, Florida; Toledo, Ohio; Oklahoma City, Oklahoma; Charlotte, North Carolina; and Charleston, West Virginia.

   She is interested in many geographic and demographic items, but asks you to begin your study with only six. Make brief (but complete) comparisons, on the topics listed below, for each of the cities. Use whatever form, headings, tables, and content you believe necessary for a complete answer. Keep your report to no more than two typewritten pages. Your report will compare

   1. Population
   2. Area size
   3. Transportation facilities
   4. Health facilities
   5. Educational facilities
   6. Major industries

   One of the best places to find such information is one of the several almanacs which are available; or perhaps you can find it in a standard encyclopedia. Whichever source you use, be certain that you footnote the reference for her information and that you use up-to-date material.

   Finally, you should remember that if you do a complete job for her on this report, she will probably call on you to do additional research on the project. With that in mind you might want to make some appropriate mention of willingness to do future research.

2. You are the manager of the purchasing department at the Dawson Company and have set up guidelines on the policies to be followed when purchasing a material or a service for the company. Write a memo report on this topic to all employees in the company who are responsible for planning orders.

   The new purchasing policy identifies three control documents that will be used in the company: (1) material or service request, (2) packing list, and (3) invoice. The purchasing policy links the processing of these documents with specific company personnel to ensure internal control and construct an audit trail.

   The approved request authorizes the purchase of a material or service. The data on this form, along with the buyer-supplied data (such as vendor, terms, shipping information, price, etc.), become the purchase order. The person initiating the request will circulate it to obtain the required data and the proper authorization, and it finally ends up in the purchasing department, where the order is placed.

   After the material or service has been received from the vendor, the signed packing list which accompanies the order (the second control document) is checked with the company's originally approved request. Both documents are inspected for proper authorization and completeness. The signed packing list provides proof of receipt.

The third control document is the vendor invoice. This represents the vendor's statement of the material or service provided, the price to be paid, and the terms of the purchase. The invoice must be checked against the material request and the packing list. The properly verified invoice will authorize payment to the vendor.

Your memorandum should include specific instructions, plus a flow chart, to illustrate the pathway of a normal material or service request. Be concise and clear. The new procedure must be followed if internal control is to be successful.

3. Assume you have received a letter from the Assistant Dean of Students, Dr. Jean Inquirer, Administration Building, your college or university, stating that you have been selected in a random sample to take part in a survey. The information gathered will be included—without student names—in an orientation booklet for entering students. She asks you to answer these questions regarding your course costs for this quarter:

a. What is your year in college and major?

b. How much did your textbooks cost you? Please mention course names and book titles, too.

c. What other required course materials did you have to pay for and how much did they cost? (Include lab fees, if any, but exclude tuition fees.) Figure only prices of new texts and materials (but you may mention any savings you gained if you bought used items).

d. What relation, if any, do you find between these total course costs and the number of credit hours your courses carry?

e. What relation, if any, do you find between these total course costs and the college (Arts & Sciences, Engineering, etc.) or department (Business, Education, Art) in which they are offered? (Answer this question if you are taking courses in more than one department or college of this institution.)

The only data you need are the prices of *new* books and materials plus lab fees, if any—for each course you are carrying *and* the credit hours of each course.

In case you feel that this quarter is exceptional for you (perhaps because you are taking only one or two courses), you may, if you wish, include information for both last quarter and this one. Indicate clearly the costs and credits in each.

Suggestions: Write your report in good business letter-report form—with heading, inside address, subject line, salutation, and closing. Use well-chosen headings to mark the main divisions of your report. Keep your report factual, objective, and well-organized.[9]

4. You are the new assistant to Mr. James Rohn, regional manager of employee relations and education (name company). Two days ago you received the following memo from him:

> Will you please look into the film "(*name*)," review it, and report to

---

[9] Actually, for a survey of this type the inquirer should send a questionnaire form on which each respondent merely fills in answers. However, for purpose of this assignment, let's assume she sent merely a stamped envelope and that she is also interested in seeing how well college students express themselves in written reports. Make yours one of the best!

me what you think of it? Specifically, I'd like (in a concise written report) to know:

1. What are the main ideas of the film?
2. What are its technical (and other) aspects--length, photography, method of presentation, quality, cost?
3. How useful would it be to our company and our branches?
4. What do you recommend we do--purchase, rent, or forget it?

Your office selects, from time to time, various instructional materials, visual aids, and other teaching materials for use in your management training program at the main office (your city). In addition, they are also available to the four branches whenever requested and when not used at the headquarters office. Each branch has its own trainees. Your company has 2,000 employees, of whom 900 are working within a radius of 300 miles from the home office. About 30 percent of your employees are in some kind of supervisory or management capacity. They communicate not only orally, but also through letters, memos, and reports.

The one communication film that the company now owns is a sound filmstrip, in black and white, shown for the past 10 years, regarding essentially letter writing. Most of the older executives think it is still adequate. It's *Dear Mrs. Somebody.* Mr. Rohn (age 59) is always on the lookout, however, for the newest and best materials regardless of cost, as long as they can be justified as to their usefulness for the firm.

Assume that yesterday you reviewed this color film about which he asked you to report. If your instructor can show a film to the entire class—or if you have seen a film in another course—use the facts and title from that film for this report. If no film is available for class showing, assume you previewed *Management Communications* at the Audiovisual Services Center in your city.

This morning Mr. Rohn, in passing your desk, casually remarked he had heard of this film (the one you previewed) through a manager who sat next to him at a luncheon recently. Mr. Rohn's comments indicated, indirectly, what his hopes and preferences are about the use of this film in your company. After seeing the film, you now realize that your own honest conclusions and recommendations are contrary to Mr. Rohn's expectations. (This realization guides you in selection of an organization plan for your report.) Regardless of whether you report on *Management Communications* or another film you saw yourself in a class, you are free to recommend whatever you wish, provided you objectively consider all facts.

Facts about the film *Management Communications:*

> 25 minutes long; produced and sold by BNA Incorporated, Bureau of National Affairs, 1231 24th St., N.W., Washington, D.C. Assume it costs $450. You've also discovered that the local Audiovisual Services Center rents it for a three-day period at $18 plus postage. They require at least 24 hours' advance notice, and they will ship the films anywhere across the country, except to Hawaii and Canada.

Your rough draft notes on main ideas of the film are these:

Shows a series of modern office scenes with a manager and one, two, or three employees who are under her management. Scenes show good and bad techniques of communication by the manager. A narrator helpfully explains the differences in techniques. Color, excellent; acting, amateur.

Major viewpoints are empathy and credibility on part of management toward subordinates and customers. Empathy is crucial. The manager must be able to put him- or herself in another person's place. To change a person's viewpoint, the manager must show that the person will benefit through the change. The manager must find out what customers' or fellow employees' beliefs are, how they will change or resist the information given, and what are their interests.

To be credible the manager must be competent, dependable, and enthusiastic. Competence is attained from a communication aspect. The manager must keep well informed and communicate necessary facts to subordinates so they in turn can transfer information to their subordinates. When possible, he or she should let them make suggestions before decisions are made; let them participate.

Being dependable requires that the manager not shirk managerial duties. The manager must not "pass the buck" by assuming no responsibility for actions or blaming them on another person. If he or she has an unfavorable management decision to pass on to the subordinates, it must be done in a way that assures them they can depend on the manager to help in every possible manner.

The manager must be enthusiastic and have enough energy to see things carried through to the end without complaining when work demands are heavy. The last four letters of "enthusiasm" may stand for "I am sold myself" (on whatever topic the manager is discussing), but the manager must be sincere.

Make any other necessary assumptions for your memo report; indicate them in a separate note clipped to the top of the report you hand to your instructor.

This is the first report you've been asked to write for Mr. Rohn. Write it in memo-report format; be sure it is well organized, with appropriate headings and subheadings. Mr. Rohn likes concise and complete reports. Try to keep this one within two typed pages (elite type), single-spaced, and trimmed to basic but important essentials. Show facts and figures regarding relative costs for renting or buying; consider home office and branch needs.

5. You have been engaged to perform a communications audit of the written collection messages of a business in your area. (Select a company which will cooperate, because you will be collecting your data through interviews with employees and the examination of company policies, files, and sample collection correspondence.) Your purpose is threefold: (1) to determine the company's credit and collection policies; (2) to analyze its current collection series; and (3) to recommend specific improvements in its collection series. Use Chapter 13, Collection Messages, as your theoretical and applications base.

The evaluation of the firm's present collection series and recommendations for a new collection series will rest on a thorough survey of debtors' payment prac-

tices, company credit and collection policies (for example, time limits on installment or mortgage payments, repossession or foreclosure policies), government
regulations which the firm must observe, industry or trade practices, and the
nature of the firm's goods or services.

Prepare an analytical letter report addressed to the company official who has
the authority and responsibility to implement the changes you recommend. As
you judge most appropriate, use the logical or psychological arrangement to
execute the three purposes of your report. A chart or table might be a fine way
to tabulate the types and number of collection messages you recommend the firm
adopt. For example, your table might have captions similar to these:

			Number of messages to debtors		
Stage	Message	Appeals	Good risk	Fair risk	Poor risk
Reminder	Statements	None	3	2	1

6. You are a management trainee for Central Advertising Agency, in which the ability to write good reports is an important qualification. Two days ago Mr. James
   Sorgens, training director, asked you to find out what types of reports are written
   by account executives in this firm. He suggested you interview Ms. May Emerson,
   vice president/account executive at Central and then write him the best report
   you can about your findings. Yesterday during your interview with Ms. Emerson
   you jotted down the following notes (with her permission). Ms. Emerson also
   gave you a sample of each of the four reports most often written in the company
   and she added general comments on agency reports.

   Account executive writes reports when directly involved in the situation.
   Otherwise, person involved and a/c exec decide together who writes report.
   In all cases concerning the client, however, a/c exec is ultimately responsible
   for reports concerning client's campaign.

   Bulk of reports written by a/c exec: job memo, memo report, conference (or
   meeting) report, and recommendation report.

   Job memo report—most important in the office. An intraoffice report written
   to all depts. of the agency. Written by a/c exec as often as necessary whenever
   any action on client's campaign is called for. They give authorization and instruction concerning client's campaign. Generally, a/c exec writes these daily.

   Memo report is written as often as necessary—usually daily. Short (usually one
   page)—to communicate information to a specific person within agency. This
   report concerns information dealing with many facets of client's advertising
   campaign needed by the a/c exec in performing his job or her job.

   Recommendation reports—most extensive and comprehensive report by a/c
   exec. Written perhaps once or twice a year; gives client agency's recommendations, marketing plan, budget analysis, and advertising approach for campaign.

Agency and client both have copy of this report; many are 20–30 pages long. Not only does a/c exec receive a copy, but so does head of agency and heads of all depts. involved with a/c.

Important that a/c exec and client understand always where campaign stands and how it is progressing. So that each one has a record of all the decisions made concerning the campaign, the conference report is used. Written immediately following a conference or meeting between agency and client. Purpose: clarify discussion and the decisions made at the meeting.

General comments:

General purpose of report—no matter what type—is to ensure and expedite communication between agency and its client or between depts. of agency. Emerson pointed out several items she thought this agency's reports could be improved upon. Also those items she thought made for good reports. Also provided information on format this agency uses for reports and what they have done to improve quality of their reports.

Too many reports are not concise. Tend to be wordy and too long; lack clarity; and negative. Ms. E. thought that if reports were more objective and emphasized positive rather than neg., they would help communication more. Also desirable factors: brevity and conciseness. In general, reports should communicate entire message in fewest words possible without sounding abrupt.

Format—no particular order or format is strictly adhered to. Whether text or terminal section comes first is not a written policy, but main points of discussion should ideally precede the discussion to expedite reading of report.

Company does not use any printed forms for reports, except for the job memo report. Nature of a/c in question dictates form used for recommendation or conference reports. Headings are used to assist reader of report.

Because of volatile nature of advertising business, no formal school in better report writing techniques is conducted. However, the American Assoc. of Advertising Agencies does provide some bulletins on better writing techniques. These help improve agency reports. Also, the a/c exec attempts to stress the qualities of conciseness, clarity, and other desirable points of report writing in informal discussions with other executives and with their subordinates.

Organize these rough draft notes into a complete, well-written, concise memorandum report, using logical plan and two degrees of headings. Assume you are attaching the four exhibits; be sure to refer to them appropriately within your report text. Remember to use topic sentences for paragraphs and to introduce subheadings properly.

7. One of your duties as manager of Wilson's Manufacturing is to check the plant's suggestion box. Recently there have appeared a number of complaints about the

unsightly, unsanitary mess in the washroom. Some employees have been careless about using and disposing of paper towels. Each dispenser has a built-in trash basket and even a sticker to remind employees to place used towels in the basket. However, the problem still persists.

As a solution, you have decided to replace paper towels with a hot-air hand dryer. At your request, Haworth Inc., makers of the Jetaire Hand Dryer, sent a salesperson to evaluate your needs. The salesperson made a cost analysis of your situation and also presented an estimate of the cost for changing to the Jetaire Hand Dryer. Wilson's has 200 employees and each employee visits the washroom an average of 4 times a day. The average number of paper towels used each visit is 2½ towels at a cost of $0.002 a towel. Assuming 22 working days a month, a 3-year cost figure for towels alone was derived. Haworth's salesperson also pointed out that there are "intangible" costs involved with paper towels. These include time spent in filling out purchase orders and the cost of mailing the order; cost per square foot of storage of the paper towels; costs in distributing, collecting, and carting away paper towels; and plumbing expenses for toilets and sinks clogged with paper towels. These intangible costs usually amount to 50 percent of the 3-year total cost of paper towels for any business.

According to the salesperson, each of the four washrooms in your plant should have three Jetaire units. The units cost $120 apiece and together use about $4 in electricity per month. There is also an installation fee of $84 (for all machines).

Because the estimated acquisition cost of the Jetaire Hand Dryers is over $500, it is necessary to receive authorization from Mr. Steve Wilson, the plant super-intendent. He is a very busy person and often does not have the time to sort through a lengthy cost analysis report. He likes to know immediately what the cost and savings are in the company. Write a memo report bringing to Mr. Wilson's attention these points as well as other facts such as employee benefits. Include one or two concise, easy-to-read tables in your discussion section. For your organizational plan will you use 2 (a), (b), or (c) (pages 580–583)?

8. As assistant sales manager, you have been delegated the responsibility of evaluating sites for the company's sales conference in your city. Each April your company's 225 sales representatives from all over the state attend a four-day sales meeting to study product improvements, discuss marketing strategies, set sales quotas, and develop selling techniques. You are to investigate two hotel-motels and evaluate each on suitability of facilities. The sales manager will use your analytical memo report to make her own decision and recommendations.

The sales manager has narrowed the choice down to two sites—one downtown, the other suburban. She has prepared these criteria on which each facility will be evaluated:

1. 100 double rooms, 30 single rooms, 2 bedroom-living room suites.
2. Banquet facilities and staff to accommodate 250 persons for breakfasts, luncheons, dinners—either sit-down or buffet. Provision for coffee breaks and hospitality hours.

3. Conference facilities for large group meetings of 250. Small meeting room facilities for five groups of 50. Rooms may be multipurpose (large group, small group, banquet) if set up ahead of the opening session and preparation requirements permit efficient scheduling.

4. Exhibit area of approximately 5,000 square feet.

5. "Break-out" areas for informal discussion and relaxation—lounge areas, spacious lobbies, and corridors.

6. Audio-visual equipment: film projection equipment and screen in large meeting area; overhead projectors, screens, and lecterns equipped with microphones for sound amplification in each meeting area. Capable staff for setup of all equipment and operation in the case of film projector.

7. Diversified menu, well-prepared food, good food service.

8. On-site entertainment and relaxation facilities.

9. Bar service.

10. Parking for 200 cars.

11. Adequate security, especially in exhibit and parking areas.

12. Efficient, courteous staff.

You do not need to consider cost factors in your analysis. Your company attempts to project a first-class image, and both site options fulfill that requirement. Your main concern is providing for the actual space, facility, and service needs of the sales meeting as well as possible.

Select a downtown and a suburban hotel-motel in your city; and using these criteria, systemmatically gather the relevant data on each facility through meetings with their conference and banquet managers and/or their promotional literature. Develop a graphic display in which you logically organize your facts and rate or rank each site on the 12 criteria.

Because your superior prefers the deductive approach, you will use this organizational pattern. Therefore, present your conclusions first, then your introduction, and finally your discussion of each facility's strengths and weaknesses relative to the selection criteria. Headings should orient the reader, and graphic aids will be useful for presenting your comparative data.

9. So far you have been reading the text's discussion of reports and listening to your professor's interpretations. You will now find out for yourself the types of reports you'll be writing on the job after graduation. Select an organization similar to the one you hope to be associated with after graduation and interview someone who has a job similar to the one you want. If you can't interview this person, consider her or his superior.

In preparation for this assignment, hand in to your professor the answers to the following in memo format. (The purpose of this screening is so your professor can make sure you ask appropriate questions and that no more than one student in class goes to the same firm.)

a. The name of the company. If you plan to be an accountant in a C.P.A. firm, choose a C.P.A. firm; if you intend to get into personnel work, choose an organization that has a personnel department.

b. Name of the individual you'll interview and/or that person's title. Be sure to choose someone who can tell you the types of reports you'll be writing on the job after graduation.

c. Purpose of the interview. To be sure the questions you'll ask fulfill the purpose of the assignment, jot down in one sentence the purpose of the interview: "The purpose of the interview is to find out all I can about the types of reports I'll be writing on the job in my chosen career." Keep this purpose in mind as you select your questions. All questions should relate directly to this purpose.

d. List at least 10 really pertinent questions you plan to ask the officer you will interview. Consider questions to which you want answers and arrange the questions in the order you'll be asking them. Given below are a few examples of questions you might want to ask.

(1) What types of reports does your (firm) prepare? (Please specify whether memo report, letter report, formal report, or printed form report.)

(2) Which of the above-mentioned types of reports are written most frequently? least frequently?

(3) Who usually prepares the report? (Individual versus group, lower echelon versus upper echelon.)

(4) What are some common weaknesses in these reports?

(5) What make(s) a good report?

(6) What is the most frequent arrangement of the body of the report? (Logical versus psychological.)

(7) How long a time, on the average, is spent preparing each type of report?

(8) Do employees work on the report more during working hours or more at home?

(9) What is the difference between a report going upward to management and downward to the workers?

(10) In what way do you feel your (firm's) reports may be improved?

Write a memo report to your professor about your findings. Be sure to include a subject line, body (all three parts), and necessary headings. The text should include more than one main division but perhaps no more than two or three. Also, you might need subheadings for one or more of the major divisions in the text.

10. You have just joined the staff of the newly founded Consumer Action and Information Foundation—an organization supported by private donations. The foundation's purpose is to communicate information to consumers through newsletters and news releases to the media. In some instances, the foundation also helps consumers directly by acting as an intermediary in resolving disputes between consumers and business firms, public utilities, so-called charitable organizations, governmental agencies, and so forth.

The foundation has received many requests from residents in your city for information about savings plans offered by commercial banks, savings and loan associations, and credit unions. The foundation has decided to publish a booklet describing the savings plans offered by such institutions in your city. You have been asked to collect information and write a report which compares the savings plans with regard to types of plans offered, interest rates paid, minimum deposits required, penalties for early withdrawals, etc. The report should identify each institution and clearly show the information about that institution's savings plans.

Remember that your "constituents" are private individuals and not large institutional investors. Therefore, you may wish to exclude a discussion of savings plans which require large deposits. The definition of what is a "large" deposit is left up to you.

Your report should be factual and up to date. Your comparisons between and among institutions should be restricted to savings plans which are of a similar nature. If you can present the information in tables, comparisons can be made more easily. Because your report is an "internal" document at this stage, you should use the memorandum-report format.

11. You are a college student and member of the University Church. Through your efforts and the help of the college student youth group, you designed and put into operation a special tutoring program to help foreign students—in your church and at the nearby university—get the help they needed in their conversational English.

You decided to create this program as a result of conversations with foreign students in your congregation. The foreign students said that they would like to have someone get together with them individually so they could practice conversing in English. You assigned a volunteer student to each foreign student seeking help. These two were required to meet at least once a week for a quarter (a 10-week period). This, however, sometimes did not work out and you had to ask the volunteer to leave. It hurt the foreign student more if the sessions were not regular. Some volunteer-foreign student pairs had sessions that lasted longer than one hour a week. Other pairs met for only the stipulated one hour a week.

The tutors are volunteers, which has presented some problem. Due to the intrinsic appeal of this program, many people volunteer. So far you have been able to keep up with the foreign student demand. Some tutors are poor. Some say they will contribute and don't and others contribute a lot of time.

Publicity is very important for getting the program going. Ads in the church bulletin and university papers are instrumental in recruiting volunteers and informing the foreign students.

In addition to meeting with the foreign student one hour a week, each tutor is required to meet with the other tutors one Sunday every month to discuss problems. The tutors must remember that they are talking with a student, and must not take a condescending attitude. At no time should tutors ever question the foreign students' religious beliefs. They must remember that although this is a religion-oriented program, the tutors' function is not to convert or judge other people.

Yesterday you received a letter from Mr. Floyd Lowers at another church in a nearby city asking for information about your program because he is interested in setting up a similar program.

You had some problems giving the tutors ideas for variety in meeting with their students. You created a list which was given to each tutor which had all sorts of ideas—like studying together, hiking and other sports, shopping together, and driving around in a car. There were also games suggested which would help the foreign student practice English.

When the foreign students sign up for tutors they are given envelopes which tell them the do's and don't's according to the goals. You also give both the tutor and the student a way to end the relationship if they don't get along. The student is free at any time to terminate the meeting arrangements and ask for a new tutor. The tutor can also ask for a new student. Strict confidence is maintained in this regard, and a lot of juggling does occur.

On the whole, the program has been a great success. Many new and lasting friendships have resulted. The tutors also found that they learned a tremendous amount from the foreign students. There has been a cultural exchange which has helped both the student and the tutor.

Reply to Mr. Lowers' request and report your experience—both the good and the bad—with organizing and operating the program.

12. As a follow-up to the interview discussed in Exercise 3 in Chapter 11, report your findings to your professor. Use memo-report format and a logically organized body (first the introduction, then the text, and finally the terminal section). The text should consist of at least two major divisions—but not more than three or four. If you use subsections in one or more major divisions, remember you must have at least two subsections for each division; the major division should begin with an introductory paragraph that introduces the reader to the overall division and its subsections. Single-space within paragraphs but double-space between paragraphs and before and after headings.

You should be able to say what you need to say adequately in a report between one and two pages in length. Unless your professor tells you otherwise, the purpose of the report is to inform the professor what qualifications the company (or the person you interviewed) wants to find in a graduating senior who is applying for a specific job or for a job in a specific field.

13. One month ago Henry Merry, manager (since 1955) of the clothing department of Walden's Department Store, announced his upcoming retirement. As the supervisor of all departments, you were asked by Lisa Walden (vice president in charge of personnel) to recommend a suitable replacement. For three weeks you have been interviewing applicants and compiling profiles on currently employed personnel that are qualified to handle the position. Walden's has no policy of seniority when it comes to hiring departmental managers. Emphasis is placed on individual qualities of leadership, ability to work with others, and a general knowledge of business operations. Previous management experience is not necessary, since most of the daily management routine can be quickly learned on the job.

Having carefully considered all 27 qualified employees and applicants, you have narrowed the field down to 3 main candidates, one of whom you must recommend—in an analytical memo-report—to Ms. Walden. On the basis of your recommendation, she will make the final decision.

The following are the three candidates' qualifications to consider in your report:

Joe Page:

At age 26, Joe will receive his master's degree in marketing at the end of the current quarter. From an interview with Joe and a resume he has given you, you know that he is a capable leader and has the type of personality that will get along well with employees in the department. In college he was captain of the track team. Most of Joe's working experience has been part-time or full-time summer employment. For the last three years he has worked in a small clothing store in the university district. A reference from the manager of the store was quite complimentary and noted especially Joe's ability to keep himself busy when there were no customers to wait on.

Kenneth Osborne:

At age 47, Ken has earned a high school diploma, received an honorable discharge after serving six years in the Army (two years as a master sergeant), worked four years in construction and then seven years selling magazines on the road, and has worked in Walden's clothing department the last twelve years. Among the clerks he has the most seniority. Often when Mr. Merry was absent because of illness or for business reasons, Ken was asked to act as manager. Company policy requires that each departmental manager keep a personality and efficiency inventory on all employees in her or his department. In the inventory Mr. Merry praised Ken's ability to handle the managerial duties in his (Merry's) absence, but he also noted that Ken had trouble in getting along with some of the employees. At times Ken was "bossy" toward new employees, even when he was not acting as manager.

Paula Barlow:

At age 36, Paula has a B.A. degree in history and English, taught high school English eight years, worked in the home furnishings department at Walden's for two years and in the present clothing department the last four years. The principal of the high school where Barlow taught told Mr. Merry by letter he has no unfavorable criticism of the job done at any time, but Barlow quit teaching because she had disciplinary problems. However, both faculty and students in high school liked her. In the personality and efficiency inventory, Mr. Merry wrote that Paula is one of the best workers he has ever managed. She never questions any request given her by Mr. Merry or by any of the other employees. Paula also gets along with all employees and seems to be the most popular among them. She has never been in a managerial position, but she does have a sound knowledge of the operations of the clothing department.

14. Write a job description of a job you are holding now or have held. Assume your employer needs the description for the new employees who are to succeed you. You are being promoted. If the work you do (or did) is the same day after day, describe one day's work in detail. If it differs each week or month, or there are certain special responsibilities on certain days, be sure to explain specifically. For example, on what days are various reports or activities done? Use appropriate headings to make reading easy. Your job description report will be filed permanently in both the personnel department files and in those of your department head.

chapter 17

The Formal Report

The formal (sometimes called "long") report is merely an expansion of the shorter one. The body of both a memo report and a formal report consists of an introduction, a text, and terminal section organized either logically or psychologically. Both have headings and other visual aids when desirable. *Formal* merely means the report includes certain prefatory and supplemental parts; it does not mean the level of language is formal. You should continue to use easily understood words and apply the C Qualities in Well-Written Reports, listed on pages 562–565.

The formal report generally covers a more complex problem than the "short" report. Consequently, the needed preliminary investigation plus gathering, sorting, and interpreting data, as well as the writing and editing, are often far more time-consuming and costly than for short reports. This chapter presents additional information you will need regarding the following aspects of formal report writing: proposals; working plans; prefatory parts; supplemental parts; documentation and explanatory notations; plus writing, revising, and typing.

PROPOSALS

As stated in the preceding chapter, proposals have an important part in business and industry as well as in government and education. A comparatively short proposal consisting of an informal letter plus attachments is illustrated on pages 603–607. Some projects, however, require proposals running to 50 or more pages—with comprehensive, detailed, elaborate presentations, depending upon the complexity of the problems involved.

A business or industrial firm (also an individual) that seeks the award of a large contract from a government agency or another firm must submit a proposal (bid) before being considered. Also, a researcher who needs a grant before undertaking a costly project or study culminating in a long formal report must write a proposal to the funding agency. Likewise, department heads who require extensive remodeling of their employer's facilities must usually present proposals to the executives concerned with approving funds.

In general, the best advice for writing proposals is to be sure your objectives match the philosophy and requirements of the funding individual, agency, or company. Follow *meticulously* the proposal requirements of the funding source. It may require for all proposals certain headings, details, format, number of copies, deadlines, and so forth. Adhering honestly and accurately to all requirements will work to your advantage. Whenever possible, use the outline and same words the agency has in its literature or guidelines. Don't use jargon that only you and your assistants can understand. The following suggestions for outlines, formats, and writing style are adaptable to various formal proposals.

Outline

Among the topics listed below are those you will often need to include in your proposals for complex research studies and for major business proposals regarding sales of your company's (or your) services, equipment, or extensive installation facilities. Of course, only very long, comprehensive proposals may include all (or almost all) these topics. Obviously some situations will require discussion on only a few—perhaps five or six—topics. For others, the total presentation may cover 30 or more topics and subtopics. Information required for a $2 million grant or sales contract will surely be much more comprehensive than for a $200 allowance! Therefore, *consider carefully which topics are desirable for your specific proposal outline.*

1. Problem

Clearly define the problem. If it's a community problem, is it specific for the local area or a general one? If it's a company problem, does it concern a certain branch or area—such as shipping delays, shoplifting, inventory control, poor customer relations, excessive purchase returns, inadequate communication, or what?

Background . . . what led up to the problem. Be concise.

Need for solution. Is it urgent? critical? why?

2. Purpose (Objectives)

State objectives concisely and clearly. Are they measurable? achievable?

Avoid including too many objectives or too broad a purpose.

3. Scope

Define the boundaries of your project. If you're proposing a research study, will you study one area of a community, company, department, or severe problem? What boundaries are you setting to accomplish your objectives? If your proposal is for service or equipment you are selling, in what areas will it serve the prospective buyer?

4. Procedures

What specific methods will you use? Are they scientifically sound?

What are you going to do? How?

Who is involved?

What is your plan of attack? Can your methods solve the problem?

Identify specific activities and state your time schedule for each. (For a research project state your initial plan and organization, search of literature, interviews, correspondence, questionnaires, experiments.) Include estimated calendar dates if possible.

Consider and identify variables, if any, in the project.

Make clear your sequence of steps in the project.

Allow sufficient time for data collection and for unexpected problems.

5. Equipment and Facilities Available

Show you have thought deeply enough to realize what facilities will be needed. (For a research project state what equipment and facilities you already have for use and assure that you can get the rest. Depending upon the type of project, you might, for example, need a movie camera, computer, programmer, 10 desk calculators, a nearby library, typewriter(s), duplicating machines and services for questionnaires, etc., even a car, truck, boat, or small plane!) If your proposal is for your company's bid on an enormous construction job, probably several departments will cooperate with you in presenting needed facts and figures.

6. Personnel Qualifications

Include an organization chart; perhaps a flow chart, if desirable.

Show job descriptions, names, and one-page resumes for top personnel (with their permission) who will assist on your project.

State your own experience and past successes with similar projects. Include dates and references (with permission) so that the prospective funder can verify your statements.

7. Evaluation

State how data generated in your project will be handled and stored.

If you are planning a community or a company project, state what factors will determine whether your project can be done again in another community or company branch.

If you are proposing a research study, show how you will evaluate how well the project is working while it is under way and how you'll determine whether to continue it, change directions, or terminate it.

State the likelihood of success. Do not promise more than you can do. Can you guarantee a solution within stated boundaries? Some problems (crime, cancer, drug abuse, etc.) may be so complex that no one expects any one researcher to solve them. In your proposal, protect yourself from charges of misrepresentation by honestly estimating (conservatively) what probable outcome can be expected. Even a partial solution of an adequately limited problem may be a step in the right direction.

8. Budget

If you're applying for a research grant, do *not* overbudget; funding sources quickly reject a padded budget. Be realistic.

List: Salaries and fringe benefits for all staff assistants and yourself
Equipment and consumable supplies needed to reach objectives
Travel requirements (estimate miles, type of transportation, number of persons who will be traveling)
Miscellaneous expenses and indirect costs
Allowance for the unexpected
Provide justification for each budget item.

If you're bidding on a job for your company (or yourself), consider all apsects of the proposed work (perhaps with advice of experts) to be sure your proposed price is competitive as well as economically feasible.

In general, before you agree to work on a lengthy project for any firm or agency, see that a suitable written agreement covers your costs, hours of work, time schedule; and make sure you understand what penalties, if any, apply for delayed performance or nonperformance. Sometimes consulting a qualified financial counselor is advisable.

Format

After you have written, in rough draft, your answers to all pertinent topics, arrange them in a coherent order. If your discussion under one topic is too brief, you may need to expand on it, or perhaps group the information under another, broader heading—unless of course the agency's guidelines prescribe exact headings and order of arrangement.

The format of the proposal includes many of the parts found in formal reports. Here is one possible suggested format for a formal research proposal:

1. *Prefatory parts*
   Title page
   Letter of transmittal
   Table of contents
   List of tables (if any)
   List of figures (if any)
2. *Body of proposal*
   Introduction
     Problem
     Need
     Background
   Objectives/Purpose

  Procedures
   Methods and sources
   Plan of attack
   Sequence of activities
   Equipment and facilities available
   Personnel qualifications
  Evaluation
  Budget
3. *Supplementary parts*
  Agency forms
   Budget justification
   References
  Tables or figures (if any)

Writing Style and Appearance

You will be wise to apply all the business writing principles and report writing techniques when writing the proposal—whether it is for a research grant or for a million-dollar sales contract by your company. In its digest on proposal writing, the Washington State Office of Economic Opportunity includes the following excellent advice:

First impressions are very critical. None is more so than that first impression your proposal gives to the reader when submitted to an agency or foundation for consideration. Many proposals are lost at the first look by the reader. He appraises the proposal immediately in terms of:

1. General appearance
2. Neatness
3. Specific appearance of:
 a. Table of Contents
 b. List of Figures
 c. Title Page
 d. Maps
 e. Graphs
 f. Charts
4. Consistency of Style
5. Title—is it grandiose or does it properly describe the project?
6. Completeness
7. Professionalism

Therefore, you cannot afford to skimp on the time you spend in "polishing" your proposal. Each item must be checked and re-checked. Since you have spent many hours developing the proposal idea, and further hours researching and writing before your first draft, why risk your investment over poor typing, proofing, graphics, etc. Some of the most important time spent working on the proposal will be that spent on the final draft.

If you are not an artist it might be advisable to employ one to prepare the cover, charts, graphs, etc. The cost is minimal when you consider the potential return.

Be sure you and your typist are familiar with an appropriate typing style. Learn it well and be sure to follow it consistently. . . . Select one which best fits your needs and adopt it for all your proposals.

Don't accept or be satisfied with sloppy typing or art work. Make sure it is reworked until satisfactory. You want all the final copy to be neat and clean prior to submission.[1]

The preceding suggestions on proposal outline, format, and writing style can be adapted to all kinds of proposals. If, instead of seeking funds for a comprehensive research study, you are writing a proposal which is your company's bid on a $3 million sales or construction contract, the basic characteristics of the formal proposal are similar. You will of course need to know the capabilities of your firm's products and services and be scrupulously accurate.

So important are proposals for some firms that they have spent thousands of dollars to equip their own company libraries with individual study rooms and up-to-date research facilities plus a staff of typists and designers. Their main purpose is to help their marketing representatives turn out top-quality, winning proposals. For example, one marketing executive's 28-page (single-spaced) successful major proposal has on its colorful cover an accurate sketch of the prospective customer's buildings. The proposal is attractively bound and protected by a plastic cover. Here is the body of the *transmittal letter* (with changed names), typed on the company's letterhead and bound in the report:

Thank you for the opportunity to review the communication needs of the Sun City Administrative Services Center.

In the past few years this administrative center has grown rapidly in both staff and services to the community. Because your communications system has not kept pace with your growth, a number of communication-related problems have developed.

Your department heads, receptionists, and employees have been most cooperative during our discussions to determine major communication problem areas. The problems uncovered, and the solutions to them, are discussed in the following pages.

Metrodynamic Communications looks forward to providing a telecommunications system which will grow and expand as your Center expands. To meet that goal, we recommend a Direction PBX. The Direction PBX features stored program control combined with time division switching, which provides exceptional versatility for today's needs and is easily adaptable to future requirements. As an alternative Centrex II will also respond to your needs, with capabilities somewhat different from the Direction System.

Either system will provide the Sun City Administrative Services Center with an efficient, flexible, versatile system for today and tomorrow. I am looking forward to working with you on a continuing basis.

---

[1] Lon F. Backman, Program Development, *A Digest on the Elements of Proposal Writing*, Washington State Office of Economic Opportunity, Olympia, Wash., December 1971.

The table of contents lists: Objectives, Communications Problems, Direction Benefits, Explanation of Contract, Direction Pricing, Summary of Direction Features, Centrex Benefits, Centrex Pricing, Optional Services, Summary of System Features, Appendix.

The body of the proposal is neatly, accurately typed (single-space) with helpful headings (second-, third-, and fourth-degree). Colorful illustrations and pictures help emphasize that the proposed system is "efficient, economical, flexible." Important figures, rates, charges, and other details are shown in tables both within the text and in the appendix.

WORKING PLANS

When someone—inside or outside of your company—requests that you investigate a problem and write a report, you first make sure you know what the person wants or needs. Be sure you are told, orally or in writing, clearly what is expected of you.[2] You should know the problem, purpose, scope, procedure to follow in collecting data, and deadline for completion. If your employer (or whoever has requested the report) doesn't give you complete information, you need to ask questions until you understand the assignment thoroughly.

After you receive the assignment, you use the given facts for informal talks with authorities on the subject and people associated with the problem, preliminary review of materials existing in libraries, study of company records, and so on. Use whatever sources will give you the necessary background and understanding to proceed further with the investigation—through the first three planning steps (discussed on pages 542–543). Given here are a suggested working plan outline and a sample plan.

Outline

The culmination of preliminary investigation is a working plan that you'll present to the person who asked you to make the report. If no one authorized you to take the assignment, you still should make out a working plan for your own benefit. In this working plan—perhaps a memo to the employer in your own organization or a letter to someone outside the firm—you'll include:

1. Problem
2. Purpose
3. Scope
4. Limitations
5. Use of the report
6. Type of reader(s)
7. Tentative outline (your main text and terminal section headings)

[2] In a formal report of a public nature, the one authorizing or commissioning the report notifies the report writer in a letter called a "letter of authorization." The message will be bound with the formal report's prefatory pages, usually just before the transmittal letter.

8. Method(s) of collecting data
9. Work-progress schedule

The whole idea of the working plan is to tell the one who authorized the report (or yourself) the way you understand the problem, the purpose, the use of the report, and so on, and to make sure you see eye to eye. Be sure you understand who your readers will be. Do you have both primary and secondary readers? Are they familiar with the subject or will they need background material? Are they biased, antagonistic, or favorably inclined toward the subject?

In the outline you want to show the areas you'll investigate and discuss in the report—and, if possible, subdivisions for each major area. Also indicate the type of terminal section you'll have—summary, conclusions, and/or recommendations—and whether you are arranging the parts logically or psychologically.

Example

The following working plan is from a researcher in a management consulting firm to a department head. It is typewritten on the firm's intraoffice memo stationery, in memo form.

```
TO:       Nina Vandeline              Date:  April 12, 19__
FROM:     Tom Browne
SUBJECT:  Working Plan for Study on Treelane Homeowners Association
```

Confirming our conversation of April 8, here is my working plan for the study you requested concerning Treelane Homeowners Association, a development in south XY County.

Problem
The association's programs are not meeting the needs of its members. The benefits the association affords are rarely taken advantage of by homeowners. They share assets consisting of a clubhouse, park, swimming pool, and fishing pond. In addition, the association has a charter which outlines rules and guidelines all homeowners are supposed to follow for (1) making changes in their property, (2) general regulation of pets, and (3) use of the common area.

However, rules are often ignored. Social activities are rarely attended by many homeowners. Business meetings have a very poor attendance record. Communication is poor. Some owners are hostile.

Purpose and Objective
I will determine the causes for the above-stated problems and make recommendations to help Treelane become a more effective organization.

My plan is to find the attitudes and interests of individual homeowners and apply my findings to aid officers in modifying the organization. My findings and proposals will hopefully lead to an organization which involves homeowners and helps them to receive benefits they are paying for.

Limitations
My evaluations must be limited to programs which are useful and stimulate interest and modifications of property within the budget. The study is limited in time, in that the recommendations are needed one month from today.

Scope
I will evaluate only those changes which are practical and feasible and which have apparent potential for bettering Treelane.

Procedures for Gathering Data
A questionnaire will be sent to all homeowners. In addition to the replies received from homeowners, I plan to interview all officers and to examine--with your permission--the records of the association.

Division of Problem and Tentative General Outline
The problem will be divided into three parts: (1) social activities, (2) physical property, and (3) rules.

First a questionnaire must be prepared to find out what preferences, dislikes, and ideas property owners have. The data will be analyzed, and selected recommendations will be evaluated by talking with officers and looking at the budget.

Tentative Conclusion
The homeowners association needs social activities which will involve more property owners. This change will stimulate interest in the organization and decrease the hostilities now present.

Work-progress Schedule
Data will be collected by Friday, April 22; organized and interpreted by Monday, May 6. Report outline will be ready by May 9. The final report will be submitted by May 12.

After completing the preliminary investigation—the authorizer and the report writer might have further consultations if warranted and appropriate. These additional contacts might occur: (1) at the completion of the investigation—after the writer has collected and studied the material and determined the results; (2) after the writer has made the final report outline; and (3) after the writer has written the report but before he or she officially submits the finished report to the receiver.

PREFATORY PARTS

One of the distinguishing features of a formal (or long) report is that it has some or all of the following prefatory parts: cover, title fly, title page, letter of authorization, letter of transmittal, table of contents (contents), table of tables, abstract. In the left-hand column below are the prefatory parts of the formal report. To the right of each entry is the location in the memo report where you find similar information:

Cover/title page   to, from, subject, date

Title fly   not needed

Title page	not needed
Letter of transmittal	introduction
Table of contents	plan of presentation (in introduction)
Table of tables	table(s) in text
Abstract	introduction and terminal section

Cover (Design and Wording of Title)

Many reports combine the cover and title page for the top page. But you can dress up a formal report by using both. Obviously, you need a cover to which the reader will react favorably. Sometimes a simple hard cover (both for the front and back), with a properly placed title, will suffice. You can type the title on a gummed label, or type or print it directly on the cover itself. However, with a little imagination and a subject that allows you the possibility, you can design a more complex cover—one that ties in with the material being discussed. For example, assume you're writing a report in which you're suggesting that the firm switch from its present printed personnel form to a more effectively worded and comprehensive form. The cover can consist of parts of both forms with a title superimposed. Or, if you're discussing foreign compact cars, a picture of one of the cars and an attractively arranged title could make an effective cover. But beware of overdoing—of making your cover gaudy or ludicrous.

Your title must exactly and specifically identify the overall subject of the report. As you ponder the wording of the title, here are a few suggestions to consider.

1. Keep the title short (usually about eight words maximum); omit "the," "a," and "an" whenever possible. Also wordy are "A Report on . . . ," "A Survey on . . . ," "Constructive Criticism . . . ," "Recommendations for Improvement for . . ." A long title kills interest and can cause filing errors. If you must use many words, use a short main title and a longer subtitle, as shown below:

MARKETING POLICIES OF OREGON'S HAZELNUT GROWERS ASSOCIATION

Appraisal of methods to increase demand for hazelnuts, with emphasis on value and effectiveness of advertising, sales promotion, price policies, and distribution channels.

2. Use your imagination to create a title that catches the eye.
3. Whenever possible, stress results rather than procedure or the way you collected your material.
4. Avoid an air of mystery—such as a title in the form of a question.
5. Pay particular attention to the scope of the report. For example, "Agricultural Products in (state)" is misleading if you're discussing only grains, vegetables, or fruits.
6. Include whichever of the five W's (and How) seem pertinent.

Title Fly and Title Page

Only when you have both a cover and title page can you use the *title fly*—usually a blank sheet of paper located between the two parts. As in books, it acts as a buffer or relief when the reader opens the book.

Whether or not your report has a cover, the *title page* usually contains the title, as well as names of the recipient and sender, and the completion date—each of which should have a separate focal point on the page. As illustrated on page 657, the title page should be attractively arranged. It may be in four or three sections; if the latter, you combine date with author's identification. If appropriate, you add pertinent facts about the individuals involved, such as title, department, and organization. Date of completion must agree with the date on the letter of transmittal.

With a cover, the title page uses the same weight paper as the text sheets do; as a combination cover and title page this part might have a heavier weight—similar to that for the cover.

Letter of Authorization

The person authorizing or commissioning the formal report notifies the report writer in a letter called a letter of authorization. In a formal report of a public nature, this message becomes one of the bound prefatory pages. Although it is often omitted from the business formal report, it may of course be included.

When you are in the position of authorizing a report, organize your message by the direct-request or good-news plan. And be sure to make clear just what you are authorizing. Take care of the items that you know a researcher needs to know.

Letter of Transmittal

The letter of transmittal officially conveys or transmits the finished report. When you're writing to a large group of people, you label it as a preface and set it up as one. The receiver is the individual who authorized the report or who needs the information. In the transmittal you tell the reader what you'd say to him or her if you were handing the report to him or her. Regardless of whether the body of the report talks in the third person, you can use first and second persons in the transmittal. You want to adhere to all the rules of letter writing for a transmittal. Use the good-news organizational plan. Basically, this letter includes transmittal, authorization, and purpose plus any other ideas listed below:

Main idea

Transmittal

Authorization

Purpose

Need or use of report

Explanation and/or highlights

Perhaps a brief indication of outcome—in general only. Indicate conclusions and/or recommendations *if* you think the reader will consider them good (or neutral) news and *if* an abstract or terminal section with the same information doesn't appear at the beginning of the report—just a few pages after the transmittal.

Perhaps a comment or two on an interesting matter closely related to the report but not discussed in it; or writer's comments outside the limits of the report.

Background and methodology are sometimes stated briefly.

Courteous ending

Acknowledgments to people who assisted. (In some formal reports acknowledgments are in a separate section instead of in the transmittal or preface.)

Indication that later reports may be necessary or forthcoming.

Willingness to discuss.

Offer to assist with future projects.

You need to be careful not to include the same elements in both the transmittal and the introduction or the transmittal and the abstract or synopsis, if any, for the needless repetition would be annoying.

The example that follows is a transmittal for an analytical formal report. Notice it briefly indicates the outcome and the writer's recommendation. (The 33-page report itself discusses both in detail; its terminal section is on page 32.) The letter is typed on this marketing consultant's letterhead stationery in the usual letter format. (For another transmittal with a formal report see page 658.)

```
Dear Mrs. Larson:

Here is the report you authorized October 18 regarding a survey of
market potential on Bigg Island.  The purpose of this report is to
present an analysis of data collected about the possible implementa-
tion of home-care service at Bigg View Convalescent Center.

You will be pleased to learn that our survey indicates a generally
favorable reaction to the project.  The report includes survey re-
sults in five areas:


Social structure
Age range
Percent over age 65
Financial structure of persons over age 65
Preferences for convalescent care


On the basis of the survey made, I recommend that Bigg View Convales-
cent Center initiate a home-care service and a program of extensive
informal education of the island's population.
```

```
I have enjoyed making this study and appreciate the opportunity to
help you reach a reliable decision concerning the home-care service.
Please call me if you have questions or if I may assist you in any
further analysis.
```

Sincerely yours,

(*signature, typed name, title*)

Table of Contents

The table of contents shows the major and minor divisions of the report and their respective locations within the report. On page 659 is the contents for an energy conservation report. Notice that the writer sets apart the body of the report from the letter of transmittal, appendix, and bibliography by indenting the introduction, major divisions of the text, and the summary. If you wish, you can separate the body even more by putting all its major parts in capitals. If you preface the introduction, major divisions of the text, and terminal section with Roman numerals (I, II, III, etc.), you should preface their subdivisions with capital letters (A, B, C, etc.). For further subdivisions, you use Arabic numerals (1, 2, 3, etc.).

Naturally, you must prepare the table of contents after typing the rest of the report —or at least after making a typewritten draft—so you'll know the correct page numbers. Use leaders (dot, space, dot, space, dot) to lead the eye from the name of each entry to the page column on the right. Every entry shown in the table of contents must appear exactly as it does in the body. But not every heading in the body has to appear in the contents. Usually you show no more than three degrees (first, second, and third) of headings.

If the appendix includes several different entries (questionnaire, reprint of a statute or regulation, various tables, or other visual aids) you can show them in one of two locations: (1) if you have only a few entries, as subdivisions of the appendix on the contents page; or (2) if you have a rather extensive appendix, as subdivisions of the appendix on the appendix title page.

Table of Tables

Label this prefatory page according to the type of formal visual aids shown throughout the text. If the illustrations are all tables, you'll label the page Table of Tables or List of Tables. Follow the same procedure for charts, pictures, and so forth. If you have a mixture of tables, charts, and other visual aids, consider a title that encompasses them all; perhaps a Table of Illustrations will suffice.

This prefatory page serves the same function for the visual aids as the contents page does for the coverage of the report. If space permits, you can include both the table of contents and table of tables on the same page. Whether the latter is combined with the table of contents or by itself on the page, the layout begins as shown below:

Table of Tables

Abstract

As a prefatory part, an abstract can definitely perform a vital service for the reader. An *abstract* is an abbreviated, concise, accurate representation of a report, document, or publication. Usually it is placed at the bottom of the title page or on a separage page immediately preceding the report body. This prefatory part carries various labels— Abstract, Synopsis, Introductory Summary, Precis—but they all are prefatory summaries that come before the report body. Abstracts may be "descriptive" (also called "indicative") or "informative."

Descriptive Abstract

This type of abstract merely states what the report contains. It includes purpose, methods, and scope, but omits the results. The reader must read the report to find the results, conclusions, and/or recommendations. A descriptive abstract can cover in fewer than 100 words any report, whether it is ten or a thousand pages long. Its length does not depend on the report length. For example, a descriptive abstract of the energy conservation report (pages 657–662) might be:

```
This report analyzes the energy conservation effort at Central Die-
sel, Inc., in three dimensions--based mainly on interviews: usage be-
fore the shortage, usage currently, and projected usage after pro-
posed changes within separate areas of special concentration.
```

Informative Abstract

Not only does the informative abstract include purpose, methods, and scope; it also has statements of results, conclusions, and/or recommendations. Because it contains more helpful information—the report's highlights all on one page—it is preferred by most readers. The busy manager, after scanning the abstract, can determine whether she or he wants to read further.

Besides being a useful prefatory part of a long, formal report, informative abstracts also serve other important functions. Some firms circulate to all their management personnel only the abstract *without* the report. (The person who originally authorized the report of course gets the complete, original report.) Those who receive only the abstract can decide whether they need the original report, which is then sent to them upon their request. This practice saves much time and expense, especially when reports are 50 or more pages long.

Another important use of abstracts is for reports, articles, documents, and such that are published. A well-written abstract can communicate contents to many more business associates. In brief reading time colleagues can scan abstracts in their professional and business journals, thus keeping up to date on literature in their special field. The quality of an abstract may determine who and how many ever see the full document. Those who find interest in the abstract may send for the original write-up.

If you are working in a certain professional area or industry, your long-report informative abstract may be widely circulated within the area or industry. For example:

> Reports from companies working on government contracts may have an initial distribution of less than 100. Yet, on NASA-sponsored company information for the space program, 9,000 copies of abstracts are circulated to potential users of these company reports (and this within two to four weeks after the report is released).[3]

Though the informative abstract length varies somewhat in proportion to the report length, it should be confined to fewer than 500 words (preferably on one page). To show you how abstracts vary, here are three examples:

Example 1

An informative abstract of the energy conservation *report might begin with the same sentence shown for the descriptive abstract above and then continue with sentences revealing conclusions and recommendations.*

Before last winter's energy shortage the firm, like many others, had no conservation policy. After realizing an energy crisis existed, all departments cooperated. Savings totaling about 14% energy usage were made by reducing temperatures, removing unnecessary lighting tubes, and reducing heat-loss sources plus excessive wastes in convenience electricity and company vehicles.

Five recommendations for future improvements to achieve estimated 35% total savings include: installing certain access doors, repairing an air compressor, replacing one inefficient heating system, changing diesel generator testing procedures to cut fuel consumption, and replacing older vehicles with smaller economy models.

Example 2

Informative abstract on a seven-page published report.

The authors undertook a survey of the attitudes of personnel officers of 250 large organizations concerning the need for communication courses at the graduate level.

[3] David L. Staiger, Manager of Publications, Society of Automotive Engineers, Inc., "What Today's Students Need to Know about Writing Abstracts," *The Journal of Business Communication,* 3(1):30, 1965.

The survey found that communication skills were rated of extreme importance by executives of large organizations, some believing it to be the single most important function of management personnel.[4]

Example 3

Informative abstract on a 32-page published manual.

Because of the vast increase in the scientific literature, technical writers must help the reader grasp ideas quickly. For this purpose, headings and introductions are two of the most useful devices.

Headings give the reader immediate insight into large blocks of information and help him digest them rapidly. Accordingly, they are an exceedingly valuable aid to speed reading.

Although headings are greatly helpful, they are not sufficient. They sometimes are ambiguous, they do not give reasons, and they look neither backward nor forward in the article—they are concerned only with the present. They therefore need supplementation by introductions, which supply this information that headings, because of their brevity, cannot give.

Introductions, in contrast to headings, are complex devices. They have five transitional functions; therefore, a complete introduction is made up of five parts. This manual defines the functions, names the parts, and shows how to use them.

The manual thus is concerned with the heading-introduction technique, and its aim is to show how we can use this technique to help the reader grasp our idea fast.[5]

One more, popular use of abstracts should be mentioned here. If you are invited to present a report at a business meeting (planned perhaps eight months in advance), the chairperson may ask you to send an abstract for distribution before the conference. The abstract may be requested even before you have started writing your report or talk. The well-planned abstract you write for the chairperson can contain the topic sentences you will use later to develop your report and talk. In this situation the abstract is written before, not after, the complete report.

DOCUMENTATION AND EXPLANATORY NOTATIONS

In every well-written report, as you know, writers must establish the trustworthiness of their statements. When your report contains quotations and/or specific facts from various sources, you must cite these references to document your report. Your introduction states methodology and mentions sources at least in general; your text discussion refers to them when it is desirable to clarify the origin of specific facts or figures. In addition—especially for long reports—the bibliography (see pages 649–651) lists sources as a supplemental part after the report body.

[4] James A. Belohlov, Paul O. Popp, and Michael S. Porte, "Communication: A View from the Inside of Business," *Journal of Business Communication,* 11(4):54, 1974.
[5] F. Bruce Sanford, "Heading-Introduction Technique," *United States Department of the Interior,* Fish and Wildlife Service, Washington, D.C., Circular 283, 1968, p. 1.

This section discusses three methods of presenting sources and additional explanatory or incidental comments within the text of the report. You can place them in (1) footnotes, (2) a list at the end of the report, or (3) citations within the text.

Footnotes

Of the three methods named above, footnotes are the most versatile and favored by many writers as well as readers (though some readers object to them because they interrupt their reading). To help you use footnotes correctly, you need to be informed of their purposes, superscripts, content, and placement.

Purposes of Footnotes

Include footnotes when you want to:

1. *Give credit to sources you used.* Any quotations and important factual statements that are not common knowledge or based on your experience must be supported by references to your sources. If you make a statement belonging to someone else and you don't credit that source, you are plagiarizing. By citing sources of paraphrased as well as of quoted materials, you not only give credit where credit is due, but also you help convince your readers that your data are trustworthy and you are willing to let them examine the references.
2. *Show a cross-reference*—directing the reader to another place within the report—such as a detailed discussion, examples of important principles, or perhaps a page in the appendix.
3. *Explain, discuss, or give additional information* that relates to an idea in the text but is incidental; too long, complicated, or technical to include in the text discussion; or shouldn't interrupt the flow of thought.

The first two purposes (1 and 2 above) pertain to *source* and *reference* footnotes; the third purpose, to *discussion* footnotes.

Superscripts

To refer your reader to footnotes and to number them, use superscripts. These are usually *Arabic numerals* placed slightly above the line. *They are used with footnotes that include sources, cross-references, or discussion.* You can number these superscripts consecutively throughout the report or begin a new series with each page or—the recommended practice—with each chapter (as in this book). In tables and figures superscripts are not numerals but usually special symbols, as explained later.

You need to use good judgment in placing superscripts consistently where they will be easily noticed by the reader and fair to the sources. Within the text, to avoid interrupting the reader's attention, the superscript is best placed at the end of a sentence if the reference will be clear there. When the superscript number refers to a source footnote regarding quoted or paraphrased material, it is placed usually at the end of the quotation (after the last punctuation mark).[6]

When desirable for clarity or emphasis the superscript may follow an author's name or a title. In this book superscripts for all numbered examples quoted through courtesy of *named* companies or persons follow immediately after the italicized headings preceding the quoted materials. Notice, for instance, superscript 7 after the heading for letter 1, p. 210, and footnote 7 giving credit to Armstrong Cork Company. Or see superscript 22 for letter 6, p. 377, and footnote 22 crediting Rosenfields.

Superscripts in tables and figures should be symbols (asterisks, daggers), or *lowercase alphabetic letters*, not Arabic numbers. See for example, the * and † in the letter-placement table on p. 138. The same symbols are used repeatedly for all tables or figures in an entire report (or article or book). Thus this method differs from the numbering of superscript numerals, which continue consecutively throughout a manuscript or chapter.

Content of Source Footnotes

The choice of content in source footnotes varies somewhat depending upon whether the report includes a bibliography (see page 644) and also which authority you are following.[7] To avoid confusing you with several alternatives, this section summarizes briefly the main items included in one popular (and simplified) method. Remember that others may be equally desirable for different situations. Use whatever is preferred by your instructor, employer, industry, business, editor, (or by you) and be consistent.

Source Footnotes without Bibliography. Sources may be either published materials or unpublished information. Footnotes citing sources the first time should always contain complete information if the report has no bibliography. When the same source is repeated in later references, these footnotes may be shortened.

You get most of the information about a book source from title and copyright pages. For a periodical—published quarterly, monthly, weekly, or daily—you'll find needed information on the cover page and the article itself. Though your reference materials will vary in content, try to include whatever items are available and helpful to specifically identify each source for your reader(s). Then arrange the items in the sequence shown in the following checklists, with a comma between items and a period at the end.

---

[6] For example, see superscript 10 and footnote (fn) 10 on p. 11; 4 on p. 48; 20 on p. 376; and 8 on p. 603.

[7] Space in this book allows only highlights about bibliographies and footnotes. For additional details on numerous variations in content and setup, you will find these publications helpful: William Giles Campbell and Stephen V. Ballou, *Form and Style: Theses, Reports, Term Papers,* 4th ed., Houghton Mifflin Company, Boston, 1974; *A Manual of Style,* 12th ed., University of Chicago Press, Chicago, 1969; *MLA Handbook for Writers of Research Papers, Theses, and Dissertations,* Modern Language Association of America, New York, 1977; Kate L. Turabian, *A Manual for Writers of Term Papers, Theses, and Dissertations,* 4th ed., University of Chicago Press, Chicago, 1973; *United States Government Printing Office Style Manual* (abridged, revised edition), U.S. Government Printing Office, Washington, D.C., 1973.

For published materials the following checklists outline briefly the items that may be included *in first-time full footnote references when the sources are books, periodicals, or newspapers.* Of course, not all these items are available or essential for every footnote.

CHECKLISTS FOR SOURCE FOOTNOTES
WITHOUT BIBLIOGRAPHY

A. Books	B. Periodicals	C. Newspapers
1. Superscript	1. Superscript	1. Superscript
Facts about the Composition		

2. Author name(s)
   a. 1 } normal
   b. 2 or 3 } order
   c. over 3:
      1st author plus
      "and others"
	2. Author name(s)
	   a. 1 } normal
	   b. 2 or 3 } order
	   c. over 3:
	      1st author plus
	      "and others"
	   d. Sometimes no
	      person's name
	      given
	   e. A bureau may
	      be author
		2. Author name(s)
		   a. 1 } normal
		   b. 2 or 3 } order
		   c. over 3:
		      1st author plus
		      "and others"
		   d. If no name, maybe
		      state section (Editorial, Business),
		      if any

3. Author capacity:
   (Used only if not
   really the author)
   a. editor–typed "ed."
   b. translator–"trans."
   c. compiler–"comp."
4. Book title
   a. typed: all capitals
      or underlined
   b. printed: italics
5. Edition number or
   name (if not the first)
	3. Article title
	   a. typed } in quotation marks
	   b. printed }
		3. Article title
		   a. typed } in quotation marks
		   b. printed }

Facts about the Publication		

6. Publisher name
7. Publisher location
   (usually headquarters
   city; add state if not
   well-known city; add
   country if foreign)
   Note: Items 6 and 7
   may be reversed–
   City: Publisher.
8. Publication date–
   year of latest edition
9. Volume number, if
   more than one volume
10. Page(s) of the citation
	4. Periodical name
	   a. typed: underlined
	   b. printed: italics
	5. Publisher location–
	   if desirable to include,
	   same as A-7
	
	6. Date of volume or issue } 6 and 7
	7. Number of } may be
	   volume, if } reversed
	   any
	8. Page(s) of article
		4. Newspaper name
		   a. typed: underlined
		   b. printed: italics
		5. City and state may be
		   inserted if not in name
		
		6. Date of newspaper–
		   month, day, year
		
		7. Page(s) of article

For unpublished sources–minutes of meetings, speeches, letters, theses, interviews– you will find a variety of different citations used. However, as a *general guide*, the minimum items to include are:

Name of author or sponsoring organization

Title or kind of material

Date

Page numbers, if these would be helpful to the reader.

The following examples illustrate various first-time full source footnotes. The small printed numbers in parentheses after each item in the first footnote are inserted merely to help you identify easily which items on the book checklist are included. Can you identify the items in all the other footnotes by comparing them with the checklists?

Books

1 (*1*)
 Richard Wincor (*2a*), Contracts in Plain English (*4*), McGraw-Hill Book Co. (*6*), New York (*7*), 1976 (*8*), pp. 82-85 (*10*).

[2]John R. Willingham and Donald F. Warders, A Handbook for Student Writers, 2d ed., Harcourt Brace Jovanovich, Inc., New York, 1978, pp. 293-4.

[3]Charles Burden and others (eds.), Business in Literature, David McKay Press, New York, 1977 (paper), p. 176.

Periodicals

[4]J. E. Weinrauch and J. R. Swandra, Jr., "Examining the Significance of Listening; An Exploratory Study of Contemporary Managers," The Journal of Business Communication, 13:1, 1975, p. 54.

[5]"Discretionary Justice," Business Week, March 16, 1979, pp. 15-16.

[6]Richard Weatherly, Michael Lipsky, and Thomas Jones, "Street-Level Bureaucrats and Institutional Reform," Harvard Educational Review, May 1977, p. 172.

Newspapers

[7]Editorial in the Los Angeles Times, December 4, 1979, p. B-6.

[8]Associated Press Dispatch, "Economics Seen behind Cancellation," The Jamaica [New York] Chronicle, November 30, 1979, p. 3-C.

Unpublished Materials

⁹H. Greenbaum, "The Appraisal of Organizational Communication Systems," unpublished manuscript delivered to the International Communication Association, Atlanta, 1972, p.3.

¹⁰<u>Report of the National District Attorneys Association Symposium on White Collar Crime Enforcement</u>, conducted at Battelle Seattle Research Center, 1978, p. 12.

Source Footnotes with Bibliography. When the report includes a bibliography, the footnotes may (but not *must*) be shortened to these items:

Superscript

Surname(s) of author(s)

Title of book, article, report, or manuscript

Page number(s) on which the information appears

¹Wincor, <u>Contracts in Plain English</u>, pp. 82–85.

⁴Weinrauch and Swandra, "Examining the Significance of Listening,". . . ., p. 54.

Because the bibliography gives the complete citations, readers can refer to it if they wish more details about any source.

Repeated Source Footnote References. When you need to cite the same source more than once in a paper, the citations after the first time are usually shortened. Two methods are acceptable.

a. Superscript, author(s) surname(s), page number(s).

or

b. Standard Latin abbreviations (which many readers do not understand, but are often required in academic papers):

Ibid (meaning "in the same place")—refers to the immediately preceding footnote, but a different page. Content is: Superscript, *ibid.*, page(s)—as for footnote (fn) 2 in Examples below.

Op. cit. ("in the work cited")—refers to a previously cited footnote that is followed by at least one intervening footnote about another source. Content is: Superscript, author(s) surname(s), *op. cit.*, page(s). See fn 4.

Loc. cit. ("in the place cited")—refers to same page in a previously cited footnote:
(1) when one or more other source footnotes intervene, use: Superscript, author(s) surname(s), *loc. cit.* See fn 5.
(2) When no other source footnote intervenes, content is: Superscript, *loc. cit.* See fn 6.

Examples

[1]Richard Wincor, <u>Contracts in Plain English</u>, McGraw-Hill Book Co., New York, 1976, pp. 82-85.

[2]Wincor, p. 89.	[2]Ibid., p. 89.
(Method a)	*(Method b)*

[3]J. E. Weinrauch and J. R. Swandra, Jr., "Examining the Significance of Listening; An Exploratory Study of Contemporary Managers," <u>The Journal of Business Communication</u>, 13:1, 1975, p. 54.

(Method a)	*(Method b)*
[4]Wincor, p. 100	[4]Wincor, <u>op. cit.</u>, p. 100.
[5]Weinrauch and Swandra, p. 54.	[5]Weinrauch and Swandra, <u>loc. cit.</u>
[6]Weinrauch and Swandra, p. 54.	[6]<u>Loc. cit.</u>

Content of Cross-Reference and Discussion Footnotes

As you know, besides the source footnotes discussed in detail above, you may also use footnotes for cross references and for additional discussion, as mentioned under "purposes," page 640. For examples of content, see the following (and other) footnotes in this book:

Cross References: footnote (fn) 1, p. 524; fn 8, p. 282, which includes both a cross reference and discussion; fn 11, p. 81; fn 4, p. 128.

Discussion: fn 2, p. 124; fns 14, 15, 16, p. 228; fn 12, p. 362; fn 4, p. 449.

Placement of Footnotes

The preferred placement for footnotes (except those in tables) is at the bottom of the same page on which they are cited by superscripts in the text. (Another method, less popular, is to insert the footnote immediately after the superscript reference to it and to separate it from the text by a line running across the page both above and below the footnote.) For tables the footnotes are placed at the bottom of each table.

A few typing guidelines are helpful when your footnotes are at the bottom of a page. The typist must plan carefully to allow a sufficient bottom margin for placement of the footnotes. Figure 17-1 below shows how footnotes are typed at the bottom of a page within the desired margins. Notice they are separated from the text by a line 1½ or 2 inches long (a double space below the last line of the text) beginning at the left margin. Each footnote is typed single space, usually indented three to five spaces on its first line and even with the left margin on all succeeding lines. Double space between footnotes.

Figure 17-1 A long-report page (double-spaced) showing placement of three superscripts and three complete footnotes.

List at End of the Report

A method of documentation used by many professional journals and academic writers is to place the notes and references at the end of the report or article, *not* at the bottom of each page that has a superscript. As with the "footnote method" discussed above, the raised superscript number in the text is placed after the word, sentence, or paragraphs to which a note refers. But the numbers always progress consecutively through the report or article. Each superscript number refers to a certain numbered reference in a list at the *end of the paper.*

The list may be titled Notes and References, or List of References, or, sometimes, merely Endnotes. Entries appear on the list in the same numerical order that the citations occur in the paper—*not* in alphabetical order (as in a bibliography). Each entry about a source contains the same items as the footnote.

Facts about the composition—author name(s) and book or article title . . . as listed in checklist items A 2-5 (books), B 2-3 (periodicals), and C 2-3 (newspapers), page 642.

Facts about the publication—publisher name, location, date, volume number, and citation pages . . . as in checklist items A 6-10, B 4-8, and C 4-7, page 642.

Entries containing cross-references or discussion are also the same as for footnotes (see p. 645).

Suppose a writer's report includes all 10 source footnotes in the order listed on pages 643–644, plus a cross reference and a discussion footnote. If he or she uses a list of References and Notes *instead of footnotes*, the 12 items will appear on one page at the *end of the report*, as illustrated in Figure 17-2. Notice that the cross-reference and

References and Notes

1. Richard Wincor, <u>Contracts in Plain English</u>, McGraw-Hill Book Co., New York, 1976, pp. 82-85.

2. John R. Willingham and Donald F. Warders, <u>A Handbook for Student Writers</u>, 2d Edition, Harcourt Brace Jovanovich, Inc., New York, 1978, pp. 293-4.

3. For a list of documents, see pages 21-22.

4. Charles Burden and others (eds.), <u>Business in Literature</u>, David McKay Press, New York, 1977 (paper)p. 176.

5. J. E. Weinrauch and J. R. Swandra, Jr., "Examining the Significance of Listening; and Exploratory Study of Contemporary Managers," <u>The Journal of Business Communication</u>, 13:1, 1975, p. 54.

6. "Discretionary Justice," <u>Business Week</u>, March 16, 1979, pp. 15-16.

7. Richard Weatherly, Michael Lipsky, and Thomas Jones, "Street-Level Bureaucrats and Institutional Reform," <u>Harvard Educational Review</u>, May 1977, p. 172.

8. In an industrial setting, such as an assembly line, little discretion is exercised by the laborer. Consequently, the generalization concerning the exercise of discretion, on the street-level, applies only to occupational settings like social service agencies.

9. Editorial in the <u>Los Angeles Times</u>, December 4, 1979. p. B-6.

10. Associated Press Dispatch, "Economics Seen behind Cancellation," <u>The Jamaica</u> [New York] <u>Chronicle</u>, November 30, 1979, p. 3-C.

11. H. Greenbaum, "The Appraisal of Organizational Communication Systems," unpublished manuscript delivered to the International Communication Association, Atlanta, 1972, p. 3.

12. Greenbaum, p. 4.

13. <u>Report of the National District Attorneys Association Symposium on White Collar Crime Enforcement</u>, conducted at Batelle Seattle Research Center, 1978, p. 12.

14. <u>Report</u> . . . . , p. 14.

Figure 17-2 List of references and notes (placed at end of paper). Numbers are in same order as in text discussion. *No* footnotes appear on text pages. List of 14 includes 10 different sources, 2 repetitions (#12 and 14), a cross reference (#3), and a discussion note (#8).

the discussion notes are numbered 3 and 8, respectively, in the (assumed) same order as the superscripts appeared in the text. Notes 12 and 14 are shortened because they are repetitions of reference notes 11 and 13 respectively, except for page citations.

This method of documentation, gathering all notes and references at the end, is not best for the reader. But it saves the writer time and space by not typing footnotes on the same pages as the referenced items. With this method the reader, however, must continually turn pages to the back of the report in order to read the referenced items immediately.

Citations within the Text

A third method of documentation is to place a citation within the text itself. Sometimes you can weave into a sentence the minimum essentials of a citation. For example:

> According to Lewis Benton (*Supervision and Management*, McGraw-Hill Book Company, 1972, p. 54), absenteeism can be controlled by....

> *or*

> Another writer--Leslie Bernstein (in "How to Right a Report," *Business Management*, September 1978, pp.46-48)--states that....

You can also use this method for backward or forward cross-references to save the reader's time. For example, within a text paragraph you might insert a parenthetical sentence like: "(See item 4, pages 52-53.)." This book has many such cross-references.

This placement of the citation within a sentence or paragraph is convenient for both reader and writer, but it has limitations. If the citation is long, the sentence also becomes undesirably long and the thought is interrupted by the citation. Furthermore, this method is not so easily adaptable for adding long, parenthetical explanations.

In summary, as with everything else for good report writing, use good judgment in your choice of documentation method and be consistent. All three methods have advantages in certain situations. Consider the type and length of note or reference and whether your reader would prefer reading it immediately, or as a footnote, or at the end of the report. Furthermore, if any material is definitely irrelevant, *omit* it entirely from your report text and footnotes. If you are writing a report for publication in a journal, use whatever documentation method the journal editors require.

SUPPLEMENTAL PARTS

The special parts that are added after the body of a long, formal report are called supplemental or appended parts, or addenda. They include the appendix, bibliography, and index.

Appendix

You put materials into the appendix when you need to include them somewhere in the report, but they aren't essential in developing any part of the text. The appendix permits you to avoid cluttering the discussion (text) with exhibits, copy of a questionnaire, and pamphlets that are unnecessary to read for the right understanding of the report but which may be useful as reference or as supporting information.

With short reports, you merely add the appendix sheets directly to the report. But for a formal report, you place a sheet of paper (the appendix title page) between the last page of the body and the first page of the appendix. If you have enough material in the appendix to justify a separate table of contents, show the contents below the title on the appendix dividing sheet, in order of the page arrangement. (See, for example, the appendix dividing sheet in this text, page 705.)

Each separate entry (sample forms, detailed data for reference, table, picture, questionnaire, chart, map, graphic representation, blueprint) in the appendix naturally requires an identifying title. As a rule you should refer the reader to every entry in the appendix in the report body (within the discussion itself or in a footnote).

The last page of the appendix is the ideal place for any table or illustration the reader will need to refer to throughout the report. You can set up this table on a pull-out sheet and tell the reader about the sheet in the letter of transmittal or introduction. Such an arrangement permits the reader to keep this master table—or whatever is on the sheet—in full view at all times.

Bibliography

The bibliography is a list of sources used when preparing the report or paper. It includes not only those sources cited in the footnotes but also other references you consulted that contain relevant ideas. This supplemental part usually follows the appendix. Among the published sources included in a bibliography are books, government publications, yearbooks, public documents, encyclopedias, pamphlets, bulletins, magazines, and newspapers. In addition, a business report bibliography may also include unpublished sources such as manuscripts, interviews, responses to surveys, and organization letters or documents.

You can present bibliographic entries in a single orderly list under the one heading, Bibliography, or under various pertinent subheadings. For example, if your list is long and varied, you might arrange sources within broad groups such as books, periodicals, and government publications. Furthermore, if you include unpublished sources, you might choose a broader main title like Sources Consulted instead of Bibliography (which literally refers to a list of books and articles).

Each entry in the bibliography is similar to a full footnote source reference, including essentially the same items as those shown in the checklists on page 642. The main differences are in the arrangement of items and in the page numbers shown. A popular way to arrange bibliographic entries is in *alphabetic* order by authors' surnames, and if pages are included for books, they are the total pages in those books (not the one or more pages cited).

1. *Composition*—author's full name (surname first) and title of the book, article, report, or pamphlet. For coauthors, reverse only the surname of the first author: "Thompson, Robert, John Jones, and Mary Smith." If more than three authors

are involved, reverse the first author's surname but don't list the other names: "Thompson, Robert, and others." (An alternate arrangement by some writers is to reverse all authors' names, not just the first name.)

2. *Publication*—publisher's name, location, edition, date, total pages in the publication.

For examples of two (among several) ways to set up a bibliography, see Figure 17-3 and the energy conservation report bibliography, page 662. Notice that the entries are typewritten in hanging-indention form, with only the first line of each entry starting at the left margin and all others indented (usually three to seven spaces). In these examples commas separate the items, as in footnotes. (However, some writers prefer periods between these items, and they also place the publisher's location before instead of after the publisher's name.) Also noteworthy are the different subheadings in these two bibliographies.

BIBLIOGRAPHY

Books

Burden, Charles, and others (eds.) Business in Literature, David McKay Press, New York, 1977 (paper) 318 pp.

Kornblum, Allan N., The Moral Hazards, D. C. Heath and Company, Lexington, MA, 1976, 179 pp.

Willingham, John R., and Donald F. Warders, A Handbook for Student Writers, 2d Edition, Harcourt Brace Jovanovich, Inc., New York, 1978, 348 pp.

Wincor, Richard, Contracts in Plain English, McGraw-Hill Book Co., New York, 1976, 148 pp.

Periodicals and Newspapers

Associated Press Dispatch, "Economics Seen behind Cancellation," The Jamaica [New York] Chronicle, November 30, 1979, p. 3-C.

"Discretionary Justice," Business Week, March 16, 1979, pp. 15-16.

Editorial in the Los Angeles Times, December 4, 1979, p. B-6.

Weatherly, Richard, Michael Lipsky, and Thomas Jones, "Street-Level Bureaucrats and Institutional Reform," Harvard Educational Review, May 1977, p. 172.

Weinrauch, J. E., and J. R. Swandra, Jr., "Examining the Significance of Listening; An Exploratory Study of Contemporary Managers," The Journal of Business Communication, 13:1, 1975, p. 54.

Unpublished Materials

Greenbaum, H.R., "The Appraisal of Organizational Communication Systems," unpublished manuscript delivered to the International Communication Association, Atlanta, 1972, p. 3.

Report of the National District Attorneys Association Symposium on White Collar Crime Enforcement, conducted at Battelle Seattle Research Center, 1978, p. 12.

Figure 17-3 A bibliography. This one shows how the 10 footnotes illustrated on pages 643–644 are rearranged alphabetically under three subheads, and it includes an additional source (Kornblum) that was not in the footnotes.

Some bibliographies are *annotated*. They contain, just below the composition and publication information about each entry, also a brief statement about its content and value. For example:

```
Concentrates on basic principles and techniques of writing technical
reports.  Focuses on data gathering, data analysis, and the scienti-
fic method.  Contains good examples.
```

Index

The index lists topics alphabetically and guides the reader to various places that discuss certain subject matter in the report. Only in very long reports will you need an index if it is necessary to help the reader find specific subjects and items alphabetically.

WRITING, REVISING, AND TYPING THE FORMAL REPORT

Before you begin to write the first draft of your formal-report body and other parts, you should have completed the following preliminary work—discussed in Chapter 15:

Considered the problem and purpose, reader(s), and ideas to include (see steps 1-3, pages 542-543)

Collected all needed material—secondary and primary data (see step 4, pages 543-544)

Sorted and interpreted data (step 5, pages 544-545)

Organized the data and prepared final outline for your introduction, text, and terminal section (step 6, pages 545-553)

Prepared all visual aids (pages 553-561)

If required or desirable, you may also have presented a working plan for approval by whoever assigned the report.

Writing the First Draft

With your research materials close at hand—sorted in piles or in folders under your outline headings—you can now begin writing. Perhaps you'll start with a section you consider easiest for you. That's a good way to feel comfortable with the job. Try to complete a section—or at least a subsection—without stopping. Writing a long report will seem easier if you think of it as a series of short reports (your main report sections), linked coherently by your well-planned outline and appropriate transitional devices.

In the first draft pay no attention to spelling, punctuation, grammar, or form. Just get the ideas down on paper. If you allow your thoughts to flow freely, you're more likely to have a smooth overall presentation than if you stop frequently to check on spelling or to polish a sentence. While writing your rough draft, leave wide margins and plenty of space between lines for later revisions. Also, make your first draft as complete as possible. Later, when revising, you'll find it is easier to delete material if necessary than to insert new material. Generally, it is better to allow several days to write a long report. Don't try to cram it all into one eight-hour session, for exhaustion and rushing will adversely affect the quality of the report.

Some writers begin with the introduction; others finish the text first. Either way is acceptable as long as you include those elements in the introduction that will best orient the reader to the rest of the report. If the length of your introduction to a 15- to 25-page double-spaced typewritten report is more than 1½ or 2 pages, you should find out what element causes this lengthiness. For example, if an introduction is four pages long because the problem or background material has required three of the pages, take the problem or background material out of the introduction and make it the first main section of the text.

In the text, beware of using too many major divisions; for a 15- to 25-page report you probably shouldn't have more than three or four major divisions. If you have more than that, look critically at your outline to see whether you can and should regroup or combine sections. Although the divisions don't all have to be the same length, every main division should include enough substance and length to justify its position of importance. Introduce ideas or figures at the best time in the development of the report—at the time the reader needs to know or use them. Of course, a report with a hundred or several hundred pages will have proportionately more main divisions; in fact, it may have "chapters," each with its own main divisions and subdivisions. Remember to insert footnotes where necessary, too.

The terminal section should be a logical outcome of the material in the text. As you know, you may label it Summary, Conclusions, or Conclusions and Recommendations; or you may want to consider one of the other possible titles, such as those listed on page 548.

Besides completing your first draft of the report body, you should also write a draft of the abstract, letter of transmittal, and bibliography, if you'll have one. You can also set up the table of contents and the table of tables (if any) in rough draft; but only after the final typing is finished can you know correct page numbers for these tables.

Editing and Revising the Rough Draft(s)

When you have finished the first draft, set it aside for at least one day. This "cooling off" step allows you to get away from the writing long enough to look objectively at the material and to see more clearly the weaknesses in the draft.

Editing the first draft requires cool objectivity. Searching self-criticism is a must; what seemed just right in the first writing may seem ridiculously out of place upon second reading. Remember too that the best writers revise and rewrite several times, when necessary!

A few handy supplies are useful when you revise a long report. You'll need a pencil (perhaps a red pencil, too), a stapler, cellophane tape, extra paper, and a pair of scissors or a razor blade. As you read your draft critically, you can use your pencil(s) for small corrections in the margins and between lines, or to cross out unneeded sentences. However, if you find a section that needs major reorganizing, use your scissors (or razor). A paragraph out of place on one page may be cut out of that page and stapled or taped to another page after you have cut it apart at the place where the insertion belongs. (Use a backing sheet underneath each cut page if necessary.) Likewise you may need to write an entirely new paragraph; you can insert it, too, into a section after you have cut the sheet at the right place.

Just rereading each word of the report isn't the best way to approach the all-important job of editing and revising. Instead you should:

1. Look critically at the title, abstract, introduction, and terminal section—these four areas your reader considers first. If these parts are weak or vague, the reader may reject the entire report—regardless of how good it might be. The title should tell the reader clearly and concisely exactly what the subject of the entire report is. The abstract, if any, should reveal the problem, purpose, sources used, and (usually) results. The introduction should adequately orient the reader to the material so that he or she will better understand what is covered in the text (discussion). And be sure that the terminal section doesn't contain new material, that it produces what you promised or agreed to in the introduction, and that it stems logically from the information in the text.

2. Check the letter of transmittal, introduction, and terminal section (if it precedes the introduction and text) for repetition. The reader who has to read the same information two or three times right away, will react unfavorably.

3. Check the headings throughout the report to make sure they match the entries in the table of contents. All major and minor sections in the table of contents must have headings in the text; but not all headings in the text (such as fourth- or fifth-degree headings) need to appear in the table of contents. Also check to see that you have indicated correctly the relation of major and minor parts and that headings of the same degree are parallel.

4. Examine the text for transitions. Have you tied your sentences together within a paragraph? Have you tied your paragraphs together within a section? Have you tied your sections together?

5. Now edit the entire report for the C qualities. Read again every one of the 43 items in the checklists on pages 562–565. Checking them will help you to see that your report is

   Complete and concise

   Concrete, convincing, objective

   Considerate and courteous

   Clear

   Correct

6. If desirable, read Checkpoints When You Edit . . . , in Appendix B.

Typing the Formal Report

After you have revised the draft(s) to your satisfaction, the report is ready to be typed (by yourself or your secretary). Although various authorities have different rules for typing this material, the suggestions here are for one of the acceptable methods. Whatever method you use, be consistent. An appropriate, consistent typing style is very important for the overall appearance of the report. The report should make a favorable impression in its overall appearance, spacing, margins, footnote setup, and pagination, in addition to its well-written content. Even the cover should be appropriately attractive. Depending upon length of the report, its purpose, and intended reader(s), the cover may be made of paper, plastic over paper, cloth, or other material, sometimes decorated with a specific design pertinent to the report subject.

Overall Appearance

Regardless of how well written your report is, if it is carelessly typewritten, it will create an unfavorable impression in the mind of the reader.

You can give the correct initial impression if you choose a quality bond 8½- by 11-inch white 16- or 20-pound typing paper. Next, be sure your ribbon produces a dark impression and be certain the keys are clean. If your secretary is using a manual typewriter, check to see that the typing is done evenly so that all the words make the same impression. If possible, the punctuation marks should be hit lightly enough so that they don't produce noticeably deep gougings in the paper. Erasing is okay if it is hardly noticeable. Be neat—avoid smudges, streaks, curled ends, wrinkled paper, and any other distractions that might divert your reader's attention from the message.

Double Spacing versus Single Spacing

Reports may be typewritten with double or single spacing. Those who prefer double spacing feel it is easily read; it is also preferred by printers. (Another reason, though not generally admitted, is that double spacing makes a report appear longer.) Single-spaced reports have become popular in recent years not only because they save paper, but also—with fewer pages for the same amount of report data—they save in several other ways: (a) typing time, (b) filing space, (c) expense of both duplicating time and materials when multiple copies of a report are needed, and (d) reading time, because readers have fewer pages to turn and the line spacing on them is similar to that on printed publications which they are accustomed to reading.

If you double-space the report, the first word of every paragraph should be indented (usually five spaces). In a single-spaced report paragraphs may be indented or begin at the left margin. However, always double-space between paragraphs and both before and after long quotations, visual aids, and footnotes.

Regardless of whether the report is typed in double or single spacing, the following parts should be single-spaced:

1. Transmittal letter—typed on company letterhead if you are writing it as an employee of the firm. And, of course, the letter is centered attractively on the page. If you need tips on letter layout, see pages 136–138.
2. Quotations and examples of three or more typewritten lines. (If this material consists of two or more paragraphs, double-space between them. Also, indent margins of the quote five spaces to the right and left of the double- or single-spaced text material.) Use elipses (. . .) to indicate omissions if you are quoting only parts of an author's paragraph. In long quotations you can show lengthy omissions by either a full line of periods or by four periods at the end of the paragraph before the omission.
3. Contrast—to set off or emphasize a list of items.
4. Footnotes.
5. Some tables and other visual aids.

Margins

In addition to the following suggested margins, you need to add ¾ inch for binding on each page. Although you usually bind the report on the left-hand side—like a book—you can bind at the top. Acceptable margins are as follows:

> *First page of prefatory parts* (preface or letter of transmittal, table of contents, table of tables, abstract), *body,* and *supplemental parts* (appendix, bibliography, index): Top margin of 1½ or 2 inches. All other margins are the same as for other pages.

> *Other pages:* Top, bottom, and side margins are 1 or 1½ inch (plus the ¾-inch allowance for binding at either left side or top).

Footnote Setup

As Figure 17-1 illustrates, a footnote goes at the bottom of the same page on which it is cited (by the superscript number within the text). Separating the last line of the discussion and the first footnote on the page is a line (usually 18 strokes long) flush with the left margin, with double spacing before and after the line. Single-space within footnotes and single- or double-space between footnotes.

Pagination

Every page in the report—except the cover and title fly—should have a number but not all numbers are actually typed on each page. For the prefatory sheets use small Roman numerals; for the body and supplemental sheets use Arabic numbers, according to these guidelines:

1. *Prefatory parts page numbers* are centered and placed ½ inch below the imaginary line that frames the bottom of the typewritten material. Count and number the prefatory pages as shown below.

Cover	don't count or number
Title fly	don't count or number
Title page	count (i) but don't insert number
Letter of transmittal	count, but usually don't insert, number. A one-page letter is page ii at the bottom; a second page of the transmittal is page iii.
Table of contents	count and number each page
Table of tables	count and number
Abstract	count and number

2. *Body and supplemental parts page numbers*—for the report bound at the left—are usually placed near the upper right corner of the page, aligned with the right margin and ½ inch (or a double space) above the top imaginary line that frames the typewritten material. The exception is that the numbers for first pages of parts are either omitted (though counted) or placed ½ inch (or a double space) below the imaginary line that frames the bottom of the typed material. They are centered with the typing on the page (as for prefatory parts pages).

3. If your report is bound at the top, page numbers are placed usually in the center at the bottom of the page, ½ inch or a double space below the imaginary line that frames the bottom of the typewritten text.

EXAMPLE OF PAGES FROM A FORMAL ANALYTICAL REPORT

The following pages from an energy conservation report within a company apply many of the suggestions in this chapter and Chapter 15 for writing a formal report. They are illustrated not as models of perfection but as one way of presenting parts about which students most often have questions:

Title page (Figure 17-4)

Letter of transmittal (Figure 17-5)

Table of contents (Figure 17-6)

First and second pages of the text (typed single space) (Figures 17-7 and 17-8)

Bibliography (Figure 17-9)

Figure 17-4   Title page.

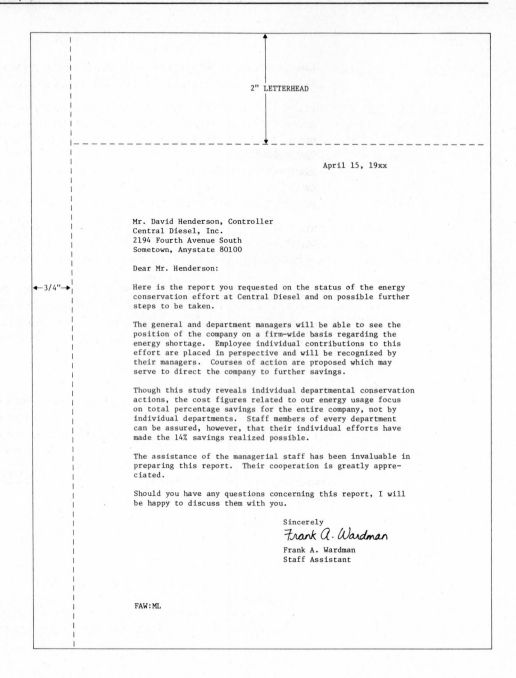

2" LETTERHEAD

April 15, 19xx

←3/4"→

Mr. David Henderson, Controller
Central Diesel, Inc.
2194 Fourth Avenue South
Sometown, Anystate 80100

Dear Mr. Henderson:

Here is the report you requested on the status of the energy
conservation effort at Central Diesel and on possible further
steps to be taken.

The general and department managers will be able to see the
position of the company on a firm-wide basis regarding the
energy shortage. Employee individual contributions to this
effort are placed in perspective and will be recognized by
their managers. Courses of action are proposed which may
serve to direct the company to further savings.

Though this study reveals individual departmental conservation
actions, the cost figures related to our energy usage focus
on total percentage savings for the entire company, not by
individual departments. Staff members of every department
can be assured, however, that their individual efforts have
made the 14% savings realized possible.

The assistance of the managerial staff has been invaluable in
preparing this report. Their cooperation is greatly appreciated.

Should you have any questions concerning this report, I will
be happy to discuss them with you.

Sincerely

Frank A. Wardman

Frank A. Wardman
Staff Assistant

FAW:ML

Figure 17-5 Transmittal letter.

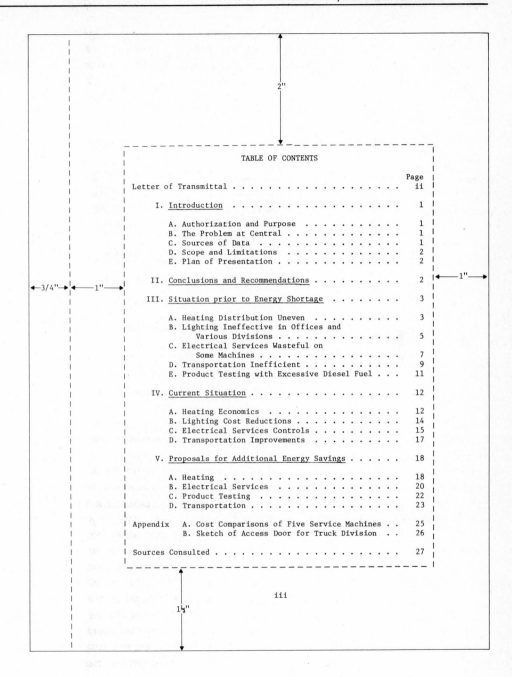

Figure 17-6 Table of contents.

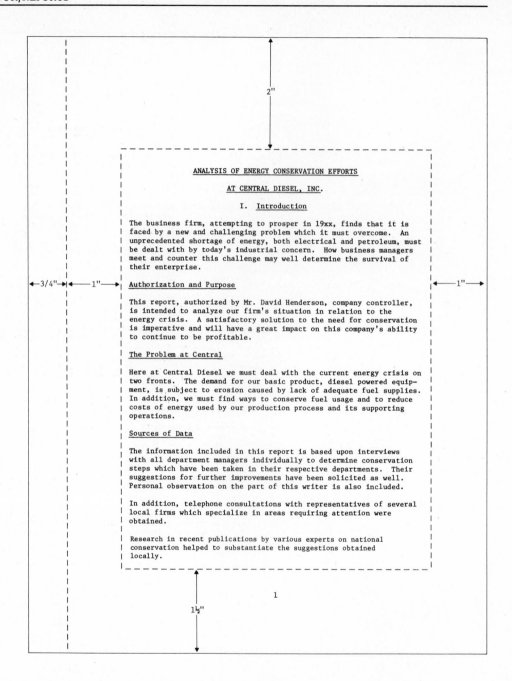

2"

ANALYSIS OF ENERGY CONSERVATION EFFORTS

AT CENTRAL DIESEL, INC.

I. Introduction

The business firm, attempting to prosper in 19xx, finds that it is faced by a new and challenging problem which it must overcome. An unprecedented shortage of energy, both electrical and petroleum, must be dealt with by today's industrial concern. How business managers meet and counter this challenge may well determine the survival of their enterprise.

Authorization and Purpose

This report, authorized by Mr. David Henderson, company controller, is intended to analyze our firm's situation in relation to the energy crisis. A satisfactory solution to the need for conservation is imperative and will have a great impact on this company's ability to continue to be profitable.

The Problem at Central

Here at Central Diesel we must deal with the current energy crisis on two fronts. The demand for our basic product, diesel powered equipment, is subject to erosion caused by lack of adequate fuel supplies. In addition, we must find ways to conserve fuel usage and to reduce costs of energy used by our production process and its supporting operations.

Sources of Data

The information included in this report is based upon interviews with all department managers individually to determine conservation steps which have been taken in their respective departments. Their suggestions for further improvements have been solicited as well. Personal observation on the part of this writer is also included.

In addition, telephone consultations with representatives of several local firms which specialize in areas requiring attention were obtained.

Research in recent publications by various experts on national conservation helped to substantiate the suggestions obtained locally.

3/4" 1"   1"

1

1½"

Figure 17-7 First page of this formal report. (Either single or double spacing is acceptable.)

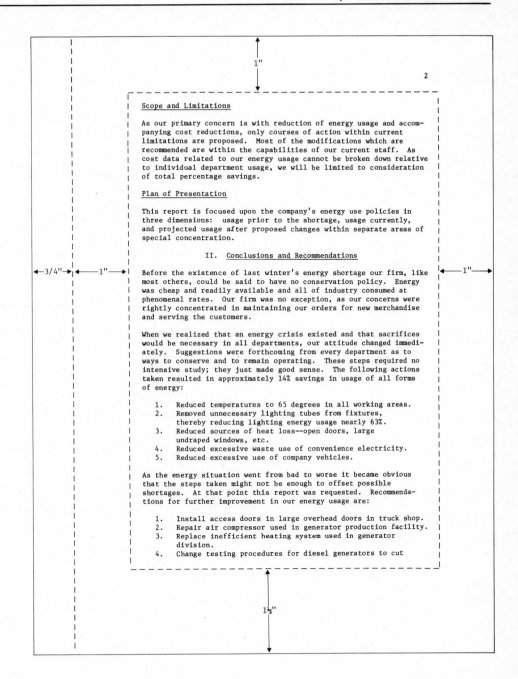

2

Scope and Limitations

As our primary concern is with reduction of energy usage and accompanying cost reductions, only courses of action within current limitations are proposed. Most of the modifications which are recommended are within the capabilities of our current staff. As cost data related to our energy usage cannot be broken down relative to individual department usage, we will be limited to consideration of total percentage savings.

Plan of Presentation

This report is focused upon the company's energy use policies in three dimensions: usage prior to the shortage, usage currently, and projected usage after proposed changes within separate areas of special concentration.

II. Conclusions and Recommendations

Before the existence of last winter's energy shortage our firm, like most others, could be said to have no conservation policy. Energy was cheap and readily available and all of industry consumed at phenomenal rates. Our firm was no exception, as our concerns were rightly concentrated in maintaining our orders for new merchandise and serving the customers.

When we realized that an energy crisis existed and that sacrifices would be necessary in all departments, our attitude changed immediately. Suggestions were forthcoming from every department as to ways to conserve and to remain operating. These steps required no intensive study; they just made good sense. The following actions taken resulted in approximately 14% savings in usage of all forms of energy:

1. Reduced temperatures to 65 degrees in all working areas.
2. Removed unnecessary lighting tubes from fixtures, thereby reducing lighting energy usage nearly 63%.
3. Reduced sources of heat loss--open doors, large undraped windows, etc.
4. Reduced excessive waste use of convenience electricity.
5. Reduced excessive use of company vehicles.

As the energy situation went from bad to worse it became obvious that the steps taken might not be enough to offset possible shortages. At that point this report was requested. Recommendations for further improvement in our energy usage are:

1. Install access doors in large overhead doors in truck shop.
2. Repair air compressor used in generator production facility.
3. Replace inefficient heating system used in generator division.
4. Change testing procedures for diesel generators to cut

Figure 17-8 Page 2 of this formal report.

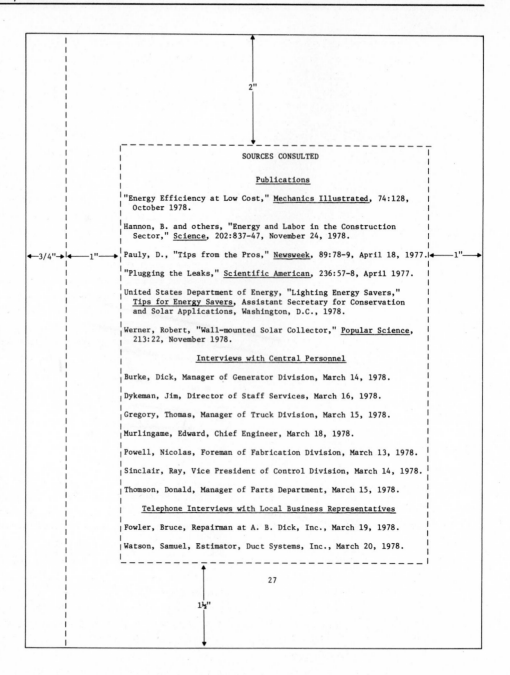

2"

SOURCES CONSULTED

Publications

"Energy Efficiency at Low Cost," Mechanics Illustrated, 74:128, October 1978.

Hannon, B. and others, "Energy and Labor in the Construction Sector," Science, 202:837-47, November 24, 1978.

Pauly, D., "Tips from the Pros," Newsweek, 89:78-9, April 18, 1977.

"Plugging the Leaks," Scientific American, 236:57-8, April 1977.

United States Department of Energy, "Lighting Energy Savers," Tips for Energy Savers, Assistant Secretary for Conservation and Solar Applications, Washington, D.C., 1978.

Werner, Robert, "Wall-mounted Solar Collector," Popular Science, 213:22, November 1978.

Interviews with Central Personnel

Burke, Dick, Manager of Generator Division, March 14, 1978.

Dykeman, Jim, Director of Staff Services, March 16, 1978.

Gregory, Thomas, Manager of Truck Division, March 15, 1978.

Murlingame, Edward, Chief Engineer, March 18, 1978.

Powell, Nicolas, Foreman of Fabrication Division, March 13, 1978.

Sinclair, Ray, Vice President of Control Division, March 14, 1978.

Thomson, Donald, Manager of Parts Department, March 15, 1978.

Telephone Interviews with Local Business Representatives

Fowler, Bruce, Repairman at A. B. Dick, Inc., March 19, 1978.

Watson, Samuel, Estimator, Duct Systems, Inc., March 20, 1978.

27

←3/4"→ ←1"→   ←1"→

1½"

Figure 17-9 List of sources consulted, including both published materials and interviews.

Succeeding pages in the text section of this report are arranged and numbered as shown on its page 2. The main headings—III, IV, and V—are centered (horizontally) on pages 3, 12, and 18 as stated in the table of contents. They do not begin new pages, but merely follow the preceding text paragraphs. Subheadings for them are third-degree headings placed at the left margin like those on its page 1—Authorization and Purpose, The Problem at Central, and Sources of Data.

Though the report is a long formal report with prefatory and supplemental parts, the wording throughout is appropriately informal because the writer is a staff assistant in the company discussed by the report. It is typed single space in keeping with his company's preference. (The broken lines and arrows are inserted in these illustrations only to show you the widths of the imaginary margins.) The bibliography is titled Sources Consulted, because most of the information came from interviews rather than publications. If you are wondering how footnotes are typed on single-spaced pages, the answer is that they are placed at the bottom of pages with the same spacing as shown in Figure 17-1—though it is a double-spaced report. (See also the guidelines for footnote setup on page 645.) To protect anonymity, the names of persons and of the company as well as some numbers in the illustrated pages have been changed.

In summary, the formal business report is "formal" because of its parts—not because it uses formal language. Each prefatory and supplemental part should serve a useful purpose for the reader; if it doesn't, it should not appear in the report. Writing a formal report becomes easier for the writer when the writer has performed carefully and thoroughly the research steps before writing. And he or she is certain to have a better piece of writing when he or she has properly revised the first draft and considered the importance to the reader(s) of the report's overall presentation.

EXERCISES

1. Assume that after graduating from college you have worked in a responsible job related to your chosen major field. Because of your high-quality work in a certain area, your employer gave you more and more responsibilities helping other employees. The past two years this firm has paid you a generous extra salary for conducting seminars two evenings a week for various groups of employees (5 to 15) that need to improve their skills in . . . . (Choose an area in which you can excel. For example, it might be memo or letter writing, English fundamentals, selling, accounting, a technical skill, or even an indoor sport activity helpful in the company's employee recreation program.) Recently your company's vice president personally complimented you on your good seminars (which are now completed) and on the substantial improvement he has noticed in the work of employees who attended them.

   Your success has also come to the attention of an executive friend in another firm that has been considering a similar training program for its employees. You have conferred with this executive, thoroughly assessed that company's needs, and decided you would like to conduct a seminar for its employees. Now you must prepare a well-written proposal that will win the contract for this consulting job.

Begin by reviewing the suggestions in this book regarding outline, format, writing style and appearance of well-written proposals. Choose the topics that apply to your particular proposal. You might also provide answers to these and similar questions:

a. Specifically what will your seminars or workshops cover? And *how will they meet the needs of this firm's employees?* Be careful not to promise more than you can accomplish, and do not bind yourself to too many specific functions that you may find later are unnecessary. You will be legally bound to fulfill your commitments to the firm's satisfaction.

b. Will you require a textbook or any other purchases by the participants?

c. Will you provide handouts as needed?

d. How many total hours will you probably devote to these seminars? Consider hours for:

> Teaching or consulting—two nights a week, two hours for each session
>
> Preparation before each session
>
> Reading and commenting on employees' work
>
> Conferences with individuals or small groups (three or four) on their specific problem areas

e. Because the workshop will meet in a classroom within the employer's building, what facilities will you need? (Consider blackboard, chalk, screen, projector, tapes, tables, armchairs, etc. Will you need use of that firm's Xerox or other duplicating equipment to reproduce materials for class discussion?)

f. What will you charge for your services? This is, of course, a difficult and very important decision. You want your price to be reasonable, neither too high nor too low. (Assume the firm is well able to pay most any fair amount, and that your present employer paid you $40 an hour even though you were a "beginner" at consulting.)

g. What other legitimate expenses should your client expect to meet? (Consider transportation costs, meals, materials, duplicating, typing, etc.)

h. What payment method does this firm prefer? Will you be expected to submit an itemized statement monthly and to be paid shortly thereafter; or will payment be a lump sum at the end of the workshops or perhaps a part payment before they begin?

i. What parts of your own training and experience should you include in your resume?

After a complete analysis you will write, revise, and type the final copy of your winning proposal. Include a letter of transmittal and follow the other pertinent guidelines on pages 624–630.

2. Choose a problem which you can solve by experimentation, survey, and/or observation, and write your proposal to the organization that is concerned with the problem. Or (if more appropriate) assume your proposal goes to a funding agency whose philosophy is in keeping with the problem you propose to research. Here are suggestions for topics—but feel free to choose your own.

   a. Try to solve a problem related to a firm's product development; plant expansion; improvement of a sales, accounting, or purchasing system; or curtailment of shoplifting.

   b. Analyze a problem in your community—crime(s) in a certain area, a traffic snarl situation, poor citizen involvement in local issues, need for attracting new industry or keeping young, educated persons in the community.

   c. Undertake a project in one of your college classes—or survey a sample of the student body regarding an important campus problem.

   Follow thoughtfully the suggestions in this chapter regarding proposal writing. Organize your topics under appropriate headings and write a proposal that meets all requirements as to content, format, and writing style. Then submit your complete proposal to (a) your instructor and/or (b) your class in an oral presentation. Be prepared to defend your proposal and to have the class critique it.

3. If you need practice in organizing topics under meaningful headings, try this assignment. Assume the sales manager of ABC New Car Agency in your city has asked you, a management consultant, to review and evaluate the agency's sales system. The internal control seems to be weak and something is causing problems.

   The main purpose of your study is to determine the strength of the internal control and its effect on the financial papers for new-car sales.

   You have just finished both secondary and primary research. Two new accounting books (assume names) substantiate your concept for internal control. In your primary research you interviewed four middle managers and 15 or 20 employees. You studied the personality of the sales staff and the viewpoints of other personnel. You observed the personnel performing their duties and their interactions. Up to now you have information under the following topics, jumbled and in no useful order.

   File clerks' job

   Keypunch operator's responsibility

   Dealership's environment

   Title clerk's functions

   Salesperson's personality

   Internal control by buyers' orders

   Personnel system's internal control

Dealership's history

Sequence of signatures in sale of a car

Accounting clerks' duties

Control system's procedure

Title clerk's work

Sales staff's functions

Flow chart of new vehicle sales system (You have drawn this on seven pages)

Dealership's new vehicle sales system

Introduction

Conclusions

Sales manager's part

Bibliography

Choose the main headings for the text of this report (three or four should be sufficient). Then organize these 19 topics under the main headings and wherever they belong in a complete outline of the well-planned formal report.

4. Your assignment is to write a formal report whose body is approximately 15 to 25 double-spaced pages. Choose a topic that is broad enough to justify the length. Yet beware of a topic so broad that it would require volumes. If possible, consider a subject that you know something about, or one that especially interests you.

Try to find a topic that involves a business problem. (For example, you might know there's too great a turnover of employees in a certain department.) From the problem, and with some thought on your part, you can determine the purpose of your report. Other ideas that you can use as a springboard for a topic are listed below, pertaining to problems involved in:

Accounting, Credits, Collections

The accountant's role in cost reduction and analysis

Computer programming and errors in monthly statements

Problems and progress of accounting in X Company

Accounting contributions to the effective management of X Company

Problems involved in a bank's converting to a computerized operation

Policy or procedure and degree of communications used by X Company in collecting retail accounts.

General Management and/or Labor

The functioning and problems of your campus student-body governing organization; accomplishments and recommendations for greater effectiveness

A profit-sharing plan for X Company

Would hiring handicapped workers be charity or good business for X Company

A program for achieving optimum discipline in X Company

Business outlook for Y industry or X Company

How X Company (or your campus) has met the energy crisis and what should still be done

A proposed program (or plan) for hiring and training of minority groups in X Company

Development of a profitable ski area on a certain mountain

Suggestions for X Company's response to Z Union's attempt to organize workers

Recommendations for a formal salary scale for X Company

Personnel Administration

Development of a personnel testing program for X Company

Analysis of the merit rating system of X Company

A safety program for X Company

The performance of women in top executive positions

Survey, interpretation, and recommendation—after a study on attitudes toward certain recent troublesome problems:
a. Opinion of X Company's employees regarding wages, working hours, parking, food services, promotion plan
b. Opinion of students in your school regarding grading, credit hours for certain courses, student parking, housing
c. Opinion of X Organization's members regarding membership dues, requirements, privileges, new clubhouse

Marketing

A promotional program for introduction of X product

A new plan for X Company to offer incentives to sales personnel

Where should X Company locate its next supermarket

How can X Company measure effectiveness of its advertising

How downtown merchants can cope with suburban shopping centers

After you have clearly determined the purpose of your report, state it in one sentence. Continue your preliminary investigation (steps 1, 2, and 3 on pages 542–543). At this point in your research submit to your professor (or anyone he or she suggests) a memo report of your working plan. Be sure to include in this memo at least the following: problem, purpose, methodology, readers (both primary and secondary), and suggested outline. In this outline show the order for the introduction, major divisions of the text, subheadings for each major division, and the type of terminal section.

After you have approval of your working plan, you can begin to collect your data; then organize this material and interpret it. With the completion of this last stage—interpretation—you can draw conclusions and make recommendations. Naturally if you're writing an informational report, you'll skip interpretation of material and merely summarize. Also at this time you should prepare (at least in rough-draft form) your tables and any other necessary visual aids. If your professor requests it, submit the final outline that you'll follow in writing your report—the one that will become your table of contents.

Now you should be ready to write. Choose the right time and place and follow the rules outlined in the chapter—both for the first draft and the revision. After your final revision, you can type (or have typed) the body of the report in final draft, or you can first write the necessary prefatory and supplemental parts. In this report assignment include at least the following: cover, title fly, title page, letter of transmittal (or preface), and table of contents. Also, you'll need to include other parts—especially appendix and bibliography—if your report requires them. If the transmittal may affect part of what's included in the body, you should at least plan the transmittal before the final typing of the body.

Although the content and presentation of the material are most important, also remember the role that mechanics play. Be sure you have nothing that detracts your reader from concentrating on what you want to tell. Thus, be sure the spelling, grammar, punctuation, and appearance are acceptable.

NONWRITTEN COMMUNICATIONS

chapter

18

Oral Communication within Groups

The ability to communicate effectively orally as well as in writing is, as you know, highly valued in business. Throughout each working day businessmen and business-women use words and gestures to convey ideas and impressions to customers, colleagues, and others.

Though this textbook has discussed mainly written messages—letters, memorandums, and reports—several chapters have also prepared you for oral communication. Important concepts useful for both oral and written communication are discussed in Chapter 2, The Process of Communication and Miscommunication; Chapters 3 and 4, Business Writing Principles (the seven C's); and Chapter 5, Planning before Communicating. In addition, Chapter 12 includes suggestions for the job applicant's interview and Chapter 13 discusses collection techniques using the telephone.

This chapter briefly covers various aspects of oral communications within groups: speaking and oral reporting, listening, and leading and participating in conferences.

SPEAKING AND ORAL REPORTING

The preparation for writing letters, memos, and reports is similar to the preparation for giving a business talk. Yet oral and written communication also have their differences. This section first discusses similarities and differences in speaking and writing, then preparation for the oral presentation, and finally the presentation itself.

Similarities and Differences in Oral and Written Presentation

When you're reporting to someone on paper, you need first of all to remember the purpose and the reader. The same is true for business talks. The purpose determines what you say, and the audience dictates how you'll say it. In both a written report and an oral presentation you need to collect, classify, interpret, and organize your material. In both you need, many times, to use visual aids and indicate to the reader or audience the points of transition. In both you orient the reader (or audience) in the introductory remarks, give details in the discussion (text), and summarize or conclude at the end. Throughout you apply the writing principles (seven C's).

In many ways communicating orally is easier than writing a letter, memo, or report. In the first place, you have had more practice in expressing your ideas orally. Furthermore, you don't need to bother with troublesome mechanics such as spelling and punctuation. And you have the aid of facial expressions, tone of voice, and gestures to make meaning clear. Finally, you have immediate feedback from the audience. If you notice raised eyebrows, excessive coughing, blank expressions, or other signs that indicate boredom or lack of understanding, you can clarify your point by restating or using an illustration or you can simply ask if the listeners understand.

Although communicating orally may be easier for the reasons just mentioned, giving a speech or oral report to a group does deserve special attention for both the preparation and the presentation.

Preparation for the Oral Presentation

Preparing for a speech or oral report requires these steps, most of which—as you will recall—are similar to those for writing reports, letters, and memos.

1. Determine the purpose.
2. Analyze the audience and the situation.
3. Choose the ideas to include in the message.
4. Collect and interpret data.
5. Organize the data.
6. Plan visual aids.
7. Rehearse the talk and revise where necessary.

Determine the Purpose

Just as in written communication, the purpose determines what you say. Are you merely informing? Are you trying to secure belief or action through persuasion? Or are you simply trying to entertain? In business you'll probably use either of the first two of these goals.

Whenever possible, choose a topic that interests you and that you know something about. Then you'll have more incentive to tackle the assignment, won't have to spend so much time in collecting your material, and will possibly even enjoy the challenge of giving the best presentation possible.

Analyze the Audience and the Situation

As with letters, memos, and reports, you need to consider the people you'll be talking to. In addition to deciding why you're talking to them, you need to consider the size of the group, age range, sex, and occupation. Whenever possible, also estimate their attitude toward your subject, their interests, capabilities, prejudices.

If you're talking to a small group, you can be relatively informal, omit using a microphone, and use small visual aids. If you're to speak at a regional or national meeting in a large auditorium, you'll have not only a microphone but also different visual aids that you can use with either a stationary or a mobile speaker system.

Ages, occupations, and capabilities of the group determine the educational level of your presentation and the choice of words and illustrations. For example, you will prepare a different talk to college students than to company management trainees or to retirees, even if the general subject is the same. Also, if you're talking only to accountants, you can use appropriate technical expressions and tie in your illustrations with their professional background. But if the audience consists of individuals from various occupations, you need to prepare your speech so that everyone will clearly understand what you're saying—in this case you'll avoid technical expressions and use general examples. If the composition of your audience makes it necessary for you to give background so they will understand your main points, by all means give this background early in the presentation.

Furthermore, you should find out the attitude as well as prejudices your listeners have toward your subject. If you're talking about a controversial topic, giving bad news, or persuading, you need to be careful not to say anything bluntly, crudely, or inappropriately—in a way that will irritate the audience or turn them off so they don't listen further.

Choose the Ideas to Include
Collect and Interpret Data

Because the speaker follows the same research procedure as the writer does when preparing a written report, it is unnecessary to dwell on these steps here. See Chapter 15 for suggestions.

Organize the Data

One of the most important planning steps is organizing your materials so that the audience can easily follow you throughout your talk. You organize your talk like a report—introduction, text (discussion of details), and conclusions. (For suggestions on logical or psychological arrangement, see pages 549–550.) In the introduction you catch the listeners' attention with the problem (if any), the purpose, and often with a promise of an answer to the problem. You orient the audience with the same introductory elements you use for a report. Near the end of the introduction, you state your plan of presentation—what you are going to say. Then you say it—by discussing the details of your text. And you end your talk with a terminal section, in which you tell what you've said.

As you organize your data you need also to consider what method you will use for presenting the talk. Of the four methods available—*impromptu, extemporaneous, read,* or *memorized*—the *extemporaneous* is usually preferred. In this method you speak from a previously prepared outline and choose phraseology appropriate to the audience. Note cards may be used. But the speech is *not* read from a manuscript nor committed to memory. (*Impromptu speaking*, on the other hand, is speaking without specific preparation. You use this method when called upon without prior notice, as happens frequently in business meetings and conferences.)

Plan Visual Aids

To help get your message across to the audience, you may also need to plan meaningful visual aids for display at appropriate times. First decide whether you will distribute handouts for each person in the audience or whether you will display all visual aids from one spot. The latter procedure is usually better, because your audience will focus attention on what you are displaying instead of shuffling papers and reading when you would rather have them listen. (However, if you think they would benefit from taking copies home, you can distribute them after your talk.)

The most common devices for "one spot" displays are chalkboards, flip sheets, cards or posters, and projectors. Each has some advantages, depending upon subject matter and audience size.

Chalkboards. When you wish to write brief, significant points or figures either before your talk begins or while you are talking, a chalkboard is useful. If you will have much material for the board, plan if possible to place it there before your talk session begins. The board can be covered until you wish to reveal your display. However, if you prefer to draw or write as you talk, do it without turning your back to the audience. The chalkboard visual aids are usable only, of course, when the audience will be seated near enough to see and easily read the notations on the board.

Flip Sheets. A variety of material on large separate pages can be on flip sheets, fastened at the top and attached to an easel or stand the right height for easy audience viewing. The size of sheets as well as the words, charts, tables, or drawings on them can be modified somewhat, in keeping with expected audience and room size. One advantage of using flip sheets instead of a chalkboard is that you can prepare them before you come to the room where you'll be speaking. Another is that they can be larger and of better quality than when material is written with chalk. Furthermore, during your talk you need merely flip pages in any order you wish and more quickly focus your eyes again on your audience. Also, you can skip pages or add facts on sheets whenever desirable.

Cards or Posters. To serve the same purpose as flip sheets, cards or posters are also useful. They can display the same kinds of drawings and materials, provided they are large enough to be easily read by the audience. An advantage is that you can arrange them easily in any sequence. They are not attached to an easel. Disadvantages are that when they are large and of heavy posterboard, they are cumbersome both to carry and to hold up for display. Pointing to pertinent parts is also difficult unless the speaker has someone else to help hold the poster while he or she talks.

Projectors. Most adaptable for displaying business materials are the opaque and the overhead projectors. Both project images on a screen or wall for clear viewing by any size audience. The opaque projector must be used in a darkened room. The overhead has the advantage of being usable in daylight or a lighted room.

With the opaque projector you can use any typewritten, handwritten, or printed materials or various specimens just as they come from your files. You can project the exact charts, tables, letters, graphs, or pictures from your written report. And you can point (with any pencil) to the parts of them as they are projected on the screen.

To use the overhead projector you must first convert your display materials into transparencies. These can be prepared quite inexpensively either on your company's spirit duplicating or Xerox machine, on one of the various other modern transparency makers, or by professional photographic methods. While projecting the transparencies to your audience you can write on them (usually with black grease pencil). You can also add overlays of more drawings when necessary—as, for example, when explaining the development of a certain manufacturing or marketing process.

Rehearse the Talk and Revise Where Necessary

After you have considered all the steps discussed above, you are ready to apply them by rehearsing your talk. This step is vital for a beginner and is also used occasionally by some experienced speakers. Here you want to simulate the forthcoming talk. Know your opening sentence word for word. Also be sure you can deliver the talk within the time limit allotted you on the program. You may need to revise or shorten some parts.

How can you practice in a physical and psychological atmosphere close to that of the actual performance? To begin with, find a room that approximates the one you'll be speaking in. And if possible, practice aloud. Talk so that a friend (real or imaginary) in the back row can easily hear and observe you. Have thorough command of your subject; and use cards, an outline, or a list of points if you'll be using them before your audience. Know what to say and then determine how to say it. Use transitional phrases and sentences to show your listeners the relationships between various sections of your report. Use the bodily action you plan to use for the actual performance. Even include the actual visual aids you'll need to accomplish the purpose of your presentation.

Remember, your real audience will be judging you mainly on your attitude, bodily action, voice, speech content, and choice of words. Whether the main purpose of your oral presentation is to inform, explain, and/or persuade, your own sincere interest in the subject, audience, and task has an important influence on your effectiveness. Be eager to share your thoughts with your audience. Have a friendly, confident, courteous attitude toward your listeners.

Bodily action—posture, movement, gestures, and facial expressions—and voice must be natural and contribute rather than detract from your message. Occasionally, while speaking you may need to change your position—to relax, to indicate a transition between one portion of the talk and the next, or to secure a desired reaction from your audience. Your voice should be loud enough so everyone can hear, but not so loud that a blast on the microphone irritates listeners. A pleasant variety in tone is appreciated by the audience. Also desirable is an occasional pause to give the audience an opportunity for your ideas to "sink in."

Presentation of the Talk or Report

When you reach the podium, place your notes in a usable position. Also, pause to make eye contact with your audience, and show you're a friendly individual by having a sincere, pleasant expression before you begin to talk. If you have prepared yourself well, you should experience little or no stage fright. But if you are nervous, remember that you feel more nervous than you appear to others, and that after the first few moments you will feel more comfortable.

Introduction

Your audience will already know the title of your talk because it is on a printed program and/or stated by the person who introduces you. You may begin with a greeting like "ladies and gentlemen," "ladies," "gentlemen," "members of _____," "fellow _____," or whatever is appropriate to the group and the occasion.

Before making your planned introductory statements, acknowledge the comments of the person who introduced you and perhaps ad-lib a few brief, appropriate, good-natured remarks. Then proceed with your introduction. State the problem (if there is one) and your purpose—always. Also include other introductory elements that adequately orient the group to your talk. If you are reporting on a study, briefly describe your methodology. A natural transition to your text is stating your plan of presentation.

In addition to using an opening that begins with the problem and perhaps promises an answer, you have other ways to catch the attention of your audience.

Tell a story that is related to your subject or that establishes background for development of the purpose.

Make a startling statement—perhaps indicating briefly a surprising outcome of your study.

Ask a question that makes the audience start to think.

Give a familiar quotation that leads into your subject.

Tell a humorous story or joke related to the subject.

Use an illustration that relates directly to the subject.

Refer to the subject, its timeliness, its importance.

Refer to the occasion, the audience, or reason for meeting.

Naturally, the right opener depends upon the purpose of the talk and the audience. Be especially aware that humor is effective only when it occurs naturally as the talk develops. Also remember—as you must for letters and memos—that what is humorous to one person may be offensive or boring to another.

Discussion (Text)

When you have completed your introduction, you begin developing the text orally in the same way you develop the written formal report. (However, because of a specified time limit, you usually must omit most of the detailed data of a long written report and concentrate on perhaps one or two phases.) Remember to apply the following:

1. Lead your audience through the speech or report. Since you don't have headings, you must clearly indicate when you complete one section and begin another. You can do so by:
   a. Changing your bodily position,
   b. Using topic sentences or introductory paragraphs,
   c. Checking off a major heading already on the chalkboard as you begin the discussion of that section.
2. Use visual aids, when desirable, to get across your point.
3. When you do present a visual aid, be sure you face your audience; at the same time don't obstruct the audience's view of the visual aid.

4. It's perfectly correct to use notes or an outline as a guide. But avoid leaning on such aids too much. Also, don't read long passages—especially the entire report—since you are sure to turn off your audience this way.

5. Pay attention to your audience. If you notice restlessness, excessive coughing, side conversations, excessive doodling, whispering, or dozing, you need to adjust your material and delivery. Other helpful clues on how the audience reacts to your talk are their facial expressions, shoulder shrugs, smiles, laughs, nods, and applause.

6. Your emphasis should be on your audience; use proper eye contact throughout your talk.

7. Avoid any unfavorable bodily actions that might distract the audience.

8. If you still feel nervous at this stage of your presentation:

   a. Introduce some physical object in your speech—talk about it, demonstrate it, or use the chalkboard. Once you're occupied and doing something with your hands, you'll calm down.

   b. Move about the platform—be active. Bodily actions help conceal nervousness.

9. Instead of sprinkling "uh's" in your talk, hesitate between sentences without uttering a sound.

Summary or Conclusions

When you have finished discussing the text portion of your talk, you begin the terminal section—a summary or conclusions. As for a written report, you'll list conclusions when you have more than one and, naturally, will not introduce new material.

In some talks you can end with a story that highlights or illustrates your main ideas. If your purpose is to persuade, urge the audience to take the recommended future action and include suggestions to make their action easier. When you begin this terminal section, let the audience know you have completed the last major section of the text and are now starting the conclusions. Keep them concise. Saying "In conclusion" is usually a welcome signal to listeners—who then expect the speaker to finish within a few minutes.

In summary, you need to prepare for your oral presentation by considering the purpose of the talk, your audience, the situation, the material and the way you organize it, and by rehearsing thoroughly. With the right attitude, knowledge of the content, and the right rehearsal you can give an interesting talk; also, you can reduce or eliminate possible stage fright by

1. Choosing a topic that interests you and that you know something about.

2. Preparing well—thoroughly know your material, make notes, and rehearse in an atmosphere like the one for your actual speech.

3. Memorizing your opening sentence.

4. Introducing some material object in your discussion, talking about it, demonstrating it—or using visual aids.

5. Moving about the platform to help cover up nervousness, indicate transitions, and/ or to secure audience reaction.

6. Having the right attitude toward yourself and your audience. Forget yourself and concentrate on your audience.

LISTENING

Because an individual in business spends most of the day listening and talking, listening plays a vital role. When someone speaks, he or she is attempting to inform, persuade, or entertain one or more individuals. But most individuals hear—they don't listen. Just what is listening, then? It means to see the expressed idea and attitude from the speaker's point of view, to sense how it feels to him or her to achieve that frame of reference in regard to the thing the speaker is talking about. Good listening requires various responsibilities of the listener and brings valuable results.

Responsibilities of the Listener

The speaker has the responsibility to communicate as effectively as possible, but listeners also have responsibilities. They cannot sit back and contentedly assume they have nothing to do. Like a speaker, listeners need to prepare themselves (before they listen); then, as they listen, they must concentrate on both the verbal and nonverbal message of the speaker.

Prepare for Listening

As a listener in a group you are influenced by the speaker, the message, other listeners, physical conditions, and your own attitudes and opinions. The first three you cannot control, but the last two you can do something about before the talk.

To give complete attention to the speaker and the message, you must choose whenever possible a position that allows you to see his or her gestures and clearly hear the tone of voice and the emphasis he or she gives to certain parts of the presentation. Also, sit up straight and look directly at the speaker. Should you become too relaxed, you might not give your full attention to the message. If you find that you're sitting near disturbing individuals in the audience, or are distracted by bothersome noise, you should move to another location. Also consider other negative factors—such as a draft from a window or door, excessive heat from a register, and undue glare—that might distract your attention from the speaker and the message.

Concentrate on the Verbal Message

Because good listening is correctly decoding what the speaker says, you must concentrate on the verbal message. Once the talk begins, be attentive to everything the speaker does or says. Don't let your mind wander—although that's not an easy task because the mind thinks much faster than one can talk. You should use this "spare time" to think about what is being said. If the speaker hasn't organized the material well, try to figure out the purpose and understand how the major points and their subdivisions develop that purpose. Also, check facts for soundness and accuracy, and separate facts from opinions.

Furthermore, exercise emotional control by withholding evaluation of the speaker's ideas until the end of the talk or until you understand his or her viewpoint. Decode the words as the speaker meant them. Put aside your bias. Keep your mind open—

don't turn him or her off because you disagree with a statement or object to physical appearance. Don't allow yourself to make frozen evaluations. Try to keep your personal attitudes, opinions, and emotions from affecting your listening.[1] Naturally, there's a danger involved if you try too hard to understand the speaker's viewpoint, because you might accept the speaker's reasoning to the point when you abandon your beliefs—without sufficient reason. But in general, adopt a positive rather than a negative attitude and an objective rather than a subjective outlook.

In conferences good listening requires all the qualities already mentioned plus a few virtues. Do not succumb to the temptation of talking too much. Listen to *all* participants, not just those you like. Respect the viewpoint of those you disagree with and try to understand the points they emphasize. Evaluate the discussion of all participants objectively and avoid heated arguments.

Also Concentrate on the Nonverbal Message

In addition to the actual message, you want to observe the speaker's gestures, tone of voice, and physical movements. Do they seem to reinforce or contradict what he or she is saying? If trying to paint a portrait of a sincere, dedicated person, does the speaker show some dishonesty? Is this person actually timid when trying to play the role of an individual full of confidence? If the speaker tries to tell the audience one thing and at the same time uses gestures that betray his or her true feelings, the nonverbal message may be the one to believe.

Results of Good Listening

Good listening pays valuable dividends. It

1. Permits the speaker and listener(s) to improve communication because each side is more receptive to the other's viewpoint.
2. Leads to positive attitudes.
3. Shows the speaker that the listeners are interested; in turn, the speaker tries harder to give his or her best presentation.
4. Results in obtaining useful information so that the listener can make accurate decisions.
5. Creates better understanding of others and thus helps the listener to work with others.
6. Helps the one speaking (especially in an interview) to talk out problems. Remember that a person needs to receive as well as give help.

LEADING AND PARTICIPATING IN CONFERENCES

As a manager you may—for various reasons—call a conference of selected department heads, supervisors, and/or employees. Or you may be one of those invited to attend

---

[1] For a discussion on frozen evaluations and the influence of attitudes, opinions, and emotions, see Chapter 2, pages 24–26.

a conference. The number of participants may range from 5 or 6 to 15 or 20. An effective number may be 10 to 15. The purpose of such a meeting may be to inform, to suggest a solution to a problem, or to discuss ways to solve a problem.

The *informational conference* is called only when the conference leader wants to check to see that the conferees understand certain information he or she has for them. Generally, however, written memos—without a meeting—suffice to bring the needed information to those concerned.

In the *suggested solution conference* the executive presents at the beginning of the conference a solution which is definitely only a suggestion for solving a company problem. The conference discussion then centers about the suggestion. All those attending contribute their ideas.

The *problem-solving conference* is called when the executive has no adequate solution to suggest regarding a problem and seeks suggested solutions from the conferees. Because this type of conference requires the most careful planning and presiding by the leader, as well as challenging participation by the conferees, this section discusses the planning steps and procedures for the problem-solving conference. You can use most of the suggestions, of course, for all types of conferences.

Planning Steps for the Problem-solving Conference

The preliminary steps in planning a conference are basically similar to those taken before writing a report:

1. Analyze the problem and determine your purpose.
2. Decide who the participants (conferees) will be and notify them appropriately.
3. Choose the topics (ideas?) to be considered and distribute information to participants sufficiently before the conference so they may prepare.
4. Take care of the physical arrangements for the meeting place.

Analyze the Problem and Determine Purpose

A good conference topic must be timely, genuine, really important, and meaningful for the conferees. It must present a difficulty or controversial question that is within the experience of the conference attendants. Also, it should be limited adequately so that conferees are able to solve it—at least partially—within the conference time. It should be about a matter that can be acted upon after the group has arrived at a solution or conclusion.

Decide upon Participants and Notify Them

When you inform the conference participants about the meeting, try to stimulate their interest in the problem. State the importance of the topic before they come to the meeting. Your memo—or letter to those outside the firm—may include suggested reference materials and whatever brief background explanation may be desirable to motivate the conferees. If you think they should bring any materials from their department, your message should invite them to do so. Follow the *direct-* or *persuasive-*

request plan in your message, depending upon the motivation you think the conferees need.

Choose Topics to be Considered and Distribute Information

Although this step is not always possible, it is desirable if you have useful information (perhaps background material for the problem) that the conferees should have before they come to the conference. Mail copies of the information to the conferees at least several days before the conference so they may have time to prepare their understanding and thoughts on the matter.

Take Care of Physical Arrangements

Regarding the meeting room, consider thoughtfully such physical arrangements as seating, materials, and atmosphere. Have someone arrange chairs in a circle—perhaps around a conference table—or in a diamond or "V" shape, so all conferees can easily see one another. Chairs should be sufficiently comfortable (but not too soft so that participants slouch while seated).

Among the possible needed materials to consider are: chalkboard(s), chalk, eraser, pencils, paper, charts, and perhaps a projector or visual aids such as charts, tables, graphs. Drinking water, glasses, and ash trays, if smoking is allowed, should be handy. Name cards may be desirable if the conferees come from different firms or widely separated departments and are not personally acquainted. The room itself should, of course, be adequately lighted, heated, ventilated, and quiet so it is conducive to free discussion.

Procedures during the Problem-solving Conference

Plan to start the conference on time and end it on time. The following steps which the conference leader should take during the problem-solving conference are also basically similar to those you take when writing the analytical report:

1. Introduce the problem and purpose of the conference.
2. Stimulate discussion to gather facts.
3. Sort, select, and interpret the data.
4. Arrange facts in order of importance and make a decision.
5. State the conclusion(s).

Introduce the Problem and Purpose

For the success of the conference, the right introductory statement is critically important. Obviously you should prepare your introductory statement before the conference, but neither memorize nor read it to the conferees. Present it in a natural, informal way.

As the leader, sell the topic to the conferees by showing why it is both interesting and significant for their serious consideration. If true, impress the conferees with the fact that they have a personal stake in the success of the conference. Show genuine enthusiasm yourself. Make clear the importance of the solution to the company and therefore to the conferees' own jobs.

State the problem clearly and concisely. Use as many of the five W's as are pertinent—what, when, who, why, when—and the how. Write the statement of the problem on the chalkboard. If desirable, give adequate background for the problem and state the scope and limitations of the conference. Define any unusual terms that will be used.

Stimulate Discussion to Gather Facts

In general, try to encourage all conferees to participate, and do keep the discussion "on the beam." Write subtopic headings on the chalkboard (or overhead projector) to help spark discussion on each topic in turn. List on another board the possible solutions of the problem as conferees suggest them. Ask questions and keep participants from wandering onto irrelevant paths or from chatting among themselves while someone else is expressing his or her views. Get conferees to analyze their own thinking as much as possible. Sometimes if the original contributor of an idea cannot add to it, another conferee may be able to carry it further. If a participant's statement is vague, rephrase it clearly before you write it on the board.

Maintain an atmosphere of goodwill and cooperation throughout the conference. If a situation becomes tense or some members are reluctant to speak or are annoying or antagonistic, apply the techniques you have learned for handling bad-news situations. Try to be tactful, considerate, understanding; and show a sense of humor. Sometimes an appropriate interesting or humorous short story can quickly revive flagging interest. Here are other tips for handling difficult conferees:

The reticent, nonparticipating member may respond if you first ask a question he or she can answer by a simple "yes" or "no." Then whenever possible, ask this member to give the conferees some information which he or she is sure to know because of job, training, or experience. Thank and praise the person as much as you can; he or she may then be more likely to enter the discussion confidently.

The "know-it-all" may be forced to justify every statement he or she makes. Whenever possible, ask other conferees for their opinions of these statements. Sometimes, if necessary and you feel the majority are annoyed by this arrogance, you may tactfully quiet the person by asking for a show of hands from the group, which strongly outvotes these suggestions.

The long-winded conferee who talks on and on, you may thank when he or she is at the end of a sentence, and then recognize someone else. Or you might move the discussion to another highly important point, perhaps with a statement like, "Well, we have two more points to consider before we wind up this meeting, so let's move along to the next topic now."

The erroneous member whom the other members—out of respect—are reluctant to correct, may require an especially tactful comment by you, the leader. As with any bad-news message, avoid direct criticism, sarcasm, or ridicule. Shield the person's pride. "When praising people, single them out; when criticizing them, put them in a group." Perhaps analyze a similar case, without referring to the speaker personally.

The conferee who shows personal animosity toward another member or members may be turned off by your directing a question to another conferee.

Sort, Select, and Interpret the Data

After you have listed conferees' suggestions on the board, encourage participants to consider advantages and disadvantages of each suggested course of action. List them separately on the board. As leader, be careful not to impose your own opinions on the group. Encourage each group member to feel a sense of responsibility for the success of the analysis. Good listening by everyone to what others offer is extremely important. (The suggestions on pages 679–680 about good listening apply in a conference as well as in a large auditorium!)

Get members to feel they are working as a group toward the collective solution to the problem, rather than allowing each member to force his or her views upon the rest. Regroup suggestions, as desirable; get the group to select the important ones, to interpret them, to compare, and to evaluate.

Arrange Facts in Order of Importance and Make a Decision

This step is comparable to writing the final outline and arriving at conclusions before you write a report. But in a conference you invite the conferees to determine the order of importance of the facts. Some suggestions may belong together under a main heading; some may need to be eliminated entirely because of irrelevance or disadvantages. Depending upon the problem, conferees may have to consider various criteria—costs, safety, employee relations, union rules, and so forth.

State the Conclusion

As with any written analytical report, the terminal section is of crucial importance. Before you dismiss the conference, review what the group has accomplished. Summarize what part(s) of the problem conference members have solved or partially solved. Mention only the highlights. Don't merely repeat the details of the discussion or those on the chalkboard. State the decision (conclusion) clearly and definitely. You might begin your statement of the conclusion by saying, "You have agreed . . ." or, "You have suggested . . ." rather than, "I think this is what should be done." If the group arrived at several conclusions, list them, preferably in order of importance.

EXERCISES

1. For a four-minute speech, select any topic you are familiar with—a sport, favorite food, event, place, gadget. Introduce yourself to the class, tell what your topic is,

develop it (in any instructive or entertaining way you wish), and summarize your talk. After you have finished, your class members will make constructive suggestions.

2. Using either one of John T. Molloy's books (*Dress for Success* or *The Woman's Dress for Success Book*), prepare a two-minute extemporaneous talk on one of the following topics:

Men

The best type and color of a suit for a young businessman's first full-time job after graduation.
The two colors of suits a businessman should not wear—and why.
Shirts and ties for the businessman.

Women

What research shows is the best business attire for the businesswoman "on her way up."
Correct accessories for the young businesswoman.
Clothing advice for the executive's wife.

3. Assume you have been asked to present your long formal report orally at an informal conference attended by 10 managers in your company. (See Exercise 4, pages 666–668.) Their work is closely concerned with the subject matter of your report. Prepare your report presentation thoughtfully. Usually a mere "summary" of the report is not the best method, because it may be too general to be meaningful to your listeners. In addition, if appropriate, select specific highlights about the problem and its solution. Choose the ideas that are most likely to be of interest and importance to your audience. For example, you might introduce to them the three or four most important factors you considered in the report. Be well informed about the overall highlights of your report and be prepared to defend your findings in a question-and-answer session (by your class members) immediately after you have presented your report. (In your presentation, you will of course, *not* read many parts of the report to the audience.) Make your talk businesslike with the right tone—neither lecturing nor "entertaining."

4. Present to your class orally the proposal you prepared for Exercise 1 or 2, pages 663–665. Assume the class members are a committee or council representing the company or agency with which your proposal is concerned. Be ready to answer their questions, to defend your proposal, and to have the class critique it. If possible, plan to display it on an opaque projector.

5. Body language is a popular topic in almost any part of today's society. There are many who write on the subject, and much research has been done. Some refer to it as one phase of nonverbal communication and others use the correct technical term, *kinesics*.

   You may need to use more than one of the terms as you look up material for your two-minute talk on one of the following topics.

1. Body language as it applies to the modern business career
2. Body language as it applies to one's modern social life
3. Body language as it differs from one country to another

6. Pair off with another class member with a similar major and select a mutually agreeable topic which you will develop in two separate four-minute talks. The topic must be a recent development in your business major. Choose one you both will find interesting to research, build a talk around, and present to your audience. You and your partner will carry out the same purpose in your talks, but each will adapt it to specialized audience needs. One speaker will assume his or her listeners are laypeople, who have no technical knowledge or experience with the subject. The other speaker will assume his or her listeners are businesspeople who possess considerable background knowledge and experience with the general subject. The first audience will be confused or apathetic unless the speaker captures, develops, and maintains its interest; the second audience will be receptive, but critical. Toss a coin to determine who presents to whom.

   Careful audience analysis is required to adapt your talk to each group of listeners. You should consider these factors as you tailor your talk to the needs, interests, and backgrounds of your audience: presentation design (especially introduction); selection of main points, subpoints, and interest material; vocabulary and definition of terms; use of audience-related examples and applications; and use of visual aids.

7. In this assignment you are a member of a five-person group which is a panel on a conference program. The chairperson your group selects will coordinate your group's activities. Together the five of you will select a topic for your group's study. (Preferably select one related to business communication or an assumed company problem.) On the day of the conference, your group will have twenty-five minutes to report on its study. You, like every other member on the panel, have five minutes to present the one project area assigned to you. Your chairperson might (or will, if your instructor assigns it) prepare and hand to the instructor a one-page outline of your group's topic and show what phase each panel member will speak on. This summary may also show what research each group member did and the bibliography of his or her secondary research. The chairperson introduces the panel members to the class before they make their presentations. Afterward, your group will have a five-minute question-and-answer period with audience participation. By any method your instructor specifies (written or oral) the class members can then evaluate each panel member's presentation—perhaps on a 1 to 5 scale.

8. The corporate annual report is perhaps the best-known and most widely circulated business report. Virtually every public, college, and university library receives copies of annual reports from business and industrial firms. Some libraries catalog the printed reports and store them in filing cabinets; others store annual reports in some other form, such as microfiche or microfilm.

Your assignment here is to make an oral report, using information collected from corporate annual reports. You will concentrate on a comparison of certain key financial ratios for the company or companies chosen. Information on computing ratios (such as the current ratio, the acid test ratio, the net profit to net sales ratio, and the inventory turnover ratio) can be found in most financial management textbooks or in *Key Business Ratios*, a booklet available free from Dun & Bradstreet, Inc.

You have your choice of two options in making the comparisons. The first option is to choose *one* company and make a comparison of at least three ratios computed for each of two recent years. Of course, you will compute the ratios yourself. Obviously, your comparisons must be between ratios which compare the same things. For example, you could choose to compare the current ratio, the acid test ratio, and the inventory turnover ratio for Company X for the two most recent years.

The second option is to compare the ratios computed for *two* companies, using annual reports for the same fiscal year. For example, you could compare the current ratio, the acid test ratio, and the net profit to net sales ratio for Company A for the most recent year to the same ratios of Company B for the same year.

In order to make your presentation complete, you should explain how the ratios were computed and what the ratios mean. For this purpose, you should prepare a visual aid (such as a poster or a transparency for use with an overhead projector). A visual aid should also be used to enhance your comparison of the ratios computed.

The time limits for your report will be assigned by your teacher. In most instances, the report called for here will fall in the four- to six-minute range.

9. Prepare an oral presentation for members of the class, who will assume the role of salespersons attending a sales meeting. They are present at this meeting in order to gain helpful tips on how to be persuasive when giving sales presentations.

As the basis for your persuasive talk, use an unsolicited sales letter that you prepared in Chapter 10. Give specific attention to benefits that the customer will receive. Supplement your presentation with appropriate visual aids when you stress the importance of creating a desire in the customer to do what it is you want done. The visual aids you could use might include one or more of the following: transparencies, flip charts, posters, chalkboard, flannel board, slides.

The following is a sample persuasion problem for your talk:

Make a presentation to a group of college students and extend to them an invitation to become a subscriber to a popular magazine. Place emphasis on items such as the savings of 50 percent off the regular newsstand rate; features in the magazine; how it will supplement their textbooks; and the ease in placing the order.

10. Prepare a 10-minute lecture on one of the chapters in this textbook. Or, if your instructor approves, choose a recent magazine article on business communication

or in your major field of interest. Bring with you an appropriate aid which is large enough to be legible to every member of the class to see while you are speaking. Make it neat, clear, and as attractive as possible. Plan to refer to the aid during your talk. Be careful to keep your listeners' attention so they won't continue to look at the aid after you are through with it! Plan to speak from note cards; do not memorize your talk. Invite your audience members to interrupt you (by raising hands) if they have questions. Sometimes the questions may be antagonistic, just to give you the opportunity to handle such a challenging matter and to show how quickly you can gain composure.

chapter

19

Interpersonal and Other Nonwritten Communications

As a business or professional person, you will communicate orally not only within groups (as discussed in Chapter 18) but also on an individual person-to-person basis. Your work will likely at some time include interviewing, dictating, and giving various instructions or demonstrations. This chapter includes suggestions for handling these communications more effectively.

INTERVIEWING

Interviewing is a conversation with a purpose; it uses all the forms of communication already discussed in this text—speaking, listening, and writing (notes during or after the interview and the interview write-up). Some of the different types of interview are:

Selection and placement interview—to hire the right person for the right job

Vocational guidance interview—to help an individual find his or her best vocation

Counseling interview—to help the emotionally disturbed

Survey interview—to help marketing persons find answers to their assignments and problems

Group interview—used for problem solving

Diagnostic interview—used by clinical psychologists

The discussion here concentrates on interviewing candidates for employment in business. Employment interviews include the screening or preliminary interview, final interview, follow-up interview, direct interview, indirect (or nondirective) interview, and the patterned interview. The material in this section covers the patterned interview, because it is used most often and is considered most effective in getting truthful responses from the candidate. It is a combination of both the direct interview (in which the interviewer keeps very close control at all times by directly limited, specific questions) and the indirect interview (in which the interviewer makes little or no attempt to direct the applicant's conversation). In the patterned interview the interviewer guides and controls the conversation but encourages the interviewee to speak freely and at length about relevant topics.

This section focuses on interviewing from the *interviewer's* standpoint. Chapter 12 includes suggestions for the applicant who is the interviewee. (See pages 441–448.) The topics here include objectives of the patterned interview, interviewer's preparation for the interview, procedure during the interview, and the evaluation. Appendix A mentions some legal aspects regarding interview questions.

Objectives of the Patterned Interview

The fourfold objective of the patterned interview for a job applicant is to

1. Match the applicant and the job by judging qualifications and areas that other sources cannot assess.
2. Give the applicant essential facts about the job and the company—to help the candidate decide whether to accept the job if it is offered or to look further.
3. Instill a feeling of mutual understanding and confidence in the applicant who accepts the job. (If the employee begins work with the right attitude toward the firm, he or she will be happier.)
4. Promote goodwill toward the company—whether the applicant does or does not receive or accept the job. It is especially important to give the right impression to the candidate who is disappointed by a turndown.

Interviewer's Preparation for the Interview

The interviewer must prepare for the interview—as thoughtfully as if he or she were going to give a talk.

As an interviewer, you need to have a clear picture of your company's organizational structure and detailed information about the job(s) for which you are interviewing. Knowing organizational structure permits you to talk with confidence and give the applicant necessary facts about your company. If possible, you should have a job analysis for each position so you know what to look for in the applicant.

> This job analysis is an orderly and systematic study of the characteristics, duties, and responsibilities of a specific job. Included also are job operations and working conditions; training needed; aptitudes; attainments; type of personality, character, or temperament required.

If a job analysis isn't available, at least be familiar with the work environment, requirements for the position (including personality) and salary.

Your next step is to decide the areas you must cover in the interview (and the necessary questions) so that you can determine what qualifications a successful candidate should have. These areas usually include the critical requirements for the job, character, personality, general makeup of the individual. Then think how each applicant can demonstrate the skills and qualities that the job requires. Usually you attain your goal by use of questions about what the applicant has done; what he or she thinks about what he or she has done; his or her interests and hobbies; relationship to friends, school, and work; his or her colleagues and family. Finally set the interview up so that you can gain the most information possible from the candidate.

In addition, you need to consider the physical setup of the interview. Choose a quiet room where there will be little or no interruption. Arrange the furniture so that a desk does not separate you from the applicant. The ideal arrangement is to have the chairs for you and the applicant on one side, to break down the formal roles of questioner and questioned. Arrange your schedule so that no one has to wait very long. Furthermore, check the waiting facilities. If possible avoid having applicants stand in the hall—especially in long lines. A quiet waiting room with chairs and magazines gives a much more favorable impression and is more relaxing.

Procedure during the Interview

The interview itself consists of a warm-up period and a planned period of information seeking and giving.

Warm-up Period

You should react to the applicant at the beginning of the interview in the same way you would to a friend who visits you at your office or home; especially important are a firm handshake, warm smile, and friendly tone of voice.

Because the applicant is probably nervous—or at least unfamiliar with the surroundings—you want to begin the conversation with small talk. You might refer to the weather (that it's cold, fair, rainy, or humid), to an event of the day, or to a topic relating to the applicant's outside interest (athletics, sailing, mountain climbing). This is the time to begin to develop rapport and to show you are friendly and sincerely interested in the applicant. With the proper warm-up, you gain the applicant's respect and (hopefully) confidence.

Outline and Content of the Interview

After the brief warm-up period, you start the interviewee talking on the subject you want to know about. A good outline to follow is a straight chronological sequence.

You begin with the applicant's education and activities and then move through work history and off-the-job activities to self-evaluation. In this coverage you check technical qualifications (ability to do the job), drive and aspirations (willingness to do the job), social effectiveness and emotional balance (relations with others and self), character (trustworthiness), and other factors you need to measure for success on the job. They might relate to physical vigor and energy, spouse's attitude toward the job, financial stability, willingness to travel, willingness to make permanent moves.[1] Especially important are those aspects of the candidate's personality that relate to interest patterns, attitudes, character, and temperament.

When you have learned the necessary qualifications and behavior of the applicant, you can turn your attention to telling about your company—salary, fringe benefits, and other facts of interest. (Some interviewers reverse this pattern by first discussing the firm.) Also, give the applicant the opportunity to ask you questions relating to the job or company.

At all times you need to keep control of the interview and at the same time get the applicant to talk. The ideal interview should *seem* like an unstructured conversation, but you should not permit it to proceed aimlessly. As a critical listener, you must notice gaps and omissions in the applicant's discussion and observe reactions, comments, and gestures. Listed here are suggestions you need to follow to be an effective interviewer:

---

[1] Theodore Hariton, *Interview: The Executive's Guide to Selecting the Right Personnel,* Hastings House Publishers, New York, 1970, pp. 25–34.

1. Let the applicant do most of the talking. If you talk more than 50 percent of the time, you are interviewing yourself—not conducting an interview.
2. Use brief verbal responses that will keep the applicant talking—prod with questions such as "Tell me more," "That's interesting," "What happened then?"
3. Give your entire attention to the interviewee and respond by encouraging facial expressions, movement and expression of the eyes, and nods of the head.
4. Allow pauses in the conversation if you think the applicant will reveal important information. But avoid lengthy pauses or a pause when the applicant has definitely finished a topic.
5. Try to understand the applicant, who in turn may volunteer really useful information.
6. Make self-expression easy for the applicant.
7. Respect the feelings of the other person even though you might consider the person wrong.
8. At all times accept what the applicant says. Never frown, show surprise, or show disapproval.
9. Avoid the impulse to cut the applicant off or change the subject abruptly.
10. Never argue.
11. Sit on the same side of the desk as the applicant and use informal, plain language.

Checklist for Effective Interviewing

Following is a checklist that should help you review whether you are carrying out the role of interviewer well.[2]

1. Try to make a favorable impression on the candidate during the first few minutes of the interview.
2. Refrain from making any judgment about the candidate during the first few minutes of the interview.
3. Put the candidate at ease.
4. Pause after the candidate has seemingly finished a remark to give him or her a chance to talk further.
5. Occasionally repeat parts of the key sentences of the candidate in a questioning tone to secure elaboration.
6. Ask one question at a time. (For a list of questions frequently asked during interviews, see Chapter 12, pages 445–447.)
7. Make your questions clear, tactful, and pertinent to information you need.
8. Avoid wording questions so as to suggest the answers wanted.
9. Appear interested in the candidate and give him or her full attention.
10. Avoid expressing approval or disapproval of the candidate.
11. Avoid indicating your own attitude.
12. Use language appropriate to the candidate.
13. Ask no personal questions until after rapport has been established.
14. Allow the candidate to digress briefly without abruptly returning him or her to the point.

[2] Milton M. Mandell, *The Selection Process: Choosing the Right Man for the Job,* American Management Association, Inc., New York, 1964, pp. 220–221.

15. Talk as little as possible.
16. Control the direction of the interview.
17. Obtain maximum information on all relevant points.
18. Follow up leads the candidate makes.
19. Spend most of the time exploring areas on which information could not be obtained as well from other sources (reference check, for instance).
20. Get a complete work history.
21. Take notes of important points.
22. Avoid taking notes when the candidate is under stress.
23. Hear and see the vocal and physical mannerisms of the applicant as well as listen carefully to all statements.
24. Give the candidate an opportunity to ask questions.
25. "Sell" the job if this is deemed desirable.
26. "Sell" at the right time.
27. Continue observing until the candidate leaves the room.
28. Give the applicant a good impression of the organization before leaving.
29. Allow the candidate ample opportunity to do himself or herself full justice.

A good interviewer asks questions that are revealing—questions concerned with attitudes. The interviewer might ask, for example:

What would you say was the most promising job you ever had?

What did you like least about that job?

What kind of people do you work with best?

Given below are other suggestions about the use of questions.

1. You can learn more about the applicant from the "why's" of actions than from "what's."
2. Broadly worded lead questions that introduce a new topic steer the applicant in the right direction and permit you to sit back, evaluate statements, and throw in only occasional probes or comments: Example: "What are some of the things you like to do off the job when you are not busy working—your outside interests and activities?"
3. Follow-up questions should also be broadly worded.
4. You need to phrase each question carefully to elicit the desired information.
5. Use of the implied question—silence—tells the applicant you feel he or she has more to say and places the burden on the applicant to take it from there.
6. An indirect question such as the following encourages further elaboration without asking a direct question: "Please explain that in a little more detail."

The Nonverbal Message. Blushing, stammering, casting eyes downward, or barking out an angry reply—these are among the nonverbal messages and can be as revealing as anything the applicant actually says. You can partially but reliably judge any statement from the tone and inflection of the person's voice, gestures, hesitations, and general conduct. Behavior tells much about personality and social skills.

Pitfalls to Avoid. The following biases, prejudices, and other weaknesses within the interviewer are to be avoided:

1. Halo effect—tendency of the interviewer to form an overall opinion about the applicant on the basis of a single aspect of his or her makeup.
2. Stereotype error trap—tendency to categorize the applicant on the basis of a few surface clues.
3. Expectancy error—inadequately aware that the applicant anticipates the needs and preferences of the interviewer and responds accordingly.
4. Ideal image error—interviewer's mental picture of the ideal person may not necessarily coincide with the person who can actually be most effective on the job.
5. Personal bias of the interviewer—poor handshake, biting of fingernails, gum chewing, loud clothes, poor eye contact.
6. Pseudoscience and myth—judging the applicant's character, mental ability, attitudes by means of handwriting, outward features, date of birth, number of letters in the name, lines or marks on the palm of the hand, and shape and bulges of the skull.
7. Stereotyped, mechanical interviewing—same questions in same order, no adaptation to the individual, no stimulating exchange of ideas, no interplay of attitudes. In turn, the interviewer receives stereotyped answers that don't appraise qualifications.
8. Illusion that previous experience, of itself, guarantees ability to do the job well.
9. Being swayed because the applicant needs a job—even though the necessary qualifications are lacking.
10. Talking too much by interviewer—not listening.
11. Poor preparing for interview.
12. Asking inappropriate questions.
13. Being discourteous and rude toward the applicant.
14. Jumping to conclusions.
15. Accepting facts without probing to determine meaning and accuracy.
16. Leaving unexplored gaps.
17. Allowing applicant to guide the interview.
18. Depending on memory to conduct interview and to evaluate the applicant's qualifications.
19. Asking another question when the applicant merely hesitates a moment.
20. Appearing to be critical and cold toward the applicant.
21. Not observing nonverbal clues (gestures, voice changes, hesitations).
22. Poor questions:
    a. Leading questions that invite a given response: "Would you agree that . . ."; "Are you in favor of . . . ."
    b. Loaded questions—use of language that reveals one's own biases and prejudices; in turn, the applicant will slant answers accordingly.
    c. Dead-end questions that elicit only "yes" or "no" answers.

Evaluation of the Information

When you have drawn the desired information from the candidate, you must form an overall opinion of what the applicant said during the time with you and supplement it with vital facts from other sources.

Here is a list of clues which often serve as indicators of the applicant's state of mind and general makeup.[3] They should prove useful to you as an interviewer in your evaluation.

1. Behavioral and psychological symptoms

   Positive
   a. Early arrival
   b. Alert, responsive attitude
   c. Emphatic attitude
   d. Relaxed manner
   e. Smiles
   f. Clear voice

   Negative
   a. Late arrival
   b. Inattentive, dull attitude
   c. Condescending or withdrawn attitude
   d. Tenseness, fidgetiness, body tremors
   e. Frowns
   f. Choked voice, mumbling

2. Verbal symptons

   a. Sticking to the main point
   b. Incisiveness
   c. Relevant responses
   d. Well-organized presentation
   e. Appropriate use of humor
   f. Spontaneous replies
   g. Speaking well of people
   h. Candor

   a. Changing the subject
   b. Overgeneralizing or too much detail
   c. Irrelevant responses
   d. Disorganized presentation
   e. Uncalled-for levity
   f. Long pauses before replying
   g. Criticism of others
   h. Rationalization, evasiveness

After the interview you may prepare an "interview write-up," consisting of a one- or two-page report with a paragraph on whatever areas are pertinent to the interview. It may cover such items as education and training, work experience, current off-the-job life, personal characteristics, and overall summary. The beginning of the body shows blank lines for interviewee's name, date, the topics considered, and name of interviewer. At the end (you might call it "conclusion") is a scale where the interviewer checks his or her overall rating of the applicant or others interviewed.

No one candidate will usually possess all the requirements you are measuring. One might not have all the work experience you'd like, but might compensate for this weakness with an abundance of drive and personality. You must select the right person for the job. But if you choose someone whose ability is far above or below the job level, you'll be doing a disservice in three ways—to the applicant, who will not remain on the job very long; to the company, which will lose money for the time the em-

---

[3] Hariton, *Interview: The Executive's Guide to Selecting the Right Personnel*, p. 58.

ployee remains on the job; and to yourself, who will lose face with yourself, the applicant, and the company.

In summary, your job as interviewer is to find out if the applicant is the individual for the job. After the interview you consider the facts gained from the interview about the applicant's qualifications, attitudes, personality, mannerisms, appearance. You will then evaluate this information, along with facts from other sources (references, tests, and so on) and decide whether or not to invite this candidate to join the company or to invite him or her to the home plant for further interviews with other officials.

DICTATING

After you have planned a letter, memo, or report, you will probably type it yourself, dictate it to a secretary, or write a rough draft in longhand. Should you dictate, you are expressing your ideas orally. Because a frequent complaint of secretaries pertains to the poor dictating habits of executives, this section focuses on both the importance of good dictation and suggestions for better dictation.

Importance of Dictation

The executive who can dictate messages clearly and quickly (instead of writing them all out in longhand) saves time and money for the employer and also, indirectly, helps build goodwill with customers. If the dictation is on tape recorders, other voice-writing machines, or the company telephone (instead of face to face), still more time is saved; the secretary can be doing other tasks while the executive is dictating. Also, such machines can be used effectively when the dictator is away from the office.

The importance of good, clear dictation is especially noteworthy when one considers the enormous costs of errors resulting from poor dictation. Transcription errors because of dictators' lack of care have ranged from embarrassing or comical to costly and disastrous. Three examples are mentioned here.

1. A department supervisor, intending to write to the Dungeness Crab Company, began his dictation (to a new secretary) with this statement: "Send the following letter to Dungeness Crab Co." (He pronounced the last word as "ko.") The result? His letter—which he unfortunately signed and mailed without reading the inside address—was addressed to "Mr. Dunjen S. Crabco."
2. Another dictator's poor enunciation and omission of spelling on an unusual name resulted in a $4,000 damage suit. Her firm's wrecking crew—instead of razing an empty house at 560 McDonough Street—had begun to tear down an empty house at 516 McDonald Street!
3. A chief engineer had a habit of uttering "huh" and "er" between phrases while dictating into a microphone, and of dropping off word endings—saying, for instance, "hund" instead of "hundred." On one important materiel requisition for this international construction company a new typist misinterpreted this engineer's "uh" for "hundred," and thus she typed 111,000 feet of a certain dimension of

lumber instead of the intended 11,000 feet. The requisition with the unnoticed error was duplicated and mailed to the company's 50 construction engineering branch offices. Can you estimate the cost of that error causing all those offices to buy 100,000 extra feet of unneeded lumber?

Suggestions for Better Dictation

To help you be sure you'll be signing your name to the message you want to mail (or to use effectively as basis for a speech or report), here are good oral practices to follow while dictating:

1. Prepare an outline and dictate from it.
2. Enunciate clearly. Very few persons can speak clearly with candy, gum, or cigarettes in their mouths. Be especially careful with plurals, and words that sound alike, such as fifty and sixty. ("Five o" and "six o" are much more definite.)
3. Spell unusual words and names when using them for the first time.
4. Dictate—at the beginning of the message—any special instructions such as extra carbon copies for certain persons, unusual tabulation of figures, or your desire for a rough draft only. For a complicated message—report, letter, memo, speech, etc.—you will surely want to edit and revise before it is mailed. Thus be sure to ask for a rough draft, double-spaced. Otherwise your assistant may unknowingly type the usual, say, five carbon copies. Your correct instruction can save precious time as well as paper and supplies.

   If your office has a magnetic card or magnetic tape typewriter, you and your typist can save still more time. You can then make changes or additions easily without having an entire report draft retyped. Text as originally draft-typed is "played out" automatically to each point of revision. Changes or additions are typed manually, and then automatic playout of the corrected copy resumes.
5. Always dictate as much punctuation as your transcriber needs to turn out an accurate, attractive message quickly. At least dictate "paragraph" to indicate each new paragraph; "quote," "unquote"; "parenthesis," "close parenthesis."
6. Dictate at a normal rate, just as you talk. Avoid long pauses followed by rapid dictation. It is thoughtful to slow down a little when reading, for instance, an inside address or a policy number.
7. Let your secretary use his or her initiative as to grammar corrections, additional punctuation, and arrangement of your letters, memos, and reports.
8. When dictating a reply to a letter received, you can save both your time and your stenographer's time if you dictate only the name of the addressee. Your stenographer can later copy the full address from the letter you return after you have dictated your reply.
9. If you have many important figures to be tabulated, write them on paper from which the stenographer can copy them.
10. Keep the mail you are answering in an orderly pile by turning each letter (or memo) upside down when you have finished answering it. After all your dicta-

tion is completed, your entire pile of answered incoming correspondence will be in order for your stenographer to obtain needed information, attach file copies, and so forth.

11. In addition to these dictation tips, you can save yourself and your company time and money by having definite dictation periods (for instance, a set time each morning and/or afternoon) with no interruptions by telephone or callers.

12. See also Suggestions for Cutting Correspondence Costs, later in this chapter, for pointers regarding dictation efficiency when you give instructions.

GIVING INSTRUCTIONS AND DEMONSTRATIONS

Another important reason for oral communication in business and industry is to give instructions and/or to demonstrate. Whether you are a relatively new employee being moved to a different job in another department, or a supervisor in charge of many employees, you will need to give various, clear, person-to-person instructions. In some jobs—such as selling, computer programming, and numerous technical jobs—you will also need to demonstrate. Your oral communications can be crucial for efficient company operations.

Clear Instructions on Individual Jobs

Perhaps you have at some time started on a new job and been "trained" by an employee whose explanations were "as clear as mud." After hearing her or him race through incoherent comments, you were not only uninformed, but also confused. By asking numerous questions, you may have eventually learned enough to perform the job. Many needless and costly errors are made, however, because of faulty and vague instructions and because the listeners are reluctant to ask questions.

Whenever you have the responsibility of training someone in the duties for a job, be sure you have a clear understanding yourself of the job description. Preferably write it out clearly first and then present it orally step by step. Follow also the seven C principles (Chapters 3 and 4) to make your instructions complete, concise, concrete, considerate, clear, courteous, and correct. Demonstrate, whenever desirable, and help your listener to follow your instructions. Welcome questions by asking, "Now what questions have you?" Answer them tactfully.

Suggestions for Cutting Correspondence Costs

In an effort to help cut the ever increasing costs of written communication (see Chapter 1, pages 9-10) you can do your part within your own company. Briefly, here are suggestions to get you started.

1. To eliminate needless repetition of basic instructions, standardize them and put them in writing for your transcribers. Develop simple code words to indicate

frequently used instructions—such as "CEPO" for "Send a carbon copy with enclosure to our Portland office."

2. Expand the efficiency of your secretarial help. As a guideline, a good stenographer using an electric typewriter and transcribing machine can turn out 30 to 35 one-page letters in a seven-hour day. See that these assistants receive helpful instructions.

3. So that typists can do other work while you dictate, and thus save time, use machine dictation and stenographic pools as much as possible (except for the top executives who have private secretaries). Dictation equipment operates about twice as fast as a secretary can write in shorthand.

4. Adopt a word processing system if your company's correspondence is large enough to warrant it. Form letters may be run entirely automatically at 1,000 wpm.

5. To speed replies and save time and money—on correspondence between branches and departments, and sometimes to outside inquirers—use the short-note-reply technique. Merely jot down your answers to written inquiries on the bottom of incoming messages; then make copies of the sheets and send them out as the answers; file the originals. See that all concerned employees have proper instructions.

6. Dictate less and delegate more. Develop effective interchangeable form paragraphs and use them wisely to handle your repetitive situations. Dictate only the basic ideas and let your subordinate compose the routine letters. Be sure he or she has adequate information.

7. Increase your use of typing pools, electric typewriters, and automatic machines.

8. Use modern, high-speed metering devices.

9. To save on paper, carbons, and miscellaneous supplies, whenever possible and desirable use a smaller-size paper—even postcards. For interdepartmental messages requiring a certain number of carbons, try using carbon sets instead of onion-skin and regular carbon paper to save the time usually required for handling and inserting the individual sheets.

10. Use form letters and memos whenever desirable. (See pages 152–154.)

11. Instruct employees to use the telephone to convey short messages. You can say a full 450 words in three minutes. The maximum charge for a daytime station-to-station three-minute call dialed within the continental United States is under $3 and considerably less after 5 p.m. and weekends. If your firm has a WATS line (wide area telephone service) you can save still more on various long-distance calls.

12. Accurate postal addresses and ZIP codes save time and costs (caused by delays if mail is inadequately zipped). See that your mail-room employees have access to correct ZIP designations.

13. Instruct employees to be careful to place sufficient postage on mailed materials—based on weight and class of mail. (Collection of additional postage, either from the sender or from the addressee, is costly to the postal service and offers a potential for delayed delivery.)

14. If your firm originates and receives large volumes of mail, instruct someone to periodically review mail-room activities, especially when mail-room employee turnover rates are high. Assure that there is continuity of understanding of com-

pany policies and postal mailing requirements. This is particularly true for bulk rate mailings which have presorting and sack labeling requirements.

EXERCISES

1. This project involves an interview (for information-gathering purposes) and an oral presentation (for information-dissemination purposes). Your first task is to identify and interview a person who has a type of job or career which you hope to enter upon graduation. The purpose of the interview is to determine what kinds of communication activities that person must engage in during a typical week. You should cover not only the types of written messages sent and received, but also determine the volume or frequency, the job title of the originator of the incoming messages, and the disposition of the messages (what does your interviewee do when he or she receives each type of message?). Don't forget to cover oral communication messages (verbal orders or directives, telephone requests, etc.). For outgoing written or oral messages, find out to whom (title of person) the messages are directed. Unless the interviewee keeps a log of such activities, you will have to depend on the interviewee's estimates for some of the information.

   The second part of this assignment requires you to make a formal oral report of your findings in class. A three- to five-minute time limit should be sufficient; however, your teacher may wish to establish other limits.

2. For efficiently handling a situation in which your oral communication skills are important to a company, you must do some preliminary planning and practice.

   Assume that you work for a firm with high employee turnover. Your responsibility is to gather information that will be useful to management in determining why so many employees leave. This information will be gathered in an exit interview procedure used by your company and conducted with every employee who leaves. You are to establish specific objectives to be followed during the interview, set up strategies that can be followed, and develop a specific list of questions that you will ask during the interview.

   Try these questions out in an interview setting in class, using another member of the class as the employee who is leaving the company. In your interview, you should first express appreciation to the employee for his or her service. (This should be done in order to set the tone for a positive and relaxed interview.) You should then emphasize to the employee that in no way will the information gathered be used against the employee when seeking employment elsewhere. Stress the fact that the information will be used to help management improve working conditions in the company and perhaps help cut down on employee turnover. Use any technique that you believe will assure a nonthreatening situation.

   Your primary functions during the interview are to solicit the information your company needs and to provide information that will be helpful to the employee.

3. For this project choose two questions from the list of preemployment questions

on pages 445–447 and assume your interviewer has asked you to answer them. Then prepare a three-minute presentation to your class (or to smaller groups). Your instructor and/or your class members will "interview" you on what you said or on any other pertinent question. They will offer constructive criticism on your persuasiveness in answering the two questions that you assumed they asked you, and will comment on both your verbal as well as nonverbal expressions. An alternative to this assignment is to divide the class into groups of two to five persons. Each student will then be "interviewed" by the group instead of by the whole class. The other members of each group will take turns being the interviewee—to present their three-minute talks answering their two chosen preemployment questions.

4. For practice in impromptu speaking, follow the assignment in Exercise 3, except that instead of preparing a three-minute presentation on two questions of your choice, you will be asked to speak three minutes on any of the questions your instructor (or class members) select for you—without previous "warning."

5. For practice in handling an oral communication situation for which you have no opportunity to prepare in advance, try this assignment. It is comparable to the performance-appraisal interview you may have some time on a job, either as an employee being appraised or as a supervisor who does the appraising. Assume that in your company each supervisor fills out every six months a personnel appraisal form similar to Figure 16-2, page 595. On the day this assignment is due your instructor will select two students at a time to come before the class. One of them will be asked to be the employee and the other, the supervisor. Your instructor will hand to the supervisor a rating form which she or he presumably filled out on the employee. It has some favorable and some unfavorable entries. It contains also a short paragraph of details on why he or she has rated the employee as he or she has—preferably with specific examples on each topic. The employee receives from the instructor a separate paragraph stating some reasons the employee may give as to why he or she performed as he or she did. Both the supervisor and the employee will have a few minutes to read these statements before the interview. Then the supervisor will open the interview. Both supervisor and employee will have a businesslike discussion for 10 (or more?) minutes. Some comments will be on touchy subjects. Prepare yourself well by reading the suggestions for interviewer on pages 690–697 and for interviewee on pages 441–448.

6. You are correspondent for a company with a centralized word processing department. By dialing a special number, you dictate correspondence from your desk telephone. This dictation is recorded in the word processing department on tape for later transcription. The typed document is routed to you for signature and mailing—or editing and retyping if necessary.

   Dictate a solution for a letter-writing exercise in Chapter 7 or 8. To simulate dictating to a word processing department, use a tape recorder. Experienced dictators can dictate routine correspondence from nothing more than a mental outline; however, you probably will need to consider the best organizational pattern to use, jot down a brief outline with major points for development, and then dictate. Be sure to indicate your name and department. Then, using the dictation suggestions on pages 697–699, dictate your letter from inside address to name and title.

7. After several years of "getting started" in the motel business, the Goodrest Motor Hotel enterprise is reaching a level of income stability. A rule of thumb in the industry is that the break-even point is somewhere between 55 and 60 percent occupancy rate and Goodrest has now surpassed that minimum figure.

   In addition, the Goodrest Motor Hotel enterprise has motels in Big City, Alabama; Production City, Texas; Oil City, Texas; Wheat City, Kansas; Coal City, Kentucky; and Cotton City, South Carolina. More motels are in the planning stage, especially in the West and Southwest.

   One of the problems that has not been overcome is that of employee turnover. Not all hotel/motel jobs, of course, are glamorous but the pay is competitive and the hours are reasonable; in fact, many of the guests also leave a tip of $1 or more for the maid if the room has been kept clean and neat during the traveler's stay. A check has been made on supervision, too, and it appears as if the style of the supervisors and managers is as good as or better than most other places of similar employment. What, then, is the reason for such high employee turnover? (The problems involve desk clerks, maids and janitors, kitchen and dining room workers, night auditors, and others. No one type of employee appears to have more problems than the others.)

   Mr. Dye M. Nickel, the president of the Goodrest Motor Hotel group, is convinced that a good employee communication program would be a possible solution and is willing to commit $50,000 out of his 198__ budget to experiment on the project. You are asked, as a member of the management team, to prepare a report for Mr. Nickel which would make suggestions for starting the effort. And, as communication involves such a wide area of possible items, you will have to do deep, serious, innovative thinking—all within the limits of the $50,000 commitment.

   Keep in mind certain factors such as: this is communication to employees, not the general public (Goodrest has an advertising agency to take care of that communication effort); one person is to be hired to head the program and that salary will have to be part of the $50,000 allocation; Goodrest has in-house printing facilities which are currently being used for printing stationery, guest postal cards, registration forms, menus, special bulk mailings to customers and prospective customers, and so forth; employee suggestions and letters would be not only welcomed but encouraged; pictures of employee participation in outside activities could be printed; the communication could be either in the form of a newsletter, a tabloid-type newspaper, or a house organ of some other type; and a certain frequency of publication should be determined.

   Your job is to make recommendations, in a report to Mr. Nickel, as to how the program should begin. Both oral and written communications should be involved and you do have time because this is May and the program would not begin until January. Mr. Nickel has also said that he would be agreeable to hiring a person to head the program as soon as a suitable and qualified individual could be found. Use proper headings to allow the reader to follow the report; use a correct introductory statement; and end with a section titled Summary, Conclusions, and Recommendations.

Remember: this is an important responsibility and is part of your job as a member of the management team of Goodrest Motor Hotel. You cannot afford to let Mr. Nickel down.

8. Present to the class a five-minute instructive explanation on how to perform the duties of a particular job you are familiar with. After you finish, call on a class member to tell as well as possible what she or he learned. (This procedure tests not only your instruction clarity but also the listener's attentiveness.)

9. Demonstrate (in five minutes) the use of a small appliance, hobby tool, or toy. If possible, have another class member stand behind you, back to back. He or she will follow your instructions as you state them orally. At the completion of your communication, see whether your listener's result is what you intended it to be.

10. One type of interpersonal communication involves group processes and experiences. There are many of these—round table, cracker barrel, brainstorming, buzz group, posting, Phillips 66, and others—which can be used to advantage. Such a session, at times, is proof of the adage that "two heads (or more) are better than one."

The Phillips 66 plan was developed by an individual by the name of Phillips, who originally planned to restrict the size of the group to six persons and the time of decision making to six minutes. From this he formed the name which is used to describe the activity. Experience has also shown that it is sometimes necessary to use a larger group or more time; however, size and time limits are important.

In the Phillips 66 group plan the following criteria are to be followed: (1) the participants must feel qualified to discuss or question the primary discussion group or the primary problem; (2) the group must know what is expected of it; (3) the assignment is to formulate *questions* dealing with the discussion topic.

For the present situation the class should be divided into groups of no more than seven and no fewer than five persons, who must select a chairperson and a recorder. The groups will then be given a primary problem and each group will be charged with the responsibility of preparing a list of pertinent questions about it. After the specified time (at the beginning it could be more than six minutes) the class will reassemble and compare results. An additional evaluation could also be made on the participation of each of the individual members of each group—not on quality, necessarily, but on quantity—for one important goal is to achieve individual participation.

Because topics quickly become dated (e.g., a petroleum crisis, a predicted recession, a war) the Phillips 66 discussion should be assigned so as to match the current local, national, and international news and events.

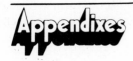

Appendixes

- **APPENDIX A: Legal Aspects of Your Business Communications**
  Defamation
  Invasion of Privacy
  Fraud
  Some Pertinent Laws regarding Employment, Credit, and Collections
  Other Areas of Caution in Business Communications

- **APPENDIX B: Mechanics and Style**
  Abbreviations
  Checkpoints When You Edit Sentences and Paragraphs
  Dangling Participles
  Numbers as Figures or Words
  Punctuation Makes Sense
  Syllabication (Division of Words)
  Transitional Words and Phrases to Help Tie Sentences Together
  Trite Expressions

- **APPENDIX C: Symbols Used in Marking Letters, Memos, and Reports**

APPENDIX A:
LEGAL ASPECTS OF YOUR BUSINESS COMMUNICATIONS

When you apply integrity, honest consideration for your reader, and the golden rule in your business communications, you should be safe in the eyes of the law. Yet as a cautious, sensible businessperson—and as a consumer—you need to realize that there are legal dangers even in some true statements. On the other hand, not all untrue words that appear to be libelous will lead to a lawsuit.

Thousands of statute laws and court decisions have been passed in the 50 states and our federal government. The laws of one state have no effect in other states, but federal laws apply throughout the country and have precedence over conflicting state laws. The U.S. Constitution is the supreme law and takes precedence over conflicting statutes passed by Congress. The right to freedom of speech versus the individual right not to be libeled have led to various legal privileges under various conditions. Furthermore, changing social and business conditions necessitate changing laws from time to time. Thus, even while books about laws are being prepared for publication, many new laws may be enacted. No single chapter or book can begin to cover even partially all specific legal interpretations applied to business communication.

The purpose of this appendix is to call to your attention some of the legal risks and complications that may occur in business communications. An overview of pertinent legal concepts should be helpful to you both as the writer and the recipient of business messages. Remember, however, that statutes in various states differ, that numerous new laws and interpretations are made from time to time, and that each legal case must be analyzed individually upon its facts. Ignorance of the law excuses no one. For advice on specific details that apply to some complicated situations, you may need a lawyer. The discussion here is necessarily a brief general introduction only; no liability is assumed for its completeness. Yet if you are aware of the risks discussed here, you can avoid harmful utterances and costly misunderstandings. This section briefs you on:

1. Defamation
2. Invasion of privacy
3. Fraud
4. Some pertinent laws regarding employment, credit, and collections
5. Other areas of caution

Defamation

The unconsented and unprivileged "publication" of a false and malicious statement which tends to injure one's character, fame, or reputation is *defamation*. Oral defamation is *slander*. Written defamation is a *libel*. Truth is usually a complete defense to a defamation suit. Also, some false statements may be either absolutely privileged or conditionally privileged. Because the words *publication* and *privilege* have important legal significance, they are discussed first; then follows a sampling of defamatory terms.[1]

Publication

In the legal sense, the unconsented intentional or negligent communication of defamatory matter to a third party is *publication*. Any means of communication by which some third party (anyone other than the person attacked) actually receives the defamatory idea can effect a publication.

If you tell Mr. X to his face privately that you consider him incompetent or a swindler, you are within your legal rights; only he has heard your statement. But if you intentionally communicate the defamatory statement to at least one other person who is not "privileged" (as defined later), you can be in serious trouble. The derogatory qualities that make a statement defamatory are the same for libel and slander. Because libelous statements are more permanent, laws pertaining to libel are more severe than those about slander. The writing (for libel) may be any permanent communication—such as a letter, postcard, telegram, circular, picture, photograph, cartoon, newspaper, recorded tape, or phonograph record.

Even a sealed letter addressed and mailed to the person you are accusing can result in actionable publication if you knew or should have known that it would be intercepted by or shown to a third person. For this reason, a letter containing unfavorable information about a person (or organization) and any collection message about past-due payments should be mailed only in a sealed envelope and addressed so that it will be read only by the addressee. Adding the words *Personal and Confidential* or *Personal* is a good precaution. Another precaution is to use an opaque envelope and to fold the message into the envelope in such a way that it cannot be easily read when held up to a light.

Accidental communications to third persons (by eavesdroppers or unauthorized letter readers) are not actionable unless you knew of or should have foreseen such possibilities. A mere possibility that someone may have seen or overheard the statement is not enough.

Dictation to a stenographer is considered by most authorities to be a publication which is conditionally privileged with respect to matters reasonably related to the ordinary conduct of the business.

Privilege

A legal right to communicate defamatory information in certain situations is *privilege*. The privilege may be "absolute" or "conditional."

[1] Unless otherwise footnoted, this discussion on defamation is based on Arthur B. Hanson, *Libel and Related Torts*, vol. 1, The American Newspaper Publishers Association Foundation, Inc., New York, 1969, pp. 21–195; Harold J. Grilliot, *Introduction to Law and the Legal System*, 2d ed., Houghton Mifflin Co., Boston, 1979, p. 501.

Absolute Privilege. In these three general areas absolute privilege applies: judicial proceedings, legislative proceedings, and the acts of important government officials, usually executives. Thus judicial officers, attorneys, and all parties participating in a judicial proceeding are absolutely privileged to make defamatory statements and to file such papers during and as part of the trial, if they bear some relationship to the matter under consideration. Letters between parties or attorneys relating to a controversy are also privileged. However, defamatory statements about a case made outside the ordinary course of a judicial proceeding, such as comments to reporters in the hallway, are not entitled to the absolute privilege for judicial proceedings.

Similarly, legislators and government officials are absolutely privileged to make defamatory statements in the performance of their official functions, but not if the statements are irrelevant to the public matter then under consideration. For example:

> A member of the highway commission in New Mexico made a defamatory statement about a highway contractor at a commission meeting with reporters present. A superintendent of banks in California made libelous statements concerning his former attorney. In each case the Supreme Court of the respective state held that these public officials were protected by an absolute privilege in the exercise of their executive function. In contrast, a public official would not be absolutely privileged to defame his subordinates when publicly explaining why he dismissed them.[2]

The risk of liability for criticism of public persons has decreased significantly in the United States since the Supreme Court decided the *New York Times* case in 1964. Under the *Times* rule, criticism or comment about the public conduct or fitness for office of public officials, and statements about the public conduct of other voluntary public figures, are privileged even if they are based on or include erroneous material—unless there was actual knowledge of falsity or reckless disregard for whether the material was true or false. Two prongs to the rule are: (1) the inclusion of both fact and opinion within the privilege of fair comment, and (2) the degree of "malice" (intent to injure) necessary to defeat the privilege, constituting knowledge of falsity or reckless disregard for truth. The Supreme Court has included within the public official designation: a city commissioner; a group of parish judges; a county attorney and chief of police; an elected court clerk; a deputy sheriff (and others). The "public figure" to which the rule applies is a person "intimately involved in the resolution of important public questions" or one who by reason of his or her fame shapes events in an area of concern to society at large, and as a result, already has as much access to the mass media "both to influence policy and to counter criticism" of his or her views and activities as does a "public official." The Supreme Court has found a university athletic director and a retired army general who was actively involved in a federally enforced school integration to be within the class of public figures covered by the *Times* rule.

However, the media are on more uncertain ground in commenting on private in-

---

[2] Paul P. Ashley, *Say It Safely: Legal Limits in Publishing, Radio, and Television,* University of Washington Press, Seattle, 1966, pp. 43–47.

dividuals who are involved in matters of public or general concern. In a 1974 case (*Gertz v. Robert Welch, Inc.,* 418 U.S. 323) the U.S. Supreme Court held that each state is permitted to establish its own standard for libel actions brought by private individuals over stories relating to matters of public concern.

Conditional (Qualified) Privilege. In several kinds of situations a conditional (qualified) privilege applies when the interest of either the participants or society dictates that communication in good faith should not be hampered by fear of lawsuits. Thus defamatory statements made in the ordinary commercial activity are qualifiedly privileged, whether they are interoffice messages or sent to persons outside the company, when the recipient has a lawful interest in the topic of discussion. This aspect of conditional (qualified) privilege is significant regarding recommendations of applicants.

The person who answers an inquiry about the performance of an employee or the credit record of a customer is obligated to take reasonable precautions that the information sent is accurate. He or she must *avoid intentional deceit or malice.* "In a personnel report it is generally believed that the writer owes a moral duty to state what is known about a former employee. What is stated honestly and in good faith is privileged communication even if it is subsequently shown to be untrue."[3]

Thus whenever you send requested information to an inquirer (prospective employer or creditor, for instance, who might suffer a loss if he or she employs or lends to an unworthy applicant), make every effort to *tell the truth and to reply in good faith without malice.* If a respondent intentionally or carelessly misleads the inquirer who seeks information about another person (for instance, a job or credit applicant), he or she may be sued for damages. The reply should neither mislead the recipient into hiring or lending to an unworthy applicant nor maliciously deprive a worthy applicant from being considered fairly for employment or credit. *When the truth about an individual or an organization is unfavorable and directly related to a question you are asked to answer, try as much as possible to protect the good name of the one involved.* Also indicate in your reply that the information was *requested* and ask that it be kept *confidential,* if possible. Remember, however, that under public disclosure laws some information cannot be kept confidential.

Some employers have been reluctant to state unfavorable but true and relevant information about an employee because they fear facing a lawsuit threatened (or implied) by the applicant. Nevertheless, the prevailing view is that the employer's right to freely express his or her opinion should not be restricted by another person's insinuations. If an employee threatens legal action in an attempt to restrain an employer from stating or committing to writing what is true, the threat is a baseless attempt to intimidate. An employer certainly can state "It is my opinion that the employee has failed to live up to the quality of work we require at this institution. We have certain standards and we feel he (or she) did not meet those standards." It

[3] Iris I. Varner and Carson H. Varner, Jr., "Business Communications and the Law," presented at the International Convention of the American Business Communication Association, Atlanta, Georgia, December 28, 1978, pp. 7 and 8.

is always desirable, of course, to specify what the expected standards are and to have records and documentation which will support the statements made.[4]

When you *request* someone *to send you information* about another person, show in your letter that you have an interest to protect and promise to keep the received information confidential if this is permissible. Also, to receive all the important facts you need, it may be advisable to include a question like, "Do you have any other information (or . . . know of any personal habits) that might help or hinder this applicant's success in the position for which we are considering her (or him)?" Such statements help protect the informer against a libel suit.

Is it illegal to provide unsolicited information in a personnel report (or recommendation letter)? No, but in this case the standard for truth is higher. Dr. Carson Varner has presented the following example:

> Suppose you are writing a recommendation for an employee who has worked as a janitor and is applying for a job as bank teller. The inquiry to which you are responding is: "How has the candidate been as an employee?" You know the janitor has been in jail, and it is generally believed the janitor was convicted twice for embezzlement, and you write this in your recommendation. Suppose it turns out the janitor has been in jail for involuntary manslaughter not embezzlement (the distinction might be critical for a bank job) and the janitor sued you for libel. Normally, the recommendation is privileged, but does it apply here? Here you were only asked to comment on the janitor's performance on the job and not about the background; therefore the information is not privileged, but subject to another standard.
>
> Were you careless or negligent in stating what you knew? If so, you could be held liable for damages caused. On the other hand, let us assume the janitor had started the rumor or everyone had believed it for years and the janitor had made no attempt to correct the rumor. In this case the jury could find you were not careless in your statement and therefore not liable.[5]

In summary, if one responds to an inquiry, one should basically have no fear of saying what one knows or adding relevant information in good faith. The response to such an inquiry is qualifiedly privileged, and truth is generally an adequate defense. But if one speaks or writes maliciously (for example, because of a desire for personal gain against a competitor or to hold an applicant up for ridicule), one may be held liable in any case. Privilege does not extend to defamatory statements unrelated to the purpose of the particular privilege (as, for instance, defamatory remarks not relevant to job qualifications). Also, the former employer may lose the privilege if the response uses such violent or abusive language that the real motive in the reply is evidence of malice or some other improper purpose. Furthermore, if the former employer knows the statement is false, clearly the privilege is defeated. If he or she is negligent or unreasonable in believing it to be true, jurisdictions differ as to whether the privilege is lost.

---

[4] S. G. Tenney, Assistant Attorney General, University of Washington, interview, February 13, 1979.
[5] Varner and Varner, *Business Communications and the Law*, pp. 7–10.

Privilege does not apply to unreasonable disclosure and publication of particulars concerning a debtor to his or her employer, relatives, and to the public by such devices as "deadbeat lists" or obvious communications forms which may be read by others who have not requested the information and have no immediate need of it.

Defamatory Terms

Among the terms that have been judged libelous, the following are a representative (but incomplete) sampling of words to be avoided or used with caution when you refer to a person or an organization:

bankrupt	drug addict	incompetent	quack
blackmailer	faker	inferior	racketeer
Communist	falsified	insolvent	shyster
corrupt	forger	kickbacks	swindler
crook	fraud (fraudulent)	misappropriation	thief
deadbeat	gouged money	misconduct	unchaste
dishonest	grafter	misrepresentation	unworthy of credit
disreputable	hypocrite	profiteer	worthless

In the collection of debts or in attempts to collect any claim alleged to be due or owing, the collector should not unreasonably oppress, harass, abuse, or intentionally cause mental distress to any person. Harassment and abuse include abusive language, anonymous or repeated telephone calls at odd hours, and anonymous c.o.d. communications.

Some statements are defamatory because they malign a characteristic necessary in a person's work (provided the occupation is legal). Thus, in most jurisdictions, it is defamatory to impugn the financial responsibility of a merchant, but not of a teacher, because ability to obtain credit is essential only to the merchant. Also it has been held defamatory to attribute communist sympathies to a public official, but not to an engineer. And, as already discussed, it is defamatory to impugn the competence of an employee to perform duties required by his or her job. But such statements may be conditionally privileged if made in the ordinary course of business activity, as discussed above under Privilege.

The truth is usually adequate defense in a libel suit, especially if there is no evidence of malice. But if the writer cannot prove his or her unprivileged statements to be true or prove that there was adequate reason for writing them, he or she may have to pay large money damages.[6]

---

[6] Philip Wittenberg, *Dangerous Words—A Guide to the Law of Libel*, Columbia University Press, New York, 1947, pp. 282–308.

Invasion of Privacy

The unconsented, unprivileged, and unreasonable intrusion into the private life of an individual is *invasion of privacy*. Unlike defamation, privacy can be violated although no publication to third persons takes place and even though the matters delved into are true or not particularly harmful to reputation. The concept of right of privacy is analogous to that of trespass, which gives one the right to keep unwarranted intruders off one's land not because of any resulting emotional distress or loss of rents, but merely to ensure the solitude of landowners. Though the boundaries in this concept have not been definitely determined, its primary concern is the protection of a mental interest—such as freedom from mental anguish resulting from invasion of one's privacy.[7]

This section discusses two aspects of invasion of privacy: use of a person's name, photograph, or other identity without permission; and physical surveillance of records, reports, and letters by persons not entitled to examine them.

Use of a Person's Identity

If a person's name, photograph, or other identity is used without permission on a sales letter or advertisement (or other permanent publication—not word of mouth), that person may have cause for legal action because his or her right of privacy has been violated.

Recovery and monetary awards have also been granted for publication of x-rays and other medical pictures, for pictures of a deformed infant, and for undue publicity of a delinquent debt.

Yet, not every use of another's likeness or identity is actionable. In some states it must be unreasonable under the circumstances, as well as unprivileged. Using pictures of an all-American football team on a beer company's calendar which also contained advertising was held (in one case) not to be an invasion of team members' privacy, because they were public figures and there was no false implication of endorsement. But using a person's picture to illustrate a story about dishonest tactics of cab drivers would shed false and unfavorable imputation on the person and would be an invasion of privacy.

Unreasonable publicity of private life may also result in legal action and costly money awards to the offended person, as in these two cases:

> A former prostitute and the acquitted defendant in a notorious murder trial had reformed, married, and pursued a respectable life in a new community which knew nothing about her former life until the defendant revealed the whole story in a movie, using her name. She was allowed a cause of action for publication of these true but embarrassing personal facts.[8]

---

[7] Hanson, *Libel and Related Torts*, pp. 197–206.
[8] Hanson, p. 203.

In the "pink letter case" a suggestive letter bearing a woman's signature was mailed to 1,000 men. Handwritten in a feminine hand, the letter was mechanically reproduced on pink stationery and mailed by a mailing agency. The name signed to the letter was that of the principal character in a motion picture the letter was advertising. Unfortunately, it also turned out to be the name of a woman living in Los Angeles—the only person by that name listed in the City Directory or the telephone directory. When the letters began arriving (in hand-addressed, pink envelopes), many wives must have looked at their husbands with a quizzical eye. But it was worse for the plaintiff, who began getting telephone calls from the men. She also worried for fear that some irate wife might shoot her—for the letter invited the men to meet the signer in front of a certain theater on a certain day and to look for a girl "with a gleam in her eye, a smile on her lips and mischief on her mind." The court felt that the plaintiff should be compensated for invasion of right of privacy.[9]

If you wish to use the picture or identity of an individual for your advertising or sales letters, for instance, be sure first to get previous consent and make clear just how the picture or identity is to be used. An individual may have indicated consent by willfully posing for a photograph, but alteration of the photograph or using it in a way to carry objectionable implications is an invasion of privacy.

Physical Surveillance of Records, Reports, and Letters

The right of privacy may also be violated if records, reports, and letters are read by persons not entitled to examine them.

Powerful binoculars, long-range telephoto cameras, and "zoomer"-type television cameras have been used effectively (and illegally) in recent years to look through windows at important papers lying face-up on desks, at models of new products and designs, and at charts displayed at conferences. These techniques have become so common in certain areas of industrial espionage that elaborate security precautions are taken to keep designs and models in windowless rooms and to keep blinds drawn at all times in certain offices.

Modern technology has added to these existing situations the possibility of passing visible light or reflected infrared energy through an envelope and taking pictures of the contents. These pictures can then be read (deciphered) by persons skilled in reading handwriting or typing where lines are inverted or superimposed. Also available is a needle-thin "flashlight" that can be inserted in a sealed envelope to "light it up" for quick reading by a trained investigator. You can help to greatly reduce or even prevent this type of surveillance by using—when desirable on certain very confidential material—envelopes with a random pattern printed on them to make them opaque and/or inserting more than one sheet of paper in them.[10]

[9] Kenneth and Irene Donelson, *When You Need a Lawyer*, Doubleday & Company, Inc., Garden City, N.Y., 1964, pp. 245–249.
[10] Alan F. Westin, *Privacy and Freedom*, pp. 78–79; copyright 1967 by The Association of the Bar of the City of New York. Reprinted by permission of Atheneum Publishers, USA.

Fraud

The intentional misrepresentation by one party to a contract of a material existing fact which is relied upon by the other party to her or his injury is *fraud*. Both as a seller and a buyer you need to be aware of the elements of fraud as well as the significance of warranties so that you can better detect and avoid fraudulent practices.

Elements

Fraud in the law of contracts requires that the party alleging it prove these elements:

1. A *misstatement* was made with the *intent* to deceive.
2. The misrepresentation was of a *material existing fact.*
3. The deceived person was justified in *relying* on the statement.
4. This person was *damaged* (in the legal sense) by the false statement.

If the misstatement was innocent misrepresentation, the victim may rescind the contract.

The misrepresentation need not be a direct falsehood for fraud to be present. In fact, failing to reveal defects or confirming false impressions by remaining silent can be sufficient. Any physical act intended to conceal true facts is in effect a misstatement. For example, a seller who sets back the mileage on a car conceals an important fact and asserts an untruth as effectively as if she or he were speaking. To be actionable fraud (for lawsuit), the misrepresentation must be of a *material* fact. False statements of opinion or of conditions to exist in the future do not constitute fraud. Before a false statement can be considered fraudulent, the person to whom it was made must reasonably believe it to be true and rely on the statement to his or her damage (injury). If he or she investigates before entering into the contract, and the falsity is revealed, no fraud exists.

Section 5 of the Federal Trade Commission (FTC) Act as amended, outlaws practices which deceive or are otherwise unfair to consumers. Included are (among others) false advertising regarding prices, performance capability, quality, and character of goods or services. Also included are endorsements by persons misrepresented as "experts" or "doctors," and many other misstatements intended to deceive.[11] A test for fraud is to ask, "Would the other party have entered into the contract had he or she known the truth?"

Warranties

In most sales contracts the seller undertakes certain obligations concerning the nature, title, and quality of the goods being sold. When these obligations are expressly stated or implied and when they actually induce the sale, the obligations are called *war-*

---

[11] Robert N. Corley, Robert L. Black, O. Lee Reed, *The Legal Environment of Business*, 4th ed., McGraw-Hill Book Company, New York, 1977, pp. 515–520, and Michael P. Litka, *Business Law*, Harcourt Brace Jovanovich, Inc., New York, 1970, pp. 152–153.

ranties. They are guarantees by the seller with respect to the goods sold. Warranties may be "express" or "implied."

An *express warranty* affirms a fact or a promise the seller made to the buyer in bargaining concerning the nature of the goods—description, grade, or model. Such a promise becomes a basis for the contract even though the term *warranty* or *guaranty* is not used.

Implied warranties are considered part of the bargain even though the parties themselves say nothing about them. For instance, the seller warrants that he or she is conveying a good title to the goods. Also, under the Uniform Commercial Code (adopted by all 50 states) if the seller is a merchant with respect to goods of that kind, he or she warrants that the goods are salable and are fit for the ordinary purposes for which such goods are used. If the seller knows the buyer intends the goods for a particular purpose and that the buyer is relying on the seller's judgment as to their suitability, there is an implied warranty of fitness for that particular purpose.

The federal law on warranties (enacted in 1975) requires that warranties on products costing $5 or more must disclose the warranty terms in simple and readily understood language. For products costing over $15 the warranty must be labeled "full" or "limited." "Full warranty" products must be repaired or replaced by the seller without charge within a reasonable time if there is a defect. If a warranty is limited, the limitation must be conspicuous so that buyers are not misled. Since passage of the new law, many sellers have chosen the limited warranty. Some have even eliminated their warranty entirely, rather than become involved with all the law's requirements.[12]

According to the U.S. Postmaster General, in the Post Office Department's informative booklet *Mail Fraud Laws*, fraudulent schemes sent through the mail are costing American consumers an estimated $500 million a year. Among the many dishonest rackets to trap the unsuspecting consumer are: fake contests, home improvement offers, auto insurance frauds, charity appeals, missing heir schemes, fake business opportunities, worthless medical cures, and fake correspondence-school programs promising "exciting, high-paying jobs."

The U.S. Chief Postal Inspector lists the following ways you can help enforce mail fraud laws:

To stop a dishonest scheme, inspectors must find that you and others buying a product or service were cheated as a result of claims the seller made in an intentional effort to defraud. Mail fraud violations occur when a general scheme or pattern of fraud exists.

When you believe mail fraud exists, hold all letters, including envelopes and other evidence related to the questionable scheme. See if your neighbors or business associates have also received similar material.

Bring such information to the attention of a postal inspector in your area by contacting him directly or through your postmaster.

Inspectors cannot investigate a case simply to force a supplier to speed up deliver-

---

[12] Corley, Black, and Reed, *The Legal Environment of Business*, pp. 524–528.

ies, obtain refunds, or to otherwise act as an intermediary in settling unsatisfactory transactions. In such instances the dissatisfied buyer should:

Seek an adjustment or settlement with the seller.

Bring his complaint to the attention of the Better Business Bureau, Chamber of Commerce, Trade Association, or publication which carried the ad.

Seek relief through civil suit if a breach of contract may be involved.[13]

Most states now have consumer protection divisions in the Attorney General's office, and they can be very helpful too.

Some Pertinent Laws regarding Employment, Credit and Collections

Here are some of the acts that affect business communications in various ways.

Employment

Title VII of the Civil Rights Act of 1964, with amendments in 1972 and 1978, prohibits discrimination in employment as to hiring, firing, compensation, termination, and conditions or privileges of employment on the basis of *race, color, religion, sex,* or *national origin.* (Exceptions are allowed in some businesses or enterprises—such as church organizations, modeling agencies, entertainment producers—when religion, sex, or national origin may be bona fide occupational qualifications necessary for normal operations.)

The law forbids discrimination, *not* the asking of certain questions. But some questions may be unfair or risky to ask because they appear to be for the purpose of discriminating, and in fact do discriminate. They might later be the basis for legal action. Even if an employer wins the court case, the damage in public relations may be extremely serious. Thus most large firms have policy guidelines with narrow rules on what recruiters may or may not do when interviewing.[14] Chapter 12 lists questions which may usually be asked during the interviews. This appendix section now presents some kinds of questions that should not be asked because they may be considered unfair and discriminatory.

Subjects	*Unfair Preemployment Inquiries*
Citizenship; national origin; relatives	Requirement before hiring that applicant present birth certificate, naturalization or baptismal record. Any inquiry which would divulge ancestry, national origin, descent, or birthplace.
Convictions	Inquiries which would divulge convictions that (1) do not relate reasonably to fitness for performing the particular job or

---

[13] *Mail Fraud Laws—Protecting Consumers, Investors, Businessmen, Medical Patients, Students;* U.S. Post Office Department, Washington, D.C., June 1969.

[14] Varner and Varner, *Business Communications and the Law,* pp. 9–11.

(2) do not relate solely to convictions within seven years of the job application date.

Family; marital status; original name (if changed by court order or marriage)	Specific inquiries concerning spouse, spouse's employment or salary, children, child care arrangements, or dependents; whether married, single, divorced, separated, engaged, or widowed. (Fair questions are whether applicant can meet work schedules or has commitments, activities, or responsibilities that might prevent meeting work attendance or job duty requirements; same questions asked of both sexes.)
Height; weight; handicaps; pregnancy; sex	Any inquiry not based on actual job requirements; overgeneral inquiries ("Do you have any handicaps?") which would tend to divulge handicaps or health conditions not reasonably related to fitness to perform the job.
Organizations; religion or creed	Requirement that applicant list all organizations, clubs, societies, lodges to which he or she belongs; inquiries about religious affiliations, church, parish, pastor, or religious holidays observed.
Photographs; race or color	Request for a photograph before hiring; any inquiry about color of skin, hair, eyes, etc.
Residence	Names or relationships of persons with whom applicant resides; whether owns or rents home.[15]

Credit and Collections

Because of the widespread use of credit by consumers, the federal government and the states have enacted a series of laws to protect consumers and try to assure that they are treated fairly in credit transactions. Space here allows only a brief introduction to some of these laws. They are detailed in the United States Statutes at Large. (Volume and page numbers are in parentheses after each act described below.)

Equal Credit Opportunity Act requires that financial institutions and other firms engaged in credit extension make that credit equally available to all creditworthy customers without regard to sex or marital status. Subsequent amendments have extended the act's protection to all persons regardless of race, color, religion, national origin, or age. The credit extenders have certain rights to make necessary inquiries for determining credit worthiness. (88:1521-5)

Fair Credit Billing Act aims to protect the consumer against inaccurate and unfair credit card practices. It applies to any existing open-end consumer credit account having an outstanding balance of more than $1 at or after the close of the creditor's

---

[15] Adapted from *Pre-employment Inquiries and Screening*, Washington State Human Rights Commission, July 1977.

first full billing cycle. The act specifies procedures for consumers to challenge any charge-account statements they believe are incorrect. Creditors must send to customers printed instructions twice a year explaining the procedures. (88:1511-17)

Fair Credit Reporting Act requires that consumer reporting agencies adopt impartial, fair procedures for meeting the needs of consumers regarding consumer credit, personnel, insurance, and other information. It specifies guidelines with regard to confidentiality, accuracy, relevancy, and proper use of such information. It stipulates the circumstances under which consumer reporting agencies may furnish consumer reports, the type of information they may and may not furnish, and the requirements for disclosing to the consumers the substance and sources of information as well as for reinvestigating to correct disputed information or errors. (84:1114-16)

Federal Truth in Lending Act aims to assure meaningful disclosure of credit terms so that consumers will be able to compare more readily the charges by different credit sources. It requires lenders and creditors to disclose the terms, conditions, finance charges, and service or carrying charges (including annual percentage rate) before a consumer signs a contract. It also gives a consumer the right to rescind within three business days after signing a contract that will result in a security interest being acquired in his or her residence. If the transaction is rescinded, the borrower (consumer) has no liability for any finance charge. (82:146-158)

Other Areas of Caution in Business Communications

Among the many unmailable materials that may violate United States postal laws are letters and printed matter concerning lotteries, obscene literature, extortion threats, and solicitation of illegal business. Space does not permit discussion of these items here. You can obtain booklets on most of these subjects through your local postmaster or the U.S. Government Printing Office, Washington, D.C., 20402. And if you are in doubt about the mailability of any particular material, you may submit a request to the Office of the General Counsel, Mailability Division, Post Office Department, Washington, D.C., 20260. A ruling will be furnished as promptly as circumstances permit.

The sending of unordered merchandise through the mail does not violate postal laws unless it is sent c.o.d. However, persons receiving such unordered items can:

If the package has not been opened, write "Return to Sender" and put it back into the mails.

If the article is not wanted, set it aside for a reasonable period of time and if unclaimed, destroy.

Treat unordered merchandise as an unconditional gift if living in a state where the laws apply.

The sending of unsolicited credit cards is illegal, as specified in the Consumer Credit Cost Disclosure Act.

Another caution pertains to the copying of certain documents. Congress, by statute, has forbidden the copying of the following documents and items under certain circumstances: United States government obligations or securities, such as Treasury and Federal Reserve notes, National Bank currency, certificates of indebtedness, silver and gold certificates, paper money, and others; also United States savings bonds (except for campaign publicity for their sale), Internal Revenue stamps (except in copying for lawful purposes a legal document on which there is a canceled revenue stamp), postage stamps canceled or uncanceled (except for philatelic purposes, provided the reproduction is in black and white and is less than ¾ or more than 1½ times the linear dimensions of the original); postal money orders; bills, checks or drafts for money drawn by or upon authorized officers of the United States; and other representatives of value issued under any act of Congress.

Also forbidden is the copying of copyrighted material without permission of the copyright owner—except for certain limited "fair use" privileges and single copies made for noncommercial purposes, as specified in the Copyright Revision bill, effective January 1, 1978; certificates of citizenship or naturalization (except foreign naturalization certificates); passports (except foreign); immigration papers; obligations or securities of any foreign government, bank, or corporation; draft registration cards, selective service induction papers bearing certain information; badges, identification cards, passes or insignia carried by military, naval personnel, or members of the various federal departments and bureaus such as FBI or Treasury (except when ordered by head of such department or bureau). In some states copying auto licenses, automobile certificates of title, and drivers' licenses is also forbidden. For these items—and others not listed here—penalties of fine or imprisonment are imposed on those guilty of making illegal copies.

As a final caution, in general, remember to:

Be honest and fair in all your business transactions and correspondence.

Avoid any statements and acts that may be considered defamation, invasion of privacy, or fraud.

Keep yourself well informed on responsibilities regarding various laws and in other areas of concern.

Consult an attorney when in doubt about the handling of any complicated situation that might involve legal risks.

APPENDIX B:
MECHANICS AND STYLE

Abbreviations

In business letters and reports, abbreviations are appropriate for the following titles: Mr., Mrs., Ms., Messrs. (as for a law firm of Messrs. White, Green, and Black). Other common abbreviations are: Jr., Sr., Mt. (Mount), St. (Saint), Inc. (Incorporated), Ltd. (Limited), D.C. (District of Columbia); compound directions, NW or NW. or N.W. (Northwest) with similar variations for SW, NE, SE; and the professional degree symbols such as B.B.A., Ph.D., M.D., C.P.A. The title Dr. (Doctor) is usually abbreviated, especially when the first name or the initials are used with the surname. [Some authorities suggest abbreviating "Doctor" when the first name or initials precede the surname (Dr. John Brown) but spelling it out in a salutation (Dear Doctor Brown). Business-persons, however, feel that applying two rules is impractical, and they abbreviate "Doctor" in both situations.]

The following words should be spelled out whenever possible: *president, superintendent, honorable, reverend, professor, building, association, department*; as well as *street, boulevard, avenue, east, west, north, south.* City names, and generally state names, should also be spelled out. It is best to use abbreviations sparingly within messages. A good rule is: "When in doubt, spell it out." However, if you are using the U.S. Post Office Department two-letter state abbreviations on envelopes, you may wish to abbreviate the state the same way in the inside address for consistency. (See footnote 9, page 140.)

Checkpoints When You Edit Sentences and Paragraphs[1]

For clarity and concreteness:

1. Use words your readers (or listeners) will understand.

	Say:	*Not:*
Choose conversa-tional, simple words when possible	use understand	utilize comprehend
Avoid Latin terms that many persons don't know. Instead, use synonyms.	about following that is for example	circa sequents i.e. e.g.

2. Use strong, vigorous words—active verbs, concrete nouns, specific adjectives and adverbs.
3. Guard against misplaced modifiers and dangling participles. (See also pages 723–725.)

---

[1] For additional suggestions see also the C qualities, Chapters 3, 4, and 15.

```
Incorrect:        As one of our best customers, we invite you to....

Correct:          As one of our best customers, you are invited to....or
                  As you are one of our best..., we invite you....
```

4. Make verb tenses say what you mean.
   a. Use the present tense wherever you can logically do so. It applies to things that existed in the past, still exist, and apparently will continue to exist.
   b. Use the indicative mood—not the subjunctive—whenever possible. Many times you can change "would" to "will," "could" to "can," and "might" to "may."
5. Avoid "this," usually, unless a noun follows.

```
Mr. Lucas once lost $5,000 that he had invested in farm mortgages
and this made him question all types of investments.
```

Improve clarity by adding "experience" after "this."

6. Use punctuation to help the reader. (See pages 729-737.)
7. Keep the average sentence length 17 to 20 words. The maximum paragraph length in a formal report should not exceed 15 typewritten lines; maximum paragraph length for a letter, 10 typewritten lines.
8. Tie your writing together with transitional words, phrases, clauses, and paragraphs.
9. See that a paragraph has a topic sentence. Also a section—especially with subheadings—should have an introductory paragraph.

For conciseness:

1. Shorten wordy phrases.
   a. Instead of *"for the purpose of,"* use *"for."*
   b. Instead of *"due to the fact that,"* use *"because."*
   c. Instead of *"in the event that,"* use *"if."*
2. Remove needless repetitions.
   a. Use a shortened form for a very long noun, after using the complete noun once; for example, American Telephone and Telegraph becomes AT&T.
   b. Substitute "it" or another appropriate pronoun for the noun.
   c. Omit repeated numerals (unless in a legal document or on a check). Use "11," not "eleven (11)."
3. Eliminate "which" clauses whenever possible.

```
She ordered desks which are of the executive type.
She ordered executive-type desks.
```

4. Limit "it . . . that" constructions.

```
It is known that we must reduce pollution versus We must reduce
pollution.
It is clear that... versus Clearly....
```

5. Avoid overusing "it is," "there is," and "there are" at the beginning of sentences.

Wordy: There are four rules which should be observed.

Concise: Four rules should be observed.

6. "Rescue" verbs that are smothered or hidden in nouns and infinitives.

	Wordy	*Concise*
In nouns		
	take a look	look
	held a meeting	met
	had a discussion	discussed
	The function of this office is the <u>collection</u> of accounts	This office <u>collects</u> accounts
In infinitives		
	The duty of a clerk is <u>to check</u> all incoming mail and <u>to record</u> it.	The clerk <u>checks</u> and <u>records</u> all incoming mail.

For correctness:

1. Avoid switching from third person to first, and/or second person. If you write in the third person (impersonal writing), don't use "I," "me," "we," "us," and "you."

2. Vary your sentence structure. Instead of beginning most sentences with the subject followed by the verb, you should begin some sentences with a different sentence structure—such as a dependent clause. Also, sandwich some short sentences among longer ones.

3. Be sure subject and verb agree.

> A <u>study</u> of these two reports <u>shows</u>--(*not show*)
> The <u>details</u> in this memo <u>confuse</u>--(*not confuses*)

4. Use parallel construction.

Incorrect: We will be glad to answer any questions you may have if you <u>write</u> to the above address or by <u>calling</u> us at 679-6622.

Correct: We will be glad to answer any questions you may have if you <u>write</u> to the above address or <u>call</u> us at 679-6622.

Incorrect: clerk, manager, selling

Correct: clerk, manager, salesperson

5. Spell every word correctly. Always use the dictionary when you are in doubt.

6. Avoid ending a sentence and beginning the next sentence with the same word(s).

Not good: Your son will enjoy using a portable electric typewriter. A portable electric typewriter....

Better: Your son will enjoy using a portable electric typewriter while he is attending college. This machine....

7. As a rule, most verbs of the senses—"taste," "feel," "see," "smell," "hear"—take an adjective, not an adverb.

Not correct: The dinner tastes deliciously.

Correct: The dinner tastes delicious.

Also correct: I feel well. (*In this sentence "well" is an adjective.*)

8. Don't overuse a word in the same sentence or paragraph unless you do so intentionally to emphasize it.

Not good: The important subject on which I am going to write is the subject of inflation, a subject of great importance to ordinary citizens.

Improved: I'm discussing inflation—a subject that is important to most people.

9. Have at least two or more lines of a paragraph on a page.
10. Syllabicate between syllables and limit your word division to no more than four words on one page. Also, don't syllabicate the last word on the page or on three consecutive lines.
11. Type quoted material of three or more lines single-spaced without quote marks, indented from left and right margins, and leave a double space (blank line) before and after the quotation.
12. If a major heading of a paper has subheadings, it must have two or more—never just one—subheadings.

Dangling Participles

A *participle* is a word that ends in "ing" or "ed" and looks like a verb; yet it actually is an adjective that must modify a specific noun or pronoun. If it doesn't, it is called a *dangling participle.*

The three most common forms of dangling participles are caused by the writer not observing the following rules:

1. The participle should be placed close to the word to which it refers, and there should be no intervening noun to which the participle might seem to refer.

Unclear: A complete <u>report</u> is submitted by our branch office, <u>giving</u> details about this transaction. (*"Giving" is the participle; it should modify "report," but it seems to modify the intervening noun "office."*)

Clear: Our branch office submitted a complete <u>report</u>, <u>giving</u> details about this transaction. (*Now the participle clearly modifies "report."*)

2. A participle at the beginning of a sentence (or at the beginning of a second independent clause in a compound sentence) should refer to the subject of the sentence or independent clause.

Unclear: Having been boiled for the proper length of time, the homemaker took the shrimp off the stove. (*"Having" modifies the subject "homemaker" when the participle should modify "shrimp."*)

Clear: Having been boiled for the proper length of time, the shrimp were taken off the stove by the homemaker. (*Now "having" modifies the right word--"shrimp," which is the subject of the sentence.*)

or

After the shrimp had boiled for the proper length of time, the homemaker took them off the stove. (*This sentence discards the participle.*)

Here's a simple way to see if the participle beginning the sentence properly modifies the subject: State the subject "shrimp" and follow it with the participial phrase, "having been boiled for the proper length of time." If the two parts give you the meaning you want, "shrimp, having been boiled for the proper length of time," then the participle is modifying the right word. But if you are boiling the homemaker, something is wrong.

3. A participle following the main clause should refer to a definite noun, not to the general thought expressed by the clause.

Unclear: These accounts disappeared from the vault, thus causing us very much worry. (*Instead of modifying a particular word, "causing" modifies the entire clause that appears before the comma. Suggestion: Reword so that you don't have the participle in the sentence.*)

Clear: Because the accounts disappeared from the vault, we are very much worried.

Clear: These accounts disappeared from the vault, a fact which caused us much worry.

Exercises. Indentify all dangling participles in these sentences, tell whether each one violates form 1, 2, or 3 just discussed, and then correct all errors.

1. Being an old customer, we know that you are familiar with our Christmas displays.
2. The check arrived six days late, causing me to write a collection letter.
3. Realizing our mistake, a new check was immediately sent to replace the first one.
4. Being larger and more attractive, these offices should make your work more pleasant, thus enabling you to work better.
5. Being a savings association, our customers do not have checking accounts here.
6. Please go down to the main office, and lying on the manager's desk you will find a copy of the latest report.

7. Having been run through the computer, the clerk used the figures for his report.
8. Changing your monthly loan payments, it will be necessary to
   get approval from the loan department.
9. Having been an outstanding keynote speaker, we can offer you
   this special award.
10. Enjoying 5% earnings, a savings account should be opened.

Numbers as Figures or Words

In general—use the figure instead of the word, because the reader can more easily read the figure and grasp its meaning. In invoices, tabular materials, purchase orders and the like, always use figures. In letters and reports—use the rule of 10 (spell out numbers 1 through 9; use figures for numbers 10 or higher) except for amounts of money and for isolated cases, as shown below.[2]

1. *If a sentence begins with a number, express the number in words:* This rule is used when the sentence cannot be effectively revised.

   Fifty applicants were interviewed for the position.

2. *When a number standing first in the sentence is followed by another number to form an approximation, express both in words:*

   Fifty or sixty will be enough.

   Note: Try not to begin a sentence with a number. Rewrite the sentence to place the number within or at the end of the sentence.

   The confirmation request was answered by 559 businesses.

3. *When a sentence contains one series of numbers, express all members of one series in figures.*

   We had 25 applicants from Arkansas, 15 applicants from Texas, and 6 applicants from Oklahoma.

4. *When a sentence contains two series of numbers, express the members of one series in words and those of the other series in figures:* If this rule is not followed, confusion results because of too many groups of numbers.

   Five students scored 95 points; seventeen students scored 30 points; and eleven scored 75 points.

[2] Most of these rules have been adopted by the Committee on Teaching Materials and Aids of the American Business Communication Association.

Three senior accountants made $100 a day; twelve semiseniors made $80 a day; and five junior accountants made $40 a day.

Note: For clarity, tabulate more than two series of numbers.

Name of accountant	Daily rate	Estimated working days	Total estimated earnings
Barlow, Helen	$80	3	$240
Dickinson, Al	70	2	140
Oman, Charles	80	1	80

5. *When one number immediately precedes another number of different context, express one number in words; the other, in figures:*

The specifications call for twenty-five 2 x 4's.
The deposit slip listed four 5's as the only currency.
You ordered 275 three-inch bolts.

6. *When an isolated number is below 10, express it in words.* This rule does not apply to exact dimensions or amounts of money.

The new salesperson sold eight refrigerators last month.
She hit a 6-foot pole.
This paper is 8½ inches wide.

7. *When numbers are expressed in words, as at the beginning of a sentence, use a hyphen to join the compound number, twenty-one through ninety-nine:* A compound number usually acts as a compound adjective.

Fifty-six accounts; twenty-one women; ninety-three men.

8. *When a numerical quantity contains more than four digits, each group of three digits should be set off by a comma (starting at the right).* (Obviously, this rule does *not* apply to dates, street numbers, serial numbers, and page numbers.)

1,000; 1,021; 5,280,000; 60,000; 600,000

9. *Express amounts of money in figures.* The following practices are recommended.
   a. *When an amount of money consists of dollars and cents, always express the amount in figures:* The dollar sign should precede the amount (unless in a tabulated column).

The invoice total was $5.51. The bonds were sold at $999.50.

   b. *When an amount of money consists only of dollars, omit the decimal point and the double zero:* Exceptions: (1) When the amount is tabulated in a column which includes both dollars and cents, include the double zero.

The invoice is $150. The check is for $5. $ 250.80
                                                       200.00
                                                       312.70
                                                       286.50
                                                   _____
                                                   $1,505.00

(2) When a series of money amounts contains mixed figures, include the double zero for consistency on all even figures.

The committee raised amounts of $15.00, $33.75, and $75.00 in the three rummage sales.

c. *When an amount of money consists only of cents, write the amount in any of the following ways:*

The piggy bank yielded $.57. The piggy bank yielded 57¢.
The piggy bank yielded 57 cents. The piggy bank yielded 9 cents.

d. *As a rule, do not write an amount in both figures and words. This procedure is necessary only in legal and financial documents.*

The check is for $7.   The total assets are $23,000.50.

In financial and legal papers write:

Ninety-five dollars ($95.00)
seven dollars ($7.00)
twenty-three and 42/100 dollars ($23.42)
twenty three dollars and forty-two cents ($23.42)

10. *Express the following numbers in figures, unless otherwise indicated:*
   a. *Dates:*

October 3, 1980
3d of October
Your letter of October 3 was most welcome.

b. *House or room numbers:* (except number one)

1503 Thomas Street
One Lenox Drive

c. *Numerical names of streets:*

Over 10:	315 69th Street or 315 – 69th Street (*Note two spaces or space hyphen space to separate house and street number.*)
Under 10:	2930 Third Avenue or 2930 3d* Avenue

*Many people prefer to use figures for all street numbers.

d. *Numbered items such as page numbers, chapter numbers, figure numbers, table numbers, chart numbers, serial numbers, and telephone numbers:*

page 10	Table X	Policy #V9109815
Chapter 10	Table 10	Policy V9109815
Chapter X	Chart 10	Claim No. 13189756
Figure 8	Chart X	Telephone 543-1111
Fig. 8	Service Serial No. 01845283	Phone (206) 333-1111

e. *Decimals:*

10.25   3.1414   .3535

f. *Dimensions and exact age:*

8½ x 11 inches   2 x 4 inches   He is 24 years, 5 months, and
8½ by 11 inches   2 by 4 inches   8 days old.

g. *Time:*

7 A.M. (reserved for headings)   7:35 P.M. (reserved for headings)
7 a.m. (more commonly used)   7:35 p.m. (more commonly used)
seven o'clock   seven in the morning

h. *Percentages:*

35%   6%
99.99%   6 percent
0.09%

i. *Fractions:*

1/32	one-half	4 3/4
3/64	two-thirds	or
25/64	one-fourth	4.75
25/100	three-fourths	

Listed below are sentences that contain numbers in the form of figures and words. If any number is used incorrectly, cross out what's wrong and add the correct usage directly above the error. Don't mark any number that is used correctly.

1. 5 policies lie on my desk.
2. Two men and 8 women work in this office.
3. The insured's car hit a 10-foot pole.
4. 10 men scored 94 points, 17 men scored 110 points, and 3 men scored 143 points.
5. May I have 100 12-inch rulers?
6. This morning I answered 17 letters.
7. You'll find the answer on page 8.
8. Mary came home at 7 o'clock.
9. She works from 8 a.m. until 5 p.m.

10. Thanks for the $50.00 loan.
11. The car hit a ten-foot pole, rolled over, and then fell down a 20-foot embankment.
12. The gate is six feet, three inches tall.
13. Your lot is 45 feet wide and one hundred thirty-two feet deep.
14. Please send the policy to 1 South Fifteenth Street.
15. Thank you for your check for twenty dollars.
16. Please buy 17 3-cent stamps.
17. The 3 items are on sale for $15, $16.95, and $20.

Punctuation Makes Sense

Punctuation is important because it helps the reader understand what you are saying. That's the whole purpose of commas, periods, dashes, and all those other little marks—to make reading easier and clearer.

Comma is used:

1. When you address the reader directly.

   Please let me know, Mr. Jones, when you will be in Tucson.
   I'll certainly appreciate your taking care of this assignment, John.
   Ms. Smith, that was a fine speech you gave to our group last week.

2. When you mention a person's title after his or her name or the name after the title.

   This person is Mrs. A. B. Jackson, President of Acme Company.
   Mr. Julius Roller, Jr., has done a splendid job.
   Our representative, Ms. Hall, will see you next week.

   Note: You omit commas in an expression like "my brother George" when a one-word name ("George") follows the title ("brother") and you have more than one brother. If you have only one brother: "my brother, George, . . ."

3. When the year follows the month and the day.

   On October 4, 1978, I started working for this company.

   but

   I was born in July 1958.

4. When the sentence contains a series or list of more than two things or persons.

   He raises turkeys, chickens, and geese.
   Mr. Smith, Mr. Snow, and Mrs. Hull appeared in court.

But in the names of business firms, follow the usage of the particular firm.

```
Merrill Lynch, Pierce, Fenner & Smith Inc.
```

5. When you can add "and" between two words that describe something.

```
You are an efficient, hard-working fellow.  (You are an efficient and
hard-working fellow.)
```

but

```
A right mental attitude makes for happiness.  (It doesn't make sense
to say "A right and mental attitude makes for happiness.")
```

6. When a sentence has two clauses separated by "but." (A *clause* is a group of words that includes a subject and verb; on the other hand, a phrase is a group of words that does not include a subject and verb.)

```
I like this car, but it is too expensive for me.
```

7. When a sentence has two clauses separated by "and" and one clause or both clauses are long.

```
You need a thorough knowledge of forestry, and you can get that knowl-
edge from on-the-job training.
His name is John, and he told me some of the most fascinating tales
about the South Pacific.
```

but

```
I like you and you like me.  (No comma is necessary when both clauses
are short--say, usually no more than five words each.)
```

8. When a sentence begins with a long dependent clause (one that cannot stand alone and that starts with such words as *although, since, because, as soon as, after, when*).

```
As soon as your letter reached me this morning, I called Mr. Doe.
Although his plan was incomplete, he received general approval.
```

but

```
His plan received general approval when the president read favorable
comments to all his department heads.  (When the dependent clause
comes after the main clause and is closely connected with it, no
comma is used.)
```

9. When a word or clause that follows the name of a person or thing isn't necessary to identify that person or thing.

```
This man, who went without sleep for two days, fell asleep at the
wheel.
Boston, the capital, is the largest city in Massachusetts.
```

but

```
A man who went without sleep for two days fell asleep at the wheel.
(Here the "who" clause is necessary to identify "man.")
Buy the book Investments the next time you go to the bookstore.
```

10. When a sentence includes a loosely connected word or phrase, called a parenthetical word or expression.

```
You will agree with me, however, that he is a great risk.
Yes, I agree with you.
You did a fine job, to be sure.
```

11. When two verbs come together.

```
Whatever is, is right.
```

12. When two figures come together in a sentence.

```
In 1979, 432 employees took their vacations in July.
```

13. When two sentence elements may be misunderstood or look strange if read together.

```
Wrong:       Ever since we have enjoyed working with him.
Right:       Ever since, we have enjoyed working with him.
Confusing:   That that is is that that is not is not.
Clear:       That that is, is; that that is not, is not.
```

14. When a sentence contains a quotation.

```
"Rules," he said, "are made to be broken."
He said, "Rules are made to be broken."
```

15. When the first word of a sentence ends in "ing" and modifies the subject.

```
Looking into this man's record, we find he was arrested twice.
```

16. When a sentence omits a word (usually a verb).

One of the persons involved in the accident is a mill operator; the other, a logger.

17. When the state follows the city.

Denver, Colorado, is called the mile-high city.

Period is used:

1. To end a sentence.

This firm has several branches throughout the state.

2. To show omission of words from a quoted sentence. (Periods indicating the omissions are called *ellipses*.)

"Fourscore and seven years ago our fathers brought forth on this continent a new nation,...dedicated to the proposition that all men are created equal ...." (*The fourth period stands for the period that ends the sentence.*)

3. To indicate abbreviations. *But* omit period after many organizations or government agencies.

Mr. Dr. Inc. a.m. p.m. N.E. NE. J. E. Doe

AFL, RCA, TVA, AT&T

4. For decimal sign.

13.5%, .04, $374.22.

5. In tabulation.

1.
2.   (*only one space after the period.*)
3.

Semicolon is used:

1. Between clauses that can stand alone and the second clause begins with words such as *however, nevertheless, consequently, therefore, moreover, hence, likewise, furthermore,* and *namely.*

He has an excellent background in education and work experience; however, I cannot find much information concerning his extracurricular activities on or off campus.

2. Between closely related clauses that can stand alone and don't have any word between them.

```
I prefer a person who has worked her or his way through school; he
prefers an individual who has devoted the entire time to schooling
and has a high grade point average.
```

But, you may use a comma to separate very short main clauses not joined by words listed in number 1 above.

```
I stopped, I aimed, I fired.
```

3. Before expressions such as *for example, that is, namely, for instance,* and *in fact* when they fall in the middle of the sentence.

```
Three of our offices have been redecorated; namely, Everett, Long-
view, and Bellville.
```

4. When a comma is in at least one of two clauses, both of which can stand alone and a word such as *but, and,* or *or* lies between the clauses.

```
On January 16, 1979, you mailed your report to us; but it didn't
arrive until January 27.
```

5. When a sentence contains a series and at least one part of the series has a comma.

```
The speakers included Ms. Roberta Jule, Vice President of Sales;
Mr. Dennis Greiner, Secretary; and Mr. Jack Blue, Comptroller.
Note: You could place a colon after "included."
```

Colon is used:

1. To introduce any lengthy quotation, list, or a table after such words as *the following, as follows, as, these, this*—stated or implied.

```
This is what he said: "Choose a job you'll enjoy living with for the
rest of your life, and then . . . ."
That house has four rooms: front room, dining room, kitchen, and
bedroom.
```

Note: To show emotions or greater emphasis, you should use dashes instead of colons.

2. To separate hours and minutes.

```
4:50 a.m.
8:35 p.m.
```

3. After the salutation in a business letter.

```
Dear Mr. Jones:
```

Dash is used:

1. To emphasize.

```
When you don't know how to spell a word--use a dictionary.
```

2. To set off a series within the sentence.

```
These people--Mr. Smith, Mr. Jones, and Mrs. Peterson--asked me
about this type of account.
```

Hyphen is used:

1. To break a word at the end of a line.

```
sub-        knowl-
stantial    edge
```

2. To tie together words thought of as a unit.

```
well-written report; is well written
letter-writing contest
secretary-treasurer
his take-it-or-leave-it attitude
40-foot pole
short- and long-run objectives.
```

But, don't hyphenate when the first word is an adverb ending in "ly."

```
slowly moving object
```

3. In numbers 21 through 99 when spelled out.

```
fifty-five
ninety-nine
one hundred seventy-six
```

4. To separate "ex," "elect," and "self" from the next word.

```
ex-president  ex-President Ford
president-elect
self-control
re-cover (cover again)
```

5. To avoid an ambiguous or awkward combination of letters.

```
re-address, pre-election (Some authorities use readdress, preelection)
```

Exclamation mark is used:

To indicate strong emotion.

```
What a beautiful car!
What a mess!
```

Question marks are used:

1. For direct question.

```
What have you found out about this individual?
```

But, use a period or a question mark after a request.

```
May we hear from you within the next 10 days.
May we hear from you within 10 days?
```

2. To show doubt.

```
In 1592 (?) Columbus discovered America.
```

Quotation marks: Here are three good suggestions to remember about punctuation before and after quotation marks.

1. All periods and commas go within the quotes.
2. Semicolons and colons always go outside the quotes.
3. Question marks, exclamation marks, and dashes
   a. Go outside the quotes when they punctuate the entire sentence.
   b. Go inside the quotes when they punctuate only the quoted matter.

Quotation marks are used:

1. Around a direct quotation.
2. Around unusual, substandard, or inexact terms.
3. Around titles of magazine articles and book chapters (but not titles of magazines, books, and pamphlets).
4. Around words to be set off.
   ```
   The "please" in a request.
   ```

Apostrophe is used:

1. To show possession.
   ```
   child's, women's, anybody's, Jones's, Moses', father-in-law's,
   someone else's
   ```

2. For omission of a letter or number.

```
I'll, you'll, we've, don't, can't, hasn't, o'clock, isn't, it's
the blizzard of '79
```

3. For plural of figures,   `7's look like 9's`
      letters,   `p's and q's`
      words used as words.   `You have five "hope's" in this letter.`

Sentences to punctuate:

```
 1.   The price is high but the quality is low
 2.   Washington Lincoln and Franklin Roosevelt were well known presidents
 3.   Youll find up to date information in that book
 4.   My sister Mary now attends college
 5.   The person who finds my watch gets a $20 reward
 6.   The boys are smiling the girls are laughing
 7.   As we agreed on the telephone this policy will run until May 6 1984
 8.   What system of bridge do you play
 9.   The price is high and the quality is poor
10.   You did a fine job John in handling this situation
11.   When you come to the meeting you should see Mr. John Narver our per-
      sonnel manager
12.   It is wise therefore to trade with reputable merchants
13.   A stitch in time saves nine says an old proverb
14.   You can be certain Ms. Corbett that you'll have our answer within a
      week
15.   In 1970 72 persons from our office enrolled
16.   Among those at the conference were Mr. A B Moe Superintendent Mr.
      Harris Lobe Sales Manager and Ms. Rollow Butts Educational Director
17.   Having read the policy twice he was familiar with its contents
18.   There was nobody there in fact when I arrived
19.   His suggestion was this Think before you write
20.   I always thought he was looney
21.   This person who found my watch gets a $20 reward
22.   When she talks she lisps her ss and rolls her rs
23.   Enclosed is a copy of our letter of February 12 1979 regarding the
      endorsement dated January 30 1979
24.   Seattle Washington is the largest city in the Northwest
25.   Please send the following Form A Form B and Form C
26.   Be certain to read pages 4 15 17 22 and 30
27.   This is your desk that one is mine
28.   Nothing has been done according to Joe to change the picture
29.   John said that he would do it
30.   It takes guts to publish that report
```

31. As Pete ate John gave him an account of the accident
32. For the next two weeks send my mail to 441 South Estelle Wichita Kansas
33. I saw this man hit that pale blue four door automobile
34. In 1939 when World War II started you were only several months old
35. People who live in glass houses shouldn't throw stones
36. They asked me whether I had taken any courses in finance
37. My sister you will be pleased to hear is now an accountant
38. A person who is honest will succeed
39. Three students Henry Pete and Mary invariably have their assignments well prepared every day
40. Its true that plenty of practice with proper guidance will improve your writing ability

Syllabication (Division of Words)

Syllabication is the division of words at the ends of lines to avoid a ragged right margin. In general, avoid this division of words, because the material isn't as easy and as clear to read. The following rules will help you to syllabicate words correctly.

1. Divide words between syllables only. Examples: prod-uct, knowl-edge.
2. Do not divide at the ends of more than two consecutive lines of typing.
3. Limit the number of syllabicated words to no more than four to a full page of typewritten material.
4. Divide hyphenated words at the hyphen only. Examples: self-control, half-brother.
5. Never divide words of one syllable or words pronounced as one syllable. The addition of past tense does not necessarily add an extra syllable. For example, "guessed," "slammed," "learned," "backed," "seemed," and "glanced" cannot be divided, because they are all one syllable.
6. Do not divide a four-letter word. If possible, avoid dividing words of five or six letters. Examples: upon, final, avoid.
7. In words having three syllables or more, a one-letter syllable should be typed on the preceding, rather than the succeeding, line. Example: sepa-rate, not sep-arate.
8. Avoid separating a one- or two-letter syllable at the beginning of a word from the rest of the word. Example: apti-tude, not ap-titude; enough, not e-nough. Exception *if necessary*: two-letter prefixes—ad, de, en, ex, im, in, re, un, up, etc.
9. Never carry just two letters of a word to the next line. Example: newly, not new-ly.
10. When two vowels coming together are pronounced separately, divide between the two vowels. Example: cre-ated, gradu-ation.

11. As a rule, divide between a prefix and the rest of the word. Examples: transpose, con-sign.
12. As a rule, divide between suffix and the stem of the word. Examples: lov-able, announce-ment.
    a. Note that in such words as "ame-na-ble," "fea-si-ble," and "de-fen-si-ble," the termination is "ble"—and the vowel preceding it is considered a part of the preceding syllable.
    b. When a root word ends with a double consonant, separate the suffix from the root word. Examples: guess-ing, tell-ing.
    c. When a final consonant is doubled before a suffix, the additional consonant goes with the suffix. Examples: trip-ping, strag-gling, stop-ping.
    d. Note that the endings "cian, cion, gion, sion, and tion" are kept as syllables, regardless of word derivation. Example: expres-sion.
13. When a consonant is doubled within a word, divide the word between the consonants. Examples: fer-ret, tal-low, shut-ter.
14. Do not divide the last word on a page.
15. Do not divide abbreviations, contractions, figures, or proper names.

Transitional Words and Phrases to Help Tie Sentences Together

Addition:

again	equally important	in addition	next
also	finally	last	nor
and	first	lastly	secondly
and then	further	likewise	thirdly, etc.
besides	furthermore	moreover	too

Comparison:

better yet	in like manner	similarly
here again	likewise	still worse

Contrast:

although this may be true	however	on the other hand
and yet	in contrast	on the contrary
at the same time	nevertheless	still
but	notwithstanding	yet

Instances and Lists:

in particular   for example   for instance   to illustrate

Place:

adjacent to	here	on the opposite side
beyond	nearby	opposite to

Result:

accordingly	consequently	therefore	thus
as a result	hence	thereupon	

Summary:

as has been stated	in brief	on the whole
as I have said	in other words	to be sure
for example	in short	to sum up
for instance	in sum	

Time:

afterward	following	in the meantime	soon
at length	immediately	meanwhile	

Trite Expressions

above captioned (loan)
above numbered
acknowledge receipt of
advise (when you mean "tell" or "inform")
allow me to
and oblige
as a matter of fact
as of this date
as per (your account)
as per our (agreement, request, letter)
assuring you of our prompt attention
as the case may be
at an early date
at hand
at the present writing
at this writing
attached find, attached please find
attached hereto
avail yourself of this opportunity
awaiting your further orders (reply)
be that as it may
beg to (state, advise, inform, differ)
by return mail
come to hand
contents noted
date of July 1
Dear Madam, Dear Mesdames
Dear Sir, Dear Sirs

deem it advisable
dictated but not read
don't hesitate to (call, write)
due course
due to the fact that
duly (credited, entered, noted)
e.g. (avoid this and other Latin abbreviations)
enclosed herewith
enclosed please find
esteemed
even date
favor (meaning letter)
for your information
has come to hand
henceforth
hitherto
hoping to hear from you, I am (remain)
I have your letter of (date)
in accordance with (your request)
in re
in reply wish to state
in the amount of
in this connection
it has come to my attention
kindly (when you mean please)
Latin abbreviations
our Mr. Jones
party (when you mean an individual)
per (your request)
permit me to say
please be advised that

please be assured (informed)
please do not hesitate to
please find enclosed
prior to
pursuant to (your request, inquiry)
receipt is hereby acknowledged
re your letter of recent date
reference loan number
regret to advise
reply to yours of
replying to your letter of
said (the said individual)
same (as a pronoun--thank you
for the same)
subject loan
take pleasure
take the liberty

take this opportunity
thank you for your attention in
this matter
thank you in advance
thanking you, we remain
the undersigned
the writer
this is to advise you
this will acknowledge receipt
under separate cover
undersigned
under the above subject
valued (letter, account)
we are in receipt of
we regret to inform you that
we transmit herewith
wise (cost wise, product wise,
personality wise)

APPENDIX C:
SYMBOLS USED IN MARKING LETTERS, MEMOS, AND REPORTS[1]

Ac	Check accuracy.	P	Use correct punctuation.
ACE	Avoid copying examples.	Pos	Use positive language.
ACP	Avoid copying problems.	PC	Use parallel construction.
AV	Use an active verb.	PH	Place letter higher on the page.
BC	Be consistent.	PL	Place letter lower on the page.
BMS	Be more sincere.	PRI	Put reader into this.
BNF	Give best news first.	Psy	Use good psychology here.
BP	Follow good business practice.	PV	Keep the correct point of view.
Cap	Capitalize.	RA	Recheck assignment.
Cl	Make meaning clear.	RB	Show reader benefit.
CSAD	Give clear statement of action desired (tell what and how).	Refs	List references.
		Reo	Reorganize.
DA	Date the action if desirable.	RPF	Recheck problem facts.
DP	Avoid dangling participles.	Sal	Use appropriate salutation.
Ds	Double space.	SL	Avoid stereotyped language.
EA	Remember "easy action."	SO	Spell out.
Fig.	Use figure(s).	Sp	Use correct spelling.
FW	Use fewer words; condense.	Spec	Be specific.
GRF	Give reasons first.	SR	Strengthen resale material.
HCA	Hyphenate compound adjectives.	SS	Improve sentence structure for unity, coherence, emphasis.
H&E	Is this honest and ethical?		
HHE	How can you help employer?	STP	Subordinate this point.
ITI	Interpret this idea (give concrete evidence to illustrate).	TAP	Improve tone and/or psychology.
		TNT	Include typed name too.
K	Eliminate the awkward expression.	UA	Strengthen you-attitude.
		UAC	Use antecedents correctly.
Lc	Make lowercase (don't capitalize).	UAW	Use appropriate word(s).
		V	Use correct verb.
Log	Make this logical.	#	Insert space.
M	Improve margins.	ℒ	Delete.
MII	Place most important idea first.	tr	Reverse (transpose) order of letters or words.
Na	Insert name or initials.		
Neg	Can you eliminate negative?	⌣	Close up (leave no space).
NNITS	Include nothing new in terminal section.	↑↓←→	Move copy (up, down, across).
		/syl	Divide word correctly.
NR	Avoid needless repetition.	plan	See text for proper planning.
Om	Insert omitted word(s).	¶	Make a new paragraph.
OS	Avoid obvious statements.	X	Serious error; paper unmailable.

[1] To help you recognize the symbols easily, note (a) in those that are composed of two or more capitals, each capital letter represents the first letter of an important word in the comment; for instance, BNF—*best news first*. (UA is an exception.) (b) the symbols with only one letter capitalized represent a part of one important word; for example, Log—*logical*.

Index

I–1